MW01088401

THE
COLLEGE
PRESS
NIV
COMMENTARY

ROMANS
VOLUME 1

THE COLLEGE PRESS NIV COMMENTARY

ROMANS
VOLUME 1

JACK COTTRELL

New Testament Series Co-Editors:

Jack Cottrell, Ph.D.
Cincinnati Bible Seminary

Tony Ash, Ph.D.
Abilene Christian University

COLLEGE PRESS
PUBLISHING COMPANY
Joplin, Missouri

Library of Congress Cataloging-in-Publication Data

Cottrell, Jack.
    Romans / Jack Cottrell.
      p.   cm. — (The College Press NIV commentary)
    Includes bibliographic references.
    ISBN 0-89900-632-9
    1. Bible. N.T. Romans—Commentaries. I. Title. II. Series.
BS2665.3.C68 1996
227'.1077—dc21   96-46296
                                                CIP

A WORD
FROM THE PUBLISHER

Years ago a movement was begun with the dream of uniting all Christians on the basis of a common purpose (world evangelism) under a common authority (the Word of God). The College Press NIV Commentary Series is a serious effort to join the scholarship of two branches of this unity movement so as to speak with one voice concerning the Word of God. Our desire is to provide a resource for your study of the New Testament that will benefit you whether you are preparing a Bible School lesson, a sermon, a college course, or your own personal devotions. Today as we survey the wreckage of a broken world, we must turn again to the Lord and his Word, unite under his banner and communicate the life-giving message to those who are in desperate need. This is our purpose.

ABBREVIATIONS

AG . . . . *Arndt and Gingrich, Greek lexicon*
ASV . . . . *American Standard Version*
GC . . . . *God the Creator, by Jack Cottrell*
GRe . . . . *God the Redeemer, by Jack Cottrell*
GRu . . . . *God the Ruler, by Jack Cottrell*
KJV. . . . . *King James Version*
LB . . . . *Living Bible*
LXX . . . . *Septuagint (Greek translation of the OT)*
MP . . . . *McGarvey-Pendleton Romans commentary*
NAB . . . . *New American Bible*
NASB . . . . . . *New American Standard Bible*
NEB . . . . *New English Bible*
NIV . . . . *New International Version*
NRSV . . . . . . *New Revised Standard Version*
NT . . . . *New Testament*
OT . . . . *Old Testament*
RomDeb . . . . *The Romans Debate, by Karl Donfried*
RSV . . . . *Revised Standard Version*
TDNT. . . . . . *Theological Dictionary of the NT, ed. Kittel*
TEV . . . . *Today's English Version*

For fuller titles and publishing information on books, see the Bibliography.

BIBLIOGRAPHY

The following bibliography includes commentaries, books, and articles cited in the text and footnotes of this work. Citations include a minimum of information; the reader must use this list for full titles and bibliographical data.

When commentaries are cited, only the author's name and page number are given. When other sources are cited, usually just the author's name and an abbreviated title (in **bold print** below) are given.

I. COMMENTARIES

Barclay, William. *The Letter to the Romans*, 2 ed. The Daily Study Bible. Edinburgh: Saint Andrew Press, 1957.

Barrett, C.K. *A Commentary on the Epistle to the Romans*. Harper's New Testament Commentaries. New York: Harper & Row, 1957; reprint, Peabody, MA: Hendrickson, 1987.

Bartlett, C. Norman. *Right in Romans: Studies in the Epistle of Paul to the Romans*. Chicago: Moody Press, 1953.

Batey, Richard A. *The Letter of Paul to the Romans*. Austin: R.B. Sweet, 1969.

Black, Matthew. *Romans*, 2 ed. New Century Bible Commentary. Grand Rapids: Eerdmans, 1989.

Boice, James Montgomery. *Romans*, 4 vols. Grand Rapids: Baker, 1991ff.

Brokke, Harold J. *Saved by His Life*. Minneapolis: Bethany Fellowship, 1964.

Bruce, F.F. *The Epistle of Paul to the Romans*. Tyndale New Testament Commentaries. Grand Rapids: Eerdmans, 1963.

Calvin, John. *Commentaries on the Epistle of Paul the Apostle to the Romans.* Tr. by John Owen. Grand Rapids: Eerdmans, 1947 reprint.

Cranfield, C.E.B. *A Critical and Exegetical Commentary on the Epistle to the Romans.* 2 vols. The International Critical Commentary, new series. Edinburgh: T. & T. Clark, 1975 (1990 corrected printing).

DeWelt, Don. *Romans Realized.* Joplin, MO: College Press, 1959.

Dodd, C.H. *The Epistle of Paul to the Romans.* New York: Harper & Brothers, 1932.

Dunn, James D.G. *Romans.* 2 vols. Volume 38 in Word Biblical Commentary. Dallas: Word Books, 1988.

Edwards, James R. *Romans.* New International Biblical Commentary. Peabody, MA: Hendrickson, 1992.

Erdman, Charles R. *The Epistle to the Romans: An Exposition.* Philadelphia: Westminster, 1925.

Godet, Frederic L. *Commentary on the Epistle to the Romans.* Tr. by A. Cusin. Ed. by Talbot W. Chambers. Grand Rapids: Zondervan, 1956 reprint of 1883 ed.

Greathouse, William M. *Romans.* Vol. 6 of Beacon Bible Expositions. Kansas City, MO: Beacon Hill Press, 1975.

Grubbs, Isaiah Boone. *An Exegetical and Analytical Commentary on Paul's Epistle to the Romans.* Ed. by George A. Kingman. 6th ed. Nashville: Gospel Advocate, n.d.

Harrison, Everett F. "Romans." In *The Expositor's Bible Commentary.* Volume 10. Ed. by Frank E. Gaebelein. Grand Rapids: Zondervan, 1976. Pp. 1-171.

Hendriksen, William. *Exposition of Paul's Epistle to the Romans.* 2 vols. New Testament Commentary. Grand Rapids: Baker, 1980-1981.

Käsemann, Ernst. *Commentary on Romans.* Tr. by Geoffrey W. Bromiley. Grand Rapids: Eerdmans, 1980.

Lard, Moses E. *Commentary on Paul's Letter to Romans.* Cincinnati: Standard Publishing, n.d.

Lenski, R.C.H. *The Interpretation of St. Paul's Epistle to the Romans.* Columbus, OH: Wartburg Press, 1945.

Lipscomb, David. *Romans.* Vol. I in A Commentary on the New Testament Epistles. 2nd ed. Ed. by J. W. Shepherd. Nashville: Gospel Advocate, 1965.

Lloyd-Jones, D.M. *Romans: An Exposition of Chapters 3.20–4.25– Atonement and Justification.* London: Banner of Truth Trust, 1970.

_____ . *Romans: An Exposition of Chapter 6–The New Man.* Grand Rapids: Zondervan, 1973.

_____ . *Romans: An Exposition of Chapters 7.1–8.4–The Law: Its Functions and Limits.* Grand Rapids: Zondervan, 1973.

Luther, Martin. *Luther: Lectures on Romans.* Ed. & tr. by Wilhelm Pauck. The Library of Christian Classics. Vol. XV. Philadelphia: Westminster, 1961.

MacArthur, John, Jr. *Romans.* 2 vols. The MacArthur New Testament Commentary. Chicago: Moody, 1991, 1994.

McGarvey, J.W., and Philip Y. Pendleton. *Thessalonians, Corinthians, Galatians, and Romans.* Cincinnati: Standard Publishing, n.d.

McClain, Alva J. *Romans: The Gospel of God's Grace.* Ed. by Herman A. Hoyt. Chicago: Moody Press, 1973.

Mitchell, John G., with Dick Bohrer. *Right with God: A Devotional Study of the Epistle to the Romans.* Portland, OR: Multnomah, 1990.

Moo, Douglas. *Romans.* 2 vols. The Wycliffe Exegetical Commentary. Chicago: Moody, 1991.

Morris, Leon. *The Epistle to the Romans.* Grand Rapids: Eerdmans, 1988.

Moser, K.C. *The Gist of Romans,* revised ed. Delight, AR: Gospel Light Publishing Company, 1958.

Moule, H.C.G. *The Epistle of Paul the Apostle to the Romans.* The Cambridge Bible for Schools and Colleges. Cambridge: The University Press, 1918.

Mounce, Robert H. *Romans*. Vol. 27 in The New American Commentary. Nashville: Broadman & Holman, 1995.

Murray, John. *The Epistle to the Romans*. 2 vols. New International Commentary. Grand Rapids: Eerdmans, 1959, 1965.

Newell, William R. *Lessons on the Epistle of Paul to the Romans*. No publisher given, 1925.

Newman, Barclay M., and Eugene A. Nida. *A Translator's Handbook on Paul's Letter to the Romans*. London: United Bible Societies, 1973.

Nygren, Anders. *Commentary on Romans*. Tr. by Carl C. Rasmussen. Philadelphia: Fortress Press, 1949.

Reese, Gareth L. *New Testament Epistles: A Critical and Exegetical Commentary on Paul's Epistle to the Romans*. Moberly, MO: Scripture Exposition Press, 1987.

Robertson, A.T. *The Epistles of Paul*. Vol. IV in Word Pictures in the New Testament. Nashville: Broadman, 1931.

Sanday, William, and Arthur C. Headlam. *A Critical and Exegetical Commentary on the Epistle to the Romans*. 2nd ed. The International Critical Commentary, old series. New York: Charles Scribner's Sons, n.d.

Schlatter, Adolf. *Romans: The Righteousness of God*. Tr. by Siegfried Schatzmann. Peabody, MA: Hendrickson, 1995.

Shedd, William G.T. *A Critical and Doctrinal Commentary on the Epistle of St. Paul to the Romans*. Grand Rapids: Zondervan, 1967 reprint of 1879 edition.

Shields, Bruce. *Romans*. Standard Bible Studies. Cincinnati: Standard Publishing, 1988.

Smith, Sherwood. *Thirteen Lessons on Romans*. Vol. 1 (1979); and *Thirteen Lessons on Romans*. Vol. 2 (1981). Joplin, MO: College Press.

Stedman, Ray C. *From Guilt to Glory, Volume I: Romans 1–8*. Waco: Word Books, 1978.

Stott, John. *Romans: God's Good News for the World*. Downers Grove: InterVarsity, 1994.

Williams, William G. *An Exposition of the Epistle of Paul to the Romans*. Cincinnati: Jennings and Pye, 1902.

Wuest, Kenneth S. *Romans in the Greek New Testament for the English Reader*. Grand Rapids: Eerdmans, 1955.

II. MISCELLANEOUS BOOKS AND ARTICLES

Arndt, William F., and F. Wilbur Gingrich. *A Greek-English Lexicon of the New Testament and Other Early Christian Literature*. 4th ed. Chicago: University of Chicago Press, 1957.

Augustine, *The Confessions of St. Augustine*. Vol. XIV in The Works of Aurelius Augustine. Ed. by Marcus Dods. Tr. by J.G. Pilkington. Edinburgh: T. & T. Clark, 1876.

Balz, Horst. "ἀποκαραδοκία." *Exegetical Dictionary of the New Testament*. Ed. by Horst Balz and Gerhard Schneider. Grand Rapids: Eerdmans, 1990. I:132-133.

Bartchy, S. Scott. *MALLON CHRESAI: First Century Slavery and the Interpretation of 1 Corinthians 7:21*. Society of Biblical Literature Dissertation Series, #11. Missoula: Scholars Press, 1973.

Beker, J.C. "The Faithfulness of God and the Priority of Israel in Paul's Letter to the Romans." *RomDeb*, 327-332.

Boers, Hendrikus. *The Justification of the Gentiles: Paul's Letters to the Galatians and Romans*. Peabody, MA: Hendrickson, 1994.

Bornkamm, Günther. "The Letter to the Romans as Paul's Last Will and Testament." *RomDeb*, 16-28.

Boswell, John. *Christianity, Social Tolerance, and Homosexuality*. Chicago: University of Chicago Press, 1980.

Bruce, F.F. "The Romans Debate—Continued." *RomDeb*, 177-194.

Campbell, William S. "Romans III as a Key to the Structure and Thought of the Letter." *RomDeb*, 251-264.

Carson, D.A. *Exegetical Fallacies*. Grand Rapids: Baker, 1984.

Coleridge, Samuel Taylor. *The Table Talk and Omniana of Samuel Taylor Coleridge*. London: Oxford University Press, 1917.

Cooper, John W. *Body, Soul, and Life Everlasting: Biblical Anthropology and the Monism-Dualism Debate*. Grand Rapids: Baker, 1989.

Corson, John. "**Faith** Alone Involves Obedience, Too!" *Christian Standard*. (10/2/77), pp. 5-6.

Cottrell, Jack. *Baptism: A Biblical Study*. Joplin, MO: College Press, 1989.

_____ . "Baptism According to the **Reformed Tradition**." In *Baptism and the Remission of Sins*. Ed. by David W. Fletcher. Joplin, MO: College Press, 1990. Pp. 39-81.

_____ . "The Biblical **Consensus**: Historical Backgrounds to Reformed Theology." In *Baptism and the Remission of Sins*. Ed. by David W. Fletcher. Joplin, MO: College Press, 1990. Pp. 17-38.

_____ . "**Covenant** and Baptism in the Theology of Huldreich Zwingli." Unpublished doctoral dissertation. Princeton, NJ: Princeton Theological Seminary, 1971.

_____ . "**Faith**, History, and the Resurrection Body of Jesus," *The Seminary Review* (Dec. 1982): 28:143-160.

_____ . *Faith's **Fundamentals**: Seven Essentials of Christian Belief*. Cincinnati: Standard Publishing, 1995.

_____ . *Gender **Roles** and the Bible: Creation, the Fall, and Redemption*. Joplin, MO: College Press, 1994.

_____ . *His **Truth***. 2nd ed. Joplin, MO: College Press, 1989.

_____ . *Thirteen Lessons on **Grace***. Joplin, MO: College Press, 1988.

_____ . *What the Bible Says about God the Creator*. Joplin, MO: College Press, 1984.

_____ . *What the Bible Says about God the Redeemer*. Joplin, MO: College Press, 1987.

_____ . *What the Bible Says about God the Ruler*. Joplin, MO: College Press, 1984.

Delling, G. "λαμβάνω, etc." TDNT, IV:5-15.

DeYoung, James B. "The **Meaning** of 'Nature' in Romans 1." *Journal of the Evangelical Theological Society*, 31 (December 1988): 429-441.

Donfried, Karl P. "False **Presuppositions** in the Study of Romans." *RomDeb*, 102-125.

_____ , ed. *The Romans **Debate***. Revised & expanded edition. Peabody, MA: Hendrickson, 1991.

_____ . "A Short **Note** on Romans 16." *RomDeb*, 44-52.

Erickson, Millard J. *The Evangelical **Mind** and Heart*. Grand Rapids: Baker, 1993.

Fiensy, David A. *New Testament **Introduction***. The College Press NIV Commentary. Joplin, MO: College Press, 1994.

Foerster, Werner. "σώζω, etc." TDNT, VII:965-1024.

Friedrich, Gerhard. "εὐαγγελίζομαι, etc." TDNT, II:707-737.

Fuller, Daniel P. *The **Unity** of the Bible: Unfolding God's Plan for Humanity*. Grand Rapids: Zondervan, 1992.

Gaertner, Dennis. "Romans: Gospel of God's **Fairness**." *Christian Standard*, part 1 (12/20/87), pp. 14-16; and part 2 (12/27/87), pp. 4-6.

Graber, Friedrich. "All, Many." *The New International Dictionary of New Testament Theology*. Ed. by Colin Brown. Grand Rapids: Zondervan, 1975. I:94-97.

Gromacki, Robert. *The **Virgin Birth**: Doctrine of Deity*. Nashville: Nelson, 1974.

Gundry, Robert H. ***Sōma** in Biblical Theology: With Emphasis on Pauline Anthropology*. Grand Rapids: Zondervan, 1987.

Harris, M.J. "**Prepositions** and Theology in the Greek New Testament." Appendix. *The New International Dictionary of New*

Testament Theology. Ed. by Colin Brown. Grand Rapids: Zondervan, 1978. III:1171-1213.

Hobbs, A. I. "**Conversion**: What Is It, and How Produced?" In *The Old Faith Restated*. Ed. by J.H. Garrison. St. Louis: Christian Publishing Company, 1891. Pp. 254-274.

Hodges, Zane C. *Absolutely Free*. Grand Rapids: Zondervan, 1989.

Jervell, Jacob. "The **Letter** to Jerusalem." *RomDeb*, 53-64.

Jeremias, Joachim. *The Central Message of the New Testament*. London: SCM Press, 1965.

Jewett, Robert. "Following the **Argument** of Romans." *RomDeb*, 265-277.

Kittel, Gerhard, and Gerhard Friedrich, eds. *Theological Dictionary of the New Testament*. Tr. & ed. by Geoffrey W. Bromiley. 10 vols. Grand Rapid: Eerdmans, 1964-1976.

Klein, Günter. "Paul's **Purpose** in Writing the Epistle to the Romans." *RomDeb*, 29-43.

Lamar, J.S. "The **Ground** of Man's Need of Salvation." In *The Old Faith Restated*. Ed. by J.H. Garrison. St. Louis: Christian Publishing Company, 1891. Pp. 98-119.

Lewis, C.S. *The Abolition of Man*. New York: Macmillan, 1947.

Luther, Martin. "Preface to the Complete Edition of Luther's **Latin Writings**." In Vol. 34: *Career of the Reformer IV*. Luther's Works (American Edition). Ed. by Lewis W. Spitz and Helmut T. Lehmann. Philadelphia: Muhlenberg Press, 1960. Pp. 327-338.

_____ . "**Preface** to the Epistle of St. Paul to the Romans." In Vol. 35: *Word and Sacrament I*. Luther's Works (American Edition). Ed. by E. Theodore Bachmann and Helmut T. Lehmann. Philadelphia: Muhlenberg Press, 1960. Pp. 365-380.

MacArthur, John F., Jr. *The Gospel According to Jesus: What Does Jesus Mean When He Says, "Follow Me"?* Revised ed. Grand Rapids: Zondervan, 1994.

Maurer, Christian. "ὑπόδικος." TDNT, VIII:557-558.

_____ . "πράσσω, etc." TDNT, VI:632-644.

Milligan, Robert. *Exposition and Defense of the Scheme of Redemption.* St. Louis: Bethany Press, n.d.

Moreland, J.P., and David Ciocchi, eds. *Christian Perspectives on Being Human: A Multidisciplinary Approach to Integration.* Grand Rapids: Baker, 1993.

Morris, Leon. *The Apostolic Preaching of the Cross.* 3 ed. Grand Rapids: Eerdmans, 1965.

Murray, John. *The Imputation of Adam's Sin.* Grand Rapids: Eerdmans, 1959.

Nash, Donald A. "A Critique of the New International Version of the New Testament." Cincinnati: Christian Restoration Association, n.d.

Oepke, Albrecht. "καθίστημι, etc." TDNT, III:444-447.

Reese, Gareth L. *New Testament History: A Critical and Exegetical Commentary on the Book of Acts.* 2nd ed. Joplin, MO: College Press, 1976.

Rengstorf, Karl Heinrich. "δοῦλος, etc." TDNT, II:261-280.

Ridderbos, Herman. *Paul: An Outline of His Theology.* Tr. by John R. de Witt. Grand Rapids: Eerdmans, 1975.

Rueda, Enrique. *The Homosexual Network: Private Lives and Public Policy.* Old Greenwich, CT: Devin Adair, 1982.

Ryrie, Charles C. *So Great Salvation: What It Means to Believe in Jesus Christ.* Wheaton: Scripture Press/Victor Books, 1989.

Sanders, E.P. *Paul and Palestinian Judaism.* London: SCM, 1977.

Schaff, Philip. "Preface." In John Peter Lange, *Commentary on the Holy Scriptures: Romans.* Tr. by Philip Schaff. Grand Rapids: Zondervan reprint, n.d.

Schneider, Johannes. "παραβαίνω, παράβασις, etc." TDNT, V:736-744.

Schrenk, Gottlob. "ἱερός, etc." TDNT, III:221-283.

Spicq, Ceslas. *Theological Lexicon of the New Testament.* Tr. by James D. Ernest. 3 volumes. Peabody, MA: Hendrickson, 1994.

Stendahl, Krister. *Paul Among Jews and Gentiles and Other Essays.* Philadelphia: Fortress Press, 1976.

Stuhlmacher, Peter. "The Purpose of Romans." *RomDeb,* 231-242.

─────────── . "The Theme of Romans." *RomDeb,* 333-345.

Thielman, Frank. *Paul and the Law: A Contextual Approach.* Downers Grove: InterVarsity Press, 1994.

Thiessen, Henry. *Introduction to the New Testament.* 2nd ed. Grand Rapids: Eerdmans, 1944.

Trench, Richard Chenevix. *Synonyms of the New Testament.* Grand Rapids: Eerdmans, 1958.

Tyndale, William. "A Prologe to the Epistle of Paule to the Romayns." In *The New Testament, Translated by William Tyndale, 1534.* Ed. by N. Hardy Wallis. Cambridge: University Press, 1938. Pp. 293-318.

Unger, Merrill F. *Unger's Bible Dictionary.* 3rd ed. Chicago: Moody Press, 1966.

Vincent, Marvin R. *The Epistles of Paul.* Vol. III in Word Studies in the New Testament. Grand Rapids: Eerdmans, 1973 reprint of 1887 edition.

Watson, Francis. "The Two Roman Congregations: Romans 14:1-15:13." *RomDeb,* 203-215.

Wesley, John. *Journal from October 14, 1735, to November 29, 1745.* Vol. I in The Works of John Wesley. Grand Rapids: Zondervan, reprint of 1872 ed.

Wedderburn, A.J.M. "The Purpose and Occasion of Romans Again," *RomDeb,* 195-202.

Wiefel, Wolfgang. "The Jewish Community in Ancient Rome and the Origins of Roman Christianity." *RomDeb,* 85-101.

Wiens, Delbert. "An Exegesis of Romans 5:12-21." *Journal of Church and Society* (Fall 1969): 5:42-54.

18

Williams, Philip R. "Paul's **Purpose** in Writing Romans." *Bibliotheca Sacra* (January-March 1971): 128:62-67.

Young, Richard. *Intermediate N.T. **Greek**: A Linguistic and Exegetical Approach*. Nashville: Broadman & Holman, 1994.

INTRODUCTION

I. ROMANS: ITS INFLUENCE AND IMPORTANCE

God's Word is a lamp to our feet and a light for our path (Ps 119:105), and no part of it shines more brilliantly than the book of Romans. The truth of God's Word sets us free (John 8:32), and Romans teaches us the most liberating of all truths. God's Word is sharp and piercing like a sword (Heb 4:12), and no blade penetrates more deeply into our hearts than Romans. Overall the book of Romans may be the most read and most influential book of the Bible, but sometimes it is the most neglected and most misunderstood book. The Restoration Movement has tended to concentrate especially on the book of Acts, which is truly foundational and indispensable. But Romans is to Acts what meat is to milk. We need to mature; we need to graduate from Acts to Romans.

In 1 Cor 15:3-4 Paul sums up the gospel as these three truths: Christ died for our sins, was buried, and was raised up again on the third day. The reality of the historical facts of the Savior's death and resurrection is stressed over and over in the book of Acts. Romans, however, is an exposition of the *meaning* of these facts. In the language of 1 Cor 15:3, Romans focuses not on "Christ died," but on the next three words: *"for our sins."* Acts explains what salvation consists of and how we may receive it. Romans does the same, but carries the explanation to heights and depths that thrill and satisfy the soul, providing it with an experience that is at the same time intellectual, spiritual, and esthetic.[1]

The unparalleled ability of Romans to convict sinners and to

---

[1] See DeWelt, 13; Moser, iii. See the explanatory note at the beginning of the bibliography for my policy regarding citations in the text and in footnotes.

motivate Christians is well attested. The comment of Sanday and Headlam (v) has often been noted: "If it is a historical fact that the spiritual revivals of Christendom have been usually associated with closer study of the Bible, this would be true in an eminent degree of the Epistle to the Romans." Leon Morris (1) concurs: "It is commonly agreed that the Epistle to the Romans is one of the greatest Christian writings. Its power has been demonstrated again and again at critical points in the history of the Christian church."

The role of Romans in Augustine's conversion is well known. In his *Confessions* he tells how a discussion of Christian commitment with two of his friends brought him under strong conviction, filling him with remorse for his sins of sexual immorality and a sense of helplessness to overcome them. Later he and his friend Alypius went into the garden, taking along a copy of Paul's writings. Augustine went off by himself to weep over his sins. While doing so, he reports, "I heard the voice as of a boy or girl, I know not which, coming from a neighbouring house, chanting, and oft repeating, 'Take up and read; take up and read.'" He took this as a sign from God to open the book of Paul's writings and read the first passage that met his eyes. He quickly returned to where Alypius was sitting and the book was lying. When he opened it, the first words he saw were these from Rom 13:13-14: "Not in orgies and drunkenness, not in sexual immorality and debauchery, not in dissension and jealousy. Rather, clothe yourselves with the Lord Jesus Christ, and do not think about how to gratify the desires of the sinful nature." This experience and these words gave him what he needed to turn completely to Christ. He says, "No further would I read, nor did I need; for instantly, as the sentence ended, — by a light, as it were, of security infused into my heart, — all the gloom of doubt vanished away."[2]

Godet (1) declares that "the Reformation was undoubtedly the work of the Epistle to the Romans." Morris (1) agrees: "The Reformation may be regarded as the unleashing of new spiritual life as a result of a renewed understanding of the teaching of Romans."

Insofar as the Reformation depends on the work of Martin

---

[2]Augustine, *Confessions*, VIII:vi-xii (¶ 14-29), 189-204.

Luther, this is surely the case. Luther confesses how in 1519 he had an ardent desire to understand the epistle to the Romans. His problem was the way he had been taught to understand the expression "the righteousness of God" in Rom 1:17. To him it meant the divine justice and wrath by which God punishes sin, which did not sound very much like *gospel*. "Nevertheless," he says, "I beat importunately upon Paul at that place, most ardently desiring to know what St. Paul wanted." Finally, by the mercy of God, he began to understand this expression in a totally different way, i.e., as the righteousness of Christ that God bestows upon the sinner and on the basis of which the sinner is justified. The effect on Luther was electrifying: "I felt that I was altogether born again and had entered paradise itself through open gates." This new understanding of this one verse — Rom 1:17 — changed everything; it became in a real sense the doorway to the Reformation. "Thus that place in Paul was for me truly the gate to paradise," says Luther ("Latin Writings," 336-337).

Luther's regard for Romans is clearly seen in this well-known paragraph from his famous preface to this epistle:

> This epistle is really the chief part of the New Testament, and is truly the purest gospel. It is worthy not only that every Christian should know it word for word, by heart, but also that he should occupy himself with it every day, as the daily bread of the soul. We can never read it or ponder over it too much; for the more we deal with it, the more precious it becomes and the better it tastes ("Preface," 365).

These words, first published in 1522, were echoed almost verbatim by the English reformer William Tyndale, in his prologue to his 1534 English translation of the New Testament. He says, "This epistle is the principal and most excellent part of the New Testament, and most pure . . . gospel, and also a light and a way in unto the whole Scripture." He also recommends learning it by heart and studying it daily, because "so great treasure of spiritual things lieth hid therein."[3]

The Swiss reformer John Calvin echoes some of Tyndale's

---

[3]Tyndale, "Prologe," 293. The spelling has been modernized.

thoughts in his own commentary on Romans (xxix): "When any one gains a knowledge of this Epistle, he has an entrance opened to him to all the most hidden treasures of Scripture."

Working indirectly through Luther's preface, the book of Romans had an effect on John Wesley similar to the way it influenced Augustine and Luther. In his journal Wesley recounts his own search for personal victory over sin and assurance of salvation based on trust in the blood of Christ alone. He tells what happened to him on May 24, 1738:

> In the evening I went very unwillingly to a society in Aldersgate Street, where one was reading Luther's preface to the Epistle to the Romans. About a quarter before nine, while he was describing the change which God works in the heart through faith in Christ, I felt my heart strangely warmed. I felt I did trust in Christ, Christ alone for salvation: And an assurace was given me, that he had taken away *my* sins, even *mine*, and saved *me* from the law of sin and death (*Works*, I:103).

Modern scholars and expositors seem unable to praise the letter to the Romans highly enough. Philip Schaff has said, "The Epistle to the Romans is the Epistle of the Epistles, as the Gospel of John is the Gospel of the Gospels" ("Preface," v). "This is in every sense the greatest of the Epistles of Paul, if not the greatest book in the New Testament," declares Thiessen (*Introduction*, 219). Newell (375) says Romans is "probably the greatest book in the Bible." "If the apostle Paul had written nothing else, he would still be recognized as one of the outstanding Christian thinkers of all time on the basis of this letter alone," say Newman and Nida (1). This familiar praise comes from Godet (x):

> The pious Sailer used to say, "O Christianity, had thy one work been to produce a St. Paul, that alone would have rendered thee dear to the coldest reason." May we not be permitted to add: And thou, O St. Paul, had thy one work been to compose an Epistle to the Romans, that alone would have rendered thee dear to every sound reason.

Godet adds, "The Epistle to the Romans is the cathedral of the Christian faith" (1).

Others add even higher praise. Batey (7) says, "Paul's epistle to the Romans stands among the most important pieces of literature in the intellectual history of Western man." "It is safe to say that Romans is probably the most powerful human document ever written," declares Stedman. Some might think this honor should go to the U.S. Constitution or to the Declaration of Independence. "But even they cannot hold a candle to the impact the Epistle to the Romans has had upon human history" (I:1-2). Boice avows: "Christianity has been the most powerful, transforming force in human history — and the book of Romans is the most basic, most comprehensive statement of true Christianity" (I:13).

Commentators often quote this statement from Coleridge: "I think St. Paul's Epistle to the Romans the most profound work in existence" (*Table Talk*, 245). Many will certainly agree, but to Coleridge such profundity was not altogether a virtue. For him it meant that Romans "undoubtedly . . . is, and must be, very obscure to ordinary readers" (ibid., 245-246). Indeed, some think that the Apostle Peter may have been referring to Romans in 2 Pet 3:16. But at the same time, perhaps paradoxically, Newell is correct when he says (vii), "There is no more simple book in the Bible than Romans, when one comes to know the book, its contents, its message, its power."

Scholars praise Romans as the clearest statement of the *gospel* of salvation. As noted above, Luther called it "the purest gospel." Nygren agrees (3): "What the gospel is, what the content of the Christian faith is, one learns to know in the Epistle to the Romans as in no other place in the New Testament." Cranfield says Romans is "the most systematic and complete exposition of the gospel that the NT contains" (I:31). The Restoration scholar Moses Lard (xx) concurs: "It is the whole gospel compressed into the short space of a single letter — a generalization of Christianity up to the hight [sic] of the marvelous, and a detail down to exhaustion." In Stott's words (19), Romans is "the fullest, plainest and grandest statement of the gospel in the New Testament."

Scholars also praise Romans for its unparalleled presentation of the essence of Christian *doctrine*. In his preface to Romans (380) Luther says that in Romans we "find most abundantly the things that a Christian ought to know, namely, what is law, gospel, sin, punishment, grace, faith, righteousness, Christ, God, good works, love, hope, and the cross; and also how we are to conduct ourselves toward everyone." Thus it seems that Paul "wanted in this one epistle to sum up briefly the whole Christian and evangelical doctrine." Schaff declares it to be "the heart of the doctrinal portion of the New Testament. It presents in systematic order the fundamental truths of Christianity in their primitive purity, inexhaustible depth, all-conquering force, and never-failing comfort. It is the bulwark of the evangelical doctrines of sin and grace" ("Preface," v).

Modern writers agree. "The truth laid down in Romans forms the Gibraltar basis of doctrine, teaching, and confession in the true evangelical church," says Lenski (8). Moo says the Puritan writer Thomas Draxe described Romans as "the quintessence and perfection of saving doctrine." Moo agrees: "When we think of Romans, we think of doctrine" (I:1). Lard (xx) calls Romans Paul's "great doctrinal chart for the future." Newman and Nida (1) declare that "above all else, the appeal of Romans is its *theology*."

Concerning its doctrinal content, MacArthur lists 49 significant questions about God and man that are answered by Romans, e.g., How can a person who has never heard the gospel be held spiritually responsible? How can a sinner be forgiven and justified by God? How are God's grace and God's law related? Why is there suffering? MacArthur points out that these key words are used repeatedly in the epistle: God (154 times), law (77), Christ (66), sin (45), Lord (44), and faith (40).[4]

Which of these assessments is correct? Is Romans the crowning presentation of the Christian *gospel*? Or is it the grandest statement of Christian *doctrine*? Actually, it is both. Romans is *the* theology of the New Testament; it is also *the* definitive statement of the gospel. In this epistle doctrine and gospel merge, and the result is a spiritual feast for Christians.

Boice (I:10) advises that "it is time to rediscover Romans." Actually, it is *always* time to "rediscover" Romans, and down

---

[4]MacArthur, I:xi-xii. Leon Morris (20) makes a similar point, but his numbers regarding frequency of occurrence are slightly different: God 153 times, law 72, Christ 65, sin 48, Lord 43, and faith 40.

through the history of Christianity individuals have been doing just this. The results have been earth-shaking. It can and does happen over and over, in the lives of individuals, in congregations, in the Church at large. F.F. Bruce (60) has well said, "There is no telling what may happen when people begin to study the Epistle to the Romans."

II. THE AUTHOR OF ROMANS

The epistle to the Romans was written by the Apostle Paul (1:1).[5] In the past a few critics challenged this, but without any real basis in fact.[6] Today, as Cranfield says, "no responsible criticism disputes its Pauline origin" (I:2). Romans was quoted by the earliest Christian writers (Clement, Ignatius, Polycarp, Justin), and was attributed to Paul by name by Marcion in the mid-second century. Since the time of Irenaeus (late second century) writers have explicitly and regularly viewed it as Pauline.

Though composed and dictated by Paul, the letter was actually written down by a Christian scribe named Tertius, who inserted his own greeting in 16:22.

A. PAUL'S JEWISH BACKGROUND

It is not necessary to go into the details of Paul's life, except for a few facts that are important in view of the content of the epistle, which relates especially to the distinction between law and grace. One relevant fact is Paul's Jewish background, which he proudly avowed: "I am an Israelite myself, a descendant of Abraham, from the tribe of Benjamin," a "Hebrew of Hebrews" (11:1; Phil 3:5; 2 Cor 11:22). Though born in Tarsus, he was reared in Jerusalem (Acts 22:3), the capital of Judaism.

Paul's education included strict and thorough religious training

---

[5]Ordinarily, citations from the book of Romans will consist only of the chapter and verse numbers, without "Romans."
[6]Sanday and Headlam, lxxxvi-lxxxvii.

in the contents of the Old Testament — especially the Law (Torah) — at the feet of Gamaliel (Acts 22:3). Gamaliel was one of the most famous and most revered of all rabbis. His knowledge of the Law was so great that he was practically identified with it, being given the title "the Beauty of the Law." A saying recorded in the Talmud declares, "Since Rabban Gamaliel died the glory of the Law has ceased."[7] "Under Gamaliel," says Paul, "I was thoroughly trained in the law of our fathers" (Acts 22:3). "Thoroughly" translates κατὰ ἀκρίβειαν (*kata akribeian*), "according to exactness, strictness, precision."

Paul's zeal for God and commitment to his Law was total (Acts 22:3; Gal 1:14). He was a Pharisee (Acts 23:6; Phil 3:5), which he properly identified as "the strictest sect of our religion" (Acts 26:5). The glory of the Pharisees was the Law; they were devoted to *akribeia* in its interpretation and observance (Dunn, I:xl). Thus Paul not only knew the Law but also devoted himself to scrupulous obedience to its commandments (Acts 26:4-5; Phil 3:6).

This probably means that he was a legalist in the proper sense of that word, i.e., one who sought acceptance by God on the basis of his obedience to the Law. This is implied in the way he contrasted his pre-Christian life (Phil 3:6) and his Christian life (Phil 3:9). This is also the way Pharisees are generally pictured in the Gospels.

Paul's zeal for the Law was expressed perhaps most vehemently in his fanatical persecution of the earliest Christians, all converted Jews whom he no doubt regarded as traitors to God and his Law (Phil 3:6). See Acts 7:58; 8:3; 9:1-2; 22:4-5; 26:9-11; Gal 1:13; 1 Tim 1:13.

B. PAUL'S CONVERSION TO CHRISTIANITY

The second relevant fact about the Apostle Paul is his conversion. The details need not be recounted here. What is important is that the one who converted him to Christianity was no human preacher, but was Jesus himself (Gal 1:15-16). Also, the gospel he

---

[7]Unger, *Dictionary*, 388.

preached was not taught to him by a human teacher; he received it by direct revelation from Jesus (Gal 1:11-12). The result was that Paul's conversion, his change, his turnaround, was complete. Whereas before he was totally committed to the Mosaic Law as a way of life and salvation, once converted he was just as totally committed to the gospel of grace.

As a Christian Paul set himself in complete opposition to everything he had stood for as a Pharisee. He now understood the way of law to be futile (10:3). He saw that his former legalistic approach to salvation was, as Murray says, "the antithesis of grace and of justification by faith" (I:xiii). Thus when Paul presents the classic contrast between law and grace in Romans, he speaks as one who knew both sides of the issue from personal experience and from the best teachers available. As Murray says, he is describing "the contrast between the two periods in his own life history, periods divided by the experience of the Damascus road" (I:xiv).

It is no surprise that Paul's preaching of the gospel and his condemnation of law-righteousness turned the Jews completely against him, even to the point that they tried to kill him (Acts 9:29; 13:45; 14:2, 19; 17:5-8; 18:12; 2 Cor 11:24-26). His opponents included "false brothers" (2 Cor 11:26), the Judaizers, or Jews who accepted Jesus as the Messiah but still clung to the Law of Moses.

In spite of all of this upheaval, Paul did not turn against the Jews as such. He still regarded them as his beloved brothers according to the flesh (9:1-3; 10:1), and as blessed by God in an incomparable way (3:1-2; 9:4-5). In fact, a major aspect of the teaching in Romans is an explanation and a defense of God's purpose for his Old Covenant people, the Jews (see especially chs. 9-11).

C. PAUL'S COMMISSION AS
THE APOSTLE TO THE GENTILES

The last detail about Paul's life that is relevant here is his call and commission to be the Apostle to the Gentiles (Acts 26:17). His appointment as an *apostle* (1:1) invested him with the full authority of Jesus Christ and with the inspiration of the Holy Spirit, so that his teachings are truly the Word of God (1 Cor 2:6-13; 1 Thess

2:13). When we read the book of Romans, we must understand it to be nothing less than this.

Also, Paul's appointment as the apostle *to the Gentiles* (1:5) completely governed his thoughts and deeds from that point on. As a Jew and a Pharisee, he had no doubt shared the typical Hebrew aversion to anything Gentile; and he had no doubt gloried in the Jews' exclusive position as God's chosen people. Thus when God revealed to him the mystery of the Gentiles — that it had been his plan all along to include Gentiles in the people of the Messiah (Eph 3:1-10), Paul was overwhelmed with awe and joy. He unhesitatingly opened his heart to the very people he had once despised. This was another complete turnaround in his life, and he devoted himself totally to his new mission.

Paul's role as apostle to the Gentiles had a direct bearing on his relationship with the Roman church and his letter to them. Paul tells us that he had often desired to visit Rome, in order to preach the gospel and have some converts there, "just as I have had among the other Gentiles" (1:13). But since there was already a church in Rome, God's Spirit directed him into other Gentile areas in Asia Minor and the Greek peninsula first (15:17-22). But now he has covered this territory with three lengthy tours of missionary service (15:19). Thus he is ready to launch out into a totally new area, namely, Spain; and his journey there will take him through Rome, as he announces in this epistle (15:23-24).

Throughout the epistle to the Romans, Paul writes with the full conciousness of his mission to the Gentiles and of the Gentiles in his audience. One point that he clarifies in the letter is the relation of the Gentiles to the Jews with respect to salvation.

III. TIME AND PLACE OF WRITING

Immediately after his baptism Paul began to preach Christ in Damascus (Acts 9:19-20), but soon went away into Arabia (Gal 1:17), which may have been the time he received his revelation from Jesus Christ (Gal 1:12). He went from there back to Damascus, then to Jerusalem (Gal 1:17-18) and elsewhere, and ultimately to Antioch (Acts 11:25-26).

From Antioch Paul launched his first missionary trip among the Gentiles (Acts 13:1-3), which was followed by two more. While in Ephesus on his third journey, "Paul decided to go to Jerusalem, passing through Macedonia and Achaia. 'After I have been there,' he said, 'I must visit Rome also'" (Acts 19:21). He shortly departed for Achaia (Greece) and arrived in Corinth, where he stayed for three months (Acts 20:1-3). This was approximately twenty years after his conversion, and ten years after the beginning of his first journey.

Corinth was the farthest point of his third trip, whence he retraced his steps back toward Ephesus. He stopped at Miletus instead, and traveled from there on to Jerusalem, with the goal of arriving by Pentecost (Acts 20:16-17). One main reason for the trip to Jerusalem was to deliver the money he had collected from the (mostly Gentile) churches in Galatia, Macedonia, and Greece, to help the poor (mostly Jewish) saints in Jerusalem (1 Cor 16:1-4; Rom 15:25-26). Though "compelled by the Spirit" to go to Jerusalem, he was apprehensive about what might happen to him there (Acts 20:22-23).

It was in the midst of this final journey, during the three months Paul spent at Corinth, that he most likely wrote the letter to the Romans. He was apparently staying at the house of Gaius (16:23), one of his converts at Corinth (1 Cor 1:14). The letter was carried to Rome by Phoebe, a Christian from the church in nearby Cenchrea (16:1).

The exact date of the writing of Romans is calculated in relation to the overall chronology of Paul's life and work. There is no unanimity on this chronology, though the differences of opinion are minor. Everyone agrees that the Apostle's stay in Corinth must have been in late winter and/or early spring, since he planned to set out from there and arrive in Jerusalem by Pentecost. Most agree also that this would have been in the middle or late 50s.[8] Thus Romans was probably written early in A.D. 56, 57, or 58.

---

[8]Possible dates suggested are A.D. 55 (Morris, 6-7); A.D. 56 (Stuhlmacher, "Purpose," 238); A.D. 56 or 57 (Cranfield, I:14, 16; Dunn, I:xliii); A.D. 57 (Bruce, 11; Edwards, 6; Fiensy, *Introduction*, 223; Moo, I:3); A.D. 57 or 58 (Hendriksen, I:14-15); and A.D. 58 (Lenski, 5; MacArthur, I:xviii; MP, 289; Sanday and Headlam, xlii).

IV. RECIPIENTS OF ROMANS:
THE CHURCH IN ROME

Rome was the largest and most important city in the Roman Empire in Paul's day. Its population was probably over one million.[9] Of this number, it is estimated that forty to fifty thousand were Jews, with as many as fifteen identifiable synagogues (Dunn, I:xlvi; Edwards, 9).

How the church in Rome originated is not known. There is no real evidence that Peter founded it, contrary to a common tradition. Some say that Rom 15:20 shows this could not have been the case. Here Paul says that he does not intend to "be building on someone else's foundation." The fact that he did plan to visit Rome and work there implies that no apostle had been there yet (MacArthur, I:xviii; Moo, I:4).

One very common speculation is that the Roman church was probably started by Jews and proselytes from Rome who were in the audience that heard Peter's sermon on the day of Pentecost (Acts 2:10), and who were among the converts baptized that day. Upon returning to Rome, they would have established the church there.[10] If so, and this seems very likely, then the first Christians in Rome were converts from Judaism.

Another likely speculation is that Christians from other churches, perhaps some of Paul's own converts from his earlier work in Tarsus and Antioch and Asia Minor, were among those who started the Roman church and helped it to grow. Perhaps some of Paul's acquaintances named in Romans 16 were among this group. Such a scenario is highly probable, given the importance of Rome and the constant travel to and from that city.

Thus the church in Rome would have begun not as the result of some formal missionary effort, but by residents converted while

---

[9]Unger, *Dictionary*, 936. Edwards (8) thinks it was closer to one-half million.

[10]Sanday and Headlam (xxviii) doubt that it happened this way, saying the new converts probably would not have stayed in Jerusalem long enough to learn enough about Christianity to evangelize others. This is a very unlikely scenario, however.

traveling (e.g., Acts 2:10) and by Christians moving there from other places. Their own evangelistic efforts would certainly have focused on the synagogues of Rome, following the pattern of evangelism reflected in the book of Acts. This would have resulted in converts not only from Judaism but also from among Gentile "God-fearers" who were commonly attached to the synagogues (Dunn, I:xlvii-xlviii).

The epistle to the Romans is addressed "to all in Rome who are loved by God and called to be saints" (1:7).[11] The main question about these saints is the relative number of Jews and Gentiles among them. In answering this question, scholars usually begin with one solid historical fact, and then draw conclusions based on inferences and a bit of speculation. This has led to the following scenario, for which there is considerable consensus among commentators today.

The one fact is that the Roman emperor Claudius issued a decree that expelled all Jews from Rome. This is recorded in Acts 18:2, and is also mentioned by the Roman historian Suetonius. The exact date of the decree is somewhat unclear, but the best calculation is A.D. 49. The reason for the decree is stated thus by Suetonius: "Because the Jews at Rome caused continuous disturbances at the instigation of Chrestus, (Emperor Claudius) expelled them from the city" (cited in Fiensy, *Introduction*, 224). Though we cannot be certain about this, most scholars agree that "Chrestus" is just a mistaken spelling of "Christus," and that the decree had to do with Jesus Christ.

In what way would Christ be instigating disturbances among the Jews in Rome? It is inferred that this refers to conflicts among the Jews stemming from Christian evangelism in the various synagogues. Because there was a wide diversity among the Jews and synagogues in Rome, it is concluded that some were more receptive to Christianity than others, and that this must have led to disputes

---

[11]Some manuscript variations in the text of Romans have led some to conclude that Romans was distributed in more than one form, possibly as a circular letter directed to churches in other areas besides Rome. The evidence for this suggestion is quite weak. For satisfactory discussions of this issue see Cranfield, I:5-11; Hendriksen, I:26-28; Moo, I:5-9.

among them. The resulting unrest was apparently unpleasant enough for Claudius to order all Jews to leave the city. It is also assumed that his decree did not make a distinction between unbelieving and believing Jews; thus even the Jewish Christians had to leave, e.g., Aquila and Priscilla (Acts 18:2). After the decree the Roman church thus would be composed almost entirely of Gentiles. (See Donfried, "Presuppositions," 104-105.)

When Claudius died around A.D. 54, the decree was no longer enforced, and Jews and Jewish Christians were free to return to Rome. Some think, however, that they were still forbidden to assemble publicly (Wiefel, "Community," 92-94). The results for the church would have been twofold. First, the problem with public assembly may have forced the Christians to set up a number of "house churches," a possibility that seems to be confirmed in Rom 16:5, 14, 15. Second, the returning Jewish Christians would find the Roman church dominated by the Gentile Christians, if not in number then certainly in power and influence (Wiefel, "Community," 94-96).

Thus the saints in Rome, to whom the letter is addressed, were almost certainly a mixture of Jewish and Gentile Christians, though there is no way to tell which group had the larger number. If the circumstances outlined in the above scenario are correct, however, it is safe to assume that there was tension if not conflict among the two groups. Wiefel refers to "quarrels about status" ("Community," 96). Bruce says, "It is implied in Romans 11:13-24 that the Gentile Christians tended to look down on their Jewish brethren as poor relations" ("Debate," 180). Dunn speaks of "at least some friction between Gentile and Jew" within the house churches, with the Jews being in a minority and feeling themselves vulnerable (I:liii).

What is obvious is that in the epistle Paul addresses both groups, with some passages being specifically directed toward the Jewish Christians and some toward the Gentile Christians (see Moo, I:10-11; Murray, I:xviii-xix). Some say the letter as a whole is directed mainly to the Jewish saints; others say it was mainly intended for the Gentiles.[12]

---

[12]Watson, e.g., says Romans was mainly to the Jewish saints ("Congregations," 212). Dunn (I:xlv) and Moo (I:11-13) say it was mainly to the Gentile Christians.

Hendriksen is surely right, though, when he says that regarding the main point of Romans this whole question is really irrelevant, since it applies equally to both groups (I:23). *All* are sinners (3:9, 23), *no one* will be saved by law (3:19-20), and *all* are equal recipients of the grace that is in Christ Jesus (3:24; 4:11-12). Hendriksen stresses Rom 10:12-13, "For there is no difference between Jew and Gentile — the same Lord is Lord of all and richly blesses all who call on him, for, 'Everyone who calls on the name of the Lord will be saved.'"

V. THE OCCASION OF THE WRITING

What were the circumstances that prompted Paul to write his epistle to the Romans? We have already noted that he wrote the letter during his three-month stay in Corinth on his final mission trip. What sorts of things were going through his mind that led him to write it at that particular time?

We are fortunate that Paul reveals his mind to us in certain statements of his desires and plans in chapters 1 and 15. These statements show us what occasioned the writing of Romans.

One main consideration was Paul's immediate travel plans, as they related to his all-determining calling as apostle to the Gentiles (15:15-24). He refers to his "priestly duty of proclaiming the gospel of God, so that the Gentiles might become an offering acceptable to God" (15:16). For twenty years he had been preaching in the eastern and northeastern sections of the Mediterranean area, and had covered it well. "So from Jerusalem all the way around to Illyricum," he says, "I have fully proclaimed the gospel of Christ"; so now "there is no more place for me to work in these regions" (15:19, 23). Thus he decided to change his focus to the northwestern section, Spain in particular (15:24, 28). In his mind he was already planning his trip to Spain.

But first he had to go to Jerusalem (15:25-31). His purpose for doing this was to deliver the funds he had been collecting from the Gentile churches "for the poor among the saints in Jerusalem" (15:26). He wanted to do this personally, to make sure that the funds were properly received (15:28). To this end he asked the

Roman Christians to offer two specific prayers for him (15:30-31).

First, he knew that he still had many enemies in Jerusalem among the Jews especially. He knew that some of these enemies had already tried to kill him. Thus he really was not sure what dangers he might be facing in Jerusalem. Nevertheless he was determined to go (Acts 20:22-23), so he requested that the Roman Christians "pray that I may be rescued from the unbelievers in Judea" (15:31). He was not afraid of losing his life; he just did not want his newly-formed missionary plans to be aborted (Acts 20:24; Rom 15:32).

Second, Paul was not really sure how the offering from the Gentile churches would be received by the Jewish saints in Jerusalem. There were still a lot of suspicions and misunderstandings between the two groups, mostly about the relation between the Old and New Covenants and the role of the Mosaic Law in the life of the Christian. Thus the money he was bringing to the poor in Jerusalem was not just an act of charity, but was also a symbol of unity between the two main factions in the church. Thus Paul was anxious that it might be received in the proper spirit, so he asked the Romans to pray "that my service in Jerusalem may be acceptable to the saints there" (15:31).

Thus Paul was ultimately bound for Spain, after an initial trip to Jerusalem. But there was a third item in his itinerary: an intermediate stop in Rome itself (Acts 19:21; 23:11), a place he had never been. So he announced to the Christians in Rome that on his way to Spain he would stop and visit them (15:23, 24, 28). This was something he had longed to do for many years and had even made plans to do (1:11, 13; 15:23), but had "often been hindered from coming to you" (15:22; cf. 1:13).

Paul had many reasons for wanting to visit the church in Rome. For one thing, he wanted to enlist their help for his mission to Spain. "I hope to visit you while passing through and to have you assist me on my journey there," he says (15:24). But he had other reasons that predated his plans for Spain. For example, he seems simply to have desired to visit with the Christians there: to have fellowship with them, to enjoy their company, to be spiritually refreshed by them (15:24, 32), and to be encouraged by them (1:12). After all, he knew quite a few of them personally (16:3-15).

Paul's principal longstanding reason for wanting to visit Rome, though, was his desire to preach the gospel there. "I am obligated," he says, "both to Greeks and non-Greeks, both to the wise and the foolish. That is why I am so eager to preach the gospel also to you who are at Rome" (1:14-15). By this means or by some accompanying means he would be able to "impart to you some spiritual gift to make you strong" (1:11). This would also enable him to "have a harvest among you, just as I have had among the other Gentiles" (1:13).

No wonder that Paul says he was praying "that now at last by God's will the way may be opened for me to come to you" (1:10).

These are the immediate circumstances that prompted Paul to write the epistle to the Romans. But a simple presentation of these facts does not in itself answer the question of exactly *why* he wrote the letter. What was his *purpose* for writing? What did he hope to accomplish by writing this *particular* letter? This is the subject of the next section.

VI. THE PURPOSE OF ROMANS

The question of Paul's *purpose* for writing the epistle to the Romans is very controversial; there is much disagreement about it.[13] Everyone agrees on the facts described above relating to the *occasion* for the writing. The problem is that these facts have to be assessed in view of the contents of the main body of the letter, 1:18-15:13. The question is not just why he wrote a letter to the Roman church, but why he wrote this *specific* letter with this particular content. Why does he write "such a lengthy and involved discussion to a largely unknown congregation"? (Dunn, I:lv).

There are two basic approaches to this question. The older and more traditional approach is that the historical circumstances as described in the previous section were not particularly relevant with regard to Paul's decision to write the letter. Neither Paul's own plans nor the state of the Roman church presented him with a

---

[13]Donfried's volume, *The Romans Debate*, does an excellent job of bringing together representatives of the various views.

pressing need or occasion that required him to write. Thus unlike his other letters, Romans is more or less non-occasional. It is regarded rather as a kind of timeless theological essay on the essence of Christianity. As Sanday and Headlam describe this view, "the main object of the Epistle is doctrinal; it is rather a theological treatise than a letter; its purpose is to instruct the Roman Church in central principles of the faith, and has but little reference to the circumstances of the moment" (xl).

The more recent approaches to the purpose of Romans take the opposite view, that it is "a situational letter rather than a doctrinal treatise" (Jewett, "Argument," 265). Paul was not simply writing an essay detached from his circumstances, but was specifically addressing a particular situation that needed his attention at that time. Thus Romans is just as much an occasional letter as 1 Corinthians or Galatians.

Those who take the latter approach usually go in one of two directions. Some emphasize that Paul wrote the letter to fulfill certain needs of his own, relating to his trip either to Jerusalem or to Spain. Others say that Paul wrote mainly to meet the needs of the Roman church at that particular time.

It is possible, of course, that Paul had more than one purpose for writing Romans, as Cranfield says: "It is surely quite clear that Paul did not have just one single purpose in mind but rather a complex of purposes and hopes" (II:815). Dunn (I:lx) and Moo (I:20) agree.

A. ROMANS IS A DOCTRINAL ESSAY

Now we shall go into a bit more detail concerning the possibilities outlined above. The first view is that Paul was not addressing a specific situation but was writing a timeless doctrinal essay. In its most extreme form this view says that Romans is a complete systematic theology, a compendium of Christian doctrine. Shedd (viii) calls it *"an inspired system of theology, . . .* a complete statement of religious truth." Romans is so "encyclopædic in its structure" that one "need not go outside of this Epistle, in order to know all religious truth."

More recently Bornkamm has taken a similar view, describing Romans as Paul's "last will and testament" — "a summary of his theology in light of the impending danger in Jerusalem" (Donfried, "Presuppositions," 103). Bornkamm says ("Letter," 27-28), "This great document . . . summarizes and develops the most important themes and thoughts of the Pauline message and theology and . . . elevates his theology above the moment of definite situations and conflicts into the sphere of the eternally and universally valid."

Many writers agree that Romans was not occasioned by some immediate need or crisis but was a kind of doctrinal essay. Nygren says (4), "The characteristic and peculiar thing about Romans, differentiating it from the rest of Paul's epistles, is just the fact that it was not, or was only in slight degree aimed at circumstances within a certain congregation." Lenski (10-12) agrees.

Most who take this non-occasional view, however, say that it is an exaggeration to call Romans a full-blown systematic theology. "If Romans is a compendium of theology," says Morris (8), "there are some curious gaps." (See also Moo, I:1; Hendriksen, I:25; W. Williams, 19-20.) It is a doctrinal essay, to be sure, but one that is more focused and limited in its scope.

Just what is the focus of this doctrinal essay? The most common view is that it has to do with the doctrines of salvation, i.e., that Romans is a summary or synopsis of Paul's *gospel*. Morris says that Paul probably thought his three-month, pressure-free sojourn in Corinth was a good time to bring together the timeless teachings that had crystallized in his thinking during his twenty years as a preacher. Thus he sets forth "a summary of the gospel and its consequences as he understood them" (pp. 18-19). Cranfield likewise says it is likely that Paul "was conscious of having reached a certain maturity of experience, reflection and understanding, which made the time ripe for him to attempt, with God's help, such an orderly presentation of the gospel" (II:817).

Vincent summarizes this whole approach quite well when he says that Romans "is distinguished among the epistles by its systematic character. Its object is to present a comprehensive statement of the doctrine of salvation through Christ, not a complete system of christian doctrine" (*Word Studies*, III:x). As Hendriksen says (I:25), "Romans is not really 'a complete compendium of Christian Doctrine.' If it had been Paul's intention to draw up such a document, he would surely have included far more material." The specific doctrine he deals with is one needed not just in Rome but by all people in all times: *"the manner in which sinners are saved."* (See Edwards, 3.)

The idea that Romans is a kind of doctrinal essay focusing on the general doctrine of salvation is correct, in my opinion. However, I do not think it is wise to separate it too sharply from the occasion or circumstances discussed in the last section. I question W. Williams' approach, for example, when he says (19), "The Epistle to the Romans is a discussion of the relation of the Gentile world to God's plan of salvation," and in the next sentence says, "This discussion was incidental to the apostle's circumstances." In my opinion this is a false choice. It *is* an essay on salvation, but its purpose was definitely related to the circumstances at that time, as we shall see below.

B. ROMANS WAS OCCASIONED
BY PAUL'S IMMEDIATE NEEDS

The second major approach to the purpose of Romans is that it was occasioned by the various circumstances relating to Paul's immediate plans in relation to his mission. In other words, it was designed to meet needs that Paul felt in his own life at the time. As Jervell says, "Its raison d'être does not stem from the situation of the Roman congregation, but is to be found in Paul himself at the time of writing" ("Letter," 54).

The main idea here resembles the modern practice of churches requesting that prospective ministers send a tape recording of one of their sermons. In this case Paul takes the initiative and sets forth in writing a "sermon" or a lengthy presentation of his gospel. He does this because he needs to introduce himself to people who are not familiar with him or with what he preaches. Or, he does this because his enemies are spreading false rumors about what he preaches, and are misrepresenting his gospel especially as to what he says about Jew-Gentile relations. Thus Romans is not just a presentation but also a defense of Paul's gospel.

This is how Moo explains the purpose of Romans. The various

circumstances that he faced "forced Paul to write a letter in which he carefully rehearsed his understanding of the gospel, especially as it related to the salvation-historical questions of Jew and Gentile and the continuity of the plan of salvation" (I:20). Bruce agrees that it was "expedient that Paul should communicate to the Roman Christians an outline of the message which he proclaimed. Misrepresentations of his preaching and his apostolic procedure were current and must have found their way to Rome" ("Debate," 182). (See Stuhlmacher, "Purpose," 236.)

Why was it crucial for Paul at this particular time to write such a presentation and defense of his gospel? The answer is that it was necessary in order to facilitate his immediate plans. For one thing, he was on his way to Jerusalem with the offering for the poor saints, and was apprehensive about how this would turn out. Thus some contend that in this letter Paul was rehearsing what he was going to say in Jerusalem in defense of himself and in an effort to seal Jew-Gentile unity. He sent the product to the Roman church in a letter, asking them to pray for him and the upcoming Jerusalem episode (15:30-32). Thus, says Jervell, Romans is Paul's "'collection speech,' or more precisely, the defense which Paul plans to give before the church in Jerusalem." He sends it to Rome "to ask the Roman congregation for solidarity, support, and intercession on his behalf" ("Letter," 56). Dunn calls this Paul's "apologetic purpose" (I:lvi; see I:xlii-xliii).

Though this is a fairly common view today, some object to it or at least doubt that it could be the only purpose for Romans (Moo, I:18). Thus other aspects of Paul's immediate plans must have elicited the letter. One of the most obvious is Paul's plan to visit Rome itself. Though he knew some of the Roman Christians, he had never been in Rome and would not know most of the people there. It must have seemed expedient, then, for him to write a kind of "letter of introduction" to himself, especially in view of the false rumors that were probably afoot.

This is how Morris understands it (16-17). Paul used his three-month interlude in Corinth "to write to the Roman Christians to let them know of his plan to visit them and to set down in order something of what the gospel meant." He wanted to give them "a clear but profound statement of the essential message of Christianity as

he proclaimed it. This will show the Romans where he stands."
MacArthur's view is similar: "Paul's letter to the church at Rome
was, among other things, an introduction to himself as an apostle.
He clearly set forth the gospel he preached and taught, so that
believers in Rome would have complete confidence in his authority" (I:xix). (See also Stott, 34.)

Those who hold this view usually take it a step further, and say
that Paul laid out and defended his gospel to the Romans as a
means of enlisting their support for his Spanish mission. In a real
sense Rome was just a means to an end, both in Paul's itinerary and
in his missionary strategy. He needed them as a kind of "base of
operations" for what he hoped to accomplish in Spain (Stott, 33).
Thus "if Rome was to be his base, the Romans would need to be
assured of his message and theological position" (Morris, 17). This
is what Dunn calls Paul's "missionary purpose" for Romans (I:lv).
This is a fairly common view. (See Cranfield, II:817-818; Jewett,
"Argument," 266, 277.)

C. ROMANS WAS OCCASIONED BY NEEDS AT ROME ITSELF

As we have just seen, those who believe the writing of Romans
was motivated by the immediate circumstances sometimes locate
those circumstances in Paul's own personal needs. Others who take
the occasional approach, however, believe that the situation in
Rome itself is what Paul is specifically addressing in this epistle.
Though he had not been there, he still would have been acquainted
with the state of the Roman church. It was, after all, a famous
church (1:8). Besides, Paul's Roman friends, such as Aquila and
Priscilla (16:3), would probably have kept him informed especially
of any problems that existed there (Sanday and Headlam, xl-xli).

Whatever the nature of those problems or needs, Paul wrote to
resolve them. Since all of Paul's other letters were "addressed to
the specific situations of the churches or persons involved," says
Donfried, we must begin with the assumption that Romans "was
written by Paul to deal with a concrete situation in Rome" ("Presuppositions," 103). This is what Dunn calls Paul's "pastoral purpose"
(I:lvi-lviii).

COLLEGE PRESS NIV COMMENTARY

1. The Need for Jew-Gentile Unity

What sorts of needs existed at Rome that would call forth from Paul's pen the most magnificent gospel tract ever written? Several possibilities are suggested, but the one most commonly held begins with the assumption that there was considerable tension in the Roman church between the Jewish Christians and the Gentile Christians. Thus the purpose of Paul's letter was to resolve this tension.

This view usually grows out of the speculations (discussed above) concerning the development of the Roman church following Claudius' decree expelling the Jews from Rome. With Jewish Christians being forced to leave Rome, the Gentile Christians became the dominant force; and this situation prevailed even after the former returned to Rome. This led to conflict between the two factions. This scenario is supported by the various references to Jews and Gentiles (Greeks) in Romans, by the discussion of the weak (Jews?) and the strong (Gentiles?) in 14:1-15:13, and by several references to unity and division within the church (12:16; 15:5; 16:17-18). Such texts seem to be evidence of a "basic division existing between the Jewish Christians and the Gentile Christians at Rome" (P. Williams, "Purpose," 64).

This view has been argued by Marxsen[14] and more recently by Wiefel, who concludes that Romans "was written to assist the Gentile Christian majority, who are the primary addressees of the letter, to live together with the Jewish Christians in one congregation, thereby putting an end to their quarrels about status" ("Community," 96). Here is Edwards' summary (15-16):

> Romans is addressed to the problems which inevitably resulted when Jewish Christians began returning to Rome following the edict of Claudius. We can imagine their trials of readjusting to churches which had become increasingly Gentile in their absence. Would Gentile believers who had established their supremacy during the Jewish absence, and for whom the law was now largely irrelevant, continue to find

---

[14]See the summary of Marxsen in Donfried, "Note," 46-49.

a place within their fellowship for a Jewish Christian minority which still embraced the law? Paul cannot have been unaware of such concerns.

In Dunn's words, "Paul wrote to counter (potential) divisions within Rome among the Christian house churches, particularly the danger of gentile believers despising less liberated Jewish believers" (I:lvii). (See also Stott, 34-36.)

2. The Need for an Apostolic Foundation

Another possible need being addressed by Paul is related to the circumstances of the origin of the church in Rome. It is inferred from 15:20 that no apostle was involved in its founding, nor as yet had even visited Rome. Thus Paul was concerned that the church did not have a solid apostolic foundation (see Eph 2:20), and he writes this epistle in order to provide that foundation. This is the view of Günter Klein ("Purpose," 39, 42), but Morris (11-12) gives reasons for doubting it.

3. The Need for Paul's Gospel

Another possibility (to which I subscribe) is that Paul did indeed recognize the need of the Roman church to hear his apostolic preaching and teaching, but not necessarily in a foundational sense. This view begins with Paul's sense of duty, based upon his special calling, to preach the gospel to everyone in the Gentile world (1:14), including those in Rome: "That is why I am so eager to preach the gospel also to you who are at Rome" (1:15).

But these people are already Christians. Why would Paul want to "preach the gospel" to *believers*? Here is a point that is often missed: the gospel is more than just the initial evangelistic witness given to unbelievers with a view to their conversion. It also includes the deeper meaning and implications of the basic facts of salvation, which are things about which even mature believers can never hear enough. That Paul wanted to preach the gospel to the Christians in Rome means that he wanted to go deeper into the meaning of

Christ's saving work "for our sins," unfolding for them the full power of the gospel in the Christian life and at the same time clearing up common misunderstandings that may arise through incomplete knowledge.

Paul's desire, of course, was to do this in person, and he had often planned to travel to Rome for this very reason. Up to this point, however, God's providence had prevented it (1:13; 15:22). Now he is once again planning to go to Rome, after his trip to Jerusalem with the offering. But based on his past experience and the uncertainty about what would happen to him in Jerusalem (Acts 20:22-24), at this point he could not be certain that he would ever reach Rome in person.[15]

This led Paul to the conclusion that if he was ever going to preach the gospel in Rome, perhaps the only way he would be able to do so was *in writing*.[16] Thus he takes the time, while staying in Corinth just before traveling to Jerusalem, to prepare a well-thought-out essay on the gospel as every Christian needs to hear it; and he sends it on to Rome in advance of his intended trip there. Thus it seems likely, says Campbell, that "the letter is the written equivalent of the oral presentation which Paul would have delivered to the congregation had he himself been present" ("Key," 258).

According to this view, then, Romans is not just a basic presentation of the gospel, written in order to provide the Roman Christians with a missing apostolic foundation. And as Nygren (7) rightly notes, "it is a misunderstanding of Romans to see in it a typical example of Paul's missionary preaching." This is contrary to those who think Paul was just introducing himself to the Roman church, hoping to win their support for his mission to Spain by rehearsing the gospel as he usually preached it. Stuhlmacher rightly notes that how Paul "preached and taught as a missionary cannot be simply inferred from the outline of Romans" ("Purpose," 242).

---

[15]See Sanday and Headlam, xlii. Later God assured him that he would indeed "testify in Rome" (Acts 23:11).

[16]"Prevented from fulfilling this desire [to visit Rome and preach in person] he pens the epistle in pursuance of his apostolic commission" (Murray, I:xv).

INTRODUCTION COLLEGE PRESS NIV COMMENTARY

According to this view, then, the primary purpose for Romans is not related to some need within Paul himself (e.g., his concern for defending himself; his missionary plans); nor is it related to some negative situation in the Roman church (e.g., Jew-Gentile disunity). It is motivated rather by Paul's loving concern for his fellow-Christians at Rome, and his desire to bless their hearts and lives with this written version of the deeper aspects of the gospel of grace. This point is brought out very well by Hendriksen (I:24):

> Paul, being an intensely warm and loving person, desires to go to Rome in order to be a blessing to his friends (Rom. 1:10, 11) and to be refreshed by them (15:32). Moreover, it is for this same reason that he, now that it is impossible for him to go to Rome *immediately*, communicates with the Roman church by means of this letter. He writes to the Romans because he loves them. They are his friends "in Christ," and by means of this letter he imparts his love to them . . . .
> It is strange that this deeply personal reason . . . , a reason clearly brought out by the apostle himself, is often overlooked. At times the emphasis is placed entirely on theological motivation or on mission incentive: Paul wants to correct errors of the antinomians and/or wants to make Rome the headquarters for the evangelization of Spain. To be sure, these matters are important, but we should *begin* with the reason first stated by Paul himself in this very epistle.

D. CONCLUSION

We have surveyed the main reasons why Paul wrote the epistle to the Romans. It should be obvious that some of these reasons may overlap or be combined; so we need not focus narrowly upon just one of them. Jewett, for example, says the immediate reason was to resolve the Jew-Gentile tensions, but this was sought in order to gain a strong and unified backing for the mission to Spain ("Argument," 266). After summarizing the missionary, apologetic, and pastoral purposes, Dunn concludes that "all three of these main emphases and purposes hang together and indeed reinforce each other when taken as a whole" (I:lviii).

In my opinion, though, the dominant reason is the last one discussed above: Paul's desire to preach the gospel to the Romans, and his decision to do so in the form of an epistle. This is the factor that Paul stresses in the introductory section of the letter, where we would expect him to say what is closest to his heart. It seems inappropriate to give priority to ch. 15 on this matter, and to pass over what Paul himself chooses to mention first of all. Just because he tells the Romans about his plans in ch. 15 is no reason to assume that his purpose for writing to Rome is specifically or directly related to these plans.

We may conclude, then, that Romans is indeed an *occasional* letter, that it was occasioned by the need of the Roman Christians to hear Paul's gospel and by the circumstances that made it expedient for him to send it to them in written form at this particular time. Thus Romans is by design a clear presentation of the deeper implications of the gospel, written not for Paul's sake but for the sake of the church at Rome. The references to Paul's own plans and needs in ch. 15 are secondary.

At the same time, just because of the nature of the situation that caused Paul to write this epistle, the purpose for Romans includes the first view discussed above, namely, that it was intended to be a kind of doctrinal essay focusing on the meaning of salvation through the grace of our Lord Jesus Christ. As noted above, it is a systematic presentation of the *gospel*: not necessarily the gospel as proclaimed in an evangelistic situation, but the gospel as unfolded to mature Christians.

When this point is understood, we can see that the epistle to the Romans is intended not just for the saints in Rome in the middle of the first century A.D., but for all Christians in all ages. It is relevant for all since it deals with salvation from sin through God's grace. As Moo rightly says (I:21),

> That Paul was dealing in Romans with immediate concerns in the early church we do not doubt. But, especially in Romans, these issues are ultimately the issues of the church — and the world — of all ages: the continuity of God's plan of salvation, the sin and need of human beings, God's provision for our sin problem in Christ, the means to a life of holiness, security in the face of suffering and death.

The circumstances contributing to the writing of this letter were far broader than the immediate situation in Rome and Paul's own immediate travel plans. They included Paul's own pre-Christian life as a Jew who sought acceptance with God on the basis of his own righteousness. They included Paul's twenty years of preaching to sinners of all types, Jews and Gentiles. They included his dealings with new Christians and new churches with all their weaknesses and problems. His experience and knowledge of human nature and human need were personal and comprehensive; thus the gospel of Romans is generic and timeless.

In most of the discussions of the purpose of Romans, a forgotten factor is the role of the Holy Spirit in the inspiration of Scripture. It is Paul himself who tells us that "all Scripture is God-breathed" (2 Tim 3:16). Whatever circumstances led Paul to compose his letter to the Romans, the choice to write and the message he wrote were not his alone. The Holy Spirit worked through Paul to produce this letter (see 2 Pet 1:20-21), and the Holy Spirit knows more than any man what is needed by every sinner and by every Christian seeking peace and power. In the final analysis it is the Spirit of God, and not just the Apostle Paul, who speaks to our hearts in the epistle to the Romans.

VII. THE THEME OF ROMANS

Almost everyone today rejects the idea that Romans is a compendium or summary of Christian theology as such. It is nevertheless generally recognized that the content of the epistle is doctrinal in nature. Its main body is an essay or treatise with a strong doctrinal emphasis and seems to be built around a particular theme. The question now is, exactly what *is* the theme of Romans? Several answers have been proposed.

A. JUSTIFICATION BY FAITH

The Reformation established a way of looking at Romans that still has considerable support among Protestants, namely, that the main theme of the epistle is stated in 1:16-17. It can be summed up in the familiar phrase, "justification by faith," i.e., justification or righteousness before God comes through faith alone. John Calvin (xxix) states succinctly that "the main subject of the whole Epistle" is "justification by faith."

Boers says this is the theme that "currently almost universally controls the interpretation of the letter" (*Justification*, 77). This is surely an exaggeration, but the justification view is still very popular. Concerning the principal content of Romans, Nygren says (16), "From the beginning evangelical Christianity has spoken clearly on that point: justification by faith. That answer is correct." Defining "theme" as "central topic" rather than as exclusive topic, Hendriksen agrees that justification by faith, "spread out into 'justification by grace through faith'. . . , is clearly the theme of Romans" (I:29). Edwards (3) says that "the driving concern throughout is *salvation* − that righteousness comes as a free gift of God and is received by faith alone." Stott (35) says two themes are woven together in the epistle. "The first is the justification of guilty sinners by God's grace alone in Christ alone through faith alone, irrespective of either status or works."

Many scholars today have rejected this traditional approach. Though justification by faith is a main topic in Romans, says Boers (88), it "never becomes thematic." Too much of its subject matter simply does not relate to this subject, he says (78). Moo agrees (I:26-27). (See Stott, 24-31.)

B. THE RIGHTEOUSNESS OF GOD

Those who are not satisfied with justification by faith as the theme for Romans sometimes opt for one that is very similar, namely, the righteousness of God (1:17). Beker says this is "the key term for the letter as a whole" ("Faithfulness," 331). Jewett says the thesis of Romans is that the gospel is "the 'power of God' to achieve the triumph of divine righteousness (Rom. 1:16-17)" ("Argument," 266).

Since the righteousness of God is integrally related to justification by faith, the two themes are sometimes confused. This is because one aspect of the theme of divine righteousness is that the righteousness of God is the basis for the personal justification of individual sinners. This is the sense in which Nygren says that the righteousness of God — in the sense of righteousness *from* God — is "the fundamental concept" and "the very foundation thought" of the epistle (9, 14-15), even though he says the "principal content" of the letter is justification by faith (16).

But most of those today who say that the righteousness of God is the theme of Romans are using the expression in a broader, more comprehensive sense. For them it includes the idea of the divine righteousness as the basis for individual justification, to be sure. For example, Stuhlmacher says the theme of Romans is "the gospel of the divine righteousness in Christ for those who believe from among the Jews and Gentiles" ("Theme," 334, 337). But in Romans, they say, the theme is more inclusive than this. It includes God's righteousness as the basis not only of his dealings with individual believers, but also of his dealings with mankind in general and especially with the Jewish nation in the context of redemptive history.

The question raised by the indiscriminate offer of justification by faith to both Jews and Gentiles is whether God is being fair with the Jews, in view of all the special treatment he has already bestowed upon them and the special promises he has given them. Does the gospel's "no partiality" principle bring God's justice or righteousness into question? "What is at stake is nothing less than the faithfulness of God," says Beker ("Faithfulness," 330); and this is what Paul is dealing with especially in Rom 9-11. Stuhlmacher explains that the "righteousness of God" refers to "the entire redemptive activity of God in Christ from creation to redemption" ("Theme," 341).

Thus according to this view the theme of Romans is not just the salvation of man but the defense of God, with perhaps the greater emphasis falling on the latter. As Fiensy says (227), "Romans is then a theodicy or defense of God in light of the Jewish-Gentile problem in the church." Gaertner says that the kinds of questions Paul raises in Romans (e.g., 3:3; 3:5; 3:29; 9:14) inquire into the nature of God's dealings with sinners, especially with his fairness and faithfulness. Thus Gaertner labels Romans "the gospel of God's fairness" ("Fairness," 1:14).

C. THE EQUALITY OF JEWS AND GENTILES

A third view is that the theme of Romans is the equality of Jews and Gentiles in God's plan of salvation. This is currently a popular view. It stems mainly from the reconstruction of the origin and development of the Roman church as described earlier in this introduction. It goes hand in hand with the idea that the letter is intended to deal with certain specific circumstances existing in Rome, especially the apparent disunity between Jewish and Gentile Christians. It recognizes that "the entire letter to the Romans is . . . permeated with Jew-Gentile issues" (Fiensy, *Introduction*, 230).

In its most general form this view says that the main emphasis of Romans is the universality of the gospel: there is just one way of salvation for Jews and Gentiles alike. The transcendent gospel goes beyond the Jew-Gentile distinction. God's salvation is given to both groups equally, favoring neither and offering favor to both.

Boers is an example of this view. He says the consistent theme of the main body of Romans is "salvation of Jews and gentiles, and the relationship between them" (*Justification*, 80). This theme is stated in Rom 1:16, "that the gospel is the power of God for all who believe, to the Jews first, and to the Hellenes" (80). That salvation is offered to the Jews *first* is important, but so is the idea that "there is no difference between Jews and gentiles" (81-82).

Dunn says, "It is precisely the tension between 'Jew first but also Greek' (1:16), which . . . provides an integrating motif for the whole letter." Paul's "repeated emphasis on 'all'" underscores the theme of universality. Even the emphasis on the righteousness of God "is primarily an exposition of the same Jew/Gentile theme," i.e., it is Paul's way of arguing that Gentiles are full recipients of the saving grace of God as much as Jews are (I:lxii-lxiii).

As noted earlier, Stott says two themes are woven together in Romans, the first being justification by faith. But since this applies equally to all people, it is the "fundamental basis of Christian unity." This provides the second theme of Romans, that "'there is no difference' now between Jews and Gentiles. . . . Indeed, 'the single most important theme of Romans is the equality of Jews and Gentiles'" (35-36).

Interpreters differ as to the nature of the circumstances that led

Paul to emphasize the theme of equality. Some say the Gentile Christians at Rome did not want to fully accept the Jewish Christians, so Romans is basically defending the right of the latter to full status in the Kingdom of God. This is how Boers understands the "Jews first" theme, as noted above. Jewett says, "Nowhere else in Paul's writings are the concerns of Jewish Christians taken up in so systematic and friendly a manner, thus counterbalancing the prejudices of the Gentile majority of Roman Christians" ("Argument," 276). The development of this theme in Rom 9-11 "is relevant to the situation in Rome," says Bruce. Here Paul "warns the Gentiles among his readers not to despise the Jews, . . . because God has not written them off" ("Debate," 183-184).

On the other hand, some say the problem in Rome was the status of the Gentile Christians. W. Williams says (19-20), "The Epistle to the Romans is a discussion of the relation of the Gentile world to God's plan of salvation." More specifically, Romans is Paul's "defense of the rights of the Gentiles against the Jewish assumption that excluded them from the Church, and from the chance of salvation." Thus "the sole intent of the apostle was to maintain the equality of the Gentiles against the assumption of the Jews." Stendahl agrees that Paul's concern is the salvation of the Gentiles. Even the subject of justification serves the purpose of "defending the rights of Gentile converts to be full and genuine heirs to the promises of God to Israel" (*Paul*, 2-4).

Either way the subject is approached, the main point is the same: the principal theme of Romans is to demonstrate the equality of Jews and Gentiles with regard to the saving grace of God.

D. SINNERS ARE SAVED BY GRACE, NOT LAW

All of the themes discussed above are certainly present in Romans, and all are important. All of them contribute significantly to the main theme. But I believe none of them as such is the main point Paul is communicating to us in the epistle. Rather than seeing 1:16-17 as the thesis statement for Paul's treatise, I see it more or less as the starting point leading up to the thesis, which is 3:28: "For we maintain that a man is justified by faith apart from observing the law."

In the most general sense Paul's thesis relates to the *gospel*, since his desire to preach the gospel in Rome (1:15) is what led him to compose the epistle as a written version of his gospel. In this sense Moo is correct: "What, then, is the theme of the letter? If we have to choose one — and perhaps it would be better not to — we would choose 'the gospel.'" Romans is simply "Paul's statement of 'his' gospel" (I:28).

But since the gospel is the good news about salvation, also in a general sense the theme of Romans is *salvation*. As Harrison says (7), "Salvation is the basic theme of Romans (cf. 1:16) — a salvation presented in terms of the righteousness of God, which, when received by faith, issues in life (1:17)." Or as Hendriksen says, the basic doctrine at stake (especially in 1:16-8:39) is *"the manner in which sinners are saved"* (I:25). And the manner in which sinners are saved, whether Jews or Gentiles, is the same: justification by faith.

But the theme of Romans is more precise than this. Yes, sinners are justified by faith, but this means they are *not* justified by works of law, which is the only alternative. It is just as important to include the negative statement in the theme as the positive one.

In actuality, then, the basic theme of Romans is the contrast between law and grace as ways of salvation. This contrast is seen especially in 3:28, which (literally translated) says, "For we maintain that a man is justified by faith apart from works of law." The contrast is stated succinctly in 6:14, "You are not under law, but under grace." *This* is the gospel, the good news of salvation. Certainly it is good news to know that God justifies us by faith in the saving work of Jesus Christ. But in a real sense it is also good news to know that we are *not* justified by law-keeping: a way of salvation which is not only futile but which sinners in their hearts *know* is futile, and which thus leads only to self-deception or to despair.

Commenting on Romans, Grubbs says, "The Gospel *versus* the Law is the one theme of which he [Paul] never loses sight in the elaboration of the details of this wonderful production" (9). Though this is a very common way of speaking — "gospel versus law" — it is not altogether accurate. The real contrast is *grace* versus law, and this message as a whole is the gospel.

Thus Paul's theme is indeed that we are saved by grace, *not* by law. Law is not a viable option as a means of salvation; the only way for sinners to be counted righteous before God is by grace. Yes, we are justified by faith, but not by works of law. Yes, the righteousness of God figures prominently in our justification, but in contrast to the righteousness of man. Yes, Romans does emphasize full equality regarding this way of salvation; Jews and Gentiles are saved the same way. Both are saved by grace and justified by faith as provided by the righteousness of God, but in contrast with every false way.

This contrast between law and grace as competing ways of salvation is not a matter of OT versus NT nor Old Covenant versus New Covenant, as if law were the way to be saved prior to Christ and grace is the way to be saved now that Christ has come. Also, the contrast between law and grace — THIS IS VERY IMPORTANT — is not simply the Law of Moses versus the grace of Jesus Christ. No sinner has ever been saved nor can be saved by the law that applies to him, whether it be the Law of Moses for Jews under the Old Covenant, or some other comparable set of God's commandments for anyone else in any other time. Every sinner who has been saved since the time of Adam has been saved by grace and not by law, and this will always be the case.

The problem that Paul addresses in the book of Romans is not one that confronts Jews only, nor Gentiles only. It is not a problem faced only by those who are under the Mosaic Law, nor only by those to whom the Mosaic Law does not apply. The problem being addressed is this: *As a sinner, how can I be saved?* It is a problem faced by Jews and Gentiles alike, and the solution is the same for both.

Perhaps even more significantly, the problem addressed in Romans is not one confronted only by unbelieving sinners. It is a problem that believers often wrestle with as well (e.g., the Judaizers). When we state the problem thus — "As a sinner, how can I be saved?" — we can break it down into two separate problems. First is the unbeliever's problem: "How can I *become* saved?" The answer is: by grace through faith, not by works of law.[17] Second is the believer's continuing problem: "How can I *stay* saved?" And the answer is: by grace through faith, not by works of law.

---

[17]How baptism fits into this answer is discussed in our comments on 1:17 and 6:1-5.

This is why the epistle to the Romans has always been and always will be in a class by itself with regard to its impact on individuals and upon the church as a whole. Its basic theme is one that is always needed and always applicable, and one that will result in the highest praise to God the Redeemer once it is understood.

VIII. OUTLINE OF ROMANS 1–8

PROLOGUE — 1:1-17

I. EPISTOLARY GREETING — 1:1-7
  A. The Author Introduces Himself — 1:1
    1. A Slave of Christ Jesus
    2. Called to Be an Apostle
    3. Set Apart for the Gospel of God
  B. The Gospel and the Old Testament — 1:2
  C. The Subject of the Gospel Is Jesus — 1:3-4
    1. The Two Natures of Jesus
    2. The Incarnation
    3. Messiahship
    4. The Two States of Jesus
    5. The Resurrection of Jesus
    6. The Son's Full Identity
  D. Paul's Apostleship — 1:5
    1. The Origin of Paul's Apostleship
    2. The Character of Paul's Apostleship
    3. The Focus of Paul's Apostleship
    4. The Purpose of Paul's Apostleship
    5. The Goal of Paul's Apostleship
  E. The Recipients of Paul's Letter — 1:6-7a
  F. The Blessing — 1:7b
II. PERSONAL REMARKS — 1:8-15
  A. Paul's Prayers for the Romans — 1:8-10
  B. Paul's Desires Regarding Rome — 1:11-13
  C. Paul's Debt to the Romans — 1:14-15
III. TRANSITIONAL STATEMENT — 1:16-17
  A. The Glory of the Gospel — 1:16a

B. The Power of the Gospel – 1:16b

C. The Scope of the Gospel – 1:16c

D. Faith and the Gospel – 1:16c

   1. Faith Is a Condition for Salvation

   2. Faith Is Not the Only Condition

E. The Heart of the Gospel – 1:17a

F. The Golden Text of the Gospel – 1:17b

PART ONE: THE IMPOTENCE OF LAW
AS A WAY OF SALVATION – 1:18-3:20

I. THE SINFULNESS OF THE GENTILES – 1:18-32

   A. Universal Knowledge of God and His Law – 1:18-20

   B. Universal Rejection of the True God – 1:21-25

   C. The Utter Depths of Gentile Depravity – 1:26-32

II. THE SINFULNESS OF THE JEWS – 2:1-3:8

   A. Jews Are Under the Wrath of God, No Less Than the Gentiles – 2:1-5

   B. God Will Be Partial to No One in the Judgment – 2:6-11

   C. Under Law, the Criterion of Judgment Is Obedience Alone – 2:12-16

   D. Jews Who Look to the Law for Salvation Are Condemned by Their Own Disobedience – 2:17-24

   E. True Jewishness Is Identified Not by Circumcision but by the Inward State of the Heart – 2:25-29

   F. Such Equal Treatment of Jews and Gentiles Does Not Nullify But Rather Magnifies God's Righteousness – 3:1-8

III. UNIVERSAL SINFULNESS AND HOPELESSNESS UNDER LAW – 3:9-20

PART TWO: THE ALL-SUFFICIENCY OF GRACE
AS A WAY OF SALVATION – 3:21-5:21

I. GRACE AS JUSTIFICATION BY CHRIST'S BLOOD THROUGH FAITH – 3:21-31

   A. Righteousness Through Faith Is Now Fully Revealed – 3:21-23

  B. Sinners Are Justified by the Blood of Christ — 3:24-26

  C. Sinners Are Justified by Faith Apart from Works of Law — 3:27-28

  D. The Way of Grace Is Available to All — 3:29-30

  E. Grace Lets Law Do Its Proper Work — 3:31

II. ABRAHAM: PARADIGM OF GRACE — 4:1-25

  A. Abraham Was Justified by Faith Apart from Works — 4:1-5

  B. David Explains and Confirms Justification by Faith Apart from Works — 4:6-8

  C. Membership in Abraham's Family Is by Faith, Not by Circumcision — 4:9-12

  D. The Inheritance Promised to Abraham Comes by Faith, Not by Law — 4:13-17a

  E. Faith Means Giving Glory to God and Believing His Promises — 4:17b-22

  F. Those Who Believe Like Abraham Are Justified Like Abraham — 4:23-25

III. GRACE AND ASSURANCE — 5:1-21

  A. Assurance of Personal Salvation — 5:1-11

    1. Justification by Faith Is the Key to Assurance — 5:1-2

    2. Tribulations of Believers Do Not Nullify Assurance — 5:3-5

    3. Christ Died for Us While We Were Still Sinners — 5:6-8

    4. Our Hope Is Even More Secure Now That We Are His Friends — 5:9-11

  B. The All-Sufficiency of the Death of Christ — 5:12-21

    1. One Sin of One Man (Adam) Brought Sin and Death to All — 5:12-14

    2. Christ and His Sacrifice Are Greater Than Adam and His Sin — 5:15-17

    3. Christ's Cross Completely Cancels the Results of Adam's Sin — 5:18-19

    4. Grace Triumphs over Sin and Death — 5:20-21

PART THREE: THE ALL-SUFFICIENCY OF GRACE GIVES VICTORY OVER SIN — 6:1-8:39

I. OBJECTIONS TO GRACE BASED ON A FEAR OF ANTINOMIANISM — 6:1-7:13

A. **Does Grace Make Sin Irrelevant? NO!** — 6:1-14
B. **Does Freedom from Law Mean We Are Free to Sin? NO!**
   — 6:15-7:6
  1. We Are Slaves to God — 6:15-23
  2. We Obey God from Our Hearts — 7:1-6
C. **Does Grace Mean That Law Is Bad? NO!** — 7:7-13
II. **GRACE GIVES VICTORY OVER SIN** — 7:14-8:13
  A. **The Christian Continues to Struggle Against Sin** — 7:14-25
    1. The Nature of the Struggle — 7:14-20
    2. The Source of the Struggle — 7:21-25
  B. **Victory over Sin Comes Through the Holy Spirit** — 8:1-13
    1. God Frees Us from Sin's Penalty and Power — 8:1-4
    2. Sin and Death Are Defeated in Us Through the Holy
      Spirit — 8:5-13
III. **THE ASSURANCE OF FINAL AND TOTAL VICTORY
OVER THE FALLEN WORLD** — 8:14-39
  A. **The Holy Spirit Marks Us as Sons and Heirs** — 8:14-17
  B. **The Redeemed Cosmos Is Our Inheritance** — 8:18-25
  C. **God Promises to Bring His Family Through Earthly Trials**
    — 8:26-30
  D. **God's Gracious Love Gives Us Unshakable Assurance** —
    8:31-39

1:1-17 — PROLOGUE

I. 1:1-7 — EPISTOLARY GREETING

In the Greek this section is one long sentence. It has the same general form as a standard epistolary greeting of the time, but is much longer. A normal greeting would have been something like this: "From Paul, to the saints in Rome, greetings." (See Jas 1:1 for something close to this.) It is lengthy even for Paul, and is the longest greeting of all his epistles. This is a great blessing to us, since it contains a wealth of doctrinal content that must be carefully unpacked.

A. THE AUTHOR INTRODUCES HIMSELF (1:1)

1:1 Paul, a servant of Christ Jesus, called to be an apostle and set apart for the gospel of God . . . . Here (see v. 5 also) Paul succinctly introduces himself to the Roman Christians by describing himself in three important ways. Perhaps he felt the need for this careful introduction because he had not yet been to Rome and was not known personally to many of the Christians there.

1. A Slave of Christ Jesus

Paul describes himself first of all as a slave of Christ Jesus. The NIV term "servant" is too weak. The Greek word, *doulos*, was almost always used of a true slave. The NASB term "bond-servant" is very close to this idea. "Bondslave" (e.g., 1 Pet 2:16, NASB) is redundant.

In the Greek world a slave was basically the property of an

owner and had no say with regard to his circumstances. He was "in a permanent relation of servitude to another, his will altogether swallowed up in the will of the other" (Trench, *Synonyms*, 30). The slave had no choice regarding his service, "which he has to perform whether he likes or not, because he is subject as a slave to an alien will, to the will of his owner." The term thus refers to "a state of affairs which one cannot escape and the consequences of which one must accept if one is not to incur punishment" (Rengstorf, 261, 270).

At the same time the OT Law presents the possibility of a person's entering such a state voluntarily. When the time came for a temporary slave to be set free, he could willingly choose to surrender himself back to his owner in a state of permanent servitude. Such a decision was usually based on love for the owner, or for family members that might be left behind if freedom were chosen (Exod 21:5-6; Deut 15:12-17).

Paul applies this term to himself here and elsewhere (Gal 1:10; Phil 1:1; Titus 1:1). The NT applies it to other individuals also (Phil 1:1; Col 4:12; 2 Tim 2:24; Jas 1:1; 2 Pet 1:1; Jude 1). Some are called σύνδουλος (*syndoulos*), or "fellow-slave" (Col 1:7; 4:7). Sometimes Christians in general are described by the term δοῦλος (*doulos*) (6:16; 1 Cor 7:22; 1 Pet 2:16).

Paul was not a slave to any human master; in fact, he was a freeborn Roman citizen (Acts 22:24-29). He tells us that he was rather a slave "of Christ Jesus." This is how he thought of his Christian existence first of all; this was the key to his self-identity.

This is true of Christians in general: being a Christian means being a slave of Jesus. This is a main implication of our confession that "Jesus is Lord" (10:9). His Lordship is his ownership and authority over his property, his slaves. Thus in our confession we acknowledge that Jesus is our owner and that we are his property. We voluntarily surrender our wills to his and put ourselves at his disposal. We accept this as our natural state and commit ourselves to unconditional service solely for the glory of God (Phil 2:11).

Such acceptance of the role of a slave is of course the very antithesis of the sinful world's ideal of autonomy or total freedom from authority. This was true in the ancient Greek world, where such freedom was prized as the basis of personal dignity. "Hence the Greek can only reject and scorn the type of service which in inner or outer structure bears even the slightest resemblance to that of the slave" (Rengstorf, 261-262). The same is no less true in the modern world, which is characterized by the spirit of autonomy, lawlessness, and rebellion against authority. Thus when we accept the basic role of "slave of Christ Jesus," we are no longer conforming ourselves to the pattern of this world (12:2).

All of this is involved in Paul's identification of himself as a slave of Christ Jesus; he thought of himself as Jesus' property. He felt himself to be under compulsion to obey Jesus and to live out his calling. In a sense he had no choice; he was totally under the authority of Jesus Christ. In this sense he calls himself a "debtor" (1:14, KJV) in reference to preaching the gospel. "I am compelled to preach," he says. "Woe to me if I do not preach the gospel!" (1 Cor 9:16).

Yet at the same time, Paul the slave served Christ Jesus willingly, from his heart. His compulsion was grounded in love, not fear (2 Cor 5:14). Not only did he say, "I am debtor" or "I am obligated" to preach (1:14), but he also declared "I am ready" or "I am eager" to preach the gospel (1:15). His heart was in it, and he would not have had it any other way. We may note that Paul also calls himself a "servant" (διάκονος, *diakonos*) of the gospel (Eph 3:7), and a "minister" (λειτουργός, *leitourgos*) of Christ (15:16). These terms do not have the connotation of compulsion or servitude, but focus on the fact that the servant is doing a specific work on behalf of someone else. The exact nature of Paul's work as a servant is given in the two other ways he describes himself in this verse.

2. Called to Be an Apostle

The second thing Paul says about himself is that he has been "called to be an apostle" (κλητὸς ἀπόστολος, *klētos apostolos*). In this phrase "called" (*klētos*) is an adjective form of καλέω (*kaleō*), and the verb "to be" has been supplied by the translator. The same is true in 1 Cor 1:1; and the same phrasing is used in Rom 1:7 for Christians ("called to be saints"; see 1 Cor 1:2). Hendriksen (I:39-40) and MacArthur (I:6) say this should be translated "a called apostle." We reject this on the grounds that there is no such thing as an *uncalled* apostle; thus such a phrase would be redundant and misleading.

In 1 Cor 15:9 Paul says he does not "deserve to be called an apostle" (because he had persecuted the church). But there the word "called" is being used in a different sense, i.e., "being named or given the title of" an apostle. Here "called" refers to Paul's Damascus road experience, the occasion when he was confronted by Jesus Christ and commissioned into his service (Acts 9:3-6; 22:6-11; 26:12-18).

The calling to which Paul refers here is similar to the way God called men to serve him in OT times, e.g., Abraham (Gen 12:1); Moses (Exod 3:1-10); and Isaiah (Isa 6:1-13). It was a call to *service*, not a call to *salvation*. The latter concept is in view in 1:6-7, but not here in 1:1. It is very important to understand this distinction, as we shall see in our discussion of Rom 9-11.

The fact that Paul was called by Jesus Christ was the basis for his self-understanding as a slave of Jesus. The call placed upon him the inescapable obligation to do what his Lord commanded him. Also, this call was important to Paul as a basis for the divine authority of his ministry. He did not choose on his own to try to be an apostle; he was *called*! He was not appointed an apostle by any human agent; he was called *directly* by Jesus Christ! See Gal 1:1.

Paul says he was called to be "an apostle." This word comes from the very common verb ἀποστέλλω (*apostellō*), which means "to send (on a mission)." In the NT it often refers to sending someone on a spiritual mission; see Matt 10:5; John 17:18. The noun itself (ἀπόστολος, *apostolos*) is sometimes used in the NT in a generic sense and means simply "someone sent on a mission," i.e., an ambassador, a messenger, a representative, or even a missionary. See Acts 14:14 (Barnabas and Paul); Rom 16:7 (Andronicus and Junias); Phil 2:25 (Epaphroditus); Heb 3:1 (Jesus himself); and 2 Cor 8:23 (unnamed "apostles of the churches").

Most often, though, *apostolos* refers to those who were specially qualified and specially appointed to the highest human office of service to the church. Apostleship is named as the preeminent spiritual gift (1 Cor 12:28-29; Eph 4:11). It is applied to the original group of twelve men chosen by Jesus (Matt 10:2) and to the post-resurrection group of twelve in which Matthias replaced Judas (Acts 1:26). This group is often referred to simply as "the twelve" (e.g., John 6:70-71) or as "the apostles" (e.g., 1 Cor 15:7; Gal 1:17).

Paul often refers to himself as an apostle. He does so in all of his epistles except Philippians, Philemon, and 1 & 2 Thessalonians. See especially 1 Cor 9:1-2; 1 Tim 2:7; 2 Tim 1:11.

What was special about those who were chosen for the office of apostle?[1] First, they were chosen personally by Jesus Christ (John 6:70). This applies to Paul, too (Gal 1:1). Second, they had to be eyewitnesses of Jesus' ministry, especially of his resurrection (Acts 1:21-22). Paul stresses that he qualifies in this respect: "Am I not an apostle? Have I not seen Jesus our Lord?" (1 Cor 9:1; see 15:8). Third, they were endowed with the Holy Spirit (John 14:26; 15:26; 16:12-15; 20:22). Paul was conscious of his own special guidance by the Spirit (1 Cor 2:7-13; 7:40). Fourth, the apostles were given teaching and ruling authority over the whole church (John 20:23; Acts 2:42; 6:6; Eph 2:20; 3:5; 2 Pet 3:2). The Apostle Paul shared this authority (1 Thess 2:6; 1 Tim 2:7). Finally, apostles were given special miraculous powers as signs of their authority (Matt 10:1; Acts 2:43; 5:12; 8:18). The same was true of Paul (15:19; 2 Cor 12:12).

While Paul shared the basic apostolic qualifications with the twelve, in some ways his apostleship was unique. As far as we know, he was not an eyewitness of Jesus' entire ministry, from his baptism by John to his ascension (Acts 1:21-22), though he saw the risen Christ: "Last of all he appeared to me also" (1 Cor 15:8). Because of the unusual circumstances of his call, he refers to himself as "abnormally born" into the office of apostle (1 Cor 15:8). Also, Paul's ministry was unique in that he was specifically appointed to be the apostle to the Gentiles (see v. 5 below).

In no case, however, were Paul's office and apostleship inferior to that of the twelve (2 Cor 11:5; 12:11). As an apostle of Christ Jesus, he spoke with the full authority of Jesus himself. We need to keep this in mind as we read the book of Romans. It is part of "the apostles' teaching" (Acts 2:42); it is Scripture (2 Pet 3:16); it is "the word of God" (1 Thess 2:13).

---

[1]See Hendrickson, I:39, for a good summary of this.

3. Set Apart for the Gospel of God

Paul's three descriptions of himself move from the general to the specific: from "servant of Christ Jesus"; to "an apostle," as the more specific form of servanthood; to "set apart for the gospel of God" as the specific focus of his apostleship.

The Greek term for "set apart" (ἀφορίζω, *aphorizō*) means "to separate, to set apart for a distinct destiny or role" (see Matt 25:32). Paul is saying that God singled him out and separated him from all other men and even from all the other apostles, giving him a special role.[2] He uses the same word in Gal 1:15, saying that God set him apart even from his mother's womb (see Jer 1:5). In his omniscience God foreknew even before Paul was born that he would respond positively to his call on the Damascus road. The special role for which Paul was set apart was to preach "the gospel of God," the "good news" of God. (Even more specifically, he was to preach the gospel to the Gentiles; but he does not mention this until v. 5.)

In what sense is it the gospel *of God*? Possibly in the sense that the gospel message is *about* God, i.e., about what he has done to save us, especially in contrast with what we try to do to save ourselves. This sense would be appropriate in view of 1:16-17, where Paul says the gospel reveals "the righteousness of God" as the source of our salvation, as opposed to our own righteousness (see 10:3). More often, though, when the content of the gospel is in view, it is referred to as the gospel of Jesus Christ (e.g., Mark 1:1; Rom 15:19; 1 Cor 9:12; 2 Thess 1:8). That is the case in this very context, which speaks of "the gospel . . . regarding his Son" (vv. 2-3), and "the gospel of his Son" (v. 9).

Thus when Paul says in v. 1 that the gospel is "the gospel of God," he probably means that it is *from* God, that God is its source. In saying this he is emphasizing the divine authority of his gospel message. It is not something he made up, nor did he receive it from any other man. It came from God himself (Gal 1:11-17).

The text does not specifically say that Paul was set apart to

---

[2]This same word is used in the LXX version of Lev 20:26, which says that God set Israel apart from all other nations.

preach the gospel; it says he was set apart "for" (εἰς, *eis*) the gospel. This certainly includes preaching (see v. 15), but it also includes the very living of the gospel. As Morris well says, to be set apart for the gospel "means to be a gospel man, to live the gospel. Preaching is important, but then so is living. Paul's call was to a way of life as well as to a task of preaching" (40). In this general sense, every Christian is "set apart for the gospel of God."

By declaring that he has been set apart for the gospel, Paul is establishing the very theme of the book of Romans from the beginning. As we saw in the introduction, the main theme of the epistle is the good news that we are saved by grace apart from works of law. Thus in view of the content of Romans we can say that Paul was set apart not only to preach and to live the gospel, but also to write it.

B. THE GOSPEL AND THE OLD TESTAMENT (1:2)

1:2 the gospel he promised beforehand through his prophets in the Holy Scriptures . . . . Here Paul's subject continues to be the gospel. His specific point is that the gospel concerning the saving work of Jesus is not some new and unexpected development in God's plan. Rather, it is something that God had already "promised beforehand" in the OT. After the initial promise in Gen 3:15, God's promises focus specifically on the role of Abraham and his descendants (see Gen 12:1-3; Gal 3:8). Indeed, the entire history of Israel was God's preparation for the coming of Christ (9:3-5), and part of this preparation was to announce ahead of time what he planned to do to save the world. Thus the gospel is simply "what God promised our fathers" (Acts 13:32).

God gave his promises "through his prophets" (see 16:25-26). A prophet is basically a spokesman for someone else, one who speaks on behalf of another. God's prophets are those whom he chooses to speak for him, to deliver his own words (3:2) to others. In this sense all biblical authors are prophets since their writings are God-breathed (2 Tim 3:16). In this functional sense, men such as Moses and David and Samuel are prophets no less than Isaiah and Amos. Sometimes the writings of Moses are distinguished from the rest of the OT since their main content is God's Law for Israel (3:21), but

Moses writes as a prophet of God (Num 12:6-8; Deut 18:15; Acts 3:21-22).

In the early years of the church, before the NT writings were generally available, the OT prophets were a main source of the gospel. Jesus cited Isa 61:1-2 to validate his ministry (Luke 4:16-21). He quoted Isa 53:12 as referring to his death (Luke 22:37). After his resurrection he twice gave a crash course on the OT prophecies concerning his death and resurrection (Luke 24:25-26, 44-46). In his Pentecost sermon Peter quoted the prophet David (see Acts 2:30) concerning Jesus' resurrection and ascension (Acts 2:25-28, 34-35). Philip used Isa 53:7-8 to preach the gospel to the Ethiopian eunuch (Acts 8:32-35).

Paul himself frequently cited OT prophecy to establish his gospel message (see Acts 13:32-35; 17:2-3). The theme for Romans itself comes from Hab 2:4 (1:17), and is undergirded with the promise to Abraham in Gen 15:6 and the promises of David in Ps 32:1-2 (Rom 4:3, 6-8).

Paul says the prophetic promises are recorded "in the Holy Scriptures." The OT is often called "the Scripture" (see 4:3; 9:17; 10:11; 11:2) or "the Scriptures" (see 15:4). In the NT the Greek word (γραφή, *graphē*) is always used for biblical writings as a category distinct from all other writings. Thus it has a kind of technical sense and is properly capitalized by the NIV.

Paul's point is that the prophetic promises concerning the gospel of Jesus Christ come to us through writings that are "the very words of God" (3:2), and thus are inspired and completely trustworthy. That Jesus died and was raised from the dead can be established by examining the NT records and other early testimony through purely scientific historical method. But the fact that "Christ died for our sins" and that "he was raised on the third day" *according to the Scriptures* (1 Cor 15:3-4) undergirds the gospel with fully divine authority.

Why does Paul emphasize the OT origin of his gospel at this point? As the book of Acts shows, the OT was often cited by the early Christians for apologetical purposes. I.e., fulfilled prophecy is a means of proving the divine origin both of the prophecy itself and of the work that fulfils it. Paul may have had this in mind here in 1:2.

It is more likely, though, that his purpose is polemical. There is no question that many Jews and even Jewish Christians had serious difficulty with the idea that anyone could be saved "apart from observing the law" (3:28), in particular the Law of Moses. However, the gospel of Jesus Christ, as known and preached by Paul in Romans, is that we are justified through faith apart from law-keeping of any kind. Thus it is important for him to show that this message is not some innovative heresy that he himself has concocted, but that it stands in continuity with what God has always taught through his inspired prophets. God has always had just one way of saving sinners, and Paul's presentation of that way is in perfect harmony with the Holy Scriptures of the OT. By stressing this point at the very beginning of the epistle, Paul seeks to deflect any criticism and skepticism that might be directed toward his teaching by Jewish readers.

Paul says that the gospel was *promised* in the OT. Does this mean that the gospel itself did not exist in OT times, and that salvation in those days came through some other means? No, not at all. God has always saved sinners by graciously forgiving their sins on the conditions of repentance and humble, believing acceptance of his forgiveness. The OT is filled with teaching concerning God's gracious nature and his promise of pardon (e.g., Exod 34:6; Ps 32:1-2; Isa 65:1-2; Hos 11:8-9; 14:1-3). Also, this forgiveness has always been based on the saving work of Jesus Christ, even when that work was only foreknown by God and not yet known by believing sinners (see 3:25).

OT saints knew and believed in God's saving grace, but they did not know specifically about Jesus of Nazareth and his role in the provision of the very grace that saved them. They had the gospel of Jesus Christ himself, but only in the form of promises to be fulfilled in the future (see Acts 13:32-35; Gal 3:18; Heb 11:8-13). They did not know who Jesus was, nor did they know exactly what he would be doing to save them. The prophets themselves — and even the angels — did not know these things (1 Pet 1:10-12). Our blessing is that we know not only the promises, but also the fulfilment. We know Jesus himself. We know the gospel in its fullness.

C. THE SUBJECT OF THE GOSPEL IS JESUS (1:3-4)

1:3-4 regarding his Son, who as to his human nature was a descendant of David, and who through the Spirit[3] of holiness was declared with power to be the Son of God by his resurrection from the dead: Jesus Christ our Lord. As we have noted above, the subject or substance of the gospel is Jesus. It is God's gospel "regarding his Son." These two verses[4] are about the *identity* of his Son, or what is usually called the *person* of Christ. The main focus here is not on his work, which is brought out more fully in the body of the epistle.

1. The Two Natures of Jesus

Though this is not necessarily its main emphasis, this passage definitely affirms the two natures of Jesus, his humanity and his divinity. The latter is seen in the naming of Jesus as "his Son," i.e., the Son of God.

When applied to Jesus this title has several connotations. Most significantly it refers to the unique relationship between Jesus and God the Father. Because of the supernatural circumstances of his virgin conception and birth, God himself designated Jesus as "the Son of the Most High" (Luke 1:31-32) and "the Son of God" (Luke 1:35). Twice the Father spoke from heaven and declared of Jesus, "This is my Son" (Matt 3:17; 17:5). In accordance with the Father's revelation, Peter confessed Jesus as "the Son of the living God" (Matt 16:16). When Jesus affirmed that he was the Son of God (Matt 26:63-66) and referred to God as "my Father" (John 5:17; 10:29), his Jewish enemies interpreted this as a claim to be equal with God (John 5:18), or a claim to actually *be* God (John 10:31-33). What is important is that Jesus did not attempt to refute this inference. Thus both the Jews' reaction to Jesus' claim to be God's Son,

---

[3]Please consult NIV original text for their footnotes here and throughout.

[4]Some think that in these verses Paul is quoting or adapting an already-existing Christian confession about Jesus (Cranfield, I:57). This is more speculation than fact, however. See Moo, I:39, 48-49; Morris, 43.

and Jesus' own response to this reaction (see the contexts), show that it is a title of deity. The title of *Son* places Jesus squarely within the Trinity (Matt 28:19).

"Son of God" is a title regularly applied to Jesus by Paul. Immediately after his conversion "he began to preach in the synagogues that Jesus is the Son of God" (Acts 9:20). Many references occur in his other epistles,[5] and in Romans itself. Besides here in 1:3-4, Paul refers to Jesus as God's Son in 1:9; 5:10; 8:3, 29, 32. That he uses it as a title of deity is consistent with his direct affirmation of Jesus as God in 9:5.

This text also emphasizes the humanity of Jesus, "who as to his human nature was a descendant of David" (literally, "from the seed of David"). The reference to the seed of David indicates that Jesus had not only divine but also human parentage. Both Joseph and Mary were descendants of David; Jesus was "from the seed of David" through his mother.[6]

The Greek text says that Jesus was from the seed of David "according to the flesh." The NIV translation ("as to his human nature") is not literal but captures the meaning of the expression quite well. Paul's use of the term *flesh* (σάρξ, *sarx*) is notoriously complex. Sometimes in Paul and in the rest of the NT it refers to the physical body as distinguished from the spirit (e.g., Matt 26:41; Rom 2:28; Phil 1:22, 24; 1 John 4:2). Sometimes it refers to the as-yet-unredeemed physical body as still ruled by sin (e.g., 7:5, 18, 25; 8:3; Gal 5:19).[7] Sometimes it refers to human nature in its earthly or pre-glorified state (e.g., 1 Cor 15:50; Heb 5:7; 1 Pet 4:1). This third meaning seems to be included here, as our discussion of v. 4 will show.

Quite often, though, the term *flesh* stands for human nature as such, in its entirety (e.g., 4:1; Eph 6:5; Phil 3:3-4; Heb 12:9). "Flesh and blood" is a fuller expression for the same thing (e.g., Gal 1:16;

---

[5]See 1 Cor 1:9; 15:28; 2 Cor 1:19; Gal 1:16; 2:20; 4:4, 6; Eph 4:13; Col 1:13; 1 Thess 1:10. Hebrews (if it is to be regarded as Pauline) uses the title even more frequently.

[6]The genealogy in Luke 3:23-38 is probably that of Mary. See Gromacki, *Virgin Birth*, ch. 17.

[7]This meaning will be discussed in more detail later. See the general introduction to Part Three (6:1-8:39), and on 7:5.

Eph 6:12; Heb 2:14). "All flesh" and "no flesh" refer to the human race in general (e.g., Mark 13:20; Luke 3:6; Rom 3:20; Gal 2:16). This last option seems to be the primary meaning in v. 3, just as the NIV understands it. The same expression and the same idea are found in 9:5, which says that Jesus came from Israel "according to the flesh." First Timothy 3:16 affirms that Jesus "was revealed in the flesh" (NASB). John 1:14 sums up this idea perfectly: "The Word became flesh"; the divine Logos became a human being.

The entire content of v. 3 is foreshadowed by Jesus' debate with the Pharisees during his final week (Matt 22:41-45). He asked them about the Christ: "Whose son is he?" They replied, "The son of David." While not denying this, Jesus went on to show that the Christ must be *more* than the son of *David*, since David confesses him as his Lord (Ps 110:1). The clear implication is that the Christ is also the Son of God. He is not only human, but also divine.

2. The Incarnation

The NIV incorrectly translates an important word in v. 3, namely, γίνομαι (*ginomai*). The NASB renders it as "born," or "born of a descendant of David." This is a possible meaning (see John 8:58; Gal 4:4), but not a common one. The KJV translates it as "made," i.e., "made of the seed of David." This is closer to the correct meaning; see John 1:3, where this word occurs three times and where the NIV translates it "made" each time.

It is best to understand *ginomai* here as "came into being" or "came into existence" (see John 1:3, NASB). The idea is that the Son of God came into existence from the seed of David as to his human nature. This is a reference to the incarnation, in which the eternal Logos "became flesh" (John 1:14, also *ginomai*), or became a human being. Prior to the incarnation, his human nature did not exist. The human person, Jesus of Nazareth, had a beginning. Jesus of Nazareth, indeed, Jesus the Christ, did not exist prior to his miraculous conception in the womb of Mary.

However, the divine person called the Logos *did* exist before the incarnation; indeed, he existed eternally along with God because he *was* God (John 1:1). But at a specific point in time the eternal

Logos "made himself nothing" (Phil 2:7) and entered into an incomprehensible kind of unity with a real human being who began to exist at this same point in time, namely, Jesus of Nazareth.

3. Messiahship

Verse 3 says Jesus "was a descendant of David." Why *David* in particular? If the point is simply Jesus' human nature, why not "from the seed of Abraham"? Why not "born of Mary"? What is distinctive about his being from the seed of *David*? One thing at stake here is the uniqueness of Jesus. All Jews were known as sons of Abraham (John 8:33, 37; Rom 11:1; 2 Cor 11:22). All Christians are Abraham's spiritual seed (4:13, 16, 18; Gal 3:29). But Jesus alone is the son or seed of David as the Bible uses that expression.

More specifically, what is at stake is Jesus' identity as the Messiah or Christ. The OT promised and the Jews universally believed that the Messiah would be a descendant of David. To say that Jesus was from the seed of David is to confess him to be the Messiah, the one promised and expected as the Savior of his people. As Jesus' contemporaries expressed it in John 7:42, "Does not the Scripture say that the Christ will come from David's family?" (literally, "from David's seed"). See 2 Tim 2:8.

This is one of the aspects of the gospel "promised beforehand through his prophets in the Holy Scriptures" (v. 2). The OT states very clearly that God would raise up a descendant of David to sit on his throne and rule his people in righteousness and wisdom and power.[8] The NT from beginning (Matt 1:1) to end (Rev 22:16) refers to Jesus as the seed and son of David.[9]

Jesus' messianic role as the son of David includes his taking care of his people as David the shepherd tended his sheep (Ezek 34:23; 37:24). The main emphasis, though, is on his kingship and lordship. Most of the promises concerning David's seed echo 2 Sam 7:13, "I will establish the throne of his kingdom forever" (see Ps 132:11;

---

[8]See 2 Sam 7:12-13; Ps 89:3-4; 132:10-11; Isa 11:1-5, 10; Jer 23:5-6; 30:9; 33:14-17; Ezek 34:23-24; 37:24.

[9]See also Matt 1:6; 9:27; 12:23; 15:22; 20:30-31; 21:9, 15; Luke 1:32-33, 69; 3:31; Rev 5:5.

Jer 23:5; Ezek 37:24). The angel who announced Christ's birth to Mary told her, "The Lord God will give him the throne of his father David" (Luke 1:32). Peter reminded his listeners on the Day of Pentecost that God promised David that he "would place one of his descendants on his throne" (Acts 2:30). David was to the Jews their "great king" (Matt 5:35), but God promised that the Messiah's kingdom would be even more glorious and that it would never end. Jesus as the Messiah is "great David's greater son."

4. The Two States of Jesus

When we get into the content of v. 4, a whole new perspective on Jesus Christ is opened up. Here we see that Paul is showing us not only the two *natures* of Christ, but also his two *states*, namely, the two stages of his messianic career. The first is his state of humiliation, which is the period of his earthly ministry from the point of his incarnation up to and including his death on the cross. It is likely that v. 3 is referring to this state, and that the term *flesh* connotes not only Jesus' humanity as such, but his human nature in its weak and not-yet-glorified state. These were truly "the days of his flesh" (Heb 5:7, NASB). This was the time when his "equality with God" was veiled by his humanness and his servanthood and his shameful death on a despicable cross (Phil 2:6-8). See 2 Cor 8:9.

But this is only his state "according to the flesh," and was followed by a state of the highest exaltation, to which v. 4 refers. The period of nothingness (Phil 2:7-8) is replaced by one of infinite and eternal glory (Phil 2:9-11): "Therefore also God highly exalted him, and bestowed on him the name which is above every name, that at the name of Jesus every knee should bow, of those who are in heaven, and on earth, and under the earth, and that every tongue should confess that Jesus Christ is Lord, to the glory of God the Father" (NASB). In the state of his exaltation Jesus is not just the Son of God, but is *the Son of God with power*.

We have two options regarding the phrase "with power." Some take it as modifying the verb, as in the NIV: Jesus was "declared with power to be the Son of God." Here the power lies in the *means* by which Jesus was designated Son of God, namely, the mighty display of power in his resurrection from the dead. The other option is to take "with power" as modifying the title "Son of God," as in the NASB [1977 ed.]: Jesus "was declared the Son of God with power." (See also the KJV and the NRSV.) I.e., in his state of exaltation Jesus is not just the Son of God, but is the Son of God *with power*. This is the better understanding. It follows the word order in the original text more closely. Also, v. 3 indicates that Jesus was already the Son of God in his state of humiliation; thus v. 4 must be pointing us to a new phase of his existence in which he is invested with unprecedented power.

What we are told, then, is that the one who came into existence from the seed of David, and who was already the Son of God in a real sense[10] has now become the Son of God with power. That is, he has entered a new state or stage of his messianic career. In his unglorified state, "the days of his flesh," Jesus of Nazareth was the divine Son of God by virtue of the incarnation. But now as the result of his messianic work he has been exalted to a new state of power and glory. This comes specifically as the result of his work of death and resurrection, in which he confronted the archenemies death and Satan (Col 2:15; Heb 2:14-15; Rev 1:18) and decisively defeated them. Thus what was his *by nature* (because he was the incarnation of deity) has now become his *by right*. He has earned it; he has achieved it by his work.

5. The Resurrection of Jesus

Paul says that the transition point where Jesus crossed the line from humiliation to glory was his resurrection from the dead. By this specific act he was declared to be the Son of God with power. The word translated "by" is ἐκ (*ek*). Sometimes this is taken in a temporal sense, i.e., "from the time of" his resurrection he was so declared (Cranfield, I:62). This is certainly true in fact, but it is not the best understanding of the preposition in this text. It is no doubt intended here to have the stronger causal meaning, "by means of,

---

[10]This is shown by the angel's testimony to Mary, by Peter's confession, and by Jesus' acceptance of his enemies' interpretation of the title, as discussed above in pages 68-69.

as the result of." As the result of his resurrection, Jesus is declared to be the Son of God with power.

A more serious issue is the meaning of the Greek word ὁρίζω (horizō), which is the one translated "declared" in the NIV. According to this understanding the resurrection is the act which reveals and affirms the fact that Jesus is the Son of God. By this act he is "seen to be" the Son of God (Morris, 47). This view emphasizes the apologetical function of the resurrection, which it certainly has. This miraculous event is proof or evidence of Jesus' true identity as deity (John 20:28). It is proof to all men that Jesus will judge the world (Acts 17:31). It shows that Jesus is more than a merely human person such as David himself, who is still dead and in his tomb (Acts 2:29; 13:36). Thus acceptance of the fact of the resurrection is an essential foundation for saving faith (10:9).

In all of these ways Jesus' resurrection certainly declares him to be the divine Son of God. But the question is, is this the best meaning of the word horizō? Many believe this meaning is too weak, and suggest that the word actually bears something close to a causal connotation. (See Cranfield, I:61; Moo, I:40.) The idea is that by his resurrection Jesus is appointed or constituted the Son of God with power; he is ordained or installed as the Son of God with power.

This latter understanding is the better one. It is closer to the actual meaning of the term (see Moo, I:40). Also, it is more in keeping with the two-states understanding of vv. 3 and 4. It is similar to the concept in Acts 2:36, which says that God *made* the crucified and risen Jesus to be both Lord and Christ. The same word (horizō) is used in Acts 10:42 and Acts 17:31 to say that Jesus has been *appointed* judge of the world.

The point is that the resurrection of Jesus is the crucial transition point in his work as Messiah. It is the deathblow to his enemies, it gives him universal authority and dominion, and it enables him to perform his continuing work of priestly intercession (4:25; Heb 7:16).

Another thought in v. 4 is that Jesus was appointed to be the Son of God with power "through the Spirit of holiness."[11] This is sometimes taken to mean *Jesus'* spirit: either his human soul, in

---

[11]See Moo, I:41-43, for a good survey of the various views of this expression.

contrast with his physical nature ("flesh," v. 3), or his divine nature, in contrast with his human nature. It is much more likely, though, that it refers to the *Holy* Spirit, who is mentioned often in Romans, especially in chapter 8. (See also 5:5; 9:1; 14:17; 15:13, 16, 19.) Since he is usually called "the Holy Spirit" or "the Spirit of God," we may ask why this unusual wording, "the Spirit of holiness," is used here. The probable answer is that Paul is using the Hebrew idiom, found in Ps 51:11 and Isa 63:10, thus reminding his readers again of his dependence on the OT (v. 2).

The main reason for taking this as a reference to the Holy Spirit is that the Spirit is often elsewhere described as the Spirit of life and the giver of life (e.g., John 6:63; Rom 8:2; 2 Cor 3:6), and especially as the one who raised Jesus' body from the dead: 8:11; 1 Tim 3:16; 1 Pet 3:18. Understanding v. 4 as a reference to the Holy Spirit fits this picture very consistently, since "the Spirit of holiness" is here said to be the agent of Christ's resurrection. The preposition "through" is κατά (*kata*); it is often translated simply "according to." It can be used in a causal sense, though, as seems to be the case here (Hendriksen, I:41).

6. The Son's Full Identity

As if to summarize his theological description of God's Son in vv. 3-4, Paul ends v. 4 with this full yet succinct identification: He is "Jesus Christ our Lord." These three appellations pull together all that has already been said.

"Jesus" is the proper name of the incarnate Son of God and calls attention to his human nature as one born in the line of David. It also points to his work as the Messiah, since it means "Yahweh is salvation" (GRe, 25-26).

The title "Christ" is the Greek equivalent of the Hebrew "Messiah." It means "the anointed one," i.e., the one appointed and anointed by God to perform the work of salvation, as promised in the OT Scriptures (v. 2). In the OT, anointing with oil was often a ceremony of ordination to an office of leadership, especially the office of king (1 Sam 16:3, 12-13), high priest (Exod 29:7, 29), and prophet (1 Kgs 19:16). As the Christ — the anointed one — Jesus performs especially the work of the great High Priest (offering himself as the atoning sacrifice) and the work of the King of Kings (in his resurrection, ascension, and enthronement at God's right hand). In relation to the latter, this title points to all that Jesus has done as the son of David.

Jesus is also called "Lord" (κύριος, *kurios*), a term applied to him often in Romans.[12] Its literal meaning is "owner," which applies in the most absolute sense to God's Son since in his divine nature he created all things (John 1:3). It is also a title that connotes the deity of Jesus, especially as used by an OT scholar such as Paul. Because he used the LXX extensively Paul must have seen that *kurios* was the Greek word used there to represent the Hebrew sacred name, Yahweh, over 6,150 times. Paul could not have used this word as his almost-exclusive title for Jesus without in his mind identifying Jesus as Yahweh. This is something he does explicitly in 10:9-13.

It is significant that Paul refers to Jesus as "*our* Lord," not just "*the* Lord." It makes all that he has said about Jesus much more personal. In particular it corresponds exactly to our own role as his slaves (see v. 1). Confessing him as "our Lord" is acknowledging him as our owner in every sense.

D. PAUL'S APOSTLESHIP (1:5)

1:5 Through him and for his name's sake, we received grace and apostleship to call people from among all the Gentiles to the obedience that comes from faith. In v. 1 Paul begins to introduce himself, especially as an apostle set apart to preach the gospel. His mention of the gospel leads him to describe it as being promised in the OT (v. 2) and as being about God's Son (v. 3a). His mention of God's Son leads him to speak in more detail of his glorious nature (vv. 3b-4). Now in v. 5 he returns to his self-introduction by further elaborating on his call to apostleship.

---

[12]See 1:7; 4:24; 5:1, 11, 21; 6:11, 23; 7:25; 8:39; 10:9; 13:14; 14:14; 15:6, 30; 16:18, 20, 24.

1. The Origin of Paul's Apostleship

He speaks first of the *origin* of his apostleship: it came "through him," namely, through Jesus Christ. This is a reference again to the call that was extended to him by the glorified Christ on the road to Damascus (Acts 9:3-6; 22:6-10; 26:13-18).

2. The Character of Paul's Apostleship

Next Paul speaks of the *character* of his apostleship: it came to him as a gift. This is the point of his statement, "we received grace and apostleship." (He says "we" only in the editorial sense, since he is talking only of himself.) The Greek word for "apostleship" is ἀποστολή (*apostolē*); it is used only here and in Acts 1:25; 1 Cor 9:2; Gal 2:8.

Why does he say that he received *grace* and apostleship? Here is where the concept of gift appears. The Greek word for "grace" (χάρις, *charis*) in its most general sense means "a gift that brings joy or gladness." It almost always includes the connotation of a gift; sometimes it is used even for the act of thanksgiving for a gift. Usually when we hear the English word "grace," the first thing we think of is the free gift of salvation through Jesus Christ. In the Bible, though, it is often used to refer to gifts of service, i.e., gifts that enable individuals to work for and serve God in special ways. See especially 1 Pet 4:10-11.

What does it mean in this verse? Some take it as a reference to the saving grace that Paul allegedly received on the Damascus road, along with but as distinct from his call to apostleship (e.g., Murray, I:13). In this sense v. 4 would be saying that Paul received from Jesus both saving grace and his apostolic calling. The more common view, and the one preferred here, is that the word *grace* refers to the apostleship itself. "Grace and apostleship" here means "the grace of apostleship" or "the gracious gift of apostleship."

This latter view is preferred for several reasons. For one thing, Paul's personal call by Jesus on the road to Damascus was specifically a call to the apostleship only. Jesus did not actually speak to him about salvation; he left that up to Ananias. Second, the gifts of service to which the word *grace* applies include the gift of apostleship (1 Cor 12:28; Eph 4:7, 11; see Rom 12:3, 6). Finally and most significantly, in many other places Paul speaks of his call to apostleship as an act of grace (15:15-16; 1 Cor 3:10; 15:10; Gal 1:15; 2:9; Eph 3:7-8).

3. The Focus of Paul's Apostleship

As an apostle Paul was told to work specifically "among all the Gentiles." The Greek word is ἔθνος (*ethnos*, most often used in the plural). Sometimes it refers to a nation or nations in general, without any particular distinctions. Often, though, as in this context, it refers only to the *Gentile* nations, i.e., the nations that are distinct from the Jews. The focus of Paul's ministry was the Gentiles (the uncircumcised) as distinguished from the Jews (the circumcised). See Gal 2:7, NASB.

We must emphasize that Paul was not meant to preach *exclusively* to Gentiles. Indeed, Jesus told him that he should declare his name "before the Gentiles and their kings and before the people of Israel" (Acts 9:15). Paul was very aware that the gospel was for "the Jew first" (1:16). Nevertheless it is clear that the *primary* focus of Paul's ministry was intended to be the Gentiles (Acts 22:21; 26:17). He emphasizes this fact in his epistles (Gal 1:16; Eph 3:1, 6-8; 1 Thess 2:16; 1 Tim 2:7; 2 Tim 4:17), and especially here in Romans (1:13-14; 11:13; 15:15-16, 18).

4. The Purpose of Paul's Apostleship

In this verse Paul tells us the specific purpose of his apostleship, namely, "to call people from among all the Gentiles to the obedience that comes from faith." The words "to call" are not in the original, though the idea is certainly present (see 2 Thess 2:14). The concept of purpose is actually found in the Greek preposition εἰς (*eis*), which can mean "unto" in the sense of "for the purpose of" (Cranfield, I:66). Paul says he was given grace and apostleship *unto* – for the purpose of bringing about – "the obedience that comes from faith."

This is an extremely important idea, one that should give every Christian worker insight into the purpose of his or her ministry. The purpose or the immediate "goal of the gospel" is to produce the obedience that comes from faith. Paul elsewhere rejoices that through his ministry Christ has been able to produce "the obedience of the Gentiles by word and deed" (15:18, NASB). In 16:25-26 he declares that the mystery revealed in the gospel "has been made known to all the nations, leading to obedience of faith" (NASB). In 1:5 and 16:26 the Greek expression is exactly the same (though the NIV without good reason translates it differently in the two verses). It is εἰς ὑπακοὴν πίστεως (*eis hypakoēn pisteōs*), without any definite articles. It literally means "unto obedience of faith." Exactly what it means is a matter of much debate.

Four things must be kept in mind when interpreting this expression. First, one must decide whether the "faith" is subjective or objective. I.e., is it the act of believing; or is it the content of our faith, the doctrine to be believed? Second, the extent of the obedience must be determined. Is it a special kind of obedience, or is it obedience in general? Third and most crucially, the exact relation between the faith and the obedience must be understood. Finally, our interpretation of this expression must be consistent with the overall message of Romans.

Some Bible translations render the expression quite literally, "obedience of faith" (NASB, NRSV). But it still has to be interpreted. Here we will briefly present five suggested interpretations, as reflected by various translations and exegetes.

The first suggestion is "obedience *and* faith." This appears in several variations in a number of translations: "obedience and faith" (Goodspeed), "faith and obedience" (NEB), "believe and obey" (LB; TEV; NIV, 16:26 only). In this view faith appears to be subjective, and the obedience seems to be general.

This view is unsatisfactory for three reasons. For one thing, it is incomplete. After translating it thus, one must still go on and explain how the faith and the obedience are related (e.g., as in Newman and Nida, 12). Also, it is not grammatically sound. Joining faith and obedience with the conjunction "and" suggests they are somehow parallel, but the Greek genitive form of *pisteōs* ("faith") indicates a non-parallel relationship. Finally, in the context of

Romans it is doctrinally misleading to place faith and obedience in such a parallel relationship, since one of the main points of Romans is that faith and obedience (good works) are not related to salvation in the same way.

The second suggestion is "the obedience which is included in faith." This is the view of Gareth Reese (*Acts*, 598-610), as summed up in Corson ("Faith," 5-6). According to this view faith includes, as part of its very essence, obedience or good works. Obedience is part of the content or definition of faith, and in terms of scope it embraces at least the further acts required by the "plan of salvation": repentance, confession, and baptism. In the Restoration Movement it is very common to hear that these acts are simply part of the content of saving faith.

This view is also unsatisfactory, however. Even though the Bible does connect faith and obedience very closely (as in the fifth view, below), it is always careful to distinguish them, especially in contexts dealing with salvation (Eph 2:8-10). Except insofar as faith itself may be considered an act of obedience (as in the next view), the two must be kept distinct. Once we go beyond this, it is difficult if not impossible to limit the scope of the obedience that would have to be included in such "faith." It may be possible to talk about (subjective) faith, repentance, confession, and baptism as "obedience *to* the (objective) faith" (as in the fourth view, below); but such a limitation cannot be made in this view, where the comprehensive or inclusive faith is itself subjective. Thus if this view were correct, the faith that justifies (3:28; 5:1) would have to include the entire obedience of the Christian life. This would simply be another version of works-righteousness or salvation by works — the very view Paul is attacking in the epistle to the Romans as a whole. Thus it must be rejected as inconsistent with the gospel of grace.

The third suggestion is that "the obedience of faith" means "the obedience that consists of faith." That is, the obedience sought by preaching is the one specific act of subjectively believing the gospel. This is the view of Cranfield (I:66-67), Murray (I:13-14), and Godet (82). Now, it is certainly correct to think of faith as an act of obedience, but it is incorrect to think that it is the *only* act of obedience God seeks to bring about through the preaching of the gospel. In Romans Paul puts great emphasis on faith, but he also stresses the obedience that must follow faith as the ultimate result of gospel preaching (see the fifth view, below). Thus this view is inconsistent with the overall message of Romans.

The fourth suggestion is "obedience to the faith" (e.g., KJV, Weymouth, Moffatt, and Phillips translations). What is distinctive about this view is that it understands "faith" in the objective sense, namely, as the body of doctrine that we believe and to which we must respond in obedience. Such a view of faith is found in the Bible (Jude 3), and so is the concept of "obeying the faith" (Acts 6:7). Also, "obedience *to* the faith" is a grammatically possible way of translating the genitive case of *pisteōs* (see 2 Cor 10:5; 1 Pet 1:22).

Is this a valid understanding of "the obedience of faith"? Perhaps. On the positive side, "obedience to the faith" or "obeying the faith" seems to be equivalent to "obeying the gospel," a concept that occurs several times in the NT: 10:16; 2 Thess 1:8; 1 Pet 4:17. What does this mean? Obedience to the gospel faith would seem to be different from obedience to the law or commandments governing the Christian life. The latter is everyday obedience, but the former would seem to be more limited in scope. How should it be understood? Most succinctly, it probably refers to what is required as *conditions* for receiving the saving grace promised in the gospel. This includes particularly faith, repentance, and baptism (Mark 1:15; 16:15-16; Acts 2:38; 5:32; 16:31; Rom 10:16-17). This required response to the gospel may be regarded as obedience, since the conditions are often presented grammatically as imperatives or commands (Mark 1:15; Acts 2:38; 16:31).

On the negative side, though, is the fact that in Romans the central concept of faith occurs overwhelmingly in the subjective sense. Since this statement in 1:5 seems to be so closely connected with the overall theme of Romans, the faith of which it speaks should probably be understood in the subjective sense also. Thus we find this view unacceptable as the intended meaning in this verse.

This leads to the fifth and final suggestion, "the obedience which results from faith." In my opinion, this is Paul's intended meaning; a wide range of commentators agree. Though it is not a strict translation, the NIV rendering is on target exegetically: "the obedience that comes from faith." According to this understanding "faith" is the subjective act of believing, and "obedience" is the whole scope of Christian good works.

This view is preferred mainly because of its contextual harmony with Romans as a whole. While faith in Jesus is stressed as the natural and necessary response to his saving work, the epistle makes it clear that this faith cannot stand alone. Paul shows in chs. 6-8 and 12-15 that the end result of the gospel is obedience or good works[13] or sanctification. His point here in 1:5 is that he was called to be an apostle *not* just to lead the Gentiles to faith as an end in itself, but to lead them to the kind of faith that produces *obedience*.

Still, the emphasis in the expression "obedience of faith" is not on obedience as such but on faith. God wants obedience, yes; but he wants the obedience of *faith*, i.e., the obedience that comes from, results from, or is motivated by faith in Jesus Christ. Continuing daily obedience to God's commandments is expected and even necessary in some respects, but the *only* kind of obedience that satisfies God is the obedience that is the expression of faith. This is the intended outcome of Paul's gospel, just as it should be for us. The purpose of preaching the gospel is to bring about obedience, but only an obedience that springs from faith rather than from legalistic requirements. God wants obedience, but he wants the obedience of *faith*. See Rom 6-8; Gal 5:6; Eph 2:8-10; 1 Thess 1:3.

In reality, true faith and heartfelt obedience (6:17) are inseparable. Abraham's example sums it up: "By faith Abraham . . . obeyed" (Heb 11:8). We cannot truly "accept Christ" without accepting him as both Savior and Lord. We accept him as Savior by trusting in his redeeming work; we accept him as Lord by committing ourselves to obey his will (see MacArthur, I:24-25).

5. The Goal of Paul's Apostleship

In the Greek the last phrase of v. 5 is "for his name's sake." While the immediate purpose or goal of Paul's gospel was to bring

---

[13]In this context there is no difference between obedience and (good) works. Paul does not choose the term *obedience* in deliberate contrast with the term *works* (of law) in 3:28, as if the gospel enjoins "obedience of faith" but rules out "works of law." This idea misses the point of both verses.

about obedience of faith among the Gentiles, its *ultimate* goal was to bring honor and glory to the name of Christ. This is a general principle of the Christian life: everything we do should be done to the glory of God (1 Cor 10:31) and in the name of Jesus Christ (Col 3:17). It is true that in the end *every* knee will bow to Christ, and *every* tongue will confess that he is Lord,[14] to the glory of God the Father (Phil 2:10-11), but our goal must be to bring the world as close to this end as we can *now*, through our life's work. Stott (53) has said it very well: "The highest of all missionary motives is neither obedience to the Great Commission . . . , nor love for sinners who are alienated and perishing . . . , but rather zeal — burning and passionate zeal — for the glory of Jesus Christ."

E. THE RECIPIENTS OF PAUL'S LETTER (1:6-7a)

1:6-7a And you also are among those who are called to belong to Jesus Christ. To all in Rome who are loved by God and called to be saints . . . . The first six verses are an expanded version of the first segment of an ordinary epistolary greeting, identifying the author. The seventh verse contains the other two segments, identifying the recipients and offering a blessing. But even before Paul gets to his formal acknowledgment of the recipients (v. 7a), he begins to address them as an add-on to his reference to the Gentiles in v. 5: "And you also are among those" Gentiles who have been called to the obedience of faith. A relative pronoun in the first part of v. 6 links the subject of this verse to the Gentiles in v. 5.

Verses 6 and 7 probably reflect the ethnic identity of the Roman church. Verse 6 definitely addresses Gentiles, but v. 7 seems to be more inclusive: "To all in Rome," i.e., *all* Christians, both Jewish and Gentile. The way the Gentiles are addressed in v. 6, though, seems to indicate that they made up a large part if not the main part of the church in Rome (see 1:13).[15]

---

[14]Those who bow and confess willingly will be saved; those who are forced to do so unwillingly by the sheer power of his unveiled presence (e.g., Rev 6:12-17) will be lost.

[15]Some suggest that Paul specifically addresses the Gentiles in v. 6 in order to call attention to his apostolic authority over them (as the apostle

The recipients of the letter — and by extension all Christians of all times — are described in three ways in these verses. Verse 6 says that we are "called to belong to Jesus Christ." The word "called" is the same as in v. 1, "called to be an apostle," and the same as in v. 7, "called to be saints." The calling itself is not the same, though. In v. 1 the call is to a specific role of service, while vv. 6-7 speak about the calling of sinners to salvation.

That God calls sinners to salvation is a Bible teaching on which all agree (e.g., 8:30; 1 Thess 2:12; 5:24; 1 Pet 2:9; Jude 1). The disagreement comes as to the nature of the call. Some say the call is selective and efficacious. I.e., God gives it only to the elect, and it irresistibly causes the recipient to believe and to accept God's grace. This is the Calvinist doctrine of the "effectual call," and commentators of that persuasion read this idea into vv. 6 and 7 (e.g., Moo, I:46; Murray, I:15; Morris, 38; MacArthur, I:28).

Others say that while God's call to sinners is gracious and powerful and necessary, it is nevertheless universal and resistible. This is the biblical view. God calls sinners through the gospel (2 Thess 2:14), which is his power unto salvation (1:16). The message of the cross draws *all* men to the Christ (John 12:32). Faith comes through the written Word (John 20:31) when that Word is faithfully preached (10:13-17). Sinners' hearts are hardened, and without the powerful message of the gospel none would turn to God (John 6:44-45; Heb 4:12). In this sense the gospel call is a *necessary* condition for salvation. The Calvinist error is to make it also a *sufficient* condition, which it is not. The sinner still has the free will either to answer the call or to resist it (Isa 65:1-7; Matt 23:37; Acts 7:51; Rev 22:17).

To say that we have been *called* to belong to Jesus and to be saints emphasizes God's gracious desire for our salvation (2 Pet 3:9) and his initiative and persistence in the whole salvation process. Because he cares, he calls — and calls, and calls, and calls.

---

to the Gentiles). This would both justify his writing the epistle and remind its recipients of their obligation to submit to it. (See Godet, 83; Moo, I:45; Cranfield, I:68; Morris, 51.) This is unlikely, though, since Paul's authority as an apostle extends equally over Jews and Gentiles alike. He is an apostle first, and apostle to the Gentiles second.

We are called "to belong to Jesus Christ." The words "to belong to" are not in the original text; they represent the NIV's interpretion of the simple expression, "called of Jesus Christ" (a genitive connection; see the NASB). This could possibly mean "those who are called *by* Jesus Christ" (Cranfield, I:68), or it could be a possessive genitive, as the NIV has concluded (also Murray, I:15; Moo, I:46; Morris, 52). Either way is grammatically and theologically correct. The latter possibility is consistent with the Lord-slave relationship (vv. 1, 4). The gospel call is a call to yield ourselves to Christ's Lordship (ownership) and to become his loving and willing life-slaves.

The recipients of the letter (and thus all of us by extension) are also "loved by God." (For other texts that speak of Christians as "loved by God," see Col 3:12; 1 Thess 1:4; 2 Thess 2:13; Jude 1.) It is true that God loves all human beings both as his creatures and as sinners who need his salvation (John 3:16; Rom 5:8; Eph 2:4-5; 1 John 2:2; 4:9-10). This is contrary to many who are of a Calvinist persuasion who say that God's love is selective and directed only toward the elect (see GRe, 329-332, 381-383). On the other hand, God *does* have a special love for those who answer his call and open their hearts to receive it (John 14:21; Rom 5:5; 8:35). Because we belong to him in a special way, he loves us as a father loves his own children, as a husband loves his own wife, and as a shepherd loves his own sheep (GRe, 343-344).

The last description of those in Rome (and the rest of us) is that we are "called to be saints" (see 1 Cor 1:2). The words "to be" are not in the original text but express the idea accurately (see "called to be an apostle" in v. 1). The word "saints" means simply "holy ones," and the word "holy" means simply "separated" or "set apart" in a special relation to God. When used in the sense of saints it does not describe a distinctively high level of Christian maturity achieved by only a few. Rather, it describes the status of every Christian: we have been separated from the "dominion of darkness" (Col 1:13; 1 Pet 2:9) and from "the present evil age" (Gal 1:4), and we have been placed by God's grace within his kingdom (Col 1:13) and family (2 Cor 6:17-18). We *are* saints, and therefore we should live like saints (12:1-2).

F. THE BLESSING (1:7b)

1:7b We finally come to the third and last segment of the letter's greeting, namely, the blessing: **Grace and peace to you**. This is Paul's standard epistolary blessing. It is exactly the same in four of his other letters (Gal 1:3; Eph 1:2; Phil 1:2; Phlm 3) and very similar in the rest (1 Cor 1:3; 2 Cor 1:2; 1 Thess 1:2; 2 Thess 1:2; 1 Tim 1:2; 2 Tim 1:2; Titus 1:4). As Bruce (75) points out, this blessing modifies and combines the standard Greek greeting, χαῖρε (*Chaire!* "Rejoice!") and the standard Jewish greeting, *Shalom!* ("Peace!"). Paul changed *chaire* to the "similarly-sounding and more distinctively Christian word χάρις (*charis*), 'grace.'" These two words together sum up the essence of the gospel and thus the essence of the message of Romans: "grace, therefore peace" (see 5:1). Because we are under his grace, we have peace with him and peace within.

The source of this grace and peace is specified; it is **from God our Father and from the Lord Jesus Christ**. Though the Father's loving and gracious heart desired from eternity past to bestow grace and peace upon his sinful creatures, it could not be done without the saving work performed by the incarnate Logos in the person of Jesus of Nazareth. Thus the Father and the Son together are the source of our grace and peace. Such a close linking of the Father and the Son is typical of Paul and is indicative of the deity of the Son (see Gal 1:1; Phil 2:11; 1 Thess 1:1; 1 Tim 1:1; see also Rev 5:13; 6:16).

Paul usually reserves the term *God* (θεός, *theos*) for God the Father, just as he ordinarily uses *Lord* (κύριος, *kyrios*) for God the Son, and *Spirit* (πνεῦμα, *pneuma*) for God the Holy Spirit (e.g., Eph 4:4-6; 1 Cor 12:4-6). This does not mean, though, that he considers only the Father to be truly God, truly divine. In 9:5, for instance, Jesus is referred to as "God over all." On the threefold name for the Son, "Lord Jesus Christ," see on v. 4 above.

This brings Paul's lengthy epistolary greeting to an end. Our commentary on it is also lengthy, not just because the greeting itself is so long but also because it is so filled with doctrinal content. As MacArthur correctly notes, "The entire thrust of the sixteen chapters of Romans is distilled in the first seven verses" (I:3). Its content thrills our souls and whets our appetites for the rest of the letter.

II. 1:8-15 – PERSONAL REMARKS

In this section Paul briefly lays aside his apostolic persona (but not his apostolic authority), and addresses the saints in Rome on a personal level. He comes down from the pulpit, walks among the people, shakes their hands, and shows them his heart. He speaks not just as Paul the Apostle, but as Paul the man, Paul the fellow-Christian.

The main thing he reveals in this section is his earnest desire to visit the church in Rome, something he had prayed about and planned to do for a long time. This would be for their mutual benefit, but Paul wanted to visit especially so that he could preach the gospel in the world's capital city. The gospel was his life and passion, and he wanted to share it on a deeper level with the Roman Christians.

Thus far, every time he had planned to go to Rome, something had come up to prevent it. But now he had a new plan that he hoped would include this long-awaited trip (15:23-24). Still, he had no assurance at this point that this plan would be any more successful than his previous ones (15:30-32). But it seems that his desire to preach the gospel in Rome was so strong (1:15) that he just could not wait any longer. If he could not preach it there in person, he could do the next best thing, i.e., write the gospel to the Romans in the form of a long and well-thought-out letter-essay. This seems to be the implication of these personal remarks, and thus we are given some insight into the purpose for which Romans was written.

A. PAUL'S PRAYERS FOR THE ROMANS (1:8-10)

1:8 First, says Paul, I want to tell you what I have been praying for. (This is not the first in a series of things, since he does not go on to a "second" and "third." It is "first" in the sense of "before I go any further, before I get into the meat of this letter or into its formal teaching.") **I thank my God through Jesus Christ for all of you.**

This first prayer is a prayer of thanksgiving. Some take it as a diplomatic gesture. I.e., by starting with this positive personal

comment the author intends to "get on the good side" of the
readers. As Barclay says, Paul "began with a compliment" in order
to "disarm their suspicions," especially since he had never been to
Rome and was a stranger to most of the Christians there (5). This is
probably reading too much into it, however. Such a statement of
personal thanksgiving or blessing or concern normally followed the
epistolary greeting in all letters of that time and culture.[16] This was
Paul's own standard practice; similar remarks appear after the
greetings in all his other letters except Galatians.

By referring to God as "*my* God" Paul reveals the close, intimate
relationship he has with the Father. For him God was not just an
academic subject but one whom he knew personally. He knew what
it meant to speak to God as "Abba! Father!" and he says that we
may do the same (8:15). Many say that "Abba" is the equivalent of
"Daddy" in English. Such intimacy is present when we begin our
prayers with "dear," as in "Dear God" or "Dear Father." (See also
2 Cor 12:21; Phil 1:3; 4:19; Phlm 4.)

Paul offers his prayer "through Jesus Christ," who is the one
and only mediator between our sinful selves and the holy God
(John 14:6; 1 Tim 2:5; Heb 4:16). This is not just a formality, but a
sincere acknowledgment that the atoning work of Jesus makes it
possible for us to be accepted by God and allowed into his presence.

Paul says he thanks God "for all of you." This includes all the
saints at Rome, from both Jewish and Gentile backgrounds (see
v. 7). This means he was praying not only for the few that he knew
personally, but also even for those whom he did not know. We are
following Paul's example when we pray for people whom we have
never met, whether it be friends' relatives or Christian workers in
all parts of the world. "The bond of Christian fellowship is not
limited to the circle described by personal acquaintance" (Murray,
I:19).

Paul says he thanks God **because your faith is being reported
all over the world**. The specific reason for his thanksgiving has to
do with the *faith* (πίστις, *pistis*) of the Christians at Rome. Why was
this so? Was there something special about their faith? Bruce

---

[16]For an example see Morris, 55, n. 97.

speaks of "the high and renowned quality of their faith" (75). Perhaps Paul means not just their faith, but their *faithfulness* (which is a valid connotation of *pistis*). This may be inferred from the fact that all people knew not only of the Romans' faith but also of their *obedience* (16:19). This is an indication of the principle that true faith always produces obedience (see 1:5).

On the other hand, many commentators deny that there was any special quality to the Romans' faith. It was just ordinary faith, like anyone else's. As Moo says, "It is the very fact of their faith that is sufficient reason for giving thanks to God" (I:52). See also Cranfield, I:75; Morris, 56-57.

If it was not an especially deep and strong faith, why would Paul give thanks for it? Some say it was appropriate to thank God for their faith since he was the author of it (Moo, I:52), a suggestion motivated more by Calvinist beliefs than by the text. Actually Paul specifies exactly why he is thankful. He thanks God not for their faith as such, but for the fact that their faith "is being reported all over the world," i.e., the known world (and still perhaps an hyperbole). Paul had traveled a lot, and everywhere he went people talked about the fact that there was a Christian church *even in Rome*.

The second part of Paul's prayers for the Roman church is a prayer of petition.[17] The next two verses (9-10) do not themselves constitute this petition, but are Paul's affirmation that he does pray for the Roman saints on a regular basis. He prays especially that he may be permitted to travel to Rome and visit with them personally.

1:9-10a God, whom I serve with my whole heart in preaching the gospel of his Son, is my witness how constantly I remember you in my prayers at all times . . . . "God is my witness" is a kind of oath, in which he calls upon God to bear witness to the truth of his statement. This is a frequent practice of Paul; see 9:1; 2 Cor 1:23; 11:31; Gal 1:20; Phil 1:8; 1 Thess 2:5, 10. He calls upon God to be his witness especially when he is affirming things that others cannot establish for themselves, especially (as in this case) revelations of his own inner thoughts and feelings (Cranfield, I:75; Morris, 57). God

---

[17]Paul not only prays for the Romans, but also requests that they pray a specific prayer for him (15:30-32).

is a true witness to these things because he knows all things, even the thoughts of our hearts, and he cannot lie (1 John 3:20; Titus 1:2).

Paul uses this oath so that he can communicate how serious he is about his concern and prayers for Rome. He wants them to have no doubt about this, especially in view of the fact that he had not yet been there, and also in view of the fact that his immediate plans are to go to Jerusalem, not Rome (15:25). The oath will help the cynics not to doubt his sincerity.

Paul cannot refrain from a parenthetical description of God as the one "whom I serve with my whole heart in preaching the gospel of his Son." The word for "serve" is λατρεύω (latreuō), which in secular use meant "to work for pay." In the NT it always has a religious sense, meaning either "worship" (either of the true God or of false gods), or "service rendered to God" (Matt 4:10; Phil 3:3; 2 Tim 1:3). The noun form is similar (9:4; 12:1).

"With my whole heart" translates ἐν τῷ πνεύματί μου (en tō pneumati mou), "in or with my spirit." The NIV captures the meaning of this phrase, since both "heart" and "spirit" are words referring to the inner part of our being, in contrast with the outward or physical part. To serve God in one's spirit is to serve him with deep, sincere motivation (see 6:17, lit. "you obeyed from the heart"). Paul is saying that his service to God is completely sincere and internally motivated. Though he served from a deep sense of duty ("I am debtor," 1:14, KJV), his ministry was not just a job, not just an obligation. His heart was in it. Some do God's work from selfish or legalistic motives (Phil 1:15, 17; 3 John 9), but not Paul. Such a testimony should cause Christians everywhere to examine their own hearts and weigh their own motives for serving God.

Paul also reminds us that he serves God "in preaching the gospel of his Son." This says literally "in the gospel of his Son"; the NIV has added the word "preaching." This is probably the right understanding. As we have seen, the whole focus of Paul's life and ministry is the gospel. His entire service to God is directed toward the end of proclaiming the gospel. The words "of his Son" echo vv. 1, 3 and refer to the content of the gospel.

Paul calls upon God to bear witness to this fact in particular,

"how constantly I remember you in my prayers at all times."
"Constantly" in this case does not mean "without interruption," but
regularly. He says that he always remembers or mentions the
Roman church when he prays. "In my prayers" means more specifically "upon the occasion of my prayers, whenever I pray." He uses
similar language in Eph 1:16, 1 Thess 1:2-3, and Phlm 4. Paul must
have had an extensive prayer list, at least in his mind.

1:10b The words at the beginning of v. 10 do seem to belong
with the sentence in v. 9, as the NIV translates (Hendriksen, I:51).
Some think they should go with the thought in the rest of v. 10 (see
the NASB), in order to avoid having two words meaning approximately the same thing in one clause, i.e., "constantly" and "at all
times" (Moo, I:53; Murray, I:20-21). This is not a problem, however;
it is just repetition for emphasis.

In the latter part of v. 10 Paul gets to his main point, mentioning the specific prayer that is on his mind: **and I pray that now at
last by God's will the way may be opened for me to come to you.**
That is, he prays that God will allow him to travel to Rome for a
personal visit with the saints there. In view of v. 13, we can surely
infer that he had no doubt prayed this prayer for many years.

Whereas v. 8 is a prayer of thanksgiving, this is a prayer of petition. The Greek word is δέομαι (*deomai*), which means "desire, ask,
beg, beseech," and is often used in the NT in that sense. The use of
such a word shows that it is acceptable and appropriate for us to
present our requests to God (Phil 4:6), contrary to the occasional
suggestion that such an act is either futile or very arrogant and presumptuous. (See GRu, 361-367.)

Since Paul had planned and no doubt prayed to visit Rome for
quite some time, he was obviously feeling a bit frustrated and maybe
just a little bit impatient because this prayer had not yet been
answered (1:13; 15:22). This seems to be indicated in the string of
short Greek words that follow: εἴ πως (*ei pōs*) — "if in any way, if by
any means, if somehow, if possibly" (the NIV does not translate
these words); ἤδη (*ēdē*) — "now," after waiting all this time, after
being denied so often; and ποτέ (*pote*) — "at some time, at last." I.e.,
"I pray that — somehow, sometime, NOW! — God may permit me to
come to you." Here we see a touch of frustration, and a sense of
urgency and eagerness, and perhaps even some uncertainty as to

whether his present plan will be fulfilled (15:23-33; see Moo, I:53; Murray, I:21).

Balancing this outburst of restlessness is an acknowledgment of God's wisdom and control over the situation. He prays that he may visit Rome "by God's will." He knows it is not wrong for him to make specific plans, but he also knows that God in his sovereign providence will either permit him to carry out his plans or else will somehow intervene and prevent it (1:13). This is the nature of God's permissive will (see GRu, 313-317). See Acts 18:21; Rom 15:32; 1 Cor 4:19; 16:7; Heb 6:3; Jas 4:15.

Paul also knows that God can sovereignly intervene and providentially cause his trip to come about, overcoming all obstacles and circumstances, specifically in answer to his prayer. Thus he prays that by God's will "the way may be opened" for his visit. The word used here literally means "to lead along a good road" (Moo, I:53-54). In the passive voice it is used figuratively to mean "to prosper, to succeed" (see the NASB), and that is probably the meaning here. Still it is a very appropriate word to use here, since he knows that if God wills he can open up the road and grant him a successful journey to Rome.

The fact is that God did answer this prayer (Acts 23:11), but certainly not in a manner that Paul would have preferred. Having been falsely accused by the Jews, he exercised his right as a Roman citizen and appealed his case to Caesar (Acts 25:10-12). Thus he went to Rome as a prisoner of the state. But since his accusers failed to show up (Acts 28:21), he was ultimately set free again. In the meantime he was held under house arrest for two years but was still able to fulfill his dream of preaching the gospel in Rome (Acts 28:15-31).

B. PAUL'S DESIRES REGARDING ROME (1:11-13)

1:11 In this section Paul explains the reason for his persistent and heartfelt prayer to visit Rome.[18] **I long to see you,** he says

---

[18]The Greek particle γάρ (not translated by the NIV) occurs at the beginning of v. 11. It is usually translated "for," and usually introduces the cause or reason for what precedes.

(15:23). This is a very intensive word and indicates very deep desire (see 2 Cor 5:2; Phil 1:8; 2:26; 1 Thess 3:6; 2 Tim 1:4). Of course Paul already knows many of the Roman Christians (16:3-15), but his desire is not limited to them.

Why is Paul so eager to see the Romans? He explains, **so that I may impart to you some spiritual gift to make you strong . . . .** Whatever the nature of this gift, it was something within Paul's power to pass along to the church, something that he himself could impart or share.[19] Paul saw himself as the source of this gift, or at least the agent by whose action it could be imparted.

The word for "gift" is χάρισμα (*charisma*). In the NT this noun is used always for gifts that come ultimately from God. We may discern two main categories of gifts: the gift of salvation itself (5:15-16; 6:23); and gifts of ministry or service, i.e., gifts that endow the recipient with the right and ability to render special service to the church. This is the more frequent usage.[20] These latter gifts may be miraculous or nonmiraculous.

The word for "spiritual" is πνευματικός (*pneumatikos*). This is the only text where it is specifically used with "gift" for the phrase "spiritual gifts"; but see 1 Cor 12:1 and 14:1, where the word "gift" seems to be understood. In what sense is a gift *spiritual?* On the one hand something may be called spiritual if empowered by or derived from the Holy Spirit (1 Cor 2:13; 15:44, 46), just as a person may be called spiritual if led by the Holy Spirit (1 Cor 2:15; 14:37; Gal 6:1). Thus a "spiritual gift" would be a gift bestowed by the Holy Spirit. On the other hand something may be called spiritual because it is related to the spirit of man or to the spirit world, in contrast with the physical (Rom 15:27; 1 Cor 9:11; Eph 1:3; 6:12; 1 Pet 2:5). In this sense a "spiritual gift" would be something relating to the spiritual life of Christians.[21]

---

[19]For the other NT uses of this word, see Luke 3:11; Rom 12:8; Eph 4:28; and 1 Thess 2:8.

[20]See 12:6; 1 Cor 1:7; 7:7; 12:4, 9, 28, 30, 31; 1 Tim 4:14; 2 Tim 1:6; 1 Pet 4:10.

[21]This latter possibility is quite valid. One cannot just flatly state, as does Murray (I:22), that "a 'Spiritual gift' is a gift emanating from and bestowed by the Holy Spirit."

Can we be sure of the exact nature of the gift Paul wished to bestow upon the Romans? Probably not. He himself does not specify what it was; he says only *some* gift (τι, *ti*, an indefinite Greek particle). Some think he spoke only in generalities because he was not certain what gift would be needed until he actually arrived in Rome. Whatever it was, it would be "a blessing or benefit to be bestowed on the Christians in Rome by God through Paul's presence" (Cranfield, I:79).

Others believe that Paul wanted to bestow gifts of service upon the Romans, i.e., miraculous gifts such as prophecy and tongues (Lard, 35). Others say this cannot be the case, since Paul said *he* would impart the gifts and since miraculous gifts come only through the Holy Spirit according to his choosing, not through a human instrument (MacArthur, I:42-43; Morris, 60; Stott, 56). Those who object thus are obviously overlooking the records in Acts 8:14-19 and 19:6, where the laying on of apostles' hands bestowed the Holy Spirit's miracle-working power. (1 Tim 4:14 and 2 Tim 1:6 are also relevant.) Perhaps since no apostle had yet been to Rome (as far as we know), Paul felt the Roman church had the same need as the Samaritan church prior to the visit of Peter and John (Acts 8:14-19). If indeed gifts of ministry were what Paul had in mind here, he would have been thinking of miraculous gifts, since there is no indication that the laying on of apostles' hands was needed for the bestowing of nonmiraculous gifts.

The other main possibility is that Paul was referring to the general spiritual benefit that he could bestow upon the Romans as the result of his own work of "preaching, teaching, exhorting, comforting, praying, guiding, and disciplining" (MacArthur, I:43). This would be "spiritual strengthening in general" (Hendriksen, I:52). I.e., it would not have to come directly from the Holy Spirit, but would be "anything that builds up the spiritual life" of the Romans (Morris, 60).

Though I do not rule out the view that miraculous gifts are what Paul has in mind, I think this last suggestion is most likely the case. We need not state it in vague and general terms, however. I believe we can be quite specific about what Paul meant, namely, the gift he wanted to bestow upon the Romans was the gospel itself (1:15). In 1 Thess 2:8, using the same verb as here (μεταδίδωμι, *metadidōmi*),

Paul says, "We were delighted to share with you . . . the gospel of God" (see v. 9). In 1 Cor 9:11 he refers to his preaching of the gospel as sowing "spiritual" things (see 1 Cor 9:14). The gospel is a spiritual gift in that it comes ultimately through the revelation and inspiration of the Holy Spirit, but Paul also calls it "*my* gospel" (2:16; 16:25; 2 Tim 2:8) since it was entrusted to him for preaching. It is also a spiritual gift in the sense that it builds up the spirit, as compared with a material gift such as the money he was taking to Jerusalem (15:27). Paul's preference was to bestow this gift of the gospel upon the Romans in person (1:13-15); but it was also possible, as a second choice, to do it by means of this epistle.

The reason why Paul wanted to give the Romans this gift was "to make you strong" (στηρίζω, *stērizō*), i.e., to strengthen you, to establish you upon a firm foundation, to confirm you in your faith. (See Luke 22:32; 1 Thess 3:2, 13; 2 Thess 3:3; 1 Pet 5:10.) Of course, the purpose of miraculous spiritual gifts was to confirm faith and build up the church (1 Cor 14:3-5, 26-33; Eph 4:11-14; Heb 2:4), so this would be consistent with the view that this was the nature of the gift. But it should be noted that the word *stērizō* is also used in Romans 16:25 to describe the effect of preaching the gospel: "Now to him who is able to establish you by my gospel." Using the same word, Peter says we are "firmly established in the truth" (2 Pet 1:12). See also 2 Thess 2:17. Thus in v. 11 Paul says he wants to go to Rome in order to bestow upon the Roman Christians a spiritual gift that will strengthen them, namely, the gospel of Jesus Christ.

1:12 that is, that you and I may be mutually encouraged by each other's faith. This verse presents an interesting addendum to the thought of v. 11. The expression translated "that is" suggests an amendment or modification of what Paul has just said. While not retracting his point about wanting to bestow some gift upon the Romans, he now graciously acknowledges that they would actually be able to give him encouragement as well: I can help you, but you can also help me.

This was not just a statement of formal courtesy or false piety or tactful diplomacy, as if he really did not mean it. No, Paul genuinely felt that he would be blessed by his visit to Rome. In 15:24 he speaks of going to Rome "to enjoy your company for a while."

"Enjoy your company" is a loose way of translating a verb that means "to be filled full." He knew that his visit would fill empty places in his own life. Paul says this mutual encouragement would take place while he was "among you" (ἐν ὑμῖν, *en hymin*) — a phrase not translated by the NIV. Of course, he was encouraged by the *report* of their faith (v. 8), and he could preach the gospel to them in the epistle; but nothing could truly take the place of a face-to-face encounter.

Such mutual encouragement made possible by Paul's visit would come, says Paul, "by each other's faith." The Romans would be able to know Paul in person, not just by reputation. They not only would be able to hear about Paul's faith through this letter or from others, but would be able to hear about it from Paul's own lips and, even better, to see firsthand how he lived his faith in his everyday life. Also, Paul would be able to observe firsthand how the Romans would mature in their faith through his own gospel preaching. He thus could receive "comfort from their settled belief" (Lard, 35).

Verse 12 closes with an expression not translated by the NIV. It is a phrase that modifies "faith," namely, the faith "of both you and me." It is simply a repetition of the phrase translated "each other's." The NASB includes them both: "each of us by the other's faith, both yours and mine." Such repetition puts even greater emphasis on the blessing of mutuality between Christian leaders and those whom they lead.

1:13 At this point some of the Romans might have been tempted to think, "Well, if Paul is really sincere, if he really wants to see us so badly, why has he not come before now?" Here Paul addresses this possible suspicion: **I do not want you to be unaware, brothers . . . .**[22] He uses this double negative for emphasis. Such an introduction means, "This is a really important point. Listen carefully. I want to make sure you understand this." He wanted no misunderstanding on this point about his desire to come to Rome.

He calls them "brothers," a term he used often to refer to his fellow Christians.[23] Though he was a physical or racial brother only

---

[22]See the similar language in 11:25; 1 Cor 10:1; 12:1-2; 2 Cor 1:8; 1 Thess 4:13.

[23]See 7:1, 4; 8:12; 10:1; 11:25; 12:1; 15:14-15, 30; 16:17. See also 1 Cor 15:58; Col 1:2; 1 Tim 6:2. Paul spoke a few times of female Christians as

to the Jews (see 9:3), as a Christian he regarded all men of whatever background as his brothers if they were fellow Christians. Thus even the members of the (mainly) Gentile church at Rome are addressed as "brothers." He thereby expresses his close relationship with them, even though he has never met most of them.

What was he so eager to have his brethren know? . . . **that I planned many times to come to you (but have been prevented from doing so until now)** . . . . He is not speaking here of simple desire to visit them, but of actual, concrete plans: not just once or twice, but often. That he had made such plans many times indicates the longstanding nature of his concern for Rome, contrary to any who might have doubted it. Lard (36-37) points out that these plans must not have been prompted by the Holy Spirit, else at some point they would have been carried out.

So far, however, they had *not* been carried out, but it was not Paul's fault; he had "been prevented from doing so." (See 15:22.) In this parenthetical statement he does not say what prevented him from coming to Rome. The demands of preaching to the unchurched eastern Mediterranean area no doubt were a main factor (15:20-22). At times God intervened to change Paul's plans (Acts 16:6-9), and sometimes Satan put up roadblocks (1 Thess 2:18).

After this parenthesis about being hindered, Paul continues his thought about his plans by stating what he hoped to accomplish by coming to Rome. In v. 11 he said he wanted to impart some spiritual gift to the Romans in order to strengthen them. Here he says he had planned to come **in order that I might have a harvest among you** . . . . The NASB is more literal: "obtain some fruit."

The question here is the nature of the fruit Paul hoped to reap from among the Romans by his presence there. One possibility is that he is referring to converts he would win to Christ through his preaching (Stott, 57). Jesus calls the lost world a harvest field where fruit may be gathered (Matt 9:36-38; John 4:35-36). Paul refers to the first converts in an area as the "firstfruit" (16:5; 1 Cor 16:15).

The term *fruit* is also used in the NT in the sense of bearing or

---

"sisters," but not as a form of address. See Rom 16:1; 1 Cor 7:15; 9:5. They are usually included in the generic reference to "brothers."

producing the fruit of mature character and holy conduct. This concept appears in the gospels (Matt 3:8, 10; 7:16-20; 12:33) and in the concept of the "fruit of the Spirit" (Gal 5:22-23). See also Eph 5:9; Phil 1:11; Heb 12:11; 13:15; Jas 3:17-18.

The terminology of obtaining or producing fruit may also refer to the more general concept of cause and effect. I.e., whenever anything produces something as its effect, that is its *fruit*. For example, whenever our lips produce praise, that is their fruit (Heb 13:15). If discipline causes righteousness, that is its fruit (Heb 12:11). The fruit or effect of slavery to sin is shame and death, but the fruit of slavery to God is sanctification and eternal life (6:21-22).

This is the sense in which we talk about the "fruit of our labor," i.e., the good results of our labor, whatever those results may be. This is precisely Paul's point in Phil 1:22, when he says in effect that the advantage of continuing to live is that his work can produce more fruit for God. He says when the Philippian church sent him material support for his missionary work, the fruit produced thereby was really to be credited to them (Phil 4:16-17). He calls the offering he collected for the poor saints in Jerusalem the "fruit" of his fund-raising efforts (15:28).

It is probable that here in 1:13 Paul is using the term *fruit* in this general sense of *results*. Thus he is saying that his desire and plans to go to Rome are for the purpose of winning converts as well as building up and strengthening the existing saints (Cranfield, I:82). He hopes first of all to preach the gospel "among you" in an evangelistic sense, thus directly reaping fruit and adding more Christians to the body there. But he also hopes to preach the deeper gospel truths that will lead to stronger faith and more mature character for the entire church, just as he has said in v. 11. In this way Paul's preaching will "get fruit" in Rome indirectly, by causing the Christians there to achieve greater depths of holiness.

In these ways Paul will have fruit in Rome **just as I have had among the other Gentiles**.[24] By the time Paul wrote Romans he had preached the gospel to a large portion of the Gentile world (15:19, 23), with much fruit being produced. See Phil 1:5-6, 10, where he

---

[24]Many take this statement as an indication that the Roman church was predominantly Gentile. See vv. 5-6.

says that the preaching of the gospel continues to produce the fruit of good works and maturity in the lives of Christians in Philippi. But somehow it would just not be fitting if he obtained fruit from all over the Gentile world but passed by its very capital and nerve center, Rome itself.

C. PAUL'S DEBT TO THE ROMANS (1:14-15)

1:14 I am obligated both to Greeks and non-Greeks, both to the wise and the foolish. Paul has spoken frankly to the Romans about his prayers and desires for them; now in these two verses he reveals another aspect of his heart. Specifically, he unveils for us all the strong sense of obligation that drove him to burn himself out in service to Christ. For "I am obligated," the text says literally, "I am a debtor." A debtor is someone who *owes* somebody something. It can be a debt of money (Matt 18:24) or a moral obligation of some other kind. In the latter sense we speak of a debt of gratitude (15:29), or of paying one's debt to society.

Every human being is a debtor to God in two ways. First, we owe him our absolute obedience (8:12) because he is our Creator. Second, because all have sinned (sins are debts: Matt 6:12), we owe him (or he owes us) a debt of punishment. Now, as Christians whose debt has been paid by the Redeemer, we also owe God a debt of eternal gratitude.[25] All of these ways of being a debtor applied to Paul, but these are not specifically what he is speaking of in v. 13. Here he refers to a debt that applied to him alone, i.e., his moral obligation to preach the gospel to the Gentiles of the world, based on his calling as God's apostle to the Gentiles (1:1, 5). Because of this, he says, "I am compelled to preach" (1 Cor 9:16). He was entrusted with the gospel as an inescapable stewardship.[26] Preaching the gospel was a debt he owed to God, because God appointed him to do it.

Actually, though, in this text Paul says he is a debtor not to God

---

[25]For a fuller discussion of these three kinds of debt see Cottrell, *Grace*, 97-103.

[26]See 1 Cor 4:1-2; 9:17; Gal 2:7; 1 Thess 2:4; 1 Tim 1:11; Titus 1:3.

but to the Gentiles themselves. His commission put him in debt to the latter as well. He *owed* it *to the Gentiles* to preach the gospel to them. How was this the case? Consider this scenario: a very wealthy man dies and bequeaths his estate to a distant relative. His lawyer is entrusted with the task of tracking down this relative and transferring the estate to him. In a real sense the lawyer owes it to the relative to make sure he receives the inheritance (see Stott, 59).

With reference to his debt, Paul says he is obligated "both to Greeks and non-Greeks, both to the wise and the foolish." There are two issues here. One, how extensive are these expressions? Do they encompass the whole world, or just the Gentiles? Second, is the second pair equivalent to or different from the first?

Some regard the first pair of terms as including the whole world, describing it as viewed by Greeks themselves. Just as Jews divided the whole world into Jews and non-Jews (Gentiles), so the Greeks divided the whole world into "Greeks and non-Greeks," as the NIV puts it. According to this view, Paul's debt is owed to the whole world.

Though Paul no doubt saw his debt as universal, this is not the best understanding of this pair of terms. There is no reason for Paul to describe the world from the perspective of Greeks. Also, in the prior context he has emphasized his apostleship to the Gentiles (vv. 5, 13). Thus we conclude that these terms are meant to be "the sum of Gentile mankind," as Cranfield says (I:83). It is true that Paul sometimes uses "Greeks" as a synonym for Gentiles (1:16; 2:9-10; 3:9; 10:12), but this is when he is contrasting them with Jews. Here the term has the more limited reference of the sophisticated, civilized, cultured Gentiles, those who were "Greek" by language and culture, whether they were born of Greek parentage or not (Barclay, 8). The word for "non-Greeks" is actually βάρβαρος (*barbaros*) or "barbarians," or the less civilized peoples who spoke strange languages that sounded like "bar-bar-bar" gibberish to sophisticated "Greek" ears.

"The wise and the foolish" also refers to Gentiles. Some see these categories as distinct from the previous ones (Cranfield, I:83-84; Morris, 65). It is more probable, though, that they are equivalent to the first pair and are just one way of explaining the difference between them (Hendriksen, I:54). Greeks are wise and learned, at least in their own eyes and with a worldly wisdom (1 Cor 1:19-20, 26-27); barbarians are foolish and uneducated and without understanding.

1:15 In this verse Paul takes the general principle stated in v. 14 and applies it specifically to the Christians in Rome. Just because he has this overwhelming obligation to the Gentile world, **"That is why I am so eager to preach the gospel also to you who are at Rome."** The expression that begins this verse can be translated either "that is why," as in the NIV, or "as far as I am concerned, as for me, for my part," as in the NASB. Paul's point is that whether his circumstances or God's providence allows him to come to Rome or not, in his own heart and mind he is ready and eager to be there and to preach the gospel.

This shows that Paul is constrained not just by a barren sense of obligation which he was resentfully determined to fulfill against his own preferences and desires. He was obligated, yes (v. 14); but he was *eagerly willing* to meet that obligation. His heart was intertwined with the will of God.

Since Paul was a debtor to all Gentiles everywhere, Rome was certainly included in this debt. Thus he wanted to preach the gospel "to you (ὑμῖν, *hymin*) who are at Rome." A question that arises here is whether *hymin* means "*to* you" or "*among* you." Some say the latter, because they think preaching the gospel is always an evangelistic effort. Thus they say Paul could not really preach the gospel to the Roman Christians; they had already heard it and accepted it. What he meant was that he was ready to preach the gospel to the unsaved in their midst or in their city (Godet, 90; Moo, I:57-58; Watson, "Congregations," 213).

This limitation on εὐαγγελίζομαι (*euangelizomai*) is not justified, however. Its primary connotation is preaching the gospel to the lost, and Paul certainly did a lot of this (15:20) and no doubt planned to do it in Rome. But it also has the connotation of explaining the fuller content of the gospel to the church, "the ongoing work of teaching and discipleship that follows initial evangelization."[27] Cranfield sees this use here (I:86), as does Dunn (I:34).

---

[27]Moo, I:57. Moo says this is an attractive possibility, but he believes there is not enough evidence to sustain it.

The latter says that for Paul the word "can embrace the whole range of his ministry, including his explication of the gospel, as in this very letter." As Friedrich says, "The Gospel is not just mission- ary proclamation . . . . It does not merely found the community; it also edifies it" ("εὐαγγελίζομαι," 734; see 719-720, 733).

This idea is clearly seen in a comparison of 1:11 and 16:25. In 1:11, as we have seen, Paul says he wants to give the Roman Christians some spiritual gift in order to establish them (στηρίζω, *stērizō*). In 16:25 he describes God as the one "who is able to estab- lish (*stērizō*) you by my gospel." There is no doubt that he means the Roman Christians in this latter verse, and that the gospel is an instrument for edifying and strengthening them. See also Gal 1:8-9; 1 Thess 2:8-9; 3:2.

One thing that seems clear from the content of this epistle is that the gospel of grace is often misunderstood and often requires a lot of follow-up clarification and explanation. This was no doubt true of the Roman Christians, and Paul "needs to correct the understanding of the gospel held by at least some of them," as Wedderburn says ("Purpose," 199). Possibly under the influence of the Judaizers, they were struggling with the role of works in rela- tion to grace and faith. This explains the emphasis on justification by faith apart from works of law (3:28). God intends the gospel to produce obedience, but it must be the obedience *of faith* (1:5).

It is clear from this verse and from earlier statements by Paul that he wanted to preach the gospel to the believers in Rome in order to clarify and establish their faith in Christ's redeeming work. This gives us our best clue as to Paul's purpose for writing his epistle to the Romans. He is under divine obligation to preach the gospel to them. He wants to do so in person; but in case his present plans to go there do not work out, he decides to preach the gospel in the form of a letter. He cannot wait any longer to pay his debt to them.

III. 1:16-17 — TRANSITIONAL STATEMENT

Most Bible students regard this section as a statement of the *theme* of Romans. Dunn says it "is clearly the thematic statement for the entire letter" (I:37). It is "the statement of the theological theme which is going to be worked out in the main body of the epistle," says Cranfield (I:87). These verses do not constitute a full statement of the theme of Romans, but are more of a preliminary or introductory statement, or (as Dunn says) a "launching pad" providing "the primary thrust and direction for the rest of the letter" (I:46). As such it is the transitional statement tying the prologue to the main body of Romans.

As has been the case throughout the prologue, the main point of this section is *the gospel*. These verses deal with its glory, its power, its scope, its relation to faith, its heart, and its golden text.

A. THE GLORY OF THE GOSPEL (1:16a)

1:16 This verse opens with a transitional word, γάρ (*gar*), meaning "for, because" (omitted by the NIV). In v. 15 Paul has declared his eagerness to preach the gospel in Rome, and v. 16 gives the reason for this: I am eager to do this, because **I am not ashamed of the gospel . . . .** (Some manuscripts add "of Christ"; those followed by most modern translations, including the NIV, do not.)

Dunn points out that "shame" is "the consequence of being shown to have acted on a false assumption or misplaced confidence" (I:38). Thus Paul is saying that he will never have to worry about having devoted his life to a false cause. He is confident that the gospel is everything it claims to be, and that he will never have to apologize or be sorry for believing it and preaching it.

Some (e.g., Bruce, 79) say the expression "I am not ashamed" is a literary device used for the purpose of emphasizing a positive point (like "I do not want you to be unaware" in v. 13). Thus Paul's real point would be that he considers it a great honor to preach the gospel; it is his pride and glory. There could hardly be any shame attached to something as glorious as the gospel.

Others doubt that this is the point, though (Cranfield, I:86; Moo, I:60; Stott, 60). They say that Paul no doubt meant this very literally, i.e., that he is not ashamed to preach a message which on the surface has all the appearances of a losing cause. In addition to

the sinful world's basic prejudice against the true God and any religious service to him at all (1:18-32), the gospel has the added liabil-
ity of focusing on an alleged "savior" who got in trouble with the
authorities and did not have enough power to prevent his being
executed in the most shameful way. Thus, according to Cranfield,
this statement by Paul is his "sober recognition of the fact that the
gospel is something of which, by the very nature of the case,
Christians will in this world constantly be tempted to be ashamed"
(I:86). Jesus himself warned us against yielding to this temptation
(Mark 8:38), as did Paul (2 Tim 1:8). Paul points out that the
message of the cross will always be ridiculed as foolishness and
weakness by those whose eyes are blinded by worldly wisdom
(1 Cor 1:18-31).

Nevertheless, Paul says he is *not ashamed* of this gospel. He is
ready to preach it anywhere, even and especially in Rome itself, the
very center of human power and pomp and presumptuousness, the
crossroads of worldly wealth and wisdom and sophistication.
Though he had no confidence in his own powers (1 Cor 2:1-3), he
had every confidence in the gospel itself, or rather in the One of
whom it speaks: "I am not ashamed, because I know whom I have
believed, and am convinced that he is able to guard what I have
entrusted to him for that day" (2 Tim 1:12).

B. THE POWER OF THE GOSPEL (1:16b)

Paul's next statement gives the reason why he is not ashamed of
the gospel: **because it is the power of God for the salvation of
everyone who believes . . . .** "Because" translates the particle *gar*,
used for the second time in the verse. Why is Paul not ashamed of
the gospel? Because it is not foolish and weak as the world thinks,
but is rather the instrument of omnipotence, the almighty power by
which God saves sinners. In some cases weakness may indeed be a
proper reason for shame, but not *power*, and certainly not the
power *of God*.

"Power" translates δύναμις (*dynamis*),[28] from which come

---

[28]See also 1 Cor 1:18, 24; 2:5; 2 Cor 4:7; 6:7; Eph 1:19; 3:7, 16, 20; Col
1:11; 2 Tim 1:8.

English words such as "dynamic" and "dynamo" and "dynamite." It means power in the sense of the ability and competence to accomplish something. Erdman rightly says, "The gospel is thus defined in terms of 'power'; it can do something . . . . It is 'the power of God'; it can therefore do anything" (27). The perception that it is weak and foolish is totally false and could not be further from the truth.

Specifically what is the power of the gospel able to accomplish? It is able to *save* those who believe. It is the power of God unto (*eis*) salvation. This recalls 1:4, which declares that the risen Jesus is now the Son of God *with power*. He is fully able to save us.

In what sense is the "gospel" God's power unto salvation? How does it save us? Here we must distinguish between the gospel as a verbal message proclaimed by a preacher, and the gospel as the actual reality of which that verbal message speaks. Strictly speaking it is not the message itself that saves, but the saving work of Christ of which the message informs us. The gospel is not just words that impact our minds, but works that impact our sinful situation and deliver us from it (see Nygren, 77).

In the Greek world the words relating to salvation were used "in the sense of an acutely dynamic act in which gods or men snatch others by force from serious peril" (Foerster, "σώζω," 966). These words could be used of rescue from a purely physical, temporal danger (Matt 8:25; Acts 27:34), but in his epistles Paul always uses them in the spiritual sense of salvation from sin by the grace of God.[29] (In v. 16 "salvation" is the same as "will live" in v. 17.)

Salvation can be described both negatively and positively, in terms of what it saves us *from* and what it saves us *to*. It delivers us from all the perils and consequences of sin (Morris, 68), e.g., "from God's wrath" (5:9). It saves us to the blessed states of grace and glory (5:2). The salvation brought by the gospel is a process. With reference to the past, we have already been delivered from the penalty of sin into the state of justification. Regarding the present, we are being delivered from the power of sin by the process of sanctification. As to the future, we will be delivered from the presence of sin in the final glorification.

---

[29] 1 Tim 2:15 may be an exception to this.

C. THE SCOPE OF THE GOSPEL (1:16c)

Another point Paul addresses in this text is the *scope* of the gospel. He says it is God's power for the salvation of everyone who believes: **first for the Jew, then for the Gentile**. In terms of its intention and potential, the gospel's power is universal. God wants everyone to receive the salvation embodied in it (John 3:16; 2 Pet 3:9). The gospel is for anyone and everyone (3:22; 4:11; 10:4, 11).

This is not a concept of universal*ism*, though, as if every human being will be fully, finally, and unconditionally saved. The actual reception and application of the gospel is limited only to those who believe in it. The world is divided into two categories: those who believe in the gospel, and those who do not. The former are saved; the latter are not.

The Jews also divided the world into two categories: themselves, and everyone else (the Gentiles). They regarded themselves as saved and all others as lost. In OT times, under the Old Covenant, there was some basis for thinking this way; but under the New Covenant this is no longer possible. The Jew-Gentile distinction is no longer relevant where salvation is concerned (10:12; 1 Cor 12:13; Gal 3:28). The gospel is intended equally for everyone alike, whether Jew or Gentile.[30] Paul's use of the expression "both . . . and" (τέ . . . καὶ, *te . . . kai*, not translated by the NIV) indicates this equality. Literally he says, "Both for the Jew (first) and for the Greek."

Although Jews and Gentiles receive the same salvation in the same way, Paul says a certain priority applies to the Jews. God's gospel of salvation is for the Jew *first* (see 2:9-10). Some think this is indicative of a permanent priority and perpetual preference to be enjoyed by the Jews as God's chosen people. Cranfield accepts this idea and sees it as a paradox in view of Gal 3:28 (I:91). Murray (I:28) has a similar view.

---

[30]In this verse Paul actually uses the term *Greek*, not *Gentile* as the NIV has it. But here he intends it to be inclusive of all Gentiles, unlike the distinction made in v. 14; and he intends the Jew-Greek combination to be inclusive of the whole human race. Paul uses this combination in other places for the same purpose (see 2:9-10; 3:9; 10:12; 1 Cor 1:22, 24; 10:32; 12:13; Gal 3:28; Col 3:11). That *Greek* and *Gentile* are sometimes used synonymously is shown in 1 Cor 1:22-24.

Others more properly see the "Jew first" principle as a temporary though significant result of God's choice of the Israelite nation
as the primary agent by which the Messiah was brought into the
world. The Jews enjoyed a place of priority in the historical process
by which God has accomplished his plan of redemption (Godet, 92;
Hendriksen, I:61). Paul's specific point is that, as a natural result of
their unique role in preparing for the Messiah (3:2; 9:4-5), the Jews
were the first to hear the gospel message and the first to have the
opportunity to accept it in faith (see Acts 2-9). Paul reflects this
"Jew first" concept in the "we" section of Eph 1 (vv. 3-12), and the
"Gentiles also" concept in the "you" section (vv. 13-19). He prac-
ticed this principle in his own ministry (Acts 13:46; 18:5-6; 19:8-9).
In view of the outstanding service rendered to God by Israel as a
nation, it was only proper that this opportunity for believing the
gospel be extended to them first.

This fits into Paul's overall message in Romans in two ways.
First, this emphasis on the divine courtesy extended to the Jews
provides balance to Paul's frequent references to the Gentiles (e.g.,
1:5, 13-14). Second, it would help to plant respect for the Jewish
Christians in the minds of the (probable) Gentile majority in the
Roman church.

It is important to remember that this historical priority enjoyed
by national Israel, with respect to the preparation for and proclamation of the gospel, was not the basis for any kind of preferential
treatment of individual Jews with regard to salvation and the final
judgment. In these matters equality prevails, as Paul will emphasize
in chapter 2 especially.

D. FAITH AND THE GOSPEL (1:16c)

The gospel is the power of God for salvation to "everyone who
believes." The references to faith in these two verses are crucial for
the theme of the letter as a whole and for the very nature of salvation by grace. (Paul has already referred to faith in vv. 5, 8, 12.) The
Greek words for faith (noun, πίστις [pistis]; verb, πιστεύω [pisteuō])
mean "to rely on, to believe, to trust, to have confidence in."

Saving faith in Jesus, of which this verse speaks, has two main components.[31] First, faith includes *assent*: acknowledging the truth of a statement, or granting the fact that a particular statement is true. This is a cognitive act, a judgment of the intellect based on sufficient evidence. In the Bible this aspect appears most clearly when the verb is used with the conjunction ὅτι (*hoti*), a combination translated "to believe that" (something is true). See especially John 8:24; 11:27, 42; 13:19; 14:10; 16:27, 30; 17:8, 21; 20:31; Rom 6:8; 10:9; 1 Thess 4:14; Heb 11:6; Jas 2:19; 1 John 5:1, 5.

The second component of saving faith is *trust*: acknowledging the trustworthiness of a person, entrusting yourself or something you value into another person's care, or surrendering yourself in some sense to that person. This is a volitional act, a decision of the will based on a combination of personal need and a confidence that the other person can meet that need. It is directed toward the person himself and not just toward statements about him. In biblical terminology this aspect of faith appears most clearly in the expressions "to believe in" and "to believe on." For the former, see especially John 3:16, 18, 36; 6:29, 40; 7:38; 9:35; 11:25-26; 14:1; Acts 10:43; Rom 10:14; Gal 2:16. For the latter, see Matt 27:42; John 3:15 (some manuscripts have *pisteuō en*); Acts 9:42; 11:17; 16:31. This concept is expressed well in 2 Timothy 1:12.

The faith of which Paul speaks here is not just a general faith in God (Heb 11:6) or a general trust in the beneficence of his providence. It is specifically faith in *the gospel*, faith in Jesus Christ as Savior, faith in his blood (3:25), faith in his resurrection (10:9). As Godet says, it is "nothing else than the simple acceptance of the salvation offered in preaching" (92).

1. Faith Is a Condition for Salvation

Two main points must be made concerning the relation between faith and the gospel as stated here. First, faith is presented

---

[31]Dunn (I:43) agrees. Some have included *right understanding* as a third component of true faith, but it is more properly a prerequisite of it. Others have included *obedience* within the very definition of true faith, but it is more properly a result of it. Thus I cannot agree with DeWelt (25), who says that faith "includes repentance, confession and baptism." This is a very common idea, but there is no basis for it.

as a *condition* for receiving the salvation provided by the gospel. This shows that salvation and grace itself are conditional.

This is contrary to the Augustinian idea that salvation is given unconditionally only to those whom God unconditionally chooses to save. According to this view, rather than being a condition of salvation, faith is itself one of the gifts bestowed upon selected sinners, who in themselves and without the gift would be totally unable to believe because of their inborn condition of total depravity.

Many Calvinist commentators use v. 16 as the occasion for introducing their belief that faith is a gift. For example, Cranfield denies that faith is "a condition imposed by God" by which a man responds to the gospel. "The faith spoken of here is the openness to the gospel which God himself creates"; it is "God's work in a man" (I:90). Hendriksen says that faith "is, from start to finish, *God's gift.*" Also, "The gift of faith is from God but so is also the power to exercise it" (I:61-63). "Paul has in mind here a supernatural faith, produced by God," says MacArthur (I:55). As Murray explains, "regeneration is causally prior to faith." That is, one must be born again before it is possible for him to believe; and God's regenerating act always produces faith, "even in the case of infants, for in regeneration the germ of faith is implanted" (I:27, n. 21).

Nygren, a Swedish Lutheran, makes the same point. He cites several interpreters who declare that faith is "a necessary condition for salvation," but then asserts that "nothing was further from Paul's mind than this" in 1:16-17 (67-69). Rather, the gospel itself "creates faith and awakens it in us" (78). Thus "one's faith is evidence that the gospel *has* exercised its power on him. . . . It is the power of the gospel that makes it possible for one to believe" (71).

Now, it is true that the preaching of the gospel induces and produces faith in the hearts of some of those who hear it. As Paul clearly says in 10:17, "Faith comes from hearing the message." The word of God is sharper than a sword and can penetrate even the hardest of hearts (Heb 4:12). The written word is able to produce saving faith in Jesus (John 20:31). Calvinists and other Augustinians, however, *do not really believe this.* They do not really believe the word of the gospel is able to produce faith in the sinner's heart. Hearing the word may be a necessary occasion for faith to arise; but they believe that what really produces the faith is a distinct and selective act of God, not the power of the gospel as such.

But gospel preaching *does* have the power to produce faith (10:17). It is not a raw, coercive, irresistible power that violates our God-given wills, but rather a drawing, persuasive, convicting power; and this power is not selective but is exerted equally on all who hear it (John 12:32). Still, the message is almost always initially met by resistance. Some eventually cease to resist, and thus allow their hearts to be moved to a state of surrender to Jesus, i.e., to faith. Others by their own choice harden their wills and continue to resist, contrary to the desire of God's own heart (Matt 23:37; Acts 7:51; 2 Pet 3:9). In other words, whereas a Calvinist says God's grace draws sinners selectively and irresistibly, Scripture teaches that the drawing is universal and resistible.

After having said all of this, I must point out that v. 16 is not talking about *how gospel preaching produces faith* at all, but rather *how the gospel events produce salvation*. That gospel preaching produces faith is true, as Scripture teaches elsewhere, but this is not the point here. The "gospel" to which Paul refers here is not the message of the gospel as preached, but the reality of the saving events of which the gospel speaks, i.e., the death and resurrection of Christ. The "power of God" lies in these mighty works of the Son of God. And Paul's point is that these mighty works produce salvation itself, not that they produce faith.

How does Paul relate faith to the gospel in this verse? He says simply that the gospel produces salvation for "everyone who believes." I.e., the saving works of Jesus do not save all sinners; they save only those who accept them in faith. In other words, Paul is most decisively asserting that faith is a necessary condition for being saved. Salvation is *conditional*. This is not by any means contrary to the concept of salvation by grace. Grace is by its very nature unmerited, but this is not the same as unconditional. We should never speak of "unconditional grace." Some conditions for salvation would definitely be meritorious and would thus contradict grace; but some conditions are not meritorious and are not "works" in the Pauline sense. Faith is certainly a condition, but it is not a work in any meritorious sense (Eph 2:8-9).[32]

---

[32]See the discussion "Is Grace Conditional or Unconditional?" in GRe, 389-399.

COLLEGE PRESS NIV COMMENTARY

As a condition for salvation nothing could be more natural than faith, and more compatible with the nature of grace as a gift (4:16; 11:6). Since our salvation is accomplished by the work of someone else (Jesus), and since it is offered to us as a free gift, the only thing we can do is accept God's word that this is so, and hold out an empty hand to receive the gift. Faith is often identified with this empty hand.

In summary the gospel is both the saving *events* or redemptive works of Jesus, and the *message* that proclaims these saving works to us. The gospel events are the power of God that works salvation in our hearts, and the gospel message is the power of the word that produces faith in those events. The former cannot take place until the latter has occurred.

2. Faith Is Not the Only Condition

Now we turn to the second main point concerning the relation between faith and the gospel. We have seen that salvation is conditional, but now we must affirm that *faith is not the only condition*. We could say that faith is a *necessary* condition for salvation, but it is not a *sufficient* condition.

A large portion of Christendom, both Calvinist and non-Calvinist, will immediately reject this statement. After all, has not Protestantism always been identified with the principle of *sola fidei*, "by faith alone"? Nygren (68) cites several scholars who declare that "nothing but faith" is required for man to be saved. For example, Althaus says, "Faith is the indispensable and only condition for salvation." As Nygren says, the issue is "the sufficiency of faith for salvation."

More recently this position has been argued by those who reject what they call "lordship salvation." This view, represented notably by Zane C. Hodges and Charles C. Ryrie, asserts the following: "Faith is the one and only condition requisite for receiving eternal life. . . . There is no mention of repentance, of good works, of commitment to lordship. It is faith, and faith alone" (Erickson, *Mind*, 109).

This idea that faith is the only condition for salvation is incorrect and is based on false assumptions and faulty hermeneutics.

Several things must be remembered. First, these two verses —
Romans 1:16-17 — do not exhaust the content of the gospel but are
a kind of introductory summary of its main points, a transitional
statement leading into the fuller exposition of the gospel.

Second, as we saw under 1:5 above, we must not only *believe* the
gospel but also *obey* it. "Obeying the gospel" is not the same as
obeying the law, i.e., "works of law" (3:20, 28). It is rather doing
those things we are instructed to do in order to receive God's
saving grace. When we examine the evangelistic preaching in the
book of Acts, we see that the gospel as preached to sinners
included not only the good news of salvation as such, but also the
necessary instructions for receiving this salvation. The latter is also
part of the good news and should never be thought of as incompatible with it, since God would never tell us to do something as a condition for receiving salvation that is in any way a violation of its gracious character.

Third, we must remember that all the conditions related to salvation do not have an *identical* relation to salvation. They are all necessary, by God's decree; but they are not necessary in the same sense.
As an analogy, food or nourishment is a necessary condition for
maintaining physical life, but the process of eating the food is also
necessary as the occasion for receiving the food into our bodies. Or,
to get light from the electricity flowing through the wiring in one's
house, a light bulb is a necessary condition; but so are a lamp and a
plug. In order to see a baseball game in person, it is necessary to
have a ticket; but it is also necessary to go to the place where the
game is played at the time it is played. In these illustrations the
food, the bulb, and the ticket are the primary conditions for achieving the desired goals (life, light, game). However, the other considerations are no less necessary; as auxiliary conditions they simply play
different roles in the process of achieving the goals.

In spite of their historical commitment to the *sola fidei* principle,
most Protestants actually acknowledge that this is so. For example,
except for those who are radically committed to the "faith and
nothing else" view, such as those who oppose "lordship salvation,"
almost all Protestants realize that *repentance* is a necessary condition
for salvation. They appeal to a universally-accepted principle of
hermeneutics, namely, that *all* the Bible says about a given subject

must be considered before we can draw final conclusions about that subject. That is, we must not take texts such as John 3:16, Acts 16:31, Rom 1:16-17, and Eph 2:8-9 in isolation from other texts that speak of the essentiality of repentance and submission to Christ's lordship (e.g., Luke 6:46-49; Acts 2:38; Rom 10:9-10).

A good example of this approach is Millard Erickson (*Mind*, 120). He asks why such men as Zane Hodges ("faith and nothing else," anti-lordship salvation) and John MacArthur (faith *plus* repentance and submission to Christ's lordship as conditions) can come to such different views. The problem, says Erickson, stems in part from the fact that "the Bible gives different formulas for conversion, different responses to the query, 'What must I do to be saved?'" Hodges emphasizes only those that specify faith. But how are we to regard those texts that specify repentance, and do not even mention faith?

The best answer, says Erickson, is that the two sets of passages must be combined and integrated in order to have the complete picture of the conditions for salvation. I.e., "both faith and repentance are necessary to salvation. In those biblical passages where only one is mentioned explicitly, the other is implicit. Repentance and faith would then be complementary aspects of a whole — conversion."

If Erickson is right, and I believe he is, then this shows that faith is not the only condition for salvation; and Rom 1:16-17 cannot be used to defend a radical "faith and nothing else" view of salvation. But I and many others will insist that Erickson has not gone far enough. He is methodologically correct to insist that we must apply the proper hermeneutical principle to this question, but he errs in limiting its application only to repentance. In view of the many passages that also include *baptism* as part of the gospel instructions on how to be saved (e.g., Acts 2:38; 8:36; 22:16; Col 2:12; 1 Pet 3:21), we cannot honestly exclude it from the list of conditions for salvation. There is no valid reason why Erickson should not treat baptism in exactly the same way he has treated repentance. The hermeneutical principle that requires us to include repentance in the list also requires us to include baptism. To criticize the likes of Zane Hodges for excluding repentance from the list of conditions and then to exclude baptism is seriously inconsistent.

It is likewise incorrect to cite the Reformation principle of *sola fidei* and to appeal to the great reformer Martin Luther in an effort to limit the conditions for salvation to faith alone. Luther was certainly committed to *sola fidei*, but this in no way prevented him from acknowledging repentance and baptism as part of the salvation process. In fact, no one has affirmed more forcefully than Luther that the act of baptism is the time when and place where God bestows saving grace upon the sinner.[33]

Since the main content of the gospel is the saving work of Jesus Christ, it is understandable that the primary condition for receiving salvation is faith in the Savior and his saving work (3:25; 10:9). We can accept Jesus as Savior only through faith; thus faith is the only *means* by which the gift of saving grace can be received. But faith in Jesus as Savior cannot be separated from a specific attitude toward the sins from which he saves us and a determination to avoid sin in the future. This necessarily involves repentance and submission to Christ as Lord. What faith is to Christ as *Savior*, repentance is to Christ as *Lord*. And for reasons known for sure only to God, he has specified that baptism is the time/place where he chooses initially to bestow the forgiveness of sins and the gift of the Holy Spirit (Acts 2:38; see below on 6:1-4).[34]

Following the analogy of the ball game as mentioned above, faith is the ticket that secures admittance to the game. At least, faith is the front side of the ticket; a ticket always has two sides, and the other side of this one is repentance. But the ticket will do the baseball fan no good unless he goes to the place where the game is to be played. Baptism is equivalent to going to the stadium, since this is where God says the action will take place.

We do agree, though, that faith is the only *means* and the key condition for salvation. It is not only necessary in the beginning for the very reception of salvation (Col 2:12), but is also necessary as an ongoing state of mind that continues to cling to and rest upon the gospel promises throughout the Christian life. This may be why Paul says the gospel is God's power unto salvation for "everyone

---

[33]See my brief discussion of Luther's view of baptism in "Consensus," 31-34.

[34]See my book, *Baptism*. See especially 18-22.

who *believes*" (present tense). The present tense of the verb implies ongoing action, "a continuing orientation and motivation for life" (Dunn, I:40). Salvation is given "to all who believe and go on believing," that is, "to all who not only come to a decision of faith, but whose whole life is characterized as a trustful acceptance of and commitment to the gospel which is God's power to salvation" (Dunn, I:47).

E. THE HEART OF THE GOSPEL (1:17a)

1:17 In v. 16 Paul says the gospel is God's power unto salvation. In v. 17 he answers the question as to *why* this is so. For the third time in this section he uses the particle γάρ (*gar*), meaning "for" or "because." The gospel is God's power unto salvation, **For in the gospel a righteousness from God is revealed, a righteousness that is by faith from first to last . . . .** That is, the source of the gospel's saving power is "the righteousness of God."[35] This is the heart of the gospel.

The Greek text does not literally say, "in the gospel." The text says "in it." But since the antecedent of "it" (v. 17) is "the gospel" in v. 16, the NIV just spells it out: "in the gospel." In any case the gospel is what reveals the righteousness of God, and this is why it has the power to save sinners.

This righteousness of God is *revealed* in the gospel, says Paul. The word *reveal* refers here to divine activity; it means "to disclose, to uncover, to unveil, to make known." Interpreters agree that this righteousness of God is revealed not just in the gospel as it is preached, but primarily in the gospel as it is enacted by Jesus Christ on the stage of history itself. That is, the very deeds of which the gospel speaks are the revelation of this divine righteousness that brings salvation. The revelation is not just a verbal disclosure to the mind, but is accomplished "in action and operation" in the historical arena (Murray, I:29). It is "the 'uncovering' of God's redemptive plan, as it unfolds on the plane of human history" (Moo, I:64). Of

---

[35]The text does not literally say "a righteousness *from* God," but uses the simple genitive case, "a righteousness *of God*."

course, the gospel *message* also reveals this righteousness of God to all those who hear it; thus the present tense is used: the righteousness of God "is revealed"; it is and continues to be revealed through the ongoing preaching of the gospel (Moo, I:65).

Certainly, whatever gives the gospel its power should be considered the heart of the gospel, and that is identified here as "the righteousness of God." To understand what this means, we must define the term *righteousness*.[36] First of all it is a mistake to translate this Greek word (δικαιοσύνη, *dikaiosynē*) as "justification" in the sense of acquittal or forgiveness, as do Lard (39-45) and Moo (I:70). Righteousness and justification are very closely related, and the justification of sinners may well be regarded either as being included in the righteousness of God (as the term is used here) or as being the direct result of it. As used here, though, the righteousness of God is a broader and richer term than simply his act of justifying sinners, as is shown in 3:25-26 especially.

Also, contrary to Dunn (I:40-41), it is a mistake to define righteousness as merely "a concept of *relation*," or specifically as faithfulness to the demands and obligations of a relationship (see GRe, 192-193). This may be one aspect of righteousness, but is much too narrow and limited to be the definition of it.

Though many today try to deny it, the biblical usage of this term demonstrates its meaning to be "conformity to the proper and relevant standard or norm" (GRe, 191-196; Cranfield, I:93-94). The proper norm for human righteousness is the law of God; thus when applied to human beings righteousness means conforming to God's law or satisfying the requirements of his law (GRe, 196-201).

What, then, is the righteousness *of God*? And in what sense is it revealed in the gospel? This latter point is important, since whatever our understanding of the righteousness of God, it must strike the sinner as *good news*. It is after all the heart of the gospel. In this connection it is important also to identify the intended contrast. The gospel reveals the righteousness of God, as opposed to — what? The answer is, as opposed to the righteousness of man, or human righteousness achieved through conformity to the law of God. This

---

[36]See my more complete analysis of this term in GRe, ch 4, especially 189-196.

contrast is the main point of Romans. It is the contrast between law and grace as ways or methods of being accepted by God. Paul's point is that we are not under law (as a way of salvation), but under grace (6:14). We are justified by faith in God's righteousness, not by works of law or personal conformity to God's law (3:28). The choice is between personal righteousness and God's righteousness (10:3). Those who have any hope of heaven are trusting in God's righteousness and not their own (Phil 3:9). Since most of us are aware of the fact that our own personal righteousness falls far short of the required norm (Isa 64:6; Rom 3:23), the revelation of the righteousness of God as an alternative way of salvation is surely gospel — good news.

But if righteousness means conformity to a norm, how can this apply to God? What is the "norm" to which he must conform? Certainly there is no law or standard apart from God with which his actions must be compared. That is true; thus the norm to which his actions must conform is *his own nature*. In the most basic sense, to say that God is righteous means that his actions are always true to his nature. Contrary to the idea that righteousness is always a relational term, i.e., faithfulness to a relationship, the ultimate essence of divine righteousness is God's faithfulness to *himself*, to his own nature and to his own word. That God is righteous means he will never act in a way that is contrary to his nature and his word. In this sense righteousness is an attribute of God's nature, and the term is used in this sense quite often in the Bible, especially in the OT (GRe, 210-215).

Is this the "righteousness of God" of which Paul speaks here in v. 17? One thing that makes this a problem is the fact that such righteousness includes the idea that God must be true to his *holy* nature, which means that he must encounter sin with wrath and retribution. This concept of wrath and vengeance and retributive justice is already amply revealed in God's *law*; in what sense could it now be revealed in the *gospel*? Indeed, how could it be revealed in the gospel at all, if the gospel is supposed to be *good* news? How can the prospect of being righteously punished with God's eternal wrath be considered "good news" to the sinner?

As we saw earlier in the introduction, this is exactly how Martin Luther as a Catholic monk had been taught to understand this phrase, "the righteousness of God," as used in 1:17. As a result he was angry with God and was completely unable to understand either the gospel or the book of Romans. Then he began to see that in this and other NT contexts this phrase refers not to righteousness as an attribute of God's nature as such, but to righteousness as something established by God and bestowed upon sinners as a saving gift. This new understanding transformed Luther's whole approach to the gospel and led to the Reformation ("Latin Writings," 336-337).

Luther was right, and most Protestants have followed his thinking on this subject.[37] The righteousness of God revealed in the gospel is the gift of righteousness that God gives to sinners, on the basis of which he accepts them as righteous, i.e., as conforming to the norm of his law, or as having satisfied the requirements of his law. It is given to us in the form of a "robe of righteousness" (Isa 61:10), and we wear it as a covering that hides our own "filthy rags" (Isa 64:6). Paul speaks of this as "the righteousness that comes from God" (Phil 3:9), and as something that becomes ours in the same sense that our sins became Christ's as he was dying for us (2 Cor 5:21). The NIV translation of 1:17, "righteousness *from* God," reflects this idea.

Specifically what is this righteousness of God, this gift of God's grace that is revealed in the gospel? We know that God *imparts* a righteous character to us through the gift of the Holy Spirit received in Christian baptism, so that we actually become more and more righteous, more and more holy as we mature in our faith. But it is generally agreed that "the righteousness of God" in 1:17 is *not* this *imparted* righteousness, but is rather an *imputed* righteousness, i.e., a righteousness established by someone else (Jesus Christ) and set down to our account and counted as our own. It results not in a righteous *character*; this comes from the Holy Spirit's working in us. It results rather in a righteous *status*. This righteous status is the state of being justified. Justification is thus not equivalent to the righteousness of God, but is the result of it.

But again, specifically what *is* this righteousness of God that is imputed to our account, on the basis of which we are justified? It

---

[37]See Cranfield, I:97-98, for arguments supporting this view.

begins with the righteousness of God in the first sense above, i.e., righteousness as the attribute of God that requires him to be true to his nature in everything he does. Thus even in the salvation of sinners he must be righteous, that is, he must be true to his nature as a just and holy God. He must be true to his law; he must be sure that the requirements of his law are satisfied. But how can God save sinners and at the same time uphold the integrity of the very law they have sinned against?

This is the heart of the reason why the Logos became flesh; this is the centerpiece of the work of Christ; this is the heart of the gospel. Jesus came as our substitute in reference to the law; he came to uphold the integrity of the divine law by *satisfying the requirements of the law in our place*. To most Protestants this means that Jesus kept all the law's commandments on our behalf; then this "active righteousness" is imputed to us so that we may be counted righteous, i.e., counted as having never sinned. But this is a serious error. Jesus did keep all the law's commandments (2 Cor 5:21; Heb 4:15), but this was something required of him just as it is of any other human being. It was something he had to do for himself; it provided no "extra merit" that can be shared with others. It was also a necessary prerequisite for his atoning sacrifice.

In what sense, then, did Jesus satisfy the requirements of the law in our place, so that God can save us and at the same time be true to his nature as a holy God (i.e., be righteous)? We must remember that law has two components: commandments we are obligated to obey, and penalties we must pay if we disobey. If we do not satisfy its requirements for obedience, we must satisfy its requirements for penalty. Either way righteousness is preserved and the integrity of the law is upheld. Here, then, is the key to understanding "the righteousness of God" in v. 17: Jesus came to establish God's righteousness by *satisfying the law's requirement for penalty* in our place. His suffering and death (his "passive righteousness") were not necessary for his own sake; thus they constitute a kind of "extra merit" that can be shared with those who need it. This is how God can "justify the wicked" (4:5), or count him as righteous: he transfers Christ's payment of the law's penalty to the sinner's account. This is how the sinner is justified, or counted righteous: he is counted as having already paid the penalty for his sins. In other words, I am *justified* not because God treats me "just if I'd" never sinned, but because he treats me "just if I'd" already paid my penalty.

No wonder "the righteousness of God" is the heart of the gospel! It is no less than the substitutionary atonement provided by the Son of God through his death on the cross. This is the sense in which the cross is the greatest demonstration of the righteousness of God that can ever be made (3:25-26). The "robe of righteousness" bestowed upon sinners is in reality the very blood of Christ that has paid the debt of penalty for our sins (1 Pet 1:18-19). "My hope is built on nothing less than Jesus' blood and [Jesus'] righteousness."

Though the good news of the righteousness of God is its central concept, it is not the sole content of the gospel. The gospel speaks also of the resurrection of Jesus, and of the saving gifts of justification and the Spirit's indwelling, and of the gracious conditions for receiving these gifts — especially faith. Verse 17 reaffirms the conditional nature of salvation and the essentiality of faith. This gift of God's righteousness, says Paul, "is by faith from first to last." The NIV paraphrases considerably here. The first part of v. 17 is translated more literally by the NASB: "For in it the righteousness of God is revealed from faith to faith." This last expression, "from faith to faith," is notoriously difficult. Does it modify *righteousness* (as in the NIV), or *revealed* (as in the NASB and as the order of the Greek words suggests)?

There are several possibilities (see Cranfield, I:99-100). Some take it as saying that the revelation of God's righteousness is given to a faith that begins in weakness but grows ever stronger, like going "from strength to strength" in Ps 84:7 (Luther, 19). Others take it to mean "from God's faithfulness to our faith" (Dunn, I:44, 48). Another very common view is that "faith" is simply repeated for the sake of emphasis, as if underlining the word *sola* in the notion of *sola fidei*. This is the view reflected in the NIV translation, "by faith from first to last." Similar suggestions are "faith through and through" (Morris, 70); "to faith and faith alone" (Nygren, 79); "faith and 'nothing but faith'" (Moo, I:71); "faith, first and last and wholly" (Erdman, 28). See also Cranfield, I:100.

A fourth possibility is that "from faith" modifies "righteousness," and "unto faith" modifies "revealed." The meaning would then be something like this: "In the gospel a righteousness of God that is ours by faith alone is revealed to our faith." This is similar in meaning to 3:22, "This righteousness from God comes through faith in Jesus Christ to all who believe." See Godet, 97; Murray, I:31-2. A variation of this view takes the latter part of the expression, "unto faith," as indicating the result of the gospel revelation: "in order to produce faith" (DeWelt, 25; see Lard, 45; Grubbs, 36). Whatever the exact meaning of this phrase, it does not add anything significant to the phrase "everyone who believes" in v. 16.

F. THE GOLDEN TEXT OF THE GOSPEL (1:17b)

Having given his preliminary and very condensed statement of his thesis, i.e., that the gospel of the righteousness of God is able to save everyone who believes it, Paul then cites a passage from the OT as a kind of proof text: **just as it is written: "The righteous will live by faith."** This is a quotation from Hab 2:4 (quoted also in Gal 3:11 and Heb 10:38). By citing this verse Paul again shows the continuity between his gospel and the OT (see v. 2). The strong connecting word καθώς (kathōs), "just as," emphasizes this sameness; and the formula "it is written" reminds his readers that he is quoting authoritative Scripture.

By citing this passage here in the transitional statement of his theme, Paul shows us that it contains the kernel or essence of the gospel. We may call it the "golden text" of the gospel. Nygren says, "The whole message of this epistle is contained in 1:17, particularly in the prophetic quotation" from Habakkuk. "On that scriptural text the apostle constructs his letter" (81).

In its original context this statement refers to the necessity for God's people to trust his purposes and his providence regarding the temporal fate of the nation of Israel. Habakkuk the prophet begins by complaining to God about the injustice being suffered by some Israelites at the hands of their own countrymen (1:2-4). God replies that he is already planning to rectify the situation by having the cruel Babylonian hordes overrun and plunder the land (1:5-11). Habakkuk swallows hard and presses on, saying, in effect, "Lord, are you sure you know what you are doing? If this happens, won't

the 'cure' be worse than the disease? Please explain" (1:12-2:1). Part
of God's reply is to this effect: I know you don't understand,
Habakkuk; but you will just have to trust me: "the righteous will live
by his faith" (2:4).

It is not clear whether "will live" by faith here means "will
conduct his life" by faith, or whether it means "will be preserved
alive" by faith when the enemy comes. If the former, it is an admonition on how to live; if the latter, it is a promise to the faithful.[38] In
any case it is the promise of earthly deliverance in the face of an
earthly threat.

When Paul cites this passage, however, he lifts it to a higher
plane. There is little doubt that he reads it as a promise and not an
admonition. He is not telling us that we ought live (i.e., to conduct
our lives) according to faith. This is a basic summary of the gospel,
and thus must be taken as a *promise*: the righteous person will be
preserved alive by faith. But in the context of the NT gospel, "preserved alive" means much more than it did for the trembling
Habakkuk in the face of the Babylonian threat. It refers to spiritual
or eternal life: the righteous will receive eternal life by faith.

This is in accord with a general biblical practice. God's New
Covenant teachings and promises are often lifted to a higher plane
as compared with his dealings with OT Israel (GRu, 143-153). For
example, OT promises regarding protection from enemies usually
refer to earthly enemies such as the Philistines and the Moabites
(e.g., Ps 37:39-40; 41:1-2). Similar NT promises focus on spiritual
enemies, however (e.g., 1 Cor 10:13; Eph 6:10-18). In the same way,
whereas Hab 2:4 originally referred to physical life, in Rom 1:17 it
refers to the gift of eternal life.[39] "Will live" means "will be saved";
it is the same as the salvation mentioned in v. 16 (see Bruce, 81).

---

[38]Cranfield assumes it is the latter, and that God is promising "political
survival" to faithful Israel (I:100).

[39]In 1:17, says Cranfield (I:101), Paul "refers not to political survival but
to the life with God, which alone is true life, the life which the believer is to
begin to enjoy here and now, but which he will enjoy in its fullness in the
eschatological future." The verb for "will live" (ζάω, *zaō*) is often used for
the gift of eternal life. See 6:11; 8:13; 10:5; 2 Cor 6:9; 13:4; Gal 2:20; 3:12;
1 Thess 5:10.

The main hermeneutical problem for this quotation is whether "by faith" is intended to modify the subject ("the righteous one") or the verb ("will live"). The word order in the Greek text favors the former: the one who is righteous by faith will live. (This is also the word order in the text of Hab 2:4.) Several English translations render it thus, e.g., the NEB, the RSV, and TEV. This seems to be most consistent with the immediate context and with the constant emphasis of the epistle (Nygren, 86; Cranfield, I:102). When understood thus, it is clear that "will live" means "will be saved." It also makes the implied contrast more clear: the one who is righteous by faith will live, not the one who tries to be righteous through his own works (3:28; 10:3). This view is defended by Lard (45-46) and Morris (71-72).

Many take it the other way, though: the righteous will live by faith (thus the NASB and the NIV). This view is defended by Murray (I:33) and Hendriksen (I:64-65, n. 31). Now, if Paul's main point is that the righteous should conduct their lives by faith, then this translation would be the more natural. But if he means (and I think he does) that the righteous *will live eternally* — be saved — by faith, then the former way is better.

CONCLUSION

The focus of Paul's apostleship and the focus of the epistle to the Romans is the gospel, the good news of God. Why is the good news so *good?* Surely if we are told that we can be saved rather than lost, this is good. But the news is even better than this. It involves not just a contrast between sin and damnation on the one hand, and salvation on the other. It is also a contrast between two entirely different ways of salvation, two ways of being right with God or of entering heaven. One is the true way that will really save us; the other is a false way that actually leads to despair and death. These two ways are *law* and *grace.* The good news — the very best news of all — is that we can be saved by grace through faith, apart from works of law (3:28). This is the gospel.

Cranfield (I:88) denies that this contrast is implicit here in Paul's transitional statement (1:16-17), but I think this is because he does not understand the true nature of this contrast. Nygren's view (66) is more perceptive: "To grasp the full meaning of the word [gospel], one ought to note how for Paul the gospel always stands in inescapable relation to the law. Wherever the gospel is, the law always stands in the background." Lard (39-40) defends a similar view, as does Grubbs (33-38). Grubbs sees Paul's thematic statement in v. 16 as standing "in opposition to the legalistic system of his opponents" at every point (33-34).

Here I want to call attention to one of the most serious errors committed by many Christians in their attempt to understand the gospel of grace. Like Grubbs, they correctly see that the gospel can be understood only as contrasted with law. But also like Grubbs, they *limit* "law" to *the Law of Moses,* and thus see the gospel as standing in contrast only with the Law of Moses. As I see it, *there is no greater hindrance to a proper understanding of the gospel of grace than this*. The actual contrast is not just between the gospel of Jesus Christ and the Law of Moses, but between grace as a method or system of salvation (on the one hand) and law as a method or system of salvation (on the other hand). The law system does not depend on the Law of Moses; it is pursued wherever human beings have any awareness at all of God's moral law, whether this be through a special revelation such as the Law of Moses or the Pauline epistles, or whether it be only through the general revelation written on the heart (2:14-15).

This contrast between grace and law as ways of salvation has been present ever since God began presenting the good news of forgiveness of sins, as far back as Eden (Gen 3:15). Everyone who has had access to God's special revelation has had the choice between law and grace. Those who lived under the Law of Moses knew the grace of God (3:21), though certainly not as fully as those who know Jesus himself. Anyone under the Law of Moses who was saved — indeed, any sinner anywhere, anytime who has been saved — was saved by grace through faith in God's promises, not by law-keeping of any sort.

As we shall see in the next section, every person who lives and has a mature rational awareness of himself and of the world knows God's law to some extent. Unless such a person comes into contact with God's special (biblical) revelation, *law* is the only system of relating to God that he will ever know. Also, many of those who do have special revelation and its message of grace (many Christians!) do not really understand it, and they still labor under the misconception that their ability to obey God's commandments is the determiner of their salvation or damnation. But Paul makes it very clear that "no one will be declared righteous in his sight by observing the law" in any form (3:20). *This is why the good news is so good!* It tells us, even those of us who want to be saved and are already struggling to be saved by our works, that the one true, effective, conscience-clearing, peace-giving, fear-banishing way of salvation is *grace*, which means putting your complete trust in the work of Jesus Christ rather than in your own works as the way of being accepted as righteous by God.

No wonder it is the *gospel* (*good* news), and no wonder Paul was so excited about it! No wonder it is dynamite! God has given us an alternative to law as a way of salvation — an alternative to law, which is a way of *human* power, or rather, human *weakness*; a way in which it is *theoretically* possible to be right with God, but which in fact will never work because it is nullified by the presence of even a single sin; a way which in fact leads only to despair or else to self-deception and false confidence.

But the gospel gives us an *alternative* to this, a way of salvation that depends not on man's weakness but on God's power, a way that depends not on human righteousness but on God's righteousness, a way that depends not on our ability to keep God's commandments but on Christ's ability to pay our penalty for us, a way that *will* lead to salvation for everyone who believes. Is this not good news?

1:18-3:20 — PART ONE

THE IMPOTENCE OF LAW
AS A WAY OF SALVATION

We come now to the main body of the book of Romans. The general flow of thought from this point on is as follows:

1. Salvation (justification, righteousness, acceptance by God) by means of *law* (works, personal righteousness) is impossible, because all have sinned. 1:18-3:20.
2. But God has provided an *alternative* to law: righteousness by faith, justification by faith, salvation by grace through faith. 3:21-5:21.
3. Justification by grace through faith does not encourage sin. Rather, the grace of God gives us victory over sin through regeneration, sanctification, and glorification. 6:1-8:39.
4. The objection that this way of salvation somehow means that God is being unfair to the Jews is without foundation. 9:1-11:36.
5. Living under grace has certain specific implications for daily living. 12:1-15:14.
6. Personal remarks addressed specifically to Rome close out the letter. 15:15-16:27.

At this point we are dealing with the first main section, 1:18 through 3:20. When we move from the transitional statement in 1:16-17 to the first verse of this section, we certainly must be surprised if not shocked. After building up our excitement and expectation with a reference to God's *good news*, the Apostle immediately drops us into the black abyss of the wrath of God! This is surely a surprising way to begin to talk about the *gospel*! Why does Paul do it this way?

First, it is a general principle that one must understand the seriousness of his predicament before he can appreciate the need and availability of its solution. In this case, we must know that we are sinners under the righteous wrath of God before we can know and appreciate God's saving grace.

Thus before Paul explains the gospel of grace in more detail, he focuses on the sinfulness and helplessness of the entire human race. But this is secondary to and supportive of the main point, which is *the impotence of law as a way of salvation*. We must not forget that the main theme of Romans involves the contrast between grace and law as ways of salvation: sinners can be saved only by grace, not by works of law. Paul will establish the reality and the glory of salvation by grace in the second main section (3:21-5:21), but first he must show that there is absolutely no possibility that anyone may be saved by the alternative, law. Thus in this first main section everything is designed to establish this point, that by works of law no flesh will be justified in his sight (3:20). Black's heading is on target: "The Failure of Law" (39).

One point must be clearly understood: strictly speaking, it is possible to be right with God by means of law, works of law, or the law system. The universe as originally created was a law system through and through; everything existed within the general framework of God's laws, both physical and moral. Man as created was "right with God" in terms of the system of law. How does this system work? How may one be right with God in terms of law? The rules are very simple. They are stated in terms of the two aspects of law as explained earlier: commandments and penalty. Here is how the law system operates:

KEEP THE COMMANDMENTS, AND (THEREFORE)
ESCAPE THE PENALTY.
BREAK THE COMMANDMENTS, AND (THEREFORE)
SUFFER THE PENALTY.

So why is 3:20 true? Why is the law impotent to save? Because *no one* has kept the commandments — all have sinned (3:9-18). A person is counted as "keeping the commandments" only if he does so perfectly; even one sin makes him liable to the penalty (Jas 2:10; Gal 3:10). In 1:18-3:20 Paul does show that all have sinned, but he does this in order to show that no one can ever be right with God by means of the law system. Thus the only way anyone will ever be saved is by the alternative provided by God, which is grace.

The main subject of this first main section, then, is *law* as such

(not just the Law of Moses). Since the very essence of sin is transgression of the law, or lawlessness (1 John 3:4), we cannot even
know what sin is, nor can we understand ourselves as sinners, until
we see ourselves in our true relation to God's law. This is the
reason why the preaching of the law must precede the preaching of
the gospel. This has strong implications for our methodology of
evangelism in general, and our concept of child nurture in particular. Before a person (such as a child) is ready to accept Christ as
Savior, he must understand that he has broken God's commandments and stands under the penalty of God's law.

Even more important is the fact that we must see that the law
system cannot make us as sinners right with God, so that we will
know that "grace through faith" is the only possible *way* of salvation. We must see the impotence of law for salvation before grace
as such can mean anything to us.

In this section and elsewhere, Paul uses the term *law* (νόμος,
nomos) in several distinct ways. Sometimes it does mean specifically
the Law of Moses, e.g., 2:12-14, 17-18, 20, 23, 25-27; 3:21b; 4:16b;
5:13, 20. But at other times it means the universal moral law or the
general will of God for all people, e.g., 2:14d-15; 3:19-21a, 28, 31;
4:13-15. Sometimes it means law as a principle or as a system of
relating to God, in contrast with grace, e.g., 3:27; 6:14-15.

This section presupposes that God's law as the basic framework
for existence is a reality with which everyone must deal. God's universal moral law, his righteous commandments, are everywhere and
demand a response from everyone who is conceptually mature
enough to understand what this means.[1] Within the framework of
law we face an inescapable choice or set of options. When confronted by God's law we must *either* keep it perfectly and thus
receive the blessings it promises, *or* we must break it and incur the
penalty it prescribes.

Obviously any rational person should choose the first option.
The awful reality, though, is that *everyone* has chosen the second
option. No one has kept God's law perfectly; all are lawbreakers
and thus have incurred the penalty of eternal death in the lake of
fire. Here within the framework of law the first choice is no longer

---

[1]This excludes young children and certain mentally handicapped people.

an option, and payment of the penalty is no longer avoidable. Thus anyone who is still counting on his record as a law-keeper (i.e., his own righteousness) for salvation is either deceiving himself with a false self-righteousness or is heading into hopeless despair.

Consistent with his holy and righteous wrath, God *could* send every human being to hell. We have all broken the commandments and all deserve the penalty. But here is where the gospel comes into the picture. Consistent with his loving and righteous grace, God has given us another choice or another set of options. Since payment of sin's penalty is now inescapable, this second set of options has to do with how this penalty will be paid. Now, because of grace, we may choose *either* to stay within the framework of law and pay the penalty ourselves, *or* we may trust someone else to pay this penalty on our behalf. This latter choice is the grace option, and it requires us to renounce the impotent and damning law system and to place ourselves under the shelter of the grace system, which is the same as accepting the gift of God's righteousness, which is believing that the blood of Christ has already paid the penalty for our sins.

The message of Romans is simply this. Within the law system ("Keep the commandments and escape the penalty, or break the commandments and suffer the penalty"), the first option is closed. All have broken the commandments and are under its penalty; thus no one can be right with God in terms of law. This is the message of 1:18-3:20. However, in his boundless love God has provided another choice for us, the choice of grace itself. This is the point of 3:21-5:21: our only hope is grace.

This first main section of Romans is thus necessary to show us that there is no hope for salvation as long as we remain in a law-relationship with God. Paul makes this point by showing us that all have sinned, which renders law impotent as a way of salvation.

Why is it necessary for Paul to take so long to make this point? Why can't he just say, as he does in 3:23, that "all have sinned"? The reason is because not everyone is willing to accept this statement at face value. Many insist that at least a few people, or a few groups of people, have not really sinned in the technical sense of that word, or at least will not be held responsible for their sins, or perhaps will be treated as exceptions to the general rule. This section is necessary because some are sure to lobby for such exceptions. Paul takes the time to show that there are *no exceptions* to the rule that all have sinned, and therefore law cannot save anyone but can only condemn. We can imagine this conversation between Paul and such a lobbyist: "Sure, Paul, we agree. No one will be saved by law since all have sinned. But surely there are some exceptions to this rule." "All right," says Paul. "Just what exceptions did you have in mind?" The objector smiles and replies, "Why, just two small groups: the *Gentiles* and the *Jews!*"

These are serious suggestions, and the content of this section of Romans is designed to show why the Gentiles and the Jews are not exceptions to the rule that law cannot save because all have sinned. First Paul addresses the possibility that the Gentiles might be exempt from judgment according to God's law (1:18-32). Then he addresses the belief that the Jews are a special case and thus will not be judged according to the rules that apply to everyone else (2:1-3:8). Finally he draws it all together and affirms the universal application of his point, with no exceptions (3:9-20).

I. 1:18-32 — THE SINFULNESS OF THE GENTILES

Paul's first point in this section is to show that the Gentiles have no basis for claiming to be exempt from the law's penalty. That the main subject of this passage is the Gentiles can hardly be denied.[2] Most commentators prefer to say that the passage refers to the Gentiles primarily or mainly, but not exclusively.[3] There is good reason for this, as we shall see.

The main problem raised about the Gentiles is this: why should they need grace, if they have never had access to law? The Jews, not the Gentiles, were chosen by God to receive the revelation of his great Law through Moses. If the Gentiles do not have this Law, how

---

[2]There is no reason to narrow the scope to a specific group of Gentiles, as do Nash (*Critique*, 26) and DeWelt (28). Nash says vv. 21-32 refer "to the heathen world outside of Judaism from Abraham to Christ." DeWelt says Paul is speaking of all the Greek legislators, statesmen, philosophers, and priests.

[3]See Cranfield, I:105; Hendriksen, I:67; Moo, I:89, 92; Morris, 74.

can they be considered as sinners? Surely God must excuse them on the basis of their ignorance. After all, does not God himself say that "where there is no law there is no transgression" (4:15)?

This is exactly the view that many people still have today about the so-called "heathen," or pagans who have never heard the gospel. Surely God has no basis for condemning them, if they have never seen or heard of the Bible. Surely God will not hold them accountable for what they have had no opportunity to know. So surely these modern-day Gentiles will not be lost. Some even question the need for missionary activity on such grounds.

This is the very issue Paul is addressing in this passage. From our perspective it does not matter whether we call these people "Gentiles" or "the heathen" or "the unevangelized." Paul calls them Gentiles (2:14) and Greeks (2:9-10; 3:9), as distinct from the Jews. But as the passage shows, what really makes them distinct is the fact that they have had no access to special revelation; their knowledge of God has been derived from *general revelation only*.

These two basic kinds of revelation are usually distinguished. *Special* revelation is that which God gives to specific people in specific times and places, either through deeds or words. All word revelation falls into this category; when God speaks to mankind in human language, he speaks into a particular place and time, usually through a spokesman or prophet. Much of such revelation has been written down for us in the Bible; all biblical revelation is special revelation. *General* revelation, on the other hand, is revelation that is given to all human beings in general, via means that make it universally available, such as the phenomena of creation and providence (Ps 19:1-6; Acts 14:17; Rom 1:19-20).

Paul's point in this passage is that even though the Gentiles may not have access to the special revelation of God's law, they know enough about God and his law through general revelation to be held accountable. They have broken the law they have, and are therefore without excuse and thus are under the wrath of God.

What is said in this passage actually does apply to all people, since general revelation by its very nature is known to all — even to Jews and others who have access to special revelation. But the specific issue with which Paul is dealing is the status of those who have been exposed to general revelation *only*. This would include most of the people who lived in pre-Christian times, and it would include anyone living today who has not yet come into contact with biblical revelation.

From the standpoint of Jews in Bible times, such people would be called Gentiles. Today they are often called "the heathen"; but this term has negative cultural connotations that do not necessarily apply, and it is offensive to a great many people. Thus many call them "the unevangelized," though this is not strictly the point. Because it is the biblical term and because of its familiarity we shall continue to use the term *Gentiles*.

In commenting on this text we will divide it thus: (1) Universal Knowledge of God and his Law, 1:18-20. (2) Universal Rejection of the True God, 1:21-25. (3) The Utter Depths of Gentile Depravity, 1:26-32. We should note that 2:14-15 also refers specifically to the Gentiles and adds to what will be said in this section.

A. UNIVERSAL KNOWLEDGE OF GOD AND HIS LAW (1:18-20)

In order to show that the Gentiles, individually and as a group, will be justly judged and condemned within the framework of law, Paul must first show that they do indeed know God and his law, and have indeed broken it. This is the point of 1:18-32, and the universal knowledge of God and his law are the subject of vv. 18-20.

The NIV fails to translate the connecting γάρ, *gar*, "for, because," at the beginning of v. 18. This word shows that Paul is introducing the reason why only the righteous by faith will live, namely, because there is no other viable option. The only other way to eternal life is through perfect obedience to God's law, and no one will qualify on this basis. Even the Gentiles have sinned and are under God's wrath, so even the Gentiles need to hear the gospel of righteousness by faith.

In other words, this section shows the universal need, not just for salvation as such, but for the specific *way* of salvation that is the heart of the gospel (1:16-17). As Sanday and Headlam say, "St. Paul has just stated what the Gospel is; he now goes on to show the necessity for such a Gospel. The world is lost without it" (40). In Hendriksen's words, "No other way to be saved is available than that of accepting the gospel by faith, *for* since the wrath of God rests by nature upon man, the latter is completely unable to save himself, whether by performing the works of the law or by any other means" (I:67).

1:18 The wrath of God is being revealed from heaven against all the godlessness and wickedness of men who suppress the truth by their wickedness . . . . Paul gets right to the point: The Gentiles are under the wrath of God.[4] God's wrath is a fearsome reality. We must never weaken its force by separating it from the nature and will of God, as some try to do. C.H. Dodd (21-24), for example, followed by Barclay (17-19), misrepresents divine wrath as an impersonal, karma-like law of nature. I.e., certain kinds of actions inevitably produce disastrous consequences. "Wrath" is not a personal attitude of God, but merely a way of describing "an inevitable process of cause and effect" in "the structure of the universe." Such a view, however, is a serious departure from the teaching of Scripture, where wrath is not an impersonal process but the deliberate penal judgment of the personal God. To say that this wrath is being revealed "from heaven" is a way of repeating for emphasis the fact that it is the wrath of the personal and holy God.

God's wrath should not be compared with frivolous, impetuous, capricious human anger. It is rather the inevitable retributive response of the eternally holy God against anything that violates his own being. It is the "consuming fire" aspect of his nature (Heb 12:29). "Wrath is the holy revulsion of God's being against that which is the contradiction of his holiness" (Murray, 35).

Paul says the wrath of God "is being revealed" (present tense). This is the same word as was used in v. 17 for the righteousness of God. As in that case, the revelation is given not necessarily in the form of a verbally-communicated message but in the reality of the punitive events themselves. Exactly what are these events that reveal to us the wrath of God?

Whenever we think of the wrath of God, it is natural to think of the end times, the judgment day, and the wrath of eternal punishment to which the damned are consigned (2:5, 8; 5:9; Rev 6:16; 16:1). Although the present tense may sometimes be used for a

---

[4]For a thorough discussion of divine wrath see GRe, 275-319.

future event, and although eschatological wrath may be a part of this picture, the main focus of v. 18 is still on the present.

Karl Barth and others have set forth the view that the wrath of God no less than his righteousness is revealed *in the gospel*, i.e., in the death of Christ as our atoning sacrifice. This seems to be Morris' view (76-77). He says Paul declares in 1:18 "that it is the cross that shows us the measure of God's wrath. It is in the events of the gospel that the revelation occurs." Now, it is true, especially in light of 3:24-26, that "the reality of the wrath of God is only truly known when it is seen in its revelation in Gethsemane and on Golgotha" (Cranfield, I:110). But the context that follows 1:18 points in an entirely different direction.

How, then, is the wrath of God being revealed throughout history, especially upon the Gentile or pagan world? It is being done "in the events of history" (Moo, I:96), "in the facts of human experience" (Bruce, 83). This includes the retributive penalties imposed by human governments (12:19; 13:4), the accusations of conscience (2:15), the pain of childbirth (Gen 3:16), the necessity for toil as the result of a sin-cursed environment (Gen 3:17-19; Rom 8:20-22), and the inescapable penalty of death itself (Gen 2:17; 3:19; Rom 1:32; 5:12; 8:10). Most significantly, the context itself suggests that the most obvious revelation of God's wrath is his judicial action of "giving over" the Gentiles to the bitter consequences of their sinful desires and depraved lifestyles (1:24, 26, 28).[5]

Paul says this wrath of God is being revealed "against all the godlessness and wickedness of men." The word "all" makes the reference universal; there are no exceptions. God's wrath is against all the sins of all people, even those of the Gentiles. That which draws the wrath of God "is repeated in every generation, by every individual" (Moo, I:93).

The word translated "godlessness" is ἀσέβεια (*asebeia*). Words from this word group that do not have the negating alpha (our letter *a*) refer to the worship that is due to the one true God (see

---

[5]This explains Paul's statement in Eph 2:3, that we are all by nature "children of wrath" (not *objects* of wrath, as the NIV mistranslates). We are not born condemned, but we are born into a condemned world where the wrath of God is exploding like bombs all around us.

Acts 16:14; 18:7, 13; Rom 1:25). With the negating alpha (similar to our prefix *un-*), as in this case, such words refer to ungodliness: opposition to and rejection of God. The other word, "wickedness," translates ἀδικία (*adikia*). This is from the word group having to do with righteousness or justice, which as we saw earlier means conformity to the appropriate norm. Human righteousness thus means conformity to God's law. With the negating alpha (as here) the meaning would be *un*righteousness, wickedness, or actions that are contrary to God's law.

Do these two terms refer to two different kinds of sin? Many have taken this view. They suggest that "godlessness" is sin against God himself, as proscribed by the first four commandments, and that "wickedness" is sin against our fellow human beings, as forbidden by the last six commandments. In accordance with the verses that follow, the latter is seen as the evil spawn of the former.[6] On the other hand, many deny that two distinct categories of sin are intended. The two words are just two names for the same thing, says Cranfield, who rightly notes that *all* sin is an attack on the majesty of God (I:112). They are synonyms, says MacArthur (I:66). "All ungodliness is also unrighteousness, and vice versa," says Lenski (92). As Moo notes, the second term certainly "cannot be confined to sins against others" but is often used very comprehensively, as in the latter part of this very verse (I:97).

The latter view is the correct one, though the terms are not completely synonymous. *Asebeia* refers to sin as a direct attack on or rejection of God himself; *adikia* refers to sin as a violation of God's law (1 John 3:4). As Hendriksen well says, "Both represent sin, rebellion against God. The first views sin as want of reverence for God; the second, as want of reverence for his ordinances, his holy law" (I:68).

Nevertheless, the distinction on which the former view is based is real, even though the reality is not reflected clearly in these two terms. The verses that follow depict the abandonment of the true

---

[6]For example, Lard (48) says, "Impiety, *asebeian*, means a failure in our duties to God; injustice, *adikian*, a failure in our duties to men." Murray (36) says the former refers to religious perversity, the latter to moral perversity. See also Stott (72) and Dunn (55, 70). Dunn says the distinction is not clear, though.

God as one kind of sin, as distinct from all the immoral and evil deeds that sinners commit among and against one another. And it seems clear that Paul is saying that the former does indeed in some way lead to the latter. It is a rule or principle that "impiety is the precursor of immorality," as Murray states it (I:36). Just as succinctly, Bruce (82) says, "Idolatry is the source of immorality."

The last part of v. 18 says that God's wrath is directed against "men who suppress the truth by their wickedness." What truth? The verses that follow show conclusively that Paul is referring to truth about God himself (see vv. 19-20, 25) and about his law or will for all mankind.

The verb translated "suppress" is κατέχω (*katechō*), which the KJV translates as "hold," yielding the concept of "holding to the truth in unrighteousness." Not only does this concept go against the very point of the next few verses; it also does not take sufficient account of the prefix *kat-* (*kata*) attached to the ordinary verb, ἔχω (*echō*), which by itself means "to have, to hold (to)." The prefix adds an emphasis which can be interpreted variously, but which in this case obviously means "to hold *down*, to suppress." God's wrath is directed against those who suppress his truth.

To say that the Gentiles suppress the truth means that they do *have* the truth and even know that it is true. In other words, the very act of suppressing the truth is evidence that they know it and are therefore without excuse and are no exception to the need for grace. The problem is that they deliberately reject it; they refuse to accept it and acknowledge it as truth. To some this may appear to be a genuine ignorance of the things of God, but Paul is saying it is only an apparent ignorance and not a real one. The knowledge is there, but suppressed. Eph 4:18 confirms this teaching when it refers to the "ignorance that is in them [the Gentiles] due to the hardening of their hearts." As Bruce (83) says, "It is a deliberate ignorance." See also v. 28.

They suppress the truth "by their wickedness." This is the word *adikia* again, as used earlier in the verse and translated "unrighteousness" in the NASB. At issue is whether the preposition ἐν (*en*) should be translated "in" or "by." If the former, then the point is that the Gentiles are comfortably ensconced in their wicked lifestyle and want to preserve it and therefore suppress all thoughts of God so as not to feel guilty. If the latter, then the point is that they suppress the truth by means of their wicked living; by their evil deeds they openly renounce the validity of God's claims on their lives. Both ideas are true, but it is difficult to tell which one Paul specifically had in mind when he wrote. Perhaps he was thinking of both.

1:19 since what may be known about God is plain to them . . . . This verse begins with "since" or "because," giving the reason for the preceding statement. God's wrath is being revealed *because* all people do know God (19-20) but have deliberately rejected him (21-25). Verses 19-20 are mainly establishing the fact that the Gentiles do have the truth (as v. 18 implies). Specifically, they have it through the *general revelation* that comes to all people through their awareness of the created universe.[7]

Paul refers to "what may be known about God" in this way. The proper translation of the Greek word for "known" is a matter of debate. Some take it as the NIV has it, i.e., "what *may be* known," or what is *knowable*, whether it is actually known or not. Thus Cranfield (I:113), Moo (I:99), and Morris (79-80). Others take it as the NASB has it, "that which *is* known." This is its meaning in all other NT occurrences, and its most common meaning elsewhere. Thus Lard (49), Lenski (95-96), and Murray (I:37). The latter is no doubt Paul's intention, contrary to the NIV. In this context his point is not about what *may* be known, but about what *is* known (vv. 20-21).[8]

The object of this knowledge is God himself. This explains the content of "the truth" of which v. 18 speaks. What the Gentiles know about God "is plain to them," says Paul. The word for "plain" is φανερός (*phaneros*), which means "manifest, evident, clear, plain, open, visible, easily seen." This is why this truth is known: it cannot be missed.

Another point of debate is the phrase ἐν αὐτοῖς (*en autois*), translated "to them" in the NIV. This is possible, since the preposi-

---

[7]For a complete discussion of general revelation see GC, 319-353.

[8]This does not make the sentence a tautology — "What is known, is known," contrary to Moo (I:99) and others. The second part of the clause (φανερός, "clear, manifest") does not refer to the Gentiles' knowing but to God's revealing.

tion *en* can mean "to" (see Murray, I:38; Morris, 80). However, *autois* without any preposition also means "to them," and it is used thus and translated thus in the latter part of this same verse. I take it as unlikely that Paul would use the two different expressions to mean the same thing so close together, contrary to the NIV. Another possibility is that *en autois* means "within them," as in the NASB (see Sanday and Headlam, 42). The connotation here is a revelation planted within the heart and known from within. Paul refers to something like this later (2:14-15), but the context is against this connotation here. The best translation of this phrase is "among them, in their midst" (see Barrett, 35; Cranfield, I:113; Moo, I:99). This is most consistent with v. 20. The first part of v. 19 thus says, "Because that which is known about God is plain to be seen in the very midst of them." ("Them," of course, refers especially to the Gentiles.)

Why is it so plain? **. . . because God has made it plain to them**. It is a matter of God's "deliberate self-disclosure," as Cranfield says (I:114). I.e., the Gentiles know this truth about God because he chose to make himself known. Their knowledge is neither an accidental discovery nor a cleverly devised speculation.

1:20 For since the creation of the world God's invisible qualities — his eternal power and divine nature — have been clearly seen, being understood from what has been made, so that men are without excuse. Verse 20 begins with Paul's favorite explanatory word, "for" (*gar*). How can we say that God has made truth about himself plain even to the Gentiles? Because, "since the creation of the world" certain truths about God have been clearly known through created things themselves. This has been the case ever since God originally created the world as recorded in Gen 1. From that time to the very present God has been revealing himself, and thus something about him has been and is known.

What is the *content* of this knowledge? Verse 19 is very general, but now v. 20 gets more specific: "God's invisible qualities" are known. This does not mean that God also has visible qualities; everything about the nature of God is invisible to his creatures. He cannot be perceived by our sight or senses (John 1:18; Col 1:15; 1 Tim 1:17; Heb 11:27; see GC, 229-233). Why is this fact about God mentioned here? It is a way of emphasizing the reality of the knowledge, expressed in the term "clearly seen" later in the verse. It is a play on words, as well as a conceptual paradox: how can "invisible things" be "clearly seen"? Cranfield (I:114) calls this an intentional oxymoron.

What specific qualities are known? "His eternal power and divine nature." It is not surprising that power should be mentioned, since God's omnipotence is the divine attribute most clearly expressed in the act and product of creation (see GC, 292-305). This is the same word used in v. 16 to describe the gospel, but that is a different kind of manifestation of God's power (see GRe, 455-458).

Paul speaks not just of power, but of *eternal* power. The word for "eternal" (ἀΐδιος, *aidios*) is rare, occurring only here and in Jude 6. There is no question that God is eternal, probably in more than one sense (see GC, 250-264). This includes the idea that he is everlasting, along with all his attributes. The question arises here, though, as to how God's eternity or everlastingness can be "clearly seen" by means of created things. Lard (52) suggests that Paul may not be saying that the eternal nature of God's power can be thus known; only the power itself can be known, but Paul as an inspired apostle characterizes it as eternal based on special revelation. Another possibility is that Paul is assuming here a basic form of what is called the cosmological argument for the existence of God (see GC, 424-433). The created universe consists only of contingent things, i.e., things that have a beginning and are perishable. From their existence we infer that their cause must be a Creator who is *not* contingent, and who is therefore eternal and imperishable. Paul later refers to this basic distinction between the immortal, imperishable Creator and mortal, perishable creatures (vv. 22, 24) as part of the knowledge for which all men are responsible.

The invisible qualities of God known through created things also include his "divine nature." The Greek word is θειότης (*theiotēs*). This is not exactly the same as the θεότητος (*theotētos*) that indwells Jesus of Nazareth (Col 2:9). The latter is deity or divinity itself in his very person, the very divine essence. The former, spoken of here by Paul, is the sum of all the characteristics or perfections of deity, in other words, all the attributes we usually associate with God: "the sum of all God's glorious attributes"

(Hendriksen, I:70). In reality there is not much difference between these words, since God's essence *is* the sum of all his attributes.

The point is, though, that other qualities of God's nature besides his power are clearly seen from the created world. These include his glory (Ps 19:1) and his goodness (Acts 14:17), as well as his righteous judgment (1:32). See GC, 339.

Having spoken of the content of the Gentiles' knowledge, the text then emphasizes the *reality* of it. These things, Paul says, "have been clearly seen." The tense of the verb is actually present: "*are* clearly seen." Herein lies the paradox, that the invisible things of God are nevertheless seen by all. How is this the case?

The base verb, ὁράω (*horaō*), is the ordinary word for seeing with the physical eyes (see John 1:18). The addition of the prefix κατά (*kata*), which occurs only here in the NT, makes the verb intensive, thus, "*clearly* seen." This emphatic word leaves no doubt as to the reality of the knowledge in question.

In this verse, though, it is appropriate to take the word in a figurative or non-physical sense. That is, the invisible things of God "are clearly seen by the eye of man's mind" (DeWelt, 28), or what Eph 1:18 calls "the eyes of your heart." The idea is that what we physically see[9] in the created universe leads the eyes of our hearts to see these invisible divine qualities. In this way all people, including the Gentiles, have true knowledge of the true God.

Next Paul identifies the *source* of this knowledge: God's invisible qualities are "being understood from what has been made." "Being understood" is the verb νοέω (*noeō*), which specifically refers to mental seeing, the activity of the mind. To say that these things "are understood" just reinforces the fact that the knowledge is real. "Are clearly seen" is the main verb; "being understood" is a participle modifying it, explaining *how* these things are clearly seen. The answer is: "from what has been made," that is, the things made by God in the activity of creation, the created visible universe.

How are the phenomena of creation a source of true knowledge of God? On a common-sense level, when we view the wonders of

---

[9]This part of the knowing process should not be limited to the sense of sight. It is not just what we *see* in the physical world, but what we experience with all our senses, or any limited number of them, that leads us to this clear knowledge of God.

nature we just instinctively infer a powerful Creator as their source. The Psalmist chastises idolaters thus: "Does he who implanted the ear not hear? Does he who formed the eye not see?" (Ps 94:9). That is, whoever made the eye and the ear can himself surely see and hear perfectly. When such data are formally analyzed by the mind, the results are what are called the cosmological and the teleological arguments for the existence of God (on the latter see GC, 433-440). These arguments assume some basic reasoning power, which all human beings have by virtue of being created in God's image. Such use of the mind "is not abstract speculation but sane and sober thought on the things made by God" (Lenski, 97).

Some would call this a kind of "natural theology" (Lenski, 99), a term and concept held in high favor by Roman Catholics but not usually by Protestants. But as long as we recognize its limitations and are not expecting to build a whole system of theology thus, we surely must admit on the basis of what Paul is saying here that we can draw some true conclusions about God based on general revelation only (see Dunn, I:56-57). Such natural theology is not a product of speculative reason, but rather of God's own revelation as thought through by analytical reason.

We agree with Moo, though, that "this knowledge is both limited and impure" (I:122). It is impure because some things present in nature (such as human disease and death) are the result of sin and do not reflect the glory of God (8:18-23). It is limited in scope because some truths about God are not revealed in natural phenomena (e.g., the fact of the Trinity). Even the cosmological and teleological arguments are limited as to what kind of Creator can be inferred from the creation (see GC, 430-432, 438). Most significantly, general revelation does not give any information about *the gospel*, i.e., about salvation and about God as Redeemer. This information comes only through special or biblical revelation and thus is not available to the Gentiles unless someone takes it to them (10:13-17).

This leads to the last point Paul makes about the Gentiles' knowledge in v. 20, namely, its *result*. Their knowledge of God is sufficient "so that men are without excuse." "Men" is not in the text, which has only the pronoun "they," whose antecedent is the men who suppress the truth in v. 18. The main reference is to the

Gentiles, but the state of being without excuse applies to all sinners, as 3:19-20 shows: "every mouth . . . the whole world . . . no one."

"Without excuse" translates ἀναπολόγητος (*anapologētos*), used only here and in 2:1. It is from the same root as the word that means "apology" in the sense of "apologetics, defense." As 1 Pet 3:15 says, the Christian can and should have an apology or defense for his hope, but Paul declares that the sinner has no defense or excuse for his sin. Why not? Because general revelation gives every person enough knowledge to be judged by (see vv. 21, 32). No one, not even the most remote Gentile, will be able to plead ignorance on the judgment day (see 3:19; Matt 22:12). To be without excuse assumes each individual's free will and personal responsibility for his actions. It also assumes adequate knowledge of the standard by which our actions will be measured, which is Paul's point here.

The Greek construction used here is sometimes taken as referring to God's *purpose* in giving creation knowledge, i.e., "*in order that* they *may be* without excuse." That is, God gave this knowledge just so no one will have an excuse if he sins. Thus the very purpose of general revelation is to condemn. See the ASV; Morris, 82-83; Murray, 40. This seems awfully harsh to some, who say instead that the Greek construction refers to the *result* of the general revelation and the knowledge it produces: "so that as a result they *are* without excuse." The NIV translation follows this view, which I believe is correct. I agree with Lenski (100), that to understand this in terms of purpose "would be monstrous."

Either way the outcome for the Gentiles is the same: they are, as a matter of fact, without excuse. Their godless and wicked behavior (v. 18) is inexcusable in view of what they know about God (vv. 19-20), and God is justified in pouring out his wrath upon them. The next section, vv. 21-25, will make this even more clear.[10]

---

[10]How does Paul's conclusion here compare with his statement in Acts 17:30, that in the time prior to the gospel "God overlooked such ignorance" (NIV)? Some take this to mean that God *will* excuse at least the pre-Christian Gentiles. This is a serious misunderstanding of the Acts passage, though. See my discussion of it in GC, 344-345.

B. UNIVERSAL REJECTION OF THE TRUE GOD (1:21-25)

To answer the objection that the Gentiles are an exception to the need for grace, Paul is showing that they stand condemned under the law. First he shows that they do have true knowledge of the true God (vv. 19-20). Now he is showing that they have refused to accept this truth and have rejected the God who gave it to them (vv. 21-25). Verses 21-23 are an explanation of how they have suppressed the truth (v. 18), as are vv. 25 and 28.

1:21 This verse begins the explanation of why "men are without excuse": **For although they knew God**, they did not respond as such knowledge requires.[11] This participial phrase sums up the point of vv. 19-20 and reaffirms the reality of the Gentiles' knowledge of God. Such knowledge in itself is not equivalent to salvation, as many mistakenly think. Even true knowledge of the true God (e.g., Acts 17:27) is not necessarily the intimate, personal, *saving* knowledge of which Jesus speaks in John 17:3. The sense here may be better conveyed thus: "For although they knew *about* God."

Despite their knowledge, **they neither glorified him as God nor gave thanks to him . . . .** These two responses — to glorify God and give him thanks — are the most basic of all human obligations toward the Creator. They are the fundamental precepts of God's law for mankind, and Paul's implication is that they are known to all people through general revelation alone.

What does it mean to glorify God as God? The Bible often speaks of the "glory" of God (GC, 446-452), a term that is meant to sum up his collective greatness. God's glory is his infinite significance, the totality of his perfections, the fullness of his deity compressed into a single concept. Most specifically, his glory is his greatness as it is manifested and as it shines forth for all to see. To "glorify" God means simply to recognize, acknowledge, and bow down before this displayed glory in the spirit of worship, and to live the kind of life that causes others to do the same. As MacArthur (I:83) says, "We glorify him by praising his glory!"

---

[11]At this point Paul switches to past tense and continues to speak thus until v. 32, when he returns to the present tense. This use of past tense does not mean that the activity being described thereby is no longer happening.

It is often observed that to glorify God is man's highest good (his *summum bonum*) and his highest obligation. It combines into one concept the requirements of the first commandment, "You shall have no other gods before me" (Exod 20:3); the greatest commandment, "Love the Lord your God with all your heart and with all your soul and with all your mind" (Matt 22:37); and the highest goal of life, "Seek first his kingdom and his righteousness" (Matt 6:33). In this last passage "kingdom" should be understood in its basic sense of *kingship* or *lordship*; our highest goal must be to honor God's lordship over all things. If glorifying God is man's highest obligation, then refusing to glorify God is man's worst sin.

The second response required by the knowledge of God received through the creation is to give him thanks. This is the only reasonable result of recognizing that this world is the product of an Almighty Creator, and that he stands behind all its bounty (Matt 5:45; Acts 14:17). Giving him thanks is simply acknowledging that he, rather than blind fortune or human merit, is the source of all life and blessings and happiness. By giving him thanks we renounce self-sufficiency and confess our dependence upon and indebtedness to him. This is the point of the simplest thanksgiving preceding a meal.

Taken together, these two basic obligations mirror God's twofold purpose for creating the universe in the first place, namely, to glorify himself and to share his goodness. See GC, 120-128.

Paul's main point, of course, is that even the Gentiles are responsible for obeying these two fundamental laws; but they have not done so. Instead of acting righteously upon the knowledge of God available to them, **. . . their thinking became futile and their foolish hearts were darkened**. The point is that they set their minds against God, and thus removed from the master plan or master program of all possible human knowledge the key element that makes sense of everything else. Their thinking is no longer the proper use of reason and logic, but is διαλογισμός (*dialogismos*), a term that is used often in the NT and almost always in the negative sense of evil, devious, useless thinking.[12] Instead of true thinking it is mere speculation and self-serving rationalization.

---

[12]See, e.g., Matt 15:19; Mark 7:21; Luke 5:22; 6:8; 1 Cor 3:20; Phil 2:14; 1 Tim 2:8.

Paul calls such thinking "futile," vain, empty, worthless, pointless. The Greek word here is from the same word group which in the LXX is sometimes used for idols (e.g., Lev 17:7; 2 Chr 11:15), i.e., they are empty nothings. The same is true of all godless thinking: it amounts to nothing; it reaches no valid conclusions. This is how the Gentiles think. Instead of building their worldviews on the reality of God, they build them on the sands of their own speculations.

Paul also says "their foolish hearts were darkened." In biblical language the heart is not just the emotional side of man, but the whole inner being encompassing all inner, spiritual activity such as thinking and willing. The "heart" is the source of thinking, and when the heart becomes "foolish" its thinking becomes futile. The word for "foolish" is also one of the sins listed in v. 31, where the NIV translates it as "senseless." It means void of understanding, or as Lard says, just plain stupid (55).

Their foolish hearts were "darkened." Since God is light (1 John 1:5), any heart that excludes God is literally in the dark. The light of God is purity, glory, and truth; when God is rejected there is only the darkness of ignorance and evil and eventually the outer darkness of hell (Matt 8:12; 22:13; Jude 13). See the parallel thought in Eph 4:17-18, which says the Gentiles live "in the futility of their thinking. They are darkened in their understanding and separated from the life of God because of the ignorance that is in them due to the hardening of their hearts."

1:22 This and the next verse continue the indictment of the Gentiles. **Although they claimed to be wise, they became fools . . . .** Wisdom is knowing how to make the right choices and decisions based on available knowledge. Basically, it is knowing how to live. Those who reject God always think they are wise, and that their rejection of God is the highest evidence of it. They always think they are wiser than believers. They consider believers to be naive, gullible, foolish, illogical, and full of wishful thinking. They consider themselves to be sophisticated, unbiased, very intelligent, and guided by critical thinking. It is the nature of worldly wisdom to confuse real foolishness with real wisdom, and vice versa (1 Cor 1:18-2:8).

"They became fools" translates a verb from the Greek word family from which our word "moron" is derived. Thus they became foolish and moronic; they became "silly," says Lenski (104). They "made fools of themselves" (NEB). This applies especially to their moral reasoning, which can never be separated from how one thinks of God.

There could hardly be a more accurate and more damning description of the godless in any age, but especially of today's self-appointed scientific "experts" and arbiters of "culture." If these people were really wise, i.e., if they really knew how to live, they would glorify God and give him thanks.

1:23 This verse explains more specifically *how* the Gentiles became fools. They did it when they **. . . exchanged the glory of the immortal God for images made to look like mortal man and birds and animals and reptiles**. Paul calls this an "exchange" (see vv. 25-26). People often measure their wisdom by the kind of deals or trades they make. Paul says the Gentiles have made a swap or an exchange, but it is not a very clever one. In fact, it is the worst possible exchange anyone could possibly make.

What have the Gentiles done? They have traded the real thing for the phony and useless. They have traded the true God for impotent idols. "The glory of the immortal God" is what they know through general revelation. The heavens declare his glory (Ps 19:1); the wonders of the earth display his power and majesty. As the true God he is immortal, which means he is eternal (see v. 20) because his nature is incorruptible and imperishable. He has always been and he always will be who he is, and therefore we can put absolute trust and confidence in him and his promises. Nothing is more valuable and precious than this. It is like the "pearl of great price": it is worth everything else to acquire and it must never be surrendered at any cost.

Yet this is what the Gentiles have exchanged — and for what? For images of men and birds and animals and reptiles! Not even *actual* men and birds and animals and reptiles, but just *images* of them. The Greek phrase is "the likeness of an image," or a likeness patterned after the form of these things. This refers to the grossest form of idolatry, the worship of manufactured statues of mere creatures.[13]

---

[13]Such idolatry is not limited to the Gentiles. God warned Israel against this very thing (Deut 4:16-18), but they often were seduced into it. Ps 106:20 sounds like Paul: "They exchanged their Glory for an image of a bull, which eats grass." See Jer 2:11.

Four kinds of idols are mentioned. Some are patterned after the *human* form, a common characteristic of pagan religions. The Greek gods of Olympus were pictured thus, as were some of the Egyptian deities. Rulers such as the Pharaohs and the Caesars were often given divine status. The other idols Paul mentions are patterned after three kinds of animals (see Acts 10:12): *birds*, such as the Egyptian gods Horus (a falcon) and Thoth (an ibis);[14] *animals* (specifically quadrupeds), such as the bull (which was widely worshiped) and Egyptian deities such as Anubis (a jackal), Bastet (a cat), and Khnum (a ram); and *reptiles*. This last category is general enough to include the serpent (also widely worshiped) and the crocodile (Sobek in Egypt).

The characteristic shared by all these categories is *mortality*; they are all corruptible and perishable. This is true not just of the idols or statues, but of the things themselves after which the idols are patterned. Man himself is mortal or perishable; only God has inherent immortality (1 Tim 6:16; see GC, 245-250). If God so willed, he could annihilate every human being, body and spirit. To reject the one true and immortal God and to worship any mortal thing is the epitome of stupidity. Isa 44:9-20 underscores the irony of such idolatry, in which a man cuts down a tree, burns part of it to cook his food and keep himself warm, then makes an idol out of the rest of it and falls down and worships it. (See Isa 46:6-7.) No wonder Paul says, "They became fools."

It would seem that Paul has already made his case by this time. He has declared that the Gentiles know truth about God, but they have suppressed and rejected it and have freely chosen to serve idols instead. Thus God is completely justified in pouring out his wrath upon them; judgment according to law shows them to be without excuse.

1:24 But Paul wants to make it perfectly clear; so now he returns to his point about the wrath of God (v. 18), and speaks of *how* this wrath is being revealed from heaven against the ungodly and unrighteous Gentiles. **Therefore God gave them over in the sinful desires of their hearts . . . .** "Therefore" means that what has

---

[14]The Egyptian deities were often depicted with human bodies and bird or animal heads.

just been described in vv. 21-23 is *why* God has acted in wrath toward them.

Exactly what has befallen the Gentiles as the result of their rejection of God? Paul says "God gave them over" to the sinful lifestyle they were intent on pursuing (see vv. 26, 28). The Greek word (παραδίδωμι, *paradidōmi*) is quite common and is used for all sorts of activities, including some works of God. In the LXX it is used for God's providential act of delivering Israel's enemies into their hands (Exod 23:31; Deut 7:23), and also for God's handing Israel over to these same enemies (Lev 26:25). God delivered Jesus over to his death (4:25; 8:32). Rom 6:17 says God hands believers over to a form of teaching. In Acts 7:42 Stephen says God gave idolatrous Israel over to her idolatry.

How does God "give someone over" to do evil? The basic answer is that in the working of his providence "he ceases to restrain them from evil or protect them against it." In other words, "he lets them alone to do as they please without hindrance from him in the matter of sin" (Lard, 57). In his permissive will he allows them to plunge headlong into what their evil hearts desire. This clearly implies, says Lard (57), "that till God gives a people up, they are always under his protecting care." He does providentially restrain individuals and even nations from going as far into sin as they would and could. We who honor him are probably not even aware of how often God has restrained us from destroying ourselves with our own folly.

But there comes a time when God withdraws his restraint, in whatever way he judges appropriate. This is probably the concept present in 2 Thess 2:6-7, which speaks of the mystery of lawlessness being restrained until that restraint is withdrawn for one last time at the end. It is reflected in Ps 78:29 and Ps 106:14-15, and in Hos 4:17, "Ephraim is joined to idols; leave him alone!" This is God's answer to the defiant sinners who mock him and challenge him to strike them dead if he is really there. God just turns his back on them. What could be more frightening than this?

Most commentators agree, though, that this "giving over" is not just a shrug of indifference by God; he is not just adopting a passive attitude while ceasing to do anything at all. In Murray's words, God's giving over "cannot be reduced to the notion of non-interference with the natural consequences of sin" (I:44). It is rather a deliberate, purposeful act by God.[15]

On the other hand, we must not go to the opposite extreme and think that somehow God is *causing* the Gentiles to fall deeper into their sin. God does not cause anyone to do evil. Thus it is, as Lenski says (108), more than permission but less than causation.

Why does God do this at all? Some say the purpose of this "giving over" is ultimately redemptive, the assumption being that when men reach the depths of sin's degradation they will see the error of their way and seek for God's mercy (Morris, 88; Cranfield, I:121). There is no indication of this in the text, though. The giving over is presented as a purely punitive act, an act of divine retribution, a penalty that is deserved (see v. 27, "the due penalty"). Cranfield is right to insist that this does not mean that "God washed His hands of them," or that he "gave these men up for ever" (I:121). It is a judicial act, but it is not the final judgment. It does not cancel the missionary imperative, but rather intensifies it.

Paul continues his thought by saying that God gave the Gentiles over "in the sinful desires of their hearts." This is not what he gave them over *to*; this is what was *already* existing in their hearts. "Finding them living in lust," God ceased to restrain them (MP, 304). In Eph 4:19 Paul uses the very same word (*paradidōmi*) that he uses here for God's act, but he uses it of the Gentiles themselves: already in their own hearts "they have given themselves over to sensuality so as to indulge in every kind of impurity, with a continual lust for more."

The word translated "sinful desires" basically means "strong desire," whether for something good (Luke 22:15; Phil 1:23; 1 Thess 2:17), or for something evil. It can be used for evil desire of any kind (1 Tim 6:9), but often connotes sexual lust in particular (e.g., 1 Thess 4:5; 2 Tim 3:6; 1 Pet 4:3). Using the word in its verbal form, this is what Jesus equates with committing adultery in the

---

[15]This is asserted especially in opposition to the view of C.H. Dodd, who says the giving over is "no more than an abstention from interference with their free choice and its consequences" (55). Also objectionable is Barclay's view, "It is not that God is punishing the man. It is that he is bringing punishment upon himself" (22).

heart (Matt 5:28).[16] The context of 1:24 shows that Paul is using the word here in the sense of sexual lust.

What, then, did God give the Gentiles over *to*? Because of their idolatry, and in their lustful condition, God gave them over **to sexual impurity for the degrading of their bodies with one another**. The desires are already there; the punitive action is that God withdraws his restraints and lets them act out their fantasies in a sexually impure lifestyle. The word is ἀκαθαρσία (*akatharsia*), which means impurity or uncleanness, and which is often used with the specific connotation of sexual impurity (see 2 Cor 12:21; Gal 5:19; Col 3:5). This is probably the case here, given the references to lust, to the misuse of the body, and to homosexuality. Thus the NIV properly translates it as "sexual impurity." This is not a condemnation of sex as such, but of sex out of control, outside the restraints of God's law.

Such unbridled, unrestrained sex is a degradation of the body, says Paul (see 1 Cor 6:18). The word translated "degrading" is ἀτι-μάζω (*atimazō*), meaning "to dishonor, to debase, to disgrace, to degrade." It is the opposite of τιμάω (*timaō*), which means "to honor, to give honor to." When God is not honored as Creator (vv. 21, 23), there is no longer any reason to respect and honor one's body as a creation of God and as a gift from God. There is no need for a sense of stewardship of the body, no acknowledgment of God's purposes for it in all its parts, including the genitals (see 6:19). Thus we see all manner of abuse of the body among those who reject God, especially all manner of sexual abuse and degradation.

We may recall here that this "handing over" to sexual impurity is a punitive act. Some may wonder how allowing someone to do what his heart desires is a penalty. But let us not forget that God hands the Gentiles over not just to their sins but also to the consequences of their sins (see vv. 24b, 27b), to which degraded and abused bodies are a witness. As Dunn says, God did not "give them their desires, rather he gave them to what they desired and the

---

[16]This does not mean that sexual desire as such is wrong, especially when it is directed toward one's spouse. It becomes *evil* desire, or lust, when its object is anyone or anything other than one's spouse.

consequences of what they desired" (I:73). As MacArthur (I:100) points out, these consequences range from the grossly physical, such as venereal disease, to spiritual ones such as "loneliness, frustration, meaninglessness, anxiety, and despair." Sinners usually do not think much about such consequences until it is too late.

The entire process described here illustrates the principle briefly mentioned earlier, that idolatry is the precursor of immorality in the sense of cause and effect (Bruce, 82). When men reject the true God, this leads to more and more excesses of immorality. "The more base the perception of God, the more base the worship and corresponding conduct appropriate to it" (Dunn, I:63). "Religious degeneration is penalized by abandonment to immorality; sin in the religious realm is punished by sin in the moral sphere" (Murray, I:43).

This is obviously true, but it is not the whole story. Paul says the lust is already in the Gentiles' hearts when God gives them over to a full expression of it. Thus it is just as true to say that immorality leads to idolatry. Why are people so anxious to exchange the truth of God for idols and false gods? Because they have evil lusts they want to act out and justify, with no sense of guilt and fear of punishment. But they cannot do this under the eye of the true God! What is the solution? Get a new god. I once asked a campus minister why Eastern (oriental) religions are so popular among college students. His reply was that, for the most part, these religions make no moral demands. As Dunn (I:73) suggests, the desire to be free from the true God is really just the desire for "freedom to indulge in immorality."

In either case MacArthur (I:86) is right on target: "Spiritual darkness and moral perversity are inseparable. When man forfeits God, he forfeits virtue. The godless philosophy of the world inescapably leads to moral perversion, because unbelief and immorality are inextricably intertwined."

1:25 They exchanged the truth of God for a lie, and worshiped and served created things rather than the Creator — who is forever praised. Amen. Before Paul continues his emphasis on the depths of sin to which God has delivered the Gentiles, he again returns to their rejection of the true God. At this point the reader might be wondering, are these people really so bad that they deserve being rejected by God as v. 24 describes? Paul stops to remind us that, yes, they really *are* this bad; they do deserve to be rejected by God, because they first rejected him.

Verse 25 begins with a relative pronoun, "who," or "the ones who." Yes, these very ones whom God gave over are the same ones who "exchanged the truth of God for a lie," as described in vv. 21-23. Here the author repeats the indictment brought against them in those verses, especially v. 23.

"The truth of God" is variously interpreted as "the true God" (NEB), truth *from* God (Lard, 58), and truth *about* God (NRSV). All of these concepts fit the context, but Paul probably had the last one in mind specifically. The Gentiles exchanged the truth about God they knew from general revelation, the truth "that God was the creator and thus the natural object of worship" (DeWelt, 30).

This truth was exchanged for a lie. Some note that the Greek has the definite article, "*the* lie" (Morris, 90). All sin is a lie, but idolatry is the supreme lie, the basic lie that leads to all other lies. In Isa 44:20 an idol itself is called a lie. On the other hand, the existence of the true God is the supreme truth (see Heb 11:6). In the title of his book *The God Who Is There* Francis Schaeffer reminds us that the very reality of God is the starting point for all thinking, the elemental framework for the only valid worldview.

In the end the Gentiles not only *suppress* the truth (v. 18), but *exchange* it for a lie. Actually one is not possible without the other. The rejection of truth leaves a vacuum which will inevitably be filled by the most convenient lie.

Paul then summarizes the practical nature of this exchange, saying the Gentiles "worshiped and served created things rather than the Creator." This repeats the idea of v. 23. The word for "worshiped" (σεβάζομαι, *sebazomai*) is used only here in the NT, but it and other words in the same word family (see *asebeia* in v. 18) all refer to the worship and adoration of God, which of course should be reserved for the true God. The word for "served" (see 1:9) refers to external religious service and worship practices.

According to God's original plan for man and the rest of creation, man was supposed to worship and serve God alone while ruling over and subduing the whole world (Gen 1:26-28). Idolatry constitutes an upheaval and reversal of this creation order. Man, the intended lord of creation, deliberately makes himself religiously subservient to some created thing and thereby becomes a slave to the material world in general.

To worship and serve any created thing rather than the Creator is again the epitome of stupidity (see Isa 44:9-20 again). The importance of acknowledging God as the transcendent Creator cannot be overemphasized. It is absolutely fundamental to everything else; it is the primary truth in the biblical worldview. To realize the distinction between the creature (including oneself) and the Creator is the basis of all piety and morality. By denying the Creator his rightful place, idolatry strikes at the very root and foundation of truth.

In the face of such impiety Paul cannot suppress words of worship for the Creator, "who is forever praised." In other places he offers doxologies directly to God (11:36; 16:25-27; 2 Cor 9:15; Eph 3:20-21). Sometimes he simply pauses to remind us of the blessed nature of God; this is called a benediction (9:5; 2 Cor 1:3; 11:31; Eph 1:3). The latter is what he is doing here. The word "praised" is literally "blessed," in the sense that he is worthy of praise, or worthy of having good things said about him.[17] As we sometimes sing, "Blessed be the name of the Lord." God is thus worthy to be praised *forever*, says Paul, in spite of man's attempts to deny him.

To this he adds an "amen" for emphasis. The English "amen" is a transliteration of the Greek word, which is a transliteration of the Hebrew word signifying solemn agreement or confirmation. Its basic meaning has to do with truth. As Paul uses it here, it is equivalent to "It's the truth!"

It is important that we pause here and remind ourselves that although Paul is primarily concerned with the Gentiles in this passage, everything he says applies just as validly to those who know God and his law through special revelation also.

C. THE UTTER DEPTHS OF GENTILE DEPRAVITY (1:26-32)

In this section Paul continues to show why the Gentiles are

---

[17]This is not the same word used in the beatitudes (Matt 5:3-11), which is often translated "blessed" but has the sense of "happy."

without excuse. He catalogs the horrible depths to which sinners sink when God abandons them to their wicked lifestyles. He stresses that even as they do these things, they know in their hearts that they are doing wrong and that they deserve the final penalty of death (v. 32).

Paul is not affirming that every individual Gentile is guilty of all the sins cataloged here. He is rather showing just how far darkened hearts can and often do go when they reject the light available to them. Not all cultures and not all individuals will fall this far, but many have and many will (Gen 6:5; 18:20; Ps 2:1-3). Tragically, as we read our newspapers and newsmagazines, and as we watch the daily news broadcasts, we cannot avoid the conclusion that many segments of our own modern culture are frighteningly close to the ugly picture Paul draws for us here.

1:26 Here the cause-and-effect relation between idolatry and God's punitive response is affirmed again. **Because of this**, i.e., because of their rejection of the Creator (v. 25), **God gave them over to shameful lusts**. This sums up v. 24. "Lusts" here is equivalent to "sinful desires" there. In other Greek literature this word (πάθος, *pathos*) does not always refer to lustful sexual passion, but it does in its three NT occurrences (here; Col 3:5; 1 Thess 4:5). The use of the modifier "shameful" makes this clear here. This word, actually a noun (ἀτιμία, *atimia*) is equivalent to the verb translated "degrading" in v. 24. It means "dishonor, contempt, shame, disgrace." Thus Paul is saying God gave them over to act out their dark passions in the most shameful and dishonorable ways.

As a prime example of these "shameful lusts" Paul specifically names homosexuality. The fact that he singles this out for condemnation, and the fact that he spells it out so thoroughly, indicate that this is the most shameful of the sexual lusts that run wild when God is rejected. MacArthur calls it "the most degrading and repulsive of all passions" (I:104). (We should note that what Paul is describing here are homosexual acts and practices, not necessarily homosexual inclination or the homosexual condition in itself. A person may exist with recognized homosexual tendencies, but not be guilty of sin unless he allows this condition to lead him into homosexual lusts and practices.)

Paul includes both female and male homosexuality in these

"shameful lusts." **Even their women exchanged natural relations for unnatural ones**. This is the only specific biblical reference to lesbianism. Paul says "*Even* their women" are guilty of this sin. The Greek particles linking vv. 26 and 27 (τε . . . τε, *te . . . te*) mean "not only . . . but also" or "both . . . and." This puts the females and the males on the same base level, says Lenski (113).

Contrary to the NIV, neither here nor in v. 27 does Paul use the Greek words for "women" and "men," since these words can also mean "wives" and "husbands." Instead he chooses the terms "females" and "males." This is probably because the kind of sex he is talking about has no relation to what God intended for human beings in the husband-wife relationship; indeed it is the very antithesis of it. Also, the terms "women" and "men" have a distinctively human connotation, but those who engage in homosexual acts have succumbed to raw animal passion.

The *exchanging* of natural for unnatural sex echoes the earlier references to exchanging truth about God for false deities (vv. 23, 25). Except for the omission of the prefix *meta* in v. 23, the same verb is used in all three verses. This shows that homosexuality is as unnatural and as worthy of condemnation as idolatry. It also illustrates the principle stressed earlier, that substitute gods and degenerate morality go together.

The term χρῆσις (*chrēsis*), translated "relations" in the NIV, is used in the NT only here and in v. 27. Its general meaning is "use" or "function" (as the NASB has it). But in secular Greek it was often a euphemism for sexual intercourse (see the NRSV). This is no doubt how Paul uses it here, as the NIV implies in rendering it "relations." The references to sexual sin in vv. 24, 26a, and the clear reference to the equivalent male homosexuality in v. 27, make this conclusive. In straightforward terms, v. 26b reads, "Their females exchanged natural sex for unnatural sex."

The term "natural" (φυσικός, *physikos*) must be understood here and in v. 27 as meaning "according to God's created order" (see Stott, 78). "Unnatural" is literally "against nature" (παρὰ φύσις, *para physis*) and means what is contrary to the natural order of things as God intended them and created them in the beginning.[18]

---

[18]The word does not necessarily have this meaning in every context.

This is the only meaning consistent with the present context. The main subject of this whole section is the Gentiles' knowledge of God as Creator and the knowledge of his basic ordinances for his human creatures. Thus the context requires us to understand natural sex as sex according to "God's creative intent" (Moo, I:109; see Cranfield, I:125-126). When one gives up the Creator (v. 25), he likewise gives up the creation ordinances, which include the husband-wife relationship as the intended context for sex. Also, we must remember that this verse says that lesbian sex is unnatural sex, and unnatural sex is the essence of the "shameful lusts" to which God has delivered the Gentiles in his punitive wrath. "When these factors are considered, it is clear that Paul depicts homosexual activity as a violation of God's created order, another indication of the departure from true knowledge and worship of God" (Moo, I:110).

It is very important to emphasize these connotations for "natural" and "unnatural," because contemporary pro-homosexual interpreters attempt to give these terms entirely different meanings here. They insist that Paul uses these words to refer to what is natural and unnatural for *particular individuals*, not for human beings in general. They say that heterosexual sex is what is natural for most human beings, i.e., it is their felt inclination. For these and these alone, homosexual sex is unnatural and therefore wrong. However, for some human beings homosexual sex is their felt inclination; therefore it is natural for them and is not wrong. Paul is not talking about this "natural" homosexuality at all. As Boswell claims, "Paul did not discuss gay *persons* but only homosexual *acts* committed by heterosexual persons" (*Christianity*, 109; see 107-114).

As we have emphasized, the context of 1:26-27 simply will not allow this interpretation. Also, Paul does not say the women exchanged what was natural *for them* for what was against *their own* nature. The terms "natural" and "unnatural" are not limited or qualified in any way. See the discussion and refutation of Boswell's view in Stott (77-78) and in DeYoung, "Meaning."

1:27 In the same way the men also abandoned natural relations with women and were inflamed with lust for one another. This verse is an impassioned denunciation of male homosexuality. This sin is clearly named and condemned in other places in the

Bible,[19] but in none as emphatically as here. The word ὁμοίως (*homoiōs*) at the beginning of the verse, translated "in the same way," indicates an equivalence between female and male homosexuality; before God one is as bad as the other.

Expanding on his description of homosexual males ("gays"), Paul says they "were inflamed with lust for one another." They "burned in their desire" (NASB); they "were consumed with passion" (NRSV). Both Greek words in this expression are used only here in the NT. "Lust" is a specific form of the "sinful desires" of v. 24, and is equivalent to the "shameful lusts" in v. 26. To be *inflamed* with such lust is to be dominated and driven by an uncontrolled and all-consuming desire for homosexual contact. MacArthur correctly remarks (I:105), "There is a burning level of lust among homosexuals that beggars description and is rarely known among heterosexuals." Anyone who can stand to read descriptions of sexual practices in the homosexual subculture will readily agree with this statement. This does not mean that everyone with homosexual tendencies gives way to them; but when this does occur, it is like a forest fire out of control. As Lenski observes (115), "The moment God is taken out of the control of men's life the stench of sex aberration is bound to arise. . . . Without God sex runs wild."

Men committed indecent acts with other men . . . ; literally, "males . . . with males." The catalog of "indecent acts" engaged in by male homosexuals is shocking and disgusting; they need not be named here. The Greek word for this expression is used in the NT only here and in Rev 16:15; cognates are found in 1 Cor 7:36; 12:23; 13:5. These words are often used to refer to the indecent and shameful exposure of the genitals (Dunn 1:65).

As a result of these indecent acts, they **. . . received in themselves the due penalty for their perversion**. This is a difficult clause, but its point is that homosexuals who indulge their wild passions get what they deserve; they reap what they sow; they suffer the deserved consequences of their perversion. This is not a reference to the final judgment, but to the infliction of divine wrath that comes in the form of historical circumstances.

---

[19]Lev 18:22; 20:13; 1 Cor 6:9-10; 1 Tim 1:8-10; Jude 7 (referring to Gen 19).

The word "received" is an emphatic form of a common word and often means, as here, "to receive back, to receive in return," i.e., to receive as the fitting result of their actions. Cranfield says it "emphasizes the deservedness of the punishment" (I:127). This verb's object, "the due penalty," also clearly refers to deserved punishment. Gays deservedly receive the recompense due to them as specified by the Creator's law.

How may we understand this "due penalty" or recompense? Some think the sexual perversion itself is its own penalty, or at least is the just penalty for their rejection of God (Cranfield, I:126-127; Morris, 93). It seems more likely, though, that Paul is referring to some punitive consequences distinct from the homosexual acts as such, consequences they experience "in themselves" or "in their own persons" (NASB) as a form of the very wrath of God (v. 18).

There is scarcely any sin that subjects its perpetrators to more severe "deserved penalties" than male homosexuality. Is AIDS an example of this? Assuredly so. MacArthur is correct (I:107): "The appalling physical consequences of homosexuality are visible evidence of God's righteous condemnation. Unnatural vice brings its own perverted reward. AIDS is frightening evidence of that fatal promise." This is not to say that God deliberately created the HIV virus as a specific penalty for male homosexuals. As it exists under the curse (8:18-22), the world is full of all sorts of bacteria, viruses, and ailments that are a threat to all of us under certain conditions. The fact is, though, that certain practices, especially sinful practices, openly invite these maladies to strike us down. Licentious, promiscuous sex has always reaped the deserved harvest of sexually transmitted diseases; AIDS is just the latest version of this and male homosexuals are especially vulnerable to it.

We should understand, then, that AIDS is just one — albeit a fatal one — of many serious health consequences homosexuals have always received back as a due penalty for their perversion. Long before AIDS entered the picture, homosexual practices focusing on the anus and excrement have kept gay men in a constant state of health crisis.[20] Lenski correctly comments (116-117) that the homosexuals'

---

[20]Rueda informs us, "Many homosexual periodicals have medical advice columns which provide information and/or answer questions. The medical information provided consists basically of advice on the nature, treatment,

"recompense is the vicious effect of the unnatural sexual vices upon men's own bodies and their minds, corrupting, destroying, disintegrating. . . . It is noteworthy that in the Scriptures as in human experience sexual sins, and not only the worst form of these, carry a special curse; they not only disgrace, they wreck; their punishment is direct, wretched, severe." This is why Paul treats this sin separately and does not just include it in the listing in vv. 29-31.

Paul speaks of the due penalty for their "perversion." The word used here is sometimes translated "error" (NASB, NRSV), but Bruce (85) is right; this is "too weak a noun" for what Paul has in mind. The word refers to wandering or roaming; figuratively it refers to wandering from the path of truth and morality. "Perversion" or "deviancy" captures the meaning very well in this context.

Except for his use of "error," Dunn's paraphrase of 27b is clearly on target: "receiving in return in themselves the penalty which matches the deed and which is proper to their error" (74). He also well sums up the thrust of this whole section: "The divinely ordered punishment for sin is to be handed over to the power of that sin, to be left to its consequences" (65).

1:28 Furthermore, since they did not think it worthwhile to retain the knowledge of God, he gave them over to a depraved mind, to do what ought not to be done. "Furthermore" translates the simple word καί (*kai*), "and." This verse does not add anything new but just reiterates what has been said thus far in vv. 18-27. It repeats the cause-and-effect principle resulting in God's giving the Gentiles over to unrestrained sin. As vv. 18, 21, 23 and 25 have already stressed, they have dismissed the true God from their worldview. This is portrayed as a deliberate decision to the effect that the whole idea of a transcendent Creator-God is not "worth-

---

and prevention of illnesses directly related to homosexual practices. Writers of these columns include physicians who specialize in the treatment of homosexuals affected by these maladies. Not only are there services available to treat homosexuals thus affected, but there is a national organization representing the interests of these services, the National Coalition of Gay Sexually Transmitted Disease Services, located in Arlington, Virginia" (*Network*, 50). This quote is from the section of Rueda's book headed, "Illness and the Homosexual Subculture" (47-59), which gives much detail about these illnesses.

while," or is worthless. The word is δοκιμάζω (*dokimazō*), which means "to test, to examine, to judge, to approve, to deem worthy, to see fit." This is stated as a negative: they did not approve of the truth about God; they did not think it worthy or fit to hold on to; they weighed the idea of God in the balances and found it wanting. Remember: "They became fools" (v. 22).

God's response to such presumptuous folly is that he gave *them* over "to a depraved mind" in return. The word for "depraved" is ἀδόκιμος (*adokimos*), which means "useless, failing the test, disqualified, worthless" (see 1 Cor 9:27; 2 Cor 13:5-7). This is a play on words and a matter of extreme irony (compare *dokimazō* and *adokimos*). They judged God to be a worthless idea, so God gave them over to their own worthless speculations. The mind that judges God to be worthless is itself worthless.

The last part of the verse, "to do what ought not to be done," again shows that faulty speculations about God directly affect moral theory and behavior. As Cranfield says, "The *adokimos nous* is a mind so debilitated and corrupted as to be a quite untrustworthy guide in moral decisions" (I:128). The fact is that the reality of the transcendent Creator-God is the starting point and the *sine qua non* of all valid ethics. Without him, there is no basis either for absolute ethical obligation or for absolute ethical norms (GC, 163-171). Without God, the only consistent ethic is some version of "might makes right."

"Ought (not) to be done" is from a word group which in the Greek philosophy of Paul's day referred to conduct proper for human beings, or "what is fitting, what is one's duty, what is in harmony with nature" (Dunn, I:66). I.e., this is how human beings act according to their nature as human beings. *Not* to do these things regarded as proper is to contradict one's own humanity. Thus the depraved mind that "banishes God not only loses godliness; he loses manhood too" (Barclay, 26).

1:29-31 They have become filled with every kind of wickedness, evil, greed and depravity. They are full of envy, murder, strife, deceit and malice. They are gossips, slanderers, God-haters, insolent, arrogant and boastful; they invent ways of doing evil; they disobey their parents; they are senseless, faithless, heartless, ruthless. In establishing the utter depravity of the

Gentiles Paul has already given specific attention to the practice of homosexuality. Now in v. 29 he begins a long list of other sins that are characteristic of those who reject God. The list is not meant to be complete, nor is every sinner guilty of all the vices listed. Those listed are not meticulously chosen and organized so as to form the basis for a handbook on ethics. The terms sometimes overlap. They are not meant to offer any new teaching about right and wrong, but are representative of what Dunn calls the "conventional morality" already widely recognized (I:67). In this context the list is meant to make an overall impression regarding the sinfulness and guilt of the Gentile world, as much as it is intended to give us moral instruction. Such a list — a "catalog of vices" — was not uncommon even in the secular literature of the time; and several such lists appear elsewhere in the NT, though none is as extensive as this one. (See references in Dunn, I:67; Hendriksen, I:80.)

Paul's list falls into three main groups in terms of grammatical form, as follows. The first four sins are the objects of the participle translated "They have been filled with" (v. 29). The next five are in a sense objects of the adjective translated "They are full of" (μεστός, *mestos*) in the same verse. (These sins do not occur just once in a while; the Gentile world is *filled* with them. This double reference to "filled" indicates the prevalence and depth of the lawlessness that permeates the world.) The remaining sins are formally parallel; they are all accusative plural forms in grammatical agreement with "them" in v. 28. The final four sins in this part of the list all share the negating alpha. What follows here are brief comments setting forth the essence of each sin.

Wickedness (ἀδικία, *adikia*). The list begins with a very general term that may be like a heading over the rest, as the modifier "every kind of" may suggest. This is the term used twice in v. 18. It is a general term for unrighteousness or transgression of God's law.[21]

---

[21]Users of the KJV will note that "fornication" is not in most modern translations. Evidence suggests that it was not in the original manuscript but was added later. None of the sins listed in vv. 29-31 are sexual sins, because Paul has already mentioned sexual impurity and has dealt specifically with one such sin, homosexuality.

Evil (πονηρία, ponēria). This is another general term, often occurring in contrast with "good." It is used often of Satan and his demons. It describes the inner nature of a person who delights in acting in ways that oppose God and goodness, and who puts his evil desires into practice.

Greed (πλεονεξία, pleonexia). This word is more specific than the first two, but is not as specific as "covetousness," which is often how it is translated. Covetousness is usually directed toward something specific (Exod 20:17), but greed is the insatiable desire to accumulate more and more things in general, without regard for the rights and needs of others. Col 3:5 says that this sin is idolatry, because acquisition of things becomes one's god.

Depravity (κακία, kakia). This is another very general term, difficult to distinguish from wickedness and evil. Barclay says it is "the most general Greek word for badness. . . . It is the degeneracy out of which all sins grow and in which all sins flourish" (27-28).

Envy (φθόνος, phthonos). As covetousness is directed toward a specific object, so envy is directed toward a specific person. It means not just wanting what another person has, but also resenting that person for having it. It is an attitude of ill-will and jealousy that leads to division and strife and even murder. (See the next few sins.)

Murder (φόνος, phonos), killing, the unlawful taking of someone's life. We should remember the NT teaching that hate and groundless anger are also forms of murder (Matt 5:21-22; 1 John 3:15).

Strife (ἔρις, eris), contention, rivalry, wrangling. This refers to someone who has a quarrelsome disposition, someone who is always looking for an argument or a fight.

Deceit (δόλος, dolos), guile, treachery, cunning, hypocrisy. Its absence in Nathaniel was so remarkable that Jesus commented on it (John 1:47), which indicates how difficult it must be to avoid this sin.

Malice (κακοηθεία, kakoētheia). This is another general term, translated variously as malignity, malevolence, spite, meanness, evil-naturedness. Barclay (29) cites Aristotle's specific definition, i.e., "the spirit which always supposes the worst about other people." Cranfield doubts Paul would use it in this special sense, though

(I:130). Hendriksen says it indicates "the desire to harm people" (I:81).

The next ten Greek words are usually taken as referring to eight different sins, the first six words all referring to six separate sins, and the last four words referring to two sins in two-word combinations. Lenski (120-122) follows an interpretation that sees all ten words as forming five two-word combinations, yielding only five sins instead of eight: slanderous whisperers, God-hated insolents, arrogant boasters, inventors of evil, and disobeyers of parents. This suggestion has merit, but most interpreters follow the former approach.

Gossips (ψιθυριστής, *psithuristēs*), literally, "whisperers," or those who whisper gossip into someone's ear behind another's back. They are talebearers, rumormongers, "whisperers-behind-doors" (Phillips) who spread their slanders secretly.

Slanderers (κατάλαλος, *katalalos*), literally, those who speak against others. Phillips translates it "stabbers-in-the-back." This is the same idea as the previous word, except the gossip or slander is open and public, not secret.

God-haters (θεοστυγής, *theostugēs*). This word usually means "hateful to God" and thus does not seem to fit in a list of sins. This is one reason Lenski and others say the sins in this section are all two-word combinations, thus, "God-hated insolents." Most interpreters just assume that Paul gives the word a new twist here, hence, "God-haters." This certainly fits the context as a whole.

Insolent (ὑβριστής, *hybristēs*). The person guilty of this sin is one who has a very high and arrogant opinion of himself, coupled with a very low and contemptuous opinion of others. It is "a lofty sense of superiority out of which the insolent person treats all others as beneath him" (Morris, 97-98). It is the attitude of a bully that leads him to use and abuse others, and run roughshod over the weak.

Arrogant (ὑπερήφανος, *hyperēphanos*), proud, haughty. This is the opposite of humble. It refers to a person who in his own mind sees himself as being far above others and as having no need of God. This is similar to the previous vice, but without the mean spirit toward others.

Boastful (ἀλαζών, *alazōn*). This refers to a person who brags about himself, often going beyond the truth in an effort to impress others. It is someone who vaunts "himself in the possession of skill . . . or knowledge, or courage, or virtue, or riches, or whatever else it might be, which were not truly his" (Trench, *Synonyms*, 99).

They invent ways of doing evil, literally, "inventors of evil." Barclay says, "This phrase describes the man who . . . is not content with the usual, ordinary ways of sinning, but . . . seeks some new thrill in some new sin" (31).

They disobey their parents. In view of biblical teaching, (e.g., Exod 20:12; Eph 6:2) we should not be surprised to see Paul include this in a list of vices. It shows how important family integrity and submission to authority are in God's plan for mankind.

The last four words in the list are rhetorically linked by the negating alpha; all are adjectives used as nouns. They lend themselves to clever translations, e.g., "without brains, honor, love, or pity" (New Jerusalem Bible); "foolish, faithless, heartless, ruthless" (RSV, NRSV).

Senseless (ἀσύνετος, *asunetos*), foolish (see v. 21). This refers not to one who *lacks* intelligence, but to one who refuses to use his God-given mind in a common-sense, God-honoring way. "It refers to those who act stupidly" in reference to God and morality (Morris, 98), or those who cannot "put two and two together in the moral life" (Lenski, 122).

Faithless (ἀσύνθετος, *asunthetos*), unreliable, disloyal, dishonest, untrustworthy, treacherous. This is a person who will not keep his word or meet his obligations, a covenant breaker.

Heartless (ἄστοργος, *astorgos*). This is an unfortunate translation, a much too general term for a specific vice. A person who is *astorgos* is one who lacks *storgē*, which means "natural family affection, love for family members," especially the love that ties parents and children together. When it is absent the results are such things as abortion, infanticide, child abuse, fratricide, and matricide.

Ruthless (ἀνελεήμων, *aneleēmōn*), merciless, pitiless, callous, unfeeling toward others. This is a person who simply does not care when others are in need or are suffering. Morris perceptively remarks, "It is significant that, in an epistle that will stress God's mercy throughout, the list of vices should be rounded off with 'merciless'. This is the very depth of evil" (99).

1:32 This brings us back to the main point of this section, and it carries the description of Gentile depravity to its final depths. First, Paul specifically affirms the fact that the Gentiles have enough knowledge of God's law to be judged and condemned by: **Although they know God's righteous decree that those who do such things deserve death . . . .** The subject of this clause is the relative pronoun οἵτινες (*hoitines*), "the ones who," i.e., "These sinners I have just been naming are the very ones who know these things are contrary to God's law." This is a participial clause and is rightly introduced by "although" in the NIV.

The knowledge Paul attributes to the Gentiles here is twofold. First, they know that such things as he has just mentioned are wrong. Second, they know that those who do such things "deserve death." In other words, they know not only the *commandments* of the moral law, but also its *penalty*. They are indeed without excuse.

The "righteous decree" of God refers specifically to the part about the penalty. God has ordained that those who commit these sins deserve to die. The word is δικαίωμα (*dikaiōma*, from the *dik-* word family, denoting righteousness), which means a decree or ordinance that is righteous and just. It is a righteous decree because those who sin are worthy of death; they deserve it. Also, the Gentiles' knowledge of this decree is not just abstract; they know it as *God's* righteous ordinance.

What kind of death is known to be ordained by this decree? The Gentiles definitely have the conviction that certain crimes are worthy of capital punishment, or physical death. This was a prominent feature of Roman law (see Luke 23:15, 41; Acts 23:29; 25:11, 25; 26:31). Could this be what Paul is referring to? The problem with this is that most of the sins in this vice list are not considered worthy of death in secular law codes. Thus the death of which Paul speaks must be more than judicially-imposed capital punishment.

Another possibility is that this knowledge is an inherent awareness that physical death as such is a righteous divine penalty for such sins, a fact affirmed in the Bible (5:12; 8:10). But Murray is right (I:51) that it must be more than this. This knowledge must also include a similar awareness that there will be a final judgment before the Creator and Law-giver, where all will have to answer for these sins and be justly condemned to *eternal* death for committing them. The concept of such a final judgment and divine retribution is widespread in pagan religions. See Cranfield, I:134.

The question is, whence comes all this knowledge in the Gentile mind? The Gentiles (by definition) have had no access to some specially-revealed form of God's moral law, such as the Law of Moses. Nor can we suppose that Paul is talking about an "unperished tradition" kept intact in every heart in every generation since Adam and Noah (contra Lard, 67). The only revelation Paul is assuming in this section is the general revelation that is available to the consciousness from the phenomena of creation. Can such revelation yield the kind of knowledge of which v. 32 speaks?

No, not by itself. But there is another aspect of general revelation not mentioned in this section but brought out later in 2:14-15. In these verses Paul speaks of the work of the law written in the heart, and of the conscience. From these two internal sources (inherent in every person by virtue of our being created in God's image), combined with the knowledge of the Creator derived from external general revelation, comes the knowledge to which 1:32 refers. The very *sense* of right and wrong, and the conviction that wrong deserves a penalty, "is ineradicably embedded in the human conscience" (Lenski, 124).[22] The *content* of the moral law, i.e., the knowledge that specific acts are wrong, also comes from within. The knowledge that these things are wrong *before God* and will be judged by him comes from the knowledge of the Creator known from his visible creation.

Thus Paul makes his case that the Gentiles are without excuse, and are no exception to the general rule that no one will be accepted by God according to the terms of law. Verse 32 just adds the capstone to his argument. As Thielman says, "The Gentile world deserves the condemnation that God's just requirement pronounces on those who sin: Gentiles are ignorant neither of God's requirements nor of the penalty for transgressing those requirements. The Gentile world, then, is without excuse" (*Paul*, 169).

Paul ends this verse and this section about the Gentiles by adding one more comment on the depth of their depravity: **they**

---

[22]Lenski adds (124), "Man's natural sense of justice is the reflex of this divine ordinance," as illustrated in Acts 28:4.

**not only continue to do these very things but also approve of
those who practice them**. Here Paul indicates that there is something worse than committing the sins named here. Some have said
that Paul means this: that *approving of* and *applauding* such sins is at
least as bad as, if not worse than, actually *doing* them. This is
because the latter may be the result of circumstantial pressures and
spur-of-the-moment passions, while the former comes from a deep-
seated and dispassionate commitment to evil. (See Cranfield, I:133-
135; Moo, 1:116.) The other approach, reflected in most translations and favored here, is that what is worse than just committing
these sins is *both* committing them *and* encouraging others to
commit them as well. (See Hendriksen, I:82; Morris, 100.)

Either way Paul makes it clear that applauding and encouraging
indulgence in sin is a serious aspect of the depravity of the Gentile
world. The word means "to be pleased along with, to consent with,
to give approval to, to applaud." Paul uses this very word to
describe his participation in Stephen's death, though he did not
throw any stones (Acts 22:20; see Acts 8:1). What makes this so evil
is well described by Cranfield: "Those who condone and applaud
the vicious actions of others are actually making a deliberate contri-
bution to the setting up of a public opinion favourable to vice, and
so to the corruption of an indefinite number of other people"
(I:135). The best modern example of this is the plethora of movies,
TV programs, books, musicians, and entertainers in general who
openly and brazenly promote all the forms of ungodliness and
wickedness described here, and more.

CONCLUSION

Another way to present the material in 1:18-32 is this: ONE:
General Revelation from the Creator to the Gentiles (1:18-20; 2:14-
15). TWO: *General Rebellion* by the Gentiles against the Creator
(1:21-32). THREE: *General Rejection* of the Gentiles by the Creator
(1:24, 26, 28).

Though 1:18-32 applies particularly to the Gentiles (or those
who have general revelation only), the fact is that every point made
in this passage applies even more emphatically to those who have

special revelation also. As far as the rejection of God and abandonment to wickedness are concerned, those in the latter group can
reject both the general and the special revelation, and can be given
over to depravity the same as the Gentiles. This has happened to
many individuals in this group, but not to the group as a whole as
in the case of the Gentiles.

Insofar as 1:18-32 is a description of the Gentile world as such,
it is not just a description of the Greco-Roman world as Paul
observed it in his time. It is a Holy Spirit-inspired description of the
condition of the pagan world from the Fall up until now. It has just
as much application today as it had in Paul's day, and the bottom
line is still the same: they are without excuse.

The implications of this are extremely relevant for missions.
Still today, many people try to find some way to excuse the many
pagan idolaters (the "heathen," the unevangelized) remaining in
the world. One view is that they do not know God so they cannot
be held responsible. Paul specifically refutes this view. A second
approach is that pagans *do* know God, and at least some have
honored and served him well enough to be saved.[23] Paul specifically
refutes this false idea also.[24] A third view grants that all pagans are
condemned by the law of general revelation, but says that God will
save them anyway if (and because) they have never had the opportunity to hear about Jesus and the way of grace.

This last view in effect misses the whole point of this passage.
Whether individuals have or have not heard the gospel is not the
issue. Whether they will be saved or lost depends not on what they
have *not* heard, but on what they *have* heard. They will be judged
according to the light they have, not the light they do not have.

---

[23]MacArthur (I:81) presents a variation of this idea: "If a person lives up
to the light of the revelation he has, God will provide for his hearing the
gospel by some means or another." There is absolutely no biblical basis for
such a speculation. In fact, it misses the whole point of 1:18-32, namely, *no
one* lives up to the light of the revelation he has.

[24]"This idea is widely held: salvation by faith in God and a moral life
without Christ and his atonement for sin. Heaven is opened to noble
pagans. But this is not biblical teaching" (Lenski, 100). "Natural revelation
leads not to salvation but to the demonstration that God's condemnation is
just" (Moo, I:101).

Paul's whole point is that they do have the light of God's moral law through general revelation; therefore they are without excuse if they do not keep it. The fact is, they *have not* kept it but have rejected God and have become thoroughly sinful. Thus they are under God's wrath (v. 18), not his grace. As Morris says, "Our condemnation in each case lies in the fact that we have sinned against the light we have, not against the light we have never received" (79).

The missionary imperative could not be made more plain than it is in Romans 1:18-32. We deceive ourselves if we hold out false hope for the unevangelized based on their non-hearing of the gospel. Listen to Moo (I:93):

> *Every person* is "without excuse" because every person — whether a first-century pagan or a twentieth-century materialist — has been given a knowledge of God and has spurned that knowledge in favor of idolatry, in all its varied manifestations. All therefore stand under the awful reality of the wrath of God, and all are in desperate need of the justifying power of the gospel of Christ. We will never come to grips with the importance of the gospel, or be motivated as we should be to proclaim it, until this sad truth has been made part and parcel of our world view.

II. 2:1-3:8 — THE SINFULNESS OF THE JEWS

INTRODUCTION

The overall subject of the first main section of Romans is the impotence of law as a way of salvation. No one can be right with God in terms of the system of law; there is no hope for salvation as long as one remains in a law-relationship with God. This is not inherently the case; a person *can* be right with God through law, as long as he does not break the law at any point. The problem, though, is that *all have sinned*; thus by works of law *no one* will in fact be justified before God (3:20). As a consequence the only possible way for anyone to be saved is through the alternative God has provided: the way of grace, the gift of righteousness made possible through the death of his Son.

Thus the main theme of this section is *law* — not just the Law of Moses, but the Creator's will and commandments in whatever form they have been made available to his creatures. In this subsection of Romans (2:1-3:8), the term "law" does primarily refer to the Law of Moses, but not exclusively so.

We should remember also that the bulk of the material in this section is Paul's response to the notion that there must be some exceptions to the otherwise universal fact that all stand condemned by the law. These exceptions are alleged to be the Gentiles on the one hand, and the Jews on the other.

The problem regarding the Gentiles is, how can they be condemned by the law if indeed they do not have the law? Paul discusses this in 1:18-32 and shows that they do have access to God's law through general revelation, and thus are without excuse. But what is the question with regard to the Jews? That is the subject of 2:1-3:8. The problem is the Jews' own belief that they surely cannot stand condemned by the law, because as a nation they have their own very special relationship with God that will shield them from the divine wrath in the day of judgment.

In this subsection, then, Paul has the objective of showing that this is a false idea, thus "deflating Jewish presumption" (Dunn, I:77). With reference to wrath and condemnation, salvation and eternal life, the Jews are *not* special; within the context of law God treats everyone alike.

1. Who Is Being Addressed in 1:1-16?

Two general questions must be discussed before we get into the text itself. The first has to do with the person or persons who are being addressed and discussed in the first half of chapter 2. All agree that the Jews are the subject of the last part of the chapter (see 2:17), but there is some disagreement about vv. 1-16. Some believe that Paul is addressing a category of people that would probably include most Jews but which also must include the more pious Gentiles, those such as Seneca and Epictetus and Marcus Aurelius, men whose superior moral character would surely separate them from the depraved degenerates of whom 1:18-32 speaks. Thus this section is about "the moralist" (Bruce, 86), or "critical moralizers" (Stott, 80). Boice believes Paul is dealing here "chiefly with the virtuous pagan" (I:235); MacArthur says he is "speaking primarily to Jews" (I:113).

The other major view on this issue, which I support, is that chapter 2 is specifically dealing with the Jews from the very beginning.[25] Murray (I:55) and Cranfield (I:138) give the reasons why this view is preferred. For one thing, the attitudes condemned in 1:1-16 (hypocritical judgmentalism toward the Gentiles; belief in divine partiality) were "peculiarly characteristic of the Jew," as Murray puts it. Also, the Jews were uniquely the objects of God's "kindness, tolerance and patience" (v. 4). Most significantly, throughout this section Paul refers consistently to only two categories of people as constituting the whole of mankind: Jews and Greeks (i.e., Gentiles).[26] It is true that Jews are not addressed by name until v. 17, but this is a matter of tactics on Paul's part. By not explicitly naming the Jews as his target in the first several verses, he can possibly avoid putting them on the defensive and perhaps secure their agreement before they realize he is talking about them.

In the section on the Gentiles (1:18-32), we saw that the most significant distinction between Gentiles and Jews in this context is that the former are those who have been exposed to general revelation only, while the latter have knowledge of special revelation also.[27] With regard to applicability to the present time, the Gentiles are equivalent to anyone today who has no knowledge of biblical revelation, and the Jews are equivalent to anyone who does have such knowledge.

It is important to keep this in mind as we go through this subsection, so that we will not miss its timeliness and relevance for the church in the Christian era. What is said in this passage applies to all who have access to special revelation, whether it be the OT or the NT or both. It applies to anyone who expects divine partiality or any kind of special privilege because of his external relationship

---

[25]Those who hold this view include Lard (71), DeWelt (34-35), Moo (I:89, 125), Morris (107), Murray (I:55), and Cranfield (I:138-139).

[26]See 1:16; 2:9-10; 3:9. See also 3:29; 9:24; 10:12; 15:8-12.

[27]We understand that some Gentiles (e.g., Cornelius), through their association with Jews, became aware of this special revelation also; but this is the exception and not the rule.

to this revelation. This is true especially of those within the general context of Christendom who consider their knowledge of the Bible, their knowledge about Jesus Christ, their membership in a local church, their baptism, or their Christian heritage in general to be their sure ticket to heaven.

Exactly what is Paul's main point here regarding the Jews? It is well known, of course, that God had chosen the Jews from among all the peoples of the earth and had placed them in a special covenant relationship with himself ever since the time of Abraham. This special relationship is a major theme of the entire OT; it is not a matter of dispute. The problem is that the Jews had drawn some false and fatal conclusions from these facts. They developed the idea that somehow they, the Jews, would be in a special category and would receive special treatment on Judgment Day. From their covenant privileges they concluded that they would not be judged by the same criteria as the Gentiles. Thus they "counted on God's partiality" (Lard, 74). They relied on their national status as God's chosen people (symbolized by the Law and by circumcision) to save them on the day of judgment. Dunn calls this "Jewish overconfidence in God's favor for and obligation to Israel," and an "assurance of a favored status based on and protected by God's election" (I:90).

Rabbinic writings reflect this attitude. These include quotes such as the following: "Circumcised men do not descend into Gehenna." "At the last Abraham will sit at the entrance to Gehenna and will not let any circumcised man of Israel go down there." "Circumcision will deliver Israel from Gehenna."[28] "All Israelites have a share in the world to come."[29] As Lard sums it up, the Jew of Paul's time "seems to have thought that the mere circumstance of being a Jew protected him against condemnation" (72).

Paul's main point regarding the Jews, then, is to show that they will *not* be treated in any special way in the final judgment. They will have no special privileges, no advantages, just from the fact that they are Jews. God will show them no partiality. As Lard says, "The aim of the Apostle is to extirpate from the mind of the Jew all

---

[28]Cited (with bibliographical data) in Cranfield, I:172, note 1.
[29]Cited in Sanders, *Paul*, 147.

thought of security based on the naked ground of being a Jew" (78). "Like John the Baptist (Matt. 3:7-10) and Jesus (cf. Matt. 21:28-32) before him, Paul denies that belonging to the covenant people per se ensures acceptance with God" (Moo, I:125; see I:89).

The reason this is so is that *the Jews are sinners, too,* no less than the Gentiles; and under God's law all sinners are treated alike. That is, under the law system every Gentile who has sinned and every Jew who has sinned will be condemned to hell. And since all Jews are sinners, the law condemns them all. The bottom line, then, is that Jews no less than Gentiles stand in need of the gospel of grace; they need the righteousness that comes through faith in Jesus Christ. They are not an exception.

2. Does Romans 2 Teach Justification by Works?

The second general question with which we must deal before turning to the text has to do with the very nature of salvation. The issue in brief is whether or not Romans 2 teaches that a sinner can be justified by his own works. Unfortunately many interpreters have wrongly drawn this conclusion from certain statements in the text, and this conclusion has the effect of derailing the proper understanding of Romans and of the concept of grace from the very beginning. Thus it is extremely important to grasp the overall perspective from which Paul is speaking in this chapter. (The commentaries I especially recommend on this point are Lard and Moo.)

The problem arises when we attempt to interpret vv. 6-10, 13, and 26. Verse 6 says God will repay every man according to his works. Verses 7 and 10 say God will give eternal life to those who persist in doing good. Verse 13 says that the doers of the law will be justified. Verse 26 suggests that Gentiles who keep the law will be saved. Do these passages somehow teach salvation or justification by works? It certainly seems that way. Citing v. 13 especially, Boers declares that "all of chapter 2 stands out as an admirable apology for justification through works" (*Justification,* 8).

The reason this is such a problem is that this seems to contradict the whole point of Romans and the whole concept of grace, namely, that we are justified by faith apart from works of law (3:28). In fact, it apparently contradicts the very point Paul wants to make in this first main section itself, namely, that by works of law no human being will be justified in God's sight (3:20). Someone with a low view of Scripture might feel comfortable affirming that Paul simply contradicts himself, but even apart from inspiration it is inconceivable that a man of Paul's obvious intelligence would have failed to recognize an outright inconsistency within a single section of an essay that is so tightly reasoned. Thus there must be another explanation.

Some take the view that in Romans 2 Paul is simply teaching the reality of justification by a conscientious response to God's law. Through hard work and serious effort, even without perfect obedience, anyone can achieve eternal life. This seems to be Boers' point. He says 2:13 "refers to the due reward for doing good in obedience to the Law" (*Justification*, 105). He says that in Rom 2 Paul "argued for a positive meaning of the Law, and justification for works done in obedience to it" (107).

Thinking specifically of vv. 7-10 DeWelt says, "There is no indication here that sinless perfection is the requirement for receiving eternal life, but rather a constant, unwavering and honest effort to attain 'glory and honor and incorruption' by doing that which they *know* is right—right according to God's law" (36-37). This applies even to Gentiles: "The Gentile will be judged according to his conscientiousness in keeping the law of nature and the Jew according to his conscientiousness in keeping the law of Moses." This implies "a certain element of mercy extended to those who never heard the gospel" (40). Commenting on 2:13 Godet says we must distinguish between our initial justification, based on the imputed gift of God's own righteousness (1:17) when we first become Christians; and our final justification on Judgment Day, based on our "*actual* possession of righteousness" through the fulfillment of the law. Thus there are "two justifications, the one initial, founded exclusively on faith, the other final, founded on faith *and its fruits*," i.e., the doing of the law (122).

In my opinion this view is false, not only because it misses Paul's point in Rom 2 but also because it is inconsistent with the overall biblical teaching on faith and works as they relate to justification.

As expressed by Godet, especially, it sounds very much like
Galatianism, or the false view of the Galatian Christians as they
were being influenced by the Judaizers (Gal 3:3; 5:4).

A second interpretation of Romans 2 has been adopted by quite
a few Evangelical interpreters. Basically this view says that in these
passages Paul is speaking of the experience of Christians who are
under the grace of God. As Christians we are indeed justified by
faith and not by works of law, but on the day of judgment our
works (our obedience to God's law) will be on display as evidence
of the faith that secures our salvation. Speaking of vv. 7 and 10,
Cranfield says the "good work" to which God gives eternal life is
probably Christians' "conduct as the expression of their faith"
(I:151-152). Verse 13, he says, refers to "that beginning of grateful
obedience to be found in those who believe in Christ, which
though very weak and faltering and in no way deserving God's
favour, is, as the expression of humble trust in God, well-pleasing in
His sight" (I:155).

In my opinion this is not the correct way to interpret Rom 2,
and doing so imports unnecessary confusion into our thinking. It is
true that in some sense every person, including Christians, will be
judged by works in the final judgment. This is a biblical teaching,
one that is thoroughly grounded in both the OT and the NT. Also,
it is true that our works will be cited in the judgment as evidence of
the presence (or absence) of saving faith. But this simply does not
seem to be the point that Paul is making here. He is not speaking
of Christian good works nor of the Christian life as such. He is not
speaking of the principles of judgment and salvation as they exist
under grace; his perspective is very different, as the following point
explains.

The final and, I believe, correct interpretation of Rom 2 in relation to the nature of salvation is as follows. In the texts in question
(vv. 6-10, 13, 26) Paul is not talking about the judgment of
Christians under grace, but about the conditions that prevail within
the sphere or system of *law*, or about how a person is judged for
either justification or condemnation under the provisions of God's
law. As already explained, the subject of this whole section is law,
and especially its inability to save sinners.

As we also saw earlier, the principles of law are this: "Keep the

commandments, and therefore escape the penalty; break the commandments, and therefore suffer the penalty." Within the context
of law, anyone who does not keep its commandments will be condemned. Likewise, anyone who perseveres in good works, who is a
doer of the law, who keeps its commandments, *will be justified*. This
is a statement of fact. Any Jew or Gentile who completely obeys the
law available to him will be justified.

But as a matter of fact — and this is Paul's whole point in this
section — there is no one at all in this category; everyone has
sinned. As a formal principle it is true that the doers of the law will
be justified. But in view of the universality of sin, it is only theoretically or hypothetically true. Not one single Jew and not one single
Gentile will in fact be accepted by God in the final judgment
because of his good works or his obedience to law. Thus vv. 7, 10,
13, 26 should not be taken as referring to any actual state of affairs.

The actual state of things is given in 3:20, that by works of law
no one will be justified, since the law judges everyone to be a
sinner. Speaking of v. 13, Lard sums it up very well: "By doers of
law we must not understand persons who keep its requirements in
part, and in part fail. We must understand perfect obedience, or
obedience to every precept without even one failure. But since
there is no such obedience, there is of course no justification based
on it. The justification of the clause, therefore, is merely potential,
not actual" (86; see also 97).

Moo explains these verses basically the same way I have explained
them here. Paul "upholds faithful obedience to God, or the law, as
a *theoretical* means of attaining justification," he says, "but he goes
on to show that no one meets the conditions necessary for this
principle to become a reality" (I:141; see I:167). This paragraph by
Moo (I:141) is especially on target:

We think, therefore, that vv. 7 and 10 set forth what is called
in traditional theological (especially Lutheran) language "the
law." Paul sets forth the biblical conditions for attaining
eternal life apart from Christ. Understood this way, Paul is
not speaking hypothetically. But once his doctrine of universal human powerlessness under sin has been developed (cf.
3:9 especially), it becomes clear that the promise can, in fact,
never become operative, because the condition for its fulfill-

ment — consistent, earnest seeking after good — can never be realized.

(See also Thielman, *Paul*, 141, 291-292; Erdman, 40.)

It is important to remember that, *under law*, there is no way to be saved other than perfect obedience. This is contrary to the Jews' false confidence in their special status within God's great historical plan of salvation. They confused their election for *service* with election for *salvation*. They did not understand that their personal sins negated the value of law as a way of salvation. They could claim salvation by law only if they obeyed it perfectly, which they did not: "Jews and Gentiles alike are all under sin" (3:9).

A corollary of this is that once actual sin enters the picture, whether in the life of an individual or in the history of mankind, the only way to be accepted by God is through his plan of grace, i.e., through trusting God's promise to forgive our sins based upon his righteousness and not our own. Anyone who is ever saved — Jew or Gentile, in OT times or NT times, under the Law of Moses or in the Christian Church — will be saved in this manner, because the only alternatives are nonexistent perfect obedience (law) and the gospel reality of righteousness through faith (grace). See Moo, I:177.

3. The Outline of This Section

In this subsection Paul's thought flows as follows.

2:1-5. First, the Jews are under the wrath of God, no less than the Gentiles. Thus they have no basis for passing judgment on the Gentiles and gloating over their fate.

2:6-11. Second, God will be partial to no one in the judgment. He will treat all alike, whether Jews or Gentiles. The principles of judgment as required by law will be applied to both in exactly the same way.

2:12-16. Third, under law, the criterion of judgment is obedience alone, not whether or how one possesses the law or knows the law. It is especially important for the Jews to know that mere possession of the law is no indication of special treatment in the judgment.

2:17-24. Fourth, Jews who look to the law for salvation are in fact condemned by their disobedience to that law. They have broken the very law they glory in and rely upon.

2:25-29. Fifth, true Jewishness is identified not by circumcision but by the inward state of the heart. Thus the Jews' reliance upon physical circumcision as the sure measure of salvation is futile.

3:1-8. Finally, such equal treatment of Jews and Gentiles does not nullify but rather magnifies God's righteousness. Those who rail at God because of this equal treatment before the law have misunderstood God's purpose for Israel and deserve to be condemned for their blasphemy.

4. The Style of Writing

A final word here has to do with Paul's writing style in certain parts of this subsection, a style known as *diatribe*. This was a common method of teaching used by writers and instructors in Paul's time. To write in this style the author engages in a dialogue with an imaginary opponent or questioner, and the writing is addressed directly to this questioner (second person instead of third person).

Sometimes the "dialogue" is one-sided, and the questions flow only from the pen of the writer. This is the case in 2:1-5 and 2:17-27, where Paul bombards the Jews with questions specifically designed to undermine their false confidence wrongly based on their special role in God's plan. At other times there is a true dialogue, as in 3:1-8. Here the questions come from the imagined Jewish partner, and Paul provides his emphatic answers.

This diatribe style surfaces in a few other places, but it is especially prominent here.

A. JEWS ARE UNDER THE WRATH OF GOD, NO LESS THAN THE GENTILES (2:1-5)

2:1 You, therefore, have no excuse, you who pass judgment on someone else . . . . Using the second person ("you") of the diatribe

style, Paul specifically addresses the Jews in the person of an anonymous representative, "O man" (not translated in the NIV). One can
imagine this typical Jew, standing slightly behind and to one side of
Paul, looking over the Apostle's shoulder as the latter continues to
heap the blazing coals of God's wrath upon the heads of the Gentiles
in 1:18-32. Under his breath he excitedly roots Paul on against these
Gentile scum: "Go get 'em, Paul! Lay it on 'em! That's right! Amen!"

Then abruptly Paul stops speaking of the Gentiles, slowly turns
toward his fellow Israelite, gets right up in his face, and says, in
effect, "You like that, don't you? 'Get those Gentiles,' right? They
really are wicked, aren't they? They deserve the wrath of God, don't
they? Well, my brother, have I got news for you! You are no better
than the Gentiles! When you point your finger at them, you have
three fingers pointing back at yourself. As Nathan said to David,
'You are the man!'" (2 Sam 12:7).[30]

The word "therefore" is a bit difficult here, since it is not clear
how the previous context in itself logically produces this (2:1) as a
conclusion. When Paul begins thus, he must be *assuming* not only
the content of 1:18-32, but also the attitude of judgment in the
hearts of the Jews whom he is addressing. "Therefore – on the
assumption that you agree with what I'm saying about the Gentiles,
and on the assumption that in your hearts you are singing the 'Hell-
to-you-all Chorus' – then you yourselves have no excuse, because
you are guilty of the same things."

The word translated "no excuse" is the same one applied to the
Gentiles in 1:20. As there, it means "without excuse, without
defense" in the face of accusation. Since both Jews and Greeks are
without excuse before the law, every mouth is thus silenced, and
the whole world stands guilty before God (3:19).

In the words "you who pass judgment," the NIV smooths out an
awkward Greek phrase that reads more literally, "O man – you
judging man – every single one of you." The word for "pass judgment" (κρίνω, *krinō*) can refer to the act of judging as such, but it

---

[30]Compare Amos' tactic in his scorching condemnation of Israel. First he
attracts the Israelites as a cheering section as he reels off a series of divine
judgments against Israel's enemies: Damascus, Gaza, Tyre, Edom, Ammon,
Moab, and even Judah (1:3-2:5). After thus getting their enthusiastic attention, Amos aims the cannon of God's wrath directly at Israel itself (2:6ff).

often has the stronger negative meaning of "condemn." The context shows the latter is intended here; it is no different in meaning from the intensified word (κατακρίνω, *katakrinō*) translated "condemning" that follows: **for at whatever point you judge the other, you are condemning yourself . . . .** "The other" refers to the Gentiles.

How can it be said that the "judging man" condemns himself? **. . . because you who pass judgment do the same things**. This assumes the principle, "Like sins deserve like condemnation" (Lard, 72), something the Jews seem to have forgotten. To say the Jews do "the same things" as the Gentiles does not mean that all Jews committed all the sins named in 1:18-32. By Paul's day idolatry was quite uncommon among the Jews, and homosexuality was always an abomination. Some think Paul is referring mostly to the fairly general and hard-to-avoid sins named in 1:29-31. In any case, the Jews are clearly guilty of the very sorts of things for which they condemned the Gentiles; thus they condemn themselves.

The problem is not just that the Jews were passing judgment as such, but they were doing so *hypocritically*. Even if there is some sense in which condemning someone else is legitimate (e.g., such as condemning his "fruit" [Matt 7:16], or deeds, in the light of the Word of God), it is never right to do so when we are guilty of the very same sins. See Matt 7:1-5.

2:2 Now we know that God's judgment against those who do such things is based on truth. Here Paul sets forth a general principle acceptable to both himself and the judging Jew: "we know," you and I, about the judging business, that the only judge whose judgment really counts is *God*, because his judgment is based on truth.

The word for "judgment" is κρίμα (*krima*), which refers not to the act of judging as such but to the verdict of a judge in the context of a court of law. More specifically, it connotes a negative judgment, a sentence of condemnation. God is a judge who will not hesitate to condemn those who practice "such things," i.e., the kind of sins named in chapter 1.

The point is that it does not matter who is committing these sins. God is an equal opportunity judge. His judgment is not based on race, sex, education, marriage status, or any other such incidental. It is "based on truth" or objective facts, not on subjective feelings, personal preferences, or favoritism.

Judgment involves three things: deeds to be judged, a standard by which to judge them, and a judge. Judgment *based on truth* involves a full, complete, objective knowledge of the relevant deeds; an objective, achievable standard known by or knowable to all; and a completely informed, totally fair judge. The final judgment includes all of these. (1) The judge will be God, specifically God the Son, Jesus Christ (2:16). He can and will judge according to truth because he knows all things, including the very thoughts of our hearts (2:16), and because he is righteous and thus meticulously fair (2:5). (2) The standard by which he will judge is his own law, which is known to all through either general or special revelation (2:12-15). (3) The deeds to be judged are our own, as exhaustively observed and infallibly remembered by the omniscient God, who will compare them objectively with the righteous standard and then reward us accordingly (2:6).

This point was intended especially to awaken the Jews to the reality of their situation. They literally expected God on Judgment Day to suspend this "judgment based on truth" and to usher them into heaven simply because they were Jews. So Paul wanted them to know that "in judgment it is not nationality or privilege that matters, but deeds" (Morris, 111).

Ideally it should be a comfort to anyone to know that on the Judgment Day we are going to receive a "fair trial." The ultimate stated goal of human judicial systems is a fair, objective trial based on the facts. The only problem with this, though, is that those who are *guilty* do not really want a verdict "based on truth." They know they are without excuse, thus they always seek to invoke some sort of special status or special circumstances that will allow them to escape their just judgment.

In God's judicial system, though, *as long as we are going by the rules of law*, there is no special status; there are no exceptions. Every deed is compared with the objective law by the righteous judge. Those who have broken the law at any point are condemned, be they Gentiles or Jews, those under general revelation only or those under special revelation also, church members or non-members.

The whole point of the gospel, of course, is that God himself has provided another, totally different system of judgment, one that is based not on the truth of the *law* but rather on the truth of *grace*. God has provided his own "exception" to judgment and condemnation according to law. One receives this exception-status not through Gentileness or Jewishness as such, but only through repentant faith in God's promise of forgiveness.

2:3 In v. 1 Paul affirmed that the judging Jew condemns himself; now in v. 3 he can repeat this point with emphasis, based on the principle enunciated in v. 2. The NIV changes the word order a bit. The verse actually begins as the NASB puts it, "And do you suppose this, O man." But the NIV begins it thus: **So when you, a mere man, pass judgment on them and yet do the same things . . . .** The NIV translates the vocative, "O man," as "a mere man," as if Paul's purpose were to compare the judging Jew's fallible humanity with God's omniscience and infallibility. This is probably not the point, though. The same vocative expression is used in 2:1; it is part of the diatribe style of writing.[31]

"Pass judgment" is again *krinō*, as in v. 1, and means "condemn." The verse literally says, "When you condemn the ones who practice such things and (then) do the same things (yourself)."[32] The repetition of these thoughts, already set forth in v. 1, is meant to help the Jews honestly see the naked truth about themselves: you *are* condemning the Gentiles, and you *are* doing the same things for which you condemn them.

The punch line is this: you who are doing these things, **do you think you will escape God's judgment?** "Do you think" is λογίζομαι (*logizomai*), actually the first word in the verse. It means "to suppose, to reckon, to consider, to conclude, to draw a conclusion based on a careful consideration of the facts." Actually, the Jews had drawn a conclusion that was *not* based on truth or facts, for this is exactly what they thought: that they were going to escape God's wrath and condemnation (*krima*). Ignoring their sins, they trusted in their special status as God's chosen people to deliver them from wrath on the day of judgment.

---

[31]Moo, with all due feminist sensitivity, translates it as "O person" (I:126, 131).

[32]There is little difference between the words "practice" (*prassō*) and "do" (*poieō*). Dunn says the former has a general sense, while the latter denotes a more deliberate act (I:81).

Thus by asking this question Paul challenges them to *rethink* their status before God. He challenges them to rethink this presumptuous conclusion that they will escape God's judgment, that God will be partial to them just because they are Jews. The wording is emphatic: "Do you think that *you* — you of all people, you who commit these same damning sins — will escape God's wrath?" Yes, they did think it; but no, it would not happen.

2:4. One might think that the Jews through their presumptuousness were showing contempt only for God's wrath and judgment. But Paul says it is much worse than this: **Or do you show contempt for the riches of his kindness, tolerance and patience . . . ?** They not only refused to take God's sternness and severity seriously; they also took for granted his kindness (11:22).

The attitude they were displaying toward God is described as "showing contempt" (καταφρονέω, *kataphroneō*). This word can have the strong meaning of the NIV, "to show contempt, despise, disdain"; or it can have a slightly weaker meaning (as in the NASB), "to think lightly of, to take for granted." Either way such an attitude is obviously unworthy to be shown toward God and is worthy of his wrath.

Exactly what were the Jews taking for granted? The "kindness" or goodness of God, represented here by two related words, χρηστοτής (*chrēstotēs*) (11:22) and χρηστός (*chrēstos*). This kindness of God is expressed especially in his "tolerance" (ἀνοχή, *anochē*) and "patience" (μακροθυμία, *makrothumia*), concepts not significantly different in this context.[33] The essence of God's patience is delay and restraint in the execution of his wrath, the holding back of his righteous judgment. OT history is full of examples of divine kindness and patience toward Israel as a nation. Thus they were thinking lightly not just of one or two isolated cases, but of the "riches," the wealth of God's kindness.

Israel seems thus to have missed the point of God's efforts: **not realizing that God's kindness leads you toward repentance[.]** The purpose of such patience, of course, "is not to excuse sin but to stimulate repentance" (Moo, I:133). See 2 Pet 3:9. The Jews, however, continued to misinterpret it as God's indifference toward

---

[33]See GRe, 357-361, for a fuller discussion of God's patience.

their sin. What was in fact intended to lead them to repentance was taken as proof that they would not be punished for their sin.

"Repentance" (μετάνοια, *metanoia*) is a change of mind toward God and especially toward one's own sin. It is the sinner's admission of the awfulness of his rebellion against God and of the heinousness of his sin. Repentance comes when one opens his eyes to the seriousness of sin in general, and begins to despise his own sin in particular. God's patience is designed to lead to this, and thus confronts the sinner with a choice: either despise your sin, or despise God's patience. Israel chose the latter.

Verse 4 implies and v. 5 declares the unrepentant state of the Jews' hearts. This refusal to repent can be explained in only two ways. Either they believed they did not *need* to repent (because they believed God would show them partiality); or they were guilty of just plain rejecting God, like the Gentiles. The former is certainly true, but there is also an element of truth in the latter. Paul says they were "not realizing" that God's kindness was trying to lead them to repent. The word used here can mean "not knowing" in the sense of ignorance, but it can also mean "not acknowledging," or refusing to acknowledge, and thus a "wilful refusal to recognize," a "thoroughly blameworthy not-knowing" (Cranfield, I:144).

Thus the Jews were guilty of *suppressing* true knowledge of God, just as the Gentiles were (1:18). But whereas the Gentiles were suppressing only general revelation, the Jews were suppressing God's special revelation. Also, whereas the Gentiles were suppressing only a knowledge of God as Creator and the Creator's law, the Jews were suppressing the overtures of his specially-revealed forgiving grace (Isa 65:1-2). This is why God said his wrath would be poured out on the Jew first (2:9).

2:5 This verse is directly related to v. 4; the paragraph break should come after v. 5 and not before it as in the NIV. The only issue is whether v. 5 is a continuation of the question in v. 4 (so Phillips; see Lard, 76), or whether it is a statement following up on v. 4 (as in the NIV and elsewhere). Either way the point is the same: "Your sinful heart is hardened, and you will experience God's wrath." **But because of your stubbornness and your unrepentant heart, you are storing up wrath against yourself . . . .**

The Jews' sinfulness is described as "stubbornness," an attitude within Israel that had tried God's patience from the beginning (Exod 33:3, 5; 34:9; Deut 9:13, 27; Ezek 3:7). Such a condition may not be as openly odious as some of the sins attributed to the Gentiles in chapter 1, but in God's sight it is no less abominable. "Stubbornness," or hardness, refers to an unyielding will that refuses to respond to God's offers of kindness and grace. Related compound words mean "hardness of heart" (Matt 19:8; Mark 16:14) and "stiff-necked" (Acts 7:51). Such hardness suppresses all feelings of guilt and sorrow for sin, and results in an "unrepentant heart."

As a direct result of ("because of") this sinfulness of heart, the Jews are described as "storing up wrath against yourself." The word for "storing up" is θησαυρίζω (thēsaurizō), which means "to treasure, to heap up, to lay up treasure." Since we usually associate treasure and laying up treasure with something very valuable and desirable (see Matt 6:19-20), it is a note of tragic irony that some choose to lay up the "treasure" of God's wrath. Perhaps by using this word Paul intends to highlight the foolishness of repudiating the *riches* of God's kindness (v. 4) and opting instead for the *treasure* of his wrath.

Paul says this "treasure" is being stored up **for the day of God's wrath, when his righteous judgment will be revealed.** "The day of God's wrath" is the general eschatological day of judgment, not the intermediate judgment of A.D. 70, when Jerusalem and the temple were destroyed. This is seen in the fact that in this context the "day of wrath" involves the Gentiles as well as the Jews (vv. 8-9, 12, 16). Rev 6:17 describes it as "the great day of their wrath."

This "day of wrath" is also called a "day of revelation" (ἀπο–κάλυψις, apokalypsis). This word is often associated with the end times and Christ's second coming (8:19; 1 Cor 1:7; 2 Thess 1:7; 1 Pet 1:7, 13; 4:13). Many things will be revealed or totally uncovered on that day, but here Paul specifies that the thing to be revealed is God's "righteous judgment." This is a judgment that will be entirely fair and just, one that is "based on truth" (v. 2).

In this paragraph Paul has not pulled any punches; he has said some very harsh things about his countrymen, the Jews. He is not motivated by unkindness, however (see 9:1-3; 10:1), and he is not gloating. Rather, as Lard (73) says, his desire and purpose for his fellow Jew are to "cut him loose from Abraham, from circumcision, from the law, and send him in despair to Christ."

B. GOD WILL BE PARTIAL TO NO ONE
IN THE JUDGMENT (2:6-11)

The transition from v. 5 to v. 6, from the first paragraph to the second paragraph of this section, seems to be this. In the first paragraph Paul declares that the Jews are under the wrath of God no less than the Gentiles. Now he is assuming that the Jews will respond to that point something like this: "Now wait a minute! How can we be under the same judgment as the Gentiles? You say we have sinned like the Gentiles. But even if that is so, remember: we are *Jews*. We are in a special category. God will not treat us as he treats others in the final judgment." In this paragraph Paul responds thus: "Yes, you *will* be treated just like all others. No, you will *not* be given a special dispensation on Judgment Day, and here's why!"

In this paragraph Paul directly addresses the root of Jewish arrogance, i.e., their assumption that they would be shown partiality on the last day. As mentioned in the introduction to this section, they confused their election to *service* with election to *salvation*. With regard to the former, God did show partiality toward Israel as a nation when he chose them, through Abraham, Isaac, and Jacob, to prepare the way for the coming of the Messiah. As means to this end God did bestow upon Israel as a nation many special blessings, including access to his special revelation (3:2), which included the knowledge of his grace.

Beginning with these facts the Jews then made an unwarranted step to a false conclusion, namely, that God would be partial to each individual Jew with regard to personal salvation. Paul attacks this false reasoning. Israel's election for service, with its attendant temporal blessings (3:2; 9:4-5), will have no direct effect on how God will treat individual Jews on the Judgment Day. On that day they will be treated in the same way as the Gentiles, with no exceptions, no concessions, no partiality. The same principles of judgment will be applied equally to all. The very nature of God demands it. God is righteous and fair, and it is contrary to his nature to show partiality. Thus God will be partial to no one in the judgment.

It is especially important to remember that in this section the main point is how individuals will be judged *under law*, not under grace. Thus — *this is very important* — we must not read this paragraph as including those who have put their trust in God's mercy or in the blood of Christ. What Paul says here applies only to those who are trusting the law (i.e., their obedience to law) to save them. His point is that in the final judgment, all those who are living within the sphere of law will be treated in the same way. For the purpose of deciding between salvation and condemnation, the rules of law will be applied in the very same way to both Gentiles and Jews.

2:6 God "will give to each person according to what he has done." This is a principle of judgment that God has always followed in handing out earthly blessings and punishments, and it will also be applied in the final judgment.[34] It even applies in a qualified way to believers who are saved solely by grace through faith in the atoning work of Christ. For them, judgment according to works will provide evidence of the presence of their faith and thus will demonstrate God's impartiality even within the sphere of grace. Also, judgment according to works will determine the degree of rewards given to individual believers.

But under the system of law this principle applies in an unqualified way. Regarding the verdict for salvation or condemnation, this is the only thing to be considered. The righteous judge will compare each person's works with the law-standard available to him. Any deviation from the standard will result in condemnation. There is nothing else to be taken into account. There will be no balance-scale judgment to see if one's good works outweigh his sins (Jas 2:10). There will be no appeal to alleviating circumstances, nor casting of oneself upon the "mercy of the court." There will be no speculation about what a person would or might have done if only he could have heard the gospel. There will be no appeal to the

---

[34]See the following passages: 2 Chr 6:30; Job 34:11; Ps 62:12; Prov 24:12; Eccl 12:14; Isa 3:10-11; 59:18; Jer 17:10; 32:19; Ezek 33:20; Hos 12:2; Matt 7:21; 12:36-37; 16:27; 25:31-46; John 5:28-29; Acts 10:34-35; Rom 14:12; 1 Cor 3:13; 2 Cor 5:10; 11:15; Gal 6:7-9; Eph 6:8; Col 3:24-25; 2 Tim 4:14; 1 Pet 1:17; Rev 2:23; 20:12-13; 22:12.

blood of Christ; that is available only under the system of grace. Here the only consideration is *law*.

For some questionable reason the NIV has decided not to translate the word ἔργον (*ergon*; pl., *erga*) as "work" or "works" here or anywhere else in Romans 1-3 (see 2:7, 15; 3:20, 27-28). "According to what he has done" should read "according to his works." "Works" are whatever a person does in response to God's law, whether in obedience or in disobedience. Acts of righteousness are works; acts of unrighteousness (sins) are works. "Works" also includes outward deeds as well as inward attitudes, desires, and decisions (which only God can see, 2:16).

As Paul uses the terms, one thing that "works" does not include is *faith* (3:27-28; 4:5; 11:6; Gal 2:16; Eph 2:8-9). Thus it is a mistake to try to interpret "works" in 2:6 as including Christian faith and the works that grow out of faith, and thus to think that in vv. 7 and 10 Paul is referring to Christians. In this section Paul is not talking about Christians, or even about OT believers. This is contrary to the view of many, including Cranfield (I:151-152). Paul's point in 2:6 is that on Judgment Day, when God renders his verdict upon an individual according to the rules of law, the only thing he will take into account is that person's works.

The word "give" is too weak as a translation for the verb in this verse, which is ἀποδίδωμι, (*apodidōmi*). "Render" is also ambiguous. The word means "to pay; to repay; to give someone his due; to give someone what he deserves, whether a reward or a punishment." Thus it is an appropriate word to use for the principle of strict retribution. Under law God will give to each person whatever his works have earned.

When this principle is applied according to the terms of law, theoretically there are two outcomes: for those who have not broken the law, eternal life; for those who have broken it, eternal punishment. As we saw in the introduction to this section, there is in reality no one in the first category, which is Paul's main point (3:20). Everyone in fact falls into the second category, that of lawbreakers. Now, some object to such a "theoretical" or "hypothetical" understanding of this verse and of other verses in Romans 2, on the basis that Paul does not use hypothetical or conditional language in 2:6. He uses the simple, straightforward future indicative:

God *will repay* each one according to his works. "The plain future indicative," says Cranfield, "is no encouragement to take these verses as merely hypothetical" (I:146). As Morris says, "Paul says God 'will render', not 'would render'. His words point to a fact, not a hypothesis" (148).

This objection misses the point. The *principle* is not hypothetical. This *is* how God will actually render judgment, namely, according to works. Paul is not saying, "*If* God judges according to works," but that he *will* so judge. The only thing that is hypothetical is the outcome, i.e., whether anyone will be in the specific categories. This does not affect the certainty and the actuality of the judgment according to the principle, as stated in the plain, simple future indicative.

The future tense does refer to the final judgment, not to any temporal or intermediate ones. The emphasis on "each person" pointedly includes both Gentiles and Jews. Wherever law is the applicable system of judgment, it will be applied to all who are under law, with no special deals for anyone.

2:7 The next four verses are a concise statement of the law system, or the principles by which God judges those who are under law rather than under grace. I have summarized these principles thus: "Keep the commandments, and therefore escape the penalty; break the commandments, and therefore suffer the penalty." Here they are stated in slightly more detail. In fact, they are stated twice, first in vv. 7-8, and then in vv. 9-10 with the main points being reversed (in an a-b-b-a, or chiastic, arrangement).

The purpose in these verses is to explain exactly *how* God will repay each person according to his works (v. 6), as dictated by the rules of law. **To those who by persistence in doing good seek glory, honor and immortality, he will give eternal life.** This is equivalent to "Keep the commandments, and therefore escape the penalty" in my summary above. "Persistence in doing good" is literally "persistence in good work." "Work" is singular; the expression means "good conduct, good behavior, commandment keeping." This refers not just to an "honest effort" to do good, but to actual sinless perfection (contra DeWelt, 36). This includes right inner attitudes as well as right external acts. It is the equivalent of "doing good" in v. 10.

Under law, such good work is the means of seeking "glory, honor and immortality." These are the rewards of heaven. "Glory" refers to living in the light and reflection of God's own glory, as the result of dwelling in the very personal presence of God (Rev 21:3; 22:4-5). "Honor" refers to God's own blessing and commendation for faithfulness, similar to Jesus' words, "Well done, good and faithful servant!" (Matt 25:21). "Immortality" is the state of incorruption, in which our bodies and spirits will never again be ravaged and destroyed by sin, disease, and death (21:4). (For creatures this immortality is acquired as a gift of God, and is not inherent as it is with God; see 1:23.)

To the one who seeks these things through his blameless conduct, God "will give eternal life." Actually there is no word in v. 7 for "will give"; this verb is rightly carried over from v. 6. As we have seen, this word refers not to the giving of a free and unearned gift of grace, but to the payment of what is due. This is the basis on which rewards are bestowed in the law system. To the person who persists in good work without breaking any of God's commandments, eternal life in heaven is what is due; it is the deserved reward.

This is the "hypothetical" element in this section. I.e., this is how it *would* happen *if* there were anyone who has persisted in good work to the point of perfection; but in fact no one has done so or will do so. Thus eternal life will in fact not be awarded to anyone on the basis of his good work.

2:8 But for those who are self-seeking and who reject the truth and follow evil, there will be wrath and anger. This is equivalent to the second half of my summary of the law system, "Break the commandments, and therefore suffer the penalty."

Commandment-breakers are described with three expressions. First, they are "self-seeking." This word is rendered "contentious" by the KJV and "factious" by the ASV, because of a supposed relation between it and ἔρις, (*eris*, "strife," 1:29). Recent studies trace the word to other roots and conclude that it has to do with selfishness or selfish ambition; hence "self-seeking" in the NIV seems to be on target. (See Gal 5:20; Phil 1:17; 2:3; Jas 3:14, 16 in recent translations.) To be selfish or self-seeking means to pursue our own desires and agendas rather than those God has planned for us. It means laying up treasures on earth — seeking earthly fulfilment (Matt 6:19), rather than seeking the heavenly treasures of glory, honor, and immortality (2:7; Matt 6:20).

Commandment-breakers are also described as those who "reject the truth and follow evil." "Evil" is ἀδικία, (*adikia*), "wickedness, unrighteousness" (1:18, 29). More literally the expression reads "those who *disobey* truth and *obey* evil." These are simply two sides of the same coin; to do one is to do the other. The language is practically the same as that used to describe the Gentiles in 1:18, "men who suppress the truth by their wickedness [*adikia*]."

It does not matter whether this truth is known through general revelation or special revelation (2:12); those who suppress and disobey it will receive "wrath and anger." These two words are objects of "will give" in v. 6. In this context both terms refer to the eschatological pouring out of God's wrath after the final judgment. The word translated "wrath" (ὀργή, *orgē*) refers more to God's constant and controlled indignation toward sin, while the word for "anger" (θυμός, *thymos*) refers more to a passionate and destructive outburst of rage. Except for here (which is clearly eschatological in reference) this latter word is used for God's wrath only in Revelation (14:10, 19; 15:1, 7; 16:1, 19; 19:15). At all times God is like a smoldering volcano, but in the end the volcano will erupt. "Our God is a consuming fire" (Heb 12:29).

This is the second of the two alternatives or the two potential outcomes when judgment is according to law. In reality it will be the only outcome, since all *are* commandment-breakers, but that is not Paul's point here. In this paragraph he is simply describing for us how judgment according to law will be conducted.

2:9 In the next two verses Paul repeats the essence of the law system, with the parts reversed. The beginning of v. 9 is equivalent to v. 8: **There will be trouble and distress for every human being who does evil . . . .** When God pours out his wrath and anger in the final judgment, the result for the condemned will be "trouble" (θλίψις, *thlipsis*) and "distress" (στενοχωρία, *stenochōria*). This is what they will experience for eternity. Some think the former refers to the outward or bodily sufferings, afflictions, and tribulations of hell; while the latter refers to the accompanying inward or mental anguish, distress, and torment.

This will be the result of God's judgment upon "every human being who does evil." Literally it says "upon every soul of man." The word "soul" is used here not in the metaphysical sense of the heart or spirit or inner man, as if only the soul (and not the body) suffers. Here "soul" means "person, individual," thus "every human being" (NIV), every single person among humankind "who does evil," who produces or brings about evil.

One new idea is added in this repetition of the thought of v. 8, namely, **first for the Jew, then for the Gentile . . . .** Here for the first time in this chapter Paul actually mentions the Jews, and he does so in a way that drives home his main point: the righteous judgment of God falls equally on both Jews and Gentiles.[35] This is enough to expose the fallacy of the myth of divine partiality toward the Jews, but Paul goes even further. Not only does God apply the principle of judgment equally to the two groups; he will actually pour out his wrath on the "Jew first." This is an application of Jesus' principle, "From everyone who has been given much, much will be demanded; and from the one who has been entrusted with much, much more will be asked" (Luke 12:48).

2:10 but glory, honor and peace for everyone who does good . . . . This much of the verse is not different in substance from v. 7; it again sets forth the first principle of law-judgment, "Keep the commandments and therefore escape the penalty." The aspects of the heavenly reward are slightly different. Glory and honor are the same as v. 7, but here "peace" is substituted for "immortality." This is not significant; neither list is a complete menu of the blessings of eternal life. Each is no more than representative of the riches to be bestowed on "everyone who does good."

This last phrase can be rendered "everyone who works good or produces good." Again, since we are working here within the law system, this means "everyone who does good all the time and never produces evil." It is the same as "persistence in doing good" in v. 7.

Again the phrase is added, **first for the Jew, then for the Gentile**. The blessings of eternal life are given "first or chiefly to

---

[35]Literally the verse says "Greeks," but this is a case where this word is used in the sense of Gentiles, with Jew and Greek intended to be inclusive of all mankind.

the Jew" because he, "through his superior advantages, hath made greater progress in virtue" (DeWelt, 34). This is not at all the same as favoritism with regard to the terms of judgment. The Jew has no "priority of privilege" (Dunn, I:93).

The point of these last four verses is to explain how the law system is completely impartial and favors neither the Jew nor the Gentile. "First for the Jew" does not mean "for the Jew on a different and more favorable basis." The basis for both is their works (v. 6), considered equally. "Paul's whole point here is that the terms of judgment are precisely the *same* for *everyone*." This undermines the Jews' belief "that God's judgment of Israel will be on different terms from his judgment of the nations as a whole" (Dunn, I:88).

2:11 For God does not show favoritism. Other familiar translations of this verse are "There is no respect of persons with God" (KJV), and "There is no partiality with God" (NASB). This is the main point of the paragraph. The justice of the law is truly blindfolded; who the person is makes no difference. Only his works will be examined. This is simply a negative restatement of the principle set forth in v. 6.

The term translated "favoritism, partiality, respect of persons" is found only in the NT[36] and in subsequent Christian writers. The same idea represented by similar terms appears in the OT. Men are exhorted not to show partiality in judgment (Lev 19:15; Ps 82:2; Prov 18:5). God is declared to be without partiality in Deut 10:17 and 2 Chr 19:7. The term and all its cognates involve a combination of two Greek words, πρόσωπον (*prosōpon*), "face," and λαμβάνω (*lambanō*), "receive." "Receiving someone's face" originally meant to accept and welcome them, but it came to be used in the negative sense of partiality (see Dunn, I:89).

While the principle applies to everyone, in this context it is a message Paul directs especially toward the Jews. God cannot be partial because his judgment is based on truth (v. 2), and because it is righteous (v. 5). A judgment that shows partiality would not be righteous. Therefore you, O Jew, cannot expect special treatment

---

[36]It is used of God in Eph 6:9; Col 3:25; Jas 2:1. Cognates are used of God in Acts 10:34; 1 Pet 1:17 (see also Gal 2:6). A cognate is used of man in Jas 2:9.

on Judgment Day. You will be no exception to the conclusion stated in 3:20.

C. UNDER LAW, THE CRITERION OF JUDGMENT
IS OBEDIENCE ALONE (2:12-16)

The next three paragraphs address two specific reasons why the Jews believed God would be partial to them in the last judgment: their possession of the Law of Moses, and the fact that they were circumcised. This paragraph (vv. 12-16) makes a very specific point about the former, namely, that the criterion of judgment within the law system is *obedience* to the law, not just possession of it or knowledge of it. Mere possession of the Law of Moses was no indication that the Jews would receive special consideration. As Cranfield sums it up, "Knowledge of the law does not in itself constitute any defence against the judgment of God" (I:139, 153).

This paragraph not only dissolves this basis for false confidence on the part of the Jews, but also defuses all possible complaints from the Gentiles that they are at a disadvantage in relation to the law since the Law of Moses was given only to the Jews. As Moo states the point, "This paragraph defends the equality of all people before God's judgment seat against the charge that the Jews' possession of the law gives to them a decisive advantage" (I:142).

In other words, the fact that the Jews had a specially-revealed form of God's law does not negate the general principle of judgment stated in v. 11, "God does not show favoritism."

2:12 All who sin apart from the law will also perish apart from the law, and all who sin under the law will be judged by the law. Two things in this verse are quite clear. First, "law" means the Law of Moses, given to the Jews by special revelation. Second, those who are "apart from the law"[37] are the Gentiles, and those "under the law" are the Jews.

But how do we know these things? There is no definite article ("the" law) in the original, but this is irrelevant. The presence or

---

[37]"Apart from the law" ("without the Law," NASB) is actually an adverb, ἀνόμως (*anomōs*), constructed from the noun νόμος (*nomos*, "law") and the negating alpha.

absence of the article is unrelated to whether "law" means the Law of Moses or the law in a more general sense. This can and must be determined by context alone; there is no other indicator. The clue in this context is the reference to people who "sin apart from the law."

What does this mean? How is it possible for a person to sin if there is no law to be broken (1 John 3:4)? Does not 4:15 say, "Where there is no law there is no transgression"? Yes, and that is the main reason why "law" in this verse must refer to the Law of Moses, and by inference to the moral law of God in any other *specially-revealed* form, unwritten (as to Adam, Noah, and Abraham) or written (as in the NT). Thus in this reference Paul must be talking about people who have no access to specially-revealed law, but do in fact have knowledge of God's law through general revelation, i.e., the Gentiles. The Gentiles do not need the Law of Moses in order to be judged according to law (as 1:18-32 has already shown).

In this context the main point is that the possession of or knowledge of the Law of *Moses* will make no difference as far as judgment according to law is concerned. As the NEB puts it, "Those who have sinned outside the pale of the Law of Moses will perish outside its pale, and all who have sinned under that law will be judged by the law."

Either way, "all who sin" will be condemned. The verb here is actually a past tense (aorist), "all who sinned or who have sinned." It is past tense from the perspective of Judgment Day, when one's past life will be considered as a whole. It means "all who have sinned, *period*, will perish," even if there has been just one sin (Jas 2:10; Gal 3:10). This is the rule when judgment is conducted according to law, and it will be applied to Jew and Gentile alike.

When judged even apart from the Law of Moses, the Gentiles "will perish." This is the verb ἀπόλλυμι (*apollumi*), which in the middle voice means "to perish, to die, to be ruined, to be destroyed, to be lost." It is often used to refer to the eternal condemnation of the wicked, as it does here.[38]

---

[38]See also John 3:15-16; 10:28; 1 Cor 1:18; 2 Cor 4:3; 2 Thess 2:10; 2 Pet 3:9; and (active voice) Matt 10:28. This word does not have the connotation of annihilation in this context, contrary to the assumption of many.

The second part of the verse refers specifically to the Jews, who sin under (within) the Law of Moses, with full knowledge of the specially-revealed law of God. Thus they will be "judged by the law" of Moses. The word "judged" is too weak to translate κρίνω (*krinō*), which here means "condemned" and is no different in meaning from "will perish." (See 2:1, 3; 3:7; 2 Thess 2:12.) Thus whether in possession of the Law of Moses or not, anyone who sins will receive the verdict of condemnation. (This is in contrast with the verdict of justification in v. 13.)

Here again is the tragic irony of the Jews' situation. The very law in which they trusted as a kind of charm guaranteeing their salvation (Morris, 122) will be the instrument of their condemnation because they have sinned against it. (The charge that they *have* sinned against it is made in detail in the next paragraph, vv. 17-24.)

2:13 For it is not those who hear the law who are righteous in God's sight, but it is those who obey the law who will be declared righteous. As this verse is examined we must remember two things. First, it relates only to the law system; it is a principle of judgment according to law. It is basically equivalent to vv. 7 and 10. "Keep the commandments, and therefore escape the penalty."

Second, whether there is anyone in this category is beside the point at this stage of Paul's argument. There does not need to be anyone in it for the principle to be true.[39] As the statement of a principle it is like the sign that warns, "Trespassers will be prosecuted" — if anyone dares. Or it is like Jonah's message to Nineveh, "Forty more days and Nineveh will be destroyed" — unless they repent (Jonah 3:4). Such statements are straightforward, but they contain unspoken conditions (see Jer 18:7-10). That is the case here: those who obey the law will be declared righteous — if anyone does. Thus those are wrong who say this principle cannot be hypothetical because the verb is a simple future indicative.

The use of the concept of righteousness here focuses our attention squarely upon the thematic statement in 1:17. There Paul sums up the *grace* system of salvation, that a righteousness of God is

---

[39]In fact, 3:20 shows that it *is* an empty category, and that the principle is hypothetical, or as Lard says, "merely potential, not actual" (86). See the discussion of this in the introduction to this main section of Romans.

revealed in the gospel, and that those who receive that righteousness by faith will live eternally. But here in 2:13 Paul is explaining the *law* system of being accepted as righteous by God, namely, by works rather than by faith. An understanding of this aspect of the law system is crucial for an understanding of Paul's main point in this section and in Romans as a whole. Under law the *only* way to be accepted as righteous is through obedience — perfect obedience — to the law's commandments. But all have sinned; therefore no one will in fact be saved by law. Thus the gospel alternative is our only hope.

Thus far we have seen several words relating to righteousness, but this is the first time the key term δικαιόω (*dikaioō*) has appeared. This is a legal term that refers to a judge's decision in a courtroom trial. It is the opposite of "condemned" (see v. 12) and is usually translated "justified," although some recent translations think this word is too theological and render it instead as "acquitted," "counted righteous," "put right," or "declared righteous" (NIV).[40] The issue is this: if our relationship with God is based on law alone, then when we think of ourselves as standing before God as judge (whether now or at the second coming), how is it possible for him to regard us as righteous? How is it possible to hear the judge say, "Not guilty!" or "No penalty for you!"?

Paul's answer is stated in both negative and positive terms. First, contrary to the Jews' assumption, one cannot be accepted as righteous before God merely by *hearing* the law. By this he means "not those who *only* hear the law," as if having the law in one's possession or even in one's mind would be enough to be counted righteous. This applies not only to the Jews but to anyone who has access to special revelation of the Creator's will for his creatures. The word "hear" in this context means "hear" in the barest sense of the term, i.e., in the sense of having some knowledge content register in the consciousness and possibly retained in the memory, but without ever acting upon that content.

Paul next states the principle in a positive way: "It is those who obey the law who will be declared righteous." As vv. 14-15 show, he means "law" in whatever form it is available to anyone; for the Jews

---

[40]This term will be discussed further under 3:24.

this would be the Law of Moses. "Those who obey the law" is literally "the doers of the law" (see Jas 1:22-25). "Doing" the law, doing God's will, doing sin, doing righteousness, doing the truth, doing good, doing evil — these are common ways of speaking in Scripture. Here "doing the law" is equivalent to obedience or good works.

The key point is that under law, the only way to be justified, or accepted as righteous by God, is to *obey* the law, i.e., by one's own personal righteousness or works. This is quite contrary to the way one is justified under grace, which is through one's own personal faith in the works of Jesus Christ. But that contrast comes later; here Paul is simply establishing how one may possibly be saved under law. The contrast for this purpose is between merely hearing the law, which will not justify, and doing the law, which will justify. Moreover, "doers of the law" is unqualified; it means "those who obey the law *perfectly*." Under law such will be justified, by their own righteousness.

2:14 (Indeed, when Gentiles, who do not have the law, do by nature things required by the law . . . .) Like the NIV, many take vv. 14-15 to be a parenthesis, with the main flow of Paul's thought being resumed again in v. 16, which will conclude the paragraph. The thought developed in the parenthesis is called for by the apparent implications for the Gentiles of the principles stated in vv. 12-13. It is easy to see how these verses apply to the Jews, but when applied to the Gentiles, one might question the *fairness* of God's judgment. Is it fair to condemn the Gentiles for breaking the law if they do not even *have* the law (v.12)? This question has already been answered in 1:18-32, but Paul answers it again here with more detail.

What the apostle is doing in these two verses is explaining the meaning of *anomōs* ("apart from the law") in v. 12. This is the category of the "Gentiles," he says, a word he has not used since 1:13. In between he has used "Greek" as its equivalent (1:16; 2:9-10), which the NIV translates as "Gentiles" anyway. These Gentiles, he says, are the ones "who do not have the law," namely, the Law of Moses, or by extension *any* specially-revealed form of God's law. He repeats this fact later in the verse.

Nevertheless these very same Gentiles, who do not have the Law

of Moses, sometimes "do by nature things required by the law."
Literally Paul says "when" the Gentiles do these things. Thus he
does not mean they do things of the law perfectly, or that they do
all of the things required by the law. He means there are times
when the Gentiles acknowledge the moral duties revealed in Moses'
law, and there are times when they even live up to them (see Dunn,
I:98; Hendriksen, I:97; Moo, I:145-146).

Paul says the Gentiles do these things "by nature," i.e., through
some kind of built-in, created instinct. That is, men's nature *as
created* includes an innate awareness of the moral law of God. This
is not the same as the knowledge of God himself, which registers
upon our consciousness from observing created things outside ourselves (1:18-21). It is something that is already inside us as a universal moral consciousness, in the form of "natural, in-born capacities"
(Moo, I:146). There will be more on this in the next verse.

As a result of this "innate or natural knowledge of God's law"
(Moo, I:147), there is a sense in which **they [the Gentiles] are a law
for themselves, even though they do not have the law . . .** in a specially-revealed form. This means that their innate knowledge of
God's law has basically the same content as the moral law revealed
in the Law of Moses.[41] That they are a "law for themselves" does
not mean that the Gentiles are free to make up whatever law code
they fancy, with God accepting that as the standard by which he will
judge them. This is a quite common idea, but it is a serious mistake
(Stott, 86). Rather, they are a law in themselves in that their inner
being bears at least the remnants of God's moral law as it was
imprinted upon human nature in the very beginning. See v. 15.

Thus Paul makes it very clear that *anomōs* in v. 12 does not
mean the Gentiles are without law altogether. They do not have
access to special revelation, to be sure, but the essence of God's
moral law is available to them in another form. Thus God's righteousness is not impugned when he condemns them for their sin.

2:15 This verse is a further explanation of how the Gentiles,
while not having access to the Law of Moses, still have a form of

---

[41]Thus, besides demonstrating the righteousness of God in condemning
the Gentiles, in these verses Paul is also deflating the Jews' presumptuousness even further by showing them that they in fact are *not* the only ones
who have God's law. The Gentiles have it, too, in another form.

God's law. Specifically, it expands on the concept that the Gentiles are a law for themselves, **since they show that the requirements of the law are written on their hearts . . . .** They show or demonstrate this in their general agreement on basic moral principles,[42] in their occasional obedience to these principles, and in their sense of guilt and hostility toward God when they disobey them.

"The requirements of the law" literally reads "the work of the law." This is an unusual expression because "work" is singular; in other places Paul speaks of the *works* of the law (3:20, 28; Gal 2:16; 3:2, 5, 10). He generally uses the plural when he is making the point that law is impotent to save (see also 4:2, 6; 9:11, 32; 11:6). Here his point is different. He is simply talking about the contents of the law's commandments. Dunn says the singular "work" means "the business of the law, what it is the law's business to produce" (I:105). A better rendering is "conduct," or "the conduct that the law demands" (Moo, I:148). Actually this "work of the law" or "conduct required by the law" is no different from the "things of the law" in v. 14.

The work of the law is "written on their hearts." This is the bottom line as to how the Gentiles have access to the law of God and how they can be justly condemned for breaking it. But what does it mean?

Some, perhaps out of an aversion to the very thought of innate knowledge of any kind, equate "written on the heart" with the generation-to-generation transmission of the moral knowledge revealed by God to Adam in the beginning. In Lard's words, it is the "unperished traditions of the divine will, communicated to the early fathers of mankind" (89). DeWelt grants this as a possibility (39). We can rule this out, however, since the language here — "by nature," "written on the heart" — seems calculated specifically to exclude the mechanics of tradition. It points unequivocally to something innate in each individual, to something "inwardly revealed" in the form of "inward, natural promptings" (MP, 312).

Some see this expression as a deliberate reference to the messianic promise of the New Covenant in Jer 31:31-34. Whereas the

---

[42]For documentation on this universal sense of basic decency and responsibility, see C.S. Lewis, *Abolition*, 29ff, 93ff. He says it is discoverable in every culture and religion in every age and place.

Old Covenant was written on stone (2 Cor 3:3), under the New Covenant, says God, "I will put my law in their minds and write it on their hearts" (Jer 31:33). If this is Paul's point in 2:15, then he is talking not about Gentiles in general, but only about Gentile Christians who have heard and accepted the gospel and whose hearts have been softened to obey God's law with "a sincere and earnest desire" (Cranfield, I:159).

This view is appealing but must be rejected on the grounds that it does not fit the context. Specifically, it does not fit the description of the Gentiles in v. 14, which says twice for emphasis that the Gentiles "do not have the law," i.e., in a specially-revealed form. Gentiles who have become Christians *have* been exposed to law in such a form, however; thus this view is inadequate.

The best understanding of how the required conduct of the law is "written on their hearts" is derived from the NT teaching on the *image of God*. Parallel passages in Eph 4:23-24 and Col 3:9-10 speak about Christian sanctification as the process that renews the image of God within us. In the context the contrast is between the Gentiles' pre-Christian moral depravity and the new way of life required of Christians. The latter is described as putting on a new self, "which is being renewed in knowledge in the image of its Creator" (Col 3:10), language that clearly alludes to the original creation in God's image (Gen 1:26-27).

Analyzing these parallel texts gives us this scenario: 1) The original creation in God's image involved *knowledge* (Col 3:10), specifically a knowledge of "true righteousness and holiness" (Eph 4:24). Since the image of God is part of our very nature as human beings, we may conclude that this moral knowledge was part of mankind's original, created nature. 2) The Fall into sin resulted in a corruption of the image of God in an unspecified manner and degree. The innate moral consciousness remains intact enough to render everyone "without excuse," but it is corrupted to the point that it cannot be completely trusted and needs to be "recreated." 3) Part of Christian salvation consists in this very thing, i.e., the recreation of the inner image of God and thus the reconstruction of the inner moral compass. This is done not from within but from the outside, through the inspired teaching of apostles and prophets (2 Tim 3:16-17), such as Paul is providing to the Ephesians and Colossians

COLLEGE PRESS NIV COMMENTARY

in these very letters. This is the fulfilment of Jer 31:33: the law is *re*written on the minds and hearts of willing Christians through the Spirit-inspired words of the New Covenant revelation.

The error of Cranfield and others, who hold the second view described above, is that they equate "written on their hearts" in 2:15 with the *third* step in the scenario above, whereas it should be equated with the *first* step. Knowledge of the basic content of God's moral law was implanted in human nature at creation, and enough of it remains in every individual to make him responsible for breaking the law. This is true of the most isolated Gentile, and also of the most rehabilitated Christian. This explains how the items on Paul's vice list in 1:29-31 are known by Gentiles to be wrong. This inward knowledge of God's law is part of God's *general* revelation since it is available to all people without exception.

Now we turn to the next part of v. 15, which focuses on another innate aspect of human nature, the conscience: **their consciences also bearing witness . . . .** The most important thing to know about the conscience is that it is *not* the same as "the work of the law written on the heart." The conscience itself has no content; it is not in itself a source of knowledge about right and wrong. It is rather an ability, a function (Murray, I:75). Specifically, conscience is the function of comparing our deeds with an accepted standard of morality, and of prodding us with a sense of guilt when a deed does not conform to the standard. It "examines and passes judgment on a man's conduct" (Bruce, 91). As Lard says, "Conscience originates no truth. It merely approves conformity to truth, or to what is held as truth, and condemns violations of it" (48-49). See Moo, I:148.

Whether the conscience functions properly or not depends on the accuracy of the standard with which it compares our deeds. To the degree to which the image of God remains intact within any individual, the conscience will work as intended by God. To the degree that the law-content written on the heart has been corrupted, the conscience will malfunction. It is similar to a spelling-check computer program. The function of the program is to compare the user's word entries with a pre-established database. Even if the program is functioning perfectly, it will not produce the right results if there are misspelled words in the database. If the words in the original database are correct, then the results can be trusted.

The only thing needed to make such a program more analogous to the conscience is the addition of a small handle the user can grip while the check is being made. If the word being checked is incorrect, the errant speller would receive a mild electrical shock. This would be equivalent to the "pangs" of conscience felt after doing wrong. This is how the conscience "bears witness" to the individual concerning the rightness of God's moral law, in addition to the witness of the internally-written law itself.

It is extremely important to remember this: wherever the knowledge of God's law has been corrupted, suppressed, exchanged, or in any way violated, the conscience will continue to function but will not produce trustworthy results. Until one has submitted to the saving work of Jesus Christ and the Holy Spirit, and has allowed the truth of biblical revelation to reinform his original moral database, the conscience will at times, perhaps most of the time, yield false results. "Always let your conscience be your guide" is bad theology. Actually, the conscience itself *needs* a guide or standard, and the only sure guide for sinners is the objective Word of God, the Bible.

The last part of v. 15, (**. . . and their thoughts now accusing, now even defending them.**), in my opinion is not different from the working of the conscience but is a clarification of how it works (so Moo, I:149; and Cranfield, I:162; contra Dunn, I:102). The functioning conscience results in an inner dialogue, forcing the mind to verbalize thoughts such as "This must be OK," or "You know that's wrong, don't you?" Our thoughts either accuse us or defend us in reference to our deeds. These are technical legal terms that suggest a courtroom trial where the individual is the defendant and his own conscience-driven thoughts are both the prosecuting attorney and the defense lawyer.

This inner witness or testimony occurs day by day, and not just at the final judgment (contra Cranfield, I:162). Also, the accusing or defending happens with reference to individual deeds, and not to anyone's life as a whole. Thus Paul is not saying that on the day of judgment there may be some Gentile whose conscience will excuse him altogether so that he is saved. This is definitely not Paul's point. He is saying only that sometimes in this life, when a Gentile does by nature what the law requires in a certain situation, his conscience will excuse him regarding that one decision. Paul hints that this is the exception rather than the rule, however, since he says their thoughts will accuse them or *even* defend them, as if the latter is unexpected.

When this inner moral consciousness (the inwardly-written law plus the conscience) is combined with the knowledge of God learned through the created universe (1:18-21), the result is that even the Gentiles know that this law is the law of the Creator-God and that they are guilty before God when they break it and are worthy of the wrath God has ordained for such lawbreakers (see 1:32).[43]

2:16 This will take place on the day when God will judge men's secrets through Jesus Christ, as my gospel declares. It is clear that this verse concludes the paragraph, but its exact connection with the preceding text is uncertain. The words "this will take place" are not in the original, where the beginning words are "on which day God will judge." The idea is that some action mentioned in the preceding verse or verses will take place on the day of judgment. What action does Paul have in mind?

Some connect this verse directly with v. 15 and say that it specifies when the "accusing" and "defending" will take place as an act of final, climactic self-judgment (Moo, I:150; Morris, 128). Others see vv. 14-15 as a parenthesis, as in the NIV, and thus connect v. 16 with v. 13. The action that will take place "on the day" is the condemning and justifying of vv. 12-13. Finally, some think v. 16 is an inclusive reference to all the main verbs pointing to Judgment Day in vv. 1-15: "will be revealed," v. 5; "will be judged," v. 12; "will be declared righteous" v. 13; and maybe "accusing" and "defending," v. 15 (see Hendriksen, I:96).

The first of these views seems much too limited to do justice to the dramatic thought of v. 16. The second view is possible. The last view is probably the best, and we should think of v. 15 as ending in a dash — with v. 16 bringing the preceding thoughts to a climax and wrapping them up in a neat package. This effect is achieved when we add the word "all" to the NIV's added phrase, thus: "All this will take place . . . ."[44]

---

[43]See my discussion of the implications of 2:14-15 in GC, 329-336.

[44]See Hendriksen's added phrase, "All this will become clear . . ." (I:96, 98).

This "day when God will judge" is the same as "the day of God's wrath" (v. 5). In v. 16 the word "judge" (*krinō*) seems to have its more general meaning of "pass judgment on." God will judge not just external and public deeds but also "men's secrets" — the hidden things of men's hearts as well as deeds done in private. The omniscience of God makes this possible (1 Sam 16:7; 1 John 3:20).[45] Jesus stressed this point especially in reference to the hypocrisy of the Jewish leaders (Matt 6:4, 6, 18; 23:25-28), an application that is relevant to the thought in the next paragraph (2:17-24).

Paul adds a Christological note at this point: the judgment will take place "through Jesus Christ" (see 1:3-4). This means that Jesus is involved not only in the gospel of salvation through grace, but also in the process of judgment according to law. For other references to Jesus as judge, see Matt 25:31-33; John 5:22, 27; Acts 10:42; 17:31; 1 Cor 4:5; 2 Cor 5:10; 2 Tim 4:1; Rev 22:12.

The words "as my gospel declares" (literally, "according to my gospel") are a bit of a problem for exegetes. Exactly what does this phrase modify? Dunn (I:103) says it means Christ will *judge* according to the gospel, i.e., that the gospel will be the measure of judgment. There is a sense in which this is so (see Rev 20:15), but that is not the point here. In this entire context Paul is explaining what it means to be judged according to law, not according to the gospel.

Others say it means, "My gospel declares that God will judge the world." It is true that God will judge the world, but is this piece of information *good news* (gospel)? Certainly it sets the stage for the good news, since the reality of the judgment is what makes the gospel all the more meaningful and welcome (see Morris, 129).

Probably the best understanding is this: "My gospel declares that the judge will be Christ Jesus" (see Cranfield, I:163). "This last alternative does most justice to the somewhat unexpected reference to the gospel," says Moo (I:151). That Jesus will be the judge is good news because it points to the fact that there is a judgment beyond that of law, a judgment according to the grace established by the judge himself in his atoning death and victorious resurrection.

---

[45]See also 1 Chr 28:9; Ps 139:1-2, 23; Jer 17:10; Mark 4:22; Luke 16:15; Rom 2:28-29; 1 Cor 4:5; 14:25; Heb 4:12-13. See 8:27 below.

D. JEWS WHO LOOK TO THE LAW FOR SALVATION ARE CONDEMNED BY THEIR OWN DISOBEDIENCE (2:17-24)

No one will be saved by his relationship to the law of God. Gentiles will not be saved by their *ignorance* of the law, because in fact they have knowledge of it. Jews will not be saved by their *possession* of the Law of *Moses*, because the only way to be saved by any law is through perfect obedience to it. There are no exceptions. God does not show favoritism, even to the Jews, when it comes to the final judgment.

In the previous paragraph Paul made the point that only doers of the law, not merely hearers or possessers, can be saved by the law system. Where does this leave the Jew? If he can no longer count on his privileged position as possessor of the law to secure his salvation, then his only hope (under law) is to obey it perfectly.

It seems that some Jews believed they were actually sinless before the law (Luke 18:9-14), including Paul (Saul) when he was a Pharisee (Phil 3:5-6). But Paul's point in this paragraph is that this is a lie. The Jews in fact are *not* "doers of the law," but are guilty of breaking the very law they glory in. The law they regard as a ticket to heaven shines like a spotlight upon their sin (3:20), thus dissolving their final hope before the law.

The first thing Paul does in this paragraph is dissect the nature of the Jews' hope in the law, the grounds for their law-based confidence as the specially-chosen stewards of the Mosaic revelation (vv. 17-20). Then in the second half of the paragraph he rips off their mask of hypocrisy and exposes their own sinfulness (vv. 21-24). This latter segment is to the Jews what 1:29-31 was to the Gentiles.

2:17 Paul returns now to the diatribe style, which he suspended in vv. 6-16, and speaks directly to the Jews in the person of their anonymous representative: **Now you, if you call yourself a Jew . . . .** The Jews have been Paul's main target all along in chapter 2, but this is the first time he addresses them specifically as Jews.

The name "Jew" comes from the name "Judah," which is related to the Hebrew verb ידה (*yadah*), "to praise" (see Gen 29:35; 49:8). It was originally used for those who occupied Judah's allotment in the Promised Land. But after the Babylonian exile this was just about all that remained of the original Israel anyway; so all Israelites came to be called Jews. By Paul's time this had been their own favored self-designation for several generations, replacing "Israelite" and "Hebrew." It was "a name accepted with pride" (Dunn, I:109).

Paul is not saying it is wrong for the Jews to call themselves Jews. In fact, most of the things he ascribes to the Jews in vv. 17-20 are not wrong in themselves. Almost all the claims and roles described here are things the Jews were *supposed* to do and be. The irony is that all these genuine privileges and prerogatives were trivialized by the Jews' false self-righteousness and hypocrisy.

Verse 17 includes two further descriptions of the Jewish self-confidence: **if you rely on the law and brag about your relationship to God . . . .** The first of these is the only inappropriate one in the whole list, and it skews all the rest. Relying on (resting upon, resting their hopes upon) the law was the Jew's root problem. "The Jew *rested upon* . . . the mere fact of having the law, as a ground of safety. In his estimation its bare bestowment on him proved him to be favored of God above all others. Confident of this favor, he had no fear" (Lard, 90). Instead of relying upon their role as recipients of the Mosaic Law, they should have relied upon the mercy of God (2:4).

The Jews also bragged or boasted about their relationship to God. The Greek expression says simply "you are boasting in God." The verb is καυχάομαι (*kauchaomai*), "to boast, to glory, to exult." The fact is that there is absolutely nothing wrong with "boasting in God," when done with the right spirit. It means to praise him and rejoice in him. Jer 9:23-24 exhorts, "Let him who boasts boast about this: that he understands and knows me, that I am the LORD." Paul twice refers to this text (1 Cor 1:31; 2 Cor 10:17). See also 5:2, 11; Gal 6:14; Phil 3:3. The problem with the Jews was that their boasting in God was selfish and exclusive, as if they alone had a claim upon God (3:27, 29). It was a kind of name-dropping, a "self-centred boasting in him as a basis for one's own self-importance" (Cranfield, I:164).

2:18 if you know his will . . . . Even those who have only general revelation know God's will to a degree, but possessing his special revelation makes this knowledge more explicit and more complete. Certainly as possessors of the Law of Moses, the Jews knew God's will more thoroughly than anyone else up to the time of the New

Covenant revelation. This is something they could rightly rejoice in.[46]

The next clause, **and approve of what is superior**, also appears in Phil 1:10. Each of the two key words has two nuances, which leads to differences in interpretation. The word for "approve" (δοκιμάζω, *dokimazō*) can also mean "to distinguish, to discern." The word for "superior" (διαφέρω, *diapherō*) can also mean "to differ." Thus one view is that the clause means, "You know how to discern what differs *from* God's will, you know how to tell right from wrong." This is the basis for the NEB's "You are aware of moral distinctions." Another view is that it means, "You know how to discern the superior elements *within* God's will, the things that matter, the essentials" (Cranfield, I:166; Phil 1:10, NIV). The last view is the one the NIV gives here in 2:18, "You approve of what is superior" (see also KJV, NASB). Either of the last two meanings is acceptable.

Both of these things — knowing God's will and discerning the essentials — are possible **because you are instructed by the law . . . .** This is the law's proper function, and the Jews would have been much better off if they had left it at that. Also, both of these things are commendable, as long as they are not considered to be a replacement for obedience. The error "lies not in knowing God's will, but in regarding this knowledge, by itself, as a mark of superiority, and ground of acceptance with God" (Lard, 91).

2:19 In this verse and the next Paul lists four basically similar things the Jews considered themselves to be. Because you know the Law of Moses so well, he says, **. . . you are convinced that you are a guide for the blind, a light for those who are in the dark . . . .** In Scripture both blindness and darkness are used figuratively to represent ignorance, especially ignorance of spiritual things. Both are dispelled by knowledge of the truth, which comes from the Word of God (Ps 119:105; John 17:17; Rom 2:20).

It was Israel's great privilege and responsibility to be "a light for the Gentiles" and "to open eyes that are blind" (Isa 42:6-7; 49:6). They were not commissioned to do this through worldwide mis-

---

[46]The Greek says simply, "You know *the* will," with "his" being understood. "God's will is 'the will' *par excellence*" (Bruce, 92).

sionary activity,[47] but were meant to accomplish this indirectly through their faithful preparation for the coming Messiah, who himself would be the direct source of light and sight to the world (Luke 2:32; 4:18). The problem was that the Jews refused to accept their secondary role in this plan, and regarded themselves as the ultimate and final source of truth.

2:20. The Jew also considered himself to be **an instructor of the foolish, a teacher of infants . . . .** These are slightly different ways of saying the same thing, and, like the two roles in 2:19, are in themselves commendable. An "instructor" is an educator, a teacher; the verb form often refers to correction and chastisement. "The *foolish* strictly are the unintelligent (NEB, 'stupid'), those lacking the ability to think things out," says Morris. This is not talking about IQ as such, but "perception in spiritual things" (133). Someone can be MENSA material or a scientific genius, and still be foolish in his thinking about God and morality.

The word for "infants" means literally just that: infants, babies. It is often used figuratively for the spiritually immature, as in the case of new converts or those who have lagged behind in spiritual growth. The NT uses it of immature Christians (1 Cor 3:1; Eph 4:4; Heb 5:13). The Jews of course regarded all Gentiles as foolish, and as spiritual infants or simple-minded children. Thus it is probable that Paul means in both these expressions that the Jews considered themselves to be proper teachers of the Gentiles, especially those who might be new converts to Judaism.

All of these elements of Jewish self-confidence were grounded in one thing: the law. You are convinced you can do these things, says Paul, **because you have in the law the embodiment of knowledge and truth . . . .** Indeed, the law possessed by the Jews — not just the Pentateuch but the entire OT — was an embodiment or repository of inspired knowledge and truth, and was therefore "useful for teaching, rebuking, correcting, and training in righteousness" (2 Tim 3:16). The Jews' mistake was the arrogant assumption that their Scriptures were the only source of knowledge and truth (contra 1:18-25, 28, 32) as well as the final source (rejecting the Christian revelation).

---

[47]Dunn is correct: "None of these phrases necessarily implies an actively outgoing missionary concern" (I:112).

2:21 Verse 17 begins with the conditional word, "if," with all of vv. 17-20 depending on it. The expected matching "then" is not explicit at the beginning v. 21 but is only implied: "If this is how you see yourself as a Jew, then why don't you *act* as a real Jew should act?" **. . . you, then, who teach others, do you not teach yourself?** This is the beginning of a series of "accusatory rhetorical questions" (Cranfield, I:167), dropped like bombshells into the midst of the smug Jewish complacency. They are based on the moral law as represented by the Ten Commandments.[48]

Phillips renders this first question thus: "But, prepared as you are to instruct others, do you ever teach yourself anything?" The implied answer is "No, you are *not* teaching yourself." You are not "practicing what you preach." The Psalmist leveled the same accusation against wicked Israelites (Ps 50:16-20), and Jesus accused the Jewish leaders of the same thing (Matt 23:3). In Gal 6:13 Paul declares, "Not even those who are circumcised obey the law." All these references, especially the present text, emphasize the terrible danger of using expertise in the law and ability to teach the law as a cloak or an excuse for breaking it.

From here to the end of v. 22 Paul gives several examples of "practicing what you preach against." None of these accusations implies that all Jews do all of these things all of the time. They are simply meant to drive home the point that every Jew has broken the law at some point, thus erasing all distinctions between Jews and Gentiles in reference to the judgment. Jews who break their law are sinners, no less than the Gentiles who break their law. "The argument is that the transgression of any individual Jew is enough to call in question the Jewish assumption that as a Jew he stands in a position of privilege and superiority before God as compared with the Gentile" (Dunn, I:116).

You who preach against stealing, do you steal? We usually associate *preaching* (κηρύσσω, *kērussō*) with preaching the gospel, and this is indeed how the word is used most of the time in the NT. On a few occasions, though, it means simply "proclaiming a message" (see Gal 5:11; 1 Pet 3:19; Rev 5:2). To a Jew who gloried in the law

---

[48]Grammatically they could be read as sentences, but most translations properly put them in question form.

(2:23), what greater message could there be than the law? This question, like the others in this series, is meant to stimulate the Jew's slumbering conscience.

2:22 You who say that people should not commit adultery, do you commit adultery? Again this is a straightforward question meant to stir the conscience and call for self-examination. As Jesus showed in his Sermon on the Mount (Matt 5:17-48), the Jews tended to look at a commandment with a very narrow tunnel vision, seeing it as prohibiting a single act. One obeys "Do not murder," for example, as long as he avoids actually killing someone. But Jesus says that rash anger and demeaning words also violate this commandment (Matt 5:21-22). The same is true of the seventh commandment, "Do not commit adultery." To the Jews this commandment was obeyed as long as one avoided physical sexual contact with someone else's spouse. But Jesus says adultery can be committed in the heart, through lusting after someone who is not your spouse (Matt 5:27-30). In that light Paul's question may not be so easily answered, and few could really answer "Of course not!"

The next question is the most difficult to understand: **You who abhor idols, do you rob temples?** The first part is easy; the monotheistic Jews took the first two of the ten commandments seriously and in principle hated idolatry. The noun form of the word "abhor" is equivalent to the Hebrew word for "abomination," which was commonly used for idols and idolatry.

But what does Paul mean when he accuses the Jews of robbing temples (ἱεροσυλέω, *hierosuleō*)? Several views have been suggested, and it is difficult to be dogmatic about any one of them. Some see this word as referring to the literal theft of idols from pagan temples (see Acts 19:37), especially those made of precious metals, which could be melted down and sold for gain. This practice is specifically forbidden in Deut 7:25. Also, throughout OT history the Jews were constantly being seduced by the idolatrous practices of their pagan neighbors, so Paul could also be referring to the theft of idols for personal worship.[49] If the robbing of pagan temples is Paul's point, the latter purpose would seem to be what

---

[49]See Schrenk, "ἱερός," 255-256.

he has in mind, since stealing as such has already been mentioned, and since it would contrast better with "abhorring idols."

Another suggestion is that Paul is talking about some kind of practice that robs the temple of the true God rather than temples of pagan gods. One such possibility is the misappropriation of tithes brought to the temple for the service of God and used instead for personal purposes (see Stott, 91), or perhaps the withholding of one's own tithes, which Mal 3:8 describes as stealing from God. One problem with this view is how this could be parallel to idolatry, but perhaps the equation of greed with idolatry in Col 3:5 answers this.

A third view takes the word to mean "commit sacrilege" against the true God in some general, unspecified sense, without any literal temple theft being involved (Cranfield, I:169-170). In this sense it could be a reference to the next two verses, which accuse the Jews of bringing dishonor upon God by their hypocritical disobedience. The contrast then would be something like this: "You make a big deal of defending God's honor by attacking the reality of all false pagan gods, then turn around and bring shame upon his name by your sin."

The three sins of stealing, adultery, and sacrilege are only a few examples of Jewish hypocrisy; others could no doubt have been cited. Paul's purpose in mentioning these three was to lead the Jews to examine their lives on all matters of the law, and ultimately to realize that they were sinners no less than the Gentiles.

2:23 Some take this verse as a statement: "While you take pride in the law, you dishonour God by breaking it" (NEB). Others (like the NIV) take it as a question, the last in the series beginning in v. 21: **You who brag about the law, do you dishonor God by breaking the law?** Either way, along with the proof text cited in v. 24, it sums up the point of this paragraph and exposes the tragic contradiction in the Jews' relationship with the law.

Just as the Jews boasted (bragged) about their relation to God (v. 17), so they boasted about their relation to his law.[50] Again, the law of God no less than God himself is something believers ought to boast about, in the sense of giving it honor and taking pride in it

---

[50]This is the same word that was used in v. 17; see the discussion there.

and rejoicing in its truth and guidance. The whole of Ps 119 is a testimony to this, e.g., "Oh, how I love your law! I meditate on it all day long" (v. 97). The Jews' boasting, however, was self-centered. In Cranfield's words, they sought to use the law as a means of putting God in their debt, and regarded their knowledge of it as making them better than their fellow men (I:170).

In any case all their positive claims regarding the law were negated by their transgression of it. Their sin brought disrepute not only to the law but also to God himself, since the law cannot be separated from the Lawgiver. To show contempt for the law by breaking it is to show contempt for God as well (GRe, 270-271). This is made even worse when the lawbreaker makes such a big display of the law and his privileged relation to it.

2:24 As it is written: "God's name is blasphemed among the Gentiles because of you." This verse begins with the Greek particle *gar*, "for, because," not translated by the NIV, and thus explains how lawbreaking dishonors God. Not only is it a personal insult against God on the part of the sinner himself, but it also causes others to blaspheme God and make fun of him. Specifically, the sins of the Jews caused the Gentiles to blaspheme God's name.

In ancient cultures one's *name* was the embodiment of the whole person; in Scripture the name of God stands for everything that God is. Thus to blaspheme God's name is to blaspheme God himself. "Blaspheme" means to speak against or say something bad about; to blaspheme God is to speak against him, to mock or ridicule him, to curse him or rail against him.

"As it is written" indicates Paul is referring to OT Scripture. He seems to be thinking of two texts, Isa 52:5 and Ezek 36:20-23. In each case Israel is enduring the shame of exile, and their Gentile conquerors are pictured as mocking the allegedly great and powerful God whom the Jews bragged about and trusted in, but who could not deliver them from this humiliation. "Some God!" they sneered. "All day long my name is constantly blasphemed," says the Lord (Isa 52:5).

The kind of thing to which Paul is referring is not quite this dramatic, but it is just as damaging to God's "reputation." The Jews portrayed themselves as "the people of the law." Being the recipients and guardians of God's law gave them a bad case of spiritual pride and a sense of superiority over the Gentiles. This also made them and their law and their God very vulnerable to criticism and ridicule when they sinned against the very law they gloried in. "If you think your law is so hot, how come you don't obey it? If you think so much of your God, why do you break his law? They don't really mean all that much to you, do they? Ha! Some law! Some God!"

The bottom line of this paragraph is that the Jews can forget about appealing to the law in any way as the basis for their hope on the day of judgment. Under law nothing but obedience counts, and in this department the Jews' record is no better than that of the Gentiles.

E. TRUE JEWISHNESS IS IDENTIFIED NOT BY CIRCUMCISION BUT BY THE INWARD STATE OF THE HEART (2:25-29)

The Jews considered themselves to be safe from wrath and condemnation because they saw themselves as encircled with the protective shield of the law. But thus far in chapter 2 the Apostle Paul has thoroughly dismantled this defense, showing that the Jews' own sin renders it ineffective. Now in vv. 25-29 he pictures the Jews as regrouping and retreating within their final stronghold, behind their final line of defense: circumcision. Circumcision was their concrete, physical evidence that they were children of Abraham and were thus protected by the covenant that God had made with Abraham *and his descendants* (Gen 17:1-14). Moo well sums up the attitude Paul is addressing here: "How can we be treated the same as Gentiles (vv. 6-11), even to the point of being in danger of the wrath of God (cf. v. 5), when our circumcision marks us as belonging to God's chosen people, heirs of the Abrahamic promises?" (I:163). (See page 173 above for quotations from rabbinic literature regarding the saving efficacy of circumcision.)

Paul's purpose in this paragraph, then, is to do with circumcision what he has already done with the law, namely, show that it is no basis for special treatment on Judgment Day. I.e., the Apostle "turns his fire so as to dislodge the Jew from this deceptive stronghold. He drives him from his hope and trust in circumcision" (MP, 315).

Paul accomplishes this in two steps. First (vv. 25-27), continuing in the diatribe style, he shows that circumcision does not take precedence over the law's more fundamental requirement, obedience itself. As he has done throughout the chapter thus far, here he continues to speak of judgment according to the rules of law. When God renders his final judgment for those under law (not under grace), he will divide them into two groups. But, contrary to the Jews' expectation, those two groups will *not* be the circumcised and the uncircumcised (equivalent to the Jews and the Gentiles). Rather, God will say, "All those who have *obeyed* the law as you have known it — circumcised or not — come over here. All who have *disobeyed* the law — circumcised or not — go over there." Thus under law uncircumcised persons could conceivably be saved and circumcised persons lost.

Second (vv. 28-29), Paul abandons the diatribe style and brings all of chapter 2 to a climax. For the first and only time in this first main section of Romans (1:18-3:20), he steps outside the sphere of law and sets forth a basic principle of grace salvation, i.e., true Jewishness is identified not by circumcision but by the inward state of the heart. Physical Jewishness, marked by physical circumcision, is not the measure of salvation; spiritual circumcision is.

2:25 Circumcision has value if you observe the law . . . . To his anonymous Jewish dialogue partner Paul succinctly sums up the circumstances under which physical circumcision will profit or be of value on Judgment Day. He says in effect, "To be sure, your circumcision does identify you with the family of Abraham, the chosen people, which gives you certain advantages and reasons to rejoice on an earthly level (3:1-2; 9:4-5). And there is even a sense in which your physical circumcision can help to usher you into heaven. You will remember that circumcision was incorporated into Moses' Law; therefore your reception of circumcision identifies you with that law and obligates you to keep the whole law (Gal 5:3). Because of this, circumcision viewed as a saving act cannot be separated from obedience to the entire law as the ground of your salvation. Thus we are back to the principle set forth in 2:13 — the doer of the (whole) law will be justified. Thus circumcision can save you 'if you observe the law,' i.e., if it is part of a life of complete and total obedience to the law."

We must be very careful *not* to read into v. 25a any reference to Christian faith or salvation by grace. The false covenant theology created in Reformed circles in the sixteenth century has caused some interpreters to transform "observe the law" into "believe in and live by the gospel" (e.g., Murray, I:85-86). But this misses the whole point. In vv. 25-27 Paul is still talking about the conditions of salvation under law, not grace; and the saving efficacy of law is clearly conditional upon perfect obedience: "*if* you observe the law." As in the earlier parts of this chapter, though, such an accomplishment is treated only as hypothetical. (See Moo, I:164.)

The other side of this coin, which represents reality, is then given: **but if you break the law, you have become as though you had not been circumcised.** "If you break the law" must be seen in light of Gal 3:10 and Gal 5:3, and thus understood as meaning "if you break the law *even once*" (see Jas 2:10). As a lawtruster, if you break just a single commandment, you will be under the curse of God's wrath. Your circumcision will be irrelevant; you will be in exactly the same boat as an uncircumcised person (a Gentile) when he breaks *his* law.

2:26 If those who are not circumcised keep the law's requirements, will they not be regarded as though they were circumcised? Here Paul continues to show the irrelevance of circumcision by showing how it affects the uncircumcised person, the Gentile. In what sense might such a person "keep the law's requirements"? Some say Paul is talking about Gentile Christians and their humble faith and faithful obedience to God under grace (Cranfield, I:173; Murray; I:86). This is a serious mistake, however. As in the previous verse Paul is still talking about final salvation or condemnation on the day of judgment, as determined by the principles of law. *If* a Gentile keeps *all* the righteous ordinances of the law, he will be saved even though he has not been circumcised. This is a conditional statement which never becomes actualized, though, because of the universality of sin.[51]

Paul does not make this statement in order to give the Gentile

---

[51]See Moo, I:166-167, for an excellent defense of this view. He says, for example, "It is impossible that Paul would have described any Christian as having been granted his status as a result of obeying the law."

217

hope under the law. He says it to the Jews, in order to doubly emphasize the irrelevance of circumcision under the judgment of the law. Not only is circumcision impotent as "a certain passport to heaven" (Barrett, 58) for any Jew who has sinned (v. 25), but its absence will not prevent the salvation of any Gentile who obeys every law of which he is aware by means of general revelation (v. 26). This of course would not include circumcision, since the circumcision requirement was known only through special revelation.

The whole point is to show the Jews that, as sinners, it is futile to trust their physical Jewishness as their key to salvation. Physical descent from Abraham, membership in the Abrahamic covenant, physical circumcision, possession of the specially-revealed Mosaic Law — all will be of no avail under law without a perfect record of personal righteousness, which they did not have.

2:27 In the beginning of this verse Paul mentions again the hypothetical Gentile who keeps the law: **The one who is not circumcised physically and yet obeys the law . . . .** That the category is empty is shown by 1:18-32; 3:9.[52] This does not affect Paul's point, though, since the mere possibility that a Gentile could ever sit in judgment on a Jew was an abomination to the Jewish mind. Yet this is exactly what Paul says could happen, in principle: that the obedient Gentile **will condemn you who, even though you have the written code and circumcision, are a lawbreaker.**

The Gentile here is called uncircumcised "by nature" (translated "physically"). This does not mean simply uncircumcised *at birth*, since this is true of everyone, Jew and Gentile alike. The term for "not circumcised" is simply a shorthand for "Gentile," who is indeed *born* a Gentile, while the Israelite is physically a Jew by birth.

The verb κρίνω (*krinō*) probably does have its stronger meaning of "condemn" in this verse, as the NIV says. The obedient Gentile will condemn the disobedient Jews not as a judge as such, but "as a witness for the prosecution" (Cranfield, I:174). It is "probably the indirect judging of comparison. On the day of judgment, the Gentile, with his poor advantages, will condemn, by his superior conduct the lawlessness of the Jew" (MP, 316). In fact, as Lard

---

[52]"We must not suppose that the Gentile, any more than the Jew, ever actually fulfilled the law. This no one did. The case is a hypothetical one" (Lard, 97).

notes (97-98), this will be true even when a Gentile is not perfectly righteous and therefore not saved, but at the same time is relatively more righteous than certain Jews. This may be hinted at in Matt 11:21-22; 12:41-42. "Their obedience to the law itself will stand as accusatory evidence against the disobedient Jew" (Moo, I:168).

Paul says the Jews are transgressors of the law in spite of the fact that they had "the written code and circumcision." These are the two great advantages the Jews had over the Gentiles: the law of God in its objectively written form, not just as subjectively written on the heart (v. 15); and circumcision as the symbol of the great covenant God made with Abraham. Yet in spite of these advantages the Jews sinned against God. In fact, these two great blessings were major instruments of their sin, since the Jews used them and presumed upon them as artificial bases for their hope, thus opening the floodgates of hypocrisy and bringing dishonor upon God. No wonder Paul says the Gentiles will condemn them!

2:28 The point of this main section of Romans is that no one can be saved when judged according to the rules of law. The Jews were willing to accept this as true for everyone except themselves. "This does not apply to us," they thought. Why not? "Because we are *Jews*. We are special. We are Abraham's children. We are circumcised. We have, not just any law, but the Law of Moses. God does not treat us as he treats other people."

In one sense, and on one level, all of this is true. On the physical level God used this one nation of mankind for the greatest mission imaginable: He used them to prepare for the coming of the Messiah, and even to supply his human nature (9:5). Just to *be* a Jew was to be involved in this mission, however marginally.

As I have indicated earlier, the Jews' critical error was to assume that this privileged status with regard to service also gave them a privileged status with regard to salvation. They assumed that their mere physical identity as Jews, marked by circumcision, was all they needed to be right with God. Romans 2 specifically refutes this idea. The picture here is of the Jew, sitting in stunned silence, contemplating the force of what Paul has just said, feeling the confidence he has had in his physical identity as a Jew melting away. We may picture him crying out in desperation, "If Jews are not special, who is? If my circumcision doesn't please God, what does?"

Even though Paul is not quite ready to get into this sort of question in detail, he does pause in these two verses to give us a foretaste of the message of grace.[53] The person who is truly accepted by God, he says, is right with him on a different level — not the flesh, but the spirit. The things that make him special to God are not on the outside, such as physical birth as a Jew, physical circumcision, and mere outward obedience to the law's commands. Rather, they are on the inside, where God alone can see them.

This has always been true, in OT times as well as now in NT times. Paul states this truth specifically for NT times in Phil 3:3, "For it is we who are the circumcision, we who worship by the Spirit of God, who glory in Christ Jesus, and who put no confidence in the flesh . . . ." But since in 2:28-29 Paul is still basically addressing Jews, he makes this point using the terminology of Jewishness. In these verses the word *Jew* is a metaphor for saved persons of all ages. Not all Jews (by birth) are *real* Jews (9:6). Not all circumcised people have had the circumcision that really counts.

A man is not a Jew if he is only one outwardly, nor is circumcision merely outward and physical. This verse is the negative side of Paul's point; it states what true Jewishness is not. It is not based on external circumstances, such as physical birth to Jewish parents. Likewise, the circumcision that counts for eternity is not the outward circumcision of the male genitals.

2:29 No, a man is a Jew if he is one inwardly . . . . Here is the positive description of true Jewishness. "Inwardly" is literally "in secret," which is a way of describing either actions or states of the heart which only God can see (Matt 6:4, 6; Mark 4:22; 1 Cor 14:25; 1 Pet 3:4). In this case it refers to the latter, as the following statement explains: **and circumcision is circumcision of the heart, by the Spirit, not by the written code.**

"The heart" refers to the soul or spirit, the inner man. "By the Spirit" probably refers to the Holy Spirit (as in the NIV), not the human spirit. There is no reason for Paul to mention the human

---

[53]I agree with Moo that "it is likely that Paul is thinking in this verse specifically of Christians. For the first time, then, in Romans 2, Paul alludes explicitly to Christians" (I:172). I think, though, that he is referring not exclusively to Christians, but also to true believers in the OT era as well.

spirit as the locus of this spiritual circumcision since he has already specified this as the heart, which is the same as the human spirit. Circumcision "by the written code" (literally, "by the letter") means physical circumcision in obedience to the commands of the law.

The distinction between external circumcision as the sign of membership in the covenant people, and inward circumcision as that which makes the individual acceptable to God, is found both in the Law of Moses and in the prophets (Deut 10:16; Lev 26:41; Jer 4:4; 9:25-26; Ezek 44:7; see Acts 7:51). There was no inherent connection between the outward and the inward forms of circumcision. Physical circumcision was a prominent and familiar phenomenon in Jewish experience; thus Moses and the prophets found it to be a convenient and appropriate analogy for the inward change God required for acceptance by him. The relation between the two is purely illustrative, and referring to this inward change as "circumcision" is situational and incidental.

In pre-Messianic times the inner circumcision was limited to the individual's own spiritual heart-cleansing, his turning from sin and his surrender to God's will through faith and repentance. A person whose heart was hardened toward God and set on sin was "uncircumcised of heart and ears" (Lev 26:41; Jer 6:10; 9:26; Acts 7:51). God's prophetic word exhorted such people to circumcise their hearts (Deut 10:16; Jer 4:4). In OT times the Holy Spirit was not directly involved in this act of spiritual circumcision; a spiritual circumcision performed by God himself was prophesied as a blessing associated with the Messianic age (Deut 30:6; see Ezek 36:26-27; John 7:37-39).

True circumcision in the Messianic age, in fulfilment of Deut 30:6, includes the working of the Holy Spirit upon our hearts.[54] Since Paul is speaking from the perspective of the Messianic age, he describes this inner circumcision as it takes place now, not as it occurred in the OT era. How does the working of the Spirit make the inner circumcision different in the NT age? On the one hand, it

---

[54]The very fact that Paul refers here to the Spirit's role in this spiritual circumcision shows that he is referring in vv. 28-29 not to law salvation (the letter), but to grace salvation; and it shows that he is including the NT age as well as the OT age.

does *not* change the requirement for the individual to circumcise his own heart (as in Jer 4:4) by surrendering his own will to God in faith and repentance. The Holy Spirit has always been indirectly involved in this human decision as he prods the heart through the inspired Word of God, but the individual must still make the decision for himself. This is nothing new for our time.

On the other hand, the Holy Spirit does add a new element to this spiritual circumcision, a work of salvation unique to the Messianic age. We call it the new birth (John 3:3, 5), regeneration (Titus 3:5), and resurrection from spiritual death (Col 2:12-13). This is an inward change worked directly upon our hearts (see Col 2:11), helping us to cut our ties with sin and to obey God's will from the heart out. (This will be discussed further under chapter 6 below.)

Such a man's praise is not from men, but from God. The true Jew's praise is not from men, because other human beings cannot see the heart, where the true circumcision occurs. Sometimes in our fallible evaluations of others based on externals, we praise or think highly of some individuals whose hearts warrant otherwise. Also, sometimes we ignore or think little of someone whose heart makes him a force for God. It is a comfort to know that the infallible God, who is greater than our hearts and knows all things (1 John 3:20), is able to discern and praise the true Jew, both now and in the final judgment (2:16).

An issue that requires comment is the supposed relevance of this paragraph, especially vv. 28-29, to the question of baptism. The suggestion is that the word "Christian" can be substituted there for "Jew," and the word "baptism" for "circumcision." This suggestion is sometimes based on the supposed equivalence of circumcision and baptism, especially as taught in Reformed theology. Sometimes it comes from the assumption that what Paul says in these verses applies to all externals as such. As Morris says, "Many commentators point out that Christian readers should remember that what is said here of circumcision applies with equal force to baptism" (140). Stott is an example: "What Paul writes here about circumcision and being a Jew could also be said about baptism and being a Christian. The real Christian, like the real Jew, is one inwardly; and the true baptism, like the true circumcision, is in the heart and by the Spirit" (94).

Now, it is true that some church members rest their hope of heaven on the fact that they have been physically baptized, even though their hearts and lives are far from God. In this sense there is a parallel with what Paul says about nominal Jews. Not all those who are *physically* circumcised/baptized are *spiritually* circumcised/baptized.

But here is where the parallel stops. The reason it cannot be pressed further is that, contrary to the widely-held assumption, Christian baptism is *not* the New Covenant equivalent of or successor to Old Covenant circumcision. Concerning the latter, we can say (indeed, it is Paul's point) that physical circumcision can exist without spiritual circumcision, *and* vice versa. The NT does not warrant our saying the same thing about baptism, though. We definitely should say that physical baptism can occur without spiritual baptism (contrary to the view called "baptismal regeneration"). But we cannot be true to NT teaching and say that in ordinary Christian experience spiritual baptism can occur without physical baptism.[55]

We must remember the context in which Paul's remarks are made. He is speaking of true salvation, whether in the OT age or in the NT age; and he is speaking of it as it relates to the Jews' false trust in their physical heritage, especially circumcision. It is a serious mistake to try to draw a general principle from this that would go against every NT comment as to the meaning of baptism. (See my book, *Baptism: A Biblical Study*.)

But what about Col 2:11-12? Does this not show a connection between baptism and circumcision? Actually, no. The only connection here is between the *spiritual* circumcision performed on the repentant believer by the Holy Spirit (v. 11) in the NT era, and the *time* God has appointed for this spiritual circumcision to take place, namely, "in baptism" (v. 12). There is no connection at all between baptism and Old Covenant physical circumcision. In the OT the latter is merely a handy analogy of the spiritual circumcision individuals were exhorted to perform on themselves; and

---

[55]Pentecost (Acts 2) and Cornelius (Acts 10) do not disprove this, because these experiences were not ordinary. They are significant not because of their ordinariness (their imitability, their paradigmatic nature), but because of their exceptionality.

even this self-accomplished OT spiritual circumcision is not equivalent to the Holy Spirit-produced spiritual circumcision of the
Messianic age. Christian baptism was established by God (for one
thing) to be the appointed time when this *new kind* of spiritual circumcision would take place.

F. SUCH EQUAL TREATMENT OF JEWS AND GENTILES
DOES NOT NULLIFY BUT RATHER MAGNIFIES
GOD'S RIGHTEOUSNESS (3:1-8)

This paragraph answers anticipated misunderstandings and
objections especially from Jewish readers, objections growing out of
the things said about the Jews in chapter 2, especially in vv. 25-29.
Here Paul returns to a modified diatribe style, posing questions and
disposing of them with answers that are emphatic and to the point.
They are questions Paul (a former Pharisee) knows are bound to
arise, or which perhaps have already been "flung at him" in earlier
face-to-face discussions with his former brethren (Stott, 95).

The discussion begins with a question about the role of the Jews
in God's plan (vv. 1-2), then quickly moves on to the issue of the
character of God himself (vv. 3-4). The thought is that what Paul
says about the Jews in chapter 2 seems to nullify the apparent
Jewish privilege and exclusiveness enjoyed since Abraham's day,
and this in turn calls into question the truthfulness and faithfulness
of God. Paul's response leads to a series of somewhat frivolous
questions which may be interpreted as one last desperate attempt
at Jewish self-justification (vv. 5-8).

Paul deals with these issues very briefly, knowing that he will
return to them in more detail in chapters 9-11.

**3:1 What advantage, then, is there in being a Jew, or what
value is there in circumcision?** Here, as Dunn says (I:138), "The
slightly agonized cry of Jewish self-identity responds in bewildered
protest" to the teaching of chapter 2. The protester's thought is
this: "If being a Jew gives us no advantage over the Gentiles on
Judgment Day, then what's the big deal about being a Jew at all?
Have we just been spinning our wheels for the last 2,000 years? Are
the covenant and its special sign – circumcision – God's idea of a

practical joke? Or is he just now changing his mind about the Jews? Is he going back on his word? What's the use of being a Jew, then?"

3:2 Paul's answer is brief: **Much in every way! First of all, they have been entrusted with the very words of God.** The Jews' basic problem was the assumption that their election to God's service gave them a kind of automatic pass to heaven. Chapter 2 shows that this was false. But here Paul explains that even though this was not the case, there were many great and glorious privileges shared by every person born into Abraham's covenant family, whether he will ultimately be saved or not. The Jews' advantage is "much in many a way" (Lard, 101).

How are we to understand "first of all"? Ordinarily the word "first" (πρῶτον, *prōton*) indicates the first of a series of events or the first item in a longer list, leading us to expect other items to follow. However, Paul mentions only this one advantage. This has caused some to interpret *prōton* to mean "first in importance, chiefly" (KJV; Calvin, 113). This seems inappropriate, though, since even what Paul mentions here could hardly exceed in importance the Jews' ultimate privilege of bringing the Messiah into the world (9:5). We conclude that Paul does intend to present a longer series of advantages, but decides not to list them at this point. He waits instead until 9:4-5.

The one advantage mentioned here is that the Jews "have been entrusted with the very words of God." It is important in this context to stress this point, even if reference to the others can be delayed until later. This is because of what Paul has just said about the Law of Moses in chapter 2, namely, that mere possession of this specially-revealed law was no basis for any Jew's personal salvation. Does this mean that the Jews' possession of God's special revelation was a trivial and inconsequential thing? No! On the contrary, it is a unique and glorious privilege, and one that is appropriately emphasized at this juncture.

What are the "very words of God" with which the Jews were entrusted? The Greek term is λόγιον, (*logion*), used here in the plural with the definite article. (See also Acts 7:38; Heb 5:12; 1 Pet 4:11.) In classical Greek this term was used for divine utterances, or oracles supposedly spoken by the gods through their inspired messengers. This is surely the sense in which Paul is using it here to rep-

resent the inspired utterances of the true God. It is variously translated as "the oracles of God" (KJV, NEB, NASB, NRSV), "the words
of God" (NAB), and "God's messages" (Phillips). It is basically equivalent to *ho logos tou theou*, "the word of God," and occurs in this
sense often in the LXX, especially in Ps 119. The NIV translation is
excellent. It is proper to understand it as referring to the entire
written OT, the "Holy Scriptures" (1:2) as possessed by the Jews.[56]

That *ta logia tou theou* is referring to the written OT is shown by
Paul's assertion that these oracles were "entrusted" into the care of
the Jews. Murray rightly says, "It is as Scripture that these oracles
were committed to the Jews; only in this form could the *Jews* be said
to have been *entrusted* with them" (I:93). To be entrusted with
something means to be given possession of it in order to see that it
is protected and put to proper use.[57] That the Jews were "entrusted"
with the OT means that God chose them to receive his special revelation in written form, and he charged them with being its
guardians or custodians. They were God's chosen stewards of this
exceedingly precious gift to mankind; they were "entrusted with the
stewardship of safeguarding and preserving" it until the time for its
fulfillment should come (Dunn, I:138).

To be entrusted with the oracles of God gave the Jews a privilege and an advantage that far surpassed anything enjoyed by the
Gentiles, who knew the Creator and his law through general revelation only. (See Deut 4:8; Ps 147:19-20.) Because they had his special
revelation also, the Jews knew God not just as Creator, Lawgiver,
and Judge, but also as a loving Savior. They knew not only his law,
but also his grace; and they had the blessed opportunity to believe
in his promise of forgiveness.

Of special importance is the fact that the Jews knew God's
intention to send a Messiah, a Redeemer. They possessed the many
predictive prophecies of his coming, and they nurtured the hope
for his appearing. Thus those who happened to be living at the
time of his coming would be the first to know him and to have the

---

[56]Cranfield, I:179; Godet, 133; Moo, I:182; Morris, 154; Murray, I:154;
Stott, 96.

[57]For comparison see other uses of this term in 1 Cor 9:17; Gal 2:7;
1 Thess 2:4; 1 Tim 1:11.

opportunity to believe in him and receive his salvation (1:16). Who could ask for greater advantages than these?

3:3 But [w]hat if some did not have faith? Will their lack of faith nullify God's faithfulness? These questions reflect the fact that many if not most[58] Jews did not in fact put their saving faith in God's gracious promises in Old Covenant times, and did not believe in their Messiah when he came. Some did have faith (and thus were true Jews in terms of 2:29), but most did not.

The words translated "did not have faith" and "lack of faith" can also mean "were unfaithful" and "unfaithfulness." Some (e.g., Dunn, I:131-132; Hendriksen, I:110) think the context favors the latter meaning. This would mean that (some) Jews were unfaithful to their covenant obligations; they were unfaithful to their duties as stewards of the oracles of God. However, others take these words in their more usual sense of "disbelieve" and "unbelief" (e.g., Cranfield, I:180; Murray, I:94). This latter view is preferred, since belief and unbelief are key themes in Romans.[59]

The point is that the Jews through their stewardship of the *logia* of God had God's covenant promises all along, but many of them habitually, generation after generation, refused to put their heart's trust in these promises. Then when the prophecies and promises of the Messiah were fulfilled in Jesus Christ, many of Paul's Jewish contemporaries refused to believe in him.

This reality of Jewish unbelief raises the question or possible objection concerning God's faithfulness. Does the unbelief of some Jews mean that God's covenant purposes have failed? Does God's condemnation of the Jews who do not believe (strongly implied in the preceding chapters, especially in 1:5, 16; 2:28-29) mean that he is breaking his promise to them and thus proving to be unfaithful? As Morris (152) words the objection, "Since God has promised to bless his people, he must do this irrespective of what the Jews do"; otherwise he is not being faithful to his promise.

---

[58]Paul says "some," but it is clear from other places, e.g., chs. 9-11, that he includes most of his contemporary countrymen in this number. See Dunn, I:131; Moo, I:183.

[59]The question of Jewish unbelief is a major theme in chs. 9-11, where Paul takes up the subject of 3:1-4 in greater detail. See especially 9:32-33; 10:16; 11:20, 23.

The word for God's "faithfulness" is πίστις (*pistis*), which in reference to human beings can mean either faith or faithfulness. Since there is no legitimate sense in which God can be said to have faith, it is properly understood here as faithfulness. The word for "nullify" is καταργέω, (*katargeō*), which has a strong meaning ("abolish, destroy"; see 1 Cor 6:13; 15:26; Eph 2:15), and a weaker meaning ("nullify, make ineffective, render powerless"; see 3:31; 4:14; 6:6). The latter is intended here, as the NIV has it.

The fact that Paul includes in this question the Greek particle μή (*mē*) shows that he expects a negative answer: "The unbelief of some Jews does not mean that God is unfaithful, does it?" Thus even before he gives his strong negative reply in v. 4, he shows what the answer will be. The sense of the verse as a whole, as Cranfield says (I:181), "is that it is unthinkable that God's faithfulness to his covenant with Israel should be rendered ineffective even by the Jews' unbelief."

3:4 Is God unfaithful? **Not at all!** This is Paul's first use of the strong negative expression, μὴ γένοιτο, (*mē genoito*),[60] literally, "May it not be!" It is usually translated with a strong English colloquialism, as in the NIV.[61] This is an emphatic "No!" answer to the preceding question.

Let God be true, and every man a liar. The verb "be" is γίνομαι (*ginomai*), which usually means "to become." Since God's nature does not undergo change, we take this to mean, "Let it become evident or obvious that God is always true" (Lard, 102), or "Let God be recognized as true." God is always reliable, faithful and true to his word. He always keeps his promises, both for blessing and condemnation. Because of his very nature he cannot lie (Titus 1:2).

The NIV connects this clause to the next with the simple copulative, "and." This does not properly reflect the stated contrast. Instead it should read "though" (NASB), "although" (NRSV), "even

---

[60]See 3:6, 31; 6:2, 15; 7:7, 13; 9:14; 11:1, 11. See also 1 Cor 6:15; Gal 2:17; 3:21.

[61]Other translations and suggestions are "God forbid!" (KJV); "By no means!" (6:2; RSV; NRSV); "Certainly not!" (3:6; 7:7); "Never!" (1 Cor 6:15; Moffatt); "Of course not!" (Phillips); "Absolutely not!" (Gal 2:17; 3:21); "May it never be!" (NASB).

though," or "even if." The idea is that we should always acknowledge that God is true, even if every human being turns out to be a liar (see Ps 116:11). This does not refer to some specific lie, such as the Jews' denial of Jesus' messiahship. It is rather a general principle about the susceptibility of all men to lying and unfaithfulness.

Paul then quotes the second half of Ps 51:4, following the Septuagint: **As it is written: "So that you may be proved right when you speak and prevail when you judge."** In the Psalm this statement follows David's confession of his sin with Bathsheba, "Against you, you only have I sinned and done what is evil in your sight . . . ." Why does the second half of the verse (quoted by Paul) begin with "so that"? Is David saying that the very *purpose* of his *sin* is to prove God to be true and just (Stott, 96)? Hardly. Rather, he is saying that the purpose of his *confession* is to prove that the sentence of condemnation God pronounced upon him (2 Sam 12:9-14) is justified (Hendriksen, I:111-112; Moo, I:198-199).

The word for "proved true" is δικαιόω (*dikaioō*), usually translated "justified" (NASB) and a key word in the doctrine of salvation. Its use in this verse helps establish its precise meaning as "declared righteous" rather than "made righteous," since we cannot *make* God righteous though we can acknowledge and declare him to be righteous (see the parallel in Luke 7:29). "When you speak" is literally "in your words." In the Psalm David is saying that God cannot be faulted for his words of condemnation against him. Paul gives the statement a more general application, saying that *whenever* God speaks, he will be proved right and his words will be found true.

The last line in the verse is difficult, since the Hebrew for "judge" is active voice, while the LXX and Romans 3:4 appear to be passive. Thus the NIV (incorrectly) says, "when you judge," while the NASB says, "when Thou art judged." It is likely that neither is exactly correct, and that the verb (κρίνεσθαι, *krinesthai*) should be taken as being in the middle voice: "When you go to law" (Moo, I:187), "When you contend in a law-suit" (Cranfield, I:182). Thus the statement can apply both ways: God always prevails when he brings suit against another, as in the case of David; and he always prevails when someone brings suit against him, as his Jewish accusers are doing in this paragraph. As Bruce says (96), God always wins his case when he enters into judgment.

This verse has two main applications. First, we must not ignore its implications for the nature of God's word in general, and especially for the nature of the Bible. Because it is the Word of God, the Bible will always prove to be true. Critics are constantly taking God to court, as it were, accusing his word of containing errors. But they will always be proved wrong, and God's word will always be vindicated.

The more specific application is Paul's main point, that God's promises to Israel will be fulfilled even if every individual Jew is unfaithful to God. Even if every Jew rejects God and is condemned to hell, God will still be faithful and his covenant will be fulfilled. This is so because God's covenant purpose for Israel did not guarantee the salvation of individual Jews. The basic covenant promise was not to individuals as such, but to Israel as a *nation*. The promise was not that all Jews would be saved, but that through the nation the *Messiah* would come. God promised to bless and preserve the nation as a nation *until* the Messiah came, but not beyond that. (See GRe, 391-395.) This is exactly what he did, and thus he was true to his word and covenant in every way.

3:5 Beginning in this verse Paul sets forth and replies to several anticipated objections to (misunderstandings of, false inferences from) his point in 3:3-4, speaking from the standpoint of the Jewish objectors. Here is the first objection: **But if our unrighteousness brings out God's righteousness more clearly, what shall we say? That God is unjust in bringing his wrath on us?** "Our unrighteousness" is the Jews' unbelief (v. 3), though the point would apply in principle to the sin and unbelief of all men (see 1:18). "God's righteousness" in this case is not the gift of righteousness of which 1:17 speaks, but God's own righteous character in contrast with the unrighteous character of sinners. To say that God is righteous means that his deeds are always consistent with his nature and his words (GRe, 194-196). This includes much more than his faithfulness to his covenant promises, and is not limited to his promises to bless and deliver his people. It also means God is true to his holy nature and to the ensuing necessity for punishing unbelievers.

The objector suggests that our unrighteousness "brings out more clearly" God's righteousness. This is an implication from v. 4a, "Let God be true, and every man a liar." The idea is that every

sin of man forms a dark background upon which the corresponding divine virtue shines forth in contrasting brilliance and glory.
This is definitely true, but "what shall we say" about it? That is,
what conclusions might we draw from this? The false inference suggested by the Jewish objector is this: "If our sin magnifies God's
righteousness, this is to his advantage and glory, and thus he really
ought to reward us rather than condemn us. And if this is so, then
God's condemnation of us is really unjust."

This question seems to reflect the Jews' refusal to come to grips
with the point Paul made in chapter 2, that sinful Jews cannot be
saved simply by being Jews, contrary to their misguided assumptions. It is another futile effort to avoid God's judgment, and one
that has no merit whatsoever. This is shown by the way Paul words
the question. He again uses the particle *mē*, anticipating a negative
answer: "We really can't say that God is unrighteous when he
inflicts wrath, can we?" This reflects the fact that all sinners know in
their hearts that they really do deserve God's wrath.

(I am using a human argument.) Paul is here making it clear
that he is not speaking for himself or for the Holy Spirit, and that
he regards the question as the product of faulty human thinking.
His statement is "a parenthetic apology for having presented . . . a
thought which is all too human in its weakness and folly," and it
underlines his own repudiation of the thought (Cranfield, I:184).

3:6 Paul then gives his standard emphatic reply, **Certainly not!**
(*mē genoito*), and words a brief reason for this answer: **If that were
so, how could God judge the world?** What is his point here? One
possibility is that he is stating a *reductio ad absurdum* argument. That
is, if we grant the objection in the case of the Jews, we would have
to grant it in the case of everybody ("the world"), since everyone
else's sins also cause God's righteousness to stand out all the more.
But this is absurd, because we know there *will* be a judgment, and
that the wicked will be condemned. (See Lard, 104.)

A better understanding is that Paul is saying the question is
absurd simply because "to impugn God's justice is to undercut his
competence to judge" (Stott, 97). An unjust God is simply not
worthy of judging the world. This is why the fact "that God who
shall judge the world is just is a fundamental certainty of all theological thinking" (Cranfield, I:185). Abraham sums up this intuition:

"Will not the Judge of all the earth do right?" (Gen 18:25; see Job 34:17). Indeed, if God were not just and righteous, why would he even *want* to judge the world? Thus the objection is worthless.

3:7 But the objector persists: **Someone might argue, "If my falsehood enhances God's truthfulness and so increases his glory, why am I still condemned as a sinner?"** This is basically a restatement of the objection in v. 5, as if the debater just refuses to give up on this point. The contrast between God's truthfulness and man's lies (see v. 4) is representative of the general contrast between the holy God and sinful man. The argument is still the same as before: "How can it be fair for a man to be blamed for his falsehood, when it has actually redounded to God's glory?" (Cranfield, I:185). Morris' comment is to the point: "We sinners display incredible ingenuity when we try to justify ourselves" (161).

3:8 Verse 8 asks another question: **Why not say . . . "Let us do evil that good may result"?** This can be taken two ways. Some see it as the Jewish objector's continuation of the point he tries to make in v. 7, as he presses it to its logical and general conclusion. This, says Moo (I:194-195), is the best understanding of the word "and" (καὶ, *kai*), which begins the verse, though untranslated by the NIV. One problem with this view is that it leaves the objection basically unanswered, unless v. 6 serves as a reply to both v. 5 and vv. 7-8a (Murray, I:99). This would be somewhat obscure, though. Moo says the very absurdity of the suggestion shows it does not deserve a reply (I:195).

It is better to take this question in another way, namely, as Paul's own question, in which he states the logical yet absurd outcome of both v. 5 and v. 7. Thus the objection in v. 7 does have a response, and this is it (Cranfield, I:187). The force of the question is this: "Well, if that [v. 7] is the case, then we might just as well say, 'Let us do evil that good may result' — which we all know is absolutely ridiculous." Again, the question begins with the particle *mē*, which implies a negative answer.

This question is basically a statement of the principle that "the end justifies the means." This verse is a repudiation of that principle.

Paul notes parenthetically that he himself was being accused of teaching this lie: **as we are being slanderously reported as saying and as some claim that we say . . . .** A clear presentation of the gospel of grace sounds so radical to most people that they may indeed assume it implies a kind of indifference to obedience. As far as Paul himself was concerned, "experience had shown that his proclamation of the gospel could be perverted in an antinomian direction" (Thielman, *Paul*, 176). Here Paul calls this accusation slander or blasphemy. In chapter 6 he discusses this inference in more detail and clearly shows it is not validly derived from the gospel.

Their condemnation is deserved. Of whom is Paul speaking? Perhaps those (the "some") who are slandering him, but more likely those who are pressing the absurd objection voiced in vv. 5 and 7 (Murray, I:98). It is not enough that Paul ridicules their view by showing its logical yet absurd end; now he turns his indignation upon the objectors themselves.

This is a fitting conclusion to this subsection (2:1-3:8). In chapter 2 Paul declares that the Jews are without excuse before God. They assumed their possession and knowledge of the Law of Moses, plus their physical descent from Abraham marked by circumcision, would be sufficient to save them in the final judgment. Paul says no: God will not be partial to the Jews. Anyone counting on law as his mode of salvation can be saved only by perfect obedience, and the Jews are *sinners* like everyone else. Therefore under law they stand *condemned* like everyone else. Their convoluted arguments (3:1-7) do nothing to alter this judgment. If anything, such twisted thinking only serves to demonstrate the fact that their condemnation is quite deserved. As Dunn paraphrases this last statement, "They deserve what's coming to them" (I:137).

III. 3:9-20 – UNIVERSAL SINFULNESS AND HOPELESSNESS UNDER LAW

Paul's main point in the first main section of Romans is to show that no one can be saved by law or law-keeping. Only a perfect person can hope to be accepted by God under the law system. The sad fact is that no such person exists. Every person is a law-breaker and is thus without hope under law.

In the first two main points of this section Paul has dealt with the two alleged exceptions to this rule: the Gentiles, or those without special revelation (1:18-32); and the Jews, or those who do have special revelation (2:1-3:8). Now in this final point (3:9-20) he pulls all of this together and draws his intended conclusion. He reaffirms the reality of universal sinfulness (v. 9), provides OT confirmation of it (vv. 10-18), and stresses the impotence of law as the result of it (vv. 19-20).

3:9 What shall we conclude then? Literally, "What then?" The NIV rightly takes this short phrase as introducing the conclusion of this section. **Are we any better? Not at all!** This brief passage of three Greek words is very difficult and is open to several interpretations. Three questions must be answered. First, whom is Paul including in the "we"? Does he mean "we Jews"? This is the most common understanding, and is based on the probability that the whole previous section (2:1-3:8) refers particularly to the Jews. Several interpreters believe Paul means "we Christians," however.[62] Cranfield says it means "we human beings in general" (I:147).

Second, what does the verb (προεχόμεθα, *proechometha*) mean? In the active voice it means "surpass, excel, be superior to, have an advantage, have a head start." But here it is either middle or passive voice. Seen as passive, it would mean, "Are we surpassed? Are we at a disadvantage?" Seen as middle, it would mean, "Are we trying to excuse ourselves? Are we trying to put forward a defense?" Another possibility is that it has a middle form but an active meaning: "Do we excel? Are we any better (off)? Do we have any advantage?"

Third, how should we interpret the negative phrase, οὐ πάντως (*ou pantōs*)? Some say it is an emphatic negative: "Not at all! Certainly not! By no means!" But the word order lends itself to another interpretation: "Not entirely," or "Not in every respect."

It is obvious that the above variables could be combined in many ways. E.g., "Do we human beings have any defense? None whatsoever!" "Are we Christians any better off than the Jews and Gentiles? Not at all!" "Are we Jews at a disadvantage, then, in light of 3:4-8? No, you are still no worse off than the Gentiles." "Do we Jews have an advantage, then? In light of 3:1-2, you have an advantage in one way, but not in *every* way." "Do we Jews have an advantage, then? None at all!"

---

[62]See Morris, 165; MacArthur, I:180; Lenski, 227-228.

The fact is that any of these views is compatible with Paul's main point; but in light of the context and the flow of his argument, either of the last two views is preferred. As the next sentence shows, in this whole section Paul has been using the two categories of Jews and Gentiles as inclusive of the entire human race. Of these two groups, Paul naturally identifies himself with the former. Also, a comparison seems to be in view, i.e., between the two groups. Thus: "Are we Jews any better off than the Gentiles?"

This query is stimulated by 3:1-2, where Paul affirms that the Jews have a great advantage over the Gentiles, especially in their possession of the oracles of God. Just so no one will misunderstand, Paul asks this question in v. 9 so that he can reemphasize the point made in chapter 2. That is, no matter what privileges the Jews may have enjoyed in relation to their unique role as the people through whom the Messiah would come, in reference to sin and judgment and their standing before God, they have no advantage whatsoever.

Paul's next sentence shows that this is the main point: **We have already made the charge that Jews and Gentiles alike are all under sin.** Thus the Jews have no "superior standing of righteousness" in the eyes of God (Hendriksen, I:120). With reference to sin and guilt the Jews are on the same level as the Gentiles. Paul has already made this charge against the Gentiles in 1:18-32 and against the Jews in 2:1-29.

"Made the charge" is a legal term that refers to the act of filing charges against someone, or accusing them before a court of law. He has charged both Jews and Greeks (used in the sense of non-Jews, or Gentiles) of being "under sin." To be "under sin" is more than just committing sins; it is more than just being a sinner. It means to be under the power and dominion of sin. Sin is thus represented as a slave master, "a power controlling man" (Cranfield, I:191); and sinners are seen as "helpless slaves to the power of sin" (Moo, I:204). See 6:16-22 for further reflection on this idea.

The main point of this summary statement is the emphasis on *universality*. Paul says "*both* Jews and Gentiles are *all* under sin," with no exceptions. As Dunn says, this "sums up the overall conclusion of 1:18-3:8" (I:148). Thus we have "Paul's own comment on his purpose in this section of his letter" (Moo, I:203). He will draw his final conclusion from this universality of sin in vv. 19-20.

3:10 In v. 9 Paul says he has "made the charge" that all are under sin. Now in vv. 10-18 he offers proof of this charge in the form of citations from Scripture: **As it is written**. These words introduce a "quotation-chain" (Hendriksen, I:121) of fourteen short and sharp statements from several places in the OT. The first six (vv. 10-12) are general affirmations of the sinfulness of all men. The next four (vv. 13-14) reinforce these general statements by emphasizing sins of the tongue, or the spoken word. The next three (vv. 15-17) zero in on sins of violent acts. The last one (v. 18) gives the root cause of all such sins.

The quotations are not verbatim but are usually quite close to the LXX and give the general meaning of the texts cited. In their original OT contexts some of these statements had a limited application,[63] but Paul applies them to all people in general. It is especially significant that he applies them to the *Jews* as well as to the Gentiles, since a major "object of these citations is to prove the undoubted guilt of the Jews" (Lard, 108).

"There is no one righteous, not even one . . . ." (From Eccl 7:20; see Ps 14:1.) Here the word "righteous" (δίκαιος, *dikaios*) is used in its basic sense of "conforming to a norm." The norm to which every human being must conform is the law of God, in whatever form it is available and relevant to him. This text says that *no one* is righteous; no one has conformed to this norm; everyone has broken God's law; everyone has sinned (3:23). That is, no one is righteous in an absolute sense, in the sense of sinless perfection, which is the only way we could be accepted by God on the basis of our own righteousness. Thus the need for the gift of righteousness revealed and offered in the gospel (1:17).[64]

3:11 "there is no one who understands . . . ." (From Ps 14:2; 53:2.) No creature can have infinite knowledge and know all possible truth about God. However, God gives every human being sufficient knowledge of himself and his law, even through general revelation

---

[63]See v. 13, for example, where the quotations originally referred to the Psalmists' enemies.

[64]On the distinction between absolute and relative righteousness, see GRe, 201-209. The Bible often speaks of people who are righteous in a relative sense, when compared with "the wicked." But no one is righteous when compared with the standard of God's law.

(1:18-21; 2:14-15). This is the kind of understanding to which this texts refers. The problem is that no one receives this knowledge with a pure and open heart (Jer 17:9); hardness of heart leads to darkened understanding and willful ignorance (Eph 4:18). We tend to suppress the truth in favor of foolish and futile speculations (1:18, 21), and exchange truth for lies (1:25). This is a universal problem; everyone is guilty of it to some degree.

There is **"no one who seeks God."** (From Ps 14:2; 53:2.) Since "seeking for God" presupposes a state of separation from God, it is something only sinners need to do. But the sinner's guilt causes him to run away from God (v. 12) and attempt to hide from him (Gen 3:8; Rev 6:15-17). In the light of 1:21-25, we understand that even the many false religions of the world are not efforts to *seek* God, but efforts to *escape* from him (MacArthur, I:184). Thus if any are to be saved, God must take the initiative and seek sinners, which he does through special providence, special revelation, and the redeeming work of Jesus Christ (Luke 19:10).

3:12 "All have turned away" from God. (From Ps 14:3; 53:3.) As previously mentioned, it is characteristic of sinners to turn *from* God rather than toward him. The verb (ἐκκλίνω, *ekklinō*) means to avoid or to deliberately turn away, not just to accidentally lose one's way (Morris, 167). See 16:17; 1 Pet 3:11. "We all, like sheep, have gone astray, each of us has turned to his own way" (Isa 53:6).

"they have together become worthless . . . ." (From Ps 14:3; 53:3.) As sinners, all have become unprofitable or useless. The Greek word translates a Hebrew word used to describe milk that has turned sour and thus cannot be used for its intended purpose. Likewise sinners have lost their usefulness and cannot fulfill their intended purpose of bringing glory to God. They are like milk that has turned sour, fruit that has rotted, or meat than has gone bad.

"there is no one who does good, not even one . . . ." (From Ps 14:1, 3; 53:1, 3.) "Good" here refers to acts of obedience to God and acts of kindness toward one's fellow men. This does not mean that no one *ever* does acts of goodness; it means that no one *always* does them. There is no one who does good, and *only* good. The universality of this indictment is underscored by the addition of "not even one." This is an appropriate way to end the series of six quotations that emphasize this universality.

3:13 "Their throats are open graves . . . ." (From Ps 5:9.) After a series of statements about the general sinfulness of mankind, Paul now begins to cite OT verses that refer to specific representative sins as illustrations of the general point. This citation is the first of four that focus on "the sinfulness of human speech" (Moo, I:206). A grave contains the rotting and putrid remains of a corpse; when it is opened, it emits a horrible stench. The sinner's throat (λάρυγξ, *larynx*) is like this grave. When he opens it to speak, all sorts of ugly, rotten, obscene words pour forth. (See Eph 4:29.) This follows Jesus' specific teaching in Matt 12:34: "Out of the overflow of the heart the mouth speaks" (see Matt 12:35; 15:18-20). Nothing reveals the state of the heart more consistently than how a person talks. A rotten heart produces rotten speech.

"their tongues practice deceit." (From Ps 5:9.) This reads "They smoothed their tongues" in the Hebrew, says Robertson (345). That is, their speech is filled with smooth, oily talk, "the deceptive flatteries of those who intend evil" (Moo, I:206). In Scripture the tongue is commonly linked with speech and especially with lying and evil talk (see Prov 6:17; 12:19; Micah 6:12; Jas 1:26; 3:1-12).

"The poison of vipers is on their lips." (From Ps 140:3.) Understanding this to refer to the Egyptian cobra, Robertson says, "The poison of the asp lies in a bag under the lips" (345). This vivid analogy refers to those who use their words to destroy others, e.g., through lies, false accusations, slander, or gossip. Such words are like the poisonous venom of a snake.

3:14 "Their mouths are full of cursing and bitterness." (From Ps 10:7.) To curse someone is to verbally call for harm to befall him. It usually springs from a heart that is full of bitterness or hostility or anger toward that person. The sinner's heart is "full of" such bitter curses, i.e., it is not just an exception but is typical of his lifestyle in general.

Some have suggested that v. 13 refers to evil speech directed against mankind, while this verse refers to evil speech directed against God. There is no real basis for such limitations, though. The "cursing" mentioned here is likely directed toward both, though the context of Ps 10:7 particularly refers to harm done to others.

3:15 "Their feet are swift to shed blood . . . ." (From Isa 59:7.)
This and the next two citations stress sinners' evil deeds, even to
the point of shedding blood in violent assault and murder. Here
the focus shifts from the organs of speech to the feet, the means of
mobility by which a person is able to put his purposes into action.
Being "swift" to shed blood suggests that such evil is carried out
with eagerness and perverse delight.

3:16 "ruin and misery mark their ways . . . ." (From Isa 59:7.)
This highlights the depravity of the sinner's heart by describing the
wreckage he leaves in his wake. He pursues his selfish desires and
purposes with no concern for others and without caring how he
may be harming them. The picture is that of a village devastated by
a killer hurricane that has passed through. "Ruin" describes the
shattered wreckage itself; "misery" refers to the pain and suffering
experienced by those over whom the sinner has run roughshod.
"Wherever they go, they leave behind them a trail of destruction
and misery" (Cranfield, I:195).

3:17 "and the way of peace they do not know." (From Isa 59:8.)
"Peace" here is not primarily a state of inner peace, or peace with
God. In line with the previous citations, it seems to be talking about
peace and harmony among men, or human beings getting along
with each other. Living in peace is something sinners do not know
how to do, says Paul. Their way is "discord and strife" (Lard, 110).

3:18 "There is no fear of God before their eyes." (From Ps
36:1.) The "fear of God" in the sense of reverence and awe toward
the Creator should be the most fundamental attitude of the human
heart. The "fear of God" in the sense of terror and dread before
the Lawgiver and Judge should be the most immediate effect of sin
upon the sinner's heart. But this citation says the sinner is charac-
teristically devoid of both.[65]

"Before their eyes" probably means the eyes of the heart (see
Eph 1:18), or the spiritual consciousness. The analogy is appropriate, because as Cranfield says, by his eyes "a man directs his steps.
So to say that there is no fear of God before his eyes is a figurative
way of saying that the fear of God has no part in directing his life,
that God is left out of his reckoning, that he is a practical, whether

---

[65]For a complete discussion of the fear of God, see GC, 443-467.

or not he is a theoretical, atheist" (I:195). "To be destitute of the fear of God is to be godless, and no indictment could be more inclusive and decisive," says Murray (I:104-105). It is "the very essence of their sinfulness" (Cranfield, I:195), "the root error that gives rise to the manifold sins of humanity" (Moo, I:207). Thus this indictment is appropriate as the conclusion of the list of quotations used by Paul to prove the universal sinfulness of man.

The total picture of mankind drawn here is very dark and somber indeed. But while it shows that every knowing person is definitely under the power of sin (v. 9), it does not mean that all individuals are *equally* guilty of all the vices here named (the same as for the Gentiles in 1:18-32). Nor does it provide support for the Calvinist doctrine of *total depravity* contrary to the claims of Stott (101). This passage demonstrates the reality of depraved behavior and depraved hearts, to be sure, but there is nothing here to suggest that even the worst of sinners cannot be convicted by the gospel and respond to it in repentant faith (1:17; 10:17). That and that alone would be the essence of total depravity.

3:19 Now we know that whatever the law says, it says to those who are under the law . . . . This verse and the next are crucial, since they draw the conclusion toward which the whole first section has been pointing. Also, a right understanding of this first half of v. 19 is crucial for a proper understanding of the two verses as a whole.

"We know" does not specify a particular group; it is simply a way of introducing an item of common knowledge, a generally-accepted principle. It is equivalent to "everybody knows." In this context it means "Everyone who is spiritually informed knows."

What is it that everybody knows? That whatever "the law" says is relevant only to those who are subject to that law. This is a general principle and applies to every sort of jurisdiction, large or small. The ordinances of one local township apply only to those who live or visit there. The building codes of one county do not apply in other counties. The laws of the U.S.A. apply to everyone who is within its borders.

What law or jurisdiction does Paul have in mind here? Many will immediately think of the Law of Moses, since Paul is especially concerned to demonstrate the sinfulness of the Jews. But most commentators take him to mean the OT in general, since he has just quoted from the wisdom literature and the prophets. Indeed, the same phrase (without the definite article) is used in 2:12 to refer to the special revelation given to the Jews.

In my opinion, though, the term "law" in this verse and the next has an even broader scope than this. Because of the absolute, universal language used in these two verses, I believe it refers to God's law in a very general sense, including (1) the demands and judgments of the OT as it speaks to the Jews; (2) the requirements of the "work of the law" written on the hearts of all, including the Gentiles; and (3) the requirements for holy living revealed in the NT Scriptures. This view is supported by the contrasting phrase in 3:21, "apart from law." There "law" cannot be equated with either the Mosaic Law or the OT as such, since it is distinguished from "the Law and the Prophets" (i.e., the OT).

What, then, does it mean to be "under the law"? The phrase is actually ἐν νόμῳ, (en nomō, see 2:12), which means "in the law, within the law, within the sphere of the law" (see Moo, I:200). A similar phrase is ὑπο νόμον, (hypo nomon), literally "under the law" (6:14-15; 1 Cor 9:20; Gal 3:23; 4:4-5, 21; 5:18). Only the context of each passage can determine if nomos means the OT law specifically or God's law more generally. Here, as we have seen, it means the latter. To be "within the sphere of God's law" in 3:19 basically means first of all to be subject to its commands and penalties. But more significantly it means to be under the system of law as a standard of judgment and a means of being right with God.

What group of people is meant, then, by "those who are under the law"? Since most interpreters say "law" here means the OT, they say Paul is referring only to the Jews. Murray (I:106-107) and Hendriksen (I:124) agree that "law" means the OT, but they declare that it applies to both Jews and Gentiles. This application is correct, but "law" here is God's law in any form (in the heart, in the OT, in the NT). Thus "those who are under the law" are indeed both Jews and Gentiles, or all people in general.

Thus "whatever the law says" is addressed to all. Exactly what does the law say to us? It is taken for granted that it speaks God's will in the form of commandments. It has been established that the law also says that commandment-breakers are worthy of death

241

(1:32). Those who break the commandments will suffer the penalty of the law; those who keep the commandments will escape that penalty (2:7-10). In this immediate context Paul refers to the point made by the series of quotations in vv. 10-18, i.e., the law of God says that everyone — EVERYONE — is a sinner.

This is relevant to the Jews, to be sure, since they considered themselves as exceptions to the rule that no one can be saved by law. But they are not the only ones who need convincing on this point. The whole world has the tendency to view salvation in terms of making oneself acceptable to God by one's own efforts (GRe, ch. 3). Thus this passage speaks out "against every attempt at self-salvation" (Stott, 104).

. . . **so that every mouth may be silenced and the whole world held accountable to God.** The word for "so that" is ἵνα (*hina*), which expresses purpose but also result. The reason why God's law stresses the reality of universal sinfulness is "so that every mouth may be silenced." The word for "silenced" evokes a courtroom scene in which the accused defendant is unable to respond to the charges brought against him (Cranfield I:196-197). See Ps 63:11; 107:42. When confronted by the evidence every person is "silenced by the indictment of being absolutely guilty and unable to make even the least defense" (Lenski, 241).

"*Every* mouth" means every individual, whether Jew or Gentile. Paul has already shown that the Gentiles (those with general revelation only) are "without excuse" (1:20), and that the Jews (those with special revelation also) are also "without excuse" (2:1). This is the sense in which every mouth is silenced. The same universal language is used in the next clause: the "whole world," without exception.

"Held accountable" translates ὑπόδικος, (*hypodikos*), used only here in the NT. "Accountable" is really too weak a translation, since it does not necessarily imply guilt. We are all accountable for our deeds, whether we actually do anything wrong or not. But *hypodikos* refers to someone who *has* done something wrong and has been brought before the court to answer for it.[66] The picture, says Cranfield, is "of men standing at God's bar, their guilt proven beyond all possibility of doubt, awaiting God's sentence of condemnation" (I:197).

---

[66]See Maurer, "ὑπόδικος," 557-558.

The law reveals that all are accountable "to God" or guilty "before God" (dative case). In secular Greek the dative is used after *hypodikos* "for the court one comes before or more commonly the person to whom the right of complaint belongs" (Maurer, "ὑπόδικος," 557). In God's court, he is both the accuser (the One wronged) and the judge (Moo, I:208).

All in all, Paul represents all humanity as sinners under the law who are standing in a hopelessly terrifying situation. Why does he make this point? In order to show the universal need for grace, for the gift of God's righteousness.

3:20 Therefore no one will be declared righteous in his sight by observing the law . . . . Here Paul draws the conclusion toward which this whole section has been pointing: the impotence of the law as a way of being right with God. This is "the grand conclusion for which the Apostle has been preparing the mind of his readers" (Lard, 112). The word "therefore" (διότι, *dioti*) refers back not just to v. 19 but to the whole section, 1:18-3:19. "Therefore," given what has been established in this section as a whole, it is plain that "no one will be declared righteous in his sight by observing the law." The only way to be saved by law-keeping is through perfect obedience, but all have sinned. Thus, as Bruce well puts it, "Because of the universal fact of sin, the way of acceptance with God by reason of our works of righteousness is closed — the notice is clearly worded: 'No Road This Way'" (98).

This part of v. 20 echoes Ps 143:2b, "For no one living is righteous before you." The universal language in v. 19 is continued; "no one" leaves room for no exceptions. The Greek actually says "no flesh," a Hebraic way of saying "no human being."

"Declared righteous" is from δικαιόω (*dikaioō*), which is the word usually translated "justified" (see 2:13; 3:4). It is a courtroom term and thus follows naturally upon the previous verse. It refers to the judge's decision to drop the charges, and his declaration that the accused person may go free without suffering any penalty. In other words, it means to be declared righteous before the law. It does not mean "to make righteous," nor does it necessarily imply that the person *is* righteous. It simply means that the person is considered and declared to be right with the law.

"Observing the law" is a poor translation of the important

expression "works of law" (ἔργων νόμου, *ergōn nomou*). The word
"law" should not be capitalized here, as if it means the Mosaic Law.
As in the previous verse it means God's law in general, in all its
forms.[67] "Works of law" is also used in 3:28, another key verse in
Romans. There is no article before either "works" or "law" in either
verse. This expression refers to *all* responses to whatever commandments of God's law apply to any given person. Efforts to limit
this phrase to the works required by the Law of Moses only, or to
OT commandments only (as in Dunn, I:154-9), are seriously misguided and are a grave hindrance to a right understanding of Paul's
main point in Romans and of grace in general. The same is true of
efforts to limit this phrase to works done from wrong motives (as in
Barrett, 70).

Paul's point is that *no one* will be declared right with God on the
basis of his obedience to God's commands. This would require
absolute perfection, which no one has achieved or will achieve. (See
Moo, I:213; Cranfield, I:198.) The universal fact of sin absolutely
rules out the law system as a way of justification. In theory such justification is possible, as 2:13 declares; but in reality it never occurs,
as this verse affirms.[68]

"Will be declared righteous [justified]" is future tense but does
not refer just to some specific future event such as the final judgment. It is stated rather as a general principle. Because of sin no
one will *ever* be justified before God on the basis of his own righteousness or works. Once sin enters a person's life, henceforward
that door will be closed forever. See Murray, I:107.

. . . rather, through the law we become conscious of sin.
"Rather" is not a good translation of the transitional word γάρ
(*gar*), which means "for" or "because." The latter well suits Paul's
meaning here. No one will be justified by works of law because the
law reveals all of us to be sinners. As Phillips translates, "Indeed it
is the straight-edge of the Law that shows us how crooked we are."

---

[67]See Lenski, 243; Lard, 112; Moo, I:209-210; and Morris, 171. As Morris
says, what Paul says "is true of 'law works' of any kind. No one will be saved
by the way of law."

[68]Thus there is no contradiction between 2:13 and 3:20. See Murray,
I:107.

(See 5:20; 7:7.) The very law by which many assume they will be vindicated will actually be the instrument of their condemnation.

The point is that we need to use God's law for something that it
can do rather than try to use it for something it can never do,
which is to make any sinner right with God. It has other proper
functions, to be sure, but one thing the law can do is show us how
sinful we are and thus how much we need God's gift of righteousness through grace.

All in all the contents of this first main section of Romans are
anything but *gospel*. From beginning (1:18) to end (3:20), the
message is one long dirge of sin, wrath, and judgment. The essence
of this section is as Hendriksen sums it up: "Man is doomed,
doomed, doomed. His condition is one of thorough hopelessness
and despair. And the law, with its demand of nothing less than
moral and spiritual *perfection* . . . creates in him a dreadful, mortifying sense of sin; hence, a presentiment of doom, total and everlasting" (I:125).

"Good news"? Hardly. But the fact is that self-righteous, complacent people must be convinced of their desperate and hopeless
plight under law before they can acknowledge their need for grace.
Thus this section is a necessary prelude to the one that follows,
which presents us with the way of *grace* as God's marvelous and
powerful alternative to the impotent and futile way of law.

3:21-5:21 — PART TWO

THE ALL-SUFFICIENCY OF GRACE
AS A WAY OF SALVATION

The first main section of Romans demonstrates the seriousness of the human predicament under law. A person *could* be saved under the law system *if* he obeyed God's law perfectly. But 1:18-3:20 shows conclusively that all have sinned; therefore no one can be justified by obedience to law. Under law there is only condemnation. For those who remain under law the holy side of God's nature, the "consuming fire" of his wrath (Heb 12:29), will prevail in the end. Indeed, "it is a dreadful thing to fall into the hands of the living God" (Heb 10:31).

But God is not only a consuming fire; he is also love (1 John 4:8);[1] and out of his boundless love he has provided another way or system of salvation, the way of *grace*. Whereas the rules of the law system allow for the justification only of the sinless, the grace system allows God to justify the wicked (4:5). Indeed, it is the *only* way a sinner can be justified.

The purpose of this second main section of Romans (3:21-5:21) is thus to set forth the essence of grace as a way of salvation, a way provided by the love of God as an alternative to law. Saving grace is the free, unmerited gift of salvation to sinners who have no claim on it and who in fact deserve its opposite. It is "favor bestowed when wrath is owed" (GRe, 375-377).

In reference to salvation from sin the term "grace" is used in several ways. First, grace is an attribute of the divine nature. It is the way God's love responds to sin.[2] It is his willingness and desire to accept us in spite of our sin. It is his readiness to forgive (Ps 86:5) and his desire to "graciously give us all things" (8:32) — the

---

[1]On holiness and love as two equally ultimate sides of God's nature, see GRe, 238-240, 255-257.

[2]Just as wrath is how God's *holiness* responds to sin.

247

very things we have forfeited through our sin. In his love he wants us back, even though we have sinned against him. This is the heart of God's nature as a gracious God.

Second, the term "grace" is used for the gift of salvation itself. The content of this gift of grace is actually a "double cure," which is God's remedy for the "double trouble" caused by sin.[3] Sin affects the sinner externally or objectively, causing the legal problem of guilt and subjecting him to the penalty of the law. It also affects the sinner internally or subjectively, causing the heart to become evil, weak, depraved, and spiritually sick. The gift of grace includes justification or forgiveness of sins to resolve the former; it includes regeneration and sanctification to overcome the latter. The former is accomplished through the power of the redeeming blood of Christ; the latter is effected through the power of the indwelling Holy Spirit. In general this section of Romans deals with the former, while the next section (6:1-8:39) deals with the latter.

Finally the term "grace" is used for the system of salvation given by God as the alternative to law. "You are not under law [as a way of salvation], but under grace [as a way of salvation]" (6:14). The contrast between law and grace is striking; they are in fact opposites. In the introduction to 1:18-3:20 the rules of the law system were stated thus:

KEEP THE COMMANDMENTS, AND (THEREFORE)
ESCAPE THE PENALTY.
BREAK THE COMMANDMENTS, AND (THEREFORE)
SUFFER THE PENALTY.

But the rules of the grace system, i.e., the way to be "right with God" in terms of grace, may be stated as follows:

KEEP THE COMMANDMENTS, BUT SUFFER THE PENALTY.
BREAK THE COMMANDMENTS, BUT ESCAPE THE PENALTY.

---

[3]See the fuller treatment of these concepts in Cottrell, *Grace*, chs. 5 and 7. The expression "double cure" comes from the gospel hymn, "Rock of Ages": ". . . be of sin the double cure; save from wrath, and make me pure" (or "save me from its guilt and power").

Whereas the rules of the law system are set forth in 2:7-10, the rules of the grace system are stated succinctly in 2 Cor 5:21, "God made him who had no sin to be sin for us, so that in him we might become the righteousness of God."

Under the law system a person is treated with utter fairness; he gets exactly what he deserves. But the grace system is just the opposite. It is neither fair nor just; under grace a person gets the very opposite of what he deserves. The first half of the grace formula, of course, applies only to Jesus Christ, since he is the only one who will ever keep the commandments with sinless perfection. He "had no sin." But at the same time he suffered the penalty; it was God's plan for him "to be sin for us," and in our place to suffer the divine wrath we deserve because of our sin. This was the exact opposite of what he deserved.

This is what makes the second half of the grace formula possible, namely, the part that applies to us. Under the grace system we who have broken the commandments also receive the very opposite of what we deserve. Through our faith in Jesus "the righteousness of God" — Jesus' payment of the penalty for sin in our place — is counted as our own, enabling us to escape the penalty we deserve.

This grace system, God's wonderful alternative to law, is the main focus of this section of Romans, with special attention being given to the first part of the double cure, or justification. The rest of chapter 3 (vv. 21-31) is the actual explanation of grace as a way of salvation. Chapter 4 provides OT confirmation, with Abraham being set forth as a paradigm of grace. Chapter 5 deals with the most immediate practical result of a right understanding of grace, namely, assurance of salvation. The first part (vv. 1-11) explains the relation between justification by faith and assurance; the latter part (vv. 12-21) emphasizes the all-sufficiency of the death of Christ as the source of saving grace.

I. 3:21-31 — GRACE AS JUSTIFICATION BY CHRIST'S BLOOD THROUGH FAITH

Paul has just declared that the whole world has sinned and stands guilty before God (3:19). The fact of guilt raises the problem of justification. How can sinners be justified, or brought back into a right relationship with God and his law? Can a person work himself back into a proper relation with this law? Perhaps with a little extra effort, we can go "above and beyond the call of duty" and do enough good works to make up for our sins. Is this possible? No! In the parable of the unprofitable servant (Luke 17:7-10) Jesus teaches that every good work we can possibly do is already owed to God (required by his law) and therefore cannot be used to pay the debt incurred by our sin. There is no such thing as extra merit; this is why works of law cannot justify sinners.

What, then, can we do? How *can* we be justified, be counted righteous, be accepted by God, escape the wrath and condemnation we deserve? Does any provision of the law allow a sinner to go unpunished? Can we remain under law and still be justified? No! If we are to be justified, we must leave the framework of law and enter the sphere of grace. This subsection of Romans shows us what this means by explaining that sinners can be justified by the blood of Jesus Christ through their faith in him. We can be justified only by faith apart from works of law (3:28).

In establishing this point the Apostle Paul produces what Morris declares to be "possibly the most important single paragraph ever written" (173). He is referring to 3:21-26. This is, indeed, the "centre and heart" of the letter, as Cranfield says (I:199). In one compact manifesto Paul brings together the heavy theological concepts of the righteousness of God, faith, sin, justification, grace, redemption, propitiation, and the blood of Christ. By emphasizing the righteousness of God and faith, he elaborates on 1:17, the key verse in the epistle's introduction.[4]

A. RIGHTEOUSNESS THROUGH FAITH
IS NOW FULLY REVEALED (3:21-23)

3:21 Paul's first words in this section emphasize the contrast between the two ways of salvation: **But now a righteousness from**

---

[4]Some critics have suggested that Paul is citing or adapting some already-existing sources in parts of vv. 24-26. This view is mostly speculation and need not concern us here. For details see Dunn, I:163-164; Moo, I:220; Morris, 173.

God, apart from law, has been made known . . . . Under law, salvation is based on perfect human righteousness. Herein lies the impotence of the law system; 1:18-3:20 has shown man's righteousness indeed to be "filthy rags" (Isa 64:6) and futile for justification. But under grace, salvation is based on the righteousness *of God*, the meaning of which was discussed fully under 1:17 above. Here, as in 1:17, it does not mean God's own personal righteousness, the attribute of his nature that requires him always to be faithful to himself. It is rather the gift of righteousness that God gives to sinners, on the basis of which he accepts them as righteous. Specifically, it is Christ's satisfaction of the law's requirement that sinners be punished, which he accomplished in our place, as our substitute. This righteousness is bestowed upon us as a gift. The NIV reflects this interpretation when it translates the simple genitive "of God" as "from God."

The gift of God's righteousness is directly related to justification. These words have the same Greek root (*dikai-*). "Righteousness" is δικαιοσύνη (*dikaiosunē*), and "justification" is δικαίωσις (*dikaiōsis*). "To justify" means to count righteous or declare righteous (see 2:13, and 3:24 below). To say that the righteousness of God has been made known is to say that the means by which God justifies sinners has been manifested.

In what way has this righteousness been "made known"? This is the same idea as 1:17, namely, that the righteousness of God has now been *revealed* in the gospel. This refers not just to the spoken message of the gospel, but primarily to the saving events upon which that message is based. "Made known" is perfect tense, referring to the decisive past events of the death and resurrection of Jesus Christ. See 3:26.

A key part of this sentence is the phrase "apart from law." "Apart from" is χωρίς (*chōris*), a preposition indicating distinct separation from something. "Law" is the law system or the law of God in general, not specifically the Law of Moses. Thus the phrase means "without relation to the law system, without any connection to law." See 3:28.[5]

Exactly what does this prepositional phrase modify? Some say it

---

[5]See Godet, 146; Murray, I:109; Morris, 174.

modifies the verb, "made known." I.e., while law can manifest God's righteousness in the sense of his personal purity and integrity, only the gospel can make known his righteousness in the sense of his gift to sinners. Thus it is revealed "apart from law."[6] The other possibility is that it modifies "righteousness of God." I.e., the kind of divine righteousness on the basis of which sinners are justified is not a righteousness measured by law but one that is defined and established outside the law system. It can be understood only in relation to a totally different way of salvation, the way of grace. While both views are possible, the latter is preferred.[7] This righteousness that is apart from law is God's gracious alternative to the unattainable righteousness that comes by works of law (3:20).

Paul says this righteousness of God that is apart from law has been made known "now." The main question here is whether this "now" has a logical or a temporal, chronological sense. If the former, it is just a rhetorical device meaning something like "on the other hand." If the latter, it is setting up a contrast between what was known in the OT era and what has been manifested "now," in this NT age, through the work of the Messiah. The divine grace-righteousness has been revealed here and now, in our time, in our day. See 3:26; Gal 4:4. This latter meaning seems to be the intended sense.

This does not mean that this way of salvation is only now just beginning, and is only now for the first time being applied. It does not mean that people were saved only by law up to this point, and that Christ introduced grace as a new and different way of salvation.[8] Salvation through grace, by means of the gift of the righteousness of Christ, has always been the only possible way sinners could be saved and have been saved. If Adam was saved, he was saved thus, "apart from law." Paul's primary example of this way of salvation is Abraham (ch. 4), who predated even Moses. What has happened "now" is that this grace-righteousness has been

---

[6]See Godet, 146; Cranfield, I:201; Moo, I:222.

[7]See Morris, 174; Murray, I:109-110.

[8]McGarvey and Pendleton (321) say this verse means "there was no justification under the Mosaic dispensation." Bruce (99) says it shows that "a new way to acceptance with God has been opened up." Godet (146) calls it "the new way of justification." Such language is unjustified and misleading.

manifested as never before in the substitutionary death of Jesus
Christ. This is not the first knowledge of grace itself, but the first
clear knowledge of the *basis* for it in the blood of Christ. (See
Murray, I:108-109; Morris, 173.)

This does not mean that there was no knowledge of this at all
prior to Christ's coming. Thus to preclude a possible misunderstanding Paul says this was something **to which the Law and the
prophets testify**. See 1:2; 4:1-25. "Law" here means the Law of
Moses or the Pentateuch; "the Law and the prophets" together represent the entire OT (see Matt 5:17; 7:12; 11:13; 22:40; John 1:45;
Acts 13:15; 24:14; 28:23). They testify to justification by faith (cf.
Gen 15:6 [Rom 4:3]; Hab 2:4 [Rom 1:17]) and to the taking away of
sins through the sacrifice of a substitutionary sin-bearer (cf. the
Mosaic sacrificial system and Isa 53). But now through the cross
this way of grace has been laid open for all to see.

3:22 Here Paul further clarifies the nature of the righteousness
that is apart from law: **This righteousness from God comes
through faith in Jesus Christ to all who believe.** Here again the
implied contrast is between law and grace as systems of salvation.
Grace-righteousness is not given to sinners by works of law (v. 20),
but "through faith in Jesus Christ." This is the same thought
expressed in v. 28, that "a man is justified by faith apart from works
of the Law" (NASB). For a discussion of the nature of faith, see
1:16.

Because the words "Jesus Christ" are in the genitive case, some
have argued that Paul is speaking of "the faith *of* Jesus Christ," or
more specifically, the *faithfulness* of Jesus in fulfilling his saving
mission on our behalf (Shields, 40-41).[9] Most agree, though, that
this is an objective genitive, i.e., that Jesus Christ is the *object* of the
faith which receives the gift of God's righteousness.

As noted under 1:16, the faith by which sinners receive the gift
of righteousness is not just a general faith in God's existence and
providential care, but is a specific faith in the person and work of
the Savior, Jesus Christ. In OT times, since Jesus was not yet
known, the object of saving faith was God's gracious promise to
forgive sins. Now that the Redeemer himself has come and has

[9]See Moo, I:224-225, for a presentation and refutation of this view.

purchased us with his own blood (Acts 20:28), we cannot be saved unless our faith is specifically directed toward him.

The role of faith is asserted twice: "through faith . . . to all who believe." When Paul says "through [διά, *dia*] faith," he is designating faith as the necessary *means* by which the gift of God's righteousness is received by sinners. As such, faith is never to be understood as a meritorious act, or as something we do that in some way deserves to be rewarded by God. The source and basis of grace-righteousness is not our faith but the one toward whom it is directed, namely, Jesus Christ.

"To all who believe" is not just a repetition for emphasis. The stress here is not on the word "believe" but on "all." Perhaps the point once again is to erase all distinctions between Jews and Gentiles and to show that they have equal access to the gospel (1:16). In any case the "all" serves "to highlight the universal availability of God's righteousness," which is "available to *anyone* who has faith in Christ" (Moo, I:225).

The rest of v. 22, **There is no difference**, goes better with v. 23 and along with that verse forms a parenthesis that sums up a main conclusion of 1:18-3:20. The NIV does not translate the particle γάρ (*gar*), meaning "for" or "because." This little word introduces the *reason* why the righteousness of God is available to everyone on the same terms, namely, because "there is no difference" in their starting point or their status before God: all have sinned.

3:23 for all have sinned and fall short of the glory of God . . . . This verse also begins with γάρ (*gar*), "for," explaining why there is no difference among human beings as to the manner of their salvation. *None* can be saved by law through works; *all* must be saved by grace through faith — because all have sinned, and grace through faith is the only possible way for sinners to be saved. Once a person has sinned even once, he has forfeited all possibility of salvation by law-righteousness (Jas 2:10).

Because the language is the same as 5:12, some say this is a reference to Adam's sin and to the idea that all sinned in Adam (e.g., Shedd, 76-77). Whether this is so or not, the main emphasis must be upon the personal sins of all people of accountable age. Following this closely upon the first main section (1:18-3:20), this verse surely refers to the "all" described in 3:9-20. To say that all "have sinned" (aorist tense) means that all who have ever lived up to this point have sinned, and by implication the same will be true from any vantage point all the way up to the final judgment (see Dunn, I:167).

"Fall short" is a good translation of the second verb (ὑστερέω, *hystereō*). It means "to lack, to be deficient in, to come short of, to be wanting, to fall behind." It is present tense, which suggests that it refers to a condition and not to action (Murray, I:112). I.e., once a person has sinned, he is in the condition or state of being destitute of the glory of God.

The difficult part of this verse is determining what is meant by "the glory of God"[10] in this context. Both Murray (I:112-113) and Hendriksen (I:128-129) set forth four possible understandings. (1) It means the honor and glory due unto God through our perfect obedience (Lard, 115). By sinning we fail to glorify him as we should. See 1:21; 4:20; 1 Cor 10:31. (2) It means the honor and praise God would give us if we lived perfectly before him (DeWelt, 55; Calvin, 140). By sinning we become unworthy of such praise. See 2:7, 10; John 5:44; 12:43. (3) It means the glory of God's presence in the future eschatological kingdom, from which sinners are excluded. See 5:2; 8:18, 21; Phil 3:21; Rev 21:23. (4) It means the reflected glory of God that creatures made in his image are supposed to display by imitating his perfect moral character (Moo, I:226-227; Murray, I:113). See Matt 5:48; 1 Pet 1:15-16. This glory is bedimmed by sin, as a light bulb controlled by a rheostat becomes dimmer and dimmer when turned down. Salvation reverses this process and in the last day completely restores us to this image and glory of God. See 1 Cor 11:7; 2 Cor 3:18; 2 Pet 1:4.

All of these are possible meanings. The weakest is the third one, since the present tense suggests the falling short is a present condition and not just a future one. I have a slight preference for the fourth view, where the "glory of God" is "his image or glory in which all were made but which all fail to live up to" (Stott, 109). This goes well with the context. Paul's point is that the fact of sin disqualifies us from being acceptable to God on the basis of our own personal righteousness; thus we stand in dire need of the righteousness that comes from God through faith.

---

[10]For a discussion of the glory of God, see GC, 446-452.

B. SINNERS ARE JUSTIFIED BY THE BLOOD OF CHRIST
(3:24-26)

These three verses, says Godet (149), form "the most important passage in the whole Epistle." Arguably, it is the most important in the whole Bible. It is like the Hope Diamond in a setting of gold. From its depths shine forth the most glorious and most welcome truths of God's revelation.

3:24 and are justified freely by his grace . . . . The verb "justified" is actually a participle and is translated literally by the NASB: "being justified." This presents a difficulty because a participle usually relates to and modifies a word or phrase in the adjacent context. Thus grammatically it would seem to relate to "all have sinned" in v. 23, as the NIV translation suggests. (See the NRSV also.) But this makes the "all" in v. 23 the subject of "justified," and suggests universal salvation unless some awkward paraphrasing is done, e.g., "All have sinned and will not be saved unless they are justified freely by his grace."

Because of this difficulty many take vv. 22b-23 as a parenthesis and connect the participle back to "all who believe" in v. 22a (e.g., Murray, I:114; Hendriksen, I:129). This yields the quite valid thought that all who believe are thus justified freely by his grace. This is probably the way it should be understood. Because of the intervening parenthesis the participle can be translated as a main verb, thus: "Those who believe are justified freely by his grace."

Thus in this unusual way v. 24 introduces one of the most important of all doctrines, justification by grace. The verb has appeared already three times in Romans (2:13; 3:4, 20), but this is its first use for the act of God by which sinners are saved through Christ's blood.

As stated under 3:21 above, justification and righteousness are closely related. "To justify" means "to declare righteous." It does not mean "to make righteous," contrary to the traditional Roman Catholic view. These two distinct definitions of justification are one of the key differences between Catholics and Protestants.

Justification is a legal or judicial term; it has to do with one's relation to the law (see 2:13). It is best understood as the declaration made by a judge once his final decision as to guilt or inno-

cence has been made. When he justifies a defendant, the judge
declares that he is in a right standing with the law. Some say it is
equivalent to the judge declaring the defendant "not guilty"; I
prefer to say it means that the judge declares "No penalty for you!"

That this is the true meaning of justification is seen by the way
the Bible uses it in legal contexts, and especially in contrast with
condemnation. See Deut 25:1; Prov 17:15; Isa 5:23; Matt 12:37;
Rom 5:16; 8:33-34. When a judge condemns someone, that does
not *make* the latter unrighteous or guilty; it is simply a *pronouncement* that he is guilty. Likewise when a judge justifies someone, this
does not *make* him righteous; it only *declares* his righteousness. This
is also illustrated by the way the term is used in Luke 7:29, which
literally says that the people justified God. This cannot mean that
they made him righteous; they were only acknowledging his righteousness.

All of this shows that justification is not strictly a salvation
concept; whether it is or not depends solely on the *basis* upon
which a person is declared to be righteous. When God is "justified," this obviously has nothing to do with his salvation; he is
declared righteous because he *is* righteous. When a person who is
truly innocent stands trial and his innocence is demonstrated, the
law requires the judge to justify that person on the basis of his
actual righteousness. If anyone could live a perfect life before God,
God would justify him on the basis of his own works of personal
righteousness (2:13). Such a person would merit or deserve to be
justified.

However, because all have sinned, this will never happen (3:20).
Thus God has provided an alternative to justification by law; he
offers to justify sinners "freely by his grace." That it is done "freely"
means it is a free gift, totally undeserved, unmerited, and
unearned. (See the use of this word in Matt 10:8; 2 Cor 11:7; 2
Thess 3:8; Rev 21:6; 22:17.) That it is "by his grace" is the very same
idea repeated for emphasis. It is the very opposite of justification in
accordance with law.

We are talking now about justification as a salvation concept,
because it is the justification of *sinners*. The God who saves sinners
is, indeed he must be, a God who "justifies the wicked" (4:5).
Perhaps we have read this verse so often that we forget what a

shocking concept this is. "No expression in Romans is more startling," says Stott (112). Think about it: God the all-knowing and all-
holy Judge looks the wicked sinner square in the eye and *justifies*
him, declares him righteous, acquits him, pardons him, sets him
free, cries "No penalty for you"!

This raises the question of the *basis* for the justification of
sinners. How is it possible for the truly righteous God to declare
sinners to be righteous? Here is the grace element: only on the
basis of the gift of righteousness which he freely gives to those who
put their faith in Jesus. As we saw under 1:17 above, the specific
content of this gift of righteousness is Jesus' satisfaction of God's
law's requirement for penalty in our place. Jesus paid the penalty of
eternal condemnation for us — a point that is elaborated in vv. 24b-
26; and on this basis God releases us from this penalty and sets us
free.

This is the heart of the concept of imputation. "To impute"
(λογίζομαι, *logizomai*[11] and ἐλλογέω, *ellogeō*) is basically a word used
in the context of commerce and bookkeeping. It means to apply an
amount of money or something equivalent to someone's account
(see Phlm 18), either as a charge or as a credit. Our situation as
sinners is that we owe God the debt of eternal punishment; but
God applies Christ's righteousness (his payment of the penalty in
our place) to our account. This is "the righteousness of God" that
comes to us as a gift (1:17; 3:21-22); on the basis of this imputed
righteousness he justifies us, declaring "No penalty for you!"

Because such justification is a free gift, it must be received by
faith rather than by works (1:16-17; 3:21, 28). When God asks us if
we want Jesus' payment of God's righteous penalty for our sin
applied to our account, all we can do is humbly and gratefully say
yes. This is the essence of saving faith.

For all practical purposes justification is the same as forgiveness
or remission of sins. A justified person is a forgiven person. In 4:6-
8, the imputation of righteousness is equated with forgiveness.
Forgiveness in and of itself bestows a righteous status upon the
sinner, and reinstates him in the favor and fellowship of God (see
Stott, 110); nothing more is needed.

---

[11]This word occurs 11 times in ch. 4; see vv. 3-11 especially.

The second half of v. 24 begins Paul's detailed explanation of the death of Jesus as the basis for the sinner's justification: we are justified **through the redemption that came by Christ Jesus.** This and the next two verses tell us more about the basic meaning of the death of Jesus than any other NT passage. They are absolutely fundamental for a proper understanding of the cross.

That which "came by Christ Jesus," and specifically by his cross, is called "redemption."[12] The Greek word is ἀπολύτρωσις (*apolytrōsis*), which comes from λύω, which means "to loose, to set free, to ransom." Related words are λυτρόω (*lytroō*), which means "to ransom, to rescue, to redeem, to liberate"; and λύτρον (*lytron*), which is "a ransom, a ransom price." The basic idea of redemption is to set something or someone free from some kind of bondage, slavery, captivity, or obligation. Under the OT law consecrated property, the firstborn, and slaves could be redeemed or "bought back" (see Exod 13:11-13; Lev 25:47-49; 27:11-19; Num 18:14-16). In NT times the terms were used for the act of ransoming slaves, prisoners of war, and condemned criminals.[13]

What is the price by which sinners are redeemed from their sin? It is stated most vividly in 1 Pet 1:18-19, "It was not with perishable things such as silver or gold that you were redeemed . . . , but with the precious blood of Christ." Because the Son of Man came "to give his life as a ransom for many" (Matt 20:28), "we have redemption through his blood" (Eph 1:7). See Acts 20:28; 1 Cor 6:20; Rev 5:9.

To whom is this ransom price paid? The answer depends on the kind of captivity from which we are redeemed. Certainly we are set free from slavery to sin (6:16-18; 2 Tim 2:26), but this is not the main point of redemption. As sinners we owe to God the debt of eternal punishment, and thus are captive to that obligation as surely as if we were in a kind of debtors' prison (Matt 18:30). Hell itself will be the ultimate debtors' prison (Matt 18:34). Thus the ransom price paid by Jesus was paid to God himself, the one to whom we owe this debt of eternal punishment (GRe, 439-440). This is how Christ's act of redemption is the basis of our justification or

---

[12]For a discussion of the Hebrew and Greek terminology related to this concept, see GRe, 15-21, 438.

[13]See Dunn, I:169; Moo, I:229.

forgiveness. Our debt of eternal penalty is forgiven or set aside because Jesus has paid it in our place. Thus from our point of view justification comes to us "freely," but from God's side it is anything but free. God the Son paid the ultimate price, the equivalent of eternity in hell for the whole human race.

3:25 Paul states this same truth in v. 25, where he uses another word parallel in significance to redemption: **God presented him as a sacrifice of atonement . . . .** The word translated "sacrifice of atonement" is ἱλαστήριον (*hilastērion*), which is also used in Heb 9:5. This term and its equivalent, ἱλασμός (*hilasmos*) (1 John 2:2; 4:10) stand for one of the most important concepts in the Bible.

Unfortunately, there is no unanimity as to the meaning of *hilasterion*. Because it is used often in the LXX and in Heb 9:5 to refer to the lid of the ark of the covenant, i.e., the "mercy-seat," many find that meaning figuratively here in 3:25. Just as the mercy-seat was the place where the atoning blood of sin-offerings was sprinkled in OT times, so also is Jesus in a sense the place where the final atonement has been made for all times (Bruce, 105-107; Nygren, 156-158; Weymouth).

While this view presents no doctrinal problems and is very close to Paul's meaning here, it does not seem to capture the full significance of the term (Moo, I:232-235). Consistent with its use in non-biblical Greek, Paul more likely intends it to mean the atoning sacrifice itself, in the sense of a *propitiation*.

The key element in the concept of propitiation is the averting of wrath. To say that Jesus is a propitiation means that he offered himself as a sacrifice that turns God's wrath away from deserving sinners by accepting that wrath upon himself in our place. Thus he is a "wrath-removing sacrifice" (Hendriksen, I:132), a "wrath-averting sacrifice" (Moo, I:237). Any interpretation of this concept that excludes the removal of the divine wrath from the purpose of the cross has missed its point and must be rejected.[14] The substitution of the ambiguous "sacrifice of atonement" for "propitiation" in the NIV and elsewhere is to be regretted.

Some interpreters reject the concept of propitiation because they deny that any true wrath exists in God; thus the atonement

---

[14]See Morris, *Preaching*, chs. 5 & 6, for the most detailed explanation of why this is so.

can have nothing to do with averting wrath. The idea of propitiation, they say, reduces God to the level of pagan deities whose fickle wrath is appeased and whose mind is changed by the offering. Instead of "propitiation" they translate *hilastērion* as "expiation" (NEB, RSV), which connotes the removal or covering of sins themselves rather than wrath.

This view is totally mistaken. The Bible clearly presents the wrath of God as an undeniable reality (see 1:18; 2:5; GRe, 275-319). When the propitiatory sacrifice of Jesus Christ turns God's wrath away from sinners, it does not do so after the pattern of pagan sacrifices that are intended to placate, appease, or bribe God, or in any sense change his mind. Verse 25 makes this clear when it says that "God presented him" as a propitiation. God's own initiative provided the sacrifice that satisfied his wrath; his already-existing love for sinners both planned and executed the propitiation (1 John 4:10). Rather than being unworthy of the love of God, propitiation is its most glorious manifestation. (See Moo, I:235-237.)

The word translated "presented" has two distinct connotations. It can mean "to plan, to purpose," as it does in 1:13 and Eph 1:9 (its only other NT uses). Some see that meaning here: God purposed or designed Jesus to be a propitiation; it was part of his eternal purpose of grace.[15] This is acceptable, but the context favors the other meaning, "to set forth, to display publicly" (Dunn, I:170; Moo, I:232; Murray, I:118). Verse 21 asserts that the righteousness of God has been "made known"; vv. 25b-26 say the cross is God's public demonstration of his righteousness. "Presented" in 25a fits this pattern, and refers to the openly historical event of the cross as explained by the gospel.

God presented Jesus as a propitiation **through faith in his blood.** As in v. 22, faith is a necessary condition for the actual application of the results of Christ's propitiatory sacrifice to the individual sinner. These results are not automatically and unconditionally applied to all sinners with a resulting universal salvation. But neither are the conditions meritorious in nature and thus inconsistent with grace (4:16; 11:6).

A point of dispute is the placement of "in [ἐν, *en*] his blood."

---

[15]Hendriksen, I:131; Cranfield, I:208-210; NEB. See 2 Cor 5:21.

Some take it as modifying propitiation.[16] It would then read that Christ is "a propitiation in his blood through faith" (NASB). However, the word order favors the view that this phrase modifies faith, i.e., "through faith in his blood" (NIV).[17] One reason Dunn and Moo reject this latter view is their claim that Paul does not anywhere else link "faith" (πίστις, *pistis*) with the preposition "in" (*en*). This is simply wrong, since Paul does this very thing in Gal 3:26; Eph 1:15; Col 1:4; and 2 Tim 3:15 (a fact that Moo himself notes in another context, I:223).

The fact that Jesus is a propitiation through faith in his blood implies that his blood, i.e., his substitutionary death on the cross, is what actually accomplishes the propitiation. It does so in the same way that it accomplishes redemption: it satisfies the penal wrath of God in the place of the sinners who actually deserve it. To have saving faith means we specifically believe that Christ's death on the cross is the basis for our forgiveness, even if we do not understand all the details about how this is so.

He did this to demonstrate his justice . . . . I.e., God presented Jesus as a propitiation for this purpose, to "demonstrate his justice." Some take the word "demonstrate" in the sense of "show forth, set forth, reveal publicly." This would make it similar to "presented" in 25a. Others say it means to demonstrate in the sense of "prove." Either view is possible; in fact, it is difficult to separate them in this context.

The cross as a propitiation specifically demonstrates God's "justice." The Greek term (δικαιοσύνη, *dikaiosynē*) is the same one used in 1:17; 3:5; and 3:21-22. In each of these instances it is translated "righteousness." The reason the NIV translates it "justice" in 3:25 is that its connotation here is different from 3:21-22. In the latter passage (and in 1:17) it refers to God's gift of justifying righteousness; here (as in 3:5) it means God's own righteous character, his inner integrity that requires him to be completely true to himself in all ways.

In this context it is clear that the aspect of his nature to which

---

[16]See Godet, 153; Bruce, 104, 107; Cranfield, I:210; Dunn, I:172; Moo, I:238.

[17]See Calvin, 143; Lard, 118; DeWelt, 55-56; Hendriksen, I:132.

his righteousness requires him to be true is his perfect holiness. God's holiness in turn requires him to uphold the full integrity of his law, and this requires him to punish those who violate that law by their sin. This specific attribute of God is often called his *retributive justice*.[18] Thus the translation "justice."

Why is such a demonstration needed? Because it would seem that God, in justifying sinners, is not being true to his law's requirement that sin must be punished. (See especially Exod 23:7; Deut 25:1; Prov 17:15.) But when Jesus is set forth *as a propitiation*, it is clear that God *is* punishing sins after all, albeit in the person of his only-begotten Son, who suffers the penalty in our place.

Such a demonstration was especially important **because in his forbearance he had left the sins committed beforehand unpunished . . . .**[19] God's "forbearance" is his patience and longsuffering, which in essence means "delay and restraint in the execution of wrath." (See GRe, 357-361.) Paul's point is that God's failure to consistently punish sin throughout the OT era may have raised questions about his integrity. How could he claim to be a righteous and holy God, and at the same time forgive sins and leave them unpunished?

"Sins committed beforehand" does not refer to the sins an individual commits prior to his baptism, but to sins committed and forgiven prior to the cross. The only basis upon which sins may be forgiven is the propitiatory sacrifice of Jesus Christ, and it was upon this basis that God forgave sins even in the OT era, even before the historical event of the atonement had occurred. It was absolutely certain that the cross would occur (Acts 2:23); thus God freely dispensed its benefits before the fact. An analogy is a person who knows his paycheck is going to be deposited tomorrow, so he writes checks on it today, knowing the funds will be there when the checks reach the bank.[20]

The problem was not God's ability to forgive pre-cross sins as such, but the appearance this gave as to God's violating his own righteousness or justice in doing so. But, says Paul, any doubts

---

[18]See Godet, 154; MP, 322; Moo, I:338-342.

[19]Some Greek texts put the Greek phrase for "in his forbearance" at the beginning of v. 26.

[20]This point is very important for a proper understanding of 5:12-19.

concerning the integrity of God's justice that were thus raised are completely dispelled by the actual event of the cross, which was a public event presented before the whole world.

There is considerable debate about the meaning of the term πάρεσις (*paresis*), used only here in the NT and translated "left unpunished" in the NIV. The question is whether it means remission or forgiveness of sins in the full sense of the word (KJV, NAB), or whether it means merely passing sins over or passing them by in the sense of leaving them unpunished (NASB, NRSV, NIV). Lard (120) says it is the same as remission, but most modern interpreters take the latter view (e.g., Murray, I:119; Cranfield, I:211; Moo, I:240-242). The point would be that God did indeed leave sins unpunished prior to the cross, but this was not because of a breakdown in his justice. Rather, it was because he knew these sins would be punished later, in the person of Jesus Christ on the cross.[21]

One point must be carefully noted here. Even if we take *paresis* to mean only the "passing over" of sins in the sense of delaying their punishment, this in itself does not imply that God was not truly forgiving the sins of OT believers. We know that he did so forgive them because other biblical texts declare that forgiveness was a fact in OT times. Paul's main paradigm for justification (i.e., forgiveness) here in Romans is Abraham (ch. 4). See also the quote from David in 4:7-8.[22] There is no basis for the idea of a "limbo" for OT saints until Christ came, or for the idea that the sins of OT saints were just "rolled back" until the time of the cross.

3:26 Whereas v. 25 relates the demonstration of propitiation to sins committed prior to the cross, v. 26 makes the same point as a general principle that applies especially to the Christian era. **He did it**, i.e., he set Jesus forth as a propitiation, **to demonstrate his justice at the present time, so as to be just and the one who justifies those who have faith in Jesus.** What has God done in this

---

[21]Whatever 25b means, it is not parallel to Acts 17:30, contrary to Godet, 156; Murray, I:119; Bruce, 108; and Morris, 183. Acts 17:30 refers primarily to those who were *lost* in OT times, especially the Gentiles; Rom 3:25 refers primarily to those who were *saved* in that era, despite the fact that the basis for their salvation had not yet occurred. On Acts 17:30 see GC, 344-345.

[22]On forgiveness of sins in the OT, see GRe, 367-375.

"present time"? He "sent his Son" (Gal 4:4) to establish and demonstrate the basis for the forgiveness he freely bestows in every era.

The latter part of v. 26 is a purpose statement, and expresses in no uncertain terms the ultimate purpose of the death of Jesus, i.e., so that God can be both *just* and *justifier*. This shows that the cross was not merely a *demonstration* of the fact that the forgiving God is just (as the RSV and NRSV imply), but was necessary in order that God might *be* just, even while he is justifying sinners (see Lard, 121). Because the cross in its nature and meaning was an act of redemption and propitiation, God is able to forgive righteously. Because Jesus on the cross was paying our debt of eternal punishment and bearing the full force of the wrath of God in our place, God is able to fully cancel our punishment and declare "No penalty for you!" without compromising his nature as a holy God who must punish sin. (See GRe, 450-455.) Such justification "at the present time" is offered only to those "who have faith in Jesus" (see 3:22).

Such is the nature of the righteousness of God that is "apart from law" (3:21). Even though from God's perspective both his law and his love are satisfied by the cross, this is not something that could have been done within the framework of the law system as such. Law alone requires that the person who sins suffer his own penalty (Ezek 18:4). Only grace, which is the opposite of law, can turn this principle upside down and provide for us one who for himself kept the law's commandments, but who for us suffered the law's penalty.

C. SINNERS ARE JUSTIFIED BY FAITH APART FROM WORKS OF LAW (3:27-28)

In the rest of this chapter Paul returns to the question-and-answer format used in 3:1-9. This does not mean he is once again counteracting an exclusively Jewish viewpoint, contrary to Moo (I:247-248). Nor does it mean that the "law" of which he speaks here is exclusively the Jewish Law. Paul moved beyond that limited perspective in 3:9. What he has been saying since then, and what he says here, is certainly applicable to Jews and to the Mosaic Law, but it is also intended to apply to all people and to the law of God as such.

In 3:21 Paul begins to explain a way of justification that is "apart from law," i.e., the way of grace. In vv. 24-26 he sets forth the basis or ground of justification by grace, namely, the propitiatory sacrifice of Jesus Christ. From 3:27 through the end of ch. 4, the main theme is *faith* as the means of appropriating the benefits of Christ's sacrifice. From the human side this is the key difference between law and grace: the *means* of justification is *faith*, not works of law (3:28). This antithesis is not intended to set faith apart from every other human act, but rather to set it apart from works as the means of justification within the law system.

3:27 Where, then, is boasting? It is excluded. The word "then" (οὖν, *oun*) introduces a conclusion drawn from vv. 24-26, namely, that the grace system excludes boasting.[23] Those under law, whether Jews or Gentiles, are given to boasting since both the ground and means of justification in that system are human works (1:30; 2:17, 23). But the way of grace is not consistent with boasting since the total package of salvation from beginning to end was conceived in the mind of God and made possible only through the work of Jesus, and is offered to sinners in the form of a free gift. (See Eph 2:8-10.)

"Excluded" is aorist tense: "it has been excluded" once for all. **On what principle? On that of observing the law? No, but on that of faith.** The exclusion of boasting is not just an arbitrary divine decree, but is true from the very nature of the human predicament and its resolution by grace. Justification through the law system would permit boasting, but such justification is not possible since all have sinned. The grace alternative excludes boasting since the only meritorious works that produce salvation within this system are done by God himself through Jesus Christ. The only thing sinners can do is react to and respond to these divine works, and passively receive the benefits generated by them. The defining element in this completely unmeritorious response is faith. Even the greatest OT saints — Enoch, Noah, Abraham, Moses, David, Elijah — were sinners whose relative righteousness fell short of the divine standard and who were saved only by God's grace. Even they had no room for boasting (4:2).

---

[23]On the meaning of "boasting," see 2:17.

The latter part of v. 27 reads literally, "Through what law [νόμος, *nomos*]? of works? No, but through a law [*nomos*] of faith." The exact sense of *nomos* here is debated. Some say it means the Torah, or Law of Moses (Cranfield, I:220; Dunn, I:186). But this requires a strained interpretation of "a law of faith" (see Moo, I:251) and is very unlikely. For similar reasons it cannot mean the law system as such. This means that Paul here is using *nomos* in a still more general sense, with a connotation that has not yet appeared in the epistle. The NIV translation, "principle," adequately reflects this understanding. Related suggestions are "method, norm, arrangement, order, system, rule, set of rules" (Murray, I:122-123; Moo, I:259; Reese, 126). The word seems to be used in a similar way in 7:21; 8:2. Moo gives examples to show that "this general use of *nomos* was very much a live meaning in first-century Greek" (I:259; see 252).

It seems, then, that Paul is using *nomos* in 3:27 the way I have been using "system of salvation." His words "of works" (NIV, "observing the law") refer to the law system as such, and his words "a law of faith" refer to the grace system as such. We may paraphrase v. 27 thus: "Where, then, is boasting? It has been excluded. Through what system of salvation? The law system, in which one is justified by works? No, on the contrary, through the grace system, in which one is justified by faith."

3:28 For we maintain that a man is justified by faith apart from observing the law. It is tempting to translate λογίζομαι (*logizomai*) as "conclude" here (KJV; Lipscomb, 78; Wuest, 63), but "maintain, hold, deem" is probably better. It is the same word that is translated "reckon, count, impute" throughout ch. 4. The word "for" (*gar*) shows this statement is not a conclusion from v. 27, but is rather the basis for it (Lard, 123). The plural "we" probably refers to Paul and his Christian readers, and thus by implication to all believers: "we Christians" (Moo, I:253; Morris, 187; Cranfield, I:220-221). "A man" refers to *any* man or *any* person, i.e., anybody who is actually justified. "Observing the law" is literally "works of law" and should be translated such, contrary to the NIV's unacceptable paraphrase (see 3:20).

This verse says nothing that has not already been said, especially in 1:16-17; 3:21-22; but it says it more succinctly and thus sums up the main thesis of the epistle. Anybody who is actually justified is justified only under the grace system, not under the law system. "Faith" is a kind of shorthand for the grace system as a whole, and "works of law" (like "works" in v. 27) is shorthand for the law system as a whole.

It is extremely important that we understand this verse aright since it is one of the main passages used to support the widely-held "faith only" doctrine of salvation. It is recognized that this contrast between "faith" and "works of law" creates two categories. Then it is assumed that the *only* thing in the first category is faith, and faith alone. *Everything* else — every other possible human act, thought, attitude, or state of mind — goes into the second category as a "work of law." Thus under the grace system the sole condition for justification is faith. (See 1:16 above.)

The consistent result of this view is to exclude even *repentance* as a condition for justification, a position held by those who oppose what is called "Lordship salvation." Many who hold the "faith-only" view object to such an exclusion and argue that both faith and repentance are necessary conditions for justification, contrary to their "faith-only" interpretation of 3:28. Both groups then proceed to exclude *baptism* as a condition for justification. To avoid antinomianism it is usually added that the faith which, alone, justifies us is not *completely* alone, in the sense that it will naturally produce good works, even if these works are not directly involved in justification (Bruce, 109).

How may we respond to this view? The key point is a right understanding of the expression "works of law." It should be carefully noted that in this verse the only things specifically set apart from faith are whatever is meant by "works of law." But does this verse imply that *everything* that is not faith is automatically included in this category? The answer is no, as will now be explained.

At this point we must note that there are some things that the expression "works of law" does *not* mean. First, it does not mean works of obedience to the Law of Moses only, contrary to Dunn (I:172), and Newman and Nida (70). The use of the example of Abraham in ch. 4 is clearly against this. The "law" in the expression "works of law" is any law or commandment given by the Creator through either general or special revelation. Thus "works of law" are "law works of any kind" (Morris, 187; Murray, I:126).

Second, the expression "works of law" is not strictly equivalent to "perfect obedience to all the law requires," contrary to Reese (110). It is true that the only way to be saved under the law system is by "sinless (perfect) obedience." And since all have sinned, it is also true that anyone who is actually saved will be justified "without perfect obedience to any law" (Reese, 128, 136). But "works of law" here in 3:28 (like "works" in 4:6) means something different, as will be explained below.

Third, "works of law" does not refer to acts of obedience done from legalistic motives, or the motive of meriting God's favor thereby. This view excludes all "meritorious" works, or "acts of human obedience viewed as satisfactory, or meritorious, in regard of salvation" (Moule, 85). According to this popular understanding the real problem with "works of law" is the wrong *motive* with which they are done. This view is unacceptable, however, because it implies that the very same works done from right motives *would* justify, which undermines Paul's very point.

What, then, is meant by "works of law"? Law itself, as said above, means God's commandments or law in general, and not just one limited version of it (such as the Law of Moses). It is composed especially of the moral law, which applies equally to all people in all ages, even though it is revealed in different forms and under different covenants. "Works of law," then, must mean any response to any such law, without restriction in terms of dispensation, form, or motive.

The preposition "apart from" is χωρίς (*chōris*), a term which emphasizes separation: "apart from, without, separated from, without relation to, without regard to." "Apart from works of law" thus means "without regard to one's response to the law, apart from a consideration of how one responds to the law." But one may respond to law either positively or negatively, either in obedience or in disobedience. In 3:28 Paul has in mind *both* kinds of response: "Apart from a consideration of one's obedience and disobedience to law."

We know that "works of law" is intended to have this all-inclusive meaning here because of the parallel with "apart from works" in 4:6. In the latter passage Paul cites David in Ps 32:1-2 as evidence that a man is justified (reckoned righteous) "apart from works." But what "works" does David mention in these verses? Only transgressions and sins! To be justified apart from works thus includes the idea of being justified apart from a consideration of our sinful deeds. The similarity of meaning between 3:28 and 4:6 thus requires us to include sinful works in our understanding of "works of law" in 3:28. (This is why we cannot simply equate "works of law" with "perfect obedience to all the law requires." This is also why the NIV translation, "observing the law," is wrong; it refers only to a positive response to the law.)

On the other hand "works of law" cannot be expanded to mean "anything a person does." Even if faith is excepted, this is too broad because not everything a sinner does is a response to law. God gives his human creatures law in his role as Creator and Lord, and we as creatures respond to this law either by obeying it or disobeying it (i.e., in "works of law"). But once we have disobeyed it, God then begins to relate to sinful mankind in a wholly new role: that of Redeemer. As Redeemer he works out our salvation; as Redeemer he offers it to sinners with instructions on how to receive it. Such redemptive instruction is *not* "law," and our response to this instruction *cannot* be called "works of law."

Thus "works of law" cannot be broadened to include "anything a person does" besides faith. We cannot posit two categories of human acts, where faith alone is one category, with everything else constituting a second category called "works of law." Sinners are instructed, yea, *required* to do other things that cannot be labeled "works of law," because they are not responses to the law given by God as Creator to man as creature. The most obvious example of this is repentance, and an equally clear example is baptism. Both repentance and baptism are the sinner's response to God as Redeemer, not the creature's response to God as Creator. They are neither "works" nor "works of law," any more than saving faith is.[24]

This does not mean that we are justified *by* repentance and baptism, in the way that we are justified *by* faith. As discussed above, faith alone is the sole *means* by which justification is received. It does mean, though, that "faith" in 3:28 (as in 3:27) is an

---

[24]See the discussion of "obedience to the faith" under 1:5 above.

abbreviated way of referring to the grace system as a whole, and that repentance and baptism are legitimately understood within the grace system as conditions for receiving justification that are fully compatible with faith. They are not "works of law" any more than faith is.

D. THE WAY OF GRACE IS AVAILABLE TO ALL (3:29-30)

3:29 In vv. 29-30 Paul returns to a continuing theme of the epistle, that God's grace makes no distinctions among sinners; it is equally needed by all and equally available to all on the same conditions (see 1:16; 3:22). No one group has an advantage over any other; especially, the Jews have no advantage over the Gentiles. **Is God the God of Jews only?** This is the question Paul addressed at length in ch. 2. It reflects the mistaken Jewish attitude that their privilege of service implied a unique access to God and his salvation. But has not Paul clearly shown that the Jews do not have a monopoly on God? **Is he not the God of Gentiles too? Yes, of Gentiles too . . . .**

The general principle of v. 28 is given a specific application here. Under grace sinners are justified apart from their response to any given version of God's law, and this applies especially to the Law of Moses. God did not give the Law of Moses as an exclusive means by which Jews alone could be justified. That was not its purpose. If it had been, then he could have simply left that law in place and continued to ignore the Gentiles (Acts 17:30). But God is God of all men, including the Gentiles; and now in the fulness of time (Gal 4:4) he has made it clear that he has always intended to include the Gentiles as full partners in salvation by grace (Eph 2:11-3:12).

3:30 Indeed, he *must* be the God of both Jews and Gentiles, **since there is only one God . . . .** The existence of only one God was a basic OT revelation (Exod 20:3; Deut 6:4), and a basic Jewish belief. Moo's comment (I:254) is appropriate: "Paul's contention is that the oneness of God requires that God be God of the Gentiles as much as of the Jews; otherwise, the Gentiles would be left with no God. In arguing in this manner, Paul takes one of the most basic Jewish beliefs, monotheism, and turns it against Judaism." I.e., he turns it against their false exclusivism.

. . . who [the one God] will justify the circumcised by faith and the uncircumcised through that same faith. Here Paul calls attention to the other main symbol of Jewish exclusivism, circumcision, and declares that within the grace system it makes no difference whatever (see 2:25-29). Both the circumcised (the Jews) and the uncircumcised (the Gentiles) are justified in the same way, i.e., by a common faith in a common Redeemer. Now that Christ has come, the Gentiles are specifically said to have *the (same) faith* as the Jews (πίστις [*pistis*] with the definite article). Stott (120) reminds us that "this identical truth applies to all other distinctions, whether of race, nationality, class, sex or age. . . . At the foot of Christ's cross and through faith in him, we are all on exactly the same level."

The future tense of "will justify" denotes the change in circumstances reflected by the Great Commission. From that point onward the gospel will be preached to Jews and Gentiles alike to the end of the age, and throughout this time God will continue to justify Jews and Gentiles alike. Though two different prepositions are used for "by (ἐκ, *ek*) faith" and "through (διά, *dia*) faith," no significant difference in meaning is intended (Lard, 125; Cranfield, I:222; Dunn, I:189; Moo, I:255).

E. GRACE LETS LAW DO ITS PROPER WORK (3:31)

3:31 Some readers (especially Jewish) may by this time be thinking thoughts similar to those voiced in 3:1. There, following Paul's long attack on the Jews' false concept of their own exclusiveness in God's plan (2:1-29), the question of the very meaning of Jewishness and the futility of their very existence is raised. Likewise, after Paul has emphatically rejected the ability of law to justify (3:20), and has declared that justification can be received only apart from law (3:21, 27-28), some are no doubt thinking that law must be rather obsolete. Paul voices this concern in the question, **Do we, then, nullify the law by this faith?**

This is not just a reference to the Mosaic Law or to the OT as a whole, contrary to Cranfield (I:223). The contrast throughout this

•

section has been between grace on the one hand and law in general on the other hand, and it is no different here. As Morris says (189), "What Paul says has reference to the Jewish law, but also to law in general."

The question is, does grace abolish law, or render it ineffective and purposeless? Does it set the law aside so that it has no relevance to the Christian? Does faith "nullify the law"? (On the word "nullify" [καταργέω, *katargeō*], see 3:3.) **Not at all! Rather,** by it **we uphold the law.** A right understanding of grace and justification by faith actually establishes and confirms the law.[25] How does it do this? By setting law free from a burden it is not able to bear and was never intended to bear, namely, function as a means of justifying sinners. When we stop trying to use the law and its commandments in such an impossible way, we can then let it perform its proper functions.

One such function is that it serves to show us our sin (3:20) and thus shows us our need for justification by faith (MP, 324; Hendriksen, I:137-138). Also, it properly functions as a norm or standard for holy living. As DeWelt says (59), under grace we can "preach and teach the real value of the law which is to point out right and wrong." As Lard says (126), "Law may be wholly useless for one purpose, and yet indispensable for others."

Here is a point we must not forget: as a revelation of God's will to us, his law is absolutely binding upon us and we have an absolute obligation to obey it. Grace does not change this fact. We are not under law as a way of *salvation* (6:14), but we are always under law as a way of *life*. To put it another way, law is not involved in the first part of the double cure, which is justification; but it is absolutely necessary for the second part of the double cure, which includes sanctification.[26]

---

[25]Paul's answer makes it clear that he is not referring to the Mosaic Law as such, since, in view of Eph 2:11-15 and the whole of Galatians and Hebrews, he has no desire to "establish" it. These texts state that the civil and ceremonial contents of the Mosaic Law have purposely been set aside or nullified. Thus we conclude that Paul is talking about the law as such, especially the moral law.

[26]On the concept of the double cure, see page 248 above.

II. 4:1-25 — ABRAHAM: PARADIGM OF GRACE

This next section of Romans (the entire fourth chapter) is a presentation of Abraham as a paradigm or pattern for grace. Throughout this discussion of the great patriarch, Paul seems to have several purposes in mind. Most generally he uses Abraham's example to explain what it means to be justified by faith apart from works of law (3:28). Thus by studying this chapter all Christians may better understand grace as the only way of salvation, as contrasted with the way of law.

More specifically, this appeal to Abraham provides OT confirmation for Paul's teaching. This does not mean that Paul is citing the OT merely to give "scriptural proof" for what he is saying, since his own writing is Scripture and is fully authoritative in itself (2 Pet 3:16). However, Paul feels it is important to show the continuity between his teaching and the OT in general (1:2; 3:21). This is surely accomplished here, especially with the added citation of Ps 32:1-2 in 4:6-8.

Perhaps Paul's most specific purpose in this section is to make it easier for the Jews to accept the gospel of grace. In their minds Old Covenant circumcision and the Mosaic Law added up not only to legalism but also to Jewish exclusivism where salvation is concerned. However, one of Paul's main points in Romans is that salvation by grace through faith makes no distinction between Jews and Gentiles. A proper understanding of Abraham would help the Jews to understand this.[27]

An appeal to the life of Abraham is ideally suited for these purposes. He is indeed an object lesson of the main truth that Paul is explaining in these chapters, i.e., that God's way of saving sinners is by grace, which means that we are justified by faith apart from works of law. Paul sees Gen 15:6 as a summary statement of this truth, and Romans 4 is basically an exposition of this verse.

With regard to the Jews, their supremely high regard for Abraham makes an appeal to his life a perfect means for correcting

---

[27]Since Paul alludes to or specifically mentions a number of the details of the life of Abraham as recorded in Gen 12:1-25:11, a study of that section of Genesis will help the student of Romans 4 to get the most out of this chapter.

their legalism and exclusivism. Showing that Abraham was in fact accepted by God on the basis of grace, i.e., that he was justified by faith apart from works of law, will be a major step for Paul in breaking down Jewish resistance to the gospel.

In keeping with the thesis statement in 3:28, the major theme throughout this section is the contrast between law and grace as ways of salvation. The categories of law and grace are represented by the following concepts:

LAW	GRACE
works (vv. 2, 4, 6)	faith (vv. 3, 5, 9, 11-14, 16-20, 24)
boasting (v. 2)	glorifying God (v. 20)
wages (v. 4)	imputation (vv. 3-6, 8-11, 22-24)
obligation/debt (v. 4)	gift/grace (vv. 4, 16)
sin (vv. 5, 7, 8, 15)	imputed righteousness (vv. 3, 5, 6, 9, 11, 13, 22)
law (vv. 13-16)	promise (vv. 13, 14, 16, 20, 21)
wrath (v. 15)	forgiveness (vv. 7-8)

While the contrast between the corresponding items is not as precise in every case as this chart might suggest, viewing the two lists together makes it clear that Rom 4 is indeed showing us the difference between these two possible ways of relating to God.

The law-grace distinction can be seen in the way faith is set over against a series of opposite concepts as Paul's argument progresses through 4:22. He first contrasts faith and works (4:1-8), then faith and circumcision (4:9-12), then faith and law (4:13-22).[28]

Sometimes Rom 4 is seen as addressing primarily or even exclusively the false rabbinic beliefs of Paul's day with regard to the role of the Jews and the place of the Law of Moses in God's plan of salvation. References to "law" (4:13-16) are taken to mean the Mosaic Law only, and the chapter as a whole is seen as having little or no

---

[28]Some see a parallel between these major sections of Rom 4 and the concluding section of Rom 3. For example, Reese (125) says 3:27-28 is explained in detail in 4:1-8; that 3:29-30 is worked out in 4:9-12; and that 3:31 is expanded in 4:13-22. There does seem to be a general correspondence in the subject matter of these sections, but this may be more incidental than intentional. For example, the material in 4:13-22 is clearly more than just an expansion of 3:31.

relevance for Christians living today. This is a serious mistake. With the exception of v. 16, "law" seems to refer to God's law in general and especially to law as a way of salvation. Trusting in one's own obedience (works of law) as the means of being right with God is far from being an exclusively Jewish problem. Thus the teaching of this section is relevant for us all, especially for Christians who are still plagued by legalistic tendencies.

The content of this section seems to fall into six paragraphs, thus: Abraham was justified by faith apart from works (4:1-5). This is explained and confirmed by David in Ps 32:1-2 (4:6-8). Membership in Abraham's family is by faith, not by circumcision; thus Abraham is the spiritual father of both believing Gentiles and believing Jews (4:9-12). The inheritance promised to Abraham comes by faith, not by law or works of law (4:13-17a). Abraham shows us what this justifying faith is like: it means giving glory to God and believing his promises (4:17b-22). Finally, all this is relevant for Christians today because anyone who believes like Abraham will be justified like Abraham (4:23-25).

A. ABRAHAM WAS JUSTIFIED BY FAITH
APART FROM WORKS (4:1-5)

4:1 Paul begins this section on Abraham with a question: **What then shall we say that Abraham, our forefather, discovered in this matter?** How does he fit into this picture? Regarding this matter of justification, what did he find to be the case?

A major exegetical issue in this verse has to do with a phrase not even translated by the NIV, namely, κατὰ σάρκα (*kata sarka*), "according to the flesh." This phrase occurs at the end of the verse. The question is whether it modifies the verb "discovered," or the noun "forefather."

Some take it to modify the verb.[29] In this case "flesh" would refer to human nature as such. The question then would be, "What was Abraham able to accomplish (regarding justification) by his own unaided human effort, by his own works apart from grace?" Jewish tradition in Paul's day viewed Abraham as justified by his

---

[29]E.g., Godet, 168; Lard, 128; MP 324; DeWelt, 61.

own works. A writing called *Jubilees* says, "Abraham was perfect in all his deeds with the Lord, and well-pleasing in righteousness all the days of his life" (23:10; cited in Moo, I:260). The apocryphal writing "Prayer of Manasseh" declares that Abraham (along with Isaac and Jacob) never sinned and thus needed no repentance (v. 8). Abraham "kept the law of the most High" (Ecclesiasticus 44:20); he "performed the whole Law before it was given" (*Mishnah Qiddusin* 4:14; cited in Morris, 195).

However, if this question is indeed asking what Abraham found according to the flesh, Paul's answer is — *nothing!* "Surely, he obtained nothing whatever in this manner" (MP, 324). Even Abraham was justified by faith, apart from works of law. This is the main point of the whole chapter.

This way of interpreting "according to the flesh" makes good sense and is true to Paul's point. Others take it a different way, however. They see this phrase as modifying "forefather." The question would then be, "What was the case regarding Abraham, our forefather according to the flesh, our physical ancestor?"[30] (See 1:3; 9:3, 5.) The word order makes this the preferred interpretation.

Why would Paul describe Abraham thus? Along with the possessive pronoun "our," this suggests that he is referring to Abraham as the "forefather of us Jews." The "our" is natural because of Paul's own identity as a Jew and thus as a physical descendant of Abraham. The main reason for referring to Abraham this way here in v. 1 is that it helps to set up a contrast that is important later in the chapter, namely, the contrast between Abraham's role as the physical ancestor of the Jews only, and his role as the spiritual ancestor of all believers, whether they be Jews or Gentiles (4:11-12, 16). Paul's question thus means, "What shall we say with regard to Abraham, the illustrious ancestor of us Jewish people? How was he justified? By works, or by faith?"

4:2 In response to the question in v. 1, Paul considers the possibility that Abraham may have been justified by his works. **If, in fact, Abraham was justified by works, he had something to boast about . . . .** This assumes that if *any* person *were* justified by his works, then he would have reason to boast — a principle suggested

---

[30]E.g., Reese, 133-134, Hendriksen, I:143; Moo, I:263; Stott, 124.

also by Eph 2:9. In the Jews' opinion, Abraham was such a person. 1 Maccabees 2:52 asks the question, "Was not Abraham found faithful in temptation, and it was imputed unto him for righteousness?" One of the Dead Sea Scrolls says that Abraham "was accounted a friend of God because he kept the commandments of God" (Cairo Damascus Document, 3:2; cited in Dunn, I:200). If this was the case, then Paul's main thesis in 3:28 would be false; and boasting would not be excluded after all, contrary to 3:27.

Well, says Paul, in the eyes of some this may be the case, **but not before God.** The reader must be careful not to misunderstand this very terse statement. One might think Paul is setting up a contrast between "justified before men" and "justified before God." If so, he would be saying that Abraham, if justified by works, could boast before men, but not before God. But this is not the point. If Abraham were in fact justified by his works, he would have to be perfect, and would thus have a right to boast before both men and God.

What, then, is the point? "But not before God" is a denial of the whole hypothesis that Abraham was justified by works. Regardless of what the Jews may think, this is not how God looks at it. From God's point of view, this is simply not the case. The way God sees it, Abraham did not find or discover justification by works. (See Cranfield, I:228; Hendriksen, I:146; Moo, I:261, 264.)

4:3 What, then, is the answer to the question in v. 1? What did Abraham find to be the case with regard to justification? Paul passes by all human opinions and goes straight to "the very words of God" (3:2): **What does the Scripture say?** The testimony of Scripture is the basis for his denial of the hypothesis in 4:2a. *Was* Abraham justified by works? No! How do we know? Because of what "the Scripture" (ἡ γραφή, *hē graphē*) says. The words of Scripture are the final authority for this and every other question.

Here is what the Scripture says: **"Abraham believed God, and it was credited to him as righteousness."** This statement, taken directly from Gen 15:6, is equivalent to saying that Abraham was justified by faith; this verse is quoted with the same meaning in Gal 3:6 and Jas 2:23.

The nature of Abraham's faith is explained later in the chapter (4:17-22), with an emphasis on the way he believed God's promises (4:21). Obviously the promises given to Abraham could not refer specifically to his future seed, Jesus Christ, and to his saving work. Nonetheless God gave him several promises of staggering import, all of which ultimately culminated in Christ's redeeming activity (Acts 13:32-33; Heb 11:8-13). First, God promised Abraham that he would be the father of a "great nation" with numberless offspring.[31] Second, he promised him and his offspring possession of the land of Canaan.[32] Third and most significantly, God promised Abraham that "all peoples on earth will be blessed through you"[33] — a reference, of course, to the messianic purpose for which God called Abraham in the first place.

The point is that with regard to all these promises, Abraham humbly believed that God could and would keep his word. Consequently he surrendered himself to God and rendered to him the obedience of faith (1:5).

The statement quoted by Paul from Gen 15:6 occurs specifically upon one of the occasions when God promised Abraham numberless offspring (Gen 15:5). We must not conclude, however, that this was the only time when Abraham believed, nor that it was the only or even first time when "it was credited to him as righteousness." Jas 2:23 also quotes Gen 15:6, but applies it to the occasion when Abraham offered Isaac as a sacrifice, an event which occurred much later (Gen 22:1-18). This implies that Abraham's faith and the resulting justification were present from the day he was first called (Gen 12:1) and to the end of his life.[34]

The word translated "it was credited" is a very important word that stands for an even more important concept, often called the doctrine of imputation. The term is λογίζομαι (*logizomai*), and it is used a total of 11 times in this chapter. Its meaning here seems to be rooted in the way it was used by Greeks in the field of business or commerce.[35] It was a technical term used to describe the procedure of entering a credit or a debit to someone's account. It is properly

---

[31]Gen 12:2; 13:16; 15:5; 17:2-6; 18:18; 22:17.
[32]Gen 12:2, 7; 13:14-17; 15:7, 18-21; 17:8; 22:17.
[33]Gen 12:3; 18:18; 22:18.
[34]See Fuller, *Unity*, 310-311, 315.
[35]See 2:3 for another main connotation of the same word.

translated "to credit [NIV], to set down to one's account, to impute, to reckon, to count as, to regard as."[36]

It was credited or counted to Abraham "as righteousness." The righteous character of God and thus the righteous requirements of his law must be fully satisfied before a person can be saved (3:26). In this sense righteousness, or the satisfaction of the requirements of God's law (see 1:17), is the very basis for salvation. Theoretically one may satisfy the law's commandments through perfect obedience and thereby be saved on the basis of his own personal righteousness, but universal sin makes this impossible. This is why God must credit or impute something else to sinners as the righteousness by which they are saved.

Exactly what is reckoned to Abraham, or credited to his account? In this verse (as in vv. 22-24) the passive verb has no specific subject, and is simply translated "it was credited." What is the "it"? Verses 5 and 9 specifically say that Abraham's *faith* was credited as righteousness. "In God's judgment, his faith is righteousness" (Schlatter, 110). Faith is thus presented as a form of righteousness that stands over against perfectly righteous character and behavior, i.e., works (vv. 4-5).[37] This does not mean, however, that faith itself is a meritorious act that is equal to a life of perfect obedience, thus making a person *worthy* of salvation.[38] Again, in vv. 4-5 Paul makes it clear that when God credits faith as righteousness, this is a gift of grace and is something quite distinct from a merited or deserved reward for works.

In fact, strictly speaking, it is not faith itself that is credited to a sinner's account, but the ultimate *object* of his faith, namely, the atoning blood of Jesus Christ that satisfies the law's requirement

---

[36]See Cranfield, I:230-231. The term is used with the same or similar meaning in 2:26; 2 Cor 5:19; Gal 3:6; 2 Tim 4:16; Jas 2:23. The meaning of ἐλλογέω is very close; see 5:13; Phlm 18. The Hebrew word in Gen 15:6 (חשׁב, *chashab*) has a similar connotation; see Moo I:265.

[37]We must reject Lard's notion that the faith credited to Abraham "contained the whole future obedience of the man" (129), and Reese's similar contention that Abraham's faith included "works of faith" and "consistent obedience" (136). Such ideas violate Paul's very point in vv. 4-5.

[38]Such a view was a popular rabbinic interpretation of Gen 15:6. See Cranfield, I:229; Moo, I:266; Morris, 196, n. 13.

for penalty in our place (see above, 1:17; 3:21-26). This and this alone is the righteousness that saves, and this is the righteousness that is credited to us. This is the significance of the language of 4:6 and 4:11, which says that *righteousness itself* is credited to believers. I.e., what is credited to us is not something we *do*, but something we *receive* as a gift. To say that Abraham's or anybody else's *faith* is credited as righteousness is shorthand for this basic gospel truth.[39]

Of course, since Abraham lived about 2000 years before Christ, his faith in the Redeemer's blood was only indirect and not direct. Nevertheless God credited the full effects of the atonement to Abraham's account, since the cross and the resurrection of Jesus were the ultimate outcome of the promises that were the object of his faith.

The result of God's crediting Abraham's faith — or the ultimate object of it — to his account was that he was fully justified. "Faith credited as righteousness" is the same as *justification by faith*, or full forgiveness of sins. The idea that OT saints received only an "IOU" instead of full forgiveness, and that they were held in a limbo-like state instead of being taken directly to paradise when they died, is without foundation of the Bible. All of Romans 4, especially vv. 3-8, shows that Abraham and other OT saints were justified in the fullest sense of the word. Their sins were not just "rolled back" until Christ actually died, but were fully forgiven in view of the certainty of that future event.

4:4 The next two verses clarify the nature of justification by faith as it applies to Abraham specifically and to all believers in general. They set forth a main difference between salvation by law (v. 4) and salvation by grace (v. 5), namely, the former is by works and the latter by faith. More precisely, these verses declare that these two ways of salvation are opposite to one another and thus are mutually exclusive. As such they are an elaboration of 3:28.

Verse 4 describes what it would be like to be justified by works of law, as some thought Abraham was (4:2a). It does so by setting forth a basic principle of economics, namely, the relation between

---

[39]See Hendriksen, I:146; Murray, I:353-359. "The righteousness contemplated in justification is not faith itself but something that comes into our possession by faith" (Murray, I:358).

work and wages: **Now when a man works, his wages are not credited to him as a gift, but as an obligation.** When anyone contracts to do a certain job and then completes that job, on what basis does he request his wages? Does he ask his employer to give it to him as a *gift*? Of course not! The wage is something that is owed to him; he has worked for it and he deserves it. From the employer's point of view he is obligated to pay the wage; it is a *debt* that he owes to the worker.

The implied parallel is clear. "When a man works" refers to anyone who is seeking to relate to God under the system of law. This is like working for wages, says Paul. Under law a person will receive from God exactly what he deserves or what he has earned by his works. The wages or reward, whatever that may be, is bestowed by God as a matter of debt or obligation, not as a gift. The word for "gift" is χάρις (*charis*), or *grace*. Thus when a man approaches God on the basis of law, he shuts himself off from grace. What is credited to his account, to be received on the day of judgment, is credited not according to grace but according to debt.

This has two serious implications. First, since only sinless obedience deserves heaven, and since all have sinned, neither Abraham nor anyone else will actually receive salvation as a reward for his works (contrary to the hypothesis suggested in 4:2a). Under law the only wage that can be expected by sinners is death (6:23), including the second death in the lake of fire (Rev 20:14-15).

Second, those who expect to receive their reward according to the terms of grace ("gift") cannot make their plea on the basis of their works. Works receive wages, and wages exclude grace. The only way to avoid receiving the wages we deserve is to lay hold of the gift of justification by faith apart from works (3:28). If it is by grace, it must be by faith (4:16) and not by works. As Moo says (I:267), "The faith that gained righteousness for Abraham was a faith that excluded works." This point is explained and emphasized in the next verse.

4:5 However, to the man who does not work but trusts God who justifies the wicked, his faith is credited as righteousness. Whereas in v. 4 Paul stated a basic economic principle with an implied theological application, here he skips the illustrative principle and goes straight to the theological point. Just as justification by works excludes grace, so does justification by grace exclude works. Who will be justified? "The man who does not work but trusts God."

What is meant by the provocative phrase, "the man who does not work"? Does it mean "the man who never obeys"? Is Paul saying that works are completely irrelevant for salvation, even to the extent that a person can be saved by bare faith even if he has no acts of obedience whatsoever? This cannot be his meaning, as chapter 6 shows. Does it mean, then, "the man who does not obey perfectly," as some suggest?[40] This would make good sense if v. 5 could be taken in isolation from v. 4, but it is not consistent with the obvious contrast between the two verses. Specifically, the "man who works" in v. 4 is not necessarily "the man who obeys perfectly."

"The man who does not work" is best understood as "the man who does not look upon his works as a means of laying hold of justification," or "the man who does not trust his works or depend upon them for his standing before God" (see MacArthur, I:239; Moo, I:267). It means "the man who has renounced the law system, in which works are rewarded in terms of wages earned." As Morris (198) says, the contrast between v. 4 and v. 5 is not between one who works and one who does not work at all, but between one who trusts in his works and one who trusts in God.

The most striking part of this verse is the description of God as one "who justifies the wicked." Such a description, says Bruce (115), "is so paradoxical as to be startling — not to say shocking." The word for wicked (ἀσεβής, *asebēs*) and its cognates (see 1:18) are strong terms describing a state of ungodliness and lawlessness. In the OT God demanded that human judges in human courts of law should always condemn and never acquit (justify) such wicked persons (Deut 25:1; Prov 17:15; 24:24; Isa 5:23). God himself declares, "I will not justify the wicked" (Exod 23:7, KJV). Rom 1:18 pictures him as directing his wrath toward all human wickedness. But here in 4:5, he is pictured as the one who *justifies* the wicked!

How can this be? How can the righteous God justify the wicked? He cannot, within the parameters and constraints of *law*. Human courts are ordained to operate according to the principles of law,

---

[40]Lard, 132; DeWelt, 62; Reese, 138-139.

and God's own holy nature is bound by these principles. But here in 4:5 the perspective is not law but *grace*, and the principles of grace are the very opposite of law! Thus whereas the holy God who is a consuming fire (Heb 12:29) must *condemn* the wicked, the same God who is also loving and gracious can also *justify* the wicked! Because of his grace Christ died for all the wicked (5:6), and the wicked who put their faith in his saving death will be justified. This description of God thus epitomizes the very essence of grace.

In this context "the wicked" of course includes Abraham along with everyone else. All are sinners, and when we ask God to justify or forgive us, we must believe that he is a God who justifies the wicked, since that is exactly what we are asking and expecting him to do! Also, when we approach God and ask him to justify us, we are in effect asking him to justify us apart from our works – our *sinful* works. That is to say, the God who justifies the wicked *is* a God who justifies by faith apart from works. Paul explains this in vv. 6-8 by citing the testimony of David.

B. DAVID EXPLAINS AND CONFIRMS JUSTIFICATION BY FAITH APART FROM WORKS (4:6-8)

In the midst of his discussion of Abraham as a paradigm of salvation by grace, Paul inserts another relevant biblical quotation, this one from Ps 32:1-2a. This citation from the writing of David serves as further evidence of the unity between OT Scripture and Paul's teaching. It also provides crucial insight into the meaning of Paul's basic theme, that we are justified by faith apart from works of law (3:28). Also, in case there is any doubt, the quotation from David serves to generalize the assertion made concerning Abraham in 15:6 as quoted in 4:3, showing that it applies to all believers.

4:6 Paul introduces David's prophetic word thus: **David says the same thing when he speaks of the blessednesss of the man to whom God credits righteousness apart from works . . . .** "Says the same thing" is the NIV's translation of the conjunctive phrase καθάπερ καί (*kathaper kai*), "just as also." This links the two OT quotes (Gen 15:6 and Ps 32:1-2a) closely together in meaning.

We must never try to understand "justification by faith apart from works" without a consideration of the meaning of these words of David. This is evident from the very way Paul describes David's testimony. Of whom is the Psalmist speaking? Of "the man to whom God credits righteousness apart from works." This language is directly tied in with the "righteousness of God" of which Paul speaks in his thematic statement in 1:17, and of which "the Law and the Prophets testify" (3:21). It refers to the gift of God's righteousness established by Jesus in his atoning sacrifice and received by sinners through faith (3:22-25). It echoes 4:3. "Credits righteousness" is the same as "justifies." "Apart from works" (χωρὶς ἔργων, *chōris ergōn*) is the same as "apart from works of law" (*chōris ergōn nomou*) in 3:28.[41]

What does it mean to say that God credits righteousness apart from works, and why is this a blessing? Before answering these questions we must examine the content of the quotation from David.

4:7-8 Blessed are they whose transgressions are forgiven, whose sins are covered. Blessed is the man whose sin the Lord will never count against him. This is an almost exact[42] quotation from Ps 32:1-2a (LXX), a Psalm attributed to David both by the OT text and by Paul (4:6). Each segment of the quote begins with the adjective μακάριος (*makarios*), just as the beatitudes do (Matt 5:3-11). It means "happy, fortunate, content"; in a theistic context it is properly translated "blessed, favored." It is "the highest term which a Greek could use to describe a state of felicity" (Sanday and Headlam, 102).

The blessing of which David speaks is attributed to a general category of people in v. 7, "they" or "those." Verse 8 applies the blessing to a specific representative of this category, "the man," in the sense of "any man." In the latter verse the Greek term is ἀνήρ (*anēr*), which means "a male human being" and is properly translated as "man." This does not exclude women from the blessing, of course. The singular *anēr* simply stands for all who belong to this group, whether male or female.

---

[41]The fact that Paul does not mention faith in 4:6 shows that 4:3 and 4:5 refer to the crediting of the *object* of faith, not to the faith itself.

[42]Or an exact quotation, according to some textual variants.

What is the nature of the blessing of which David speaks? Three separate expressions are used, all of which basically refer to the same thing: the way a person's sins are regarded by God under the grace system. Under grace, our "transgressions are forgiven"; our "sins are covered" and will never be counted against us. Two different words are used for sin. One (v. 7a) is ἀνομία (*anomia*), from *nomos* ("law") with a negating alpha, thus "lawlessness, transgression of the law" (see 6:19; 1 John 3:4). The other term (vv. 7b-8) is the common ἁμαρτία (*hamartia*, used 48 times in Romans), which refers to missing the mark or falling short of the standard (see 3:23). The connotations are similar if not the same.

The blessing of grace is that the engraced person's sins are *forgiven*. This is the common word ἀφίημι (*aphiēmi*). This word and its noun form, ἄφεσις (*aphesis*, "forgiveness, remission") are used in this theological sense quite frequently in the NT, though very seldom by Paul.[43] In secular Greek it meant (among other things) "to release someone from an obligation, from a debt, or from punishment; to pardon; to leave behind." Thus when used in the religious sense of forgiveness, *aphiēmi* means "to release from the debt of punishment owed to God because of sin." A person whose sins are forgiven is a person for whom the debt of eternal punishment has been left behind.

Another way of saying this is that our sins have been *covered*. See Ps 85:2 for the parallel use of forgiveness and covering with respect to sin. To say that our sins are covered means that God himself has blotted them out of his own sight (Heb 8:12). When he looks at us in Jesus Christ, our sins are hidden from him in the sense that he does not hold them against us.

This is indeed the third way of expressing this blessing: for the man who is under grace, the Lord will never count his sins against him (v. 8). We are sinners, without question; but the gracious God will not make us pay for our sins. The term is λογίζομαι (*logizomai*) again, i.e., God will not reckon our sins against us; he will not enter them into our own personal accounts as debts for which we must render payment to God in the form of eternal punishment in hell.

---

[43]This is probably because he prefers to speak of justification, which is almost synonymous with forgiveness, as we shall see below.

The emphatic certainty of this blessing is underscored by the use of a double negative, οὐ μή (*ou mē*): the Lord will by no means, he will not ever, he "will never" (NIV) hold our sins against us.

To say that such a person is blessed implies that he *knows* that his sins are forgiven and covered. Who can deny that this is indeed the greatest blessing we could ever desire or imagine? The knowledge that the gracious God has released us from the debt of punishment and will not hold our sins against us should fill us with eternal awe and amazement, with the greatest heights and depths of gratitude and love, and with "inexpressible and glorious joy" (1 Pet 1:8).

These two verses specifically assert the second half of the grace formula or grace principle (see page 248 above): "Break the commandments, but escape the penalty." But we should never forget that the reason why God is able to bestow such an immeasurable blessing upon us, of course, is because of what Jesus has done for us through his work of propitiation on the cross. Instead of reckoning our sins to our account, God has reckoned or imputed them to Jesus Christ; he has put them down to Jesus' account, and Jesus has paid the deserved debt of punishment in full, in our place. This righteous payment of sin's punishment, rather than the sin itself, is then credited to our account; this is the righteousness of which v. 4:6b speaks. This is what it means to say that "God credits righteousness apart from works."

In a real sense this section (4:6-8) is the culmination of the explanation of justification by grace that was begun in 3:21. It casts vital and crucial light on the whole discussion and especially on the thesis statement in 3:28. It helps us to understand the meaning of justification as such, and it is crucial for our understanding of "justification by faith apart from works of law."

Throughout this whole section (3:21-4:8), the following expressions are basically equivalent: "righteousness from God . . . through faith" (3:22); "justified freely by his grace" (3:24); "justified by faith apart from works of law" (3:28, RSV); "it was credited to him as righteousness" (4:3); "justifies the wicked" (4:5); "faith is credited as righteousness" (4:5); "credits righteousness apart from works" (4:6); "transgressions are forgiven . . . sins are covered" (4:7); and "whose sin the Lord will never count against him" (4:8). Because of the basic equivalence of these expressions, we should never draw our conclusions as to the meaning of any one of them without considering them all together.

There are several implications from this. First, *justification of the wicked* is the same as *forgiveness of sins*. There is no basis for saying that "forgiveness is a very important *part* of justification," or that it is "a basic *component* of justification."[44] For sinners, this is it: justification *is* forgiveness (see Reese, 141). This is the implication of Paul's citation of Ps 32:1-2a. What David says is "the same thing" as justifying the wicked. God justifies sinners by forgiving them, by not holding their sins against them.

A second and closely related implication, is the equivalence of justification (the non-imputation of sins) with the imputation or crediting of righteousness (4:6). As we have already seen, the righteousness imputed to the sinner's account is the righteousness established by Jesus when he paid the penalty for sins in our place. There is no reason to include in this imputed righteousness anything more than Christ's payment of sin's penalty.

A final implication of the parallelism of the expressions in 3:21-4:8 has to do with the meaning of "apart from works of law" in 3:28. It is commonly assumed that this expression refers only to *good* works, or to *positive* responses to God's law, or to *obedience* to the law in some form.[45] But this is a serious error, as 4:7-8 clearly shows. The language in 4:6, "credits righteousness apart from works," shows that Paul is expanding on the expression in 3:28, "justified by faith apart from works of law." To what *works* does he specifically refer? *Sinful* works! To be justified apart from works of law means to have our acts of disobedience to law (*anomia*, 4:7) forgiven. To be justified apart from works means that God does not hold our sinful works against us. To be justified by faith apart from works of law means that God counts us righteous because of our faith (4:3), apart from a consideration of how we have responded to

---

[44]Hendriksen, I:147; Moo, I:269. Italics added.

[45]This is seen in various translations of 3:28: "observing the law" (NIV); "works prescribed by the law" (NRSV); what one "has managed to achieve under the Law" (Phillips); "keeping the law" (NEB); "doing what the law commands" (TEV); "actions done in obedience to Law" (Weymouth); "the good things we do" (LB).

his law. Our good responses to law (i.e., obedience) do not warrant our justification, nor do our bad responses (i.e., sins) prevent it.

C. MEMBERSHIP IN ABRAHAM'S FAMILY IS BY FAITH, NOT BY CIRCUMCISION (4:9-12)

Having established that Abraham is the OT paradigm for justification by faith by citing Gen 15:6, and having clarified what this means in a general way by citing Ps 32:1-2a, Paul now applies this specifically to the Jew-Gentile debate. In vv. 1-8 he shows that we are justified by faith alone, apart from a consideration of works. Now in vv. 9-12 he establishes from the Abrahamic paradigm that a person is justified by faith, apart from a consideration of whether he has been circumcised or not.

This is the second time Paul has discussed circumcision. In 2:25-29 he showed that the Jews who were attempting to be saved by law would be judged by their obedience or disobedience to the entire law, not just by their possession of circumcision. Here he shows that under grace those who share the Abrahamic blessing of justification are those who share his faith, not his circumcision. This is a direct attack on Jewish exclusivism, which linked circumcision to salvation and limited salvation to those who were circumcised (Acts 15:1).

Paul makes his point by observing that the announcement of Abraham's justification by faith (Gen 15:6) occurred many years before circumcision was introduced (Gen 17:9-14). Thus, as Bruce says, there was no way that the Jews could argue that the faith principle was valid only for Abraham's circumcised offspring. "The case of Abraham shows that circumcision or uncircumcision is irrelevant to a man's status before God" (111-112).

4:9 Is this blessedness (the forgiveness of which David speaks) **only for the circumcised, or also for the uncircumcised?** I.e., is it available only to the Jews, or is it for the Gentiles also? Cranfield says that the rabbis of Paul's day generally assumed that Israelites alone were forgiven (I:234-235). But Paul here uses the example of Abraham to show that this assumption is false. His argument continues to be based on the parallel between Gen 15:6 and Ps 32:1-2a.

In 4:6-8 he uses the latter text to explain the *meaning* of the former; here he cites Gen 15:6 again to establish the *scope* of the Psalms passage. **We have been saying** (4:3) **that Abraham's faith was credited to him as righteousness.** More specifically, as noted above, the implicit object of his faith (the righteousness of God in Christ) was credited to his account and counted as his own.

4:10 How is this relevant to the Jew-Gentile issue? Paul gets to this point by asking two questions: **Under what circumstances was it credited? Was it after he was circumcised, or before?** If Abraham had already been circumcised when his faith was taken for righteousness, then the Jews might try to argue that the blessing of forgiveness is only for them. But if this happened prior to the introduction of circumcision, then there is no way that this blessing can be limited only to those who are circumcised. The OT record is very clear. **It was not after, but before!**[46] Thus as far as the conditions for justification are concerned, "circumcision was no factor at all" (Murray, I:137).

4:11 This does not mean that there was no relation at all between Abraham's faith and his circumcision. In the first part of v. 11 Paul comments on the introduction of circumcision into the covenant relationship thus: **And he received the sign of circumcision, a seal of the righteousness that he had by faith while he was still uncircumcised.** Abraham received this sign about 14 years or more after the specific recognition of his faith (cf. Gen 16:16 and 17:1). This shows that the circumcision was not a condition for his justification.

Why then was circumcision given? Paul uses two words that relate to its purpose or function: *sign* and *seal*. The former term comes directly from Gen 17:11, where God said to Abraham that circumcision "will be the sign of the covenant between me and you." This is no doubt the only reason why Paul here calls it "the sign [consisting] of circumcision." This was its commonly-known purpose; it was "the sign of the covenant," or the sign of belonging to the covenant family consisting of Abraham's earthly descendants

---

[46]The NIV smooths out the Greek text's double reference to circumcision and uncircumcision. A literal translation would be, "How then was it [faith] credited? When he was in circumcision, or in uncircumcision? Not in circumcision, but in uncircumcision."

through Isaac and Jacob. It had this meaning not only for Abraham but for all who received it. Paul does not mean that circumcision was given as a sign of Abraham's faith (contra Murray, I:137) or of his justification (contra Hendriksen, I:150; Stott, 129). Nor could it have served such a purpose for anyone else, since it was applied in infancy before faith could be present, and was applied to every male infant whether he grew up to become a believer or not (Gen 17:12).

But Paul does say that Abraham's own circumcision functioned as "a seal of the righteousness that he had by faith" even before he was circumcised. A seal (such as a signet ring or its impression) serves as a mark of ownership or identification. Thus by extension it can mean "a confirmation, an attestation, an authentication, a guarantee" (see 1 Cor 9:2). This latter meaning is the point here. By giving Abraham the sign of circumcision, God was providing him with an "outward and visible authentication, ratification and guarantee, of the righteousness by faith which was already his while he was still uncircumcised" (Cranfield, I:236). As such it served as a source of assurance to Abraham that God had truly accepted him and counted him righteous because of his faith. Thus "to Abraham it was a guarantee of the trustworthiness of God's promise" (Hendriksen, I:150-151).

The point that Paul makes from this is that it shows that Abraham was already justified before he received circumcision, since a seal does not confer that which it ratifies, but assumes that it already exists. *"This proves that circumcision has nothing to do with being declared righteous,"* in the sense of being a necessary condition for it (Hendriksen, I:150).

It is commonly taught that what is said here of circumcision applies equally to Christian baptism, and to the "sacraments" in general.[47] Indeed, in Christian literature baptism is constantly called "a sign and a seal." The NT itself never uses this language for baptism, though;[48] calling it such is purely an inference from the supposed parallel between baptism and circumcision. Assuming

---

[47]"We have indeed here a remarkable passage with regard to the general benefits of sacraments," says Calvin (164).

[48]The NT calls the Holy Spirit the Christian's seal: 1 Cor 1:22; Eph 1:13; 4:30.

such a parallel, commentators and theologians constantly use this passage as a foundation for their doctrine of the "sacraments" in general. They use it especially in an attempt to establish that a person must already be justified (forgiven) before he is baptized, and more generally to argue that there can be no connection between salvation and "externals" of any kind.[49]

Two comments are pertinent. First, as far as its general meaning was concerned, *not even circumcision* was "a sign and a seal" pertaining to salvation. It was indeed a sign of covenant membership for all who received it, but there was no necessary relationship between covenant membership and salvation. Also, it was a seal of "righteousness by faith" *only* for Abraham. It was never intended to have this latter meaning for anyone else. Thus even if there were a parallel between baptism and circumcision in general, the concept of the seal would not be a part of it.

Second, the idea that baptism is the NT counterpart to OT circumcision must itself be rejected as a false doctrine (see under 2:29 above). It has neither a sound exegetical basis nor a solid theological rationale. It is an inference drawn from the faulty concept of covenant unity, which itself was created by Huldreich Zwingli in 1525 in the midst of his controversy with the Anabaptists regarding infant baptism.[50] The bottom line is that Romans 4:11 has nothing whatsoever to say about the meaning of Christian baptism.[51] Nor does it warrant any general conclusion about the relation between salvation and "externals" as such.

In this text the main question is this: is the blessing of forgiveness for Jews only, or for Gentiles also (v. 9a)? Paul sets the stage for his answer in vv. 9b-11a by showing that Abraham received forgiveness "by faith while he was still uncircumcised" (v. 11a). The answer is given in vv. 11b-12, where the Apostle affirms that

---

[49]For example, see Hendriksen, I:151; Stott, 129; Boice, I:456-458; McClain, 115; Lloyd-Jones, 187-188; and Mitchell, 98. Even those who do not specifically affirm a parallel usually use 4:11 as a springboard for making this point about baptism (e.g., Robertson, 351; Mounce, 126).

[50]See Cottrell, "Covenant" and "Reformed Tradition" for a detailed study of Zwingli as the originator of this concept.

[51]See Moo, I:277. He rightly says that an allusion to baptism in 4:11 is "unproved and improbable."

Abraham is the spiritual father of all believers, whether they are circumcised or not. The NIV begins this answer with **So then**, indicating simple result. The Greek is better rendered in terms of purpose, however. See the NASB, "that he might be"; or the NRSV, "The purpose was." I.e., Abraham was credited as righteous prior to his circumcision *so that* he might be . . . **the father of all who believe but have not been circumcised, in order that righteousness might be credited to them.** This of course refers to the Gentiles, and it clearly shows that Gentiles may receive justification through faith no less than Jews.

There is no question that Abraham was the father or founder of the Jewish nation (4:1), and that being able to claim him as one's ancestor was a great privilege.[52] Here, however, Paul is speaking of Abraham's *spiritual* fatherhood, which is determined not by physical descent but by imitation of Abraham's faith (Gal 3:7, 29). He is "the father of all who believe," which was God's ultimate purpose for him from the beginning (Gen 12:3). All Christians have the privilege of calling Abraham "our father" and of inheriting the salvation promised through him (4:13-17; Gal 3).

4:12 This applies to the Jews also, both the true believers under the Old Covenant and Jewish Christians under the New Covenant. **And he is also the father of the circumcised who not only are circumcised but who also walk in the footsteps of the faith that our father Abraham had before he was circumcised.** Jews have the privilege of being children of Abraham in two senses. First, all are descended from him physically, an involuntary circumstance marked by circumcision. No promise of eternal salvation is attached to this relationship. Second, any individual Jew may choose to "walk in the footsteps of the faith" of Abraham. This choice is unrelated to circumcision as such; and this choice alone is the way of salvation, even for Jews.[53]

The bottom line is that membership in Abraham's larger and permanent spiritual family is by faith in the blood of the Redeemer, not by blood relationship as marked by circumcision.

---

[52]See Matt 1:1; 16:22-31; Luke 1:73; 13:16; 19:9; John 8:39, 56; Acts 7:2; 2 Cor 11:22; Jas 2:21.

[53]To "walk in the footsteps" of Abraham's faith is a graphic way of describing how we must all follow Abraham's example of faith if we want

D. THE INHERITANCE PROMISED TO ABRAHAM COMES BY FAITH, NOT BY LAW (4:13-17a)

The salvation of sinners comes not in accordance with works done in response to law, but on the condition of faith in God's grace. This contrast between law and grace, between works and faith, has been Paul's overriding theme thus far (3:20-22, 28; 4:2-5), and it continues to be so in this section. In chapter 4 the theme develops thus: we are justified by faith: apart from works (vv. 1-8); apart from circumcision (vv. 9-12); and apart from law (vv. 13-17a). These are not different points, but different aspects of the same point.

4:13 It was not through law that Abraham and his offspring received the promise that he would be heir of the world, but through the righteousness that comes by faith. The NIV fails to translate the connecting particle *gar,* "for," which connects this section with the previous one. The flow of thought is this: Abraham is "the father of all who believe" (4:11), *because* the blessing that God promised to give through him comes "not through law" but through faith.

The promise did not come "through law." To what law does this refer? Some say it must refer to the Mosaic Law, since "law" in vv. 14-16 seems to refer to this (Cranfield, I:239; Moo, I:279). This would certainly make sense, given the fact that the Mosaic Law did not even exist until over four centuries later (Gal 3:17-18). The form of this argument would thus be the same as the argument about circumcision in 4:9-12. Since the promise preceded circumcision by 14+ years, it cannot be dependent on circumcision; and since the promise preceded the Mosaic Law by 400+ years, it cannot be dependent upon the Law, either.

Others say the "law" in v. 13 refers to any and every form of law, including the Law of Moses but not limited thereto (DeWelt,

---

to be his true offspring. "Walk" is the Greek verb στοιχέω (*stoicheo*), "to form a line, to march in line." Faith itself is personified as the leader of the march, the one in whose footsteps we walk. This is a figure for imitating or conforming to Abraham's faith. See Gal 5:25; 6:16; Phil 3:16 for other uses of the verb in this sense.

85; Sanday and Headlam, 110; Murray, I:141).[54] This is not contrary to the context, since νόμος (*nomos*) in vv. 14-15 is better understood in this same general sense, and since this has been Paul's main connotation for it in the preceding context. The promise did not and does not come through obedience to whatever form of law one possesses, i.e., through law-keeping.

The focus here is on the concept of promise,[55] which is a natural corollary of grace and faith. Grace focuses not on what man can do (i.e., works), but on what God has done and promises to do, and on what he promises to give to sinners as a result. All the sinner can do — and must do — is believe God's promises and accept his gifts.

The full scope of God's promises to Abraham was laid out under 4:3 above. He was promised possession of the land, numberless offspring, and the role of being a source of blessing for all nations. The OT text does not use the exact terminology used here — that Abraham "would be the heir of the world." This is probably a summary of the three main promises as they are now understood in the light of NT revelation. "The world" is first of all Abraham's innumerable family of spiritual children, drawn from "all peoples on earth" (Gen 12:3; see 18:18; 22:18). It probably also includes the new earth inherited by them (Matt 5:5; 2 Pet 3:13), of which the gift of Canaan (later Israel) was a symbolic type. To say that "he" (Abraham) would be the heir of the world means that he would inherit this spiritual family, and through them would inherit the (new) world itself.[56]

The "offspring" (σπέρμα, *sperma*, "seed") of Abraham here refers to all believers, as v. 16 shows. In Gal 3:16 Paul says that technically the *one* seed and heir of Abraham is Jesus Christ, but all who put their trust in Christ are joined to him and thereby become Abraham's seed and heirs as well (Gal 3:26-29).

---

[54]The requirements of God's moral law would have been known to Abraham, even if only as written on his heart (2:14-15).

[55]This is the first reference in Romans to this concept. From here on in chapter 4 it is a key word. See vv. 14, 16, 20, 21.

[56]"*Heir* strictly means someone who secures possession after the death of the owner, but in the New Testament it is often used of secure possession without regard to the way the possession is obtained" (Morris, 205-206).

The NIV says that Abraham and his offspring "received" this promise. The Greek text actually has no verb. The thought is probably that the promise *will be fulfilled* to Abraham and his offspring. How? By faith, not by law. This contrast is Paul's main point. "Not through law" stands first in the verse for emphasis, and the connecting adversative ἀλλά (*alla*, "but") expresses a very strong contrast. Abraham's family is still growing today; and any individual can have a share of their abundant inheritance "through the righteousness that comes by faith," *not* by works of law.

4:14 For if those who live by law are heirs, faith has no value and the promise is worthless . . . . This and v. 15 explain why the inheritance comes "not through law." Gen 15:6 is taken as the foundational principle, as establishing that justification is by faith. Once we accept this truth, we *must* grant that it cannot be by law, because the law principle (law as a way of salvation) is incompatible with the grace-faith system (see Morris, 205-206).

The NIV translation "those who live by law" is unfortunate. The Greek phrase is οἱ ἐκ νόμου (*hoi ek nomou*), "those of law." Everyone, even those who are saved by grace through faith, should *live* by law. That is, we should always obey the precepts of God's law. But those who are "of law" in this verse are those who are *depending* or *relying* on their law-keeping as the basis for their claim to the Abrahamic inheritance. This includes law-depending Jews, but is not limited thereto. "Law" is not just the Mosaic law, but the code of commandments available to and applicable to any given person at any given time. (See Morris, 206; and Murray, I:142; contra Moo, I:280-282.)

The two ways of salvation are incompatible, says Paul. If the inheritance comes "by law," i.e., by works, then faith would have no valid role in the process. The verb is κενόω (*kenoō*), "to empty." Faith would be emptied of its value; it would be irrelevant and ineffective (see 1 Cor 15:14). Also, the promise would be worthless; it would be nullified. Those who choose law as their way of relating to God thereby cancel his promise, since the two cannot coexist (Gal 3:18). Faith and promise go together, and they belong to an order that is distinct from law and works, namely, the order of grace. (See Stott, 131.)

4:15 because law brings wrath. The problem is not just the basic incompatibility of law on the one hand, and faith and promise on the other. The more immediate problem is the fact that all are sinners (3:23), and under law sinners have forfeited the promise and are "heirs" only of wrath (see 6:23). When sinners remain under law, the only outcome is wrath.

How does law produce wrath? By definition law includes both commandments to obey and penalties for those who disobey. The commandments of the law are the very measure of sin (1 John 3:4). **And where there is no law there is no transgression** because there would be no standard by which any particular act could be judged right or wrong. But since there is law, there is also such a thing as sin. And since there is sin, the *penalties* of the law (i.e., wrath) must be applied. In this sense law cannot help but inflict wrath upon sinners; it is its very nature to do so.

"Where there is no law there is no transgression" is a general principle that may be applied either universally or particularly. Its universal application is theoretical only, i.e., *if* there were no law at all, then there would be no such thing as transgression or sin.[57] But law does exist; therefore transgression also exists. The only practical application of this principle is in reference to particular cases, individuals, and laws. In cases where God has given us no commandments regarding a particular activity or behavior, either specifically or in terms of general principles, then that behavior cannot be called sinful. This is the category we call "matters of opinion."

Also, though law does exist, some individuals are unable (by reason of immaturity or mental handicap) to *understand* its true origin and nature as commandments of God bearing the penalty of eternal wrath. In this case "where there is no law" means "where there is no ability to know the law." This applies to those who have not reached what we call "the age of accountability." Furthermore, this principle may apply in the case of mature individuals who are

---

[57]Moo (I:282) says that "transgression" (παράβασις, *parabasis*) is not equivalent to sin in general, but refers only to a certain kind of sin, i.e., to the breaking of "clearly defined, verbally transmitted laws and commands." This is probably not the case, however. The word refers to a transgression of boundaries, in this case the boundaries set by God's law. Such is the very essence of sin as such (1 John 3:4). But see the next footnote.

involuntarily ignorant of a particular law of God. For example, those who are exposed to general revelation only will not be held responsible for obeying commandments that can be known only through special revelation. Thus this principle warrants the conclusion that God will finally judge all people in terms of their conscientious response to available light.[58]

4:16 Paul now draws his general conclusion from the preceding discussion: **Therefore, the promise comes by faith . . . .** Literally it reads, "on account of this — of faith." I.e., in light of what we have just seen, the promised inheritance can be received only through faith, not by law. Ἐκ πίστεως (*Ek pisteōs*), "of faith," is set in contrast with ἐκ νόμου (*ek nomou*), "of law" (v. 14).

It is "of faith" **so that it may be by grace . . . .** Given the reality of sin, law can only *enforce* the penalty of God's wrath; it cannot deliver us from it. Deliverance can come only in the form of forgiveness; forgiveness is possible only as a free gift of grace; and grace can be received only through faith in God's promise. Grace and faith are naturally compatible. Faith is the key that fits the lock that opens the treasure-house of grace.

Because the promise comes by grace through faith, it **. . . may be guaranteed to all Abraham's offspring . . .** i.e., to his spiritual children, or those who follow his example of faith. God's concern is to make the promise firm or secure to them all. The issue is not the objective believability of the promise, since God's power and truthfulness are a firm basis for this. The point rather is the subjective apprehension of the promise, the inner assurance that we are indeed safe and secure in "the bosom of Abraham," that "our transgressions are forgiven" and our "sins are covered" (4:7). Such assurance is possible only when we understand that the promised forgiveness is received by grace through faith. (See 5:1-11.)

This assurance comes **not only to those who are of the law but also to those who are of the faith of Abraham** — i.e., not only to Jews, but also to Gentiles. These descriptions of the two groups are

---

[58]In this circumstance as well as the previous one, an act that is truly sinful is not *counted* as transgression of law since the one committing the sinful act is excusably ignorant of the law that identifies it as a sin. Only in this sense can an act be *sinful* and at the same time not be a *transgression*. See the previous footnote.

quite condensed compared with vv. 11b-12, and present some difficulties. *Ek tou nomou*, "of the law," refers here to the Law of Moses,
whereas the other references to law in this section seem to refer to
law in general. Taken thus, the first part of this statement refers to
the Jews, but by implication only to Jews who are believers. Then
the second part of the statement refers specifically to those who are
not of the Jewish law but who are only of the faith of Abraham, i.e.,
Gentile believers. The way of grace thus makes it possible for both
categories to be included in the one redeemed family of Abraham:
He is the father of us all. See 4:11b-12; Gal 3:29.

**4:17a As it is written: "I have made you a father of many
nations."** This is taken by many to be a parenthesis (NASB;
Cranfield, I:243; Murray, I:145). The quote is from Gen 17:5, and
serves to reinforce the references in v. 16 to "*all* Abraham's offspring" and "father of us *all.*"

E. FAITH MEANS GIVING GLORY TO GOD AND
BELIEVING HIS PROMISES (4:17b-22)

In this section the focus changes from the *fact* of Abraham's justifying faith to its *nature*. Though Abraham's circumstances were
different from ours, we can learn important lessons from him as to
the kind of faith God expects from us today. He shows us "what it
means to believe" (Schlatter, 114).

**4:17b He is our father in the sight of God, in whom he
believed . . . .** If the first part of this verse is a parenthesis, then this
clause connects directly with "the father of us all" at the end of
v. 16. The NIV makes this connection simply by repeating the
thought, "He is our father," though these words do not occur in
the Greek text of v. 17. The idea is that in the sight of God
Abraham the believer is the spiritual father of all subsequent believers; this is how God sees him (Cranfield, I:243).

Though Paul's wording here may seem a bit awkward, he puts it
the way he does in order to focus our attention upon the object of
Abraham's faith, namely, God himself. Having then named God as
the one "in whom he believed," Paul then utters one of the most
basic yet most profound descriptions of God in Scripture: He is **the**

God who gives life to the dead and calls things that are not as though they were. This refers to resurrection from the dead and creation from nothing: the two masterworks in the repertoire of divine omnipotence. By his "incomparably great power" God raised Jesus from the dead (Eph 1:19-20).

That God is the one who gives life to the dead was "a general designation of God in Jewish devotion," says Bruce (118; see Cranfield, I:244). As the focus of his faith, Abraham believed that God could miraculously restore both his and Sarah's reproductive powers, a kind of figurative "resurrection from the dead" (4:19; Heb 11:11-12). He also believed that God had the power to raise Isaac from the dead if necessary, had the commanded sacrifice been completed (Heb 11:19). This sets the example for us, who are called on to believe that God raised Jesus from the dead (4:24), and to believe that he raises us from spiritual death in baptism (6:4; Col 2:12) and will raise us up from physical death on the last day (8:11, 23).

The second part of the description is more difficult.[59] Literally it says God calls the not-being-things as being-things. Or, he addresses things that do not exist as though they exist. Many take this to be a reference to God's unique power to create *ex nihilo*, "from nothing" (see GC, 97-117). "Paul is speaking of God as creating something out of nothing by his call. This applies to the physical creation," says Morris, though Paul may not have had this specifically in mind here (209). Cranfield (I:244) and Hendriksen (I:158) agree that the expression at least includes the original creation of Gen 1:1. The word for "calls" is καλέω (*kaleō*), which is often used "to denote God's creative call," says Cranfield. It can "signify to call into existence, and this is the meaning we find here" (Morris, 208; see Moo, I:286-287). See Isa 48:13.

Some deny that the original creation is intended to be included here, mainly because of the wording "*as though* they were." The Greek word is ὡς (*hōs*), "as." The argument is that if creation *ex nihilo* were intended, Paul would have said *eis* ("into"), not *hōs*. I.e., God calls the not-being things *into* being. (See Moo, I:286-287.) However, although this might certainly be a clearer reference to

---

[59]See Sanday and Headlam (113) for four ways to interpret it.

creation *ex nihilo*, the wording as it stands cannot be said to exclude it. "The idea would then be that God, in calling into being what does not exist, addresses His creating word to it, thus in a sense treating it as though it already existed" (Cranfield, I:244).

The more general language is probably used so that the concept of God's omnipotent, creative call can be applied specifically to Abraham's situation. As the object of Abraham's faith, God is surely the one who names or speaks "of things in the remotest futurity . . . , with as much certainty as if they existed" (DeWelt, 66). When God said to Abraham, "I have made you a father of many nations" (Gen 17:5), he spoke of the future, as-yet-unborn legions of believers as though they already existed (MP, 328). Thus Abraham's faith required him to believe that God controlled the future, and that he could and would bring into existence things which then existed for him only in the form of promises (Heb 11:10, 13-16). This is an example for us today, since we also must believe that God can and will one day call into being our not-yet-existing redeemed bodies and their eternal home in the new heavens and new earth.

Thus this verse declares God to be sovereign over the two things that baffle human beings most: death and nothingness (Stott, 133). To believe that God is the master of these mysteries is to believe he can do anything. Abraham so believed, and thus rested his hope in God's promises.

4:18 Against all hope, Abraham in hope believed and so became the father of many nations, just as it had been said to him, "So shall your offspring be." This is Paul's first reference to hope (ἐλπίς, *elpis*) in Romans. Hope is closely related to faith. Indeed, it overlaps that part of our faith that is directed toward the future (8:24-25). In the same way it is closely related to assurance of salvation. Hope as such is the "expectation of something desirable" (Hendriksen, I:159). The biblical connotation does not involve the element of uncertainty or "wishful thinking" often attached to it in American vernacular. In Scripture, hope is the *confident* expectation of our future possession of all that God has promised us.

Abraham's hope was focused especially on the promise of countless descendants as recorded in Gen 15:5. After calling his attention to the multitude of stars in the heavens, God said to him,

"So shall your offspring be." At this time Abraham was between 75 and 86 years old (Gen 12:4; 16:16), and was already very conscious of the fact that he was still childless (Gen 15:2-3). But God reassured him, and Abraham believed (Gen 15:6). At least thirteen years later, when he was 99 and Sarah was around 90 (Gen 17:1, 17), God again promised that he would be "the father of many nations" (Gen 17:4); and he instituted circumcision as the sign of this covenant (Gen 17:10-14). Abraham demonstrated his faith in the promise by immediately ordering circumcision for himself and every male in his household (Gen 17:23-27).

Under such circumstances Abraham's hope surely transcended all expectation based on natural processes (his own "works"); it was surely grounded in his faith that God could raise the dead and bring something out of nothing. Paul says it thus, that Abraham believed "against all hope," yet "in hope." The word for "against" (παρά, *para*) can also mean "beyond." This difficult statement may thus be understood in two ways (see Cranfield, I:245-246). If *para* means "against," this says that Abraham from the beginning had been filled with true hope even though all along it meant going against all natural expectations. If *para* means "beyond," the idea is that in the beginning (Gen 12:1-3) Abraham's hope involved his and Sarah's natural ability to have children; but God delayed the birth of Isaac so long that they simply went beyond that point. Either way, Abraham continued to have hope, but ultimately he knew that its fulfillment rested completely in the hands of the omnipotent and faithful God. He knew that without God, he would be without hope (Eph 2:12); but he knew that God's promise is always a sufficient basis for hope.

4:19 Without weakening in his faith . . . . What makes this difficult to understand are the episodes recorded in Genesis that seem to reflect a weak faith on Abraham's part. To avoid an imagined danger in Egypt, he lied about his relationship with Sarah instead of trusting God (12:10-20). When Sarah appeared barren, he followed her suggestion and sought to beget offspring through her maidservant Hagar instead of waiting on the Lord (16:1-5). When God promised him a son by Sarah at ages 100 and 90 respectively, he laughed (17:17).

These episodes do not contradict Paul's statement, though.

These are relatively minor incidents compared with Abraham's overall record of strong faith. Some people have a weak faith as such (14:1), but Abraham had only momentary lapses from which he always recovered. The Egypt event was early in his covenant relationship with God. Prior to the Hagar event God had not specifically named Sarah as the mother of his heir. Fuller says Abraham's laughter was "a laughter of faith and not mockery" (*Unity*, 307). When the greatest test of all came — the command to sacrifice Isaac, he did not hesitate (Gen 22:1-10). Certainly no one's faith, not even Abraham's, is perfect. But "despite his spiritual imperfection, Abraham always came back to the Lord in faith, and the Lord honored that faith and continued to renew his promises to Abraham" (MacArthur, I:237).

. . . he faced the fact that his body was as good as dead — since he was about a hundred years old — and that Sarah's womb was also dead. "Faced the fact" is κατανοέω (*katanoeō*), "to consider, to contemplate." Some ancient manuscripts include the word "not" at this point, which makes it read "he did not consider the fact" (see KJV). Interestingly the point is the same with or without the negative. With it the idea would be that his faith was so strong that 'he did not pay any attention to the fact that he and Sarah appeared to be past the age of natural childbearing. He did not regard that as the deciding factor, and he did not allow it to weaken his faith (Lard, 147). All that mattered was God's promise. On the other hand, without the negative (the preference of most modern critics and translations), the idea is that he was fully aware of his and Sarah's inability to have children; he took this into account but still continued to believe. (See Cranfield, I:247.)

Describing the lack of childbearing ability in terms of death highlights God's role in the birth of Isaac as a kind of resurrection from the dead (4:17, 24). In this regard Abraham's body was "as good as dead" (see Heb 11:12), and Sarah's womb was dead. Even before they left Haran Sarah was declared barren (Gen 11:30). When the promise included her specifically she was 90 years old (Gen 17:17) and definitely "past the age of childbearing" (Gen 18:11; Heb 11:11).

Because of these factors the conception and birth of Isaac were undoubtedly the working of God's supernatural power. In view of the fact that he later fathered six sons by another wife, Keturah (Gen 25:1-2), we can assume that "the procreative power granted by God to Abraham was not confined to the birth of Isaac alone but remained with him afterward" (Moo, I:293).

4:20 In spite of the state of procreative "deadness," **[y]et he did not waver through unbelief regarding the promise of God, but was strengthened in his faith . . . .** This helps explain the fact that Abraham did not "weaken" in his faith, i.e., he did not waver to the point of unbelief. Calvin (179) points out that expressions of wonder and astonishment can be expected in the face of such remarkable promises as Abraham received (Gen 17:17). No less than the virgin Mary asked, "How will this be?" (Luke 1:34). But where true faith is present, the wonder itself generates an even stronger faith.

The word "waver" (διακρίνομαι, *diakrinomai*) means "to decide, contend, be divided within oneself, be at odds with oneself, stagger, waver, doubt." Lard (148) takes it in the most neutral sense, that Abraham simply did not "decide" for unbelief. Moo gives the word a very negative connotation here, saying it "is not a passing hesitation but a more deep-seated and permanent attitude of distrust" (I:290). Either way, Abraham's faith never gave way to unbelief. This is not to deny that he sometimes had to struggle with his faith, but a struggling faith is not the same as unbelief.

That Abraham "was strengthened in his faith" does not mean that he was strengthened in his body *by* his faith (contra Sanday and Headlam, 115). It simply means he was strengthened with reference to his faith; his faith itself was strengthened. How was it strengthened? Up to the time of Sarah's actual pregnancy and Isaac's birth (Gen 21:1-2), the only thing he had as a basis for his faith was the bare promise of God, which the Lord kept graciously renewing to him. But the repetition of the promise was enough; he continued to walk by faith, not by sight. "Abraham had nothing going for him except the promise of God. But for the man of faith that was enough" (Morris, 212).

What follows in the rest of v. 20 and in v. 21 is an excellent two-part summary of the essence of Abraham's justifying faith, and it presents a pattern that all believers can and must follow. The first aspect of Abraham's faith was that **he gave glory to God . . . .** The "glory" of God is his collective greatness, his total perfection, his manifested majesty (see 1:21). It cannot be increased; it can only be acknowledged and honored. We "give" glory to God by honoring him and by calling attention to everything that makes him great. The very essence of justifying faith is that it gives glory to God, since it is faith *in God* and in what *he* has done and promises to do, rather than a reliance upon ourselves and what we are able to achieve. Faith by its very nature puts ourselves in the background and turns the spotlight upon God.

4:21 This verse sets forth the second aspect of Abraham's faith: **being fully persuaded that God had power to do what he had promised.** The verb means "to be fully persuaded, fully convinced, fully assured." Toward what was this total confidence directed? Nothing less than the *promises of God*. Everything rested on whether or not God could keep his promises; Abraham believed that he could. He believed in the promises because he believed in the power, the "wonder-working power" of God, the power that is able to raise the dead and create from nothing (4:17).

Stott rightly points out that trusting in a person's promises requires believing he has not only the *power* to keep them, but also the *will* to do so. I.e., "behind all promises lies the character of the person who makes them" (134). Though it is not explicitly stated in this verse, it is implied that Abraham was fully persuaded not only that God *could* keep his promises because of his power, but also that he *would* keep them because of his faithfulness.

The essence of justifying faith still follows the pattern of Abraham. God promises to save us by his grace through the work of Jesus Christ. We are called on to trust completely in this promise, believing in the loving intention of God and the forgiving power of the cross. This is not easy to do, just as it is not easy for a drowning person to relax and let a lifeguard hold on to him and pull him to shore. Instinctively the drowning person wants to grab and hold on, while thrashing and kicking and straining; but this only hinders and may even thwart the attempt to save him. If he really wants to be saved, he must relax and trust himself to the expertise and ability of the lifeguard. Likewise if we want to be saved, we must truly believe in God's saving grace, which requires us to let go of our works and to rest in the certainty of his promises. Such faith enables us to stop anxiously examining our personal "workometer" in order to make guesses as to our salvation status. It enables us instead simply to fix our eyes upon Jesus, the author and perfecter of our faith (Heb 12:2).

4:22 This is why "it was credited to him as righteousness." Most of the verses in this section have explored the meaning of Gen 15:6a, "Abraham believed God." Having shown us in stunning fashion the main aspects of the patriarch's faith, Paul here closes this section by simply quoting Gen 15:6b again: "It was credited to him as righteousness."

The words "This is why" indicate that there is a cause-and-effect relation between the two parts of Gen 15:6. Because Abraham's faith was this kind of faith, he was fully justified before God. As Murray says, "The grandeur of Abraham's faith makes all the more apparent why it was imputed for righteousness" (I:152).

F. THOSE WHO BELIEVE LIKE ABRAHAM
ARE JUSTIFIED LIKE ABRAHAM (4:23-25)

4:23-24 The heading over this main section (ch. 4) calls Abraham the "paradigm of grace." Throughout the entire chapter we have been applying his example to all believers who follow him and especially to Christians today. In this last brief section of the chapter we see that such a parallel is intended. God wants us to know that those who believe like Abraham are justified like Abraham. In fact, says Paul, the key words in Gen 15:6 were included in the Bible specifically for our sakes. **The words "it was credited to him" were written not for him alone, but also for us . . . .** The whole account of Abraham and the record of his strong faith were written not just to honor him but to benefit us believers today.

"Not for him *alone*" suggests that it is appropriate for such a great man to be honored. It is fitting that he should live on in the memories of his children, both physical and spiritual, and that his life of faith should be held up as an example worthy of praise.

But we must not forget its intended application to our lives today. Indeed, the NT tells us that everything recorded in the OT, including good and bad behavior, has been recorded for our sakes, for us to learn both what pleases God and what angers him. (See 15:4; 1 Cor 9:10; 10:11; 2 Tim 3:16.) The example of Abraham is special, though, because it illuminates so clearly the essence of grace, the heart of which is justification by faith. The key words of Gen 15:6, "it was credited to him as righteousness," mean simply that he was *justified* — by his faith. This sets the pattern for those today **to whom God will credit righteousness**, i.e., whom God will justify. And of whom is this blessed category comprised? **. . . us who believe in him who raised Jesus our Lord from the dead . . . .**

The reference to crediting righteousness (i.e., justifying) has a future ring to it. Paul says literally that believers are "about to be" credited as righteous. Some see this as pointing ahead to the final judgment (Morris, 214; Schlatter, 117), where God will once and for all declare us righteous through the blood of Christ. Another possibility is that "about to be" points to what was in the future from the perspective of Abraham himself. In any case there is no reason to take this as implying that believers are not yet justified. Paul in other places makes it clear that our justification is a past event (4:7; 5:1; 1 Cor 6:11; Titus 3:7) and a present reality (3:24; 5:9). Indeed, the very example of Abraham confirms this: "it was credited" is past tense (4:3, 9-10, 22).

The act of faith is here called believing "upon" (ἐπί, *epi*), which is not just bare intellectual assent to facts but also a surrender of the will and a commitment of the self to the *person* who is the object of faith, in this case God the Father. In the context of salvation Jesus is usually named as the object of faith (e.g., John 3:16; Acts 11:17; 16:31; Rom 3:22; Gal 2:16; 3:26), but not exclusively so (see Acts 16:34; Rom 4:5; Col 2:12). Here the focus is on faith in God the Father because of the prominence of the theme of resurrection from the dead (4:17, 19), and because Scripture predominantly describes the resurrection of Jesus as the work of the Father.[60]

It is clear that justifying faith must include faith in the resurrection of Jesus from the dead (10:9), in addition to faith in the

---

[60]See Acts 2:24, 32; 3:15; 4:10; 5:30; 10:40; 13:30, 33, 34, 37; 17:31; Rom 8:11; 10:9; 1 Cor 6:14; 15:15; 2 Cor 4:14; Gal 1:1; Eph 1:20; Col 2:12; 1 Thess 1:10; 1 Pet 1:21.

atoning power of his death (3:25). Abraham's faith is most appropriately paradigmatic for the former, since it was truly a faith that
God is able to raise the dead (4:17, 19). Our faith is no different,
except we now know that this holy resurrection power is ultimately
displayed in the raising of Jesus (Eph 1:18-20; Col 2:12). In this light
it is significant that the final fulfilment of God's promise to
Abraham was when he raised Jesus from the dead (Acts 13:32-34).

4:25 Paul fittingly closes this chapter with a brief summary of
the gospel facts that make salvation by grace possible and that are
at the very heart of justifying faith: the death and resurrection of
Jesus (see 1 Cor 15:1-4): **He was delivered over to death for our
sins and was raised to life for our justification.** The words "to
death" are not in the Greek text, but this is no doubt the meaning.
The term for "delivered over" is παραδίδωμι (*paradidōmi*), the same
word used for God's act of delivering rebellious sinners over to the
consequences of their sins in 1:24, 26, 28. Here the reference is to
the One who was delivered over to the cross in their place, and
ours. The One who so delivered him is the Father (Acts 2:23; Rom
8:32; see Rom 3:25).[61]

He was "raised to life" refers to the resurrection of Jesus ("to
life" is not in the original). The word for justification is the noun
δικαίωσις (*dikaiōsis*), used only here and in 5:18. Usually the verb
δικαιόω (*dikaioō*, "to justify") is used. Either way the concept is
equivalent both to the expression "crediting of righteousness"
(used throughout the chapter) and to the terminology of forgiveness (4:7-8).

The most difficult problem of interpretation in this verse comes
from the double use of the preposition "for" (διά, *dia*). The
concept is causal: "on account of, because of" (see NASB). The
problem is whether the object of each of these two uses of *dia* is the
cause or the *effect* of the action it modifies. If it is the cause, the
phrase is said to be retrospective, or looking to the past. This seems
to be the most natural way to understand the first clause: he was
delivered up as the result of our sins. Our sins are the cause, and

---

[61]On another level, of course, it was Judas who delivered or betrayed
Jesus to his executioners (Matt 10:4; 26:21-25; etc.), but here the emphasis
is on God's purpose and work.

his death is the effect. But if the object of *dia* is the effect, the phrase is said to be prospective, or looking to the future. This seems most natural for the second clause: he was raised up in order to bring about our justification. His resurrection is the cause; our justification is the effect.

The reason this is problematic is that it seems Paul would not use *dia* here in parallel clauses in such different senses. Though some interpret him thus (Moo, I:297; Hendriksen, I:161), other commentators argue for consistency and interpret both uses of *dia* in the same way. Moule (98) and Schlatter (118) say both uses are retrospective. This would require us to say that in some way the resurrection was the result of our justification, as the cross was the result of our sins. On the other hand Murray (I:155) says both are prospective. This would require us to say that Jesus' death was the cause of something relating to our sins, such as their covering or atonement.

In considering all these possibilities, the weakest concept is the idea that somehow Jesus was raised because we had already been justified, or that his resurrection was somehow the result of our justification. When we rule this idea out, that leaves us with just two options: either *dia* means different things in the two clauses, or both clauses have a prospective reference.

Though it is most natural to say that Jesus was delivered up on account of the fact of our sins (retrospective), it also makes sense to say that he was delivered up because of the need to atone for our sins (prospective). I do not know how to choose between these two meanings here; perhaps both are intended.[62]

Regarding the second clause, to say that it is prospective is the better choice; but this still leaves us with the question, in what way does the resurrection of Jesus bring about our justification? It is much easier to see how Jesus *died* for our justification, but here Paul says he was *raised* for it. What does this mean?

Bruce (119) says Jesus was raised "to guarantee" our justification.

---

[62]The latter choice requires us to add something not explicitly stated in the text, i.e., the idea of atonement. But this is not an insuperable problem; the thought may be streamlined to make it formally parallel to the second clause.

But in what sense would this be the case? One possibility is that his resurrection demonstrates the validity of his claims and proves that the apostolic teaching about the meaning of the cross is true. Anyone could make lofty claims about his impending death (see Mark 10:45; John 12:32); but if his dead body turned to dust in his grave, we would be inclined to disregard his claims. But in the case of Jesus his resurrection confirms his claims and guarantees the justifying power of his blood; thus we know that our faith in his blood is not in vain. This is the faith that justifies, and because of his resurrection we have a firm basis for it. As Murray says, "Only as the living Lord can he be the object of faith" (I:156).

This is similar to Hendriksen's suggestion (I:161) that Jesus was raised in order to *assure* us that in God's sight we are indeed justified. "The Father, by raising Jesus from the dead, assures us that the atoning sacrifice has been accepted; hence, our sins are forgiven."

One other possibility is that Jesus' resurrection brings about our justification by enabling him to complete the full process of atonement. According to the OT pattern, the High Priest not only offered the sacrifice but also sprinkled its blood on the altar in the Most Holy Place (Lev 16). Likewise, to accomplish our justification, Jesus our Great High Priest not only had to offer himself as a sacrifice by shedding his blood on the cross; he also had to enter heaven itself "once for all by his own blood," and "appear for us in God's presence" (Heb 9:12, 24; see Heb 6:19-20; 10:19-22). Therefore it was necessary for him to be raised from the dead so that he could ascend bodily into heaven and complete the work of atonement on which our justification is based. (See Lard, 151; MP, 330.)

III. 5:1-21 — GRACE AND ASSURANCE

How does Romans 5 relate to the overall development of Paul's argument in this epistle? In my opinion it should be regarded as the conclusion of the discussion that began at 3:21. The main subject continues to be the presentation of grace as the only effective way of salvation. In 3:21-31 Paul explains the essence of grace as the free gift of God's righteousness to sinners, a righteousness established by the propitiatory sacrifice of Jesus Christ and received by faith apart from works of law. In ch. 4 he shows that being counted righteous (i.e., being justified) by faith has always been God's way of saving sinners, citing especially the example of Abraham. Now in ch. 5 the Apostle sets forth one of the most important immediate results of justification by faith, namely, assurance of salvation.

In one way or another almost all commentators describe ch. 5 this way. They use a variety of terms but say the same thing, i.e., that this chapter presents the results, fruits, benefits, blessings, effects, or consequences of justification by faith. Though these benefits may be enumerated in various ways (e.g., peace, hope, joy), they all may be summed up in one word: *assurance*.

A. ASSURANCE OF PERSONAL SALVATION (5:1-11)

The first half of Romans 5 shows how justification by faith yields a genuine sense of assurance of personal salvation, a conviction of being at peace with God and accepted by God. The main point of the passage is "the certainty of Christian hope" (Moo, I:317), or the "certainty of salvation" (Erdman, 61). Its theme is that "those who have been justified by God have peace with God" (Cranfield, I:257-258). "Such peace with God, such access to a loving Father, such unclouded hope of glory, are the sure and inevitable blessings of all who are justified by faith" (Erdman, 64). This is what these verses teach.

A sense of personal assurance is the privilege of every Christian, and we cannot overemphasize the blessedness of it. Unfortunately, many Christians do not have this sense of assurance, mainly because they do not understand its proper basis. What is that proper basis? It is the knowledge that we are justified by our faith in the atoning blood of Jesus Christ. That is the point of 5:1-11.

1. Justification by Faith Is the Key to Assurance (5:1-2)

5:1 Therefore, since we have been justified through faith, we have peace with God through our Lord Jesus Christ .... "Therefore"

introduces the practical conclusion to be drawn from the presentation of grace in 3:21-4:25. "Since we have been justified through
faith" sums up the main point of that passage and states the heart
of grace. The verb is aorist (past) tense, indicating that justification
is an event that has already occurred in the experience of Paul's
Christian readers. This past act, however, produces a continuing
state of *being* justified, so that the Christian is a justified person, a
forgiven person.[63] "Through faith" indicates the means by which we
first *became* justified, and also the means by which we *remain* justified.

The main point here is the cause-and-effect relationship
between justification and peace: because we have been justified,
"we have peace with God." This refers to an objective state of
peace, a cessation of hostilities and an end of enmity between God
and the sinner. The relation between God and unbelievers is a kind
of warfare; each is the enemy of the other. The unbeliever fights
against God in rebellion, lawlessness, and fear; God's righteous
holiness is turned against the sinner in wrath and hatred (Ps 5:5-6).
But God's righteous love initiates a process of reconciliation (5:10-
11), leading to this state of peace in which we are no longer God's
enemies but are his friends. The key element in this process of reconciliation, of course, is "the death of his Son" (5:10); thus Paul
says our peace with God comes "through our Lord Jesus Christ."

This peace is an objective state, not a subjective feeling; but we
may rightly infer that peace as a subjective state of mind is the
natural consequence of being at peace with God and knowing it.

This latter point — *knowing it* — is crucial for attaining subjective
peace. The fact is that Christians truly *are* justified and truly *are* at
peace with God; but often because of confusion concerning how
faith, works, and justification are related, they do not understand
their own status before God and do not have true inner peace. This
is why it is so important to understand what Paul is teaching about
law and grace in Romans 1-4. Only when we understand that we are
justified by faith apart from works of law (3:28) can we have this
inner peace, which is a basic element of assurance of salvation.

---

[63]See the present tense in 3:24. Also, v. 2 speaks of *standing* in this grace,
i.e., in the state of justification.

Beginning with the state of enmity, the following sequence of events thus takes place: God's love sent Jesus to die in our place, removing God's own enmity toward us. We accepted God's offer of reconciliation in faith, giving up our enmity toward him. God then bestowed his gift of righteousness upon us, i.e., he justified us. This was the beginning of our objective state of peace with God. Because we understand the meaning of these events, we have a feeling of inner peace. In other words, because we know that we are in a right relationship with God, we have assurance of our salvation. We know that if we were to die now, or if Christ were to come at this moment, we would be saved, because we will meet him as friends and not as enemies.

Verse 1 contains a textual variation for the verb translated "we have." In some ancient manuscripts this verb is indicative, a statement of fact: "we *have* peace with God" (NIV, NASB, KJV, RSV, NRSV). In other manuscripts it is subjunctive, an exhortation: "*let us* have peace with God" (see Goodspeed, Moffatt, NEB, Phillips). Though the latter has better textual support, the former makes more sense in the context and is preferred by most commentators,[64] including myself. As Lard says, "Peace is a fact which results from justification, not something which the justified are merely exhorted to have, but may not have" (153).

5:2 Verse 2 continues the thought by speaking of Jesus as the one **through whom we have gained access by faith into this grace in which we now stand.** The work of Jesus is always the cause of our salvation, the meritorious ground or basis which makes it possible. "By faith" is simply the means by which we personally receive the gift of grace made available through his work.[65]

Because of the demonstrative pronoun, "this grace" must refer specifically to something named in the preceding verse.[66] Paul is most

---

[64]See, e.g., Lard, 153-154; Cranfield, I:257; Morris, 218-219; Hendriksen, I:168.

[65]Some manuscripts and thus some translations do not include "by faith" here in v. 2 (see Cranfield I:259). Some commentators accept it (e.g., Murray, I:159); some reject it (e.g., Morris, 219). The issue is not crucial since Paul has repeatedly asserted such a role for faith, even in 5:1.

[66]Thus it is probably not "the covenant of grace" (DeWelt, 74), nor the kingdom or church (Lard, 154).

certainly referring to the state of justification (Murray, I:160; Cranfield, I:259), though he may also mean the state of peace with God. Most likely "this grace" includes both, since they are inseparable.

In any case Paul describes "this grace" as a state or sphere that is *entered* and in which one *stands*. The idea of entering grace is seen in the phrase "we have gained access." This is not the best translation; the language suggests personal accomplishment ("gained") rather than a free gift. Also, "access" suggests the continuing availability of grace as needed, which is not the idea here (Mounce, 134; Moo, I:308). The word for "access" is better rendered "entry" or "introduction" (NASB); this is consistent with the preposition "into" (*eis*) before "grace" (Lard, 154; Moo, I:308). The idea is that at a certain point of time we *entered* into the state of grace; we were introduced into it by Jesus Christ.

Paul also says grace is a *state* "in which we now stand," within which we securely rest. "*We stand* translates a perfect tense, used in the sense of the present," says Morris (219). The idea seems to be that of a continuing, abiding existence within the state of grace, rather than a sporadic, revolving-door, "now you're in, now you're out" condition. The word "to stand" suggests that our position in grace is firm and secure, rather than tentative and precarious (see Stott, 140). We are standing on a firm foundation, rather than clinging by our fingertips to some weak and tattered cord.[67]

The point is that grace is like a room into which we enter by the door of Jesus Christ, a room which becomes our refuge and in which we continue to dwell. It is the sphere of our Christian existence, "the sphere of God's grace" (NEB) as opposed to the sphere of law.

Verse 2 concludes with these words: **And we rejoice in the hope of the glory of God.** This affirmation is parallel to "we have peace with God" in v. 1. "Peace" is our present relationship with God; "hope of glory" (Col 1:27) points to our future heavenly inheritance.

"The glory of God" (see 3:23) in this verse is surely a reference to the final, eschatological revelation of God's majesty and splendor

---

[67]That it means "we have taken our stand" (Dunn, I:249) is probably an unintended connotation, as is the idea that "to stand" contrasts with our *fallen* state as sinners (Schlatter, 120).

(Lard, 155; Cranfield, I:260). Our hope is not only that we will one day *behold* his glory (DeWelt, 73), but that in a limited sense we will actually *participate* in it (Murray, I:162) or *partake* of it (MacArthur, I:280). The latter will be true in the sense that we will have a glorified body like the glorified human body of Christ (8:29-30; Phil 3:21; 1 John 3:2), and in the sense that we will actually dwell in the beneficent radiance of God's glorious presence (Rev 21:3-4, 23; 22:4-5).

Paul says that we who are justified by faith and have peace with God have *hope* of this glory. As noted earlier (4:18), in the Bible the Christian's hope is not an uncertain wish or an unfounded longing, but a confident expectation of our future possession of all the elements of salvation not yet received (Cranfield, I:260; Stott, 140). Its object is not simply what we *want* to happen, but what God has *promised* will happen (see 2 Tim 1:12). See Newman and Nida, 93.

As such, biblical hope is the heart and core of the Christian's assurance of salvation. As we saw under 5:1, assurance includes first of all the subjective peace of mind that comes from knowing we are at peace with God now that we are justified by faith. We are sure of our *present* relationship with God. But here we see that our assurance also includes a blessed confidence about the *future*. We have neither anxiety nor terror as we look ahead to the day of judgment, because we know that the same justifying blood of Christ that brought us into this present relationship with God will continue to cover us and will be our passage into future glory.

No wonder "we rejoice"! The same or similar words are translated "brag" or "boast" in earlier texts (2:17, 23; 3:27; 4:2), but "rejoice" is proper and preferred in this context (as in 5:3, 11). It is a stronger concept than ordinary rejoicing. Murray calls it "exultant rejoicing and confident glorying" (I:161); Cranfield adds "jubiliation" (I:259). This "exceeding great joy" rests upon the *hope* described above; it is the natural product and companion of assurance.

2. Tribulations of Believers Do Not Nullify Assurance (5:3-5)

In this fallen world everyone suffers the general ravages of sin, sickness, and death; but Christians often suffer even more in the form of persecution from Satan and from the unbelieving world.[68] When this happens we are strongly tempted to doubt our salvation and to question the very love of God. Thoughts like these form in our hearts: "If God really loves me, why does he let these things happen to me? It seems as if God has abandoned me; he must be punishing me for my sin. Maybe there is no God, and heaven is a myth."

This seems to be the kind of potential situation Paul is addressing in these verses. He has stressed the reality of our peace and hope that are based on the knowledge that we are justified by faith in Christ's blood. But he knows that the hope of future glory is sometimes hidden by the dark clouds of present suffering. So he reminds us that within the broad scope of God's sovereignty and love, not even tribulations can nullify our assurance of salvation. In fact, they actually strengthen it.

5:3-4 Not only so, but we also rejoice in our sufferings . . . . "Sufferings" (afflictions, hardships) is a strong term and refers to the experiences of life that press down upon us and crush us both physically and mentally.[69] Here they include the kinds of suffering shared by all people (e.g., hunger, war, disease, death), as well as persecutions directed specifically toward Christians. The latter are not just end-time tribulations, but include the constant hostility and ongoing opposition of the unbelieving world.

Here Paul makes the unlikely assertion that we *rejoice* in such suffering. In v. 2 he says we rejoice in our hope, which makes perfectly good sense. But now he says we also rejoice in the very things that would seem to negate and bedim that hope. In fact, he says that in an indirect way, such sufferings even *increase* our hope!

This does not mean that we should deliberately seek such suffering, like masochists; nor does it necessarily mean that God is purposefully causing us to suffer, contrary to a popular idea.[70] It is

---

[68]See John 15:20; 16:33; Acts 14:22; Rom 8:17; 2 Cor 1:4-10; 2 Thess 1:5; 2 Tim 3:12; 1 Pet 3:14-17; 4:12-19; 5:9-10.

[69]The noun is θλίψις (*thlipsis*); it comes from the verb θλίβω (*thlibō*), which means "to press, to crush, to squeeze, to push."

[70]This idea is suggested by Stott's statement that "there is a divine rationale behind suffering" (141). Some believe that God deliberately created a world that includes suffering as a necessary means of building mature char-

rather a recognition of the fact that, now that suffering is present in the world and is inevitable for Christians, God is able to *use* it in such a way that it actually adds to our assurance (8:28). Thus the Bible consistently describes the afflictions of Christians as positive experiences that produce joy and blessing. See Matt 5:4, 11-12; Acts 5:41; 2 Cor 4:17; 12:9-10; 2 Thess 1:4-5; Jas 1:2-4; 1 Pet 4:12-14.

Paul does not go into great detail in explaining *how* tribulations produce hope.[71] He mentions only three steps: **because we know that suffering produces perseverance; perseverance, character; and character, hope.** First, suffering produces perseverance. This is ὑπομονή (*hypomonē*), often translated "patience." It means patient endurance, steadfastness, the ability to bear and to bear up under whatever comes along. The assumption is that the Christian is facing his sufferings in faith, with full confidence that God will work all things for good (8:28) and that he will provide the strength necessary for such perseverance. In other words, sufferings do not in and of themselves automatically produce endurance. Rather, when we enter into such sufferings while holding onto the hand of God, he himself works endurance within us through them and for them.

Second, perseverance works character. This is δοκιμή (*dokimē*), which belongs to a word group that refers to the process of testing or trying or proving something, and also to the state of having been tested or proved and thus of being approved. Here it means "the quality of provedness which is possessed by faith when it has stood up to testing, like the precious metal which is left when the base metals have been refined away" (Cranfield, I:261). The NASB more appropriately translates it here as "proven character." The idea is that sufferings are like a test which, when endured by the strength which God supplies, results in a quality of life and character that has been tempered and purified and demonstrated to be pleasing to God. (See Zech 13:9.)

Finally, proven character produces hope. This assumes that we as Christians are consciously aware that we have stood up under

---

acter, but I cannot accept this view (GRu, 388-397). Some suffering may be imposed by God's love as a means of chastening wayward Christians (Heb 12:1-11), but this cannot be the explanation for suffering in general.

[71]He reflects further on these ideas in 8:28-39 (see below).

the trial of our sufferings, and that God has been with us and has not allowed us to be defeated by them. This gives us even more confidence in God, and the sense that nothing, not even the worst tribulations, can separate us from the grace of God and prevent us from entering eternal life. Thus our hope is strengthened and confirmed. As Morris says (221), "The Christian who has been tested has proved God's faithfulness and will surely hope the more confidently."

5:5 Assurance of salvation is ultimately based on the assurance that God really does love us, that he is truly on our side, that he is for us and not against us. The various trials and sufferings of this life can very easily cause us to lose sight of this crucial and basic truth of God's love. Thus here Paul stresses that no matter how severe our present trials may be, our hope is still secure because we know for a fact that God loves us.

And hope does not disappoint us . . . . The word for "disappoint" is more properly translated "does not cause us to be ashamed."[72] The tense is present, but it points also to the future, especially to the end time when our hope will be fulfilled and we will be vindicated for continuing to hope "against all hope" (4:18). We will not be personally disappointed, nor will we have to feel humiliation and shame in the face of mocking and ridicule from the enemies of Christ. Our hope is solidly based; it will not let us down now and will not prove vain in the future.

. . . because God has poured out his love into our hearts . . . . Our hope is certain because it is grounded upon the reality of the love of God. The original text is passive; it reads, "the love of God has been poured out." The NIV rightly identifies "the love of God" as "God's love toward us" ("his love") rather than "our love toward God." Only the former fits the context. "Into our hearts" refers to the soul or spirit (as distinct from the body), which includes the "conscious inner life" of the person (Schlatter, 122). Thus Paul is talking about how the love of God becomes present within our inner life and in a sense present to our consciousness. It becomes present within us by being "poured out" into our hearts. The

---

[72]The same expression is used in 9:33 and 10:11 (quoting Isa 28:16). In these verses the NIV translates it "will never be put to shame."

imagery of "pouring out" represents the concept of *abundance*. God's love comes to us as a brimming and overflowing river (Bartlett, 61), in "immeasurable torrents" (MacArthur, I:283), in "unstinting lavishness" (Cranfield, I:263).

God's love is poured out into our hearts **by the Holy Spirit, whom he has given us.** This refers to the gift consisting of the Holy Spirit, who himself was poured out from heaven on Pentecost (Acts 2:17-18, 33) and who is poured out into the heart of each individual believer in the act of baptism (Acts 2:38; Titus 3:5-6). Here "given us" refers to the latter event.

The main question now is, *how* does the Holy Spirit pour God's love into our hearts? We must pay close attention to the wording. For one thing, Paul specifically says that the love of God itself is poured out, not the consciousness or awareness of it. Thus we must be careful not to limit the outpouring of love to the latter. Also, Paul does not specifically say that the pouring out occurs *when* the Spirit is given to us; the expression "whom he has given us" is simply a phrase describing the Spirit. Thus the outpouring need not be limited to the time when the Spirit is given. With these cautions in mind, we may identify three ways in which the Holy Spirit pours out God's love into our hearts.

First, as the divine author of Scripture, the Holy Spirit does pour out the *knowledge* of God's love into our hearts through the biblical testimony to the atoning sacrifice of Christ, which is the greatest possible demonstration of God's love (John 3:16; 15:13; Rom 5:8; 1 John 4:8-10). The fact that God loves us is objectively revealed in the very events of redemption; and the knowledge of this love is objectively recorded for us in the words of Scripture, which were given through the inspiration of the Holy Spirit. Our subjective knowledge or awareness of this love is thus poured out into our hearts by the Holy Spirit primarily through his inspired Word. We must be on guard here against unwarranted subjectivism.

Second, the Holy Spirit pours the love of God into our hearts as the agent by which the blessings of redemption are applied to us in the initial moment of our salvation. That God's love is poured out into our hearts somehow means that we now possess it. Exactly what do we possess? Not the love of God as the inner attribute of his nature, nor as the subjective attitude of his heart toward us.

Rather, we possess the love of God in the concrete form of the gifts and blessings produced for us by and because of his inner affection toward us. In fact, the Holy Spirit himself is one of the primary gifts of God's love to us; when God pours out the Spirit into us (Titus 3:6), he is in that very event pouring out his love into us. The Holy Spirit in turn lavishly pours out further gifts of God's love, i.e., the renewing and regeneration of the new birth (Titus 3:5; John 3:5) and his ongoing, ever-present sanctifying power (8:13; Eph 3:16). This is why our hope does not disappoint us, because the Holy Spirit as the initial gift of God's love has already been poured out in us and is already present within us as the first-fruits of the fullness of eschatological glory (8:23), and as the earnest or down payment guaranteeing our full and final salvation (Eph 1:13-14). This is Paul's primary point.

Third, the Holy Spirit pours the love of God into our hearts by strengthening our inner conviction of the certainty of God's love for us personally. Most commentators tend to ignore the first two points above and to focus entirely upon this subjective experience. Dunn says Paul is referring here to "deep emotional experiences" common to Christians, especially the "awareness of being loved" (I:265). Moo says it means "the inner, subjective certainty that God does love us," as an "internal, subjective, yes, even emotional sensation" (I:312-313). The Spirit gives us a "fresh awareness" and "the assurance" of God's love (Mounce, 135; Murray, I:165).

Certainly we cannot deny that the Holy Spirit strengthens and sharpens our awareness of and faith in God's love as a part of his sanctifying work in our hearts. But we must be careful not to separate this from the first two points above, as if some purely subjective experience of God's love were the basis for our hope. However important this inward strengthening of the Spirit may be, our hope is not based on this subjective experience as such. The fact is that this subjective experience presupposes and supplements several prior *objective* realities: the atoning death of Christ, the Spirit's inspiration of Scripture, our hearing and obeying of the gospel, and our reception of the Holy Spirit himself in Christian baptism. All of these things together constitute the outpouring of the love of God into our hearts, and together they assure us that our hope will not make us ashamed.

3. Christ Died for Us While We Were Still Sinners (5:6-8)

The next six verses are an exposition of the point stated above, that assurance of salvation is ultimately based on the assurance that God really loves us. Here Paul explains how we can know for sure that God loves us, and he explains how this knowledge is the way to assurance.

One key element in Paul's argument is the distinction or contrast between *what we were* before we turned to God for salvation, and *what we are now*, in the present state of grace. The main point is this: if, while we were God's *enemies*, he loved us so much that he was willing to die for us, how can we think that he loves us any less now that we are his *friends*?

The other key element in the argument is the comparison between the first and second transitions in the process of our salvation. The first one, already accomplished, is the transition *from wrath to grace*. The second, which is yet to come, is the transition *from grace to glory*. Which of these transitions is the more difficult, the more radical, the less likely and less expected? The first one, by far. Yet, because of his love and by the power of the cross, God has brought us through this first transition, through faith. The main point now is this: if we have already experienced the first transition, which was infinitely unlikely and even impossible from the standpoint of human expectation, how much more can we confidently expect God to bring us through the second transition as well? We came through the first one by faith apart from works of law; are we now trying to make the second one somehow more difficult than the first?

In this present section (5:6-8) Paul focuses on what we *were*, prior to the first transition. His point is that no matter how miserable and hopeless our condition was then, God still loved us so much that Christ died for us.

5:6 You see, at just the right time, when we were still powerless, Christ died for the ungodly. Manuscripts differ slightly as to the transitional words at the beginning of v. 6. Some have εἴ γε (*ei ge*), "if indeed"; others have ἔτι γάρ (*eti gar*), "for nevertheless." The latter is preferred; *gar* provides an explanatory link with vv. 3-5. The love of God has been poured out into our hearts, and we have hope, *because* we have heard the gospel of the cross.

As Godet says (191), this verse "describes the miserable condition in which we were at the time when divine love was extended to us." First, we were ἀσθενής (*asthenēs*), "powerless, weak, helpless, without strength." Here this means not the finiteness of the creature, but the helplessness of the sinner. It refers to that state of "moral sickness" in which we were mired (Godet, 192), "that helpless weakness of sin which so incapacitated us as to render us incapable of goodness" (MP, 332). Also, we were totally helpless to do anything about it; we were unable to save ourselves.

Second, we were ἀσεβής (*asebēs*), "wicked, ungodly" (see 1:18; 4:5). This means that we were in a state of opposition to God and his law, and were totally undeserving of his loving forgiveness. It means that we were standing in his wrath, since the wrath of God is against all the wickedness (*asebeia*) of men (1:18).

These adjectives describe the condition of the whole fallen human race, and the plight of each individual in our unsaved state as God viewed us in his foreknowledge from the perspective of eternity past. ("We" refers to all human beings.) Even then he loved us so much that he planned the atonement (Rev 13:8); and "at just the right time" in history (see Gal 4:4), Christ came and died for us. This explains how God is able to justify the wicked (*asebēs*), as 4:5 declares. As the saying goes, "Love will find a way."

In the expression "Christ died for the ungodly," the word "for" is ὑπέρ (*hyper*, v. 8 also). It means "for" in the sense of "on behalf of, for the sake of." Though some question this, it can also mean more precisely "in the place of, instead of." In other words, it can have the connotation of substitution; and when used here for the death of Christ it connotes the substitutionary atonement. Harris ("Prepositions," 1196) explains that the word originally meant "over" or "above." Thus the meaning "on behalf of" seems "to have arisen from the image of one person standing or bending *over* another in order to protect or shield him, or of a shield lifted *over* the head which suffers the blow instead of the person." It is easy to see how it would also come to mean "in the place of."[73]

---

[73]Harris gives considerable evidence for the substitutionary connotation of the word (1196-1197). See also Moo, I:315; Morris, 222-223; Hendriksen, I:173.

5:7 Very rarely will anyone die for a righteous man, though for a good man someone might possibly dare to die. This verse raises a number of exegetical questions. One is whether the adjectives "righteous" and "good" are meant to be neuter or masculine (in the genitive they have the same form). If the former, Paul is saying it is difficult to find anyone who will die for a just and good *cause*. If the latter, "a righteous *man*" and "a good *man*" are correct. The latter seems the better choice, since the comparison is with Christ dying for *people* rather than a cause.

Another issue is whether the "righteous man" and the "good man" are basically the same, or whether there is a significant distinction between them. Those who take the latter view usually say the "good man" is somehow better and more likeable than the other, and that Paul is thus presenting a progression of thought: "It's really hard to find anyone who would give his life for a pedantic, holier-than-thou legalist, but you might find some who would die for a nice, generous, neighborly sort of guy."[74]

I agree with Hendriksen, though, that such efforts to distinguish these words in this text amount to "over-interpretation." The distinction, he says, "should not be pressed" (I:172-173).[75] The two clauses are best understood as saying the same thing in different ways. The first says it negatively: scarcely ever will anyone die for a righteous man. The second says it positively: well, maybe — possibly, perhaps — someone could be found who would do this. And if this is such a rarity, it goes without saying that we might as well give up trying to find anyone willing to die for a wicked and unjust person!

But is this not the very point Paul is making? There is indeed someone who was willing to die for the weak and the wicked, namely, Jesus our Lord! Thus the contrast here is not between the righteous man and the good man, but between the (hypothetical) good and righteous man of v. 7, and the weak and ungodly persons of v. 6. The latter are the very ones for whom Christ died! And if it is so difficult to find someone who is willing to die for a good man,

---

[74]For this view see DeWelt, 73, 75; Dunn, I:255, 267; Morris, 223; Stott, 145.

[75]Agreeing here are Murray, I:168; MacArthur, I:285; and Bruce, 124.

then how much more *amazing* it is that he died for weak and ungodly sinners! In view of this contrast, the love of God is magnified even more, as Paul now states:

5:8 But God demonstrates his own love for us in this: While we were still sinners, Christ died for us. He died "for" us (*hyper*, see v. 6) while we were weak, ungodly sinners. This was our condition in the mind of God when he determined to give his only-begotten Son to be the propitiation for our sins. What more could he do to show us that he really and truly loves us? This actually *proves* it, says Paul. The word for "demonstrates" has the connotation of proof. That Christ died for our sins, while we were sinners, is proof of his love.

This is why Paul can say that God has "poured out" his love into our hearts (v. 5). Whenever we hear and meditate upon the message of the cross, it floods our consciousness with the awareness of just how much God loved us and still loves us.

This is why we know our hope will not disappoint us. The reality of the cross is set over against whatever sufferings may come upon us. When suffering afflicts us and tempts us to doubt God's love for us and thus challenges our assurance, we must remember the cross. The worst suffering this world can inflict cannot silence the resounding voice crying out from the cross, "God loves you! God loves you!"

4. Our Hope Is Even More Secure
Now That We Are His Friends (5:9-11)

In this paragraph Paul brings into full view the contrast between what we were and what we are, and the relative ease of the remaining transition from grace to glory as compared with the already-accomplished transition from wrath to grace. Actually Paul's point here is that there are *three* stages in the Christian's spiritual journey, marked by the two transitions. In these verses they are named thus: (1) enemies; (2) justified and reconciled; (3) saved. The point is that if God's love has brought us from the first to the second stage, it will all the more surely bring us from the second to the third.[76]

---

[76]See Godet, 194-195.

A more complete chart of these stages and transitions, based on this entire section (5:1-11) follows:

PAST	PRESENT	FUTURE
Powerless (v. 6)	Justified (vv. 1, 9)	Glory of God (v. 2)
Ungodly (6)	Peace with God (1)	Saved from
Sinners (8)	Standing in grace (2)	wrath (9)
Enemies of	Rejoicing in hope (2, 11)	(Fully) saved (10)
God (10)	Rejoicing in suffering (3)	
	God's love in our hearts (5)	
	Holy Spirit within us (5)	
	Under Christ's blood (9)	
	Reconciled to God (10, 11)	

The key words in this paragraph are "much more." We may think of this passage as teaching us the "much more" of Christian assurance. We know that God has already brought us from wrath to grace through the greatest possible demonstration of his love, even though we were his enemies at the time. Therefore, now that we are his friends, we can have *much more* confidence that his love and Christ's blood will suffice to take us on to glory.

Verses 9 and 10 are parallel in form, both making this same point in different ways. Verse 9 emphasizes justification and thus our changed legal standing before God; verse 10 focuses on reconciliation and thus our changed personal relationship with God (Hendriksen, I:174). Each is an argument from the greater to the lesser, thus: "If God has already done the most difficult thing, reconcile and justify unworthy sinners, how much more can he be depended on to accomplish the 'easier' thing, save from eschatological wrath those who have been brought into such relationship with him" (Moo, I:318).[77] As Godet puts it, "When one has done *the most* for his *enemies*, he does not refuse to do *the least* for his *friends*" (194).

5:9 Since we have now been justified by his blood, how much more shall we be saved from God's wrath through him! The opening words of this verse in the Greek are "Therefore much

---

[77]See also Lard, 157; Cranfield, I:266, 268; Hendriksen, I:174; Murray, I:175; Morris, 225; MacArthur, I:287.

more." The word "therefore" shows that Paul is drawing a conclusion from the fact stated in v. 8, which is the "greater" element in his argument, v. 9 being the "lesser." The words "much more" are put here for emphasis.

The word "now" points to the present stage of our spiritual odyssey, as compared both with the past stage ("sinners," v. 8) and the future stage ("saved," v. 9b). Where are we, *now?* In 5:2 Paul says we are "standing in grace," which he here says includes being "justified." This is an aorist participle, referring to the past act in which God declared us righteous, resulting in the continuing state of being justified (see 5:1).

"By his blood" refers of course to the blood poured out on Calvary when Christ put himself in our place and suffered the eternal wrath of God for us. It is the efficacious basis for our justification. God counts us as righteous because he accepts Christ's payment of our penalty in our place. We stand in justification because we are now standing under his blood, which is over us as a shield from God's wrath. Standing in grace thus includes standing under the blood. See 3:24-26.

Our future state is described as being saved from God's wrath. Here "saved" is future tense and refers to our final salvation on the day of judgment (see 13:11; 1 Cor 3:15; 5:5). "God's wrath" is the sentence of condemnation at the final judgment and eternal consignment to the lake of fire (Rev 20:14-15). This is the ultimate outpouring of divine wrath (1 Thess 1:10; 5:9; 2 Thess 1:7-9; Rev 6:16-17; 11:18). As Christians justified by Christ's blood, we know that this is not our destiny; "no wrath is reserved for the justified at the judgment seat" (Murray, I:171).

Paul continues to remind us that this is all because of Jesus Christ. We became and remain justified "by his blood," and we shall be saved from wrath "through him!" "There is therefore now no condemnation for those who are in Christ Jesus" (8:1), i.e., under his blood.

5:10 For if, when we were God's enemies, we were reconciled to him through the death of his Son, how much more, having been reconciled, shall we be saved through his life! Here the form of the argument is exactly the same as v. 9, with the focus being on reconciliation[78] rather than justification. The past-present-future theme is clearly stated: enemies, reconciled, saved. That the greater transition gives us assurance of the yet-to-come lesser one is emphasized by the repeated words, "much more."

The transition from being God's enemy to being in a state of reconciliation with him is as radical a transition as can be imagined. The worst possible situation a creature can be in is to be an enemy of God. This relationship of enmity includes, of course, the sinner's hostility toward and hatred of God (8:7; Col 1:21), which must be removed in the process of reconciliation. But it also includes God's hostility toward and hatred of the sinner (11:28), which must also be removed in this process.

It is a myth that God hates the sin but does not hate the sinner also. "You hate all who do wrong," says Ps 5:5. "The Lord detests men of perverse heart" (Prov 11:20). See also Deut 25:16; Ps 11:5; Prov 6:16-19; 16:5; 17:15; Jer 12:8; Mal 1:3; Rom 9:13. In the state of enmity, not only are we against God; he is also against us. "The face of the Lord is against those who do evil" (Ps 34:16; 1 Pet 3:12). "I am against you," are the words God hurls in the faces of sinners (Jer 21:13; 50:31; Ezek 13:8; 21:3; 26:3). This is the whole point of the *wrath* of God. It is his righteous judicial enmity toward those who are against him (1:18-32).

Paul's point is that, even while we were in this state of mutual hostility, God took the initiative to eliminate the enmity and bring about reconciliation between the warring parties. This means that the infinite and all-conquering love of God co-existed within his nature alongside his own enmity toward us in a kind of tension.[79] But in accordance with his eternal wisdom, his love was able to find a way for him to give full expression to his righteous wrath and enmity, while at the same time offering reconciliation to repentant sinners. This "way" of course was "through the death of his Son," which was a propitiatory sacrifice that allowed God to pour out his wrath upon Jesus instead of upon us. Thus through the death of Jesus God's wrath is satisfied and his own enmity is set aside. This is the first step to reconciliation.

---

[78]The essence of reconciliation is the removal of hostility and the restoration of peace and friendship between two estranged parties.

[79]On this concept of tension within God's nature see GRe, 313-314, 372-375, 408.

The second step is to confront sinners with the reality of what God has done, and to persuade them to give up their own enmity toward him and allow him to cancel his enmity toward them personally (5:11; 2 Cor 5:20). Only when this takes place does the reconciled state actually begin. At that point the "peace with God" of which 5:1 speaks begins to exist.

Now comes the argument from the greater to the lesser: "If God has done so much for his enemies, what will he not do for his friends?" (Erdman, 63-64). Being his friends, how *much more* can we now count on him to take us on to the final state of glory! God is no longer against us; he is *for* us (8:31), imperfect though we are. He surely will not abandon us now.

Again Paul refers to this future stage as "being saved," i.e., receiving the full and final salvation of heaven. "Through his life" refers to Christ's risen and glorified life as he exists at the right hand of the Father in his ongoing intercessory ministry (Mounce, 138). See 4:25; 8:34. This will come to a climax on the day of judgment, when Christ the Judge will himself intercede for us and continue to cover our sins with his blood and usher us into eternal life.

Paul's greater-to-lesser argument for assurance of salvation, based on the much more radical nature of the first transition as compared with the second, may be illustrated thus. The gap or chasm separating our former state (wrath) from our present state (grace) was like the Grand Canyon in its vastness; but the love of God and the cross of Christ were able to bridge that chasm, and we crossed the bridge through faith. Now, the gap separating our present state (grace) from the future one (glory) is like a small drainage ditch by comparison. Surely the same means that brought us across the first gap are more than sufficient to get us across the second one.

The three key factors mentioned by Paul as the means of bridging these gaps are first and most important, the love of God (vv. 5, 8); second, the cross of Christ as the product of that love (vv. 1-2, 6, 8-11); and finally, our faith as that which clings to the cross (vv. 1, 2). We must be especially aware of this third one. We must not think that from the standpoint of our own participation in this process of salvation, God is somehow making it harder for us to cross the second and smaller gap than it was for us to cross the first and greater one. If we made the first transition by faith apart from works, so shall we make the second. We were justified by faith in the beginning, we are justified by faith now, and we shall be justified by faith in the end.

5:11 Not only is this so, but we also rejoice in God through our Lord Jesus Christ, through whom we have now received reconciliation. "This" refers to "shall be saved" in vv. 9 and 10, namely, our future salvation. Paul is reminding us that our salvation is not just future; it has already begun. We have already received the reconciliation and possess it *now* as the result of being justified *now* (5:9).

Thus even now our lives are filled with *rejoicing in God*. This is the same word used in vv. 2 and 3, where the NIV also translates it "rejoice." In 2:17, where the word probably has the connotation of bragging or boasting in God, Paul reproves the Jews for joyfully boasting in God in reference to his Law, or more specifically in reference to their own prideful use of that Law. Here in 5:11 Paul shows us how to rightfully boast or rejoice in God, namely, in reference to his *grace*. We are constantly overwhelmed with "jubilant exultation" (Cranfield, I:268) as we think about what God has done for us through Jesus Christ. And why should God's people not rejoice, asks Bruce, when they know that "the end to which they confidently look forward is no longer the outpouring of divine wrath but the unveiling of divine glory" (121)!

Finally we must call attention to the way Paul has exalted Jesus Christ throughout this passage as the one who has made grace and assurance possible. Ten times in these 11 verses the saving role of Jesus is thrust before our consciousness: "through our Lord Jesus Christ . . . through whom . . . Christ died . . . Christ died . . . by his blood . . . through him . . . through the death of his Son . . . through his life . . . through our Lord Jesus Christ . . . through whom." He, and not ourselves — what he has done, not what we have done or are doing — is the source and basis for our assurance of salvation.

B. THE ALL-SUFFICIENCY OF
THE DEATH OF CHRIST (5:12-21)

This section, which serves as the conclusion to the second main section of Romans (3:21-5:21), has a reputation for difficulty. No passage in the New Testament, says Barclay, "is more difficult for a modern mind to understand" (77). Long ago Lard (162-163) acknowledged these difficulties, but regarded them as "exaggerated." In a real sense Lard is right. There are some genuine exegetical problems here; but once four key questions are answered, the overall meaning of the passage becomes quite clear.

The first question is this: *What is the purpose of this passage in relation to the epistle as a whole?* This passage is best understood as continuing the theme of assurance that began with 5:1.[80] In 5:1-11 Paul assures us that we can put all our hope and confidence in *one saving act* (the cross) of *one man* (Jesus Christ). We have pointed out how in those 11 verses the apostle makes 10 references to the saving efficacy of Christ and his cross. In light of this someone might begin to wonder, "Isn't this expecting an awfully lot from just one man?" This is indeed what the gospel asks us to believe, that essentially one act of just one man has the power to save the whole world from all its sins. It calls upon us to "put all our eggs in one basket," so to speak. But how can this be? Paraphrasing Winston Churchill, Stott (148-149) asks how can "so many owe so much to only one person"? As MacArthur words it (I:291), "How could what one man did at one time in history have such an absolute effect on mankind?"

In order to show that this is not as far-fetched as we might at first think, Paul calls attention to the man whose one act has already been demonstrated to have a universal effect upon the human race, namely, Adam. Then he uses this by way of comparison and contrast to show that the "one righteous act" of the one man, Jesus, will surely be just as efficacious and universal as the "one sinful act" of the one man, Adam — and even "much more" (5:15, 17). His argument moves from the lesser to the greater. If we

---

[80]I agree with Moo: "The main connection is with the teaching of assurance of final salvation in the immediately preceding paragraph" (I:327).

can accept the fact that the one sin of a mere man has brought sin and death upon the whole world, then we can surely believe that the atoning death of the Son of God has brought salvation upon the whole world. The purpose of the passage, then, is to increase our confidence in the all-sufficiency of the death of Christ.

The second preliminary question is this: *Does this paragraph teach the doctrine of original sin?* It is not wrong to raise this question. Indeed, we cannot read Paul's many references to Adam and to the universal consequences of his one sin without wondering about it. Adam's sin brought death, judgment, and condemnation upon all; by his one sin all were made sinners. Does this mean that every child is conceived and born sinful, and born condemned to death and eternal punishment? Is this the main doctrine Paul wants to establish in this passage?

The fact is that at least since the time of Augustine (early fifth century), many in Christendom have used these verses to construct this very doctrine. Because the concept of original sin has had such a profound and far-reaching impact upon Christian thought as a whole, Barclay has rightly said that no passage in the NT "has had such an influence on theology as this passage" (77). The doctrine of original sin basically teaches that, in addition to physical death, Adam's first sin brought severe spiritual consequences upon all his natural descendants.[81] The term itself refers not to that first sin but to the spiritual state in which children are conceived and born as the result of it.

Now the question is this: does 5:12-21 actually teach some form of original sin? Without doubt Paul is here affirming that Adam's sin did bring serious consequences upon all his offspring. Our understanding of the exact nature of these consequences depends upon how we interpret the terms "death," "judgment," "condemnation," and "made sinners" as used in the text. Many have tried to limit them all to physical death only, thus denying that 5:12-21 teaches any sort of original sin. Others believe that these terms, both in themselves and as compared with the blessings received

---

[81]The term "natural descendants" or something similar is usually used in order to exclude Jesus himself from the category of those who suffer the consequences of Adam's sin.

from Christ, must refer to something much more serious than physical death by itself. Thus they conclude that this text does indeed teach original sin.

The biggest problem with this whole approach is that it implicitly assumes that Paul's main subject here is Adam and his sin and its consequences. But that is not the case. Paul did not write this passage just to teach a doctrine of original sin. Yes, he does declare that Adam's sin brought all these terrible things upon the human race, but that is not his main point. His main subject is *Jesus and his cross* and the universal, all-sufficient consequences of that saving event. His purpose is not to emphasize what happened to the race as the result of Adam's sin, but to emphasize what has happened to it as the result of Christ's saving work.

The fact is that it really does not matter which view of "original sin" one holds. Did Adam's sin bring only physical death upon us? Or did it also bring spiritual depravity — partial or total? Did it also make us guilty sinners, condemned to eternal punishment in hell? In the final analysis it does not matter what content anyone feels compelled to pour into the concept of "original sin," because Paul's main point is this: *whatever the whole human race got (or would have got) from Adam has been completely canceled out for the whole human race by the gracious atoning work of Jesus Christ.* Make the Adamic legacy as dire as you want: physical death, total depravity, genuine guilt and condemnation to hell. The whole point of the passage is that Christ's "one act of righteousness" (5:18) has completely intercepted, nullified, negated, canceled, and counteracted *whatever* was destined to be ours because of Adam. All the potential spiritual consequences of Adam's sin are intercepted even before they can be applied. The only consequence that actually takes effect is physical death, and it is countered with the promise of resurrection to eternal life.

This understanding of 5:12-21 and original sin has been clearly understood at least since the Reformation, when it was taught by Anabaptist writers, and is widely accepted within the Wesleyan tradition. Also, this principle has been most clearly stated in earlier Restoration Movement writings. As A.I. Hobbs succinctly puts it,

> It should be emphasized that, under the reign of grace, whatever death was brought upon our race through Adamic sin by

reason of his federal headship was annulled by reason of the federal headship of the second Adam. . . . What, without our will or consent, we lost in the first Adam, we have regained or shall regain in the second Adam, without our will or consent ("Conversion," 269).

Robert Milligan repeats this principle and concludes that "no man need, therefore, feel any concern or anxiety about the sin of Adam and its effects on his posterity" (*Scheme*, 60). See also J.S. Lamar ("Ground," 105); McGarvey and Pendleton (336-337); and Lard (174).

What does this mean? It means that there is no doctrine of original sin taught in 5:12-21. No child is actually conceived and born under the curse of Adam's sin. If anything, this passage teaches a doctrine of *original grace*: every child is born under the grace of God, born saved, "born free" from all spiritual effects of Adam's sin, and born with the guarantee of ultimate freedom from all physical effects of that sin by means of the resurrection unto glory. God began to apply this "original grace" to the first generation of Adam's own children, in the same way that the results of the cross were applied retrospectively to believing adults in the pre-Christian era (3:25).

We are now ready for the third question: *What is the scope of the words MANY and ALL as they are used in 5:12-21?* These terms appear at crucial points in the text. "Death came to all men" (5:12). By Adam's trespass "many died," but Christ's grace overflowed "to the many" (5:15). Through Adam came "condemnation for all men," but through Christ came justification of life "for all men" (5:18). In Adam "the many were made sinners," but in Christ "the many will be made righteous" (5:19). Exactly who are meant to be included in these terms?

What is at stake here is this: if the answer given to the second question above is correct, as it so obviously seems to be, why do so many still believe and teach a doctrine of original sin? The answer lies in how they interpret "many" and "all" in the verses cited above.

Most interpreters, even those who hold to original sin, generally agree that there is no difference in scope between the two terms themselves. I.e., "many" and "all" refer to the same group of

people. The term "many" is not intended to be set in contrast with
"all," but rather in contrast with "one." Even though Adam is just
one man, his one sin had consequences that extend to *the many*
(i.e., more than one). Even though Christ is just one man, his one
act likewise applies to *the many*. The term "all" is then used to
convey the connotation of totality, but is not meant to be broader
in scope than "the many." I am in total agreement with this.

Wherein lies the problem, then? It lies in the way these two
terms are applied to Adam on the one hand and to Christ on the
other hand. The most commonly-held idea seems to be that when
these terms are used in relation to Adam's sin, they are completely
universal in scope; but when they are used in relation to the work
of Christ, they are more limited and restricted in scope and do not
really mean "all." In Stott's words, "The 'all men' who are affected
by the work of Christ cannot refer to absolutely everybody," as it
does for Adam (159). Adam did indeed inflict the entire race with
the consequences of his sin, but the atoning work of Christ canceled out these consequences only for the smaller group of those
who are actually saved. "Original sin," however understood, thus
remains intact for the rest of mankind.

One way of saying this is that Christ's one righteous act is *able* to
cancel original sin for everyone, that it has the power or potential
to do so; but in fact it does so only for those who consciously *receive*
the gift of grace through faith (5:17). E.g., MacArthur says the
passage teaches that "all *can*[82] be made righteous in Christ," that
"Christ's one sacrifice made salvation *available* to all mankind"
(I:297, 302). Mounce says, "Just as condemnation spread to all, so
also is the divine acquittal *offered* to all" (144).

More often, however, especially for those who hold to the classical Augustinian doctrine of original sin, the distinction between
Adam's "all" and Christ's "all" is stated thus: the consequences of
Adam's act extended to all who were in him or belonged to him
when he sinned—which includes the whole race; but the consequences of Christ's act extended only to "all" who were in him or
belonged to him when he died—which includes only the elect.
"Both Adam and Christ would then be viewed as inclusive repre-

---

[82]In this and the next paragraph, the italics in the quotations are added.

sentatives whose actions can be considered as the actions also of *those who belong to them*" (Moo, I:340). In v. 18, says Mounce, the contrast is between "all who are *in Adam*" and "all who are *in Christ*" (145).

What I want to emphasize, however, is that all such approaches to 5:12-21 are false; all attempts to reduce the "many" and "all" when used of Christ to anything less than their scope when used of Adam must be rejected. The reason should be obvious: such a discrepancy in the numbers would negate the whole purpose of the Adam-Christ comparison! The question of assurance is this: can I have confidence that Christ's work is sufficient for taking away all my sins — and those of the whole world as well? Paul's answer is "Yes! You *can* have such assurance! Look at what has already been done as the result of his work: his one righteous act has *already* counteracted *everything* brought upon *everyone* by Adam. This is the stepping stone for our confidence that his work is capable of 'much more' (5:15, 17), i.e., it is capable of taking away all the consequences of our personal sins as well."

Thus to maintain the basic theme of assurance, we must insist that the terms "many" and "all" when used of Christ are at least as broad in scope as when used of Adam. Adam's sin brought sin, death, judgment, and condemnation upon *every* member of the human race; likewise Christ's atoning act brought righteousness, justification, and life upon *every* member of the human race. Schlatter (126) asks, "How is the work of the one through whom *all* are what they are canceled? Through the one who acts as effectively *for all* as the first one did" (italics added). The failure to acknowledge this is the greatest hindrance to a proper understanding of this passage; it is also the single most influential reason why many still believe this passage teaches a doctrine of original sin.

This leads to the fourth and final preliminary question: *Does this passage teach universal salvation, then?* Some believe that Paul's use of "all" and the inclusive "many" do indeed suggest universalism.[83] Käsemann (157) asks, "Does not the hope of general restoration . . . come to expression here" if we take these terms seriously? Surely "all-powerful grace is unthinkable without eschatological universalism."

---

[83]See Moo, I:355-356; Dunn, I:285.

Reflecting on 5:18 Dunn opines that we should not "exclude the possibility that Paul . . . cherished the hope of such a universal salvation . . . . How, after all, can grace be 'so much more' in its effect if it is less universal than the effect of death?" (I:297).

Many of those who limit the "all" to whom Christ's work applies in 5:12-21 do so because they think that to do otherwise is to embrace such universalism. For example, Stott very clearly implies that taking "all" to mean "everybody without exception" is "to believe in universal salvation" (159). Many have uncritically assumed this to be so.

The answer to the question, however, is NO! Romans 5:12-21 does not teach universal salvation, and taking the "all" and "many" who receive Christ's grace to refer to the whole human race does *not* entail such universalism. Why not? Because the primary focus of the passage as a whole and of these words specifically is how the work of Christ counteracts and cancels in their entirety the consequences of *the one sin of Adam* for every single individual. This is not a matter of possibility or potentiality; it is not just something Christ is able to do, or something that is offered to all and accepted by some. No, this is a reality; it is an accomplished fact; it has been done and will be done for the entire race; it is a sure thing.

However, Paul here absolutely does *not* say the same thing about the consequences for all *our own personal sins*. This is another matter altogether. As Romans has already made perfectly clear, the guilt and penalty for our personal sins are removed only through personal faith. The language of possibility and potentiality and "offered" applies to our personal sins, and 5:12-21 certainly implies that Christ's sacrifice is sufficient to take care of these also; indeed, this is the ultimate conclusion to which Paul's argument leads. But the universal language in the text applies only to what we have all received from *Adam's* sin.

In other words, from a practical point of view, this passage addresses the question of the spiritual state of infants when they are conceived and born. Do infants "inherit" anything from Adam, or is anything imposed upon them as the result of Adam's sin alone? Quite obviously so, particularly physical death. Paul affirms in 5:12 that death comes to all men as the result of sin, but this cannot mean personal sins since even infants sometimes die. Therefore death must come upon all because of Adam's sin. This is Paul's point in 5:13-14, where "those who did not sin by breaking a commandment" must refer to infants. (This is the force of the word καί [*kai*], "even," in v. 14.) It is likely that the language used in other verses (judgment, condemnation, made sinners) means that Adam's sin brought serious spiritual consequences upon infants as well.

The point of the passage, though, is that Christ's one atoning act cancels out *all* of these consequences for *all* infants. Because of Jesus Christ no infant is born sinful, depraved, or condemned. All do face the inevitability of physical death, but insofar as such death derives from Adam's sin, it too will one day be canceled out in the final resurrection from the dead. Every single baby is thus conceived and born in a redeemed or saved state (original grace!). The gifts of righteousness and justification and life are received universally and automatically by every infant as the means of salvation from Adam's sin.[84] This is the only "universalism" in 5:12-21.

At the same time in this passage Paul alludes to the fact that babies grow up and reach the age of accountability and commit personal sins ("many trespasses," v. 17). Commenting on the "much more" in 5:15 McGarvey and Pendleton (336-337) say,

> If we had only Adam's sin to answer for, then the teaching of this passage would establish the doctrine of universal salvation, for Christ's act completely counteracted Adam's act. But there are other sins beside that first one committed by Adam, and other punishments beside natural death. It is in its dealings with those that the range of Christ's act exceeds that of Adam, and it is here also that salvation becomes limited.

When a child reaches the age of accountability and begins to become responsible for his personal sins, he forfeits the original grace under which he has been living since conception. He comes under the wrath

---

[84]Thus Barclay (81) is wrong to say that Paul's argument has a flaw in it, in that the parallelism between Adam's sin and Christ's gift is faulty. He says our connection with Adam is not something we can choose, but our connection with Christ is voluntary. What Barclay fails to see, though, is that the latter is true only in reference to our personal sins. The removal of the effects of Adam's sin is no more voluntary than their infliction upon us. Both, as Hobbs says, happen "without our will or consent" ("Conversion," 269).

of God and bears the full consequences of the sins that he is now
committing by his own choice. He has even forfeited the redemptive
resurrection gained through the cancellation of the death derived
from Adam. If he dies in his own sins, he will be raised from the dead,
but not redemptively in a glorified body like that of Christ.

The only way to escape the consequences of one's personal sins
is by conscious choice and personal faith. Since everyone does not
so choose and believe, there is no universal salvation.

Thus the spiritual odyssey of the individual has four possible
stages: (1) "*Original sin*," even if this is understood to involve only
the penalty of physical death as the result of Adam's sin. Many
understand it to include much more, of course. The main point
about this stage is that (except for physical death) it is theoretical or
potential only; it is never actually experienced because it is intercepted and canceled for everyone by the all-sufficient work of
Christ. Thus no one ever actually passes through this stage, and
children are certainly not born in it.

(2) "*Original grace*," which is the stage we enter when we first
come into existence and under which we stay until we reach the age
of accountability, thanks to the work of the Second Adam. All
infants and young children are here, as are those whose mental
abilities never develop beyond those of young children. This is a
state of salvation and it is universal; thus the concept of "universal
salvation" applies here.

(3) "*Personal sin*," the stage all enter when they reach the age of
accountability and lose the original grace under which they were
born. Those in this stage are the lost, the unsaved. If they die here
they will be condemned forever to hell.

(4) "*Personal grace*," a term we might use for the position occupied by all believers, or those who have personally repented and
believed God's gracious promises. This is a state of salvation, but it
is not universal. It is available to all, but is entered only through
personal choice.

This concludes our discussion of the four preliminary questions.
In answering them I have tried to present the gist of Paul's teaching
in 5:12-21 in a summary form. We are now ready to begin our
verse-by-verse study of the passage, proceeding according to the following outline: a) Verses 12-14 show how the sin of one man

(Adam) brought sin and death upon the whole world. In v. 12 Paul begins a thought that is not immediately completed. It is put on hold while he pursues some related ideas; then in v. 18 he picks it up again. b) In vv. 15-17 Paul presents a negative contrast between Christ and Adam, showing that Christ and his sacrifice are greater than Adam and his sin. c) In vv. 18-19 Paul completes the thought of v. 12 by declaring that Christ's cross completely cancels the consequences of Adam's sin. d) The final section, vv. 20-21, asserts the triumph of grace over sin and death.

1. One Sin of One Man (Adam) Brought Sin and Death to All (5:12-14)

5:12 Therefore . . . . This first word in the verse indicates that Paul is about to draw a conclusion from something that serves as a premise or basis for it. Opinions vary widely as to what this premise is. Most find it in the preceding context. For some it is the reference to the death of Jesus in v. 10 (Lard, 164). Others say the premise is the entire section, 5:1-11 (Cranfield, I:271). Still others say it includes everything from 1:18 to 5:11 (Dunn, I:272). On the other hand, some actually find the premise in v. 12 itself (Williams, 172-173).

This is a difficult question, but the connection is probably both backward and forward. As stated above, at the end of v. 12 Paul seems to break off his main argument until he can lay down some related truths; then he picks it up again in v. 18, with 18a reiterating v. 12 and 18b stating the long-awaited conclusion. The progression of the main thought, then, is this: "Therefore, in view of what has just been said about the saving power of the death of Christ (5:1-11), and also because we know that an example of such vicarious power already exists in the person of Adam (5:12-14), we may safely conclude that the one righteous act of the one man Jesus Christ is definitely sufficient to bring salvation to all people."

. . . just as sin entered the world through one man . . . . The "one man," of course is Adam[85] (v. 14), who along with Eve was

---

[85]Does the theological point of this passage depend on Adam's being an actual historical individual, and his sin's being an actual event? Dunn

responsible for introducing sin into the world (Gen 3:1-7). Since Adam was the head of his wife[86] and in a real sense the head of the whole human family,[87] he alone is singled out as the responsible party and also as a kind of pattern for Jesus (v. 14). The word for "sin" is ἁμαρτία (*hamartia*), which in this case refers not to a specific act but to the very principle or power of evil and lawlessness that enters like an invading force and takes root in the hearts of its willing victims (Godet, 204; Moo, I:331). "The world" (as in John 3:16) is the world of mankind, the sphere of human beings; sin had already entered the world of angels through the sin of Satan (1 John 3:8).

The main point of this statement is the phrase, "through one man," which is in the emphatic position in the Greek. To make his point that just one man (Jesus) is the source of all salvation, Paul is reminding us that just one man (and a lesser one at that) is the source of all sin.

. . . and death through sin . . . . This statement is highly condensed. Several words carry over from the first clause, so that the entire thought is thus: "And (just as) death (entered the world [of human beings]) through sin." In this case "sin" (*hamartia* again) seems to refer to the first specific sinful act of Adam, his disobedience to the command about the tree of knowledge of good and evil (Gen 2:16-17). Just as this one man was the channel through which sin entered, his one sin was the channel through which death entered. Again we understand the entry to be limited to the world of human beings; we can draw no conclusions from this verse about death among animals (Schlatter, 127; Stott, 165-166).

To what specific kind of death is Paul referring here? Many rightly understand the Bible to distinguish three kinds of death: physical, spiritual, and eternal (Godet, 205). Physical death of course

---

(I:289) says no, "an act in mythic history can be paralleled to an act in living history without the point of comparison being lost." I seriously disagree; the whole point of the comparison is to demonstrate the greater power of Christ's cross. This claim is empty unless Adam and his sin were real. See MacArthur, I:294; Moo, I:336, 365; Stott, 162-166.

[86]1 Cor 11:3; Eph 5:23. On Adam's headship prior to the Fall see Cottrell, *Roles*, 80-102.

[87]Most (but not all) apocryphal Jewish literature assigned this role to Adam. See Cranfield, I:280-281; Dunn, I:272, 287; Moo, I:364-365.

is the death of the body; spiritual death is equivalent to the soul's condition of sinfulness and depravity (Eph 2:1, 5; Col 2:13); eternal death is condemnation to hell or the lake of fire (Rev 20:6, 14). Some believe Paul is referring to all three kinds here (Hendriksen, I:185; MacArthur, I:295). Sometimes those who hold this view lump the last two kinds (spiritual and eternal) into the single category of spiritual death, and declare that Adam's sin resulted in both physical death and this inclusive spiritual death, or "total death" (Moo, I:332; Shields, 65; Mounce 141; Stott, 150). On the other hand, some contend that in this verse Paul means physical death only (Lard, 165-166; MP, 340; Murray, I:181-182). Morris (230) agrees that physical death is in mind, but believes that spiritual death is indirectly in view in that physical death is the sign and symbol of it.

In my judgment, Paul's primary concern in 5:12 is with physical death; this is clear from 5:13-14, where physical death is obviously in view (Godet, 205; Smith, I:85). Whether Paul considers anything else to be imposed upon the human race as a result of Adam's one sin must be determined by a consideration of 5:15-19.[88] But at this point, to focus on spiritual death misses the main point of 5:13-14, where physical death even among babies is cited as evidence for the point about the "one man" in v. 12.

Paul is not just saying that death is the result of sin in general, and he is especially not saying that each individual's death is the result of his own sin. No, his whole point in 5:12-21 rests on the fact that the deaths of all individual human beings are the penal consequence of one sin of *one man*, Adam: "The many died by the trespass of the one man" (5:15a; Smith, I:85).

. . . and in this way death came to all men, because all sinned . . . . Up to this point, based on 5:12a alone, there is no reason to extend the sin of Adam and the resulting death beyond their entry point, namely, Adam himself. But 5:12b shows that there is more to it than this — much more. This part of the verse reveals the universal consequences of Adam's one sin. "In this way," i.e., through the one sin of the one man, "death came to all men." The word for "came" means "went through," "spread," or "permeated." Paul is

---

[88]In my judgment Paul does broaden the scope of death in these verses, but that is not relevant here.

saying that death "made its way to each individual member of the race . . . like a father's inheritance divided among his children" (Sanday and Headlam, 133).

If Paul had ended his thought here and gone directly to v. 13, the task of exegetes and theologians would no doubt have been considerably lighter. But this was not to be. Led by the Spirit, Paul added these four words: ἐφ' ᾧ πάντες ἥμαρτον (*eph' hō pantes hēmarton*). The last two words are not difficult to translate; they simply state, "all sinned," or "all have sinned" (as in 3:23). Thus sin, like death, is universalized: all die; likewise all sinned. Adam sinned, but everyone else sinned as well.

This leaves two major problems to be resolved. First, what is the meaning of *eph' hō*? And second, in what sense have all sinned?[89] Regarding the former question, some have taken the *hō* in *eph' hō* to be a relative pronoun referring back to the "one man" in 5:12a. Thus it has been translated "in whom," namely, "in Adam," the whole clause then meaning "in Adam all sinned." Augustine, who was following the common Latin translation *in quo*, accepted this view and used it as a significant part of the basis for his doctrine of original sin.

Modern interpreters agree that this is a poor translation of *eph' hō*. The antecedent is too far removed from *hō*, and "in" is not a common meaning for *epi* (*eph'*). By general agreement today *eph' hō* is taken as a conjunction introducing a dependent clause, and is usually translated "because." Thus the NIV translation, "because all sinned." I see no reason to disagree.

But this does not really help a lot, because it still leaves us asking in what sense "all sinned." I.e., how is the sin of all somehow the cause of the death of all, especially since the death of all has already been stated to be the result of the *one* sin of the *one* man, Adam?

Proposed answers fall into two categories. One approach is that the statement "all sinned" must be taken as referring to each individual's personal sins, as in 3:23. In this case each person dies because of his own sins. But how is Adam's sin involved? One view

---

[89]See Cranfield, I:274-279, for an analysis of the variety of views on these questions.

is that when we sin personally we are *imitating* Adam's sin; thus Adam's sin is still indirectly responsible for every person's death (Shields, 66; Barrett, 111). Another view is that Adam's sin imposes a corrupt nature on all his descendants, which causes them all to sin and thus incur death (Dunn, I:290; Cranfield, I:278-279; Batey, 73-74). Again, the relation between Adam's sin and our death is indirect.

In my judgment neither version of this view is acceptable. Once Adam is made only the indirect cause of death, rather than the direct cause, the main point of the passage — the analogy between Adam and Christ — breaks down. The "one man Adam vs. one man Jesus" theme (5:15-19) loses its punch (Morris, 232). Also, neither form of this approach can explain the death of infants, who have not sinned personally. (See Murray, I:183-184, for these and other arguments against this view.)

The other approach to "all sinned" is to posit some kind of union between Adam and his descendants, the result being that when he sinned, we all somehow sinned in or with him. Thus "all sinned" does not refer to the subsequent personal sins of each individual, but to a kind of collective sinning of all in Adam's one act of disobedience in the Garden of Eden. (Practically speaking, this view has the same effect as translating *eph' hō* as "in Adam.")

One version of this latter approach is to see all mankind as existing within Adam when he sinned, so that his sin literally was the sin of us all; thus we all are equally accountable for it and are punished for it (MacArthur, I:293, 296).[90] An analogy is the relation between Abraham and Levi in Heb 7:9-10. When Abraham paid tithes to Melchizedek (Heb 7:1-2), Levi also "paid tithes, for he was still in the loins of his father" when Abraham tithed. In this same sense we were all in Adam's loins when he sinned; thus we also sinned.

The other version of this second approach is to treat Adam as acting as a representative for the whole race in his test regarding the tree (Lard, 167-168; Smith, 87). Thus Adam is called the "federal head" of all mankind (MP, 334). The analogy here is the relation between Christ on the cross and the whole human race.

---

[90]See Murray's discussion of this view in *Imputation*, 24-36.

We were not in him when he died; but he died representatively for all (2 Cor 5:14), and the consequences of his death are imputed to others.

In my judgment this second approach is the better one, either according to its second version or as a combination of the two. (See Stott, 151-154.) "All sinned" does not refer to our personal sins, but to the one sin of Adam in which we all participated in some form, and for which we all suffer the penal consequences. We can offer no explanation for such an arrangement other than divine appointment. "All sinned in Adam as being in him. By divine appointment, Adam . . . stood for and represented the whole of his posterity" (Lard, 167). "When Adam sinned he was not just a man, he was mankind" (Smith, 84). "In Adam all sinned; in Adam all died" (Hendriksen, I:178). Thus, as Moo points out, "all die because all sinned" and "all die because Adam sinned" are both true, "because the sin of Adam is the sin of all" (I:338).

It is wrong, though, to conclude (as many do) that this understanding of "because all sinned" leads to the doctrine of original sin. I have explained in the introduction to this section why this is not the case.

5:13 Verse 12 introduces an intended comparison between Adam and Christ that is not completed. Only the "just as" portion (the *protasis*) is given; the "so also" part (the *apodosis*) is not stated. In 5:18-19 Paul will come back to the comparison and present it in two different ways. But before then, in 5:13-17 (sometimes treated as a parenthesis, as in the KJV), he pauses in order to verify and clarify what he says in 5:12.

In v. 12 two crucial points are made: one, that death is the result of sin; and two, that the death of all is the result of the sin of one man, Adam. Paul does not try to prove the first point, but 5:13-14 seems designed to prove the second point (Godet, 209; MP, 334; Murray, I:187). The proof lies in the fact that some people die even though they have never sinned personally, including babies, young children, and some with mental handicaps. Thus if sin is indeed the cause of death, the fact that such people sometimes die proves that the one representative sin of Adam must be that cause.

. . . for before the law was given, sin was in the world. But sin is not taken into account when there is no law. This and v. 14 are very difficult, and in my opinion can be understood only as an extremely condensed argument, some parts of which are assumed. We may wonder why Paul even brings up the Adam-to-Moses period, if his main proof is going to be infants. The answer seems to be that in the minds of his Jewish audience especially, the general nature of this period as a whole ought to prove Paul's point. This would seem to be the case based upon the combination of two factors: first, "where there is no law there is no transgression" (4:15); and second, the Law[91] was not given until the time of Moses. Thus even though in the pre-Mosaic period people did things that were sinful, they could not be held accountable for them because there was no law. But the whole population in this period died anyway; therefore they must have died because of Adam's sin.

This train of thought would seem perfectly valid to many, especially to those who put such strong emphasis on the Law of Moses. So this is where Paul *begins* his argument, even though it is not where he ends it.

That "sin was in the world" before Moses' Law was given is indisputable (Gen 6:5, 11; 8:21; 18:20; Exod 9:27).[92] It is also indisputable that "sin is not taken into account when there is no law," as Paul had already said in 4:15. The word for "taken into account" (used here and in Phlm 18) is an accounting term and means "to enter into the ledger or into the account of someone." This is the concept of imputation, though in this case Paul is talking about imputing one's own sins to one's own account. He says this does not occur when no law exists by which sins can be identified as violations of God's will. In such a case God does not impute sinful acts to a person's account and therefore does not punish him. But since people between Adam and Moses did suffer the penalty of death (v. 14a), they could only have died because of Adam's sin.

This reasoning would be sound except for one thing: there *was* law between Adam and Moses! True, the Law of Moses was not yet

---

[91]Here "Law" must be understood as the Mosaic Law, in view of 5:14.

[92]In view of these and other clear references to *sins* in the pre-Mosaic era, it is incredible that many still argue that there were no truly accountable sinful acts during this period. See, e.g., Wiens, "Exegesis," 47; Dunn, I:291; MacArthur, I:298-299.

given, but Paul has already argued that law is revealed and known through general revelation (1:18-32; 2:14-15); and he has already declared that Gentiles or pagans are "without excuse" (1:20) when they go against this general revelation. Indeed, Paul named a whole list of specific sins (1:24-31) committed by pagans; and he specifically said that those who commit these sins *know* God's decree, that those who do so are worthy of death (1:32)! Also, we have every reason to believe that God instructed Adam and Eve regarding his moral law; it is ludicrous to assume that the only law they were given was the one about the trees (Gen 2:16-17). What they knew of God's moral law would thus have been handed down from generation to generation, supplemented by occasional special revelation (e.g., Gen 4:9; 6:13; 7:1; 9:1-7). Otherwise, how could Noah have functioned as "a preacher of righteousness" (2 Pet 2:5)? The fact that God destroyed the human race (except for Noah's family) because of their wickedness shows that they had law and were being held accountable for it. The same is true of Sodom and Gomorrah. Thus the idea that "there was no positive commandment" in the pre-Mosaic period except for Gen 2:16-17 is quite false (contra Bruce, 130; Trench, *Synonyms*, 244; Schneider, "παρα–βαίνω," 5:740; and Schlatter, 128-129).

But if this reasoning is not sound, why does Paul bring it up? Because the argument would no doubt have occurred especially to Paul's Jewish audience, and he brings it up to get it out of the way. Thus I am suggesting that between v. 13 and v. 14 Paul is assuming that his readers will remember what he has already said very plainly in 1:18-32 and 2:14-15, and will draw their own conclusions as to the invalidity of the argument. This unspoken caveat then sets the stage for Paul's own argument in v. 14.

The thought of 5:13-14a may be paraphrased thus: "We have said that all die because of Adam's sin. But what gives us any reason to think this? Let's consider first of all a common assumption. Some who agree that Adam *must* be the source of human death base this conclusion on the fact that people died between Adam and Moses, before the Law was given; and we know God does not hold people accountable for their sins where is no law. Thus (so this argument goes) since people died then, they must have died because of Adam's sin.

"Now, at first glance this argument seems sound, but I'm sorry to say that it does not hold together. Why not? Mainly because it assumes that there was *no law* in this period between Adam and Moses; but this is not true. You will remember my clear teaching that there *was* law during this period, and people knew that by breaking this law they deserved God's wrath. So if we are going to show that all die because of Adam's sin, we must find another argument."

5:14 "Let's stay with the period between Adam and Moses. In this era (as in all other times, of course), death came to all human beings, *even* over those not old enough to commit personal sins like the sin of Adam. The fact that infants sometimes die is all the proof we need for the truth that all die because of Adam's sins."

Nevertheless introduces Paul's own valid argument, in contrast with the abbreviated invalid argument from v. 13.

. . . death reigned from the time of Adam to the time of Moses . . . . This is clearly a reference to physical death, which is personified as a tyrant having everyone under its power in the period in question (and in all other times as well; see v. 17). To depict death as a reigning monarch emphasizes its universal scope, its oppressive domination, and its inescapable certainty.

. . . even over those who did not sin by breaking a command, as did Adam . . . . This is the key point of the whole argument in vv. 13-14; this is what proves the fact that Adam's sin brought death upon us all: death reigned, *even* over this group. The word "even" (*kai*) is important, because it focuses the argument on a group that is more narrow than the general population of the earth (contra Godet, 212; Moo, I:345-346). This group is described as "those who did not sin by breaking a command."

Who are in this group? It depends on what Paul means by the expression, "did not sin by breaking a command." The word "command" is not in the original; this participial phrase literally reads "the ones who did not sin after the likeness of Adam's transgression." The word for "transgression," παράβασις (*parabasis*), is used in the NT here and in 2:23; 4:15; Gal 3:19; 1 Tim 2:14; Heb 2:2; 9:15. Its meaning is important, since many believe it is the key to identifying the group introduced by "even."

Parabasis literally means "stepping over a boundary, a deviation from the prescribed path or norm, a trespass, a transgression." In the NT it refers to breaking God's law, a transgression of his law. Here in 5:14, the group singled out by Paul did not sin according to the likeness of the *parabasis* of Adam. I.e., they did not transgress God's law in the same way that Adam did.

Most interpreters take this statement to mean that the *law* which Adam transgressed was crucially different from the law transgressed by those who lived between Adam and Moses. I.e., it was of such a nature that he could be held responsible for breaking it, whereas the latter group could not. The law Adam transgressed (Gen 2:16-17) is variously described as a direct command, an express command, an explicit command, an expressly revealed ordinance, a positive prohibition, a clear and definite divine commandment, a prohibition known to be a commandment of God. It is implied that no other command of this nature was given by God until the Law of Moses. Some add that the command to Adam was accompanied by a death sentence, and in this way was different from any laws between Adam and Moses (MP, 334-335; Moo, I:343). Thus it is concluded (by most interpreters) that the expression "those who did not sin by breaking a command" refers to *everyone* who lived between Adam and Moses, and not just to a special group such as infants.

The reasons I cannot accept this view are as follows. First, there *were* explicit commands and prohibitions (other than the command regarding the trees) between Adam and Moses, available in the beginning and sporadically thereafter by means of special revelation, and passed along as tradition to future generations. Also, the definitions usually given to *parabasis* in this context are much too narrow. It means transgression of the law, to be sure; but limiting such law only to that given through special revelation is indefensible. For example, in light of the emphasis Paul gives to general revelation in 1:18-32 and 2:14-15, the principle set forth in 4:15 (using *parabasis*) surely cannot be limited to specially-revealed law. We should also remember that the laws known through general revelation also carry the death sentence and that this is known by those who break them (1:32).

Finally, the main difference between Adam's sin and the sins committed by the specific group in 5:14 was not a difference in the *kind* of law they transgressed, but rather in the *way* the law was transgressed. Adam's sin was indeed a voluntary, conscious, deliberate decision to disobey a command of God. But so were most sins committed by most people even before the Law of Moses came. It does not matter whether the law being transgressed was specially revealed or written on the heart; anyone deliberately breaking either kind of law was guilty of *parabasis* and thus was "without excuse" (1:20; 2:1). I.e., *all* lawbreakers during this period committed *personal* sins worthy of death.

But there is one *way* of sinning that is "not like the transgression of Adam" (NASB), i.e., not a voluntary, deliberate, personal sin. What is it? None other than the sin which everyone committed *representatively* in Adam in the Garden of Eden (5:12). This is the *only* kind of sin some people have committed, and *even they* sometimes die. Who are in this group? Infants, small children, and some with mental handicaps. These are the ones to whom Paul refers here in the "even" clause.

I am aware that many declare that Paul cannot be talking about infants here, but rather must be talking about adult sinners only (e.g., Cranfield, I:279; Dunn, I:276; Moo, I:345-346); or at least that he cannot be talking about infants only (Lard, 172). But it seems to me that this misses the whole point of Paul's argument, and severely weakens his case that Adam's sin is the cause of the death of all. Paul has made it clear that even sinners against general revelation are worthy of death and know it (1:32). Genesis makes it clear that the bulk of those who died in the Flood and in the cities of the plain deserved to die because of their own sin. Thus *only* a group (such as infants) who have committed no *personal* sins and who sometimes die anyway can truly prove Paul's point that the real cause of human death is the one representative sin of Adam.[93]

Having established his point about Adam, Paul briefly points us back in the direction his original thought was beginning to take in v. 12, i.e., a comparison between Adam and Christ. He does this by stating that Adam **was . . . a pattern of the one to come.** "The one to come" refers to Christ, who was yet to come from Adam's per

---

[93]Expositors who argue that infants are in view here include DeWelt, 78, 80; Moule, 104-105; Shedd, 132; and Murray, I:191. Murray also includes those who sinned against general revelation, but I disagree.

spective. The word "pattern" is τύπος (*typos*) or "type." Moo (I:346) explains that this word originally meant "the impression made by striking something," and that it came to mean "a form, pattern, or example." In the NT it refers to "those OT persons, institutions, or events that are seen to have a divinely intended function of prefiguring the eschatological age inaugurated by Christ." See Cranfield, I:283.

In what sense does Adam prefigure Christ? Only in this one point, namely, that just as Adam was only one man yet performed a single act that affected the entire world, so also was Jesus Christ just one man whose one act likewise affected the whole human race.

2. Christ and His Sacrifice Are Greater than Adam and His Sin (5:15-17)

The main point in 5:12-21 is the one positive comparison between Adam and Christ, as just described. In this sense Adam is a type of Christ. But before Paul actually states this comparison (5:18-19), he pauses once again, this time to make it clear that in most ways Adam and Christ are very *different*. Even though the positive comparison he is about to draw is very important, so are the *contrasts* between Adam's one sinful act and Christ's one saving act.

5:15 But the gift is not like the trespass . . . . This statement is a heading over 5:15-17, telling us that the subject is the contrast between the negative results of Adam's sin and the positive results of Christ's cross. The word for "trespass" is παράπτωμα (*paraptōma*), "a false step, straying from the path, departing from the norm." There is little difference between this and *parabasis* as used in 5:14.[94] The word for "gift" is χάρισμα (*charisma*, closely related to χάρις [*charis*], "grace"). It refers to the gracious result that flows

---

[94]Dunn, I:279, 293. In my opinion too much is made of the differences among the words used for "sin" in 5:12-21 (*hamartia, parabasis, paraptōma,* and *parakoē*). Etymologically these words have different nuances, but all are used to denote sinful acts performed in disobedience to the law of God. The one major difference is that *hamartia* is often used to denote sin as a pervading force or power that seeks to dominate the will and express itself in sinful acts.

unto all from the one saving act of Christ, in contrast with the devastating result that comes upon all from Adam's trespass.[95] What is
this gift, this gracious result? Most likely it is the "gift of righteousness" (5:17), the imputed righteousness of Christ that results in justification (5:16, 18) and life (5:17-18).

The rest of this verse is the first of three different ways Paul
expresses this contrast. Adam's side of it is stated thus: **For if the
many died by the trespass of the one man . . . .** As Murray sums it
up, "The one sin of Adam is the judicial ground or reason for the
death of the many" (I:192). This point has already been made in
5:12 and proved in 5:13-14. The word "many" (see 5:19) is equivalent in scope to "all men" in 5:12 and 5:18. Here it is used in contrast with "one," i.e., even though Adam was only *one* man, what he
did had consequences for *many* men (denoting all others as a totality).[96] The word "died" is aorist (past) tense, pointing back to the
first sin of Adam as the time when all came under the sentence of
death (Lard, 177).

The other side of the contrast is stated thus: **how much more
did God's grace and the gift that came by the grace of the one
man, Jesus Christ, overflow to the many!** The words "much more"
indicate that this is an argument from the lesser (Adam) to the
greater (Christ). Some say this expression has a *quantitative*
meaning, indicating the superiority of the power and effects of
Christ's cross as contrasted with the power and effects of Adam's
sin. It describes "the infinitely superior effectiveness" of Christ's act
(Cranfield, I:284; see Mounce, 143; Stott, 161).

The quantitative superiority of Christ's cross is suggested by the
word translated "overflow." God's grace and the gift that comes by
it overflowed or abounded to the many (see v. 17). This means first
of all that God's gracious gift reached out to embrace *all* who have
been affected by Adam's sin, and has completely canceled and nullified the total consequences of Adam's sin for the entire human

---

[95]To preserve an exact symmetry with the sinful act of Adam, Moo
(I:348) says the gift must refer to the saving *act* of Christ rather than the
effect of that act. This is an awkward use of "gift," though.

[96]See the discussion of this in the introduction to this section, above. See
Graber, "All, Many," 95-96.

race. If it has not done *at least* this, then Christ's act is not even as powerful as Adam's sin, much less *more* powerful. This is the "original grace" explained in the introduction, above.

Second, the overflowing "much more" of Christ's cross means that the saved state into which it brings us is a state far better than what was lost in Adam. It includes "a better body than Adam ever had, a better life than he ever lived, a better world than he ever lived in, a world where Satan, and sin, and death can never come" (Lard, 178).

But most importantly, the overflowing "much more" means that the one saving act of Christ not only saves the entire race from whatever consequences have come upon us because of Adam's sin; it also is able to save the entire race from the consequences of their own *personal* sins, and does in fact cancel all such consequences for those who personally accept the free gift of grace through faith (MP, 336-337; DeWelt, 82). (We will see this point made in 5:16, where Paul refers to "many trespasses.") The saving work of Christ does not *actually* and in fact set the whole human race free from the effects of their personal sins; this would be universalism. Its application to personal sins is conditional and therefore limited. But the point is that the ability of Christ's cross to counteract mankind's personal sins means that its effectiveness extends far beyond the scope of Adam's sin. McGarvey and Pendleton (336) sum up this point very well: "We are here informed that the result of the sacrificial act of Christ fully reversed and nullified the effects of the act of Adam, and that it did even much more. The effect, in other words, had in all points as wide a range, and in some points a much wider range, than that of Adam's act." If not for this "wider range," most human beings would still be without hope, for "in addition to their sin in Adam," they have "other sins of their own for which to answer. The hope of the world lies, therefore, in the 'much more.'"

But some see another sense to the words "much more," called the *logical* sense, where the point is not the quantitative contrast between the two acts of the two men, but rather the *superior degree of certainty* we can have with regard to the efficacy of Christ's act, once we understand the nature and efficacy of the one act of Adam. This approach to "much more" presupposes the quantitative superiority of Christ over Adam. As Godet put it (216), "If a slight cause could bring sentence of death on all mankind, this same mankind will experience in its entirety the salutary effect of a much more powerful cause." He states the logic of Paul's argument thus: "Adam's offence has reached down to me, having had the power of subjecting me to death; how much more certainly will the grace of God and the grace of Christ combined have the power of reaching to me to save me!" Wiens says, "If such a little act has had a great and universal effect, how much more certain is it that a greater act will also extend to all men!" ("Exegesis," 48). See also Moo, I:349.

My inclination is to see both meanings, the quantitative and the logical, in Paul's reference to "much more." The former is surely emphasized as part of the contrast between Adam and Christ in 5:15-17, especially in the references to overflowing (v. 15), "many trespasses" (v. 16), and abundance (v. 17). The latter is even more appropriate, given the assurance theme that permeates this whole chapter. In view of what we know about Adam, we have all the more reason to put our total trust in the all-sufficiency of Christ's one saving act.

"God's grace" here probably refers to grace as an attribute of his nature. His loving grace overflowed to us in his decision to come to us in the person of "the one man, Jesus Christ," whose death provided for us the gift of righteousness and life.

Because of the widespread resistance to this fact, it is necessary to repeat here that "the many" to whom God's gracious gift has come are *the same* as "the many" who died from Adam's sin, and the same as the "all men" in 5:12 and 5:18. I.e., the term includes the whole human race, and it refers primarily to the complete cancellation of the effects of Adam's sin for all men. Any limitations we may place on "the many" (e.g., believers only, those who are "in Christ" only) begin to apply only when we get past this universal application to Adam's sin and are talking about individuals' personal sins.

5:16 Again, the gift of God is not like the result of the one man's sin . . . . This repeats the heading of v. 15 and introduces the second version of the contrast between Adam and Christ. Again the emphasis is on the infinite superiority of Christ's work. His saving act is much more efficacious than Adam's sin since it not only nullifies the universal results of that one sin but also is able to cancel the consequences of the personal sins of the many. It takes away the former unconditionally for all; it takes away the latter conditionally for believers.

"The one man's sin" is better translated "the one who sinned" (NASB). The gift again seems to be the gift of Christ's righteousness, on which our justification is based.

The judgment followed one sin and brought condemnation, but the gift followed many trespasses and brought justification. One contrast here is between "one sin" and "many trespasses." The judgment unto condemnation results from the single sin of one man; but the gift unto justification applies not only to this one sin but to many personal sins as well (and thus is quantitatively superior).

Another contrast is between the results of each man's act. On the one hand, Adam's sin brought "judgment" unto "condemnation." The word for "judgment" is κρίμα (krima), which is a judge's decision or verdict, usually an unfavorable one (see 2:2-3; 3:8; 13:2). Leaving no doubt that he is talking about a negative judgment, Paul says it is unto "condemnation" (κατάκριμα, katakrima), a term used in the NT only here and in 5:18; 8:1. It refers to the sentence of punishment, not only as pronounced but also as carried out.

On the other hand, the free gift that comes from Christ, the gift of imputed righteousness (v. 17b), is unto "justification" (δικαίωμα, dikaiōma). This Greek word is used ten times in the NT, but it means "justification" only here. (In 5:18 it means "righteous act.") The only other noun translated "justification" is δικαίωσις (dikaiōsis), which is used only twice in the NT (4:25; 5:18). Exegetes think Paul used dikaiōma here because its ending matches the other -ma words in the verse: δώρημα (dōrēma, "gift"), κρίμα (krima, "judgment"), κατάκριμα (katakrima, "condemnation"), χάρισμα (charisma, "gift"), and παράπτωμα (paraptōma, "trespass").[97]

The key question concerning this verse is, what does Paul mean by "condemnation" and "justification"? He says Adam's sin brought condemnation, and Christ's cross cancelled the condemnation by

---

[97]Käsemann calls this "rhetorical assimilation" (154); Dunn, "rhetorical balance" (I:281).

bringing justification. Up to this point the apostle has mentioned only *death* as the result of Adam's sin, and contextually there has been no reason to think that he means anything more than *physical* death. But the language of this verse raises the question of whether something more serious must be added to the Adamic legacy.

Some are quick to answer *no*, nothing more than physical death is in view, even with these new terms. The "condemnation" means only the sentence of physical death, they say; and the "justification" means only the temporary suspension of this sentence allowing some time to live on the earth, then in the end resurrection from the dead (DeWelt, 78). We can agree that physical death is a judicial penalty and can rightly be called "condemnation." When *katakrima* is used in 8:1, however, it hardly seems limited to physical death, and is usually taken to refer to eternal punishment. Even the word *krima* ("judgment") is often used in this sense. Thus we are persuaded to think that by using the word "condemnation" Paul is telling us here that the death imposed upon all men because of Adam's sin is not just physical death, but includes eternal death also (see 6:23).

This conclusion seems all the more warranted when we realize that this condemnation received from Adam is counteracted with the "justification" received from Christ. In other contexts justification involves so much more than resurrection from the dead. Thus I believe we are wrong to limit it to that in this context. Here we should give it the meaning it has in other places, especially here in Romans, namely, the cancellation of eternal punishment in hell.

Indeed, this is exactly how almost everyone understands these two terms when they are applied to the "many trespasses" (personal sins) in this verse. Thus how can we give them a more limited meaning when applying them to Adam's sin and its consequences?

But when we interpret condemnation as eternal death in hell and justifiction as the cancellation of this eternal punishment, are we not opening the door to the doctrine of original sin? Not at all. But is this not the Augustinian view? No, it is not. True, the Augustinian doctrine of original sin says the condemnation of eternal death in hell comes upon all as the result of Adam's sin; but it omits the most important part of Paul's teaching, namely, that the original grace of Jesus Christ *justifies* all men insofar as Adam's sin is concerned. I.e., it completely cancels out this condemnation, so that in its eternal element it is never even applied.

5:17 For if, by the trespass of the one man, death reigned through that one man . . . . These words begin a third way of expressing the contrast between Adam and Christ, another way of explaining how the gift is not like the trespass. They add nothing to what has already been expressed in vv. 12-16. To say that death *reigns* emphasizes "the powerful and destructive sway it exercises over the affairs of human beings" (Hendriksen, I:181). The aorist tense again indicates the past point in time when death *began* to reign, i.e., when Adam sinned.

. . . how much more will those who receive God's abundant provision of grace and of the gift of righteousness reign in life through the one man, Jesus Christ. The word translated "abundant provision" (the noun form of the verb "overflow" in v. 15) points again to the fact that the benefits of Christ's cross extend far beyond the scope of Adam's sin and are able to offset the "many trespasses" (personal sins) of v. 16. This suggests that the phrase "much more" may again be emphasizing the quantitative superiority of Christ's work. There is no doubt, though, that "much more" has a logical force here and is stressing the glorious certainty or assurance we can have with regard to Christ's gift of grace. As Godet explains it, it has already been established that the weaker cause (Adam's sin) has had serious universal effects; therefore *how much more certain* it is that the more powerful cause (Christ's cross) will have an even greater effect and an even wider extension (220-223). See also Lard (182) and MP (339).

Many interpreters seriously misunderstand the identity of "those who receive" here in v. 17b. They say that this expression refers only to adults or those old enough to personally make a conscious decision to accept the promise of grace. They see this as parallel to "many trespasses" in v. 16b. Since that phrase means personal sin, "those who receive" is taken to mean those who personally believe. Some see another dimension of death being introduced at this point, too. In addition to the *physical* death (only) which came to all through Adam's sin, they see these verses as referring to *spiritual* death, which comes only as the result of personal sins (DeWelt, 82-83; Smith, I:85-86).

A principal reason why many take this view is their understanding of the verb λαμβάνω (*lambanō*, "receive"). Again and again we hear that this verb "is active, and not passive," and therefore that it must refer to a personal, conscious decision (MP, 339; see Godet, 217, 221). "The reception is voluntary and active, not passive. It is the act of him who believes in Christ and obeys him, and of no other" (Lard, 182; see DeWelt, 83). The word indicates "choice and personal decision," says Moo; it refers only to "those who respond" (I:353). "The *lambanontes* are undoubtedly believers," says Käsemann (155). The grace of Christ is for all and sufficient for all and offered to all, but only believers will receive it (see Dunn, I:295, 297).[98]

Now, we can agree that personal, conscious, voluntary, active choice is a condition for receiving grace for those who have committed personal sins. We can also agree that such persons are included in the discussion at least in vv. 16-17. But I believe it is a serious mistake to think that these are the only ones Paul has in view in these verses, and I believe it is contrary to fact to say that *lambanō* must refer only to the active, voluntary reception of grace.

Throughout these verses (15-17) where Adam and Christ are set in contrast to one another, the scope of those affected by both men is the same in all three verses. Adam's sin affected *all*, and so does the cross insofar as it cancels the results of Adam's sin for *all*. To deny this jeopardizes the main point of this whole passage, the *all*-sufficiency of Christ's cross. The reference to personal sins in this immediate text is *in addition to* the Adamic sin, but not instead of it. Also, as v. 16 indicates, it is likely that spiritual death (including eternal death) has been brought into the picture here, but there is no textual basis for regarding it as the result of personal sins only.

The key question, though, is whether *lambanō* necessarily means an active, conscious act. This seems to be a myth. Interestingly, in his TDNT article on this word, Delling (5-6) says this verb developed both active and passive meanings, and that the latter is pre-

---

[98]Sometimes this understanding of *lambanō* is used as a justification for limiting the scope of those affected by Christ's cross in the whole passage (5:12-21) and not just in these verses. This opens the door to the doctrine of original sin, since it can then be affirmed that Adam's sin brought both physical and spiritual death to *everyone*, but Christ's cross erases these effects *only* for those who personally respond to him.

dominant in the NT, especially in theological contexts. A survey of the many NT verses using this word shows that it can indeed refer to the passive reception of something, apart from a deliberate act of acceptance by the recipient. See, e.g., Luke 20:47; Acts 1:8; Rom 13:2; 1 Cor 4:7; 2 Cor 11:24; Jas 3:1; 1 Pet 4:10. The bottom line is that there is nothing in the word *lambanō* that requires us to limit "those who receive" to conscious, willing adults; the word is no less able to describe the passive reception of "original grace" by *all* those affected by Adam's sin, even in infancy or before. (See Murray, I:198.)

We conclude, then, that the primary reference in v. 17b (as in 15b and 16b) is to the universal application of grace to all mankind to counteract the results of Adam's sin, with the added assurance that this grace is abundant enough to erase the effects of our personal sins as well.

In vv. 15-16 Paul has spoken of the "gift" that comes to all through Christ; here he identifies its content as "righteousness." This is the "righteousness of God" (1:17; 3:21) established by Christ's atoning death and received by sinners through grace. Thus it is not something different from the "abundant provision of grace," but explains what this grace consists of. Receiving this gift of righteousness is the event of justification.

Those who receive the gift will "reign in life" through the power of this one man, Jesus. Rather than being slaves of the tyrant death, they themselves will reign in abundant life. "Reign" is future tense and refers to the yet-to-come resurrection of the body[99] at the end time and to the gift of eternal life to be lived in the very presence of God. As Christians we are already partaking of the abundance of grace, especially justification, and we are already reigning in a spiritual way over sin (Rev 20:4, 6); but in the life to come we shall surely reign as kings in an unprecedented way! See Rev 1:6; 5:10; 22:5. (This is true of all children who die before reaching the age of accountability, and of all accountable persons who have personally accepted Christ's saving grace.)

---

[99]Grace does not prevent us from dying. The nullification of physical death is a certainty for those under grace (original and personal), but it occurs only in the future when the redeemed receive glorified bodies like that of our risen Lord (Phil 3:21; 1 John 3:2).

3. Christ's Cross Completely Cancels the
Results of Adam's Sin (5:18-19)

Having established the fact that Christ's one act is different from Adam's sin in many ways, Paul returns to the main point he began with in v. 12. He now focuses on the one respect in which the two are equal, namely, the breadth or scope of the effects of the one act of each. *Just as* Adam's sin had a universal effect, *so also* did the cross of Christ. This point is intended to reinforce our assurance that the cross is worthy of our trust. We need not doubt its all-encompassing and all-sufficient power.

Actually this truth has been implicit throughout 5:15-17, even while Paul was emphasizing the contrasts between Adam and Christ (MP, 340). But it is necessary now to make explicit the one positive comparison Paul had in mind when he said that Adam was a type or pattern for Christ. Thus he now presents this comparison in a symmetrical, no-frills manner, stating it in two distinct ways.

5:18 Consequently, just as the result of one trespass was condemnation for all men . . . . This begins the first version of the comparison and basically sums up the content of v. 12, where Paul began to make this very argument before breaking it off for the parenthesis of vv. 13-17. No new concepts are introduced here.

The language is extremely condensed. A verb must be supplied ("the result was," NIV; "there resulted," NASB; "led to," NRSV). Also, some think the "one" refers to the one *man*, Adam, and read it thus: "through the trespass of the one man." This makes it parallel with 17a and 19a, they say (Cranfield, I:289; Dunn, I:283; Moo, I:354, 357). I believe it is best to stay with the NIV, though (Lard, 183; Hendriksen, I:182). Murray rightly says that "this rendering is more natural than 'through the trespass of one'" (I:199). Also, it makes explicit what is implicit throughout, that what is at stake is not just what *one man* can do, but what *one act* of one man can do.

The word for "condemnation" is *katakrima* again (see v. 16). Some limit this to physical death only (Lard, 185; MP, 339; DeWelt, 78, 83). But while physical death is no doubt included in the condemnation that comes from Adam, I believe that such a strong word as *katakrima* cannot be limited to that alone but must also include eternal condemnation (see 6:23; 8:1). This is all the more likely when we see that its opposite is *justification* (v. 18b). See the discussion under 5:16, above.

Through Adam's one sin this condemnation came upon "all men," the whole human race. Whether it was physical death only or both physical and spiritual/eternal death is largely irrelevant, since it has been totally nullified for "all men" by the cross, as the rest of the verse shows.

. . . so also the result of one act of righteousness was justification that brings life for all men. This is the long-delayed completion of the thought begun in v. 12. Again some say the "one" refers to the one *man*, Jesus (Moo, I:354; Dunn, I:283), but I disagree and concur with the NIV. The word for "act of righteousness" is δικαίωμα (*dikaiōma*), the same word used for "justification" in 5:16. Sometimes it means "ordinance" of the law (2:26; 8:4), but "righteous act" is also a valid meaning (Rev 15:4; 19:8). The latter is appropriate here, since it is being contrasted with the one (sinful) act of Adam (Murray, I:200; contra Morris, 239).

What is this "one act of righteousness"? No doubt it means the atoning death of Jesus on the cross (Lard, 185; MP, 340; Schlatter, 131). Many who agree that the cross is in view are not satisfied with limiting it to *just* this one act, though. They take it as embracing Jesus' whole sinless life also. As Hendriksen says, "We should not interpret this concept too narrowly: Christ's voluntary death represents his entire sacrificial earthly ministry of which that death was the climax" (I:182). Cranfield says that "Paul means not just his atoning death but the obedience of his life as a whole" (I:289). Murray apparently agrees, saying that the term represents Christ's life as a "compact unity" (I:201).

I strenuously object to this, however. The "one act of righteousness" is *one act*, the cross. We must not lump Christ's life and death together as if they had equal significance and are equally imputed to sinners as the basis for our justification (see under 1:17 above). The comparison here is between *one* sinful act and *one* righteous act. To broaden the scope of the latter to include the whole life of Christ compromises the comparison and forfeits the whole point of this passage (Dunn, I:283).

The result of this one righteous act is to offset the condemnation that came through Adam's sin. This result is called "justification

that brings life," or literally "justification of life." "Justification" is
δικαίωσις (*dikaiōsis*), used also in 4:25. What does this include?
Those who see the condemnation as physical death only must and
do limit this justification to the gift of physical life only. Lard specifically denies that it includes remission of sins here; he limits it to
temporary postponement of the death sentence and eventual
bodily resurrection (186). See also DeWelt (78) and MP (340).

As I have said in the discussion of 5:16 above, this is an unacceptable limitation to the concept of justification. Although seldom
represented by a noun (4:25, 5:16, and here), the event and the
state of justification are very often represented by the verb *dikaioō*
(e.g., 2:13; 3:20, 24, 26, 28, 30; 4:2, 5; 5:1, 9; 8:33). In these other
contexts it implicitly involves the cancellation of the full penalty of
sin, especially condemnation to hell. In my opinion limiting it to
the cancellation of physical death alone gives it an unnatural sense.
Thus I take it here to imply that Adam's sin brought full condemnation upon the entire race, but that Christ's cross brought full justification upon all men in that it releases all (in infancy) from Adamic
condemnation.

The "life" brought by this justification is therefore not just physical, bodily life, but *eternal* life in the sense of release from the
penalty of hell and entrance into heaven.

When Paul says the one righteous act of Christ results in justification of life *for all men*, he means exactly that and nothing less. In
the introduction to this section I have discussed the common view
that this "all" is somehow less than the "all" affected by Adam's sin.
This view must be emphatically rejected. Christ's original grace
cancels any potential state of original sin *for all men*. If this is not
the case, then the point and purpose of 5:12-21 as a whole are completely negated.

**5:19 For just as through the disobedience of the one man the
many were made sinners . . . .** This verse affirms the parallel
between Adam and Christ in a different way, keeping the symmetrical form of v. 18. The word "for" may mean that Paul is here explaining why it is possible or appropriate for all to receive condemnation
as the result of one man's sin. The reason is that, by this one man's
sin, the many were "made sinners." This recalls the point at the end
of 5:12, "because all sinned" in Adam. His sin was the sin of all; when

he disobeyed God's command, all became sinners. Thus it is appropriate that all should be condemned for that one sin. ("The many" is universal in scope and equivalent to "all men" in v. 18a.)

The difficult question here is the meaning of "made." The Greek word is καθίστημι (*kathistēmi*). It means "to appoint, ordain, make, constitute, render, place in a particular class or category." The issue is whether it means merely "counted as" or "declared to be something," or whether it means "actually made to be something."

How one understands it here depends largely upon what is regarded to be the subject of the action. Exactly who or what is it that "makes" us sinners? Those who take the subject to be God (Lard, 187; Shedd, 139) usually prefer the former meaning. Adam's sin is what caused all to be sinners; consequently God merely *declares* us to be sinners or places us in the category of sinners. "He pronounced them to be what they had already become by their own act in Adam" (Shedd, 139-140). On the other hand, if the subject of *kathistēmi* is Adam or Adam's sin, then this word could itself be taken in a causative sense. The point would then be that *Adam* through his one act made us all sinners. (Actually, even if God is the subject of the action, it could still be taken in a causative sense, since God is the one who decreed this connection — whatever it entails — between Adam's sin and his posterity in the first place.)

Whether the subject is God or Adam, in my opinion the second meaning given above is preferred, i.e., *made* and not just declared. This seems to be how the word is used in other contexts, even in classical Greek (see Godet, 225-226). In the NT it is most commonly used for appointing or ordaining someone to a particular position or office. Someone is "made to be" a judge, a ruler, a governor, an elder, a high priest.[100] For example, when Pharaoh "made" Joseph governor over Egypt (Acts 7:10), he was not just announcing an already-existing reality, but was actually *causing* Joseph *to become* the governor. Likewise, as the result of Adam's sin, the many actually *became* sinners; they were placed in the position

---

[100]See Matt 24:45, 47; 25:21, 23; Luke 12:14, 42, 44; Acts 6:3; 7:10, 27, 35; Titus 1:5; Heb 5:1; 7:28; 8:3.

of being sinners. This does not mean simply that "they all in their turn lived sinful lives" (contra Cranfield, I:291), or "were made liable to sin" (contra DeWelt, 78). Rather, it means that in their solidarity with Adam all men actually became sinners; that's why it was appropriate to *treat* them as sinners by condemning them (5:18).[101]

One point must be kept in mind, namely, that whatever nuance we give to "made sinners," it must be parallel to the meaning we give to "made righteous" in 19b.

. . . so also through the obedience of the one man the many will be made righteous. The obedience of Jesus is set over against the disobedience of Adam. Some err again by expanding this obedience so that it "covers his whole life, not just his passion and death" (Cranfield, I:290; see also Godet, 226; Murray, 205). But again this destroys the parallel with the *one* act of Adam's disobedience. The obedience here is the one act of righteousness, the one supreme act of obedience, the cross (Phil 2:8; Heb 5:8). See Lard, 189; and especially Dunn, I:284-285.

The key question here is the meaning of "made righteous." The issue is whether it refers to a simple forensic declaration equivalent to justification, or whether it refers to a change in the sinner's nature or status by which he is actually made righteous.[102] Our answer must take into account the parallel with "made sinners" in v. 19a, as well as the meaning of *kathistēmi* as discussed there.

Many take "made righteous" in the former sense alone. Stott says, "The expressions 'made sinners' and 'made righteous' cannot mean that these people actually became morally good or evil, but rather that they were 'constituted' legally righteous or unrighteous

---

[101]See Oepke, "καθίστημι," 445. He says the word is not used for a forensic declaration (a "judgment") alone. While this may be involved, the main point of the verb is the actual state of the thing or person that is its object; and its force is not materially different from "become." Thus he says Rom 5:19 should read "as the many became sinners . . . so the many became righteous."

[102]Lard (189-190) says "made righteous" means being raised from the dead and nothing more. This is because he limits the Adamic condemnation to physical death alone; therefore the Christic counterpart, no matter how Paul describes it, can be no more than bodily resurrection. But this is an unacceptable understanding of "made righteous." It demonstrates how untenable it is to limit this whole discussion (5:12-21) to physical death.

in God's sight" (156). The expression "basically means '*to be declared* righteous*,*" says Hendriksen (I:183). Murray equates it with the justification of v. 18b (I:205). Mounce says it is an imputed "right standing before God" (145). See also Cranfield, I:291.

Others, however, see something of the latter sense in the expression. Godet says it includes eschatological sanctification (226). MacArthur says it means "to be made righteous by nature and constitution." When a person is made righteous, "he not only is declared righteous forensically but is . . . given an inward rightousness that must and will bear fruit" (I:307). In my opinion, even if forensic righteousness is involved, the meaning of *kathistēmi* and the meaning of "made sinners," as discussed above, seem to require something of this second sense. I.e., as the result of Christ's one act of obedience, all are actually made righteous and become righteous.

The fact that this is future tense ("*will* be made righteous") may simply reflect the fact that this is an ongoing process and will continue to apply to people in the future (Murray, I:206). Or it may mean that this "making righteous" is something that will be consummated at the final judgment, when the redeemed will finally be completely sanctified (Godet, 226).

As we have already determined, "the many" who are made righteous is no less a number than the "all men" who are justified in v. 18b. More importantly, they are no less than "the many" who are made sinners by Adam. Again we deplore all efforts to reduce the number of those affected by Christ's cross to anything less than those affected by Adam's sin. That the making righteous is universal does not result in universal salvation, of course, since it applies to *all* men only in reference to the sense in which they were made sinners by the one sin of Adam. In whatever sense the latter *would* have been the case, it does not in fact happen because of the cross. Thus *no baby* is born a depraved sinner, a spiritually-weak sinner, a guilty sinner, a condemned sinner, a sinner by declaration, or a sinner in any other sense of the term. All are made righteous by the obedience of the one man, Jesus Christ.

4. Grace Triumphs Over Sin and Death (5:20-21)

This brief paragraph makes a fitting conclusion not just to this section (5:12-21) but to Part Two as a whole. Indeed, it draws together the main elements of the entire letter thus far: law, sin, and death versus grace, righteousness, and life.

5:20 The law was added so that the trespass might increase. This is most likely a reference to the Mosaic Law. Why does Paul bring it up at this point? He is probably answering a question that must have been in the minds of his Jewish audience, i.e., how does the Law relate to all of this? To the devout Jew the Law was regarded as the solution to everything. Surely it must have some part in the resolution of the problem that began with Adam. But Paul has for all practical purposes jumped directly from Adam to Christ. Where is the place for Moses? (See Moo, I:360.)

Paul's answer to such questions is not what the Jews wanted to hear. He says "the law was added." The word for "added" is not at all complimentary; the concept is closer to "temporarily tacked on." In its other NT use (Gal 2:4) it has a negative connotation ("sneaked in," NASB). That idea is somewhat harsh for this context, but the word is still unfavorable enough to suggest that the Law was definitely a secondary part of God's plan, and not an end in itself. It implies that the Law came in through the servants' door, as opposed to making a grand entrance. See Morris, 241; Moo, I:360.

But that's not all. The Law was added, says Paul, "so that the trespass might increase." Thus in a sense the Law, rather than being a part of the solution, is a part of the problem! But this is not meant to be altogether negative. We must remember that it was God himself who added the Law (see Gal 3:19), and the increase of sin was at least part of the very reason why he added it in the first place. ("So that" is ἵνα [hina], indicating purpose.) And God would not have done this unless he had some ultimately good purpose in mind.

The Law certainly was not given to prevent sin; it was too late for that. Nor was it intended to save anyone from sin; it was too weak for that (Morris, 241). But it could cause sin to increase. Certainly sins were already present in abundance, because law in other forms was already present, including the law written on the heart. And certainly the giving of the Law of Moses added to the already-present ocean of sins. It did so by increasing the very number of laws that could be broken, and by provoking specific sins (7:7-8).

But this is not exactly the point here. The Law (indeed, any law) does make sins more numerous, but that is not what Paul names here as God's purpose for adding the Law. He says the Law was added so that *the trespass* (singular) might increase.[103] "Trespass" is παράπτωμα (*paraptōma*), a word used several times in the previous verses for the *one sin* of Adam (vv. 15, 17, 18). Thus it seems likely that Paul is not talking here about the quantitative increase of sins in general, but some kind of increase in the sin of Adam.

In what sense could the Law cause "the trespass" to increase, and why would God purposely cause this to happen?[104] The best answer is that the Law served to increase man's *awareness* of the power and seriousness of sin and of the sinful condition brought upon the world by Adam's trespass. By objectively embodying God's standard for righteousness, and by unmistakably identifying sinful behavior, the Law served to magnify the reality of sin and to intensify man's sense of hopelessness as he struggles against it. "The law causes sin to stand out in all its heinousness and ramifications."[105]

But why did God *want* to thus increase the trespass? What possible good could come from this? The answer lies in the rest of the verse: **But where sin increased, grace increased all the more . . . .** God is always ready to bestow the gift of his grace; but (apart from the cancellation of the Adamic sin) this gift must be willingly accepted. Thus the only thing that prevents the increase of grace is

---

[103]This was not the only purpose for the Mosaic Law or any other law, nor even its main purpose. The ultimate purpose of the Mosaic Law was the same as God's purpose for Israel as such, namely, to prepare for the coming of the Messiah. See GRe (266-269), for the purpose of law in general.

[104]See Moo, I:360-362, for a discussion of main answers to these questions.

[105]Hendriksen, I:184. See Moo, I:361; Cranfield, I:293. MacArthur says, "The law identifies particular transgressions, so that those acts can more easily be seen as sinful and thereby cause men to see themselves more easily as sinners" (I:308).

man's denial of his need for it and his refusal to accept it. But when confronted with the law in any form, man can no longer deny that he is a sinner. So by increasing man's sense or consciousness of sin, the Law increases his sense of need for God's grace, thereby causing grace to be more readily received and thus to increase.

Actually this applies to any law from God, not just the Mosaic Law. But here Paul seems to be speaking especially of the latter. In what special sense has the Law of Moses caused sin and therefore grace to increase? The answer relates to God's messianic purpose for Israel as a whole. The Law of Moses magnified the reality and seriousness of sin within Israel as such. The chosen people's manifold violations of the law aspect of the covenant are recorded in detail in the OT. Thus the consciousness of sin increased not only for the Israelites themselves, but it increases also for all who read about them (1 Cor 10:6-11). Indeed, one of the clearest lessons we learn from the OT is the sinfulness of mankind and how we deserve to be condemned for our sins. Reading about Israel is like looking at ourselves in a mirror, and we do not like what we see.

But at the very place "where sin increased," namely, in Israel, God caused grace to increase *all the more*. Among the very people where the Law caused the trespass of Adam to explode like an atomic bomb, the grace of God exploded like the more powerful hydrogen bomb. This explosion of grace came in the person and work of Jesus the Messiah, which was the reason for Israel's existence in the first place. Thus the Law itself had a large part in Israel's purpose of preparation for the coming of the Savior. By increasing the consciousness of sin, it increased the sense of need for grace, and thereby caused at least some Israelites to welcome the Messiah all the more. This is one way the law, even the Law of Moses, should still function today.

5:21 so that, just as sin reigned in death . . . . "So that" introduces another purpose statement. It tells the reason why God wanted grace to increase, i.e., to be accepted by more and more sinners. The train of thought in vv. 20-21 is this: God added the Law so that the awareness of sin might increase (20a). He wants the awareness of sin to increase so that grace may be all the more accepted and increased (20b). And he wants grace to increase so that it might defeat sin and death and reign triumphantly in the end (21).

This thought is stated in the form of one last comparison. "Just as sin reigned in death" sums up the point about Adam in 5:12-19. Paul has said twice (vv. 14, 17) that *death* reigned through Adam's sin. But here he identifies the true tyrant, sin itself. Sin not only rules the sinner's heart in a state of spiritual death (Eph 2:1, 5; Col 2:13); it also tyrannizes man's physical existence by causing it to be permeated with the inescapable canker of bodily death. The aorist (past) tense is used in reference to the sin of Adam, at which time sin "established its reign" (Dunn, I:287).

. . . so also grace might reign through righteousness to bring eternal life through Jesus Christ our Lord. The reign of sin and death is not the final word. Adam is not the victor; Jesus is. Sin reigned in death, and still does to some degree; but grace will ultimately reign in life, and already does to some degree. Grace reigns through righteousness, the righteousness of God which is the content of the gospel (1:17) and which was established by Christ's incomparable atoning sacrifice wherein he paid the penalty for our sins. When this gift of imputed righteousness is bestowed upon the believing sinner, sin and death become defeated enemies and grace reigns triumphant unto eternal life, all because of the all-sufficient redemptive work of Jesus Christ our Lord.

This statement appropriately brings the second main section of Romans to an end. In the first section Paul showed how law cannot succeed as a way to heaven, since that could happen only if one kept the law perfectly, which no one has done. Then here in the second section the Apostle has shown how God provided an alternative way into heaven, the way of salvation known as *grace*. This he has done only through the propitiatory sacrifice of Jesus Christ, on the basis of which a believing sinner is justified or declared righteous before God. Knowing that we are justified by faith in Jesus Christ gives us a sure foundation for hope. The sin and death which once ruled over us have been forever vanquished by the power of his blood. Grace reigns!

6:1-8:39 — PART THREE

THE ALL-SUFFICIENCY OF GRACE GIVES VICTORY OVER SIN

Though some divide Paul's argument between chs. 4 and 5, with 5-8 forming a single unit,[1] I believe ch. 6 begins the new unit,[2] with chs. 6-8 being the next major section of Paul's presentation of the gospel. It would be possible to take 3:21-8:39 as one main unified section (as does Stott, 37), with 3:21-5:21 and 6:1-8:39 forming its two major subsections. However, I believe this obscures the close relation between 1:18-3:20 and 3:21-5:21 as presenting the contrasting ways of salvation, law and grace. Thus it is better to see 6-8 as a new and self-contained section that continues the theme of grace from a different perspective.

INTRODUCTION

A. THE MAJOR THEME OF THIS SECTION

The gospel addresses the question of how to be saved, or how to be accepted by God. Parts one and two of Romans are a negative and a positive response to this question. The negative response is that it is impossible to be accepted by God according to the terms of *law*, since this requires impeccable personal righteousness, and all have sinned (1:18-3:20). The positive response is that God accepts sinners according to the terms of *grace*, wherein he counts them righteous (i.e., justifies them) on the basis of the gift of his own righteousness. This gracious gift is made possible through the death of Jesus on the cross, and is given to those who accept it through faith apart from works of law (3:21-5:21).

---

[1]E.g., Nygren, Hendriksen, Käsemann (158-159), Cranfield (I:252-254), Moo (I:300-303).

[2]E.g., Godet, Erdman, Sanday and Headlam, Bruce, Morris, Dunn.

Paul's explanation of grace as justification by faith raises some further questions, however. If we are justified by grace through faith apart from works (3:28), then what about law? What about sin? What about obedience? Is God's law irrelevant under grace? Are good works optional? Does it no longer matter whether we sin or not?

In answer to such questions Paul in effect reminds us that grace is a *double cure*. It not only takes away the guilt of sin through the imputed righteousness established by the blood of Christ; it also takes away the power of sin by healing the spiritual sickness that permeates both our souls and our bodies. In other words, grace includes not only *justification* but also *sanctification*, which begins with the decisive act called regeneration or the new birth and continues through the power of the indwelling Holy Spirit. In the present section Paul's focus is on this "other side" of grace, which brings not an external change in our legal status but an internal change in our nature and character. Now that the penalty of sin has been removed through justification, we are free to focus on being rid of sin itself: serving God, keeping his law, and doing good works. Unless and until we have done the latter, we have not realized the fullness of grace.

B. THE DOCTRINAL CONTENT OF THIS SECTION

The main theme of these chapters is how the grace of God gives us victory over sin. At this point it will be helpful to summarize their basic doctrinal content before setting forth the verse-by-verse exegesis upon which it is based.

1. Key Concepts

Several key concepts form the backbone of this section. The first is *law* (νόμος, *nomos*), which is used in three major ways. Primarily it refers to the preceptive will of God, the law-code that defines right and wrong conduct, the totality of commandments and prohibitions that apply to human beings in any given time or place. At times the Law of Moses may be specifically in view, but the main point is not the distinction between the Law of Moses and the moral law in general nor even the distinction between the Old Covenant and the New Covenant. The Law of Moses as a law code is simply representative of God's laws as such, in whatever form it is available and known. The main point is still the distinction between law and grace (6:14-15), and the main concern in this section is the distinction between proper and improper uses of law by those who are under God's grace.

Second, sometimes in this section "law" means "order, pattern, system, governing principle, rule of life," especially in the sense of an all-encompassing world order or life paradigm (7:21; 8:2; see 3:27). Finally, the term *law* sometimes refers to an indwelling, compelling force, or a dominating power that seeks to control the individual, either for good or for evil (7:23, 25).

The second key concept is *sin* (ἁμαρτία, *hamartia*). This word is used over three dozen times in these three chapters, almost always in the singular in the sense of an active, alien force that seduces us, draws us to itself as into a black hole, permeates us, and makes us its captive. As such sin is not our actions nor the inert product of our actions, but a personified power that acts upon us. The key point of this whole section is that this enemy has been defeated, and thus "sin shall not be your master" (6:14).

Our relation to sin progresses through four stages. (1) At first sin is only potential (7:9). Because of original grace (5:12-19) we come into the world in a state of purity and innocence, but sin is still a possibility because of our free will. (2) Then, when we fall into disobedience, sin becomes imperial; it rules over us (6:6, 14). (3) In conversion sin is conquered but is still residual and must be consciously resisted (6:12-13; 7:17, 20). (4) In the end when we are free from this corrupted body (6:6; 7:24-25; 8:23), sin will finally be nil to us. We will be in the blessed state where all the effects of sin are completely removed from our being and our environment.

A third key concept is *death*, which appears in these chapters in a number of terms and forms, as follows: (1) Physical death as such, considered as an event (7:2, 3; 8:10, 36, 38) or as an enemy to be conquered (6:9; see 5:14, 17). (2) The physical death of Jesus Christ, considered as an event (6:10; 8:34), as an instrument of salvation (6:3, 5), or as the state from which he was raised (6:4, 9; 7:4; 8:11). (3) The spiritual death of the sinner, considered as the event of his first "fall" into sin, or as the state in which he subsequently exists (7:9-13; see Eph 2:1, 5). (4) The soteriological death of the sinner's "old [spiritually-dead] self" (6:6), his death "to sin" (6:2, 11) and "to law" (7:4, 6). This is a constitutive part of the event of regeneration or new birth and is an extremely important concept. It is an event that takes place in our own history, not in the first century and not in some transhistorical sphere. (5) The death of sins (8:13), which is a constitutive part of the ongoing sanctification process. (6) Eternal death, the ultimate penalty for sin (6:16, 21, 23; 7:5, 24; 8:2, 6, 13).[3]

A correlative concept is *resurrection*, which is threefold. First is Christ's resurrection from the dead, the event by which he conquered death and in whose saving power we participate. Second is the sinner's spiritual resurrection to new life. This follows upon his death to sin and is the climactic conclusion of the regeneration event. Third is the resurrection of the body in the end-time, which is the final stage in our victory over sin. Closely related, of course, is the concept of *life*. Those who have been raised from the dead are alive; they have "newness of life" (6:4, NASB) or "eternal life" (6:23) in two stages, spiritual and physical.

A final set of concepts that permeate this section are *slavery* and *freedom*. The sinner is pictured as a slave to law (7:1-5), sin (6:17, 19-20; 7:14; 23; 25), and death (7:24; 8:2). Redemption is described as being set free from these (6:6, 14, 18, 22; 7:6; 8:2), but also as becoming enslaved to a new set of masters: God (6:22), obedience (6:16), and righteousness (6:18-19).

2. Anthropological Dualism: Body and Spirit

Scripture in general and Paul especially describe the individual human being as a twofold creature composed of a physical body or flesh, and a spiritual entity known variously as the spirit, the soul,

---

[3]The references cited are given as examples of the various uses and are not necessarily exhaustive.

the heart, and the inner man.[4] Both body and spirit are created by God and are inherently good (Gen 1:31). They are designed to complement one another and to function holistically; there is no natural antithesis or antagonism between body and spirit. Both together form the whole human being; an individual is not complete without both. The body without the spirit is dead (Jas 2:26), and the spirit without the body is naked (2 Cor 5:3).

This view of man, known as anthropological dualism, is presupposed and asserted throughout this section of Romans. The spiritual side of man is specifically mentioned in 6:17 ("heart"), 7:22 ("inner man"), 7:23, 25 ("mind"), and 8:10 ("spirit"). It is quite possible that the "old man" in 6:6 also refers to the inner man. Likewise, the physical side of man is often referred to in this passage as both "body" and "flesh."

This dualistic view of man is a key for understanding these chapters. It is crucial for a proper view of what sin has done to us and how we are saved from its effects. It is crucial for understanding both the nature of our present struggle against sin, and the content and significance of our hope. In brief, we are saved in two stages. In conversion only the spirit or inner man is changed, through the act of dying and rising again in baptism. The body is still under the curse of death and remains a stronghold from which sin continues to assault the spirit. The result is a serious struggle between the renewed spirit and the sin-weakened flesh. Victory is ours to win, however, because of the new life bestowed upon our spirits and because of the assisting power of the Holy Spirit. We are able to control our resisting bodies even as we look forward in hope to the time when these bodies also will be set free from sin in the day of resurrection and cosmic renewal.

In my exegesis of this passage I have found it necessary to go against the conventional understanding of the term "flesh." The

---

[4]Many of these terms have other meanings also. For full discussions of this dualistic nature of man, see Gundry, *Soma*; Cooper, *Body*; and Moreland, *Perspectives*. Anthropological dualism must not be confused with cosmological dualism. The latter is a worldview that usually regards matter, including the human body, as inherently evil. The former is a view of the nature of man as such (that he is twofold), and does not necessarily view the body or flesh as inherently evil. The Bible certainly does not.

common explanation is that this term, here and in other places in Paul, refers to the whole man (body and spirit) as controlled by sin in its preconversion, sinful state. It is seen as the "old man" that dies in conversion but still exerts a drawing power upon us from its grave. I have had to conclude, however, that the "flesh" is the physical body, not the entire person. It is true that the flesh is described in very negative terms both here and in other places in the NT. But that is not because the body is inherently sinful and antagonistic to the spirit, but only because it has not yet been redeemed and is still under the influence of sin and death.

3. The Stages of the Spiritual Life

Here I will briefly describe the main stages through which a believer passes on his way to eternal life, as set forth in Romans 6-8.

Conception to Accountability

In 5:12-19 we saw that Christ's atoning death redeemed us all from the consequences of Adam's sin. Even though a child is still subject to physical death with all its mortal preliminaries (such as defects and disease), he has the guarantee of redemptive resurrection in the last day. More importantly, no spiritual consequences actually reach the child directly from Adam. Every infant is conceived and born free from guilt, condemnation, and depravity. This is the time when one is spiritually alive (7:9). Sin is only potentially present as a possible choice of the free will.

The Sinner's Life Under Law

When a young person becomes aware of God's law as *God's* law, and breaks it, he experiences his own personal fall and becomes a sinner (7:7-11). Both soul and body come under the power of sin. From this point on, he is living "under law" (6:14) and "in the flesh" (7:5).

Though the law in itself is good (7:12), to the sinner it becomes an occasion for sin (7:7-13). Because of the weakness of his spirit and the power of sin working in his flesh, the sinner looks upon the law as his enemy and is unable to obey it (8:7-8). Yet, paradoxically, he becomes a slave to law because he regards it as his only means of salvation. He is in an impossible situation: seeking salvation through flawed obedience to a law which cannot save him (8:3). Such is the futility of works-righteousness, or life "under law" (6:14).

Personified as an enslaving tyrant, sin as a dominating power invades the life of the fallen sinner and rules with an imperial presence over both spirit and body. The person literally becomes a slave to sin (6:12-20; 8:15). The same is true of death, which also takes control of the entire person (7:9-13). In the grip of sin the spirit dies in its ability to respond positively to the law. The body, already subject to physical death, becomes permeated by the seeds of spiritual death (7:5) and thus becomes "flesh" in the negative sense.

The second aspect of the sinner's "double trouble" is now in full bloom. He is "in the flesh" (7:5; 8:8), or controlled by its evil desires (6:12). He is existing and conducting his life "according to the flesh" (8:4-9, 12-13).

The Conversion Event: Saving Grace Applied

When the spiritually-dead person hears the gospel, accepts it as true, and puts his trust in the saving work of Jesus, he then submits to Christian baptism (6:3). At this specific point in time (baptism) he comes under the grace of God, not just for justification but also for regeneration or renewal.

The latter involves two distinct acts of God. The first is the *death* of the sinner's "old self" (6:6-8). This is a death to law (7:4, 6) and a death to sin (6:2, 4, 11). The second is a *resurrection* of the believer into a state of new life (6:4-5, 11).

The conversion event is also described in terms of slavery. The submissive believer is set free from slavery to sin (6:17-18, 22). He is also set free from slavery to law, both as a way of salvation (6:14) and as an occasion for sin (7:3-6). Grace does not free us from slavery altogether, though; it simply provides us with new masters: God, obedience, and righteousness (6:17-18, 22; 7:6).

A crucial point is how conversion affects the two aspects of our dual nature. At this point the whole person in principle dies and rises again, but in reality the spiritual death-to-sin and the resurrection to new life affect only the spirit. The body itself continues to be permeated with the power of sin and death (7:17-25; 8:10). Nevertheless the conversion experience includes God's promise that the body also will one day be redeemed through resurrection (6:5-8; 8:10-11).

The Believer's Life Under Grace

The believer's life under grace is summed up in three words: power, struggle, and victory. As already suggested, the regeneration event (death-resurrection) gives the believer the power to conquer sin and to submit to God's law. Though the body is as yet unredeemed, we can reign over it (6:12-13; 8:12-13). This God-restored ability is the basis for strong exhortations to stop sinning (6:12-13, 19). A desire to obey the law from the heart is also present (6:17; 7:15, 22, 25).

However, the presence of the "flesh" is the source of continuing conflict and struggle. The unredeemed body is still under the power, not just of physical death, but of spiritual death as well. "The law of sin and death" which once pervaded our entire nature is still residual in the believer's body (7:17-21, 23, 25). As such it exerts a drawing power upon the soul, pulling it back toward sin and spiritual bondage (7:23-24). Struggling against the "flesh" is the most basic form of spiritual warfare: the redeemed inner man versus the unredeemed body (7:23-25). The "flesh" is the *body itself* as inhabited by and controlled by this "law of sin and death," and as it exerts its drawing and seducing power over the inner man. Left alone, the redeemed believer would still be in a state of constant struggle, with the distinct possibility that the flesh might once more overcome the spirit (8:13).

Even in the presence of struggle we are assured of victory, however. We have already experienced victory over the guilt of our sin, through the blood of Jesus Christ (8:1, 3, 30, 33-34). And now we are promised victory over *sin itself*, through the power of the Holy Spirit (8:2). In baptism (Acts 2:38) the Spirit of the Living God enters and indwells us (8:9, 11). The purpose of his presence is to ensure our victory in this present struggle (8:4-9, 14). He enables us to "put to death the misdeeds of the body" (8:13).

The Believer's Final and Total Victory over the Fallen World

The assurance of our final victory is our adoption into the family of God (8:14, 16). The Holy Spirit is the mark of our sonship to God the Father (8:15-16). The risen Christ is the firstborn Son in this family, and our brother and fellow heir (8:17, 29).

As of now we have only a small portion of our inheritance (8:23), but one day we will inherit a new cosmos (8:19-21) as the eternal home of our new, glorified bodies (8:11, 23). Then our sonship will be complete (8:19), and the tyrant sin will be conquered forever and completely *nil* in our person and in our environment. This is our hope (8:24-25).

This hope is firm. Nothing outside ourselves can prevent us from receiving this inheritance. The Holy Spirit helps us in our struggles (8:13, 26-27), and God's providence is completely in control (8:28). In accordance with his foreknowledge God has already predestined us to glory (8:18, 29-30). Our assurance rests on nothing less than the power of the blood of Jesus Christ (8:31-34) and the security of his love (8:35-39).

C. THE OUTLINE OF THIS SECTION

The material in these three chapters falls into three major parts. In the first part (6:1-7:13), Paul names three objections to grace based on a fear of antinomianism, and responds decisively to each. (a) Does grace make sin irrelevant? NO! (6:1-14). (b) Does freedom from law mean we are free to sin? NO! (6:15-7:6). (c) Does grace mean that law is sinful or bad? NO! (7:7-13).

In the second part (7:14-8:13), Paul makes it clear that, rather than encouraging sin, grace provides the means for victory over sin. He candidly describes the Christian's inner tension between flesh and spirit, his struggle against the power of sin that lingers in his body (7:14-25). He assures us, though, that we may achieve victory over sin through the power of the indwelling Spirit (8:1-13).

In the final part (8:14-39), Paul lays down the basis for our assurance of final salvation, despite our involvement in the continuing outward tension between the old creation and the new creation. He assures us that the Holy Spirit has marked us as God's sons and heirs (8:14-17), and that the redeemed cosmos is our inheritance (8:18-25). Until we receive it, God promises to bring us through earthly trials (8:26-30). In the meantime, the knowledge of grace gives us an unshakable assurance of our ultimate victory over the fallen world (8:31-39).

I. 6:1-7:13 — OBJECTIONS TO GRACE BASED ON A FEAR OF ANTINOMIANISM

The rejection of law as a means of righteousness and salvation, and the presentation of grace as the only way of salvation, are bound to cause people to wonder whether law and obedience have any relevance at all in the Christian life. I.e., does grace lead to antinomianism? This word comes from the Greek words ἀντί (*anti*), the basic meaning of which is "against"; and νόμος (*nomos*), "law." In its most general sense an antinomian is one who believes that we are not bound by law and have no obligation to obey it; hence there is no reason not to sin. In the Christian context the radical nature of grace — especially justification by faith apart from works of law (3:28) — may cause it to be mistaken for antinomianism by those whose knowledge of it is incomplete or perverted.

Such people existed in NT times. Jude 4 refers to "godless men, who change the grace of our God into a license for immorality." Paul tells us in 3:8 that some were falsely attributing such teaching to himself. Down through Christian history, this view "has been commoner than is often realized," says Bruce (134). He and others cite especially the example of the Russian monk Rasputin (see MacArthur, I:314).

A problem perhaps even more serious than antinomianism, though, is the fear that grace *will lead* to antinomianism if it is as radical as Paul seems to make it and if it is preached and embraced in this full radicalness. Thus the legalistic mind tends to resist grace and to raise this specter of antinomianism as a way of blocking its progress. Paul alludes to this fear in 3:31 when he raises the question of whether justification by faith nullifies the law. In 5:20 he makes the provocative statement that "where sin increased, grace increased all the more." He knows that this is likely to be twisted into an antinomian doctrine; thus in this section he takes the initiative and refutes such a charge as part of his continuing presentation of grace.

How grace affects our relation to law, and the continuing role of the law in the Christian life, are main questions answered in this section. It is true that grace sets us free from law (not just the Mosaic Law, but *all* law) in some crucial ways. Mainly it sets us free from law as a way of salvation, something it cannot accomplish anyway. As corollaries grace sets us free from the condemnation of the law, and it frees us from legalistic motives for obedience. *But* — and here is the main point — it does *not* release us from our obligation to *obey* God's laws, in whatever form they are available to us and apply to us. Under grace we are all the more slaves to God and owe him our complete obedience, with the goal of achieving full personal righteousness and holiness (6:15-22).

But some, especially Jews, may argue that law is our only sure safeguard and weapon against sin. If we set aside the law, are we not opening the floodgates of sin? No, says Paul, we are not; anyone who thinks this has not yet grasped the full scope of grace. The fact is that grace is not just the only way to be justified and accepted by God; it is also the only source of victory over sin itself. Grace is what *enables* us to obey God's commandments. The first part of the double cure of grace is indeed justification through imputed righteousness (3:21-5:21), but the second part is regeneration and sanctification through imparted righteousness. Grace sets us free not only from sin's penalty, but also from its power. Because of law, we still *ought* to obey; but because of grace, we *can* obey.

A. DOES GRACE MAKE SIN IRRELEVANT? NO! (6:1-14)

The question with which this section begins suggests that grace must somehow negate our obligation to obey God's commandments. In responding to the question Paul unequivocally denies that this is the case — "By no means!" But then he shifts the discussion in a different and more relevant direction. Not only does grace *not* negate our *obligation* to obey God's laws;[5] in fact it specifically

---

[5]Nothing can negate this obligation; it is grounded in God's work of creation and our unalterable status as his creatures. See GC, 163-164.

gives us the *ability* to obey. This is the main point of this section. The first part (1-11) is mainly indicative, asserting the fact that grace has changed us and given us the power not to sin; the last part (12-14) is mainly imperative, commanding us not to sin.

In interpreting this passage we must avoid the temptation to engage in microexegesis, or to find some new and different idea in each successive phrase or statement. In these verses are three major points, each of which is stated in a variety of ways: we died to sin; we were raised up from spiritual death and are now alive unto God; therefore we can and should stop being slaves to sin.

6:1 What shall we say, then? Each of the three objections discussed in this section begins with the same form. First is a general interrogative: "What shall we say, then?" (6:1; 7:7) or "What then?" (6:15). Then comes the specific objection in the form of a question, followed by the emphatic denial, μὴ γένοιτο (*me genoito*; see 3:4 above).

In each case the general question links the objection to the preceding context. Based on what has just been said about grace and justification by faith as such, what conclusions can be drawn about law, obedience, and sin? Paul knows that some even in good conscience will be tempted to draw false inferences from the radical nature of grace. Thus he takes it upon himself to raise these questions and dispose of these potential distortions from the beginning.

Shall we go on sinning so that grace may increase? This particular objection reflects the language of 5:20b especially. In some better manuscripts the verb is subjunctive, meaning more precisely "*should* we continue" (NRSV), as if the fact asserted in 5:20b *obligates* us to keep on sinning so that God may show more grace.[6] In the phrase "go on sinning" the word for sin is a noun; literally it reads "remain in sin," i.e., in the sphere of sin. This expression is stronger than merely "continue to commit sins"; it means "continue in the state of sin or under the control of sin" (Moo, I:372; Dunn, I:306). Thus, given the nature of grace, should we not just remain where we are without making any changes in our sinful lifestyles and sinful habits? Or to use the language of 6:2, should we not just continue to "live in" sin?

---

[6]Murray, I:212; Moo, I:408.

6:2 By no means! This is Paul's usual emphatic negative, "the strongest idiom of repudiation in New Testament Greek" (Mac-Arthur, I:316; see 3:4). **We died to sin; how can we live in it any longer?** This is the answer to the objection in a nutshell; it sums up the entire answer of vv. 3-14. MacArthur calls it "the fundamental premise" of the entire chapter (I:319).

The subject of the verb, "we" (οἵτινες, *hoitines*) is emphatic: "we who died, those of us who died." It refers to all Christians and has this force: "We, of all people! We Christians, who died to sin! How could we choose to live in it any longer?"

In "died to sin" the verb is a simple aorist (past) tense, indicating a specific past event in our personal history. Speaking as Christians, at some point in the past we actually *died* to sin. Prior to that point we were dead *in* our sins (Eph 2:1), but at that point we died *to* sin. Here "sin" is singular and does not refer to the ongoing death of specific sins that is part of our spiritual growth (8:13). Rather it refers to sin as a controlling power and as an enslaving tyrant. In relation to the power of sin, we died. See Col 2:20; 3:3.

This does not mean that something *within* us died, such as sin itself or the seed of sin or the power of sin. No, *we ourselves* died. I.e., the person we used to be, the one who was dominated by sin and the flesh — this "old man" (6:6) died. Something happened to us that was so radical that it can only be called an act of dying. It was an act of saving grace, performed upon us by the power of God. It was part of the event called regeneration; along with the immediately-following act of resurrection it transformed us into new beings. This means that as Christians we have passed from under the control of sin and into the control of righteousness.

As Stott (170) points out, this does not mean that the Christian is in a state of death as far as sin's temptations and allurements are concerned, as if he were immune to them in the same sense that a corpse is totally beyond the ability to respond to physical stimuli (contra Lenski, 389-390). In this whole section it is clear that sin's drawing power still plagues Christians and must be consciously resisted. But because we have died to sin we are now resisting it from the outside rather than being overwhelmed by it within its own domain.

Our death to sin is a fact, and Paul uses this fact as the crux of

his reponse to the objection in v. 1. Shall we as Christians continue
to live in sin? How *could* we, since we have *died* to sin and have left
its sphere? If you think otherwise, says Paul, you just don't get it.
You don't yet understand what grace is all about. Grace is a *double*
cure—not just forgiveness, but also a change in your very nature
and character. For one who has died to sin to continue to live in it
is a true contradiction of terms.

It is not a physical (metaphysical) contradiction, because it is
actually possible for a believer to yield himself up again to sin's
power; otherwise the exhortations *not* to do so (6:12-13) would be
unnecessary and empty. It is rather a "moral contradiction" (Bruce,
136), a "moral incongruity" (Stott, 169). Literally Paul does not ask
"How *can* we" (contra the NIV), but "How *shall* we" (future tense,
NASB). Perhaps the sense of it is best expressed as "How *could* we?"
(Phillips).

Paul does not ask how we could continue *to sin*, as if regeneration immediately makes us completely perfect and beyond sinning.
He asks how we could continue to *live in sin* as a lifestyle, sinning
habitually and perpetually (MacArthur, I:317). As Morris says, "Paul
is not setting forth a doctrine of sinless perfection, but of freedom
from sin's domination. The Christian may sin, but sinning is out of
character. It is a declension from his norm, not his habitual practice" (245). "We die to sin in so far that righteousness becomes the
rule of life, and sin the painful, mortifying, humiliating, heartbreaking exception" (MP, 342).

6:3 Or don't you know what happened to you in your baptism?
Literally Paul says "or are you ignorant" of this. He asks this sort of
question quite often.[7] It has the tone of a mild rebuke, implying
that you *should* know this, but just in case you do not I will explain
it. In this instance his question has to do with baptism. Without a
doubt all of Paul's Christian readers would have remembered the
time and event of their immersion, since this was a part of the basic
presentation of the gospel[8] and of becoming a Christian. However,
they may not have understood the deeper spiritual significance of
this act; this is what Paul now explains.[9]

---

[7]6:16; 7:1; 11:2; 1 Cor 3:16; 5:6; 6:2, 3, 9, 15, 16, 19; 9:13, 24.
[8]Acts 2:38; 8:35-38; 22:16. See Cottrell, *Fundamentals*, 78-82.
[9]See my treatment of Romans 6:3-4 in *Baptism*, ch. 7.

Don't you know **that all of us who were baptized into Christ Jesus were baptized into his death?** "All of us who were baptized" means all Christians; in the NT there is no such thing as an unbaptized Christian. "Baptized" refers to water baptism and everything the NT includes in it. It is fairly common for expositors to claim that the baptism to which Paul refers in Romans 6 is a "spiritual" or "dry" baptism only, as distinct from water baptism. For example, Lloyd-Jones concludes "that baptism by water is not in the mind of the Apostle at all in these two verses [6:3-4]; instead it is the baptism that is wrought by the Spirit" (36). Those who hold to such a view are almost always from Protestant traditions that have adopted Zwingli's innovative separation of baptism from the time of salvation.[10] Stott's view is surely the more reasonable, namely, that in the NT "baptism means water baptism unless in the context it is stated to the contrary" (173).

On the other hand, even though Moo agrees that water baptism is in view (I:376), he wrongly concludes that baptism here "functions as shorthand for the conversion experience as a whole" (I:371). Certainly what Paul has already written (and the NT writings as a whole) make it obvious that faith and repentance are presupposed here as precursors of baptism. But what happens in the initial moment of faith and repentance, and in the conversion experience as a whole, are not Paul's point here. He specifically refers to what happens in *baptism*.

The Apostle refers to baptism as being "baptism into Christ Jesus." That he does not dwell on this point shows that it was a basic truth that any Christian would already know. To be baptized into Christ means to be baptized for the purpose of entering into a specific relationship with him, or into a living union with him. As Moo says (I:377), the preposition "into" (*eis*) has the connotation of movement from one space to another, as well as the connotation of purpose. Thus as Moo puts it, "baptized into Christ" means "baptized with a view to being united with Christ." See Gal 3:27.

This union with Christ is not effected by the ritual itself, either by the water or by the act. It is accomplished by the grace and power of the living God alone. That it happens in the act of

---

[10]See Cottrell, "Reformed Tradition."

baptism is simply a matter of God's free and sovereign choice; he has appropriately designated this event as the occasion for the beginning of this saving union with the Redeemer. It is not wrong to say that the external ritual of water baptism *symbolizes* or has a metaphorical connection with this saving union. What is wrong is to separate the symbol from the reality as if the temporal connection between them is irrelevant.

All of the above is part of what Paul assumes his Christian audience already knows. In the latter part of the verse he begins to talk about the point of which they may be ignorant, the point that he wants to stress in reply to the question in v. 1. Don't you know, he asks, that you were baptized into the *death* of Christ? If you were baptized "into Christ" as such, don't you realize that this means you were baptized into a union with Christ *in his death*? Ordinarily when we think about coming into contact with the death of Christ and its benefits, we think of the atoning and justifying power of his blood, and we think of the fact that baptism is for the forgiveness of sins (Acts 2:38), or justification. But here Paul primarily has something else in mind. He is letting us know that our union with Christ's death in our baptism had a result that is crucial for our victory over sin itself. This result is explained in the next verse.

6:4 We were therefore buried with him through baptism into death . . . . Here Paul continues to make his point by drawing a conclusion from his preceding statement, as indicated by "therefore." The main point of this conclusion is the phrase "into death." First of all, whose death does Paul mean? He has already said we are baptized into *Christ's* death (6:3). The phrase "buried with him" basically repeats this. Therefore we must conclude that "into death" means something else, namely, *our own* death to sin. When we were baptized into Christ's death (or buried with him through baptism), we were actually baptized/buried *into our own death* as well. According to v. 2, "we died to sin." This is the main point of this whole section and the main reason why grace does not imply antinomianism. The rest of this section (vv. 3-14) is meant to explain this death to sin. The introduction of the subject of baptism ("or don't you know") leads us to expect some specific reference to this death in connection with baptism. But if the phrase "into death" here in v. 4 does not refer to our personal death to sin, then this passage does not connect it with baptism at all, and there would seem to be no good reason even to bring up the subject of baptism. Also, everything in the following context presupposes such a reference to our own death to sin. Therefore I vigorously disagree with those who see "into death" as referring to Christ's death only. It may include that, but the main reference is to our own personal death to sin.

The implication is that in some true and significant sense, the death of Jesus has a death-dealing power in reference to sin. When we became united with Christ's death in baptism, our old sinful self was put to death — not by our own will power, but by the power of his holy cross. It is as if, in his death, Jesus became a flame that is capable of extinguishing everything having to do with sin and death. When we are baptized into his death (buried with him in baptism), we touch this flame; and it consumes the "old man" of sin, and sets us ablaze with a holy fire that continues to purge the residual sin from our lives.

I take the phrase "into death" as modifying the verb, "we were buried," though many take it as modifying "baptism." Some have trouble with the former view because "the idea of burial into death seems a forced one" (Käsemann, 166; see Cranfield, I:304). However, Dunn agrees that the phrase goes with the verb, and argues that the ancients would have seen nothing strange about "burial unto death" (I:314). Indeed, burial is one of the most effective methods of putting someone to death.

Why does Paul say that "we were buried with him"? Obviously in the experience of most people, including Christ, death precedes burial and is distinct from it. Burial is simply the natural sequel to death. It is assumed that this same distinction and sequence apply to the sinner's death to sin and his burial with Christ. It is assumed that the actual death to sin occurs prior to baptism, usually when faith and/or repentance begins. This is followed by baptism as a ritual burial of the corpse. The baptismal burial "sets the seal on death" (Bruce, 139) or establishes its finality (Moo, I:382) and certifies its reality (Mounce, 149).

I see an entirely different picture here, however. Paul says nothing about dying *first*, and *then* being buried in baptism. Rather, he says very clearly and pointedly that were were buried with him *through baptism, into death*. The death and the burial are not separated by time. The only sequential relationship here is that the burial precedes the death as cause precedes effect. Also, both the death and the burial occur *through baptism*. There is no significant difference between the burial and the death. To be "buried with him through baptism" is just another way of saying "baptized into his death."

Then why does Paul adjust the image in v. 4a and speak of burial at all, rather than just death as such? For two reasons. First, his main point is that by being baptized into Christ's death, we have been baptized into our own death; and it would be awkward and ambiguous to repeat "baptized into his death" in v. 4. By switching to the image of burial he can make this point in a much more smooth and unambiguous way. Second, the image of burial is naturally suggested by the reference to baptism, which as an act of immersion into water is a perfect physical symbol of the deaths and resurrections (Christ's and ours) that are represented and occurring there. It is tragic that so many would rob baptism of this, its most central symbolism. I agree with all those who understand that baptism is immersion,[11] and who declare that only in this form can its connection with the realities of death, burial, and resurrection — both Christ's and ours — have any meaning at all.

It is necessary at this point to raise the question as to *exactly when* the sinner's death to sin occurs. Paul says very clearly that we were "buried with him *through baptism* into (our) death." However, it seems that most interpreters are determined to locate it at some other point in time, *anywhere* but in baptism itself. Cranfield's view is typical. He denies that baptism "actually relates the person concerned to Christ's death, since this relationship is already an objective reality before baptism takes place." Baptism is just a pledge of "that death which the person concerned has already died" (I:303). Restoration writers often hold this view. Lard declares that "we . . . died to sin before our baptism" (195). Our death to sin was brought about "preceding our baptism," says DeWelt (90).

If not in baptism, then when *does* our death to sin occur? There are two main views. Some say we died with Christ on his cross, and

---

[11]See Lard, 198-200; MP, 343; MacArthur, I:320; and especially Sanday and Headlam, 162-163.

thus at a particular point in his history, not ours. We "died with him on the cross," says Mounce (151). "When Christ died on the cross, his true followers all died there with him," says Hendriksen (I:198). But if this is true, then there is no point of time in the sinner's own history when this death to sin occurs. If it occurs on the cross itself, then it has been infallibly accomplished once for all for those who were in Christ at that time. The result is either universal salvation or limited atonement.

The second main non-baptismal view says that the sinner's death to sin occurs at the moment of faith and/or repentance. This is a common Restoration view. Lard says, "We die to sin when we believe in Christ and repent of our sins"; baptism is just the burial of the dead man (195-196). DeWelt's view is the same (90-91); see also Moser (65) and Lipscomb (114). Of course this view is common outside the Restoration Movement. Godet's statement is typical, that "the death to sin" is "implicitly included in faith." Baptism is a burial, and "people do not bury the living" (238-239). "When we believe we die to sin, and when we are baptized the burial is carried out," declares Morris (248). Baptism just *symbolizes* what has already occurred.

At least this second view places our death to sin at a point within our own lifetime. The problem, though, is that Paul himself says *nothing* in this passage about either faith or repentance. If either or both of these are the time when death to sin occurs, why did he not just say that? Why didn't he just say, "Don't you know that all of us who believed and repented were united with Christ's death when we believed and repented? Don't you know that we believed and repented into death?" But he says nothing of the kind; he says it happens "through baptism." Nor does he say anything about baptism being only a symbol of an already-existing reality.

Paul's language is clear. He says we were *baptized* into Christ's death, and that we were buried with him into death *through baptism*. The words "through baptism" belie all notions of post-reality symbolism. They connect our baptism and our death to sin together as cause and effect. This does not mean that the water or the physical act as such produces this spiritual effect. Only the spiritual working of God himself, which he graciously performs in conjunction with the physical act, can cause us to die to sin and rise again.

387

Paul says that we are baptized into Christ's death, and that through baptism we are buried with him into our own death to sin. This means that God has so worked it that in some manner the death of Jesus Christ with all its saving benefits is literally present to the believing sinner and actually touches him in the act of baptism; and this union produces our death to sin. Käsemann well says, "Christ alone died on the cross." Baptism is "our reception of his act and participation in his fate" (166). In baptism the event of the cross "lays hold of him who submits to this act and it does so in a documentary, visible, existence-changing fashion. . . . The cross is actualized in the act of baptism" (168).

Are we saying, then, that baptism is both the *occasion* and the *means* by which the believing sinner is regenerated? In reality, it is impossible to separate occasion and means. We can say that baptism is both if we remember one thing, namely, that the one act of baptism (Eph 4:5) is a dual event in which physical and spiritual acts are taking place simultaneously. While the believing sinner's body is being immersed into water by a human agent, God himself is working the works of salvation upon the sinner's spirit, including justification and regeneration. Physical immersion is the *occasion*, and the simultaneous working of God is the *means* of producing these effects. Thus in a general way we can say yes, baptism is a means of salvation in the sense that the total event includes not just the physical immersion but also the efficacious works of God.

In what sense, then, is faith itself (and perhaps repentance also) a *means* of salvation? Col 2:12 (NASB *only*) brings all these elements together: "Having been buried with Him in baptism, in which you were also raised up with Him through faith in the working of God, who raised Him from the dead." "Buried with him" and "raised up with him" are saving acts that effect justification and regeneration. "In baptism" (physical immersion) indicates the time, place, or occasion when these saving acts take place. "The working of God" is the *active* means that brings about these saving acts, and "through faith" is the *passive* means by which we receive their results.

Without a doubt our death to sin is one of the most important events in our lives, and Paul here makes it the keystone of his reply to the first antinomian objection to grace (6:2). Yet in a real sense this death is not the main event but is itself a means to an even greater end: resurrection. This is seen in the rest of v. 4, which is introduced by the word ἵνα (*hina*), indicating purpose and translated **in order that**.[12] We were buried with Christ through baptism into our death to sin so that, **just as Christ was raised from the dead through the glory of the Father, we too may live a new life.** The death of our old man simply prepares the way for our new life.

The resurrection of Jesus is introduced here not just as an analogy of our own spiritual resurrection, but, like his death, as an essential part of his saving work with which we come into contact in baptism. The resurrection of Jesus Christ represents and generates infinite life-giving power (Eph 1:18-23; Heb 7:16), a power that produces in us the ability to walk in newness of life. "From the dead" is literally "from among the dead," but the sense is "from the state of death." That Jesus was raised "through the glory of the Father" probably means "through the Father's gloriously displayed power." (See under 1:21.) Glory and power are often closely related (Cranfield, I:304-305).

The main idea here is "in order that . . . we too may live a new life." This is a very condensed statement. Paul does not specifically say that we were "raised from the dead" just as Christ was raised. It is definitely assumed, however, since he mentions it later (6:11, 13) and elsewhere (Eph 2:5-6; Col 2:12-13). The word "too" connects his resurrection and ours.

That this resurrection also occurs in baptism, as the counterpart to burial, is implied in this verse and specifically stated in Col 2:12 (NASB only). We emphatically reject, as the tragic legacy of Zwingli's revisionist baptismal theology, such statements as this by Mounce (150): "We do not believe . . . that rebirth is in any real sense connected to water baptism." As we will see below, there is a future aspect of our resurrection with Christ, but that must not be allowed to obscure the all-important spiritual resurrection that occurs in our baptism.

The ultimate purpose and goal of both our death to sin and our resurrection with Christ is the actual living of a new life. The NIV translation "may live a new life" is too sanitized. The Greek literally reads "might walk in newness of life" (NASB). The emphasis is on

---

[12]Godet (240) says this is the main word in the verse.

life. Prior to our conversion we were *dead* in our trespasses and sins (Eph 2:1, 5), and our whole existence was under the pall of death. But in baptism all this was changed. Now the power that controls us is life, not death. Our existence is characterized by life rather than death.

This is indeed a *newness* of life — a new kind of life that transcends even that innocent state of life in which we were born and in which we existed until we sinned (7:9). It is life derived from Christ's own glorified existence, life transmitted to us by the Spirit of life (8:2), life that is in continuity with our ultimate eschatological and eternal life (6:23).

We do not just "live" this life; we *walk* in it. This word (περιπατ-έω, *peripateō*) is one of Paul's favorite expressions for one's behavior or daily conduct, good or bad. He uses it over 30 times in this sense, no doubt under the influence of a similar idiom in the OT (Dunn, I:315-316).

To "walk in newness of life" means to live a holy life, a life of obedience to God's laws. This is the whole purpose of our death to sin and resurrection with Christ. Rather than the antinomian inference that grace encourages sinning, it does just the opposite. By design and in effect it separates us from sin and sets us on the road of righteousness. The verb "to walk" is subjunctive, hence the translation "might walk." Death to sin and resurrection to life create the possibility and ability of walking in the new, holy life; but we must take the responsibility of applying this new life-power to our daily conduct. "Shall we remain in sin?" is the objection. Paul replies, "How *could* you? You have died to sin and been made alive in Jesus Christ! So *walk* in the possibilities and the power of your new life! *Just do it!*"

6:5 If we have been united with him like this in his death, we will certainly also be united with him in his resurrection. This verse basically restates the point of vv. 3-4, namely, that we died with Christ so that we might be raised up with him into a new life. If we have done the former, we must do the latter. We cannot die to sin and live in it at the same time (v. 2).

It is generally agreed that "united with" (from συμφύω [*symphyō*]) is a better reading than "planted together" (from συμφυ-τεύω [*symphyteuō*]; see KJV). The word is commonly used for the joining of two things that proceed to grow together as a unity, as in the fusing together of a broken bone or in the grafting of a branch into a tree. The latter image is especially appropriate in view of John 15:1-8 and Rom 11:17-24. When we are "grafted into" Christ, his life flows into us and we continue to grow with him into spiritual maturity.

The phrase "like this" in the NIV is a poor translation of "in the likeness of." Since there is no word for "him" in the Greek text, some take "likeness" as the object of "united with," i.e., "we are united with the likeness of his death." It is difficult to know what this would mean, however. It is better to supply "him" as the understood object, just as in v. 6 "him" is understood to be the object of "crucified with." Thus "we are united with him in the likeness of his death."

What is the meaning of "the likeness of his death"? It is not the cross itself,[13] nor the death of Christ itself. In view of the context it most probably is the act of baptism (Lard, 202; MP, 344), considered as the place where we become united with Christ in his death. On the spiritual side of the baptismal event, of course, we did not become united merely with the *likeness* of Christ's death, but with his death itself. But on the physical level, baptism (immersion) is indeed a symbolic *likeness* of that death.

The latter part of the verse is strictly parallel with the former part, as the words "certainly also" indicate. It is necessary to supply some words here, since the original says only "certainly also we shall be . . . of the resurrection." The NIV rightly adds "united with him." The parallelism suggests that we should also add "in the likeness of." Thus the thought is, "We will certainly also be united with him in the likeness of his resurrection."

Why is this a future tense? Some take it as a promise of the eschatological resurrection, when we will receive a body like Christ's glorified body (Phil 3:21). Others take it to be a statement of moral obligation (Lard, 203), and others see it as a logical future: "If *a* has happened, then *b* will also surely happen." The last two views go together and are the main idea here: "If we have joined Christ in his death, we shall certainly find ourselves also participating in his

---

[13]This view is "modern mythology," says Käsemann (168).

resurrection and shall without fail devote ourselves to living a new life free from sin's control." (See Cranfield, I:308).

The main point is that in our relation to Christ we cannot separate death and resurrection. If we have become united with Christ's *death* in the baptismal event that is the likeness of his death, then we also have become united with Christ's *resurrection* in that same event, which is also the likeness of his resurrection. In union with Christ there can be no death without resurrection. Thus how could we continue to live the old life of sin?

6:6 For we know that our old self was crucified with him . . . . "We know" can refer to what already is or should be known by all believers, or it can refer to something new that is about to be told. Here it is probably the latter. Following his general statements that we have been united with Christ's death, Paul is about to explain in more detail *how* this frees us from sin.

First of all, when we died with Christ, "our old self was crucified with him." What is "our old self"? Literally it says "our old *man* (ἄνθρωπος, *anthrōpos*)"; see also Eph 4:22; Col 3:9. This phrase is generally taken to mean the person we used to be in our fallen, unbelieving state — not a part of our being, but our whole being under the influence of sin. It means "our former self, the self that sinned before we died to sin" (Lard, 203). It is "the whole of our fallen human nature, the whole self in its fallenness" (Cranfield, I:308-309). It is "the person we once were, our human nature considered apart from grace" (Hendriksen, I:197). In Eph 4:22, 24 the "old man" is contrasted with the "new man." The same contrast appears here, as this crucified "old man" gives way to "newness of life" (v. 4). The "old man" is old in the sense of worn out and useless (MacArthur, I:323), and in dire need of replacement.

I agree with this explanation for the most part, with the following qualification. I believe that here the "old man" refers only to the soul or spirit, which is the center and seat of selfhood or personhood in the human being. Thus the "old self" that has been crucified with Christ is our fallen spirit that was dead in its trespasses and sins (Eph 2:1). In other words, in terms of the anthropological dualism discussed in the introduction to this main section, in baptism the *inner* man, or spirit, experiences death and resurrection with Christ; but the *outer* man, or body, does not. Elsewhere Paul speaks of this "inner man" (ἔσω ἄνθρωπος, *esō anthrōpos*) — 7:22; Eph 3:16; see 1 Pet 3:4, "the hidden person [*anthrōpos*] of the heart" (NASB). He also speaks of the "outer man" (ἔξω ἄνθρωπος, *exō anthrōpos*) or body, as contrasted with the "inner" (*esō*) — 2 Cor 4:16.

Thus here in 6:6 the "old man" is the "inner man" as it once existed under the control of sin. But it no longer exists as the "old man." That old man died; indeed, it was *crucified with Christ*. What does this mean? This is not a new idea; it is the same as our *death to sin* (6:2) that happened when we were baptized into Christ's death (6:3), and the same as our burial with him into death (6:4). Thus our crucifixion with Christ did not take place on Golgotha's cross, as if we were somehow literally yet mystically present there. We were not transported back in history; rather, the living Christ has become present in *our* history, specifically in the event of our baptism. The power of the cross was there applied to our fallen soul, putting it to death as to its sin-ridden existence. The old man dies "causatively and effectively by baptism," because "in baptism" Christ has "caught up all Christians into his death" (Käsemann, 165). "In the act of baptism we came into his crucifixion" (DeWelt, 90), or more precisely, his crucifixion came into us.

Lenski reminds us that crucifixion is "a violent, accursed death." Thus when our old man died, he "was literally murdered in our baptism, he did not die willingly but was slain as one cursed of God, the passive implying God as the agent" (400). That this should occur in baptism is appropriate, since, as Morris reminds us (246-247), in the first century the Greek word for "baptize" itself "evoked associations of violence." In its basic meaning of "immerse," the word was used of "people being drowned, or of ships being sunk." Thus it makes sense for Jesus to call his crucifixion a baptism (Mark 10:38; Luke 12:50), and for Paul to call our baptism a crucifixion. Thus the baptismal ceremony is not just "gentleness and inspiration; it means death, death to a whole way of life," as Morris says.

Why was our old self crucified? **. . . so that the body of sin might be done away with . . . .** What is this "body of sin"? A common view equates it with the "old man" in the first part of the verse; and since the "old man" is usually taken to mean "the whole man, as controlled by sin," that is how the "body of sin" is understood as well (Cranfield, I:309). The NEB translates it simply "the sinful self." It is "the person in his entirety, viewed as controlled by sin," says Hendriksen (I:198), or "man under the rule of sin and death," says Dunn (I:320). Many interpret Paul's use of the term "flesh" in the same way; thus all three expressions are taken as equivalent.

I think, however, that they cannot be the same, since the reason for the crucifixion of the "old man" is the destruction of the "body of sin." These are two different things. Stott rightly says, "The two expressions cannot mean the same thing, or the sentence makes nonsense" (176; see Godet, 245). Thus I have concluded, based on the way Paul uses the terms "body" and "flesh" in the entire passage, that the "body of sin" here in 6:6 refers only to the physical body. It does not denote the body as such, as if it were inherently sinful. Rather, it is the body *of sin*, the body as it has become infected by and controlled by sin. As Gundry says, "Paul writes of the body only as the victim of sin, not as the origin of sin" (*Sōma*, 204).

Thus I agree with those who say the "body of sin" means "the body so far as it serves as an instrument of sin in human life" (Godet, 245). DeWelt calls it "the body . . . which sin has seized" (88). It is "the body as the instrument, or outward organ of sin," or "the body as the place where sin materially manifests itself," or "the body which sin . . . dominates" (Gundry, *Sōma*, 39). It is "the physical body which so easily responds to sinful impulses" (Morris, 252).

The old man is crucified so that this body of sin "might be *done away with*." What does this mean? The Greek word is καταργέω (*katargeō*, see 3:3). It can have the strong sense of "abolish, destroy." Those who equate "body of sin" with "old man" may easily give it this sense here. If the "old man" is crucified, it dies and is "destroyed" (as in the KJV, RSV, NRSV). It is "done away with" (as in the NASB and later editions of the NIV). But if "body of sin" means the physical body, how would this apply? It is literally destroyed only when it dies. This may possibly be what Paul means, but this would not be very relevant to our baptismal death to sin and would do little to quench the fears of antinomianism.

It is much better to take *katargeō* here in its weaker sense of "put out of action, make ineffective, render powerless." The object of the action is not destroyed or done away with, but is defeated and disabled so that it loses its power. In this sense Satan himself was "rendered powerless" by the death of Christ (Heb 2:14). This is the sense that applies in 6:6. In fact, older editions of the NIV translated it "rendered powerless" here.

This is how MacArthur understands it: "to make something ineffective by removing its power of control" (I:325). That is the whole point. The "old man" (the soul as corrupted by sin) is crucified with Christ, and by his resurrection is transformed into a new man, so that the lusts and temptations and weaknesses that still characterize our sin-ridden body can be resisted and suppressed and controlled, rather than being allowed to control. Thus in baptism not only does the soul itself undergo healing from the sin that has infected it, but also by that very fact it gains power over the not-yet-redeemed "body of sin."

It is true that the "body of sin" continues to be a beachhead or staging point for temptations and lusts of all kinds. However, it no longer has the willing partner of a fallen spirit, and it cannot dominate and rule the "new man" raised up in the latter's place. A tension remains between the redeemed spirit and the unredeemed body, to be sure (7:14-25), but we have all that is needed for a sure victory over sin.

That is the point of the rest of the verse, which is another purpose clause. The old man was crucified with the purpose that the body of sin should be rendered powerless; the body of sin is rendered powerless with the purpose **that we should no longer be slaves to sin . . . .** Sin (through our bodies especially) continues to assault and attack us,[14] but we are no longer its slaves. "No longer" implies that we once were slaves of sin, but that has changed — *we* have changed, or have *been* changed.

This does not mean that we will never again sin. The power of sin that remains in our bodies still seeks to enslave us, and our raised-to-new-life spirits are not yet restored to full strength. Thus the threat of sin still lurks, and sometimes sin becomes the "heartbreaking exception" (MP, 342). But as Hendriksen says, "There is a

---

[14]This is why "rendered inactive" is not a good translation of *katargeō* here, contra Lard, 203; and DeWelt, 88. The same applies to Sanday and Headlam (158), who say that the body of sin is "reduced to a condition of absolute impotence and inaction, as if it were dead."

vast difference between (a) committing a sin and (b) constantly living and delighting in sin" (I:198). Being delivered from slavery to sin means being set free from the latter.

6:7 because anyone who has died has been freed from sin. The first question here is whether this is a proverb or "old saying" that Paul adapts to his point, or whether it is a truth that applies only to the specific kind of dying that is his subject here. The former is probably the case. It is a general maxim used to illustrate v. 6: a dead person is free from sin's power over him and its claims upon him.[15] The specific application, of course, is to the sinner's death to sin.

The second question has to do with the meaning of "freed." This is a problem because the word is not literally "freed, set free" (as in 6:18), but rather the word regularly translated "justified" (δικαιόω, *dikaioō*) elsewhere. For this reason many say that justification is Paul's point here: the believing sinner who has died to sin has been set free from the penalty or condemnation of sin; sin no longer has any legal claims upon him.[16] The problem with this is that justification is not Paul's subject in this paragraph. He is dealing not with the guilt of sin but with the power of sin (Käsemann, 170). So why does he use *dikaioō*? Perhaps the answer lies in the preposition attached to it, ἀπό (*apo*), "justified *from*" (see also Acts 13:38-39). This is a "strange expression" (Käsemann, 170), certainly unusual. It may be that the combination of *dikaioō* and *apo* — "justified from" — is a broader concept that includes both justification and sanctification: freed from both the guilt and power of sin. Also, if this statement is indeed a maxim from public life, in that context *dikaioō* might not have had the usual Pauline meaning, says Godet (246-247).

In any case freedom from the power of sin seems to be the main point. Dying with Christ sets us free from that power; "death marks the end of sin's rule" (Dunn, I:321).

6:8 This verse basically repeats the point of 6:5, that union with Christ in his death necessarily involves union with him in his

---

[15]Lard, 204; Moo, I:394-395. A later rabbinic proverb is similar: "When a man is dead he is freed from fulfilling the law" (Käsemann, 170).

[16]Cranfield, I:311; Murray, I:222; Stott, 177.

resurrection. **Now if we died with Christ, we believe that we will also live with him.** "Died with Christ" is the same as "baptized into his death" (v. 3), "buried with him" (v. 4), "united with him in his death" (v. 5), and "crucified with him" (v. 6). It happened in baptism.

"We believe" expresses not just Paul's faith but the faith of all Christians. This does not mean that everyone understands and consciously believes this truth; it means rather that it is a necessary part of the content of the Christian faith. If we believe that we died with Christ in baptism — and we do, then we should also believe that we shall live with him as well. The one implies the other.

"Believe that" expresses the *assent* aspect of faith (see 1:16), or the acceptance of the truth of the content of God's inspired word. See Cranfield, I:312.

We believe that "we will also live with him." Because the death and resurrection of Jesus are inseparable, with the same certainty our death with him implies our resurrection with him. But what does the future tense imply? Some see a reference to our bodily resurrection at Christ's return, "an actually glorified existence in the future" (MP, 345). While this is our ultimate hope and faith,[17] and while it is implicitly included in the baptismal symbolism, the main reference here is to our present renewed spiritual life (6:11) that began with our resurrection with Christ in baptism (Morris, 254; Cranfield, I:312-313).

Lard (204-205) calls this "the future of duty or obligation" and translates it "we *should* also live like him" (see v. 14). It is better, though, to take the future tense as emphasizing the *certainty* of our newness of life (6:5). As Murray says, it "points to the certainty of participation in the resurrection life of Christ here and now" (I:223). At this present time, our resurrection life is our holy living and obedience to God's laws. So how can the Christian "go on sinning" (6:1)?

6:9 To undergird the reality of the new life we now enjoy, Paul here goes into a bit more detail about its parallel and source, the resurrection existence of Jesus Christ. **For we know that since**

---

[17]I agree with Dunn, that "the (full) share in Christ's resurrection life is still future" (I:322).

Christ was raised from the dead, he cannot die again . . . . "We know" reflects the common Christian understanding of Christ's resurrection. If we already know this is true about Jesus, then we can have the same confidence regarding ourselves. I.e., what happened to Jesus is the basis for what has happened to us and therefore for our *assurance* that it has happened. We have confidence that God has raised us from the dead, because we know he raised up Jesus (Col 2:12).

"He cannot die again" distinguishes Christ's resurrection from all miraculous resurrections that brought other people back to life, such as Lazarus and Dorcas. Christ's resurrection was in a category by itself. It was not just a partial and temporary victory over death, but one that was total, decisive, and permanent. In his raised and glorified human nature he is the first-fruits of the eschatological resurrection itself and the first representative of the redeemed world of the new heavens and new earth. He is living a *new kind of life*, one that is beyond the reach of sin and death. . . . **death no longer has mastery**[18] **over him.** It did once, for that brief time when he took our sins upon himself and allowed himself to be over-whelmed by death in our place. But in his resurrection Jesus won the decisive victory over sin and death, and we are even now sharing in that victory.

6:10 The death he died, he died to sin once for all . . . . This reinforces the point about Jesus' complete victory over death and the endless power of his new life. "Died to sin" means that he died in relation to sin; his death had something to do with sin. The wording is the same as 6:2 and similar to 6:11, which affirm that *we* "died to sin." This does not mean that Jesus died to sin in the same way that we did (contra Dunn, I:323). His death was the cause, ours the effect.

In what sense did Jesus die in relation to sin? Paul has already affirmed that he died to bear the guilt and penalty of our sin (3:24-26). But here he seems to refer to something else, i.e., that in some way Christ died to deliver a death-blow to sin and to destroy its

---

[18]"Has mastery" (κυριεύω, *kurieuō*) is similar to the word used of death in 5:14, 17, and of sin in 5:21 (βασιλεύω, *basileuō*). The former is from the word for "lord," the latter from "king." They are basically equivalent in meaning. See 6:12, 14.

power (Murray, I:224-225). See Eph 4:8; Heb 2:14-15. Sin the usurper (5:21) has been dethroned by the instrument of the cross. This is why our union with Christ in his death is the death of our own sin (6:4). The blood he shed in his victorious battle with sin is the instrument of our sanctification (Heb 10:10; 13:12); it sweeps aside "acts that lead to death, so that we may serve the living God" (Heb 9:14).

Jesus' death to sin was "once for all." This idea is emphasized in the book of Hebrews,[19] where the point is the true efficacy of Christ's sacrifice, as opposed to the non-efficacy of the sacrifices under the Old Covenant. The latter had to be repeated often; but Christ's one act of death (5:18) was infinite in power and does not need to be repeated. In 6:10, though, the contrast is different. Here Christ's death is compared with his own resurrection. His encounter with sin was a one-time event, not an ongoing, never-ending mission. Sin has no power where Christ is concerned. It is a usurper in his universe. Jesus entered this fallen world where sin rules, fought sin on its own turf (so to speak), won the battle through the unlikely weapon of the cross, then arose and ascended into heaven (Eph 4:8). That's it; that's the end of it; he did it once and it was over. The descent so eloquently described in Phil 2:7-8 will never be repeated. "It is finished," he said as he died (John 19:30).

. . . but the life he lives, he lives to God. Here is the contrast: a one-time encounter with sin and death, but an ongoing and eternal reign in *life* through the power of God and in the presence of God the Father (Phil 2:9-11). "I was dead, and behold I am alive for ever and ever!" (Rev 1:18). The state of his earthly humiliation "was conditioned by the sin with which he was vicariously identified"; but in his death "he destroyed the power of sin, and in his resurrection he entered upon a state that was not conditioned by sin" (Murray, I:225). It is the state characterized rather by *life*, the eternal life that comes only from God, in whom life is everlastingly inherent (John 5:26).

That Jesus lives "to God" must mean more than "for the benefit of, to the glory of, God" (Moo, I:397). *Everything* Jesus did, including and especially his death, was for God's benefit and glory. This is

---

[19]7:27; 8:12, 26, 28; 10:10; see 1 Pet 3:18.

why the main idea in living "to God" must refer to the new kind of life that he lives in his resurrected and glorified state at the very right hand of God the Father.

6:11 In the same way, count yourselves dead to sin but alive to God in Christ Jesus. This verse is closely associated with v. 10, contrary to the paragraph division in the NIV. It is important to understand the nature of *Christ's* death and resurrection, because we too have been put to death and raised again with him. Our death to sin and resurrection to newness of life draw their meaning and power from his own. Thus "in the same way" refers to what has just been said in vv. 9-10 especially, though it also sums up the entire didactic section in vv. 2-10.

"Count yourselves" is an imperative, an exhortation — the first in the epistle, as Morris notes (256). Nevertheless it is not parallel to the imperatives in vv. 12-13, which form the behavioral application of the factual data laid down in vv. 2-11. Verse 11 is an exhortation to accept these data as true. The verb is λογίζομαι (*logizomai*), which was used throughout ch. 4 in the sense of "declared, reckoned, imputed." This verse (6:11) is not talking about God's imputing something to us, though. We ourselves are the subject of the verb; Paul says emphatically, "*You* count *yourselves* dead to sin but alive to God." In other words, "I have been stating this as a fact over and over (vv. 2-10); now it is time for you to put yourselves into the picture. You must not only accept this death and resurrection as true in an abstract sense; you must consider it to be true of yourselves *personally*."

We are "dead to sin," in some ways just like Jesus. His encounter with sin was a once-for-all victory; when it was over, it was *over*. He left it behind him. Likewise we must realize that we too have died to our old life; we have left it behind us. We have moved on to something better; we are "alive to God" (Col 3:1-4). Just as the risen Christ now has a new kind of existence based upon and enveloped by the glory and power of God, so we also have a new existence, a newness of life in which everything is from God and for God. In this new life we look upon sin as our hated and defeated enemy, we look upon God's law with loving reverence, and we regard obedience to his law not only as our duty but also as our delight. All this is true only "in Christ Jesus," only because he too has died to sin and for our sins and has been raised again, and only because we have been crucified and raised up with him in our baptism.

With all this being true, why should we even *want* to remain in sin, much less think that it is somehow our obligation under grace (6:1)? The very thought is ridiculous. "For the Christian to choose to sin is the spiritual equivalent of digging up a corpse for fellowship," says Mounce (153).

6:12 Therefore. Here is the significant transition from the didactic or *indicative* to the *imperative* part of this section. The former (vv. 2-11) sets forth the facts of our death and resurrection with Christ; the latter (vv. 12-13) exhorts us to live lives that are consistent with these facts. "This connection between the indicative of our incorporation into Christ and the imperative of Christian living is the real heart of Romans 6," says Moo (I:383).

. . . do not let sin reign in your mortal body so that you obey its evil desires. The focal point of these exhortations has to do with the *body*. Many see the "mortal body" here as equivalent to their interpretation of "old self" and "body of sin" in v. 6, i.e., as the entire fallen self. It is "the whole man in his fallenness" (Cranfield, I:317), "man as a whole in his belongingness to this world" (Dunn, I:336), "the whole person" (Moo, I:400). I disagree with this view and see "mortal body" as referring specifically to the physical body, just as I do "the body of sin" in v. 6. It is called the *mortal* body because it has not yet been redeemed (8:23) and thus is still under the curse of death (8:10; see 1 Cor 15:53-54).[20]

We all have two choices. We can reign over sin, or we can let sin reign over us (v. 14). Here Paul speaks of this choice in terms of the body-spirit dualism. In the unregenerate sinner, sin reigns over the whole person, body and spirit. Through regeneration (dying and rising with Christ) the spirit is set free from the corruption and power of sin, but the body remains unredeemed. The exhortation "Do not let sin reign in your mortal body" implies that sin is still present there. Our unredeemed bodies are thus a kind of weak point, a vantage point from which sin still opposes us and fights against us and tries to conquer us (Godet, 250; Hendriksen, I:201). As DeWelt (93) says, sin "is personified as a tyrant reigning in and

---

[20]"Mortal" is θνητός (*thnētos*), from θάνατος (*thanatos*), "death."

through the body" — or at least trying to so reign. Stott (180) says, "Sin can use our body as a bridgehead through which to govern us." MacArthur says the mortal body is a "beachhead where sin can attack a Christian" (I:337).

Sin launches its attack in the form of "evil desires" that press upon us, demanding us to fulfill them and obey them. The word for "evil desires" (ἐπιθυμία, *epithymia*) can mean strong desire of any kind, good or bad (see 1:24). Here the context justifies the translation "evil desires" or "lusts" (NASB). Most bodily desires are not evil in themselves, but only become so when they are not kept within the boundaries of God's laws. The very point of sin is to let these desires flow unchecked and unrestrained, as if we were no more than animals.

The very fact that we are exhorted to prevent this shows that if we do not take charge of ourselves and our bodies, and if we do not make a deliberate effort to resist sin, then it is possible for sin to regain dominion over us and reign in our bodies. If it were not possible, this exhortation would be a sham.

At the same time, the very fact that we are exhorted not to let sin reign shows that we *can* do this. Unlike animals, we are spirit as well as body and thus are more than bodily desires. And unlike unregenerate sinners, our spirits have been infused with new life and new power by which we can and must rule over these bodily desires and keep them within their God-imposed boundaries. Thus we are not helpless; *we are able* to prevent sin from reigning in and through our bodies. This is the point of this exhortation.

The central truth stated in 6:6 is the basis for this ability and this responsibility. Our "old man" (the fallen "inner man" or spirit) was crucified with Christ in baptism for this very purpose — that the body of sin (mortal body) might be rendered powerless to rule over us, so that we should no longer be slaves to sin. Thus contrary to all antinomian hopes and fears, grace does not give us an excuse to go on sinning, but instead makes it possible, even *morally necessary* to stop sinning.

6:13 The first part of this verse goes with v. 12; it continues the negative exhortation begun there concerning the body: **Do not offer the parts of your body to sin, as instruments of wickedness . . . .** "Of your body" is not in the Greek text, but this is the correct sense. The word for "parts" (μέλος, *melos*) means "limb, organ, body part, member." Some try to broaden it here to include spiritual "members" such as the mind and will, or "any natural capacity" (Cranfield, I:317). It surely is true that we should offer no part or faculty of our being into the service of sin, but that is not the point here. Paul is speaking of the physical body, in continuity with v. 12.

The image here is of someone presenting the assets under his control into the service of a monarch. "Offer" means "to place at the disposal of, to present for use in the service of." The word for "instruments" often means "weapons," and many take that as the meaning here (see Hendriksen, I:202-203). "Sin" is pictured as a tyrant or dictator who wants to use our own bodily members as instruments or weapons by which it can rule over us. "Wickedness," or unrighteousness, is the use to which our members are put when we let sin control us.

The rest of the verse contains a two-part positive exhortation about presenting everything in our control into the service of God the true King rather than sin the usurper. **. . . but rather offer yourselves to God, as those who have been brought from death to life; and offer the parts of your body to him as instruments of righteousness.** In the first part of the verse "offer" is present tense: "do not go on offering your members into the service of sin," in answer to the question in 6:1. Here in the latter part of the verse "offer" is aorist tense, reflecting "deliberate and decisive commitment" (Dunn, I:338). I.e., make up your mind and begin to do it *now*!

In my judgment these two positive imperatives reflect the spirit-body dualism. "Offer *yourselves*" refers to the spirit or inner man, the seat of selfhood, the "command center" for the whole person. This inner self is the part of us that has already "been brought from death to life" (vv. 2-11). Therefore we can and must present our whole inner being for service unto God — mind, will, emotions, desires, motives, passions, love. Only a person still dead in his transgressions and sins will continue to place these faculties into the service of sin and self.

The two parts of the positive exhortation are joined with the simple conjunction καί, (*kai*, "and"), indicating two separate ideas. The second part, "offer the parts of your *body*," refers to the physical body as distinct from the soul or spirit. The verb is not repeated in the Greek; it occurs once and has two objects: offer *yourselves* and *your parts*. "Of your body" is properly inferred from the word for "parts, members" (*melos*). Here the contrast with v. 13a is precise. Instead of presenting your bodily members to King Sin for unrighteous purposes, present them to God as instruments or weapons to be used for the cause of righteousness in daily obedience to his will.

That we have been brought from death to life is a fact; that we must now present ourselves and our bodies to God is an exhortation. That it is an exhortation means that it is possible for us to choose *not* to do it — but how could we, and why should we? (See v. 2.) It also means that it is possible for us to choose to *do* it. We *can* present our selves and bodies to God for righteousness!

We must understand exactly what is involved in this latter choice. Yes, our regenerated spirits have the power to take charge of our bodies and to direct ourselves, body and spirit, into God's service. But this is not the same as saying that we as made-alive Christians have full power *in ourselves* to suppress the "evil desires" of the body (v. 12) and to walk unassisted in the path of righteousness. The actual overcoming of sin and walking in righteousness are possible only through the power of the indwelling Holy Spirit (8:13-14), as chs. 7 and 8 show. But what we made-alive Christians *can* do is *present* ourselves and our bodies to God and allow him, in the person of his Spirit within us, to empower us for righteous living. We *can* lay ourselves before him and trust him for strength to overcome temptation and to grow in holy virtue. Sometimes we make the mistake of thinking we are supposed to do it all by ourselves, and the prospect of imminent defeat leads us to despair (see 7:14-25).

In other words we must not *underestimate* what we as made-alive Christians can do; we *can* take charge of ourselves and our bodies, and place them in God's hands and point ourselves in the direction of righteousness. But on the other hand we must not *overestimate* what we can do. Even as we continue to work out all the possibilities and responsibilities of our salvation, we must remember that it is God the Holy Spirit who works in us and gives us the power to do it (Phil 2:12-13).

6:14 For sin shall not be your master . . . . Some take this future tense as having an imperative force: "Sin must not be your master" (TEV). Others take it as an eschatological promise: "Sin will not *finally* be the victor" (DeWelt, 94). I.e., it states "a future fact made sure to a believer as a glorious promise" (Godet, 252). Murray says it is neither of these, but rather simply "expresses the certainty of that which is affirmed"; it is "a statement of assured fact" (I:228).

Murray is probably closest to the truth. It is no doubt a promise; and since it is a divine promise, it is no doubt certain. More importantly, this promise cannot be limited to the final state; it is meant to apply to Christians *now*. Christians already, even now, have been set free from sin's dominion (6:18), and this freedom will continue until it is culminated and finalized in the end. This does not mean that Christians will never commit any sins; it means that sin will not be their controlling power. Nor is the promise unconditional; it assumes that we will fulfill the imperatives of vv. 12-13.

. . . because you are not under law, but under grace. This seems to give the *reason* why sin shall not be our master. If we were under law, sin would definitely lord it over us in every way. But because we are under grace, sin will not be our master in any sense.

The contrast between law and grace is a bit surprising, since law has not been mentioned anywhere up to this point in this section. We must not forget, though, that the contrast between law and grace as ways of salvation is the controlling idea at least in the first half of Romans. In 1:18-3:20 Paul explains the nature and futility of law (law-keeping) as a way of salvation; in 3:21-5:21 he explains the alternative to law, namely, grace. In the latter section he focuses on justification as the first and primary benefit of grace, i.e., freedom from sin's *penalty*; in this present section (6:1-8:39) he is developing the second benefit of grace, i.e., regeneration and sanctification as the victory over the *power* of sin.

His point here is that law cannot set us free from sin in either sense. It cannot justify a person once even a single sin has been committed, nor can it give sinners the strength necessary to obey its own commands. Thus as a way of salvation, law is a total failure.[21] It leaves the sinner's life under the power of sin, and it

---

[21]Of course, it was never intended to be an instrument of salvation, so this failure cannot be blamed either on God or on the law itself.

cannot divert him from the inevitable destiny of (eternal) death. Indeed, it is "the law of sin and death" (8:2).

But the blessed grace of God does what the law cannot. Its double cure sets us free from both the penalty and power of sin. This is why sin shall not be the master of those under grace. Living under the prospect of the penalty of eternal condemnation is itself a form of bondage to sin, but the grace of Jesus Christ has set us free from that (8:1; Heb 2:14-15). Living under the tyranny of sin considered as an enslaving power is also a form of bondage, but the grace of Jesus Christ has set us free from that also, as this whole chapter shows.

Here the word "law" is not limited to the Law of Moses, contrary to the assumption of many (e.g., Dunn, I:339; Moo, I:405). It refers to law in any form: the Mosaic Law as it applied to Jews under the Old Covenant; the total body of commandments that make up the prescriptive will of God for all of us in the New Covenant era, including Christians; and the law written on the heart, for those who have general revelation only.[22] The point is that Christians, or believers in any age, are not under law (whatever its applicable form) as a way of salvation.

A person has only two choices. He is either under law, or under grace. The pre-accountable child is automatically under the original grace of Jesus Christ (5:12-19). The accountable sinner is under law, with its guaranteed failure in reference to salvation. Among accountable persons today only believers in Jesus Christ are under grace, which is the only possible way to be free from the terrible tyranny of King Sin.

Limiting *nomos* here to the Mosaic Law makes the verse meaningless to most people, since most have never been under the Law of Moses and do not even know what it is. In fact most sinners are *neither* under the Law of Moses *nor* under grace, and the choice between the Mosaic Law and grace is unintelligible to them. But if "law" here means law in general, when properly explained this choice will be clear to anyone.

---

[22]For this latter view see Godet, 252; Murray, I:228-229; Lenski, 418.

B. DOES FREEDOM FROM LAW MEAN
WE ARE FREE TO SIN? NO! (6:15-7:6)

The reference to freedom from law in v. 14 again raises the specter of antinomianism. If we are not under law, then are we not free from all obligation to obey any commands of God? This is basically the same question raised in v. 1, but at that point Paul did not deal with the issue of obligation as such. Instead in 6:2-14 he established the even more basic point of our *ability* to obey. Now he turns specifically to the question of *obligation*.

The spirit of antinomianism says we have two choices. We can choose *autonomy* and be a law unto ourselves, thus having the absolute freedom of self-determination. Or we can choose to submit ourselves as slaves to the *authority* of another. Only a fool would choose the latter. Why make yourself someone else's slave, when you can be your own boss?

Over against this fiction, Paul makes it clear that this choice between autonomy and authority does not really exist. *We are slaves* and always will be, whether we are under law or grace. The only choice we have is which master we will serve: God or sin. When we accept God's offer of grace, we are no longer slaves to law and sin; but we are still slaves: "slaves to God" (6:22). Grace does not diminish our obligation to obey his commands a single iota.

We must resist the continuing temptation to limit "law" to the Law of Moses. This view is quite prevalent, and it is easy to understand why. The concept of a transition from law to grace corresponds very nicely with the transition from the Old Covenant age to the New Covenant age, and with the replacement of the Law of Moses by the Gospel of Jesus Christ.[23] But this is *not the point* of "we are not under law but under grace." The transition to which Paul refers in 6:14-15 is not this general turning point in salvation history, but rather each specific individual's personal conversion experience. Prior to accepting God's gracious promise of salvation, every individual is *under law*. But upon receiving salvation he comes *under grace*, whether he be Adam, Abraham, Moses, David, Paul,

---

[23]Compare Moo, who says 6:15 refers to the fact that Christians "live in the new era where grace, not the law of Moses, reigns" (I:413).

Augustine, Luther, or Campbell. Thus we conclude that "law" in this section refers to whatever form of law is available and applicable to any given individual in any given time.

The main point, though, is that our personal transition from law to grace changes our relationship to law in significant ways, but not in every way. Because of grace we are no longer under law as a way of salvation, but we are still under law as a way of life. Even though by grace we are not under the law's penalties, we are still under its commands. Though saved by grace we are still creatures and must still obey the Creator, but grace changes our motives for obedience. Our sinful impulses are no longer held in check merely by external restraints such as the threat of eternal punishment. Rather, we are impelled to obey by our internal desire to please God and to show him our loving gratitude for his grace.

The content of this section falls into two main paragraphs. The first (6:15-23) shows what freedom from law does *not* mean. I.e., it does not mean autonomy or antinomianism. We who were slaves to sin have willfully submitted ourselves to a new master, God; and in so doing we have joyfully acknowledged our obligation to obey his law. Freedom from law is not freedom from obedience. The second paragraph (7:1-6) shows what freedom from law *does* mean, i.e., freedom from external, legalistic motives and freedom to serve God from the heart. Like a woman with a new husband, we are free to serve God in a new way with a new spirit.

1. We Are Slaves to God (6:15-23)

6:15 What then? Shall we sin because we are not under law but under grace? By no means! This verse has the same form as 6:1: a brief opening question, an objection worded as a question, and an emphatic denial. While the objection is basically the same as 6:1 in that it voices the fear that grace will lead to antinomianism, there is a slight difference. In 6:1 the problem is that the availability and abundance of forgiveness would seem to make converts indifferent toward the abandonment of sin. Why not just sin all the more, since grace will surely cover it all? In 6:15 the problem is that the absence of law as a moral restraint would seem to leave the convert with no reason not to sin. Without law to restrain behavior, won't we just keep right on sinning? In fact, without law how can any specific act even be called a sin?

So, "shall we sin[24] because we are not under law but under grace?" Paul's answer is the emphatic and decisive μὴ γένοιτο (*me genoito*), "By no means!" Anyone who thinks this does not yet understand the meaning of freedom from law. The transition from law to grace does not leave us free to sin, as if there were no longer any law at all by which sin is defined and restrained. Accepting grace means the abandonment of the law system as a way of salvation, but it does not separate us from law altogether. Under grace the commands of the law are still operative as a binding norm, identifying the limits and requirements of accepted behavior.

I stress again that "law" must not be limited here to the Law of Moses. The point is not the end of the era of the Mosaic Law and the beginning of the era of grace. Trying to be saved by law was not just a problem for Jews under the Old Covenant; it is a danger faced by all people, no matter what form of law they possess. All sinners are "under law" even where the Law of Moses is totally unknown. Countless people today who have only an intellectual acquaintance with Jesus Christ and the NT Scriptures are "under law" because they believe that living according to NT ethical principles (such as the Sermon on the Mount) will save them.

On the other hand, coming under grace is a possibility for anyone who hears the promise of God's forgiveness known through special revelation. The Law of Moses was binding upon all Jews who lived under the Old Covenant dispensation, yet some were "under law" and some were "under grace." The former were those who believed their obedience to the Law of Moses was their ticket to heaven. The latter were those who trusted in God's promises rather than in their own goodness, but who nevertheless continued to obey the statutes of the Mosaic Law as the norm God had assigned to them. Anyone today who ceases to trust in his own

---

[24]6:1 says, "Should we remain in sin?" (present subjunctive). Here the question is more simply put: "Should we sin?" (aorist subjunctive). Some think the former refers more to remaining under the power of sin, and the latter to the committing of specific sins. While this is probably true, the difference does not seem to be significant.

righteousness as the basis for his acceptance by God, and who receives Christ as his Savior according to the terms specified in the NT, is no longer under law but under grace. But he is still bound to obey the moral statutes of the entire Bible and the religious statutes of the NT.

6:16 Don't you know that when you offer yourselves to someone to obey him as slaves, you are slaves to the one whom you obey . . . ? Slavery was commonplace in the Roman Empire of the first century. In large urban areas nearly half of the population were either slaves or freed slaves, therefore the first recipients of Paul's letter would have been very much at home with this metaphor. They would have readily understood ("Don't you know . . . ?") the principle the Apostle is enunciating here. It is based on the fact that in that culture many people entered into slavery voluntarily, often to pay off a debt.[25] The principle is this: when you make a decision to obey someone, you become that person's slave.

Paul applies this principle to the individual's spiritual life. We are all slaves who serve a master, but we do have a choice as to whom we will serve. The concept of choice is seen in the expression, "offer yourselves" (see 6:13). This shows that the individual's free will is involved in both his sin and his conversion.

According to Paul your free-will choice determines **whether you are slaves to sin, which leads to death, or to obedience, which leads to righteousness[.]** These are the only two alternatives. We cannot serve both at the same time (Luke 16:13), and we cannot decline to choose (see Josh 24:15).

One choice is to be a slave of sin. Here Paul continues the image of sin as a personified power or tyrant that wants to reign over us (5:21; 6:12-14). When we decide to live a life of sin, we become its slave, for "everyone who sins is a slave to sin" (John 8:34). The result of serving as sin's slave is *death*. This is not the redemptive death of the "old self" (6:6), the death *to* sin discussed in 6:1-14. It is rather the death that comes *from* sin, the devastating effect of sinning and the divine curse upon sin. This includes spiritual death (Eph 2:1), or

---

[25]"In both Greece and Italy, large numbers of persons . . . sold themselves into slavery" (Bartchy, *Slavery*, 46). OT law also provided for voluntary slavery. See Lev 25:39-43, 47-55; Deut 15:12-17.

the present state of moral corruption that hardens the sinner toward God. It includes physical death, which is a triumph for sin since the sinner has no promise of redemptive resurrection. It includes especially the final curse of eternal death (6:23; Rev 20:14). Indeed, "sin is deathly and death in every respect follows in its wake" (Murray, I:231).

The other choice is to be a slave of obedience itself. Later Paul speaks of being slaves to righteousness (v. 18) and slaves to God (v. 22). These are not three choices, but are three ways of describing the same choice. Obedience is the means by which we live as slaves to God, and righteousness is its outcome.

Being a "slave to obedience" is an unusual expression. In effect it says that as Christians we are *obeying obedience*. Some say this refers to the initial act of faith in the gospel (Godet, 255), or "obedience to the gospel call" (Morris, 262). But this initial obedience to the gospel (see 1:5) is what we do when we "offer ourselves" to become slaves of obedience. "Obeying obedience" is what we do throughout our Christian lives. But why this awkward expression? For one thing, it emphasizes the fact that we still have the *obligation* to obey God's law, even under grace. We are still slaves (to God), and this is "a dramatic way of emphasizing that obedience is the very essence of slavery" (Stott, 183). For another thing, it shows us that slavery to sin does not deserve to be called obedience; service to God is the only true obedience.

This true obedience does lead to righteousness. But is this righteousness *forensic* (the pronouncement of a judge), or *moral* (personal ethical living)? Some take it to mean or at least include the former: being declared righteous in the sense of justification.[26] They reason that this has been the meaning of "righteousness" throughout most of Romans thus far; that this makes a better contrast with "death" in the other choice; and that obedience and moral righteousness are the same thing, so how could one lead to the other?

I think it is better, however, to take righteousness here in the moral sense.[27] It is true that the concept of forensic or imputed

---

[26]See Stott, 183; Morris, 262; Lard, 212; Cranfield, I:322.

[27]See Godet, 255; MacArthur, I:343; Moo, I:416.

righteousness (justification) dominated in chapters 1-5, but in chapter 6 the focus has shifted to sanctification or personal righteousness. This is clear in 6:13, where righteousness is contrasted with wickedness; see also 6:18-20. Also, when we see that "leads to death" probably includes the sinner's present state of spiritual death or moral corruption, moral righteousness corresponds very well with it. Also, a serious problem with taking righteousness here in the forensic sense (justification) is that it makes justification the result of obedience, which is works-righteousness, contrary to Paul's whole point in 3:21-5:21. This can be avoided only if "obedience" here is the initial obedience to the gospel, but we have seen that is not the case. Being *slaves* of obedience is not a one-time act but a lifelong state.

But if righteousness here does mean moral or personal righteousness, how is this different from obedience? In what sense does obedience *lead to* such righteousness? (A similar question arises in 6:19, where Paul says slavery to righteousness leads to holiness.) We must remember that the basic meaning of righteousness is "conformity to the relevant norm" (see 1:17), and for human beings the norm or standard is the law of God. A righteous person is one who conforms to God's law or satisfies the requirements of his law. This is in fact not very different from obedience, and the two terms could be used as synonyms. Here the distinction is probably that "obedience" refers to specific acts of obedience and "righteousness" to the spiritual state of our souls that is being brought about by such acts. This reference to righteousness (as conformity to God's law) helps Paul make his point that being under grace does not make obedience to the law irrelevant.

Paul's main point here is not to warn Christians against forsaking obedience and choosing to serve sin again (contra Moo, I:414-415), though this could happen. His main concern in these verses is to remind us that we have already made our choice as to whom we will serve. We have offered ourselves as slaves to God, "and slavery demands a total, radical, exclusive obedience. . . . Having chosen our master, we have no further choice but to obey him" (Stott, 183). Rather than being free from moral restraint, contrary to the objection in 6:15, we have placed ourselves even more firmly under it.

6:17 Now, given the two alternatives in v. 16b, where do we as Christians stand? Here is Paul's answer: **But thanks be to God that, though you used to be slaves to sin** in your pre-Christian life, **you wholeheartedly obeyed the form of teaching to which you were entrusted.** This refers to our conversion experience, when we made the choice to stop being slaves of sin and to surrender ourselves to God instead. "You obeyed" is aorist tense and refers to our initial obedience to the gospel when we offered ourselves (v. 16) as lifelong slaves to Jesus as Lord.

This initial obedience (which involved faith, repentance, and baptism) was done "wholeheartedly," or literally, "from the heart." This shows that our decision to surrender to God was our own choice and was not coerced or irresistibly imposed upon us. It also means that we gave ourselves to God "sincerely and earnestly" (Lard, 213); the decision was "deeply felt and deeply motivated" (Dunn, I:343). A slave's service is usually outward only, with the heart being in rebellion; but when we entered God's service the very first thing we surrendered to him was our heart. See 1 Pet 1:22.

The rest of this verse is extremely difficult. What is "the form of teaching," and in what sense were we "entrusted" or delivered to it? Many possibilities have been suggested, and it is difficult to discern a clearly preferable answer. "Form" is τύπος (*typos*), which "properly refers to a mold for producing a shape, or a wooden stamp for making an imprint in clay"; it is an outline or a model after which something else is meant to be patterned (Spicq, *Lexicon*, III:384-385). "Teaching" is διδαχή (*didachē*), the ordinary word for doctrine or what is taught.

This refers to the whole scope of biblical and apostolic teaching (Acts 2:42). It includes all biblical truth, and is therefore the "sound doctrine" of the biblical worldview. To say that Christians have "wholeheartedly obeyed" this form of teaching means that we have begun to allow it to mold our beliefs and our behavior. Such is the essence of our slavery to God, and it is a lifelong process.[28]

---

[28]I vigorously reject Dunn's view, that the "form of teaching" is the ethical example set by Jesus (I:334, 343, 353-354). This is an example of the Christological fallacy, a seriously false doctrine (GC, 166-171).

Why does Paul say we were "entrusted" to this form of doctrine? Would it not make more sense to say it was entrusted to us? The word is παραδίδωμι (*paradidōmi*), which in other places is used for the handing over or passing on of divinely revealed truth (1 Cor 11:2, 23; 15:3; 2 Pet 2:21; Jude 3).[29] But here the thought is different: we were handed over to this form of teaching. Some believe the concept comes from the world of slavery, the specific image being the occasion when a slave changes ownership and is "delivered over" to a new master (Cranfield, I:324; Dunn, I:343-344). This thought is appropriate in the context, but it should be supplemented by the following idea as well. When we became God's slaves, he delivered us over to the body of doctrine which he has revealed through his apostles and prophets, and instructed us to conform ourselves to it. This is our job as his slaves, and is in accord with the references to "righteousness" in vv. 16 and 18. By shaping our minds and deeds to the pattern or mold of sound doctrine, we achieve the righteousness that is characteristic of slaves to God.

6:18 You have been set free from sin and have become slaves to righteousness. This completes the thought begun in v. 17. We were once slaves to sin, but in conversion we were set free from it. This is the same event as dying to sin (6:2, 11), but here it is described in terms of slavery. Under both images the action is something done to us: "our old self was crucified" (6:6, passive), and we "have been set free" (passive). This shows that, even though we have the freedom to choose the one to whom we offer ourselves as slaves (v. 16), we cannot be delivered from slavery to sin without the liberating power of God. As sinners we make the decision that we want to change masters, but God alone gives us the power to do so when he kills our old self and gives new life to our spirits in baptism. This breaks sin's power over us.

As regenerated Christians we are now "slaves to righteousness." This is the same as the second option named in v. 16, "slaves to obedience, which leads to righteousness." It is similar to v. 17b, that we have committed ourselves to obeying the form of teaching to

---

[29]This is not the word used in 3:2, which says that Israel was entrusted with the "very words of God," the OT Scriptures.

which the Liberator has delivered us. We have acknowledged our obligation to conform our thoughts and deeds to the Lord's teaching, i.e., to become righteous. Conforming our lives to God's will has become our goal and our passion, and our feet have been set upon that road by the power of God. This is a slavery to which we willingly and joyfully submit.

6:19 I put this in human terms because you are weak in your natural selves. Here Paul explains that, when he uses the metaphor of slavery, he is using (what was then) a common, everyday human relationship to help us understand our spiritual condition. Why is this necessary? In literal translation, "Because of the weakness of your flesh."

What does this mean? One possibility is that "the weakness of our flesh" makes it difficult for us to understand spiritual things; thus an analogy from daily life, even if the parallel is not always exact, will help us to grasp their meaning. This weakness could be just creaturely finitude, in which case "flesh" would mean our (morally neutral) human nature (4:1; 9:3, 5; see 1:3). Or, it could be a spiritual dullness, in which case "flesh" would mean our unredeemed bodily natures which still exert a negative influence upon our thinking processes. In either case the weakness is a difficulty of understanding.

Another possibility is that "the weakness of our flesh" refers to our sinful desires (6:12) and impulses toward autonomy; thus it is necessary to use this harsh and graphic slave analogy as a way of helping us curb these lusts and impulses (Käsemann, 182). By describing us as slaves Paul is able to stress our "total obligation and total accountability" to God, even under grace (Cranfield, I:321). In this way he accomplishes his contextual purpose of addressing antinomian fears and tendencies.

In any case Paul continues to use the slave analogy in the next few verses: **Just as you used to offer the parts of your body in slavery to impurity and to ever-increasing wickedness, so now offer them in slavery to righteousness leading to holiness.** This is a "before and after" description of our lives, as indicated by the word "now." I.e., both before and after that point of time in which we died to sin, when our old man was crucified with Jesus (6:2, 6), our status was and is that of a slave. In our role as a slave we offer the parts of our body to a master (see 6:13, 16). "The parts of your body" is literally "your parts" or "your members," but as in 6:13 the phrase "of your body" is implied. As in that verse and in 6:16, the implication is that each individual has the responsible freedom to choose the master to whom he will submit himself as a slave.

Before our conversion it was simply a fact that we offered our bodies to impurity (or uncleanness) and wickedness (literally, "lawlessness"). What is the difference between these? Lard (215) says the former is sins against ourselves, and the latter is sins against others. MacArthur (I:350) says one is inward sin, the other outward sin. Such distinctions have little basis. Actually these words are just two ways of describing *all* sins. All sins are impure in that they contradict the purity of the holy character of God, and all sins are lawlessness in that they are disobedience to the law of God. This is just a more intense way of saying we were "slaves to sin" (6:16, 20).

"Ever-increasing wickedness" is literally "lawlessness unto lawlessness."[30] The idea is that when we yield our bodies to sin, this simply leads to more and more sin, specifically to a state characterized by lawlessness. This expression, which brings to mind the scenario of depravity described in 1:18-32, helps to make Paul's main point, that living under grace does not lead to lawlessness. Contrary to the objection in 6:15, and paradoxically, *living under law* leads to lawlessness, while *living under grace* honors God's law by leading to righteousness and holiness.[31] This latter point is made in the last part of the verse.

The end of the verse is the only imperative in this section; everything else is stated as a matter of fact: we were once slaves to sin, but we have changed masters and are now slaves to righteousness. Given these facts, we are exhorted to live lives that are consistent with this new master-slave relationship, by presenting the parts of our bodies in slavery to righteousness. The words of comparison, "just as," encourage us to be as diligent in our slavery to righteousness as we once were in our slavery to impurity.

---

[30]Some manuscripts omit "unto lawlessness," but it was probably part of the original. It makes this former part of the statement symmetrical with the latter part, "leading to holiness."

[31]By translating ἀνομία as "wickedness" instead of "lawlessness," the NIV translation obscures this important point.

The imagery in this verse (slavery) is different, but the point is the same as 6:13. The implication is that our as-yet-unredeemed bodies will not easily give up their slavery to impurity; we must make a deliberate effort to conform them to the demands of righteousness. Thus this imperative is "a summons to battle and resistance" (Käsemann, 184).

Slavery to lawlessness and slavery to righteousness are exact opposites. As we have seen, righteousness as such means conformity to the relevant norm; the norm to which human beings must conform is the law of God. Thus the essence of moral righteousness is "satisfying the requirements of the law." Before conversion we fought the law; now we are committed to conforming our entire lives to it. Jesus has already satisfied the law's requirement for *penalty*, in our place; this is our justification. Now it is our responsibility to satisfy the law's requirement for *obedience*, which is our (progressive) sanctification.

Slavery to righteousness leads to holiness, says Paul. The latter word is ἁγιοσμός (*hagiosmos*), and there is some debate as to whether it means holiness (sanctification) as a process or as a state. It is probably the latter. The *process* of (progressive) sanctification, which simply means becoming more and more holy, is the same as obedience (v. 16) and the same as offering our bodies in slavery to righteousness. The final result of this process will be a *state* of complete sanctification or perfect holiness, which will occur when our bodies themselves are redeemed in the last day (8:23). See 6:22.

6:20 When you were slaves to sin, you were free from the control of righteousness. This statement continues to emphasize the before-and-after contrast of v. 19. The NIV does not translate the initial particle, *gar*, "for, because"; and thus the connection with v. 19 is obscured. Also, this statement is very condensed; it must be supplemented by an unstated conclusion. The entire thought seems to be this: "Just as you were once fully devoted to sinning, so must you now live as slaves to righteousness instead. For when you were slaves to sin, you were free with respect to righteousness; but now that you are slaves of righteousness, you must keep yourselves free from sin."

"Free with respect to righteousness" does not mean that as sinners we were free from the obligation to be righteous. It means

we were free from the desire and from an inner sense of responsibility to be such. We were "deaf to God's righteous demands and
incapable of responding to them" even if we had heard (Moo,
I:422). This is not a happy freedom, but one that is insidious and
deadly.

**6:21 What benefit did you reap at that time from the things
you are now ashamed of? Those things result in death!** The NIV
omits the word "therefore," which actually begins the thought contained in vv. 21-22. This shows that these verses are drawing a conclusion from something in the preceding context. They seem to be
expanding the thought concerning the respective consequences of
slavery to sin and slavery to righteousness stated in v. 19. There it
was said that slavery to impurity and lawlessness results in further
lawlessness (see the NASB, not the NIV), while slavery to righteousness leads to holiness or sanctification. Now, says v. 21, in view of
that, what are the relative benefits of these two forms of slavery?

The word translated "benefit" in vv. 21-22 is καρπός (*karpos*), or
"fruit." This could be intended in the neutral sense of "result" or
"consequence"; but more likely it is intended in the positive sense
of "benefit, advantage, profit." I.e., what good and beneficial result
is produced by these respective forms of slavery?

There is some disagreement as to how v. 21 should be punctu-
ated. Some take it like this: "What was the result of your former life
of slavery to sin? Actually the result at the time was just more and
more lawlessness, things of which you are now ashamed! And the
final end of such things is death." Others, including the NIV, take it
like this: "What positive benefit did you receive from your former
slavery to the sorts of things of which you are now ashamed?
Actually, none at all, for the only end result of those things is
death." The latter is probably the better way to read the verse.[32]

The acts and habits of impurity and lawlessness, which characterized our life of slavery to sin, are things of which we are now
ashamed. Shame is not the same as the feeling of guilt or the sense
of regret with respect to sin. It is more a feeling of inner pain and
humiliation and disgrace that causes us to wonder how we could

---

[32]See Lard, 217; Murray, I:235-236. For the former view see Cranfield,
I:327-328; Moo, I:422-423.

ever have done those things which seem so repulsive and hateful to us now. Such a feeling of shame with reference to our former sins is a necessary aspect of repentance and sanctification. To be without shame is to be under sin's dominion.

The question is, what good fruit did we reap from such a life of sin? The implied answer is, none! Its only immediate result was more and more sin, as v. 19 says; and its final result (τέλος, *telos*) is death. Sin produces death in every form, but especially it results in the eternal death that follows the final judgment (see 6:16).

6:22 But now that you have been set free from sin and have become slaves to God, the benefit you reap leads to holiness, and the result is eternal life. The verbs in the first part of this verse are aorist participles, referring to the decisive past event of conversion when we as slaves were transferred from one master to another. The thought is the same as that of v. 18, with one variation. Verse 18 says we became slaves to righteousness; here we "have become slaves to God." The difference is not significant; in truth these are two ways of saying the same thing. In this context it has been appropriate to speak of slavery to obedience (v. 16) and to righteousness because the alternative is stated as slavery to sin, impurity, and lawlessness. This verse is simply indicating that the ultimate source of the standards of obedience and righteousness to which we have become slaves is God himself. True slavery to righteousness is not blind obedience to some impersonal legal code; it is loving obedience to the personal God (see 7:6).

Being "set free from sin" is not just freedom from its penalty, which is justification, but also freedom from its power over us. The latter is the point here.

The latter part of the verse states the contrast with v. 21. Whereas our slavery to sin gave us no benefits at all, as slaves to God we have fruit unto holiness or sanctification. This is the same idea as v. 19b. The fruit that we reap from being slaves of righteousness is first of all a life of obedience and virtuous character, which Paul calls the "fruit of the Spirit" (Gal 5:22-23; see Matt 5:17). This ultimately results in the complete sanctification or perfect holiness of which v. 19b speaks, and finally culminates in eternal life. The life of holiness which we have now begun will by God's Spirit progress to a state of moral perfection that will never end.

The point of the contrast between slavery to sin and slavery to God in vv. 21-22 is to show us that the latter is infinitely preferable to the former, and to encourage us to be diligent and faithful in presenting our members as slaves to righteousness.

6:23 For the wages of sin is death, but the gift of God is eternal life . . . . This often-quoted verse concludes this section on the Christian's slavery to God, adding little that is new. In general v. 23a corresponds to 6:21, and v. 23b corresponds to 6:22. As in those two verses, the final results of the two kinds of slavery are contrasted: (eternal) death and eternal life, hell and heaven.

Death is described as the "wages of sin." In NT times the term here translated "wages" often meant "a soldier's pay," and some see that special meaning here. They believe it corresponds well with the word for "instruments" in v. 13, which often meant weapons of warfare. On the other hand, the term was also used for the allowance or pocket money given a slave by his master. Either of these special meanings could be intended, but more likely the word simply means wages in the general sense of compensation justly earned and deserved for labor performed.

Many agree that "the wages of sin" means that *sin* is the one who is paying the wages, and not the labor for which the wages are paid. If so then sin is personified as the general paying his soldiers, or the slave-owner paying his slaves (v. 17), or as an employer of a less specific sort. This is possible in view of the sustained imagery of slavery, but it is by no means certain. Whatever view one takes must not be allowed to cloud the fact that on Judgment Day God himself is the one who will give to the sinner the righteous judgment that is his due (2:5-6). Strictly speaking God is the one who will pay the sinner the wages he deserves for the sins he has committed.

In any case the main point here is not the one who pays the wages, but rather the sharp contrast between the *nature* of the rewards bestowed respectively upon the slave of sin and the slave of God. The former receives *wages*, the latter a *gift*. These two terms characterize the two distinct ways a person can relate to God, and also the two systems of salvation, law and grace. Under law a person relates to God in terms of wages; i.e., he receives what he actually deserves for his works. But every man has sinned (3:23), and what a sinner deserves is death. Under grace, however, a person relates to God in terms of a gift; i.e., his reward is not what he deserves but what God desires to give him. And even though we have all sinned and deserve death, God desires to give us eternal life.

Thus our choice between slavery to sin and slavery to God is in the end a choice between being paid the deserved wages of death, and receiving the free gift of eternal life from God's heart of grace.

Paul makes it clear that this free gift is possible only **in Christ Jesus our Lord.** Though eternal life is free to us, it is not free to God. It was paid for through the blood of Jesus. Thus this chapter ends with the same praise to the Redeemer with which chapter 5 began and ended (5:1, 21).

2. We Obey God from Our Hearts (7:1-6)

Are we free from the law? Yes, we are under grace instead (6:14). Does this mean sin is irrelevant, that we can be indifferent to the distinction between sin and virtue (6:15)? No, as slaves of God we are still under absolute obligation to obey his commandments (6:16-23). But if that is the case, then it would seem that "freedom from law" is a meaningless and misleading concept. No, says Paul, that is not so. He has already established that we are free from the law *as a way of salvation*, and nothing could be more meaningful than this. Now, in this brief paragraph, Paul makes the further point that grace frees us from the law by *changing our motivation* for obedience. Like a widow who remarries, we are still "under a husband," namely, Jesus Christ; but our obedience to him is from a willing and eager heart, not from the external constraint of legalistic motives.

Some do not see this paragraph as being closely related to ch. 6. It is "a fresh start," says Käsemann (187). On the contrary, Dunn is right: there is "no real break in the flow of argument at this point" (I:367).

7:1 Do you not know, brothers . . . ? Who are these "brothers"? Some take them to be Paul's fellow Jews, or the Jewish Christians at Rome in particular (DeWelt, 100-101; MacArthur, I:359). This fits well with the view that the "law" throughout this section is the Law of Moses. I cannot agree, however. The law from which we are freed is not just the Law of Moses, but law in any form. The "brothers" are Paul's fellow Christians in general. He has already addressed the entire church at Rome by this title of affection (see 1:13). In 9:3 he does use the term for Jews specifically, but qualifies it with the phrase "those of my own race."

. . . for I am speaking to men who know the law . . . . What Paul says here about the law is true of all law. Most of the initial recipients of Romans, whether Jews or Gentiles, would have known the Law of Moses. They would also have been quite familiar with Roman law. Those living in other times and cultures will know other law codes, both divine and human. But the principle Paul states in this verse is true of all law, as is the specific example given in vv. 2-3. Thus here he simply means, "Now, brothers, I'm sure you all know how law works."

Specifically, you know **that the law has authority over a man only as long as he lives[.]** "Have authority over" is κυριεύω (*kyrieuō*), the same word used in 6:9 of death and in 6:14 of sin. The idea is not authority as such, but rather power or dominion or control. In 6:14 Paul says sin shall not be in control of our lives, because we are not under law. Now he uses this word for law itself. Though *kurieuō* is not an inherently negative concept, its use in this context for the "unholy trinity" of sin, death, and law must not be overlooked.

What does it mean to be ruled or controlled by law, as far as one's relation to God is concerned? It means to regard God's law as the dominant spiritual category in one's life. God is viewed primarily as the Lawgiver, and law is the whip in his hand by which he keeps us in line. Our immediate concern each day is to keep from breaking this law, i.e., to keep from sinning. Not sinning is the only true key to peace, because the law decrees that death in hell is the penalty for sin. This threat of eternal death in hell fills us with terror, which becomes our primary motivation not to sin. We obey the law not because we love God and want to please him, but because we want to escape the law's penalty. So on the outside we try not to sin, while on the inside we hate the law that binds us and keeps us from doing the very things we secretly want to do. At the same time the very law that forbids us to sin and threatens us with hell if we do, because of our weakness *provokes* us to sin (7:5, 8), which only increases our fear of death and our dread of Judgment Day. In brief, law dominates a person when he regards his destiny as being determined by his response to law.

The principle Paul enunciates here, though, gives hope to those who are thus controlled by law. It is true of any law that its power and authority apply to a person only as long as he is alive. When a person dies, he is no longer within the sphere of the law. In v. 4 Paul will declare that we have indeed died, alluding to our death to sin discussed in 6:1-14; and this death to sin was a death to the law. We are no longer "under law" in the sense that it is no longer in control of our lives.

7:2 In vv. 2-3 Paul's intention is simply to illustrate the principle stated in v. 1. His point is not to give instructions about marriage and remarriage; nor is he constructing an allegory in which every detail is intended to be matched with some spiritual reality. He is simply showing that death sets one free from law.

For example, by law a married woman is bound to her husband as long as he is alive; but if her husband dies, she is released from the law of marriage. The word "married" literally means "under a husband" and is used only here in the NT. Paul probably chose this word because he is still talking about what it means to be "under law" and "under grace" (6:14). To be under law is like being "under" or married to one kind of husband, while being under grace is like being "under" or married to another kind of husband.

The point is that just about any law code, human or divine, has specific laws and regulations concerning marriage. Since the main person in Paul's illustration is a wife, he speaks here literally of "the law of the husband." A wife is bound by whatever the law says about her relationship to her husband as long as they are both alive. But if death occurs, such law is no longer relevant. The wife is no longer bound by it; she has been released from "the law of the husband."

One may notice that in the illustration the one who dies does not correspond with his counterpart in reality. In general the wife represents the sinner/Christian, while the first husband represents the law itself and the second husband Jesus Christ. But in the illustration the husband is the one who dies, while in reality the one who dies corresponds to the wife. This is not a problem unless we try to press the details of the illustration beyond its one main point, i.e., the effect of death on one's relation to the law.

So then, if she marries another man while her husband is still alive, she is called an adulteress. But if her husband dies, she is released from that law and is not an adulteress, even though she marries another man. Some have taken this passage as teaching that the only thing that can break the marriage bond is death; therefore divorce for any reason is wrong, and any remarriage while one's first spouse is still alive is adultery. But this is not Paul's point. Yes, he does in effect say that death breaks the marriage bond, freeing a person to remarry. But it is not his intention to discuss whether there may be other contingencies that also break the marriage bond, and he is not denying that these may exist.[33] He is concerned only with pointing out how death affects the marriage.

As long as a woman has one husband, she cannot marry another man without becoming an adulteress; this would be bigamy.[34] But if the husband dies, she can marry another man without committing adultery, since death makes all laws concerning adultery and bigamy irrelevant.

7:4 Having stated his principle in v. 1, and having illustrated it in vv. 2-3, Paul now draws his conclusion from the principle: **So, my brothers, you also died to the law through the body of Christ . . . .** Just as death within a marriage cancels the law governing that marriage, so does the death of our "old self" bring an end to the law's dominion over us. "You also died" is definitely a reference to the death to sin emphasized in 6:1-14; here Paul is adding the fact that our death to sin was also our death to law.

We must keep emphasizing that "law" here is not just the Law of Moses, but whatever law applies to any given person. Unless this is so, then this truth does not apply to most Christians, since most

---

[33]See Matt 19:9; 1 Cor 7:12-15.

[34]This assumes that the man is still *her husband*, and that no legitimate divorce has occurred. It is important to see that the situation Paul describes here is bigamy, not remarriage after divorce.

Christians have never been under the Law of Moses and thus cannot have died to it. Also, it is significant that Paul says *we* died, not the law. If he were talking about the Law of Moses, he could have said that "the law died," because in a real sense this is true of the Mosaic law (Eph 2:15). The point, however, is not the cessation of the law, but a change within the sinner himself, the cessation of the sinner's wrong attitude toward the law and his wrong use of the law.

"Died" is passive, i.e., "put to death" or "made to die" (NASB). This indicates that the change within us was not something we could muster from our own inner strength, but was something that required the working of God.

In what sense have we been put to death with reference to law? Certainly we are not under the law as a system of salvation, and we are dead to the penalty of the law. This is true because of "the body of Christ," in that "he himself bore our sins in his body on the tree" (1 Pet 2:24). Thus our objective relationship with the law has been changed by virtue of Christ's propitiatory sacrifice.

But this is not the whole story, nor even the main point here. When we truly come to understand these *objective* changes in our relationship to the law, the result is a *subjective* change in our attitude toward it. The law no longer controls our concept of our relation to God and to salvation. We are no longer in bondage to the idea that our acceptance with God is determined by our performance as measured by the law. We are no longer under constant pressure to make ourselves "good enough" to go to heaven. We are no longer slaves to the fear of death and judgment (Heb 2:15). We are no longer constrained to obey the law from these legalistic motives.

Like a wife who remarries after her husband dies, we who are put to death with reference to the law immediately enter into a new "marriage," as it were, with Jesus Christ. You died, **that you might belong to another, to him who was raised from the dead, in order that we might bear fruit to God.** Whether we think of our relationship with Jesus in terms of marriage is not the point here. Some take it this way, and the Bible elsewhere makes ample use of the marriage metaphor as an appropriate way to picture the relation between God and his people (Dunn, I:362).

The main point is that we have come to "belong to" Christ, as the one "who was raised from the dead." Paul refers to Jesus in resurrection terms to remind us that in our union with him we also were raised from the dead (6:4-6). This gave us a whole new perspective on the law. We are like a wife who used to be bound only by duty to a mean and miserly husband, but who is now willingly and joyfully united to a new, loving, generous husband and cannot do too much to please him. Even so, instead of producing dead works from a dead heart as driven by the law's threats, we as Christians are now alive in our spirits so that we may bear the fruit of good thoughts, words, and deeds, motivated only by a love for our Lord and a desire to please him.

Some see the reference to "fruit" as a continuation of the marriage metaphor, since in the Bible children are often called "fruit" (see Smith, I:96). Others see it simply as a reference to people as trees and their works as fruit (Matt 7:16-20). The Christian bears good fruit to God through his willing obedience to God's commands. When we were dead in sin we produced bad fruit; even our works that looked good on the outside were like shiny apples filled with worms and rottenness within, since they sprang from legalistic and selfish motives. But under grace the fruit we present to God is the "obedience of faith" (1:5) motivated by love (John 14:15), which is sweet and pleasing to his taste.

7:5 For when we were controlled by the sinful nature, the sinful passions aroused by the law were at work in our bodies, so that we bore fruit for death. This and v. 6 are an elaboration of v. 4 and thus give us further insight into what it means to be dead to the law and alive under grace. Following the familiar before-and-after format, v. 5 tells us what it was like before we died to the law, and v. 6 describes how it is now.

"Controlled by the sinful nature" is literally the simple phrase "in the flesh." This expression is used in different senses in various texts. Sometimes it means life in this present world, in this present body (2 Cor 10:3; Gal 2:20). In 2:28 it refers in a neutral sense to the physical nature as distinct from the spirit. A common view is that "flesh" (σάρξ, sarx), especially in this part of Romans, means "sinful nature," or all the sinful tendencies and inclinations that were characteristic of our pre-Christian life and which still "wage war against the soul" (1 Pet 2:11). This view does not limit "flesh" to the physical body but takes it as including the whole person. As such it is equated with the "old self" and the "body of sin" in 6:6. It is "human nature as controlled and directed by sin" (Murray, I:244). This is the view in the NIV here in 7:5.

I disagree. In the introduction to this section I have stated my conclusion that *sarx* in this context is not some generalized sinful nature but is rather the physical body, especially viewed as sin-weakened and unredeemed and thus as a source of evil desires (6:12) and "sinful passions." Thus to be "in the flesh" means to be governed by our bodily desires in such a way that they are the center of our lives and are promiscuously indulged without regard for moral boundaries. This was our pre-Christian state, says Paul. Instead of controlling our bodies, our bodies controlled us. The NIV properly translates the preposition "in" (ἐν, *en*) as "controlled by."

The reference to "sinful passions" (literally, "the passions of sins") confirms this interpretation. The word for "passions" (πάθημα, *pathēma*) often means "suffering," but can mean strong desires and emotional feelings in general, as here. The word does not necessarily have a negative connotation; but here (and in Gal 5:24) it does, as indicated by the qualifier, "passions *of sins*." Paul says these sinful passions "were at work in our bodies," literally, "in our members" (see 6:13, 19). Thus to be "controlled by the flesh" means to allow sinful passions to have free reign in the members of our bodies. Such passions include those that are directly associated with the body, such as sexual lust, gluttony, and slothfulness. Hendriksen says they also include such things as anger, hatred, ill will, jealousy, envy and unreasonable fear — all of which may arise in the spirit but which "express themselves physically: the jealous eye, the clenched fist, the hateful gesture, etc." (I:217).

At the time when we were controlled by these things, we "bore fruit for death." In other words, their consequence for our lives was death in every sense (6:21, 23). This is in contrast with bearing fruit for God in v. 4.

A key question here is, what does it mean to say these sinful passions were "aroused by the law"? This is important because it is a description of our condition "under law" (6:14), before we "died to the law" (7:4). The Greek text says simply that the sinful passions

worked in our members "through the law." Some take this to mean
only that the law *reveals* certain passions to be sinful (Lard, 225; see
3:20; 7:7). Others take it to mean that the law in some sense *stimu-
lates* or excites these passions, as in the NIV's "aroused by"
(Cranfield, I:337; Moo, I:443-444). The latter is probably the
intended sense (see 7:7-13).

This does not mean that the law is *supposed* to stimulate sin, and
in the pure heart it does not do so. But in our fallen, sin-weakened
condition, this is exactly what it did. Very often, to the sinful heart,
just knowing something is wrong or against the law makes the
doing of it all the more attractive. As Prov 9:17 says, "Stolen water
is sweet." Young people who have chafed at the rules of their strict
parents, when they leave home cannot wait to indulge in what was
once forbidden to them. This is part of the power that sin *as lawlessness* has over us; it implants within us the spirit of rebellion against
God's law, so that the law itself becomes the stimulus for doing the
very thing it forbids.

7:6 This verse goes beyond a mere contrast with v. 5, and
affirms that we have died to the law in a general sense. **But now, by
dying to what once bound us, we have been released from the
law . . . .** The definitive turning point in our lives was the moment
of our death: our death to sin (6:2) and to the law (7:4). Here Paul
is thinking especially of the latter. In our pre-Christian life the law
bound us by inciting us to sin, by imposing its penalty upon us, by
limiting us to a futile effort to save ourselves by our own obedience, and thus by restricting us to legalistic motives even when we
tried to obey. But by dying with Christ we were set free from the
law in all these senses.

In the rest of this verse Paul focuses on one specific result of
our being freed from the law, namely, **so that we serve in the new
way of the Spirit, and not in the old way of the written code.** The
word for "serve" is δουλεύω (*douleuō*), which means "to serve as a
slave, to obey." Though released from the law in some ways, we are
still slaves and still owe to God an absolute obedience to his commandments. Thus freedom from the law is not freedom from obedience, but freedom from a negative, legalistic attitude toward obedience and toward the law as such.

This change is described as a transition from "oldness" to

"newness." Formerly we served "in the old way of the written code," or literally, "in oldness of (the) letter." This means that we regarded the law as a cold, impersonal, abstract code of behavior, and that we obeyed it only because it threatened punishment if we did not. We viewed it as detached from the personal heart of God, and thus our obedience was not from our own heart. We obeyed it as an unwilling slave obeys a hated master, conforming ourselves to it externally but not in our spirits.

But now we serve, literally, "in newness of spirit." The word "newness" is the same as in 6:4, "newness of life" (NASB). Many see "Spirit" as referring to the Holy Spirit, and thus capitalize it (NASB, NIV). This would mean that our new and willing service to God is possible only through the enabling power of the Holy Spirit. This is certainly true, and this point is emphatically made in chapter 8. Also, in 2:29 and 2 Cor 3:6 the Spirit/letter contrast does seem to refer to the Holy Spirit.

However, in my judgment "spirit" in this context is better understood as referring to our own spirit or soul or inner man. A major emphasis of this whole section of Romans is the fact that our conversion includes the regeneration and renewing of the spirit. Thus our "newness of life" (6:4) is a newness of our spirits, which have been made alive toward God and filled with a positive attitude toward his law.[35] This results in a major change in our motivation for obedience: from "have to" to "want to," from "got to" to "get to." We now obey as willing slaves who have voluntarily attached ourselves as life-slaves to God because of our grateful love to him (see Deut 15:16-17).

These last two verses are a general description of before-and-after as experienced by every believer. Paul is not talking here about the difference between the Old and New Covenants, the Law of Moses versus the "law of the gospel" (contra DeWelt, 100; and Moo, I:445). The change he describes took place to a degree in the hearts of OT believers; it certainly takes place in the conversion experience of every Christian, with or without reference to the Law of Moses.[36]

---

[35]See Lard, 227; DeWelt, 102-103; MP, 351.

[36]There is a sense in which the two covenants differ in terms of letter and Spirit (2 Cor 3), but that is not Paul's point in Rom 7:5-6.

C. DOES GRACE MEAN THAT LAW IS BAD? NO! (7:7-13)

This final objection to grace based on a fear of antinomianism focuses on the nature of the law as such. Is there something wrong with law? Is it inherently bad or harmful? Are its consequences purely negative?

Thus far Paul has certainly presented God's law in a less than favorable light. It is unfavorably contrasted with the Spirit or spirit (2:29; 7:6). It is unable to justify sinners (3:20, 28). It is closely associated with sin (4:15; 5:20; 7:5). Believers are not under law; we have died to it and have been set free from it (6:14; 7:4, 6). Stott observes that all of this "must have sounded to some like full-blown antinomianism" (198).

Thus the main point of this section is to defend the integrity of God's law. Despite all the seemingly negative things said about it, the problem is not with law but with sin. Sin, again personified as an opposing tyrant, uses its sinister power to abuse and exploit God's good law for its own negative purposes. Like the serpent in Gen 3:1-6, it distorts the law in a way that leads to sin and death; but this does not mean that the law itself is a bad thing. Indeed, Paul specifically declares that it is "holy, righteous and good" (7:12).

The major exegetical problems in this section stem from Paul's use of the first person singular. Who is the "I" whose experiences are being described here?[37] Some say Paul is putting himself in the place of Adam and speaking in his name. Some say the "I" stands for the collective nation of Israel; others say it stands for mankind as a whole. Still others say that Paul is speaking autobiographically, i.e., he is giving intimate details of his own personal spiritual history. I believe this last view is the correct one. It is the common-sense way of interpreting first person singular, especially in the absence of any specific reference to Adam or to Israel.

The next question is whether the spiritual events described here are true only of Paul, or whether they are true of Paul as the representative of a larger group. I along with most modern interpreters take the latter view.

---

[37]For fuller discussions of the possibilities see Cranfield, I:342-344; Moo, I:450-452; and Stott, 198-201.

But this leads to another question: what is this larger group of which Paul's experiences are representative? Some say Paul is describing his life as a Jew under the Law of Moses, and thus as a representative of all Jews under the Law.[38] Others say his experiences are those of all people when confronted by the law of God in any of its forms, be it the Mosaic Law or the moral law in general.[39] I accept the latter view, which is in keeping with the fact that Paul has been using the term *law* in this general sense at key points throughout the letter thus far.

A final question remains: what particular stage in his life is Paul describing?[40] One possibility is that he is referring to his "coming of age" as symbolized in the *bar mitzvah* ceremony, when every thirteen-year-old Jewish boy formally became a "son of the commandment" and accepted personal responsibility for his own behavior. This would be representative of the time when every person reaches the age of accountability. Another possibility is that Paul is describing the time later in his life when the law awakened in him a true conviction of the seriousness of his sins, which opened the door to his conversion. This would be representative of a similar stage through which any sinner must pass in order to become a believer.

In my judgment the former view is the correct one here. The main objection to it is that by virtue of his upbringing there would never have been a time when Paul was "apart from law" (7:9) in the sense of ignorant innocence. But unless Paul was in some sense divine, this is surely not true. Paul's psychological development as a child would not have been qualitatively different from that of anyone else. At some point (probably long before his *bar mitzvah* at age thirteen) he became accountably aware of God's nature as Lawgiver and Judge, of the Law of Moses as the law of *God*, and of his own identity as a sinner condemned by that law.

On the other hand, there is a serious objection to the other view, namely, its explanation of the *death* brought about by the law

[38]Moo defends a version of this view (I:452-456). See also Godet, 280.
[39]Others who take this view include Lard, 229-230; Cranfield, I:341-344; Murray, I:255; Morris, 277; MacArthur, I:368; Stott, 201; Smith, I:102.
[40]See Moo, I:450-451; Stott, 199-200.

(7:9-11). According to Murray (I:251, 255) and Morris (277, 282), as a self-righteous Pharisee Paul was "alive" in the sense that he had no true conviction of his sin; he was self-complacent, self-assured, and unperturbed. But at some point the law brought him under conviction and killed this sense of self-confidence and complacency; this is the death of which Paul speaks. This view is unacceptable, though. For one thing, as Stott notes (199-200), "we have no independent evidence of a spiritual crisis in Paul before his Damascus road encounter with the risen Lord," which could hardly be called a confrontation with the law. Also, "alive apart from law" would be an extremely odd way to describe the attitude of self-righteousness and false complacency, and it certainly has no parallel anywhere else in Paul's writing. But most significantly, such a definition of "death" is completely at odds with the context, in which death is pictured as a bad or negative thing. Indeed, the fact that the law in a sense produces this death is one of the very bases for the allegation that the law itself is bad (7:13). But the kind of death described by Murray and Morris, while not the saving "death to sin" of 6:2, is surely a good and positive step in that direction and thus is inconsistent with the death depicted here.

Thus we must conclude that Paul is talking here not about his or anyone else's preconversion experience, but about the time when he like all of us passed from innocent childhood to the age of accountability and personal guilt before God. This is the sense in which he says, "I died" (7:9). His main point, though, is not to present a lesson about the age of accountability but to exonerate the law from responsibility for this death and for any other evil result.

7:7 This objection is introduced with the same formula as the previous two: first the opening question, **What shall we say then?**; then the specific objection: **Is the law sin?**; finally the emphatic negative, **Certainly not!** The objection has to do with the very nature of law.[41] Given the seemingly negative things said about it thus far, is the law somehow included within the sphere of sin or things sinful? Is it in league with sin, on the side of sin? Is it bad or sinful?

---

[41]This refers not just to the Law of Moses, but to God's law in general (contra Lard, 228; and Dunn, I:379).

By no means, says Paul. There is absolutely no sense in which this is true.

Indeed I would not have known what sin was except through the law.[42] The word translated "indeed" (ἀλλά, *alla*) can be taken two ways. It can introduce a strong contrast: "on the contrary" (NASB), or it can introduce a qualification: "yet" (NRSV). Here the latter seems to be the case. I.e., the law is definitely not sinful in any way, but still it *does* have an important connection with sin: it gives us a *knowledge* of sin.

Is this knowledge purely cognitive or also experiential? God's law certainly gives us a cognitive (purely intellectual) knowledge of sin. I.e., its commandments tell us what specific acts and what kinds of acts are sinful (3:20; 1 John 3:4). Also, because the law includes penalties for disobedience, it gives us an inescapable knowledge of the wrongness of these sinful acts. And, because the law is given to us by God, we are painfully aware that sin is wrongdoing against God himself.

But the knowledge of which Paul speaks is more than this, as the rest of this section shows. Except through the law, he is saying, I would not have *experienced* the presence of sin in my own life. I may have been doing wrong things, but I would not have *known* them to be wrong without the testimony of the law. When I read in God's law that certain behavior is wrong, and when I see that very behavior in my life, I have a personal consciousness of the fact that I am a sinner; I have a sense of personal sinfulness before God.

This is not the same as being *convicted* of sin as a positive step toward repentance and conversion, though (contra MacArthur, I:366-367). It is simply the consciousness of being a sinner that makes us without excuse before God (1:20; 2:1). How we deal with this consciousness is a different issue altogether.

For I would not have known what coveting really was if the law had not said, "Do not covet." The previous sentence is a general truth; this is a specific example of that truth and explains how it is so. The example Paul chooses is the last of the Ten Command-ments: "Do not covet." Paul's first knowledge of this commandment

---

[42]As explained in the introduction to this section, the first person singu-lar describes Paul's own personal experience as typical of all men.

no doubt came through the Law of Moses, but it is amply repeated in the New Covenant Scriptures (13:9; Gal 5:16; 1 Pet 2:11). Also, even pagans know that such behavior is wrong (1:24, 32); it is part of the law written on the heart (2:15).

The word for covetousness (ἐπιθυμία, *epithymia*) means "strong desire" (see 1:24). It is used for sexual lust but can also include illicit desires of all kinds, such as are enumerated in Exod 20:17 (cf. 7:8, "every kind of covetous desire"). It is the "desire for something forbidden" (Dunn, I:379). Since desire as such is natural, without the law to tell us which desires are wrong, such desires could be present in our hearts without our knowing them as sinful.

Why does Paul choose this particular example? For one thing, the sin of *epithymia* is appropriate because it is the root of all sin, says James 1:14-15. Also, it was no doubt the particular commandment that first awakened Paul to the reality of sin in his own life. Perhaps he was like the rich young man who once told Jesus that he had kept all the commandments since he was a boy (Mark 10:20). Jesus' response (v. 21) was designed to force him to confront the tenth commandment and thus his own sinfulness.

Thus the law makes us conscious of what sin is and conscious of being a sinner. Does this make the law bad? In no way! This is, among other things, exactly what the law is supposed to do. Unpleasant though it may be, it is a necessary and holy function of God's law.

7:8 But this is not the whole picture of the relation between law and sin. Surely no one can object to the propriety of law as the source of our knowledge of sin (7:7), but now in 7:8-11 Paul describes a relation between law, sin, and death that is much more subtle and which at first glance appears to make the law responsible for the sinner's death. The point Paul makes, though, is that the real culprit is not the law but *sin itself*, which is here personified as a powerful tyrant who seeks our ruin.

But sin, seizing the opportunity afforded by the commandment, produced in me every kind of covetous desire. This is not just a restatement or an explanation of v. 7. Here the law is pictured not simply as revealing and defining sin, but as in some sense *provoking* the very sinful behavior that it condemns. However, this is neither the law's purpose nor its proper function. It does so only indirectly, as an instrument wielded deceitfully by the tyrant sin itself.

The subject of the sentence is *sin* (ἁμαρτία, *hamartia*) as a personified, purposeful power, which some see as standing for Satan himself (Lard, 230; DeWelt, 104). The word for "opportunity" (ἀφορμή, *aphormē*) has a military connotation; it means a base or bridgehead for a military operation, a springboard or starting point for an expedition or attack — and thus in a general way, an occasion or opportunity. Thus sin is pictured as an enemy who is using the law itself, specifically the command against covetousness, to launch an attack upon us.

The prepositional phrase "by [διά, *dia*] the commandment" is taken by the NIV and others as modifying "seizing the opportunity." Others take it as modifying "produced" ("accomplished, worked, brought about"), i.e., sin produced every sort of lust in me through the commandment itself. The latter seems to be the intended meaning,[43] and is more in harmony with vv. 5, 11, and 13. Either way the perversity of sin is emphasized: it seizes upon the very commandment that forbids covetousness as an instrument for producing it.

How can the commandment be an opportunity for sin? In what sense can sin produce disobedience in a person through the very means that is designed to prevent it? The most obvious answer is that of Prov 9:17, "Stolen water is sweet." I.e., prohibitions awaken the desire to break them (see Morris, 280; Stott, 203). "The prohibition has for its effect to fix the object strongly on the imagination, and thereby to lend it a new charm" (Godet, 274). This is not the fault of the commandment, but is a possibility inherent in the freedom of the will.

Cranfield (I:350) well says that the dynamic here is not merely a psychological connection between the prohibition of a thing and the desirability of the thing as such. Rather, after the pattern of Gen 3:1-6 and through Satan's temptation, the commandment (*any* commandment) is misinterpreted as taking away freedom and preventing self-realization, and therefore becomes an occasion for resentment against the Lawgiver. This arouses a spirit of rebellion,

---

[43]See Cranfield, I:350; Dunn, I:380; Murray, I:250; Morris, 280.

which then uses the commandment as an opportunity to express itself. See 7:5 above.

For apart from law, sin is dead. "Apart from law" means "in the absence of law; where no law exists." The "law" here is not just the Law of Moses, but *any* law of God. This is similar to 4:15, "Where there is no law there is no transgression." The point in 7:8 is somewhat stronger, however. 4:15 says that nothing counts as sin without a law to identify it as such. Here the point is that sin *as sin* lies dormant and ineffective, lacking in power and in this sense "dead," without the law as a weapon to use against the sinner. In such a case there is no commandment to be exploited as a temptation to further sin.

7:9 As stated in the introduction above, this verse is best understood as referring to Paul's "coming of age," or reaching the age of accountability. Also, he presents his experience not as something unique, but as representative of human beings in general. The main point is the role of law in this event.

Once I was alive apart from law . . . . This refers to "the days of innocent childhood" (DeWelt, 106; see MP, 353), i.e., the childhood of the individual, not of the human race (contra Cranfield, I:351; Dunn, I:381-382). This is the period when a child is living under the original grace of Jesus (5:12-19), before he comes to understand the significance of living in a world subject to the law of the Creator.

This is the meaning of "apart from law." It does not mean "apart from the existence of law," since there has never been such a time in human history.[44] Nor does it mean "apart from a knowledge of the law"; children can learn the ten commandments at a very young age, and can know that it is wrong to break them. "Apart from law" refers rather to that age of innocence before a child understands the law to be the law *of God*, and before he realizes that breaking God's law has *eternal consequences*.

"Alive" refers to the spiritual state of the individual (the child) before he reaches accountability. His inner man (the soul or spirit) has not yet become dead in his transgressions and sins (Eph 2:1),

---

[44]Even Adam and Eve were created with "the requirements of the law" written on their hearts (2:14-15).

and he is not yet under the penalty of eternal condemnation. The child in this state does not need conversion; he does not need baptism. If he dies in this state, he dies "alive" and thus is saved.

. . . but when the commandment came . . . . This does not refer to the command given to Adam in Gen 2:16-17 (contra Dunn, I:383), nor to the coming of the Law of Moses, including the tenth commandment (contra Cranfield, I:352), nor to the pre-redemptive conviction that prepares one for conversion (contra MacArthur, I:372; Morris, 282). It refers to the coming of the commandment into the consciousness of the child, the time when he first understands its full significance as a commandment *of God* with eternal condemnation for disobedience. In Paul's case the command "Do not covet" awakened within him this full consciousness of sin.

. . . sin sprang to life . . . . The word here is ἀναζάω (*anazaō*). The prefix *ana-* can give it the meaning "come to life *again*" (as in Luke 15:24), or "revive" (NRSV). But the word can also mean just "come to life" or "become alive" (NASB). The NIV correctly follows the latter sense. That sin "springs to life" in a child coming to the age of accountability does not mean that it was already present in the sense of a state of original sin derived from Adam. It means rather that the *potential* for sin is present in the heart of every free-will creature, just waiting to take on a life of its own.

. . . and I died. (Some texts and versions place this statement at the beginning of v. 10.) Here and in the first part of the verse ("I was alive"), Paul uses the pronoun ἐγώ (*egō*), "I." We should not make too much of this. The main point is the comparison of the self with the personified power of sin: Once *sin* was dead (v. 8) and "*I* was alive; but when *sin* came to life, *I* died" (see vv. 17, 20).

This is not the redemptive death *to* sin of 6:2, but the event of becoming dead *in* sin (Eph 2:1, 5; Col 2:13). This includes being placed under the sentence of death as a penalty for sin (Lard, 231, 233; DeWelt, 104-105); it also includes entering a state of spiritual death or separation from God, a state of helplessness before the law's demands and sin's lures. In short, it means the infliction of sin's "double trouble."[45]

---

[45]As explained in the introduction, this death is *not* the pre-conversion dawning of conviction when the old Pharisaical Paul died, along with all his false illusions of innocence and complacent self-righteousness (contra

7:10 The problem that Paul is addressing here is not the fact of this death as such, but the fact that *the law* somehow seems responsible for it. He has declared that the law is not bad or sinful (7:7a). Indeed, it performs the good and necessary function of defining sin and exposing its reality in our lives (7:7b). But the law also in a real sense provokes us to sin and brings about our spiritual death (7:8-9). This leads to an ironic paradox: **I found that the very commandment that was intended to bring life actually brought death.**

"The very commandment" refers to "Do not covet" (7:7), but it stands for the law of God in general. God's law is "intended to bring life" in the sense that obedience to it was meant to be the way of maintaining a right relationship with God and continuing in the blessings of life in his presence.[46] The law can actually accomplish this purpose only when obeyed perfectly, however. Once sin has entered and brought about spiritual death, the law is impotent to restore the sinner to a state of spiritual life. Only grace can do this.

7:11 For sin, seizing the opportunity afforded by the commandment, deceived me, and through the commandment put me to death. This verse basically condenses the ideas already presented in vv. 8-9, and thus reaffirms the conclusion of v. 10, that there is a sense in which the law brings death. (On "seizing the opportunity," see 7:8.) But Paul makes one thing very clear: the real culprit is sin, not the law. Sin is personified as a formidable and powerful enemy who attacks us and kills us. The law is only the instrument used by sin to accomplish this awful deed. Thus sin, not the law, is the true source of death.

The new element here is the idea that sin "deceived me," and that it deceived me "by the commandment."[47] How does sin deceive through the commandment? The reference to deceit draws attention to Gen 3:1-6 (see 2 Cor 11:3; 1 Tim 2:14). There Satan

---

Hendriksen, I:223; MacArthur, I:373; Morris, 282; Murray, I:251). Such a death would be a positive blessing; but in this context the death in which the law has a part is quite negative, otherwise Paul would not have to defend the law for its role in effecting it.

[46]See Lev 18:5; Deut 4:1; Ezek 20:11; Matt 19:17; Luke 10:28; Rom 10:5.

[47]"By the commandment" modifies "deceived," as the symmetrical structure of the verse shows. Literally it says, "For sin, seizing the opportunity, *through the commandment deceived me* and *through it killed me.*"

used the commandment of God (Gen 2:16-17) to raise questions about God's motives in making certain things "off limits." In this way the prohibition was used not only to stimulate a curious desire to experience what was forbidden (7:8), but also to arouse in Eve a resentment toward God for denying her something seemingly so desirable and beneficial. In the same way sin continues to use the law to deceive us, clouding our eyes to its life-giving purposes and provoking us to disobey it in resentment toward the Lawgiver and in a futile quest for self-fulfillment. The result is only death. "By thus using the divine prohibition to provoke disobedience, sin in effect made the commandment a force for death" (Dunn, I:402).

7:12 So then, the law is holy, and the commandment is holy, righteous and good. Here Paul refers to both "the law" and "the commandment." The former refers to the entire law, or the will of God in general (not just the Mosaic law); the latter refers to each individual commandment of the law, including "Do not covet." With regard to its character, what is true of the whole law is true of all its parts, and what is true of each part is true of the whole.

This verse along with v. 13 is the definitive answer to the question in v. 7. "Is the law sin?" Absolutely not! Rather, it is *holy, just,* and *good*. These attributes apply to the law because they are the attributes of God, who is its author and source. "As holy, just, and good it reflects the character of God and is the transcript of his perfection" (Murray, I:253).

To say that God is *holy* (in the moral sense) means that his nature is totally separate from sin, the very opposite from sin (GRe, 251-254). Thus the same must be true of his holy law, which is derived from and based upon his own nature. It too is the very opposite of sin; it stands "as far away from sin as possible" (Morris, 283), contrary to the antinomian accusation of v. 7.

The law in all its commandments is also *just*. To say that God is just means that his actions always are in perfect conformity with his nature (GRe, 211-215). The law reflects God's justice in that those who follow its commandments will also be conforming their actions to the perfect norm of God's nature. Thus because of its just nature it produces not sin but righteousness.

The law and its commandments are also *good*. God's goodness is his benevolence, kindness and good will toward his creatures; he desires only what is best for us (GRe, 322-323; GRu, 289-291). To say that his law is good means that it is intended in every way for man's benefit, not his ruin. When we "uphold the law" (3:31) and allow it to fulfill its proper functions, it will only bless us.

7:13[48] But does this not contradict one of Paul's main points in this section, namely, that the commandment has produced death in us? The death of which he speaks is certainly not a beneficial death. Thus how can that which produced it be called "good" in any sense?

But is it really the case that the commandment is the source of my spiritual death? **Did that which is good, then, become death to me? By no means!** Paul has already stated in vv. 8, 11 that the real culprit, the true source of death, is sin, not the law. Sin deceitfully and perversely *uses* the law as a means of provoking disobedience, which leads to death; but this is not the law's own true purpose. The blame lies with sin, not with the law.[49]

To make this point perfectly clear, Paul now reiterates this idea, as stated earlier in vv. 8, 11: **But in order that sin might be recognized as sin, it produced death in me through what was good . . . .** The "good" thing is the law of God; the "death" produced in me or to me is the inner spiritual death of a depraved spirit as well as the penalty of eternal death in hell. The instrument "through" which it is produced is the good commandment. But sin itself is the true and ultimate source of this death.

Why does God allow his law to be used in this perverted way? Is any divine purpose accomplished thereby? This verse actually contains two purpose clauses. The first is stated here: "in order that sin might be recognized as sin." I.e., by its perverse use of the law its true character *as sin* is completely exposed; it is shown to be the evil that it truly is.

---

[48]Some take this verse to be part of the next section, but its content is closely tied in with v. 12 and follows up on its thought.

[49]Actually the blame lies with the sinner, for allowing himself to be deceived by sin. If a person jumps off a building and seriously injures himself, he cannot blame the law of gravity; he can blame only his own stupidity. If a criminal is sent to prison for theft or murder, he cannot blame the law; he knew in advance that such an act would bring upon him the penalty prescribed by the law for such behavior.

This is allowed to happen **so that through the commandment sin might become utterly sinful.** This is the other purpose clause. Again this takes place "through the commandment." I.e., by using the commandment to provoke sin and produce death, sin not only simply exposes itself as sin, but magnifies beyond measure the depths of its perversity and ungodliness.

Thus Paul ends his defense of the law. Even though sin uses the law for its own murderous ends, the law itself remains pure and holy and good. A person could take a hypodermic needle and inject poison into someone's body, but this does not make the needle bad. Someone could be beaten to death with a fire extinguisher, but that would not make the extinguisher bad. The evil lies in the wielder of these instruments, and all the more so for using something designed for good to produce such a baneful result.

II. 7:14-8:13 — GRACE GIVES VICTORY OVER SIN

The previous section dealt with certain antinomian conclusions that some might think are encouraged by grace, especially by the fact that sinners are justified by faith. The idea is that somehow grace must negate the authority of the law, and must encourage and increase sin. Paul emphatically denies that this is so.

In this section the subject is still the connection between grace and sin, but with a different focus. Rather than taking a defensive stance against possible objections to grace, Paul goes on the offensive and shows that, rather than encouraging sin, grace provides the means of victory over it. He acknowledges that sin is still present in the life of the Christian and is the source of serious tension and struggle (7:14-25), but he affirms that God's grace gives us victory over sin through the power of the indwelling Holy Spirit (8:1-13).

A. THE CHRISTIAN CONTINUES
TO STRUGGLE AGAINST SIN (7:14-25)

Many see no break between vv. 13 and 14, and include all of 7:7-25 under a single heading. I see a significant break occurring at this point, however, with a new section beginning at v. 14. The change is subtle but real. In vv. 7-13 the main subject is God's law, and personal spiritual history is secondary. In vv. 14-25 this is reversed. The law is still in the picture, but the main point is our struggle to obey it and to conquer sin. As Bruce remarks (150), "There is an inward tension here which was absent from verses 7-13."

In this section Paul continues to use the first person singular. As in vv. 7-13, he is recounting his own spiritual experience as representative or typical of us all. However, a new element appears in vv. 14-25: the use of the present tense. This raises the much-debated question as to what period of his life and others' lives is in view. Is the present tense to be taken at face value, indicating that Paul is describing his present Christian experience? Or is it just a dramatic way of portraying some past stage of his life? The question is usually couched this way: do these verses apply to an unregenerate sinner, or do they apply to the regenerate Christian? This is one of the major issues in the interpretation of Romans.

Here I will summarize the major approaches to this question, which fall into three main categories. (1) The first view is that, from Paul's perspective at the time of his writing, he is describing his (and others') past history as an unregenerate person. This view has several versions. (a) The main one is that these verses refer to the life of an unregenerate, unsaved person as such. This is quite a common view, held, e.g., by most early church fathers, the early Augustine, John Wesley, Godet, and Sanday and Headlam. It is based on several significant considerations. For example, Paul's strong negative statements about himself (7:14b, 18a, 24a, 25b) seem inconsistent with the realities of the Christian life as described elsewhere (e.g., 6:2, 6-7, 11, 17-18, 22). Also, the transition from v. 13 to v. 14 does not seem to be dramatic enough to indicate a shift from the life of the unregenerate (7:7-13) to the life of the regenerate. On the other hand, the transition from ch. 7 to ch. 8 seems much more radical and is the likely point for the change of perspective (see Godet, 281-282). Also, the struggle depicted here seems more unsuccessful than victorious; the outcome suggests defeat rather than victory (see Moo, I:472). (b) A second version of this view is that Paul is describing the experience of the unregenerate or unsaved Jew living under the Law of Moses, using himself as an example (Moo, I:474). (c) A third version is that the persons described here are unregenerate but have reached the point where they are under strong conviction about their sins and are desiring salvation. Though still unregenerate, they are on the threshold of regeneration. This is the view of seventeenth-century Pietism (see Moo, I:470-471) and Lloyd-Jones (229-257, esp. 255-257). For good critiques of this first approach, see Nygren (284-296) and Hendriksen (I:226-227).

(2) The second approach also says that Paul is describing an episode from his past spiritual history, but it was a time when he was saved or regenerated. (a) One version of this is that these verses speak of the life of regenerate or saved Jews living under the Law of Moses, i.e., OT believers. This is Stott's view (208-210). (b) Another version is that the verses depict an early, immature stage in a Christian's life which is transcended when he fully surrenders to the Holy Spirit. But as long as he depends only on his own strength, he fights a losing battle with sin. This seems to be Bruce's view (150-153, 156-158).

(3) The third approach to this issue is that Paul is talking about his present experience as a regenerated, mature believer, and by extension the experience of all believers. This was the view of the later Augustine, most of the Reformers, Lard, and MP. It is the view of many modern commentators such as Hendriksen, Cranfield, MacArthur, Morris, and Murray. I believe this is the correct view and will now summarize the reasons for it.

First, the major theme of the main section in which this passage occurs (chs 6-8) has to do with the Christian life.

Second, the use of the present tense should be taken at face value. The sudden shift from past to present between vv. 13 and 14 indicates a change in perspective. If Paul were continuing to talk about some past stage of his life, he would only be confusing the issue by using present tense.

Third, the things Paul says about the law of God and about his own inner life are completely incompatible with the heart and life of an unregenerate man as described elsewhere in the Bible. He upholds the goodness of the law and affirms his joyful desire to obey it. He declares his hatred of sin and his desire not to do it. All of this is contrary to the mind of the unregenerate (1:18-3:20; 8:5-8). At the same time Paul sorrowfully confesses his weaknesses and failures in his attempts to obey, and describes himself in the most humble and self-effacing terms. This corresponds to his other humble descriptions of himself as a Christian (1 Cor 15:9; Eph 3:8; 1 Tim 1:15), and contrasts with his pre-Christian attitude of self-righteousness (Phil 3:6; Gal 1:13-14).

Fourth, the intense spiritual struggle pictured here exists only within the heart and life of a regenerate person who has the Holy Spirit (see Rom 8:13; 1 Cor 9:27; Gal 5:16-18). As noted, Paul describes his pre-Christian life as self-complacent and self-assured.

Fifth, the longing for deliverance expressed in v. 24 suggests the tender heart of the Christian.

Sixth, the assurance of triumph in v. 25a is something that only the Christian has (see 8:23).

Seventh, the order of the sentences in v. 25 is incompatible with the experience of the unregenerate. I.e., even after resting his soul upon the salvation provided by Christ, Paul once more describes his inner state as one of conflict with sin.

Eighth, as Smith observes, the experience of spiritual struggle described by Paul is consistent with the experience of countless sincere Christians, if not all of them (I:103).

But what about all the seriously negative self-descriptions: "sold as a slave to sin" (7:14), "nothing good lives in me" (7:18), "evil is right there with me" (7:21), "prisoner of the law of sin" (7:23), "wretched man" (7:24)? Surely these confessions are no worse than Paul's declaration that "I am" (εἰμὶ ἐγώ, *eimi egō*, present tense) "the worst" of sinners (1 Tim 1:15). Only a Christian would be aware of such conflict and admit it with such sorrow. We should remember that it is necessary for regenerate Christians to be exhorted and warned about sin (6:1-2, 12-13, 19; 8:12-13).

But how can we account for such an intense conflict within the life of the believer? How can a person who experiences such hatred for sin still be a slave to it? How can a person who so strongly desires to do good and who takes such joy in the law say that "nothing good lives in me"? The answer lies in the fact that our nature is twofold, i.e., in the distinction between the flesh (outer man, body) and the spirit (inner man, soul). As we have already seen, we are redeemed in two stages. First, at conversion the sinful soul is crucified with Christ and raised up into a state of spiritual life

(6:1-6). Then, at the second coming the sin-infested body will be redeemed through resurrection (8:23) or transformation (1 Cor 15:51-54). But in between these two events, while we are still living on this earth, we exist as an awkward combination of redeemed soul and as-yet-unredeemed body. In Bruce's words, we are "living simultaneously on two planes" (151). This fact is the source of the conflict of which this passage speaks, as the following exegesis will show.

This section is divided into two parts: the *nature* of the Christian's struggle against sin (7:14-20), and the *source* of this struggle (7:21-25).

1. The Nature of the Struggle (7:14-20)

7:14 We know that the law is spiritual . . . . This is a transitional statement. It sums up the basic point of 7:7-13, reaffirming the goodness of the law in response to the questions in vv. 7 and 13. It also prepares the way for Paul to begin the intimate analysis of his own spiritual life, which serves as a mirror in which every Christian sees himself.

"The law is spiritual" means primarily that it originates in the mind of God and in its written form comes to us through the inspiration of the Holy Spirit (2 Tim 3:16; cf. Matt 15:4 and Mark 7:10). It probably also means that the law addresses and has a natural affinity with the human spirit; it is "agreeable to our spiritual part" (DeWelt, 107; see Lard, 236). The law is not merely an arbitrary written code that constrains us through external coercion (7:6). On the contrary, in the law we see the very heart of God revealed (1 Cor 2:9-12); and we joyfully embrace it with our own hearts (6:17; 7:22), from the very depths of our spirits (7:6). As we gladly receive God's law and meditate upon it, it lodges within us and begins to shape (actually, reshape) our lives from within, conforming our spirits to its own moral configurations (12:2).

Despite my spiritual affinity with the law, a serious problem exists. Though I am in tune with the law in my spirit, my as-yet-unredeemed body is still a source of serious resistance. **. . . but I am unspiritual, sold as a slave to sin.** "Unspiritual" is an unforgivably poor attempt to translate σάρκινος (*sarkinos*). This word is from σάρξ (*sarx*), "flesh," and means "of flesh" (NASB) or "of the flesh" (NRSV). This is not the same idea as "in the flesh" (7:5, NASB; see 8:5, 8), which means *controlled* by the flesh. Here it means basically "composed of flesh" (Cranfield, I:357). It does not refer to the whole self, but to the physical part of the self. "I," the *ego*, am (in part) *sarkinos*. I am not only spirit; I am also body.

But this is not just a bare metaphysical statement ("I am physical"); it is also a moral statement. It includes the implication that I am still under the influence of my sin-afflicted physical part. Despite the desires of my spirit, I am still hounded by the lusts of my unredeemed body. Lard has said it well: "I Paul am fleshly; though redeemed, and pardoned, and accepted, I am still fleshly; not wholly so, but fleshly, fleshly because still in a body of flesh, from the influence of which, so long as I am in it, I can never become entirely freed" (236).

This moral implication of *sarkinos* is confirmed by the modifier, "sold as a slave to sin." The Greek says literally, "sold under sin" (KJV). One connotation of the word for "sold" is "sold into slavery" (see Matt 18:25). That is probably the picture Paul intends to draw here, as indicated by the preposition "under" (ὑπό, *hypo*), "sold *under* sin," sold to sin as a slaveowner and thus under the power of sin.

But if this is a description of the Christian life, how can it be reconciled with 6:6, 15-23, which says that we "used to be slaves to sin" (6:17), but have been "set free from sin and have become slaves to righteousness" (6:18)? The answer is that ch. 6 refers to the liberation of the spirit or inner man from slavery to sin, while ch. 7 affirms that the body has not yet been so redeemed (7:25). It is the body, the fleshly part, that is still "sold as a slave to sin."

This is not an excuse for sin, however. Because our spirits have been renewed and set free, we are now able to take control of our bodies even though they still incline toward sin, and are able to use them in the service of God (6:6, 12-13). We can do this not just because our spirits have been renewed, but because we are empowered to do so by the indwelling Holy Spirit (8:13).

Thus this statement ("I am of flesh, sold under sin") neither excuses sin nor consigns us to hopelessness. But it does explain *why* and *how* we, even as Christians, continue to be plagued by sin and are subject to constant struggle and occasional defeat.

7:15 I do not understand what I do. Paul is talking about the fact that he still sins, even though he does not want to. "Understand" is not the best translation of γινώσκω (*ginōskō*) here, since throughout this passage Paul shows that he does in fact understand why this happens (see 7:14). A better translation is "approve," in the sense of "condone, acknowledge the validity of" (see Cranfield, I:358-359; Moo, I:483). An analogy would be one government's refusal to acknowledge or accept the validity of another government established by coup or revolution in another country. The new government may be a fact, but it need not be acknowledged and recognized as legitimate. In this sense Paul says, "Yes, I admit that sin sometimes takes control of me, but I do not acknowledge sin as my true master; I do not accept the legitimacy of its rule over my life."

My true, inner self is very different, in fact. **For what I want to do I do not do, but what I hate I do.** The key words here are "want" and "hate." They represent the basic inner attitudes of the regenerate spirit. "Want" is θέλω (*thelō*), which basically means "to wish or desire something," but also has the stronger connotation of "to will or purpose to do something." In vv. 18-19 Paul indicates that the object of his desire and purpose is "the good," and in v. 16 goodness is identified with the law. Thus the basic desire and purpose of the regenerate heart is to obey God's good and perfect law (12:2).

"Hate" is μισέω (*miseō*), which means to dislike, detest, despise, or abhor something; to have a loathing or an aversion toward it; to be filled with hostility, enmity, and opposition toward it; to be repelled by it and want to avoid it. The object of such hatred is evil (v. 19) or disobedience to God's law. Just as the regenerate heart desires and purposes to do the good, so does it hate every form of sin and evil. Such hatred of sin is an essential aspect of repentance. Both attitudes are characteristic of the believing, regenerate Christian and are the opposite of the way an unbeliever thinks. This is a main reason for applying this passage to the regenerate rather than the unregenerate man.

The tragic irony, though, is that our actual practice is often the very opposite of these inner spiritual attitudes. What we *want*[50] to

---

[50]θέλω is used seven times in this context.

do goes undone, and we wind up doing[51] the very things we despise. This conflict between willing and doing is the Christian's basic inner tension.

7:16 And if I do what I do not want to do, I agree that the law is good. Some take this as an indication that Paul's main subject is still the law (e.g., Dunn, I:390). But I take it only as a parenthesis in which Paul is reaffirming the point already made in 7:7-13. When a Christian sins, that does not mean he is casting aspersions upon the law and calling it bad. On the contrary, when a Christian sins he is doing the very opposite of what his heart wants to do. What he truly thinks of the law is shown not by his unlawful deeds, which are the product of his sin-enslaved flesh, but rather by his inward desire to obey it (7:22, 25). This inward state of our hearts demonstrates that we really do accept the fact that God's law is good in every way (7:12-13).[52]

7:17 As it is, it is no longer I myself who do it, but it is sin living in me. This further explains why "I do, not what I want, but what I hate." In 7:7-13 Paul made an important distinction between sin (personified as an enemy) and the law. His point was that sin deceitfully uses the law to stimulate our disobedience to it. But the law itself does not cause disobedience; it is simply an instrument in the hands of sin itself. Now in this verse the key distinction is between sin and the *ego* or self (see 7:8-9). When I do the things I hate, says Paul, it is no longer I (ἐγώ, *egō*) who am doing them, but sin itself.

I take the words νυνί (*nuni*, "now") and οὐκέτι (*ouketi*, "no longer") to have a temporal meaning. The allusion is to the regeneration of the inner man described in ch. 6. Now that my spirit has been changed and reborn, I am not doing these hateful things with my whole being. My inner self repudiates them even as I do them. They stem from the sin that still dwells in me. This is not an excuse that relieves me of personal responsibility for my sin; it is only an explanation of why it occurs.

---

[51]In this context three words are used for what we *do*: κατεργάζομαι (*katergazomai*), πράσσω (*prassō*), and ποιέω (*poieō*). They are used here basically in the same sense, "to do."

[52]Morris suggests that καλός ("good") here means "morally beautiful" (292).

Paul speaks of sin as "living in" or "indwelling in" himself. This may seem strange for a Christian to say, but in the next few verses (esp. 18, 23) he makes it clear that sin indwells not his spirit but his body. The power and residue of sin are still present there. MacArthur's analysis is on target (I:386-387):

> After salvation, sin, like a deposed and exiled ruler, no longer reigns in a person's life, but it manages to survive. It no longer resides in the innermost self but finds its residual dwelling in his flesh, in the unredeemed humanness that remains until a believer meets the Lord at the Rapture or at death.

7:18 Verses 18-20 are a restatement of vv. 14-17, with the emphasis still upon the conflict between willing and doing in the Christian life. **I know that nothing good lives in me, that is, in my sinful nature.** This is a negative version of v. 17b and also serves as a qualifier thereof. "In my sinful nature" is literally "in my flesh" and should be so translated. Again "flesh" refers not to the whole of human nature as fallen, but only to the body (vv. 23, 25). Paul is not saying that the body is inherently evil, or that it lacks inherent goodness, a false view that is common enough (e.g., Gnosticism). He is speaking rather of the body as it has been commandeered by sin, and which in its unredeemed state is still under the power of sin even for Christians. As Moo puts it, Paul "considers the material body to be that part of the person that is particularly susceptible to sin" (I:486). Thus the statement "nothing good lives in me" is qualified by being limited to the body.

"Nothing good lives in me" is an unduly exaggerated translation. A better rendering is "Good does not live in me" (Newman and Nida, 139). In this context "good" is identified with the law (vv. 12-13, 16). Thus "good does not live in me" means that, from the standpoint of my physical nature, I am not inclined to obey God's law.

For I have the desire to do what is good, but I cannot carry it out. I.e., in my heart I want to conform myself to the law, but my body is a continuing source of resistance. Thus in his quest for holiness, the Christian is hindered by the weakness of the flesh. "'I' have the will to do good, the good which the law defines, but not the strength to translate that willing into action" (Dunn, I:408). This would be a source of unbearable agony to us (7:24) were it not for Christ's gift to us of the indwelling Holy Spirit (8:4-13). By the power of God the Holy Spirit working in us, we are able not only to will but also to do what God's good law requires (Phil 2:13).

7:19 For what I do is not the good I want to do; no, the evil I do not want to do — this I keep on doing. This is the same lament as 7:15b. "The good" is behavior enjoined by the law, and "the evil" is behavior forbidden by the law. This is not meant in an absolute sense, as if Paul were saying that he *never* does anything good, and that he *always* commits *every* evil deed that he abhors. The comparative frequency of such paradoxical behavior is not the point. For the sensitive Christian even one such incident is too much.

7:20 Now if I do what I do not want to do, it is no longer I who do it, but it is sin living in me that does it. This is the same as 7:16a, 17.

2. The Source of the Struggle (7:21-25)

In this section Paul reflects on the source of the tension between willing and doing described in 7:14-20. It lies in the conflict between the redeemed spirit and the as-yet-unredeemed body. He has already indicated as much in 7:14 ("I am of flesh") and 7:18 ("in my flesh"), but here he goes into unambiguous detail.

7:21 So I find this law at work . . . . "I find" means "When I analyze what is going on within myself, this is what I discover." What does he discover? A "law" working within him. Here "law" (νόμος, *nomos*) must mean "the controlling rule of life, the governing principle, the regulating pattern." This meaning of *nomos* appears also in 3:27 and 8:2.

What is this rule or pattern? **When I want to do good, evil is right there with me.** When I intend to keep my temper and speak only kind words, as soon as I open my mouth the angry words fly out. Though I resolve never again to commit that sin, as soon as the opportunity arises, I fall.

7:22-23a Paul now reveals the source of this constant conflict in unmistakable language: **For in my inner being I delight in God's**

law; but I see another law at work in the members of my body . . . . Here the two parts of human nature are distinctly contrasted. One is the "inner being" or literally the "inner man" (see 6:6; 2 Cor 4:16; Eph 3:16). This is the soul or spirit or personal center of every human self. In v. 23 it is called "the mind." In the Christian this inner man has undergone the transformation of regeneration and has become the "new man"; the soul of the unregenerate is still the "old man" (6:6; Eph 4:24; Col 3:9-10).[53] The other aspect of human nature is the physical or fleshly body, here simply referred to as "my members," i.e., the members of my body (see 6:13).

Another contrast in this passage is between two kinds of law. One is "God's law," which is the same as "the law of my mind" in v. 23b. It includes whatever code of divine commandments applies to any given person, whether it be written on the heart, on stone, or on paper. Over against this is "another law," which is the same as "the law of sin" in v. 23b. It is called the "law" of sin for the sake of symmetry with the "law" of God. It is a law in the sense of a power or compulsion that exercises control over us.

Spiritual conflict is present in the Christian's life because one part of our being follows the law of God, while the other part follows the law of sin. On the one hand, the regenerated inner man (mind) is fully committed to God's law, and delights in it. We "joyfully concur" in it (NASB). It is the good thing our hearts want to do. (See Ps 119:14, 16, 24, 35, 47, 97.) It should go without saying that only the regenerate man willingly embraces the law of God with such enthusiasm and joy.

On the other hand, the law of sin is "in my members," i.e., in the members of my body (cf. "in my flesh," v. 18). This law or power of sin still "lives in" the body (vv. 17, 20), still permeates it and exploits its appetites and weaknesses.

7:23b This other law is **waging war against the law of my mind and making me a prisoner of the law of sin at work within my**

---

[53]Thus, contrary to some, the "inner man" is not equivalent to "the real regenerate me" (Stott, 213), or "the 'new man' in Christ" (Bruce, 154), or the "better self" (DeWelt, 108). We had this inner man even before we were regenerated. Every person has it, whether saved or unsaved. It is an element of human nature as such.

members. This description of the Christian's inner conflict is couched in military metaphors. The law of sin ensconced in my body "wages war" against the law of God which I have embraced with my inner being. My every inclination to do right comes under attack, not just from outside enemies such as ungodly cultural forces and Satan's devices, but from within my very own self.

Not only am I attacked, but sometimes I am defeated. This is the implication of "making me a prisoner," another military metaphor used of taking prisoners of war in battle. This is not a constant state of incarceration, but an occasional defeat. To be sure, the fact that the body is still a captive of sin is a more-or-less constant condition and will be so until its death and resurrection. My soul, however, has been rescued from the enemy and set free. But until the final victory is achieved, I face the danger that my soul may be temporarily recaptured with respect to individual sins.

7:24 This thought is the "last straw" for Paul. He has been describing his struggle against sin in very dark and bleak terms, but this confession that his better inclinations are sometimes overwhelmed by the sin that remains in his body evokes from him a highly emotional outburst: **What a wretched man I am! Who will rescue me from this body of death?**

Here he once more identifies the source of the struggle: "this body of death." "Body" must refer to the physical body, in view of the references to bodily members in v. 23. The Greek may be read either as "this body of death" or "the body of this death." It is probably the former, since the body has just been mentioned. If it were the latter we would expect another reference to death in the nearby context, but none occurs.

To call the body a body "of death" means first of all that it is still under the curse of physical death as the result of our union with Adam in his sin (5:12-19). But in this context the body's *spiritual* death is in view also. To be a slave to sin (7:14); to be indwelt by sin (7:17-18); to be used as an instrument of warfare against one's own soul (6:13), putting it in danger of eternal death — what is this but a state of spiritual death? Thus even though our inner man has already been raised up from its own spiritual death, the body is still so much in the grip of sin's power that it can be called a "body of death" in a spiritual sense of the word.

No wonder Paul cries out, "What a wretched man I am!" Is this a cry of despair? Many prefer not to use this word, since it implies hopelessness. But surely it is a cry of distress, anguish, and frustration, all of which Paul experiences as he reels under the power of the sin that still resides in his flesh. This is not the wretchedness of someone who is lost, but of someone who in his heart wants so desperately to be fully obedient to the law of God but finds himself still assaulted and overwhelmed by an opposing power that is still a part of himself.

Paul's distress is expressed in the form of a question: "Who will rescue me from this body of death?" This does not imply that he did not know the source of his deliverance. It is rather a humble confession that he *needs* deliverance, that he is unable to win the battle alone, even though his inner man has already been renewed. Thus he cries out for rescue not from bodily existence as such, but from this corrupted body from which sin still wages war against his spirit. He yearns to be free from the constraining power exerted upon him by the lusts of the body (6:12; 7:5).

7:25 In the next chapter Paul shows that deliverance from "this body of death" is possible now through the indwelling of the Holy Spirit (8:13), and is guaranteed ultimately (eschatologically) through the redemption of the body (8:23). But here he pauses, in response to his own question, in order to answer it on the deepest level: **Thanks be to God — through Jesus Christ our Lord!** Here Jesus is presented not as the mediator of this prayer of thanksgiving but as the source of the rescue sought in v. 24b. Both the indwelling Spirit and our new resurrection bodies are gifts from the resurrected and exalted Christ.

After his somewhat premature outburst of anguish and praise, Paul now introduces a summary of the struggle described in vv. 14-23: **So then, I myself in my mind am a slave to God's law, but in the sinful nature a slave to the law of sin.** "I myself" is the emphatic αὐτὸς ἐγώ (*autos egō*). This does not mean "I by myself, apart from Christ," as some think (especially those who see this section as referring to the unregenerate Paul; cf. Godet, 291-292). The point rather is the unity of his person or self. Even though there is a basic division within him, he is still one person, one *ego*, the man Paul. Though his inner man and outer man are now in a state of conflict, each is an authentic part of his essential self. The inner conflict is indicated by the untranslated particles μέν (*men*) and δέ (*de*), "on the one hand . . . on the other hand." Both sides of the conflict are described by the same verb, δουλεύω (*douleuō*), "to serve as a slave," as a δοῦλος (*doulos*).

On the one hand, says Paul, he is a slave to the law of God with his mind. Here the mind represents the entire inner man, the spirit or soul. In his spirit the Christian has already been delivered from slavery to *sin* (6:6), and from *unwilling* slavery to the law (7:6). Nevertheless he still submits himself as a slave to God's law; but he does so freely, from his heart (6:17), because he delights in the law in his inner being (7:22). This kind of slavery is surely the mark of a Christian.

On the other hand, Paul says he is still a slave to the law of sin with his σάρξ (*sarx*), his flesh (*not* his "sinful nature," contra the NIV). His as-yet-unredeemed body is still under sin's sway and thus is at cross-purposes with his mind. Before conversion we served sin with our whole selves (6:17); we willingly offered up our bodies as slaves to wickedness (6:19-20). But now as Christians our spirits have switched allegiance from the law of sin to the law of God, and are committed to obeying the latter. Even though it is now our responsibility and desire to control our bodies and offer up their members as slaves to God (6:19), the body itself resists and clings to the law of sin. Thus the inner turmoil, the inner conflict, the inner struggle — and the all-too-frequent defeat. Is there a sure way to victory? This is the subject of the next section.

B. VICTORY OVER SIN COMES THROUGH
THE HOLY SPIRIT (8:1-13)

For many people Romans 8 is the high point of the Bible, especially because of its emphasis on the Christian's assurance of victory over all opposing forces. Godet (295) remarks that this chapter begins with *no condemnation* and ends with *no separation*. It is truly the logical climax of the gospel of grace.

Many commentaries treat Romans 8 as one unit under a single heading. For most, the unifying theme is the Holy Spirit. My approach is slightly different. I agree that the main theme of vv. 1-13 is the sanctifying work of the Spirit, but I think the emphasis shifts in v. 14 to the general subject of glorification, or the Christian's assurance of eternal glory. Thus I see vv. 14-39 as a separate unit.

This helps us to see more clearly how 8:1-13 relates to what precedes it. The opening word of ch. 8, "therefore," indicates a conclusion drawn from something in the earlier context. In 7:7-25 Paul describes the Christian's continuing battle against sin, especially as it indwells the body. In 8:1-13 he shows us that Christ has provided us with what it takes to win this battle, especially the gift of the indwelling Holy Spirit.

1. God Frees Us from Sin's Penalty and Power (8:1-4)

Paul's heart-cry in 7:24, "Who will rescue me from this body of death?", was immediately answered in brief: "Thanks be to God [because he has rescued me] through Jesus Christ our Lord" (7:25a). While the main concern of this question and its answer is freedom from the *power* of indwelling sin, we need to be reminded again of the main point already established in 3:21-5:21, that the *penalty* for our sin has been paid in full by Jesus. In the midst of our intense spiritual struggle against sin, in which we are sometimes on the losing end, we need not fear that our forgiveness is in jeopardy. Christ has already secured this for us on the cross.

The decision to interpret 8:1-4 as including a reference to justification (the absence of penalty) is not difficult in view of such phrases as "no condemnation" (v. 1), "a sin-offering" (v. 3), and "he condemned sin" (v. 3). These expressions have a decidedly judicial or forensic connotation. However, other parts of the paragraph seem to refer to sanctification, or overcoming sin's power and living a holy life through the Spirit (vv. 2, 4b). These verses thus include freedom from both sin's penalty and sin's power.

8:1 Therefore, there is now no condemnation for those who are in Christ Jesus . . . . "Therefore" shows that a conclusion is being drawn, most likely from the reference to the saving work of Christ in 7:25a. "Now" points to the same event: "Now, in view of what Christ has done." "Condemnation" is κατάκριμα (*katakrima*), used only here and in 5:16, 18. This is a judicial or forensic term. It refers to a judge's sentence upon a guilty person, not only as pronounced but also as carried out. I.e., it means "penalty, punishment, doom." The word for "no" (οὐδέν, *ouden*) is emphatic and means "not a single one" of any kind (Lenski, 494). "In Christ Jesus" identifies those to whom this wonderful blessing applies, namely, those who have entered into the saving union with Christ described in 6:1-11.

The point of the verse is this: even though sin still lives in our bodies, causing us at times to do sinful things that we hate, we can be assured that these sins will not condemn us because Christ has already died for them and we belong to Christ. Though we may still sin, we are "justified by his blood" (5:9); there is "no penalty" for us,[54] none of any kind. No disaster or tribulation suffered in this life should now be interpreted as a punishment sent by God. No damnation to eternal hell awaits us after death, and even the sting of physical death has been blunted by the promise of resurrection from the dead (1 Cor 15:53-57).

Some interpreters, especially those who believe 8:1-4 refers equally or solely to the overcoming of sin's *power*, expand the meaning of "condemnation" to include sin's enslavement of the flesh. Thus they interpret "no condemnation" as including freedom from sin itself, i.e., freedom from its enslaving power.[55] There is little basis for this expanded meaning of *katakrima*, however. In 5:16, 18 it is clearly opposed to justification (which itself is a forensic concept). There is no good reason or basis for extending its meaning beyond that connotation here.[56] Thus "no condemnation" is the equivalent of "justification" (Stott, 217).

In the KJV 8:1 ends thus: "who walk not after the flesh, but after the Spirit." However, these words are not found in 8:1 in the earlier and better manuscripts and are omitted from most modern translations (such as the NIV). The same words appear in 8:4b, though, and will be discussed there.

---

[54]See Dunn, I:435.
[55]See Godet, 296; Hendriksen, I:245; Bruce, 159; Murray, I:274-275.
[56]So say Moo, I:504; and Morris, 300.

8:2 because through Christ Jesus the law of the Spirit of life set me free from the law of sin and death. "Because" (γάρ, *gar*) implies that this verse gives the *reason* for the statement in v. 1: "There is no condemnation *because* we have been freed from it by the law of the Spirit of life." At first glance it seems that v. 2 is talking only about the sanctifying work of the Holy Spirit. This is why many expand the meaning of "condemnation" in v. 1 to include the indwelling power of sin; otherwise Paul would appear to be saying that we are *justified* (v. 1) because we are *sanctified* (v. 2), which would be equivalent to justification by works.

But if we do limit "condemnation" to the penalty for sin, and "no condemnation" to justification (as I have done above), how do we avoid this conclusion? By seeing that v. 2 itself is not limited to the sanctifying work of the Spirit. It speaks rather of freedom from "the law of sin and death" in every respect, including death as the *penalty* for sin.

Through Christ Jesus we are set free from the law of sin and death. This in itself points to the comprehensive nature of this liberation. By applying to us the full scope of the redeeming work of Jesus Christ, the Spirit of life sets us free from every aspect of sin and death, including its penalty.

It is difficult to decide exactly what the two uses of "law" (νόμος, *nomos*) mean here. We know that it does not mean law in the sense of a set of commandments, whether it be the Mosaic law or God's law in general. The latter connotation appears in vv. 3-4, and the context shows it has a different sense in v. 2.

Also because of the context, I conclude that *nomos* here has the general sense of "order, rule, pattern, system," as applied on a cosmic scale. The two "laws" named here are the two competing world orders, the two rival life paradigms. The first is the life system in which the Spirit of life operates and dominates; the second is the life system controlled by sin and death. They are related to the contrasting spheres of flesh and Spirit as discussed in vv. 4b-13.

As understood in this general sense, the *nomos* of v. 2 includes both the conceptual and the concrete, or the connotations of both "governing principle" and "controlling power." It cannot be limited to power alone; this would limit the liberating activity of v. 2 to sanctification, and raise problems regarding the relation between v. 1 and v. 2 (see above). Thus we conclude that *nomos* also includes the governing principles according to which this power operates (see Bruce, 160; MacArthur, I:403).

Thus in 8:2 Paul is referring to two exclusive and competing world orders. One is the order of the flesh, in which sin is the dominant power and death the inevitable outcome. It is governed by the principle that sin and death are inseparable: wherever *sin* rules, it always brings *death* in all its ruinous varieties. The other world or life system is the order of the Spirit, in which the *Holy Spirit* is the dominating power and *life* is the inevitable outcome. It is governed by the principle that the Holy Spirit and life are inseparable: wherever the *Spirit* enters, he always brings *life* in all its abundance (John 6:63; Rom 8:11; 2 Cor 3:6; Gal 6:8).

Paul's point in this section is that, through Jesus Christ, the governing principle and the controlling power of sin and death have been driven out of our lives by and replaced by the governing principle and the controlling power of the Spirit of life. In 8:1-4 the main point is that the regulating principle that sin always brings death has been shattered by Christ's propitiatory atonement, allowing for the justification of the wicked (4:5). In 8:5-13 the point is that the dominating power of the Spirit overcomes the dominating power of the flesh (the body of sin and death – 6:6; 7:24) in the lives of Christians.

How does v. 2 relate, then, to v. 1? Why is there no condemnation for those who are in Christ Jesus? Because, through Christ and the world order that he has made possible, my life is no longer governed by the rules of sin and death. Yes, my sin deserves the penalty of death, but Christ's death has paid that penalty for me, and the Spirit has applied that redemptive act to my life. *This breaks the connection between sin and death!* It has set me free from the principle that sin always brings death, and has restored me – a sinner – to the role of a child of God and heir of eternal life (8:15-17). Thus the liberation of 8:2 is the basis for the justification of 8:1.

But it is also the basis for the sanctification of which 8:5-13 speaks. The indwelling Spirit has broken the power of the indwelling sin which seeks to drag me back down into the pits of spiritual death. When Christ gave me his Spirit, the principle and power of life took over, thus ending the illegitimate reign of those usurping tyrants, sin and death.

We should note that the verb "set free" is aorist (past) tense. The act of liberation that set us free from sin's penalty and power (the "double cure") is a past event for any Christian. Specifically, it happened in our Christian baptism, in which we received not only forgiveness of sins (justification) through Christ's blood, but also the indwelling presence of the Spirit of life (Acts 2:38). In that event the course of our lives as well as our ultimate destiny were totally recast or reprogrammed; the sin-brings-death system was replaced by the Spirit-gives-life paradigm.

In this verse some translations read "set *me* free" (KJV, NIV), and some read "set *you* free" (NASB, NRSV). The former fits better with the first person singular in 7:7-25 (especially 7:24), but the latter has better manuscript support, according to Cranfield (I:377).

8:3 For what the law was powerless to do in that it was weakened by the sinful nature, God did . . . . The Greek speaks literally of "the impossible thing of the law." What is this "impossible thing"? The answer is in v. 2: the law (God's commandments as such) cannot set a sinner free from the tyranny of sin and death. The law was "intended to bring life" (7:10), and it can do so when followed completely. But once a person has sinned, the law cannot set him free from sin's penalty and power; it cannot restore him to the sphere of life.

That the law cannot give life to sinners is not due to some inherent flaw or failure in the law itself, since it was not designed for this purpose. This weakness is due rather to "the sinful nature"; literally, "it was weak through the flesh." This may refer to the flesh as incapacitated by sin (cf. the NIV), or it could refer to the inherent limitations of human beings simply as finite creatures. I.e., in the hands of mere men, the law can never deliver us from the consequences of our sins.

But what the law cannot do, God can; and he can do it without violating the integrity of his law. As we have seen (1:17), God cannot disregard his own righteousness in his dealings with men; he must always be true to himself and to the requirements of his law. But once sinners have broken the law's *commandments*, the only way God can be righteous is to satisfy his law's requirement for *punishment*. And this is exactly what Jesus came to do — in our place.

The substitutionary atonement of Jesus is the point of vv. 3-4a.[57] Though sin still lives in our bodies, we are not condemned thereby (8:1), because we have been set free from the "sin brings death" principle (8:2). How is this possible? Because God sent his divine Son to suffer the penalty of death in our place (8:3), thereby satisfying the law's requirement (for penalty) and maintaining his own righteousness (8:4a).

God did this **by sending his own Son in the likeness of sinful man to be a sin offering**. This simple statement contains deep Christological concepts. To say that God "sent" his Son does not in itself imply the Son's pre-existence with the Father in heaven, since the OT often speaks of God's "sending" the prophets. But as Godet suggests (298), when this is combined with the description of Jesus as God's "own Son" (see 8:32), it indicates not only the pre-existence of Christ but his divine nature as well.

On the other hand, "in the likeness of sinful man" refers to the incarnation and human nature of Jesus. "Sinful man" is literally "sinful flesh" or "the flesh of sin." Paul is *not* saying that flesh is inherently sinful or evil, as dualistic philosophies such as Gnosticism taught. Rather, he is alluding to his consistent teaching in this context that the human body has come under the power of sin and remains so to some extent even for Christians. It is "sinful flesh" because it harbors sin.

But what does it mean to say that Jesus came in the "likeness" of sinful flesh (likeness implying "similar but different")? He came in real flesh, but only in the "likeness" of *sinful* flesh. His body was fully human in the truest sense. It had everything a human body is supposed to have, but it did not have the corruption caused by sin.[58] It was not necessary for him to assume a sinful human nature

---

[57]MacArthur says that 8:3 is the most succinct statement of the substitutionary atonement in the Bible (I:405).

[58]Some go too far at this point, saying that Christ was incarnated in a *sinful* human nature, or in *sinful* flesh with all its corruptions and sinful tendencies (e.g., Lard, 249; Hendriksen, I:247). The only way he was different from us is that he never committed personal sins. See Cranfield's critique of this view (I:381).

in order to be able to redeem us; he only had to have a genuine and complete human nature, which he did.

The purpose of the incarnation is then stated: "to be a sin offering." In the Greek this is a simple prepositional phrase, "concerning sin." Many give it a very general sense, i.e., Jesus came "to deal with sin" (NRSV). The reason for the NIV translation is that the Septuagint regularly uses this very phrase to translate Hebrew terms meaning "as a sin offering" (see Dunn, I:422; Moo, I:512). The following context suggests it is reasonable to think this is how Paul is using it here.

And so he condemned sin in sinful man, or more accurately, "in the flesh." Some take "condemned" in the general sense of "destroyed" or "destroyed the power of." They say Jesus destroyed sin's power by living a sinless life, thereby showing that sin can be resisted and setting a precedent for our sanctification.[59] But this fits neither the context nor the meaning of the word "condemned" (κατακρίνω, *katakrinō*), which is the verb form of the word "condemnation" in 8:1. This term refers to a judicial act (Moo, I:513). It means that God's judicial sentence against sin "was passed and executed" (Bruce, 161), that "the full weight of God's wrath against sin" was poured out (Cranfield, I:383).

What does the phrase "in the flesh" modify? Some say it goes with "sin," i.e., God condemned the sin that dwells in our flesh, or the sins committed by "sinful man" (NIV). The context, however, favors the view that "in the flesh" modifies the verb, and that it refers to the flesh (human nature) of Jesus Christ. I.e., the very thing the law could not do because of "the flesh" of sinners (v. 3a), God himself has done in "the flesh" of Jesus. The only way we human beings can gain eternal life through the law is to obey its commandments completely, but in our weakness we have all sinned. But Jesus came to earth in our very same flesh, though untainted by sin; and in his flesh he restored us to the sphere of life by allowing sin to be condemned in himself instead of us.

The nuance of the last sentence is significant. It does not say that God condemned Jesus Christ himself, as if he were a sinner.

---

[59]Godet, 299-300; Lard, 250-251; DeWelt, 115-116. See Moo's discussion of this, I:513.

Nor does it say that God condemned us in Jesus Christ. Rather, it says simply that God "condemned sin in the flesh," i.e., he condemned *our* sin in the flesh of *Jesus*. This is how God has set us free from the law of sin and death (8:2) in reference to its penalty, namely, through the substitutionary (vicarious) atonement of Jesus.

8:4 This substitutionary atonement was necessary **in order that the righteous requirements of the law might be fully met in us . . . .** The word ἵνα (*hina*), "in order that," shows that this is the intended result or purpose of God's condemning sin in the flesh. The main question is whether this intended result is our *justification* (8:1) or our *sanctification* (holy living).

The key to this question is the meaning of δικαίωμα (*dikaiōma*), translated "righteous requirements" by the NIV. Basically it means "an ordinance, a decree, or a requirement that expresses or upholds righteousness." In 2:26 it is used for "requirements" of the law in the sense of commandments; that is how many take it here. God condemned sin in the flesh in order that the law's requirements for holy living might be fulfilled in us. He set us free from the *power* of sin, enabling us to live in obedience to his law.[60] A variation of this is that Christ is the one who fulfilled these requirements vicariously for us; his perfect obedience was then imputed to us.[61]

I believe this whole approach to be wrong, however. The first clue is that, unlike 2:26, *dikaiōma* here is singular (*not* plural, contra the NIV). The second clue is the connection between the *dikaiōma* and the act of condemnation in v. 3b. I.e., that which fulfills the righteous requirement of the law is a judicial act, an act of condemnation. The third clue is that this act of condemnation enables this righteous requirement to be be fulfilled completely, or "fully met" — something we can never personally do with the law's commandments.

These considerations together show that the *dikaiōma* of the law is not its various commandments, but its decree that sin must be punished. This is how it is used in 1:32 ("righteous decree"). And as we have already seen (1:17), the very essence of the "righteousness

---

[60]E.g., Bruce, 162; Stott, 221; Hendriksen, I:248.

[61]Moo, I:514-516. I have denied the validity of this concept under 1:17 above.

of God" which is the content of the gospel is that Jesus came to satisfy the law's requirement for penalty in our place. Here the words "in us" do not mean "by us personally," but as accomplished by Jesus Christ and *imputed* to us, as the basis for our justification.

Thus far the main emphasis of this paragraph has been on the first part of the double cure, or justification. We have been reminded that, in the face of sin's vicious opposition to us and in the process of our fighting against it, we must not forget that Christ has broken the connection between sin and death; we have been set free from condemnation. In our effort to implement the second part of the double cure (sanctification), we must not allow ourselves to be distracted by doubts about the first part.

But Paul is now ready to leave this subject, and at the end of v. 4 he makes a transition to the main subject of this section on victory (8:1-13), namely, the sanctifying power of the Holy Spirit. "The law of the Spirit of life" not only sets us free from sin's *penalty* of death; it also delivers us from the *condition* of death as it exists in our souls and bodies. This latter aspect of grace has been prominent in chs. 6-7, and will now become the main point in 8:5-13. In ch. 6 Paul shows that our "inner man" or soul has already been set free from sinful corruption. In ch. 7 he laments the fact that our as-yet-unredeemed bodies are still indwelt by sin and are a beachhead for sin's continuing war against our souls. Now he is ready to show us how God himself intervenes in this battle and rescues us from "this body of death" (7:24), namely, through the power of the Holy Spirit.

The words at the end of v. 4 are not intended to present a *condition* for justification; rather, they simply *identify* those to whom the vicarious suffering of Jesus applies. It does not apply to everyone, but only to those **who do not live according to the sinful nature [*sarx*] but according to the Spirit.**

The word for "live" is "walk," a term often used in Scripture for conduct or behavior regarded from a moral point of view. As MacArthur well says, one's "walk" is his lifestyle or his "habitual way or bent of life" (I:410). There are only two kinds of people: those whose lifestyle is based on the *sarx*, and those whose lifestyle is based on the Spirit.

Most people walk according to the *sarx*. Here *sarx* refers not to some nebulous "sinful nature" (contra the NIV), but to the flesh or material body which in its fallen state is indwelt by and enslaved to sin, and thus is the source of sinful lusts and inclinations. Those who are "in Christ Jesus," however, walk according to the Spirit. Though some take *pneuma* here to mean the human spirit,[62] it much more likely means the Holy Spirit (as in 8:2). What it means to walk according to the flesh or Spirit is explained in the introduction to the following section.

2. Sin and Death Are Defeated in Us
Through the Holy Spirit (8:5-13)

Fighting against sin is an intense struggle (7:7-25), but Jesus has provided us with the means for victory through his gift of the indwelling Spirit. Our deliverance comes through Jesus Christ (7:24-25a), because through his redeeming work the energizing power of the Spirit of life enables us to overcome the insidious power of sin and death that remains in our bodies (8:2).

This is what Paul now explains in detail. First he describes the difference between the two "laws" or world orders (8:2) as a contrast between *flesh* and *Spirit* (8:5-8). Then he affirms the reality and the nature of the Spirit's victory over the flesh in the life of a Christian (8:9-11). Finally he reminds us that we have a personal responsibility to resist the flesh and to surrender ourselves to the Spirit's power (8:12-13).

Two translation notes are in order. First, where the NIV has "sinful nature" (also "sinful men" and "sinful mind"), the Greek word is σάρξ (*sarx*) and should be translated "flesh." Also, the Greek uses several expressions to describe the two ways of life as lived within the two world orders: walking according to flesh/Spirit, v. 4; existing according to flesh/Spirit, v. 5; existing in flesh/Spirit, vv. 8-9; and living according to flesh/(Spirit), vv. 12-13. The NIV translates vv. 4, 5, 12-13 the same, i.e., as "live." This may be misleading, especially in v. 5, since there seems to be a difference between being/existing in (according to) flesh or Spirit, and walking/living according to the flesh or Spirit. See v. 12.

---

[62]Lard, 252; MP, 358; Smith, I:108-111.

Existing in (according to) the flesh or the Spirit refers not to certain specific acts as such, but to a person's life orientation or state of being. On the one hand, a person existing in or according to the flesh is someone whose life is determined by all the things that relate to bodily life in this world. It is someone whose whole being, both body and soul, is basically controlled by the sinful lusts and inclinations of the flesh, e.g., for food, comfort, sex, and pleasure in general. On the other hand, a person existing in or according to the Spirit is someone whose life is oriented around and determined by "the law of the Spirit of life." It is someone who is committed to Spirit-inspired Scripture as his authoritative moral and spiritual compass, and who is committed to using the Spirit's power to live the holy lifestyle prescribed therein.

Walking or living by the flesh or Spirit is different in that it refers to the way a person actually lives. It refers to the lifestyle or conduct that a person chooses to actualize (v. 12). While a person who exists according to the flesh cannot live according to the Spirit (vv. 7-8), a person who exists according to the Spirit *can* choose to continue to live according to the flesh, to his eternal peril (vv. 12-13).

8:5 Those who live according to the sinful nature have their minds set on what that nature desires; but those who live in accordance with the Spirit have their minds set on what the Spirit desires. The literal NASB translation is better: "For those who are according to the flesh set their minds on the things of the flesh, but those who are according to the Spirit, the things of the Spirit." "To set the mind on" (φρονέω, *phroneō*) means "to think," "to have a specific opinion or attitude" about something. It also means "to focus the mind or attention upon, to be preoccupied with." As MacArthur says, it refers to "the basic orientation, bent, and thought patterns of the mind" (I:416).

Thus a major difference between those existing under the two world orders is the content of their minds. This includes one's daydreams, conscious goals, interests, desires, attitudes, and points of view. One whose life orientation is the flesh is constantly preoccupied with the things of the flesh, i.e., things having to do with one's bodily nature as it exists in this physical world. The one whose life orientation is the Holy Spirit, on the other hand, is preoccupied with the things of the Spirit. His desires, goals, and points of view are determined by the truth revealed in Scripture by the Spirit of God.

8:6 The mind of sinful man is death, but the mind controlled by the Spirit is life and peace . . . . Literally, "For the mind of the flesh is death, but the mind of the Spirit is life and peace." "Mind" (φρόνημα, *phronēma*) is the noun form of *phroneō* (v. 5) and conveys the same idea. It thus means the content of the mind in terms of one's worldview, mindset, and thought patterns.

This verse names a second major characteristic of those who are of the flesh or of the Spirit. On the one hand, the mind of the flesh is *death*. This refers both to one's present state and to his eternal destiny. The person controlled by his flesh is in a state of spiritual death; he exists according to "the law [world order] of sin and death" (8:2). This is the state of spiritual depravity (not *total* depravity), which is the second half of the sinner's "double trouble." It is death in the most serious sense, i.e., separation from God (Isa 59:2). Also, to be controlled by the flesh means that one's final destiny is eternal death in the lake of fire (6:23; 7:5; Rev 20:14-15), where separation from God is eternal.

On the other hand, the mind of the Spirit is *life* and *peace*. This also refers to one's present state and to his eternal destiny. At conversion we were raised from spiritual death to spiritual life (6:4, 11; 8:10; John 5:24), and we began to exist in a state of objective peace with God and internal peace of mind (5:1-2). This peace with God is in contrast with the mind of the flesh, which exists in a state of enmity toward God (8:7). We should note that it is a state of peace with *God*, not peace with *sin*. Thus such peace is consistent with the state of battle against sin described in 7:14-25.

Also, "life and peace" are the final blessings of eternal life and of eternal peace in heaven. To have the mind of the Spirit is to exist according to "the law [world order] of the Spirit of life," and the Spirit's final gift of life is a new body designed for glory (8:11, 23).

8:7 the sinful mind is hostile to God. "Sinful mind" is literally "the mind of the flesh," exactly as in v. 6. This statement is preceded in the Greek by διότι (*dioti*), "because" (untranslated by the NIV). This connects with the first part of v. 6. I.e., the mind of the flesh is death, *because* it is hostile toward God. "Hostile" is a noun, ἔχθρα (*echthra*), that means "hostility, hatred, enmity." It is the state that exists between enemies, in contrast with the state of peace in v. 6.

The mind devoted to the flesh is enmity against God because it is committed to everything that God is against. The "carnal mind" (KJV) may not consciously sense itself as being an enemy of God, and may deny that it is so. But the fact remains that "friendship with the world is hatred [*echthra*] toward God" (Jas 4:4). As the maxim says, "The friend of my enemy is my enemy."

The nature of this enmity is explained in the rest of the verse: **It does not submit to God's law, nor can it do so.** This is connected to v. 7a by *gar*, "for, because" (untranslated in the NIV). This shows a causal relation between 7a and 7b. The mind focused on the flesh is an enemy of God *because* it does not and cannot submit to God's law.

"Law" in this context is the general law of God in any and all of its applicable forms. That peace with God and enmity against God are measured by one's attitude toward his law is significant. It shows that God and his law cannot be separated. To reject God's law is to reject God himself.

The choice between the mind of the flesh and the mind of the Spirit is the choice between the attitude of lawlessness, which is the essence of sin (1 John 3:4), and the attitude of submission to God's law (see 7:22). "Submit" is ὑποτάσσω (*hypotasso*), which in the passive voice means to surrender oneself to the authority of someone or something. To submit to the law of God means to acknowledge its authority and to make a conscious effort to obey it. This is precisely what the mind of the flesh does not do. More significantly, it *cannot* do so. This theme of inability is continued in the next verse.

8:8 Those controlled by the sinful nature cannot please God. Literally, "And those who are in the flesh cannot please God." On the phrase "in the flesh," see 7:5. The translation "controlled by" gives the proper sense of it.

This verse is simply reinforcing the point of v. 7b. "Cannot please God" is directly related to "cannot submit to God's law." This shows that what pleases God is inner submission to and external obedience to his law. On the subject of pleasing God, see 12:1-2; 1 Cor 7:32; 2 Cor 5:9; Eph 5:10; 1 Thess 4:1; 2 Tim 2:4; Heb 11:5-6; 13:21; 1 John 3:22.

Paul says that the one whose mind is set on the flesh cannot submit to God's law (v. 7) and cannot please God. What is the nature of this inability? Calvinists and others use these verses as proof-texts for the idea of total inability, which is the core of the doctrine of total depravity (see Murray, I:287; Moo, I:521). These verses are taken to mean that sinners are unable to repent and believe the gospel without the sovereign and irresistible grace of God, which he gives to those whom he unconditionally chooses.

It is important to see, though, that these verses do not teach this kind of inability. They obviously teach that the person controlled by his flesh is unable to do something, but his inability is clearly related to the law, not to the gospel. This is the key to understanding this text.

Basically, such a person is unable to obey any command of the law as God wants it done and as the law requires. He may obey it outwardly; but as long as he exists according to the flesh, he cannot submit to God's law in his heart (Gal 5:6; Heb 11:6). One simply cannot do both at the same time: he cannot set his mind on the flesh *and* submit to God's law simultaneously (Morris, 306). Thus as long as he is in the flesh, he cannot please God with respect to his law.[63]

The key words are "as long as." A person cannot be pleasing to God in obedience to his law *as long as* his mind remains set on the flesh.[64] But here is the crucial point: there is no indication whatsoever in this text that a sinner is unable to respond to the gospel, or unable through the power of the gospel to redirect the set of his mind from flesh to Spirit. The context shows that "cannot please God" refers only to an inability to be subject to the law, and does not imply an inability to respond to the gospel. The failure to make

---

[63]Of course, if a person committed to the flesh cannot please God in relation to the law's commandments, then he cannot achieve personal righteousness by his efforts at law-keeping (10:3). Being thus unable to satisfy the law's requirements for obedience, he cannot be justified by his works.

[64]See Lard, 255-256; DeWelt, 119. See the parallel idea in Heb 6:4-6.

this distinction is the main error of Calvinists' interpretation of these verses. In other passages it is clear that sinners are able and expected to respond to the gospel in faith and repentance (John 3:16; Rom 1:17; Rev 22:17; see Matt 23:37).

8:9 In vv. 5-8 Paul gives an objective description of the two orders of flesh and Spirit. Now he begins a personal application to the Roman Christians and Christians everywhere. His point is this: despite the law of sin and death that continues to work in and through your as-yet-unredeemed bodies, and despite the reality of your continuing struggle against its enslaving power, you need not despair, for God has given you a gift of grace second only to the gift of justification through Christ's blood. This second gift of grace is the indwelling Holy Spirit himself. His very presence within you gives you all the resources you need for victory over your flesh now, and for ultimate victory over death in every sense.

You, however, are controlled not by the sinful nature but by the Spirit, if the Spirit of God lives in you. Literally, "you are not in the flesh but in the Spirit." The "you" is emphatic and draws the Christian reader personally into the sphere of the truth enunciated in the text. Paul flatly states that you (Christians) are not "in the flesh," or "controlled by the flesh." Your life is not oriented to this world; your mind is not set upon the things of this earth. Rather, you are "in the Spirit." Some take this to mean the human spirit. I.e., you are not governed by the desires of your bodies but by the higher inclinations of your spirits.[65] As in the preceding verses, however, it is best to take this as referring to the Holy Spirit. That is, your life now falls within the sphere of the Spirit's influence and power.

This is true, of course, only *if* the Spirit of God indeed dwells in you. The word "if" is εἴπερ (*eiper*), which sometimes means "since" (3:30; 2 Thess 1:6). Some take it thus here, in order to eliminate all uncertainty as to the status of Paul's readers.[66] "If" or "if indeed" is probably the intended meaning, though, as in 8:17 (see 1 Cor 15:15). It simply states the condition for being in the Spirit. The point is not to create uncertainty as to one's status, but rather to

---

[65]E.g., Sanday and Headlam, 196; Lard, 256; DeWelt, 119.
[66]E.g., Hendriksen, I:252; Cranfield, I:388; Moo, I:523.

eliminate other conditions, especially those having to do with human achievement. The fact that we are "in the Spirit" depends not upon what we have accomplished in ourselves, but upon what God has accomplished in us through his Spirit.

The word for "lives" is οἰκέω (*oikeō*), and is related to the word for "house, dwelling place." The word implies not a temporary, transient visit, but a permanent settling down. When the Holy Spirit is given to us in baptism (Acts 2:38), he takes up permanent residence and makes himself at home within us. He comes to dwell in our very bodies (1 Cor 6:19), which continue also to be indwelt by sin (7:17, 23). Thus he is in position to do battle for us in the very place where we need him most.

And if anyone does not have the Spirit of Christ, he does not belong to Christ. This makes the same point in a negative way. Those who do *not* have the Spirit are outside the sphere of the redeemed. This is not applied personally to Paul's readers, but is stated of the impersonal "anyone." That the Spirit is called both the Spirit of *God* and the Spirit of *Christ* suggests that Christ as God the Son is on the same level as God the Father; it implies his deity.

How can we know whether or not the Holy Spirit is dwelling in us? First we must ask whether we have done that which God has specified as the condition for receiving the Spirit: Acts 2:38; 5:32; 19:1-7. Then we must look for the signs of his continuing presence. These signs do not necessarily include the possession of miraculous powers, since these can be present even where Christ and his Spirit are absent (see Matt 7:21-23). The best sign is the presence of the fruit of the Spirit in our character and conduct (Gal 5:22-26), though even this is not an infallible indicator. What we can say is this, that where such fruit is absent, the Spirit is also absent.

This verse clearly ties our relationship to the Spirit with our relationship to Christ. When the Spirit lives in us and we thus "live in the Spirit," we belong to Christ. (This is the implication from the negative statement that one who does *not* have the Spirit does *not* belong to Christ.) This same connection is made in 1 Cor 6:19-20.

8:10 But if Christ is in you . . . . Here Paul returns to second person, indicating his confidence that this condition is indeed the condition that applies to his Roman readers. Verse 9 says the Holy Spirit dwells in us; now Paul describes our saved state by saying that

Christict dwells in us.[67] This does not equate Christ with the Spirit, but shows the intimate interrelation between them. It also indicates how difficult it is to give an exact or literal description of the Christian's own intimate relation with both Christ and the Spirit. The Spirit is in us; we are in the Spirit. Christ is in us; we are in Christ.[68] Some say the Holy Spirit dwells in us personally and directly, while Christ dwells in us only indirectly *through* the Spirit (Lard, 258). This is not necessarily the case, however. Both may certainly dwell in us, each for his own purpose.

If Christ is in you, here is where you now stand. First, **your body is dead because of sin . . . .** The body here no doubt is the physical body, as in v. 11. In what sense does Paul say that "the body is dead" (present tense)? The primary and most obvious reference is to physical death (see v. 11), the idea being that the body is subject to death, under the curse of death, "irrevocably smitten with death" (Godet, 305). It is doomed to die. "Because of sin" must then refer to the sin of Adam (5:12-17), since even sinless infants and young children sometimes die.

But it is also true that the Christian's body is even now still permeated with the spiritual effects of his own sin and thus with a kind of *spiritual* death (see 7:24). I.e., the physical body is spiritually dead because of the sin that indwells it (7:17-18, 23). Because the Christian's body has not yet been delivered from the power of this spiritual death, it is thus the source of constant struggle.

That we still have "this body of death" is the bad news, but there is also some very good news: **yet your spirit is alive because of righteousness.** The most difficult question here is whether *pneuma* ("spirit") means the human spirit or the Holy Spirit. Many say the latter, the strongest argument being that the Greek does not say "the spirit is *alive*" but rather "is *life*." In view of the close connection between the Holy Spirit and life (8:2), the affirmation that "the Spirit is life" makes very good sense. On the other hand, to say "the redeemed human spirit is life" is somewhat problematic. (See Cranfield, I:390; Hendriksen, I:252-253.)

Nevertheless many do believe *pneuma* refers here to the human

---

[67]See 2 Cor 13:5; Gal 2:20; Eph 3:17; Col 1:27.
[68]For "in Christ," see 8:1; 16:7, 11; Eph 1:1; Phil 1:1.

spirit,[69] the strongest argument being the apparent parallel between "body" and "spirit." I believe the case for this view is stronger, and that the NIV translation is appropriate: "your spirit is alive." Either way the phrasing is a bit awkward.

Whichever view was intended, the other is still true and is actually present by implication. If Paul is saying "the Spirit is life," since this is in contrast with "the body is dead," then we must understand that the Spirit's first and best gift of life was the life he gave to our spirits in the act of regeneration. If Paul is saying "the spirit is alive," then we must understand that the source of this life is the Holy Spirit. (See Titus 3:5.) Either way, the Holy Spirit is the source of our power over sin and our ability to stand against its attacks. This is the main point.

The spirit is alive "because of righteousness." Many take this to mean the imputed righteousness that is the basis for justification.[70] This would mean that in some sense our regeneration is grounded in our justification through the blood of Christ. This is not at all unlikely since "the law of the Spirit of life" is able to operate only "through Jesus Christ" (8:2). Others take it to mean a kind of imparted righteousness. This is not as likely, since it is difficult to separate imparted righteousness from our own righteous living, and since our spirit's being alive seems in no way attributable to our righteous living. It is rather the opposite: we can live righteously because we have been made alive by the Spirit.

8:11 The Christian is a combination of "a dying body and a living spirit," as Stott says (226). But this is not the whole story. Just as our spirits have already been raised from the dead, so also will our bodies one day be rescued from the grip of sin and death and restored once more to a state of pure life. This "body of sin" (6:6), "this body of death" (7:24), is appointed to undergo physical death (Heb 9:27); but after that we shall be raised in new bodies that are no longer susceptible to such death and are no longer infected with sin and spiritual death. While the resurrection of Christ has certainly paved the way for this bodily resurrection and has made it possible, its immediate agent is the Holy Spirit.

---

[69]See Lard, 260; DeWelt, 115, 119; Smith, I:111; Godet, 305; Sanday and Headlam, 198; MacArthur, I:420; Stott, 226.

[70]E.g., Lard, 260; Hendriksen, I:252; Cranfield, I:350.

And if the Spirit of him who raised Jesus from the dead is living in you . . . . Paul has already established that the Spirit of God dwells in all who exist according to the Spirit (v. 9). The word "if" (εἰ, *ei*) does not suggest uncertainty but is simply establishing the basis for our hope regarding the resurrection of our bodies. Some would translate it "since."

We may note that this clause reflects the Trinitarian nature of God. "Him who raised Jesus" is God the Father; "the Spirit" of the Father is God the Holy Spirit; Jesus is God the Son.

. . . he who raised Christ from the dead will also give life to your mortal bodies . . . . If God raised Jesus from the dead, he can also raise up our bodies as well (see 1 Cor 6:14; 2 Cor 4:14). The resurrection of Jesus is thus a basis for our assurance that we too will be raised up in the day when Christ returns. "Mortal bodies" refers to the physical body; it is mortal in the sense that it is subject to death and pervaded by death both physically and spiritually (6:12; 8:10). But no matter how strong a grip death has on our bodies, its power will be completely broken **through his Spirit, who lives in you.** The present indwelling of the Spirit is a further assurance of our future resurrection. See 2 Cor 1:22; Eph 1:13-14.

It is significant that our promised rescue from this body of sin and death (7:24) does not consist merely of physical death and freedom from bodily existence as such, as many pagan religions teach. According to the Bible physical death itself is something to be rescued from, and the human spirit was not designed to exist apart from a body. Thus our rescue comes only through "the redemption of our bodies" (8:23) in the form of resurrection.

8:12 The approach here is similar to 6:1-13, where a description of the fact of regeneration (1-11) was followed by exhortations to Christians to live consistently with their new inner life (12-13). Here, vv. 5-11 are likewise descriptive. They describe the difference between existing for the flesh and for the Spirit, and affirm that Christians do indeed exist according to the Spirit. Now vv. 12-13 set forth the *personal responsibility* resting upon those who are in the Spirit.

The facts that we have been regenerated, and that we have received the gift of the indwelling Holy Spirit, do not in themselves guarantee holy living. They make holy living possible; this is one of the great gifts of grace celebrated in the gospel. But they do not make it automatic and inevitable. Grace does not make us robots; we are still freewill creatures who must personally seize the opportunity and actualize the possibility created by grace.

Therefore, brothers, we have an obligation . . . . This is directed specifically and personally to Christians (brothers). It is not a formal exhortation, but it has the force of one. Literally it says "we are debtors" (see 1:14). We *owe* it to God to live a holy life. It is an absolute obligation based on the fact that he is our Creator, and it is a debt of gratitude based on the fact that he is our Redeemer.

. . . but it is not to the sinful nature, to live according to it. Literally, we are debtors "not to the flesh, to live according to the flesh." We owe nothing to the flesh, to our as-yet-unredeemed bodies. We do *not* "owe it to ourselves" to experience as much physical and earthly pleasure as possible (Phil 3:19).

Actually Paul does not finish his sentence. He tells us we are *not* debtors to the flesh, but he stops before stating the obvious, namely, that we *are* debtors to the Spirit, to live according to the Spirit. Without hesitation we can assume that this is his point, in view of the contrast between flesh and Spirit pervading this context. I.e., we owe it to God to take full advantage of the power and the potential existing within us through the Spirit — the power to overcome the sinful cravings of the flesh and the potential to obey God's commandments to the fullest.

Contrary to the NIV, this is the first use in 8:1-13 of the terminology "*living* according to the flesh" and (by implication) "*living* according to the Spirit." In 8:4 "walking" is basically the same as "living." But vv. 5, 8-9 speak of *being* in the flesh or Spirit. Unbelievers *are* in the flesh, just as Christians *are* in the Spirit. This is our status, our position, our nature. "Are" describes a reality that exists. But now, given this reality, it is our responsibility to *live* in accordance with it. Now that we exist in the Spirit, we owe it to him to live up to the potential he provides. (See 6:2.)

8:13 The reason Paul breaks off his sentence is so that he can pursue the theme of living according to the flesh. He issues a solemn warning, stressing the danger of continuing to live the lifestyle of the flesh now that we are in the Spirit. **For if you live**

according to the sinful nature [literally, "flesh"], **you will die . . . .**
"Die" cannot mean die physically, for that will happen regardless.
Thus it means die spiritually by reverting to an unsaved condition;
or die eternally in hell. Actually these cannot be separated; those
who are spiritually dead will die the eternal death. This is the "law
of sin and death" (8:2).

This verse is a strong affirmation of the real possibility that a
Christian can fall from grace and lose his salvation. Those who
cling to the dogma of "once saved, always saved" deny this, of
course. Moo (I:528) says he favors the "Calvinist" interpretation,
i.e., that "the truly regenerate believer, while often committing
'fleshly' acts, will be infallibly prevented from living a fleshly lifestyle by the Spirit within." This view, he says, "in no way mitigates
the seriousness of the warning Paul gives here." MacArthur (I:422)
agrees: "The apostle is not warning genuine believers that they may
lose their salvation and be condemned to death if they fall back
into some of the ways of the flesh. . . . He is rather saying that a
person whose life is characterized by the things of the flesh is not a
true Christian and is spiritually dead."

Such comments are incredible in view of the fact that Paul here
directs this warning specifically to his "brothers" (v. 12). He is not
speaking of an anonymous "anyone" (v. 9) who is not a true
Christian, but is speaking directly to these brothers in second
person plural: "If *you* live according to the flesh, *you* will die." To
say that it cannot really happen "in no way mitigates the seriousness of the warning," and to say that the Spirit will "infallibly
prevent" the very thing he warns against, approaches the limits of
spiritual confusion. *Of course* it mitigates the seriousness of the
warning! If living according to the flesh is impossible for Christians,
then this "warning" is *meaningless* to the very ones to whom it is
addressed, and it can be totally ignored.

The warning is serious and relevant: if believers continue to live
according to the flesh, they will die. But the warning is balanced by a
glorious promise: **. . . but if by the Spirit you put to death the misdeeds of the body, you will live . . . .** This is the Christian's other
possibility. He can continue to live the fleshly lifestyle, yes (and die!);
or he can put to death the sins of the body (and live!). "Misdeeds" is
the word *praxis*. It means "acts, deeds" or "evil deeds," depending

on the context.⁷¹ The latter is the connotation here; hence "misdeeds" (see Acts 19:18; Col 3:9). The misdeeds "of the body" are the sinful deeds that result from the law of sin that resides in the flesh, i.e., the as-yet-unredeemed body (6:6; 7:18, 23-25).

These and any other sins are to be "put to death," mortified (KJV), killed. This is the opposite of *living* according to the flesh. We can either let these sins continue to live in us and kill us, or we can kill them (see Col 3:5). The latter must be our choice. The sins of the body must be attacked at their very root, where they are imbedded in our flesh on the level of our inclinations and desires. Like Paul, we must beat or buffet our bodies and make them our slaves (1 Cor 9:27), gaining control of our passions. We must train ourselves not only on the level of acting but also on the level of willing or desiring (Phil 2:13).

The point of this is not to punish the body as such, as an end in itself, but to do what is necessary to squelch the *sins* of the body. This requires spiritual discipline, not necessarily asceticism.

We must note here again the Christian's personal responsibility for this discipline: "if . . . *you* put to death." Again, this is not automatic and inevitable; we must personally will it and do it. As Lard says (263), "The will is to be your will, the effort your effort, and the result your deed." After all, our spirits have been regenerated and in principle set free from the enslaving power of sin that remains in our bodies, and thus we should be able to bring our bodies under control in the service of righteousness (6:6-7, 12-14).

But this is not the whole story; it is not even the main point of the story. Yes, we have been renewed in our spirits, but we still find ourselves locked in a discouraging struggle with our indwelling sin (7:14-25). So what is the key to victory in this struggle? Whence comes our rescue from this body of death (7:24)? The key to victory lies in these three words: "*by the Spirit*"! The Spirit's power alone ensures victory in our battle against sin; this is why he lives within us. He gives us the power to put sin to death. "The Spirit of God — and only the Spirit of God — is to be the means of the destruction

---

⁷¹Maurer says most of the 7 NT uses of *praxis* seem to have a "derogatory nuance." In Rom 8:13 "it has a strong inclination to the ethically negative side" (πράσσω, 6:643).

of the flesh and its activities" (Cranfield, I:394). On a conscious level we are aggressively putting sin to death, but below the level of our consciousness the Spirit is empowering us for this victory. See Lard, 263; MP, 360.

The promise to those who succeed, by the Spirit, is eternal life: "You will live." This can be nothing less than the glory of heaven. This promise is a fitting conclusion to the section on our struggle with and victory over sin (7:14-8:13); and it is also a fitting transition to the next section, which emphasizes our assurance of ultimate victory in the end (8:14-39).

One last question must be raised concerning v. 13. If Paul is here warning Christians that they will lose their salvation if they persist in living according to the flesh, and if he is promising eternal life to those who overcome sin, does this not compromise the basic gospel truth that we become, are, and remain justified *by faith*? Does this not make *remaining* justified dependent on works? No, but it does show the very close connection between faith and works (obedience). Justification is always by faith; but this faith must produce the "obedience of faith" (1:5). Otherwise the faith itself will die, and so will the individual. Faith produces works; but good works also strengthen and nourish faith, while sinful deeds poison and strangle it (see Matt 13:20-22). A Christian who continues to live according to the flesh is like a person who deliberately drinks poison. His faith will die, then he will die. But the Christian who puts sin to death and lives obediently is keeping his faith robust and strong. He will surely live.

Grace is a double cure, and it is all or nothing. One cannot accept the justification that comes by faith, and then refuse the sanctification made possible by the Holy Spirit. That is one of Paul's main points in this whole section (chs. 6-8).

III. 8:14-39 — THE ASSURANCE OF FINAL AND TOTAL VICTORY OVER THE FALLEN WORLD

The theme of this third main part of Romans (chs. 6-8) is that the all-sufficiency of grace gives us victory over sin. The focus is on the second aspect of the double cure: regeneration and sanctification through the Holy Spirit. In sections I and II of Part Three, it has become clear that sanctification cannot be completed until our *bodies* have been brought within the scope of Christ's redemptive work.

This leads to the subject of glorification, which is the final step of sanctification and the climax of the entire salvation process. When Jesus returns in the last day, the state of glory begins. It will include first of all and primarily the resurrection of believers' bodies into a glorified state (8:23), but will also include the renovation of the universe to be an appropriate home adapted to the eternal needs of glorified human beings (8:20-21; Rev 21:1-7). This is the unifying theme of this present section.

Paul approaches the subject in terms of *inheritance*. In 4:11-18, where believers are identified as Abraham's heirs (see Gal 3:1-4:7), the emphasis is upon the *means* of receiving the inheritance, namely, faith in the promises of God. Here the emphasis is upon the full content of this inheritance (a glorified body in a glorified universe), and the assurance that it will indeed be ours, based on our status as God's adopted children.

A. THE HOLY SPIRIT MARKS US
AS SONS AND HEIRS (8:14-17)

The inheritance of glory will be ours because we are sons or children of God. If we have the Spirit of God, we are his children; and if we are his children, we are his heirs. That is the point of this paragraph in a nutshell.

The Spirit plays a key role in this picture, but it is important to define this role carefully. In general, the Spirit provides God's people with two kinds of benefits: those relating to *knowledge* (e.g., the inspiration of Scripture), and those relating to *power* (e.g., sanctification). Most interpreters approach vv. 14-17 in terms of knowledge. They think this passage teaches that the Holy Spirit affects us cognitively, directly implanting knowledge in our minds concerning our status as children of God. I believe Paul's main point is quite different, namely, that the Spirit gives us the power to live the kind of life indicative of a child of God, and the power to confidently claim our filial relationship with the Father.

Thus the point is not that the Spirit *makes* us children of God as such, nor that he makes us *aware* that we are children of God through some mysterious inner revelation. The idea rather is that the Spirit *marks* us as God's children indirectly through what he enables us to do. By objectively observing his mark upon our lives, we ourselves as well as others can have assurance that we belong to God's family and are heirs of his glory.

8:14 because those who are led by the Spirit of God are sons of God. This section expands on the promise at the end of v. 13, "You will live" in eternal glory. You will live, that is, *if* by the Spirit you put to death the sins of the body. But how does putting sin to death lead to eternal glory? Because those who do this "are sons of God," which makes them heirs of eternal life.

The key is to see that putting sins to death by the Spirit in v. 13 is the same general idea as being led by the Spirit in v. 14 (Cranfield, I:395, 401). Those who ignore this connection tend to give "led by the Spirit" a cognitive meaning; i.e., the Spirit leads us by enlightening our minds in some subjective and mystical way. He "guides" us by inwardly showing us the right thing to do or by helping us to know God's will in specific circumstances.

But this is not the point. The Spirit leads us not by subjective enlightenment of our minds, but by inward empowerment of our wills. He "strengthens the human spirit, to enable it to control the flesh" (Lard, 264), i.e., to "put to death the misdeeds of the body." He leads not by overriding our wills and driving or dragging us along.[72] Rather, his leading is an inward prodding of the conscience, an influence upon the heart, an empowerment of the will to do what we already know is right based on the teaching of Scripture. Our problem after all is not ignorance as such but moral weakness. The Spirit leads us by taking our hand and giving us inner strength to walk in the paths of righteousness.

Being led by the Spirit is another term for walking or living according to the Spirit (8:4, 12-13), and includes producing the fruit of the Spirit (Gal 5:18, 22-25). It refers to one's lifestyle, and means "to have the direction of one's life as a whole determined by the Spirit" (Moo, I:534).

---

[72]Contra Godet, 309; Käsemann, 226; Dunn, I:450.

The main point of the verse is this: those led by the Spirit are "sons of God,"[73] and *that* is why they can be sure they will live in eternal glory. The Spirit-led lifestyle is a sign of sonship, and in this way the Spirit's influence upon our lives marks us as God's sons. By enabling us to live the distinctive lifestyle of the redeemed, the Spirit becomes our seal (Eph 1:13-14), our distinguishing mark, our "family crest." Being led by the Spirit is not what *makes* us children of God; we "are all sons of God through faith in Christ Jesus" (Gal 3:26). But by allowing the Spirit to lead us, we *show* ourselves to be sons of God; we demonstrate that it is so (see Morris, 313; Moo, I:534). We demonstrate it not just to others but to ourselves, and thus we become strengthened in our confidence and assurance of our acceptance with God.

8:15 For you did not receive a spirit that makes you a slave again to fear, but you received the Spirit of sonship [literally, "Spirit of adoption"]. (See 1 Cor 2:12; Gal 4:6; 2 Tim 1:7.) The first question here is whether πνεῦμα, (*pneuma*, "spirit") refers to the Holy Spirit or to a disposition or attitude of the human heart. The NASB says, "a spirit of slavery" and "a spirit of adoption," meaning the attitudes of a slave and of a son respectively. Most expositors reject this interpretation and rightly see this word as a reference to the Holy Spirit. The verb "received" is aorist (past) tense, indicating a single past event when the Spirit was received, namely, baptism (Acts 2:38). See Cranfield, I:396; Lard, 264.

The idea is this: the Holy Spirit, whom we received in our baptism, is *not* a spirit who marks us as slaves and thus engenders a slave's servile and cringing approach to God: obedience motivated by fear of punishment. Rather, the Holy Spirit is one who enables us to see ourselves as true sons of God, whose obedience is motivated by loving gratitude and a genuine desire to please him. Just as the Spirit empowers us to put sin to death and obey God's law, so also does he enable us to change our deepest desires and motives and dispositions, and to adjust them from those of a slave to those of a son. As Phil 2:13 says, God (the Holy Spirit) works in us to empower not just our doing but our very willing itself.

The word "again" refers to our pre-Christian lives, where our basic identity was indeed that of a *slave* to sin and lawlessness (6:17-

---

[73]See 8:19; 9:26; 2 Cor 6:18; Gal 3:16; 4:6; Heb 2:10; 12:5-7.

20) and to the law (7:6). Though the sense of enslavement to sin is still present in us to some degree because of the influence exerted upon us by the sin that still indwells our bodies (7:14-25), we have been set free from sin's inevitability (6:17-22; 8:2), and our basic identity now is that of a *son*. The Spirit does not rescue us from one kind of slavery just to entangle us in another. True, our present relationship to God is that of slave to master (6:22; Eph 6:6). This imagery is still appropriate as a reminder of our absolute *obligation* to obey God's will. But regarding our *motivation*, we now have the freedom of sons. We no longer obey because we feel the yoke on our necks and the whip on our backs. We no longer fear death (Heb 2:14-15); we have no fear of judgment and condemnation. God's fatherly love for us, and our reciprocal love toward him, combine to cast out such fear (1 John 4:18).

The reference to *adoption* distinguishes our sonship from the unique Sonship of Jesus Christ, the only-begotten Son of God (John 3:16), but it does not suggest that ours is a mere pseudo-sonship. In the Greek and Roman cultures of Paul's day, those adopted into a family became sons in every sense of the word, and possessed the same rights as natural sons (see Dunn, I:460; Moo, I:536), especially with regard to inheritance. In fact, one of the main reasons for adopting a son was to appoint an heir for an otherwise sonless father. Now of course, God is not Sonless, and he does not need more heirs in the normal sense of that word (since he is not going to die!), but he *wants* to add as many as possible to his family so that he can share his unlimited "estate" with them, as an earthly father bestows his goods on his children through his will.

As the Spirit of adoption, the Holy Spirit does not cause the adoption and *make* us sons of God. Again, his coming into our lives *marks* us as sons by engendering within us the attitude of sons rather than slaves.

And by him — by the Spirit — **we cry, "*Abba*, Father."** "Cry" is κράζω (*krazō*), a term used often in the LXX for sincere and urgent prayer, and for heartfelt praise to God (e.g., Isa 6:4). Here likewise it indicates a deeply-felt and emotional acknowledgement of our sonship, poured forth from the heart as a positive counterpart to the mournful outcry of 7:24.

The word *abba* is Aramaic, which was the Hebrew-like language spoken by Jews in NT times. *Abba* was the intimate term used by a child to address his male parent, similar to "Dada" or "Daddy" in English. By the time of Jesus it was not limited to the speech of children (Cranfield, I:400); but it was still a term of intimacy and endearment, not one the Jews would presume to use in addressing God. But Jesus used it (Mark 14:36), and from Rom 8:15 and Gal 4:6 it is apparent that Christians were taught to do the same in imitation of their Lord.

Use of this term in addressing God has several implications. First, it is "a family word, expressive of family familiarity and intimacy" (Dunn, I:461). When we use it, we are acknowledging that God is our Father and we are his children. Second, it indicates that our relationship to our Father is one of closeness, tenderness, and childlike confidence. It shows that even the transcendent God is not distant and alien from his children (see 1:8). Third, it expresses our family solidarity with Christ, since *our* "Abba" is *his* "Abba." He is "the firstborn among many brothers" (8:29). In a real (though not complete) sense we have a shared sonship and joint heirship with Christ (8:17).

In all three NT passages where the term is used, the full expression is ἀββά ὁ πατήρ (*abba ho patēr*); that is, the Aramaic word is followed by the Greek equivalent. Some think the biblical writers added *ho patēr* in order to translate *abba* to those unfamiliar with Aramaic. Others think the entire phrase was "an established formula in the churches," a "single dual-form ejaculatory cry" (Dunn, I:453, 461). Today we would say "Abba! Father!"

To be able to address God as "Abba! Father!" is an indication of our assurance that we are truly his children. By doing so we bear witness to both God and man that we are sons and daughters of God. That we do so *by the Spirit* reflects the Spirit's role in empowering us to live the kind of life expected of a member of God's family and in enabling us to do so in the spirit of sons and not slaves. In this way the Spirit empowers us to declare our sonship and to claim all the rights and privileges related to it: "Abba! Father!" Again, the Spirit's role is not to add content to our knowledge, but strength to our wills.[74]

---

[74]See 1 Cor 12:2, where the Spirit gives us the strength also to confess "Jesus is Lord!" even in threatening circumstances.

8:16 The Spirit himself testifies with our spirit that we are God's children. Most agree that this verse speaks of the Holy Spirit bearing witness in relation to our personal spirit (the soul or inner man). But exactly what does this mean? The verb is συμμαρτυρέω (*symmartyreō*), which combines *martyreō*, "to testify, to bear witness," and *syn*, "with." Does this mean the Spirit "bears witness *with*" our spirit, or "bears witness *to*" our spirit? Most agree that the former is the literal meaning of the word, but they treat it as if it means the latter. In truth, the crucial question is this: *to whom* is the Spirit's witness addressed? Most commentators say this verse refers to the inward, experiential, subjective testimony of the Spirit directly to our spirit, a testimony that gives us assurance that we are indeed children of God. It is "a direct operation of the Holy Spirit on our spirit," says Morris (317).

Whether the Spirit's testimony is distinct from our testimony is a matter of dispute. Some say v. 15 ("Abba! Father!") is *our* testimony, while v. 16 is a separate witness altogether. Others combine the two more or less into a single witness. Our cry of "Abba! Father!" is itself the Spirit's testimony, they say, since we could not utter this cry apart from the Spirit. Some versions translate vv. 15b-16 to reflect this idea: "When we cry, 'Abba! Father!' it is that very Spirit bearing witness with our spirit that we are children of God" (NRSV, endorsed by Stott, 232).

I strongly disagree with this view. For one thing, v. 16 does not begin with the common particle indicating a causal connection with the previous verse (γάρ, *gar*, "for, because"). Paul uses *gar* thirteen times with this meaning in 8:1-26. Why would he omit it here if he wants us to see a causal relationship between the Spirit's testimony (v. 16) and our cry of "Abba! Father!" (v. 15)?

Also, a main point of Romans, especially in 3:21-5:21, is that assurance of salvation is not only possible but is the expected result of a right *objective* understanding of grace and of what it means to be justified by faith in the atoning blood of Christ. (See the "much more" theme in 5:1-11.) In addition, through his sanctifying power as it affects both our outward lives (v. 14) and our inward consciousness (v. 15), the Spirit has already given us reason to cry "Abba! Father!"

In what way, then, does the Spirit testify *along with* our spirit, that we are children of God? The natural understanding of the word is that his testimony is directed toward the same audience as our own, namely, to the Father. When we cry "Abba! Father!" we bear witness to him that we are his children. Then the Spirit adds his own testimony to ours, likewise bearing witness to the Father that we are his children.[75] See Smith, II:5.

We have assurance that someone besides ourselves is confirming our testimony to the Father. The fact that Paul is here *telling* us that the Spirit likewise testifies to the Father that we are his true sons and daughters makes our assurance even more firm. This is similar to the Spirit's intercession between us and the Father in 8:26-27. This is not necessary for the Father's sake, but knowing that it happens gives *us* a sense of calmness and assurance.

The content of the Spirit's testimony is that we are "children of God" (see 8:21; 9:8; Phil 2:15). This is probably not meant to imply anything different from "sons of God" in v. 14. The point is that we are part of his family (see 2 Cor 6:18).

8:17 Now if we are children, then we are heirs — heirs of God and co-heirs with Christ . . . . Here we come to the main point of this paragraph, that we are God's *heirs*. The argument is very simple: if we are led by God's Spirit, then we are God's children; and if we are God's children, then we are his heirs. This builds upon the prominent OT theme that the Jews were heirs of the "promised land." We now see this as pointing to the higher reality of all believers' ultimate inheritance of all the glories of heaven (1 Pet 1:4).

Our identity as heirs of God involves three emphases. The first is the sheer amount or *content* of the inheritance, which includes all the riches and wealth of the entire creation. The second point is that our possession of this wealth is still *future*. We are heirs, but we do not yet possess the full inheritance; we have only a foretaste of it (see v. 23). The third emphasis is the *certainty* of our ultimate possession of it all. This seems to be the main idea in the concept of "co-heirs with Christ." Our right to be heirs of God is based on our relationship to Jesus, the one true Son and heir (Gal 3:16-29); and our assurance of ultimately receiving the inheritance is as firm and

---

[75]Some link this with the need for two or more witnesses to convict a criminal under Moses' Law (Deut 19:15), but this connection is doubtful.

secure as that of Jesus himself. "Whatever inheritance . . . awaits him as Son, also awaits you as children" (Lard, 267; see Cranfield, 1:407).

We are heirs of God and co-heirs with Christ **if indeed we share in his sufferings in order that we may also share in his glory.** As in 8:9, εἴπερ (*eiper*) means "if, if indeed." This specifies a particular condition for heirship, namely, the same one that applied to Jesus: first suffering, then glory. Jesus necessarily followed this path (Luke 24:26; Phil 2:6-11; Heb 2:10; 12:2). If we want to be co-heirs with him, we must be willing to accept this same sequence, since "participation in Christ's glory can come only through participation in his sufferings" (Moo, I:543).[76]

What kind of sufferings are indicated here? The text says simply "if we suffer with, in order that we may also be glorified with." Neither verb has an object ("him"); but both have the prefix *syn* ("with"), which implies an object. This object is no doubt Christ: "if we suffer with Christ." The concepts of suffering for righteousness' sake and suffering for Christ's sake are found in many passages.[77] The main point, though, is not that being a Christian guarantees suffering. It is rather this, that faithful suffering with Christ guarantees that we will share in his glory (2:3-4; 2 Cor 4:17). On "glory," see 2:7, 10; 3:2. As MacArthur has well said (I:448), "The more a believer suffers in this life for the sake of the Lord, the greater will be his capacity for glory in heaven."

B. THE REDEEMED COSMOS IS OUR INHERITANCE (8:18-25)

This paragraph is a brief explanation of at least part of the "glory" that constitutes our inheritance. The main focus is the promise of redeemed bodies (v. 23). This is appropriate and expected in view of the fact that thus far only our spirits have been regenerated, and the fact that our as-yet-unredeemed bodies are a major source of the sin against which we still struggle. The redemption of our bodies will

---

[76]See John 15:20; 16:33; 2 Cor 1:5; 1 Pet 4:13-16; 5:10.

[77]Generally, Matt 5:10-12; 1 Pet 4:14, 17. Specifically, 2 Cor 1:5; Phil 1:29; 3:10; Col 1:24; 2 Tim 3:12; 1 Pet 4:1, 13-16.

mean that our entire being has finally been redeemed, and that our victory over sin is complete. Moreover, the redemption of our bodies will be accompanied by the redemption of the entire universe.

8:18 I consider that our present sufferings are not worth comparing with the glory that will be revealed in us.[78] The point here is the contrast between our present suffering and our future glory. The former includes everything we suffer specifically as Christians, and possibly (in this verse) all the other suffering that we must endure just because we live in a fallen world. The latter includes such things as natural disasters, disease, frustration, and death (see Moo, I:548; Morris, 319). These sufferings are said to belong specifically to the "now time," which refers not to any one period in earth's history but to the whole era of fallenness, from the sin of the first Adam to the return of the second Adam (12:2; Gal 1:4). This is what Scripture calls "this age" in contrast with "that age" (Luke 20:34-35) or "the age to come" (Matt 12:32; Mark 10:30; Eph 1:21). The bad news is that such sufferings exist; the good news is that they will end when we pass into the age to come. Just knowing they are temporary helps us endure them.

Just as this age is marked by suffering, so (for believers) the coming age is the age of glory (see v. 17). This glory will be "revealed in us," or more accurately, "revealed *to* us." This act of revealing is not a "manifestation of that which already exists" (contra Moo, I:549), since in this context the reference is mainly to our new bodies and the new universe. These exist now only in the mind and plan of God (Murray, I:301), and will be unveiled to us upon completion at the time of the second coming. Even though we are already sons and heirs, we do not yet have our full inheritance. There is still plenty to hope for (8:24-25).

The Greek describes this glory as "coming" or "about to come" (μέλλω, *mellō*, not translated in the NIV). Some take this as an indication that Paul expected this eschatological revelation to happen very soon ("about to be" revealed, NRSV). Others take it as emphasizing the certainty of this future revelation, but not necessarily its imminence. The latter view is probably correct (see v. 13), and the

---

[78]For "I consider" (λογίζομαι) see 3:28.

translation should read "the glory that will surely be revealed to us" in the age to come.

The main point is the contrast between the present suffering and the coming glory. While the former may seem serious and odious while we are in the midst of it, we should try to "step back" and view it from the perspective of eternal glory. In terms of weight, the sufferings hardly show up on the scale at all, while the coming glory presses it all the way down. See 2 Cor 4:17.

8:19 The creation waits in eager expectation for the sons of God to be revealed. The focus here seems to shift abruptly to "the creation." Though some have included more, the most common and most likely view is that this refers to the physical or natural world, or all of creation except human beings and angels.[79]

This verse depicts the physical universe as earnestly, breathlessly expecting something. This is emphatically stated in rather unusual wording, literally: "the eager expectation of the creation is eagerly awaiting." The noun translated "eager expectation" is usually identified as a compound word that means "to stretch out the head, to crane the neck forward" in an attempt to see something.[80] Phillips translates, "Creation is on tiptoe." Whatever the etymology, the word represents an especially strong sense of expectation. This is compounded by the verb, which itself means "to await eagerly."

What is striking here is that the impersonal creation is pictured as having a personal sense of deep longing and earnest expectation. It is also described as being filled with frustration (v. 20) and groaning (v. 22). In each case nature is being *personified*, or treated as a personal entity for rhetorical purposes. The OT precedent for this is abundant; see, e.g., Ps 96:12; 98:8; Isa 35:1; 55:12; 65:12-13; Jer 4:28.

Exactly what is the object of the creation's "earnest expectation"? Literally, it is "the revelation of the sons of God." A common explanation of this is that believers are already sons of God, but this sonship is now veiled. At the second coming it will be revealed and will become a matter of public knowledge. (See Cranfield, I:412-413; Dunn, I:470.) This is not the point, however. We are

---

[79]Lard speculates that this probably includes animals (270).
[80]Balz has doubts about this meaning ("ἀποκαραδοκία," 132).

already sons, yes; but until we get our new bodies, our sonship is not complete. Not even we know all the glory that our sonship entails (1 John 3:1-2). Thus not only we, but the whole of creation is eagerly awaiting the unveiling of the "new model" of the human body.[81]

8:20 For the creation was subjected to frustration . . . . This carries the connection between mankind and the creation back to the Fall. The reason the creation's ultimate deliverance is linked to that of mankind is because its fallenness was caused by man's sin. When God placed the human race in charge of the rest of the material creation (Gen 1:26-28), from that point on the fate of the latter was tied to that of the former. When Adam sinned, God declared, "Cursed is the ground because of you" (Gen 3:17). Instead of man's servant, the earth became his antagonist. Instead of perpetuating man's life indefinitely, it is forced to engorge man's dead body into its dusty maw (Gen 3:18-19).

Through this curse the creation was subjected to frustration. "Subjected" is ὑποτάσσω (*hypotassō*), "to place under the power or authority of." Figuratively, the creation was placed under the power of "frustration." This is the word ματαιότης (*mataiotēs*), which is used 37 times in the LXX version of Ecclesiastes ("Vanity of vanities; all is vanity," 1:2, KJV). It conveys the idea of futility, emptiness, purposelessness, and meaninglessness.

The main idea is that the physical universe was originally created to play the role of servant under the lordship of man (Gen 1:26-28). Under this benevolent dictatorship it was intended to serve man's needs and in so doing to glorify God. Man's first sin, however, included an attempt to manipulate the creation and to misuse it for vainglorious purposes. As a result of this sin and its subsequent curse, man became the creation's slave instead of its master. Thus the creation itself was wrested from its original role in the intended order of things and can no longer fulfill its intended function or purpose. Thus the concept of *mataiotēs*: "lacking the purpose for which it was designed, it has no purpose" (Morris, 321; see Dunn, I:470).

---

[81]The body Jesus had during the forty days between his resurrection and his ascension was not "the resurrection body" in its glorified state (Cottrell, "Faith"). See 1 John 3:2.

"Frustration" presumes the personal ability to understand this condition of meaninglessness and to feel a sense of helplessness to do anything about it. The NIV translation thus continues the personification of nature, as in v. 19. Understanding it thus, Cranfield (I:413) says, "The sub-human creation has been subjected to the frustration of not being able properly to fulfill the purpose of its existence." This is why it is eagerly awaiting the revelation of the sons of God. When man's redemption fully comes, the creation will then be able to fulfill its own original purpose.

Exactly *who* subjected the creation to this state of futility? Paul says it occurred **not by its own choice, but by the will of the one who subjected it, in hope . . . .** Its state of meaninglessness is not its own fault; it did not choose to rebel against its Maker and abandon its intended role. Its present state is the result of someone else's choice. Indirectly it came from Adam and Eve's decision to sin. Thus some say "the one who subjected it" is Adam. Others rightly see this as referring to God, however. "Subjected" (ὑποτάσσω, *hypotassō*) is an authoritative action, a judicial decision, and thus something only God could rightfully have done (Cranfield, I:414). Man committed the sin, but God pronounced the curse and brought it about. Also, attaching the element of hope to the curse is something only God could have done (Murray, I:303).

The phrase "in hope" more likely modifies "subjected," whether one begins v. 21 with "that" or "because," and whether or not we include a comma after "subjected it." At the very beginning of this age of the curse and of suffering and frustration, God saw fit to include the promise of redemption through the seed of the woman (Gen 3:15). This provided a basis for hope, and this hope in turn became the basis for the creation's eager anticipation (v. 19).

The NIV says the creation was subjected "by the will of the one who subjected it." The Greek says it was subjected "because of" or "for the sake of" the one who subjected it. In what sense was God's action of subjecting the creation to meaninglessness and frustration *for his own sake*? It was necessary in order to uphold the integrity of his holiness in the face of sin; he did it to glorify his holy character (see Lard, 272).

8:21 What is the content of this hope that causes the creation to eagerly await the revelation of God's sons? It is the hope **that the creation itself will be liberated from its bondage to decay and brought into the glorious freedom of the children of God.**

The universe is not only "subjected to frustration"; it is also in a state of "bondage to decay." "Decay" (φθορά, *phthora*) can mean moral corruption (2 Pet 1:4; 2:19); or, as here, it can mean breakdown and decay in the physical world (2 Pet 2:12). Some decay is natural and was no doubt a part of the good creation from the beginning. For example, the growth and seasonal cycles of plants and trees, and their production of edible fruit, vegetables, seeds, and leaves, will necessarily leave a residue that is reabsorbed by the earth through the process of decay.

The cosmic Fall, however, resulted in a *bondage* to decay. This means that death and decay overran their intended boundaries and engulfed what was never meant to die and dissolve — especially the bodies of human beings (Gen 3:19b; 1 Cor 15:42). It also means that the entire universe is undergoing an inexorable process of cosmic decay, which is sometimes called the law of entropy. This "refers to the constant and irreversible degradation of matter and energy in the universe to increasing disorder," says MacArthur. Indeed, "the natural bent of the universe — whether of humans, animals, plants, or the inanimate elements of the earth and heavens — is obviously and demonstrably downward, not upward" (I:455-456). I would hardly call it "natural," though. Rather, it is quite unnatural, being the result of God's curse and the source of the frustration noted in v. 20.

The bad news is that the entire cosmos has fallen with Adam; the good news is that the whole thing "will be liberated" from the consequences brought upon it by sin. The final glory that will be revealed to God's children will include not just new and glorified bodies, but also a completely renewed universe to serve as our eternal home. "Creation itself must be redeemed in order that redeemed man may have a fitting environment" (Dunn, I:471). Thus the second coming of Christ will be the time of "the renewal of all things" (Matt 19:28), or the "restoration of all things" (Acts 3:21, NASB). Out of the cleansing cosmic fire will come new heavens and a new earth, completely purged of sin's effects and fully indwelt by righteousness (2 Pet 3:10-13; see Isa 65:17; 66:22;

Rev 21:1). In that day the meek will inherit the new earth, in which there will no longer be any curse (Matt 5:5; Rev 22:3).

No wonder the entire universe is eagerly waiting "for the sons of God to be revealed" (v. 19). That will be the day of its own redemption, a *cosmic redemption* through which it participates in "the glorious freedom of the children of God." The latter phrase is better translated literally, "the freedom of the glory of the children of God," where *glory* stands in stark and utter contrast with *decay*. The glorified universe will be the inheritance of every believer. It is in a sense God's gift to Christ and his new bride (Rev 21:1-2), the ultimate wedding gift of a new universe!

8:22 We know that the whole creation has been groaning as in the pains of childbirth right up to the present time. This verse adds one more description of the (personified) universe's present fallen state. The frustration resulting from being in bondage to decay is depicted as expressing itself in groaning and suffering as if in pain. Two parallel verbs describe this idea: "to groan with" and "to suffer agony with." The prefix "with" (σύν, *syn*), attached to both verbs, signifies that all parts of the creation are jointly participating in the pain of purposelessness.

Without its prefix the first verb means to sigh or groan or even complain because of undesirable circumstances from which one longs to be free (see v. 23). The second verb means especially to be in travail or to suffer the pains of childbirth. This is appropriate in view of the fact that pain in childbirth is part of the very curse which is the source of the creation's pain (Gen 3:16). The main point in referring to "the pains of childbirth" is to emphasize the seriousness of the curse under which the creation groans. "Right up to the present time" indicates that the pain of the curse was constant from Eden up to the very moment of Paul's writing. As the context shows, it will continue without relief until the day of our resurrection.[82]

8:23 Not only so, but we ourselves, who have the firstfruits of the Spirit, groan inwardly as we wait eagerly for our adoption as

---

[82]This simple phrase, as well as this whole section, shows the fallacy of the notion that believers receive their resurrection bodies as soon as they die. The resurrection of our bodies and the renewing of the universe are interrelated.

sons, the redemption of our bodies. Not only does the whole creation groan out of frustration at not being able to fulfill its intended purpose, but so do we also ourselves. "We also ourselves" (the literal Greek wording) is stated twice in this verse for emphasis. We Christians — yes, even *we Christians* — groan inwardly. That is, we also have an inward sense of pain and frustration growing out of our own inability to conform to God's will for us. Having the firstfruits of the Spirit gives us the desire and the ability to live holy lives, but we are still locked in mortal combat with the law of sin that dwells in our unredeemed bodies. To use Stott's term (242-243), as yet we are only "half-saved." Thus we groan because of our own fallenness and sin, and we groan especially out of longing for the completion of our redemption, the gift of a new body. (See 2 Cor 5:2, 4).

The contrast between the "already" and the "not yet" is strong here. The main verb is "we groan," but it is modified by two parallel participles, "having" and "eagerly awaiting." In other words, we already have part of our salvation, part of our inheritance as God's sons; but part of it is still in the future, and we can only look forward to it in earnest hope.

What we already have is called "the firstfruits of the Spirit."[83] The idea of firstfruits was common in Bible times. As the choice part of the harvest, it constituted an appropriate sacrifice or offering to God (Exod 23:19; Lev 23:10-11; Deut 18:4; 26:1-4). The first converts to Christ in a particular area were called "firstfruits" (16:5; 1 Cor 16:15). Christ himself is the firstfruits in reference to the resurrection (1 Cor 15:20, 23).

To say that we have the firstfruits of the Spirit means that even though we do not yet have our complete inheritance as God's children, we have already received a significant portion of it in terms of the gift of the indwelling Holy Spirit, along with all he has already accomplished for us in the way of regeneration and sanctification. This is the sense in which the Spirit is the *"earnest* of our inheritance" (Eph 1:13), i.e., the down payment, the first installment, the

---

[83]We also already have forgiveness or justification, but here the emphasis is on the second part of the double cure, in which the Holy Spirit is especially involved.

deposit, the pledge of the fullness of glory (see 2 Cor 1:22; 5:5). In this sense the "firstfruits" are not simply the beginning of the harvest, but are also the guarantee that much more will follow. And as this context shows, the complete inheritance includes the redemption of our bodies and a liberated, glorified universe.

On the other side of this picture, what does Paul say we do not yet have but are eagerly expecting? Our "adoption as sons." This raises a minor problem of interpretation. In vv. 14-16 Paul seems to be saying that we have *already* been adopted as sons; we *are* sons and children of God. So how can we be "waiting eagerly" for this adoption? Again, some say our sonship is real but not yet mani-fested; all we are waiting for is a public announcement of it (e.g., Bruce, 171; Cranfield, I:419). This does not do justice to the inten-sity of the expectation described in this paragraph, however. The idea is rather that we already have the *status* of adopted sons, but we do not yet have the full *inheritance* that goes with our adoption (Moo, I:537, 557). See 8:29. Even though our spirits have already been redeemed by the regenerating power of the Spirit, we will not be fully redeemed until we are clothed with our new bodies. Until then we are only half-saved.

The phrase "redemption of our bodies" has two important implications. First, physical bodies are a natural and necessary part of human existence. We are not complete human beings without them; our spirits are naked without their bodies (2 Cor 5:1-5). Contrary to most religions, we are not redeemed *from* our bodies; our bodies themselves are redeemed. Second, what will happen to our bodies in that event called "the resurrection" will truly be an act of *redemption*. This means that (just as in the physical universe as a whole) all the effects of sin will be gone; all defects and imperfec-tions will be corrected: the blind will see, the deaf will hear, the lame will run, the mentally handicapped will understand, and amputees will be made whole.

But the redemption of the body means much more than this. In the context of Rom 6-8, the true glory of the resurrection body is that it will be totally cleansed not just from the *effects* of sin but from *sin itself*, i.e., from its evil desires (6:12), its sinful passions (7:5), its indwelling sin (7:17-18), and the law of sin (7:23). It will no longer be a "body of sin" (6:6), a "body of death" (7:24), and "sinful flesh" (8:3). Thus the resurrection of the body is not just the issuing of a new and updated model to replace one that is old and worn out. It is a true act of *redemption*, an act of deliverance from sin itself. No wonder Paul depicts us and the entire universe as eagerly awaiting this final inheritance. It will be God's final answer to the question of 7:24.

8:24 For in this hope we were saved. "Were saved" is aorist (past) tense; it refers to the conversion event when we entered the sphere of grace. (For similar language see Eph 2:5, 8; 2 Tim 1:9; Titus 3:5.) At that time we were saved, but not completely so. That is why Paul says that we were saved "in hope." This should not be rendered "saved *by* hope" (contra KJV and Schlatter, 189). The point is that at first our salvation was only partial, but even then we knew that one day it would be made complete. Thus the element of hope has been present in our minds and hearts from the beginning, and we groan and hope at the same time. We groan because part of our salvation is still lacking, but we have the confident expectation that the missing part will one day be ours. (The distinctive element in hope is not uncertainty but *futurity*.)

But hope that is seen is no hope at all. Who hopes for what he already has? Here "hope" refers to the *object* of our hope. If we already see it, or have it in our possession, it can no longer be the object of hope. That would be a contradiction of terms. We only *hope* for things that are still in the future, things we know we will have one day but do not have yet.

The main point of this explanation of the futurity of hope is to remind us that a major aspect of our salvation is still in the future. This is meant to give us encouragement in the midst of our present sufferings (v. 18) and our present struggles against sin. Yes, we have been saved, but not completely so; so do not expect perfection and paradise yet. It will come, but in the meantime do not be discouraged and do not give up.

8:25 But if we hope for what we do not yet have, we wait for it patiently. The latter part of the verse literally reads, "Through patient endurance (ὑπομονή, *hypomonē*) we are eagerly expecting." (The latter word is the same one translated "wait eagerly" in v. 23.) These two aspects of our present attitude correspond to the two elements of hope.

First, since hope involves *futurity*, it is always for something we do not yet have. Thus hope requires patient endurance. On the meaning of *hypomone* see 5:3-4; it can also be translated "steadfastness" or "perseverance." As Moo says (I:559), it is basically the ability to bear up under pressures in order to attain desired goals. Thus it is not just a passive waiting as if in a vacuum, but an active confrontation with all that would derail our hope. See 1 Thess 1:3; Heb 10:36; Jas 1:3-4; Rev 13:10; 14:12.

Also, since hope involves *certainty*, it is always a matter of eager expectation. We can endure the delay, and we can endure the interim struggles and pressures, because we are sure the day of final glory is coming! As Dunn says (I:476), "The Christian perspective is determined not by the frustrations of the present, but by its future hope." To have redeemed bodies, to live forever in God's presence in the redeemed universe — what joyous expectations!

C. GOD PROMISES TO BRING HIS FAMILY
THROUGH EARTHLY TRIALS (8:26-30)

Overall this main section (8:14-39) assures us of ultimate victory over the fallen world. The key to this assurance is our membership in the family of God. The Holy Spirit working in us marks us as God's sons and heirs (8:14-17). Our inheritance is the fullness of glory, including redeemed bodies and a redeemed cosmos (8:18-25). But what about the present, with all its sufferings (8:17-18)? If we are truly God's family — his sons and daughters, why does he let us endure them? And how do we know that they will not overwhelm us and rob us of our victory over sin and the fallen world in general?

This brief paragraph addresses these questions. Paul reassures us that our heavenly Father does not expect us to cope on the basis of our own weakness; he has given us his Spirit to help us. He assures us that it has always been God's purpose to have a large family with many children; he will not allow any amount of earthly obstacles to thwart this purpose. In his omnipotence and wisdom he is able not only to help us overcome such obstacles, but also to use them for our ultimate benefit. He has been from the beginning, is now, and always will be in control of this family-building project. He will see us through it until its intended goal is accomplished.

8:26 In the same way, the Spirit helps us in our weakness. We do not know what we ought to pray for, but the Spirit himself intercedes for us with groans that words cannot express. "In the same way" indicates a comparison with something just preceding. Many think Paul is comparing the Spirit's groaning for us with the groaning of the creation and of ourselves (vv. 22-23).[84] While the idea of a threefold groaning is very interesting, this is probably not the point. More likely the comparison is between the way *hope* sustains us in the midst of present sufferings (vv. 18-25), and the way *the Spirit* sustains us by personally aiding us in our weakness.[85] The idea is that we have more than enough resources to keep us going in the midst of earthly trials.

What is the nature of "our weakness"? The word refers, as MacArthur says, to "our human condition in general" (I:466). This includes not only our natural finiteness, but also especially our spiritual weakness or sin-sickness, the second part of our "double trouble."[86] This includes weaknesses related to living in a not-yet-redeemed body and in a sin-corrupted world.

While acknowledging that such weakness exists, Paul's main point is that the Holy Spirit comes to our aid and gives us inward spiritual power at exactly those points where this weakness puts us in danger of doubt and sin. He shoulders the burdens of our suffering and fills in the breaches in our defenses against our spiritual enemies. This is his ongoing work of sanctification, and the very reason for his indwelling. See 8:13; Eph 3:16; Phil 2:13.

One weakness is that we are not even aware of all our weaknesses. Thus we do not always know exactly what to pray for in the prayer aspect of our spiritual warfare (Eph 6:18). The NASB says that "we do not know how to pray," but this is too ambiguous. Paul is not talking about the manner of prayer, but its content (not the "how," but the "what"). Also, he is not talking about all prayer, for

---

[84]Cranfield, I:421; Hendriksen, I:276.

[85]Moo, I:559; Murray, I:310-311; Stott, 244.

[86]The word for "weakness" is closely related to the word translated "powerless" in 5:6. In each case a spiritual condition is in view.

surely we know to pray for such things as our daily bread and workers for the harvest, and we know to intercede for the sick. Even in our spiritual warfare, we may know in general what to pray for, but in this and other things we may not know *exactly* what to pray, or how to word our prayers. In such matters there is a proper kind of petition, one that is within God's will ("what we ought"), but we simply may not know what it is or may not be able to articulate it.

Here is one of the ways the Spirit comes to our aid. In our feeble attempts at heartfelt prayer, he intercedes for us, standing between us and the Father. "Intercede" means to make an appeal to someone on another person's behalf. The same combination of words is used in v. 27, "the Spirit intercedes for the saints"; and in v. 34, "Christ Jesus . . . is also interceding for us." Thus we have two divine intercessors between us and the Father: Jesus intercedes for us in heaven at God's right hand (v. 34), and the Spirit intercedes for us from within our hearts.

This does not negate Christ's role as a unique intercessor or mediator (1 Tim 2:5-6), because he is the only one who stands between us and the Father's wrath, the only one who secures for us the decree of justification. The Spirit's intercession is in the realm of our sanctification and is specifically related to our prayer life. By his divine power he looks upon the deepest levels of our hearts and gives content to our unspoken and uncertain prayers, then he lays these prayers before the Father's throne. Knowing that this happens alleviates the frustration and despair that might otherwise arise out of our uncertainty concerning God's will and our inability to know what to pray for.

The Spirit's intercession takes the form of "groans that words cannot express." "Groans" is the noun form of the verb used in vv. 22-23. It refers to the nonverbal vocalizing of deep inward feelings, as in a sigh or groan. Some think these are our own groanings, as stirred up and enabled by the Spirit,[87] but this does not fit the concept of intercession. Others[88] rightly see them as the Spirit's own groanings, as he extracts the deepest unformed prayers from

---

[87]Lard, 277; DeWelt, 129; MP, 365; Dunn, I:492; Murray, I:312.
[88]Hendriksen, I:275; Moo, I:562-563; Stott, 245.

our hearts and presents them to the Father in a kind of intradivine communication that does not need words.[89] This communication is described as "groans" because it conveys to the Father not only our thoughts but also the deep feelings associated with them.

Exegetes debate whether ἀλάλητος (*alalētos*; "that words cannot express") means "unutterable, inexpressible, unable to be spoken"; or simply "unspoken, unexpressed, wordless." In the final analysis this does not matter, since the reference is to the Spirit's communication and not ours. We assume that whatever is in our hearts *could* be expressed in words if we knew exactly what to pray for. What the Spirit carries to the Father may or may not be adaptable to human speech; the point is that this communication is not on that level in the first place.

8:27 And he who searches our hearts knows the mind of the Spirit, because the Spirit intercedes for the saints in accordance with God's will. This continues the thought of the Spirit's intercession for us in our prayers. Just as the Spirit reads our hearts and translates our uncertain petitions into meaningful prayer (v. 26), so does the Father know the mind of the Spirit and thus receives these prayers into his own bosom (v. 27).

"He who searches our hearts" refers to an aspect of God's omniscience or universal knowledge, namely, the fact that he knows the contents of the hearts of all human beings. The "heart" is equivalent to the soul or spirit or inner man, which includes the mind. The Bible often states that God knows what is in our hearts. The argument here is from the greater to the lesser, or from the less likely to the more likely. If God knows what is in the minds of created beings who are qualitatively different from him and relatively independent of him, then surely he knows what is in the mind of the Spirit himself, who is qualitatively equal with God and one in nature with him.[90] What he sees in the mind of the Spirit are the nonverbal groans that convey the contents of the saints' uncertain and unspoken prayers.

---

[89]This shows that Paul is certainly not referring here to glossolalia or speaking in tongues. Glossolalia is man's speech, not the Spirit's as such; it is not a form of intercession; and it is expressed in words that some can understand (Acts 2:1-11).

[90]1 Cor 2:10-11 says the Spirit knows the mind of the Father also.

If God the Father can directly search our hearts, why is it necessary for the Spirit to intercede for us? It is not a matter of necessity
but of choice. In relation to our redemption the triune God has
chosen to divide the various aspects of his redemptive activity
among the various persons of the Trinity (see GRe, 159-161). Since
the Spirit is specifically responsible for our sanctification, and since
this weakness in our prayer life is a matter of sanctification, this
intercession is part of his distinctive work; i.e., it is "in accordance
with God's will"[91] that the Holy Spirit should intercede for the
saints. (On "saints," see 1:7.)

**8:28 And we know that in all things God works for the good of
those who love him, who have been called according to his
purpose.** The verb here is συνεργέω (*synergeō*), "work together"; but
how to translate the verse is complicated by a significant textual
variation regarding its subject. Some manuscripts include ὁ θεός (*ho
theos*), "God," as the obvious subject of the verb; this accounts for
the NIV and NASB translations. But many believe that *ho theos* was
not in Paul's original text.

This leaves three alternatives. (1) The subject of *synergeō* is the
Holy Spirit, carried over from vv. 26-27. Most reject this view
because it interrupts the flow of thought into v. 29, where the
unnamed subject seems clearly to be God. (2) The subject is *panta*,
"all things." This is grammatically possible, and is the view found in
the KJV, the NRSV, and the NIV margin. Some object that this
seems to leave the fate of Christians in the hands of some sort of
positive karmic force rather than the hands of God. (3) The subject
of *synergeō* is "he," i.e., God, carried over from the phrase "to the
ones who love God," which precedes the verb in the original. *Panta*,
"all things," would then be the object of the verb, and the meaning
would be exactly the same as the NIV. The main objection to this
view is that this verb is usually intransitive; it does not take an
object.

Despite this objection (3) seems to be the best choice. The only
one that is not an option is (1), which makes the Holy Spirit the
subject of the verb. Even if we accept (2), "all things work together

---

[91]Literally this reads "according to God," but most agree that it means
"according to God's will."

for good," it is certainly implied that they do so only because God is in control of history and providentially directs all things toward a good end. As the NASB says, "God causes all things to work together for good." Whether or not this is the best translation, it is surely Paul's thought.

How much is included in "all things"? This must be determined by the context, which specifically deals with the ills and adversities of our present earthly life, "our present sufferings" (v. 18; see vv. 33-39). This includes trials and miseries suffered as the consequence of others' sins, but not necessarily our own (Godet, 322).

The promise is that God will bring good consequences out of all adverse circumstances, including persecution and death itself. This is important: Paul does not say that God *causes* all these circumstances, but that he causes good to *come out of* them (GRu, 407-409). This is a function of his special providential control of all things. Also, this promise does not guarantee that each individual adversity will have an "immediate good result" (Smith, II:10). All things *working together* will *ultimately* produce good, but not necessarily for us personally or even in our own lifetimes.

What is the "good" toward which God directs all things? It is surely not the shallow materialism of the "health and wealth" gospel, as Moo rightly points out (I:566). On the other hand, we should not limit it only to the ultimate good of "our completed salvation" (contra Stott, 247). It certainly includes this, and some adversities may produce their benefits only at this final stage. But we should include also a whole host of present or intermediate goods (Moo, I:566), spiritual in nature, that contribute toward our sanctification and our ability to serve God and others more effectively (see 5:3-4; 2 Cor 1:3-6; Jas 1:2-4). See GRu, 143-153.

This wonderful promise is not made to all human beings, but only to "the saints" (v. 27), i.e., the adopted children of God (vv. 14-16). Here they are described as "those who love God." This is not intended to make a distinction among Christians, as if some love God and some do not. Rather, it is simply a way of distinguishing Christians from unbelievers. Christians are "those who love God," while non-Christians are those who do not.

The persons to whom this promise applies are also described as those "who have been called according to his purpose." On the concept of calling, see 1:6. Calvinist commentators see this as a reference not to the gospel call that goes out to all, but to an inward, selective, irresistible enabling that inevitably produces saving faith in its chosen recipients. As such it is part of what is called "irresistible grace." Scripture is clear, however, that sinners are called not by a secret, inward operation of the Spirit but by the gospel itself (2 Thess 2:14), and that faith comes by hearing the word of this gospel (10:17). Whether or not this outward call is accompanied by an inward operation of the Spirit, both on the outward and inward levels the call is universal (John 12:32) and resistible (Matt 23:37). See Godet, 323-324.

But why are Christians distinctively described as "the called ones," if others have also received the same call but have just refused to accept it? The answer is that it reminds us of who actually took the initiative in our salvation. Even though we believe the gospel and love God, God loved us first (1 John 4:19) and *called* us unto himself while we were still in our sins. We did not go looking for God and persuade him to love and accept us. He came looking for us, calling us into his family and inviting us to come to him for salvation (10:13).

Paul declares that we have been called "according to purpose." Many early church fathers took this as a reference to human purpose, i.e., to man's free choice to answer God's call. Today it is almost universally, and rightly, understood as referring to *God's* purpose, and most versions insert "his." Calvinists usually interpret this as a reference to God's eternal decree to save only the elect (e.g., MacArthur, I:487), but that is not the point.

What does it mean to be called "according to (God's) purpose"? The purpose includes both the ultimate end or goal God has in mind in issuing his call, and the means he has devised for achieving this end. These are explained in vv. 29-30. The goal (v. 29) is that some will "be conformed to the likeness of his Son, that he might be the firstborn among many brothers." In other words, God has purposed to gather together a family of believers who will love him as their heavenly Father and glorify him forever, and whom he can love and bless as his own children. This is not just God's eternal purpose of *redemption*, but was originally his eternal purpose of *creation* itself. But because mankind has fallen into sin, this purpose can now be accomplished only through Jesus Christ as the firstborn of this family, and only through the process of redemption as summed up in the fivefold process of foreknowledge, predestination, calling, justification, and glorification (vv. 29-30). See 2 Tim 1:9.[92]

Thus again v. 28 is meant to give us comfort and assurance in the midst of earthly trials. No matter what adversities may befall us, God's providential power will cause good to come from them for his called ones. We can be sure of this because God's whole purpose for creation and redemption is a glorified family of loving children. The fact is that God wants us saved into his family even more than we do. This is why we know that he will work all things together for our good, and for the ultimate accomplishment of his purpose — because these are the same thing.

8:29 For those God foreknew he also predestined to be conformed to the likeness of his Son, that he might be the firstborn among many brothers. Here Paul gives more detail about God's purpose. He states exactly what this purpose is (v. 29b), and sums up the *means* by which God will accomplish it: the act of foreknowledge and the decree of predestination. The relation between this act and this decree may well be the most controversial as well as the most crucial exegetical question in the book of Romans.[93]

The word for "predestined" combines ὁρίζω (*horizō*), "to determine" (see 1:4), and πρό (*pro*), "before," yielding προορίζω (*proorizō*). This means "to determine beforehand, to predetermine, to foreordain." The translation "to predestine" suggests the nuance "to predetermine the destiny of." When used of persons with reference to salvation it is closely related to the concept of election (v. 33). The prefix *pro* indicates that the determination in view took place before the world was created (see Eph 1:4; Rev 17:8).

In this verse the predetermination of an individual's destiny is the point. God predetermined that those whom he foreknew would

---

[92]This general purpose should not be confused with God's specific purpose for Israel as related to the Gentiles. This is another issue and is dealt with in other contexts (see 9:11; Eph 1:11; 3:11). In fact, the Jews' failure to recognize this distinction is what lies behind Paul's difficult dissertation in chs. 9-11.

[93]For a fuller treatment of predestination see GRu, ch. 9.

one day "be conformed to the likeness of his Son." This is often
taken as referring to our spiritual re-creation in the moral image of
God as perfectly embodied in Jesus Christ. As such it would include
our present and continuing sanctification.[94] But this is not the
point. In this context the emphasis is on our final inheritance, the
eschatological glory of the redeemed body (vv. 11, 23). "The likeness of his Son" refers to the fact that our resurrection bodies will
be like that of Christ. It is the same thought and language as Phil
3:21, which says (literally) that our body "will be conformed to the
body of his glory." See also 1 Cor 15:49; 2 Cor 3:18.[95]

This interpretation is confirmed by the reference to Christ as
"the firstborn among many brethren." In Col 1:15 "firstborn" signifies the unique preeminence of Christ, but the point here is that he
is "the firstborn from among the dead" (Col 1:18; see Rev 1:5), i.e.,
the first to be raised from the dead in a glorified body. (See Acts
13:34; 26:23; Rom 6:9; 1 Cor 15:20.) As such he is the first "among
many brethren," i.e., among many others who will also be raised in
glorified bodies to constitute God's eternal family. This will be, as
Dunn says, "a new race of eschatological people in whom God's
design from the beginning of creation is at last fulfilled" (I:484).

This is what is predestined: our final salvation, our conformity
to Christ's resurrection body, our inheritance of glory. In other
words, even before the world was created, God had already predestined that some individuals would go to heaven, and that the rest
would go to hell. It is important to see that such predestination
applies to specific individuals and not just to an impersonal plan or
group. (See GRu, 338-343.) Thus far we can agree with Calvinism.

But now comes the crucial question: *on what basis* did God so
predestine us? Here is where non-Calvinists part company with
Calvinists and other Augustinians. For the latter, God's predestination of certain individuals to salvation is an *unconditional election.*
Prior to creation, they say, in one all-encompassing, efficacious
decree, God laid out in detail everything that would take place
within the created universe. He decided that he would create X
number of human beings, and he unilaterally and unconditionally

---

[94]So Cranfield, I:432; Hendriksen, I:283-284; Bruce, 176.
[95]So Lenski, 561; Murray, I:319; Moo, I:571; Lard, 282-283.

determined that some of these would ultimately be part of his heavenly family, and that the rest would not.

The key word here is *unconditional*. That is, for Calvinists, when God was predetermining which individuals would go to heaven, his decision was not contingent upon whether or not these individuals would meet certain conditions, such as faith and repentance. God never *responds* to human contingencies; this would be contrary to his sovereignty (see GRu, 217-228). This does not mean that he will save anyone apart from faith and repentance. It means rather that when God predestined some to salvation, he not only determined their heavenly destiny but also determined that he would sovereignly bestow upon them the faith and repentance that are prerequisites for heaven. He predestined not only the end but also the means.

This is where Calvinism goes wrong. It is biblical to say that God predestines certain individuals to salvation's end result, heaven; but it is contrary to Scripture to say that these individuals will meet the conditions for going to heaven only because God has predestined them to do so. God predestines the end, but not the means. He predestines all believers to heaven, but he does not predestine anyone to become a believer. Salvation is conditional (see 1:16), and individuals must meet these conditions by their own free-will choice. Therefore predestination itself is conditional; God predestined to heaven those whom he foreknew would meet the required conditions. (See GRu, 343-345.)

Here we come to the crucial point in this verse, i.e., the relation between foreknowledge and predestination. "Those God foreknew he also predestined." We should note that v. 29 says only that God foreknew certain *persons*; it does not say specifically what he foreknew about them. In view of the Bible's teaching about salvation in general, many assume that God foreknew "that they would comply with the conditions of justification" (Lard, 282). As Godet puts it (325), they are "foreknown as sure to fulfil the condition of salvation, viz. *faith*; so: foreknown as his *by faith*."

This answer is not at all unreasonable, but I suggest that v. 28 has already revealed the object of God's foreknowledge. We must not overlook the connection between these two verses, as if v. 29 exists apart from any context. Verse 29 begins (after the conjunction) with the relative pronoun "whom" (translated "those" in the

NIV). Ordinarily we would expect an antecedent for this pronoun, and here we find it in v. 28, namely, "those who love God." God foreknew those who would love him. He foreknew that at some point in their lives they would come to love him and would continue to love him unto the end. See the parallel in 1 Cor 8:3, "But if anyone loves God, he is known by him" (NASB). This is exactly the same idea as Rom 8:29a, the former referring to knowledge and the latter to foreknowledge.

We should also note that v. 29 begins with the causative conjunction ὅτι (*hoti*), "for, because." This most likely goes with "we know" in v. 28. Thus the thought is quite simple: We know that God works all things for the good of those who love him and are called into his eternal family according to his purpose. How do we know this? Because, having foreknown from eternity that they would love him, he has already predestined them to this state of eternal glory! Thus we can be sure that the temporary trials of this life are not able to nullify what the Almighty God himself has already predestined will occur! Rather, he uses them in ways that prepare us to enjoy eternity even more.

Calvinists reject this simple explanation, of course. At issue, they say, is the meaning of the word "foreknow" (προγινώσκω, *proginōskō*). Since *ginōskō* means "to know," and *pro* means "before," it would seem obvious that *proginōskō* means "to know beforehand" in the sense of prior cognitive or mental awareness. God certainly has such precognition. Because of his unique relation to time, his knowledge is not limited to the now; he knows the past and the future as well as he knows the present (GC, 255-259, 279-289). The verb "foreknow" is used here and in four other places in the NT: Acts 26:5; Rom 11:2; 1 Pet 1:20; 2 Pet 3:17. (The noun is used twice: Acts 2:23; 1 Pet 1:2.) Everyone agrees that in Acts 26:5 and 2 Pet 3:17, where it refers to human foreknowledge, it has this simple meaning of precognition or prescience.

But Calvinists argue that in all the other passages, in which God is the subject, both the verb and the noun have another connotation altogether, namely, *distinguishing love*.[96] Included here are two

---

[96]Προγινώσκω "is not the foresight of difference but the foreknowledge that makes difference exist . . . . It is sovereign distinguishing love" (Murray, I:318).

concepts: loving and choosing. Since the word "know" itself at times is "practically synonymous with 'love,' to set regard upon, to know with peculiar interest, delight, affection, and action," foreknowledge in 8:29 must mean "whom he knew from eternity with distinguishing affection and delight," or "whom he foreloved" (Murray, I:317).[97]

The key word, though, is "distinguishing." For Calvinists the foreknowledge of 8:29 is an act by which God (unconditionally) *chooses* some people out of the mass of future mankind to be the sole recipients of his saving grace. This says "foreknowledge" is the same as "election."[98] As Moo sums it up, "The difference between 'know or love beforehand' and 'choose beforehand' virtually ceases to exist" (I:569). For 8:29 Arndt and Gingrich (710) give the definition of "choose beforehand." Newman and Nida (167) translate it "Those whom God had already chosen." It has the "connotation of electing grace," says Bruce (177).[99]

On what do Calvinists base this peculiar definition of foreknowledge? Mainly they base it upon a few selected biblical uses of the verbs for "to know," in which they find the connotations of "choose" and/or "love." These include the places where "know" is a euphemism for sexual intercourse, and they include a few other OT uses of יָדַע (*yada'* — Hebrew for "know"), usually Gen 18:19; Exod 2:25; Jer 1:5; Hos 13:5; and Amos 3:2. Also cited are these NT texts: Matt 7:23; John 10:14; 1 Cor 8:3; 13:12; Gal 4:9; and 2 Tim 2:19. Since "know" in all these passages allegedly means much more than simple cognition, we may conclude that "*fore*know" in 8:29 and elsewhere also means much more, namely, "distinguishing love bestowed beforehand." Thus, "whom He *chose* beforehand, he also predestined."

---

[97]For this equation of "foreknown" and "foreloved," see also Hendriksen, I:283; Moo, I:569; Stott, 249; MacArthur, I:496.

[98]It is not the same as predestination itself, though, contrary to criticism by non-Calvinists such as Godet (324) and Lenski (560). As Calvinists see it, "to elect or choose in advance" means God is simply picking out the ones he will bless, while "to predestine" means he is determining exactly *how* he will bless them (Murray, I:318; MacArthur, I:497; see Cranfield, I:432). Thus the equating of foreknowledge with election does not make predestination redundant.

[99]See also Cranfield, I:431; Dunn, I:482; Morris, 332; MacArthur, I:495.

How may we respond to this? By a thorough study of the way the Bible uses the words for "know" and "foreknow." Such a project is outside the scope of this commentary, but we may offer a summary analysis.

First, noncognitive connotations for *ginōskō* are virtually nonexistent in secular Greek. Moo admits that the Calvinist definition of foreknowledge sounds "somewhat strange against the background of broad Greek usage" (I:569).

Second, the use of "know" as a euphemism for sexual relations contributes nothing toward this Calvinist view, since it refers specifically to the sexual act and not to any love that might be associated with it. Also, the act of sexual "knowing" in no way includes the connotation of choosing, but rather presupposes that a distinguishing choice has already been made (via marriage). Finally, the use of "know" for this act is much closer to cognition than either loving or choosing; it connotes cognitive knowing at the most intimate level.

Third, biblical texts where "know" and "foreknow" seem to have a connotation of love or affection (e.g., Exod 2:25; Hos 13:5) prove nothing, because they usually do not specify the *reason* for God's love-knowledge, and they certainly do not suggest that it was unconditional. In fact, 1 Cor 8:3 seems to say it is conditional: "The man who loves God is known by God."

Fourth, an analysis of the NT texts where the words for "know" have persons as their objects, i.e., where the action of knowing is specifically directed toward persons and not facts as such, shows that in such cases these words never have the connotation of "choosing" or "imposing a distinction." This applies to *ginōskō* (used c. 52 times in this way), *epiginōskō* (c. 15 times), and *oida* (c. 43 times).

Such an analysis yields very helpful insights into the meaning of God's foreknowledge. In order of increasing specificity, the three basic connotations of "know a person" are as follows. (1) *Recognition*. In this case "to know" means to recognize someone, to know who he is, to know his identity or his true identity, to be able to identify him for who he is, to be acquainted with him, to be familiar with him, to understand him, to know his true nature. This is by far the most common connotation.[100] It is a purely cognitive act. It

___
[100]"Know" with a person or persons as its object occurs in this sense at least 80 times. A few examples are Matt 11:27; 14:30; 17:12; 26:72, 74;

does not impose an identity upon someone, but perceives that identity. This includes the idea of recognizing someone as belonging to a particular group, as distinct from those who do not. This is the sense in which Jesus "knows" his sheep (John 10:14, 27), even as his sheep know him (John 10:14; see 2 Tim 2:19). This is the connotation of "know" that applies to "foreknow" in 8:29.

(2) *Acknowledgment.* Here "to know" means not only to have a cognitive knowledge of someone's identity, but also to admit or acknowledge that identity. As such it is an act of will, though it presupposes an act of cognition. The most important thing is that this acknowledging does not impose a particular identity upon anyone, but simply confesses it.[101]

(3) *Experience.* The third and most intense connotation of "to know" when a person or persons are its object is to know experientially, to experience a relationship with someone. Again, it presupposes cognition but goes beyond it. Most significantly, such knowing is not an act that initiates a relationship but simply experiences it. This connotation is found especially in 1 John.[102] Matt 7:23; 1 Cor 8:3; and Heb 8:11 could be either (1) or (3).

In each case the act of knowing does not create a person's identity or his distinction from other people. It rather presupposes an already-existing identity or distinction; the act of knowing perceives and in some cases acknowledges that identity or distinction. These connotations for knowing fit the term "foreknowledge" very well as it is used in 8:29 and elsewhere. Those whom God from the beginning recognized and acknowledged as his own, he predestined to be members of his glorified family in heaven. (The connotation of experiencing a relationship does not transfer well to the concept of *fore*knowledge, since foreknowledge as such precedes the existence of its object, precluding an experienced relationship.)

In any case, an analysis of *all* the uses of "know" with persons as the object undermines the notion that it means "choose," and thus

---

Luke 7:39; 10:22; 13:25, 27; 24:16, 31; John 1:10, 26, 31, 33, 48; 7:27-28; 14:7, 9, 17; Acts 7:18; Rom 1:21; 1 Cor 13:12; Heb 10:30; 1 John 4:2, 6.

[101]A few examples of this connotation are Mark 1:24, 34; Acts 19:15; 1 Cor 1:21; 16:12; 1 Thess 5:12. (This is almost all of them.)

[102]Examples are John 17:3; Phil 3:10; 2 Tim 1:12; Titus 1:16; 1 John 2:3, 4, 13, 14.

does not support the Calvinist idea that foreknowledge is the same as election or choosing beforehand.

The four other NT uses of "foreknow" and the two uses of "foreknowledge" do not comfortably bear the connotations of "forelove" and "choose beforehand." Acts 26:5 and 2 Pet 3:17 do not refer to God's foreknowledge, but they clearly refer to precognition. Rom 11:2 refers to God's foreknowledge of Israel as a nation and not to any individuals within it. The context suggests that Paul is referring to God's precognition of Israel's rebellion and idolatry. Despite the fact that he foreknew all of this (see 9:22, 27-29; 10:16-21), it was never his plan to reject his people altogether.

In 1 Pet 1:20 Christ is the one foreknown from the foundation of the world; and in the context precognition, not choosing, is the preferred meaning. The contrast is between the hidden and the revealed. Even though the Father knew from the foundation of the world that Christ the Son would be our Redeemer, he did not reveal it until the last days.

The two uses of the noun "foreknowledge" are likewise consistent with the non-Calvinist understanding of "foreknow" in 8:29. First Peter 1:1-2 says that the chosen (are chosen) according to the foreknowledge of God the Father. Thus a clear distinction is made between foreknowledge and choosing, and there is no reason to see in foreknowledge anything other than its basic meaning of precognition. Thus the relationship between foreknowledge and election here is exactly the same as that between foreknowledge and predestination in 8:29.

Acts 2:23 refers to the foreknowledge of God the Father; its object is Jesus Christ and the circumstances of his death. Jesus was delivered up "by God's set purpose and foreknowledge." "Set purpose" is equivalent to predestination; the NASB translates it "predetermined plan." I.e., God had already determined from eternity that Christ would die for our sins. That he was delivered up "according to foreknowledge" means that God foreknew all the human acts of participation in Christ's betrayal and death, such as those of Judas and Herod. God did not predetermine these acts, but he knew them in advance and therefore could work his plan along with them and through them.

Sometimes Calvinist exegetes try to equate the foreknowledge and predetermined plan in Acts 2:23 by invoking a rule of Greek grammar. Here is how MacArthur (I:496) argues:

> According to what Greek scholars refer to as Granville Sharp's rule, if two nouns of the same case (in this instance, "plan" and "foreknowledge") are connected by *kai* ("and") and have the definite article (the) before the first noun but not before the second, the nouns refer to the same thing . . . . In other words, Peter equates God's predetermined plan, or foreordination, and His foreknowledge.

Wuest (143-144) puts it almost exactly the same way, that in such a case the second noun "refers to the same thing" as the first; therefore Acts 2:23 shows that predestination and foreknowledge "refer to the same thing."

This argument, however, is seriously flawed. Both MacArthur and Wuest misquote Sharp's rule. The rule does not say that the two nouns in the construction described above "refer to the same thing." It says only that in such a case the second noun "always relates to the same person that is expressed or described in the first noun." There is a huge difference between *relating* to the same person (or thing) and *referring* to the same person (or thing). Carson says it is an exegetical fallacy to assume that the latter or strict form of Sharp's rule has universal validity. He says, "If one article governs two substantives joined by *kai*, it does not necessarily follow that the two substantives refer to the same thing, but only that the two substantives are grouped together to function in some respects as a single entity" (*Fallacies*, 84-85). Also, Sharp states his rule as applying only to persons, not to things. As one Greek scholar says, "Non-personal nouns disqualify the construction"; he cites Acts 2:23 as a specific example of this (Young, *Greek*, 62).

In conclusion, the preponderance of evidence shows that "foreknowledge" is not equivalent to election or choosing, and that in 8:29 it refers to nothing more than the cognitive act by which God knew or identified the members of his family (as distinct from all others) even before the foundation of the world. He identified them by the fact that they were (would be) the ones who loved (would love) him, and who met (would meet) the required conditions for salvation. Knowing through his divine omniscience who these individuals would be, even at that point he predestined them to be part of his glorified heavenly family through resurrection from the dead after the pattern established by the firstborn brother, Jesus Christ.

8:30 And those he predestined, he also called; those he called, he also justified; those he justified, he also glorified. Exegetes speak of a "golden chain" or "unbreakable chain" of divine acts in vv. 29-30: God foreknows, predestines, calls, justifies, and glorifies. Each of these is a distinct act, and in the redemptive process they do follow one another in this sequence. However, we must resist the temptation to bind them together into too neat a package.

For one thing, these five acts do not give a complete picture of salvation. There are no overt references to man's part in the process, which is of course consistent with Paul's purpose here; but not even all of God's redemptive acts are named. Notably missing are regeneration and sanctification.

For another thing, the progression of thought in vv. 29 and 30 is not that of one linear chain. Verse 29 is the main point in itself; grammatically and doctrinally it is a complete thought. It refers to two divine acts, foreknowledge and predestination. The latter is primary and is linked directly to one of the chief elements of glorification, specifically, the resurrection. It could be shortened thus: whom he foreknew, he predestined to be glorified.

Verse 30, instead of simply lengthening a chain begun in v. 29, is intended to expand v. 29b by adding a couple of details: the redemptive process does not go directly from predestination to glory; there happen to be a few other steps in between! This verse does not name them all, but mentions two that are representative of the entire process.

Thus the first and the last redemptive acts of v. 30 are carried over from v. 29. "Predestined" has already been explained. "Glorified" refers to the final stage of salvation, eternal life in heaven. This has been a prominent theme in this whole context, and is the point of v. 29b. "Conformed to the likeness of his son" refers to our resurrection in a glorified body.

Why "glorified" is in past tense is a matter of debate, since it has not happened yet. Some say it actually has been accomplished, in the person of Jesus as our representative (see Cranfield, I:433;

Godet, 327). But most agree that the past tense refers to the fact that God has already *predestined* it; therefore it is as certain as if it had already occurred (e.g., Bruce, 178; Moo, I:573).

This verse adds two steps between predestination and glorification, probably to show us that God's predestining believers to glory does not make a mockery of the intervening process. Some have wondered why, in the Calvinist view, the intervening steps are necessary. But when the biblical concept of free will is retained, we see that what comes between the beginning and the end is what makes it possible for God to predestine some to glory in the first place.

The two divine acts given as links between predestination and glorification are *calling* and *justifying*. We have already examined the meaning of these concepts; the question now is, why specifically are they inserted here? One reason, as indicated, is to show that intermediate steps *such as* calling and justifying are necessary. Another reason, possibly, is to indicate that human decisions are not totally absent from this process but are implicitly present as the objects of the divine foreknowledge in v. 29. As we have already seen, the connection with v. 28 shows that the most likely object of God's foreknowledge is believers' love for God. Now, in v. 30, calling and justification are mentioned. Both of these divine acts are necessarily linked to human decisions: God's call must be answered, and justification is given only to faith. These human decisions may thus implicitly be included here as other objects of the divine foreknowledge by which God predestines us to glory.

The primary reference, of course, is to calling and justification as acts of God himself. Calling (see 1:6; 8:28) is the act by which God initiates personal contact with those whom he foreknew and predestined before even the earth existed. As we have seen, this is not some special, irresistible call that goes out only to the chosen few, but the general call of the gospel (contra Dunn, I:485; MacArthur, I:498). Those whom God foreknew and predestined are those who not only hear the call but also accept it (Lard, 283; Godet, 327). "For many are called, but few are chosen" (Matt 22:14, NASB). Lenski comments (562-563),

> If it be asked why God did not foreknow, foreordain, call, justify the rest, the biblical answer is found in Matt. 23:37 and similar passages: God did not exclude them, but despite all

that God could do *they* excluded themselves. "These he called" includes the acceptance of the call; and it in no way excludes the extension of the same call with the same power of grace to the rest.

This raises the question of whether "these five links in the chain of God's saving work are unbreakable," as MacArthur avers they are (I:494). According to this understanding, *all five* of these divine works are applied to the elect and *only* to the elect as an inseparable package. Only the predestined are called; all those called will be glorified; no one is ever justified except those who are foreknown and predestined to glory. "All five elements are co-extensive," says Murray; "there cannot be one element without the others" (I:320). For example, says Moo, there is an "exact correspondence between those who are the objects of predestining and those who experience this calling" (I:572).

The language of vv. 29-30 does not require such a view, however. Indeed, this chain is unbreakable and its elements co-extensive only if the Calvinist system of unconditional election, irresistible grace, and "once saved, always saved" is true. Once we break away from this system, we can see that some are called but do not respond; thus only one of the five elements applies to them. Since it is possible for someone to become a true believer and become justified, and then to fall away, only two of the elements apply to this group. In the latter case one may be called and temporarily justified, but never foreknown and predestined to be glorified. Such situations are not contrary to 8:29-30. Paul does not say that *only* those who are predestined are called, but that those who are predestined will without fail be called. Nor does he say that *only* those who are predestined to glory are justified; those who are so predestined will without fail be justified, though.

In a similar way, Paul does not imply that *everyone* who is called will be justified — since some refuse the call; nor does he explicitly state that *all* who have ever been justified (by faith) will without fail be glorified — since some will lose their faith. Here the key to certainty about glorification is predestination, not the intervening links. The point is that all those *who are predestined* will without fail be glorified, and that they will without fail be called and justified prior to glorification.

513

Paul has in view here only an audience of sincere believers ("us all," v. 32) who need assurance that God will never fail them or forsake them, and that he can and will see them through to the end. Unlike in the Epistle to the Hebrews, he is not warning wavering believers who are seriously considering apostasy. His purpose here is to assure those who have no intention of abandoning Christ that Christ will not abandon them.

D. GOD'S GRACIOUS LOVE GIVES US
UNSHAKABLE ASSURANCE (8:31-39)

This paragraph is considered by many to be the most blessed and glorious in the entire Bible. In a way that is both spiritually satisfying and poetically pleasing, it sets forth the believer's unshakable assurance and its unassailable foundation in the love of God.

This theme was developed earlier in 5:1-11, where the Apostle tied personal assurance to three items: God's love, Christ's cross, and our faith. At that point Paul's main polemical purpose was to show that we are justified by faith apart from works of law (3:28), therefore he was emphasizing the necessity of a right understanding of justification by faith as the key to a sense of assurance. Here the polemical theme has faded into the background, and the emphasis falls simply on God's love as expressed in the cross as the actual foundation upon which our faith and hope can rest.

Not surprisingly, we find many commentators attempting to use this passage as a basis for the "once saved, always saved" doctrine. Since the theme here is that *nothing* can separate us from the love of God in Christ, this supposedly means that not even anything we ourselves can do will cause us to lose our salvation (see v. 39 below).

However, this view ignores the element of personal responsibility implicit in the very theme of justification *by faith*. God's love gives us justification through the blood of Christ, and keeps us justified in the same way, but not apart from our continuing active trust in his blood. In 5:1-11 the role of faith was explicit (5:1-2); here it is implicitly assumed that those whom nothing can separate from the love of God are *believers* who *want* to stay within the family of God.

Whether a believer can or cannot lose his faith is not the point in this section. The point is simply this: not even the worst earthly disaster, and not even the strongest spiritual enemy can place us into a circumstance that is so negative that it nullifies and overwhelms the reality of God's love for us as infallibly demonstrated in the propitiatory sacrifice of Christ Jesus our Lord. Not even the worst suffering can outweigh the intrinsic power of the cross to assure us that God loves us and is for us and wants us in his eternal family.

8:31 What, then, shall we say in response to this [literally, "to these things"]? What are "these things"? In a real sense they include the argument of the entire epistle thus far (Cranfield, I:434-435). Thus this paragraph is a fitting climax to everything that has been presented about the central facts of the gospel, such as grace, the cross, and justification. I think, though, that "these things" refers especially to the subjects of sonship, heirship, and predestination in 8:14-30. In view of the facts about these things, what conclusion can we draw?

If God is for us, who can be against us? "If" does not imply some sort of uncertainty, but is stating an unassailable argument: "If A, then B." And, based on everything we have just said, we know A is a fact; therefore B is also a fact.

"God is for us" is an excellent way to draw together everything Paul has been teaching about the plan of redemption, all the way from God's precreation purpose to our final glorification. It summarizes perfectly God's attitude toward us, his work on our behalf, and our relationship to him. As Cranfield says (I:435), it is "a concise summary of the gospel."

Basically this brief statement means that *God is on our side*. He is not only "with us," in the sense that he is present alongside us (Ps 23:4; see Isa 7:14, "Immanuel"); he is also "for us" in the sense that he wants "our side" to win. In our conflict with all the personal and personified enemies who desire to drive us back into unbelief, God is on our side and will protect us and defend us from these enemies (Ps 56:9). In the following verses this conflict is presented in the image of a courtroom where we are on trial. That "God is for us" means that he is our Defender, or more specifically he is the Judge who has already decided the case in our favor (8:1).

"Who can be against us" does not mean that we will never have any opposition in our Christian life. It means only that none of our adversaries stands a chance against the one who is our Champion, the one who is defending us. Certainly, we do have enemies, but they are nothing compared with God. Therefore it really does not matter who is against us, since none can prevail against God. "There is no one whose hostility we need fear" (Cranfield, I:435), especially in light of 8:28. See Ps 27:1.

8:32 He who did not spare his own Son, but gave him up for us all . . . . This recounts the lengths to which God was willing to go to ensure our ultimate victory and our presence in heaven with him, and thereby it establishes the infinite depths of his love for us (John 3:16). Even though his Son, prostrate, cried out for some alternative to the mission that was about to lead him through the very agonies of hell itself (Matt 26:39), God did not spare *him* so that he might spare *us*!

God "gave him up for us all" (see 4:25) describes the substitutionary atonement of Christ, his propitiatory sacrifice on Calvary (see 3:24-26). Paul's purpose for bringing this up is to highlight the divine love embodied therein (1 John 4:9-10), so that we might be assured that God is indeed on our side.

"His own Son" means God's *unique* Son (see 8:3; John 5:18), as distinct from his adopted sons (8:14-16). "Us all" in this context refers to the believers who will constitute the completed family of God. By using first person plural Paul applies this truth especially to the readers of his epistle. This does *not* support the Calvinist idea of limited atonement; it does not deny that Christ was the propitiation for the sins of the whole world (1 John 2:2). Paul does not say God gave Jesus up for "us *only*." Since Christians are his audience, he simply speaks directly to and about them at this point.

. . . how will he not also, along with him, graciously give us all things? The argument here is from the greater to the lesser (see 5:9-10). God has given us the greatest possible gift when he gave up his Son for us. Why should we think he will now for some reason withhold the rest of our inheritance, or allow anything to prevent us from receiving it? Along with Jesus will surely come all the gifts of glory promised in the previous context, including a glorified body and a redeemed universe. These are immeasurably precious, but still they are nothing alongside God's gift of his own

Son. Since he has already given the latter, how can we doubt that he will give us the former also?

8:33a Who will bring any charge against those whom God has chosen? In vv. 33-34 Paul uses explicit courtroom imagery to undergird our assurance of final victory. He continues to press the contrast of v. 31b, "If God is for us, who can be against us?" Christians are pictured as defendants in a judgment scene, with the possibility that witnesses may appear who will bring charges against us and accuse us of being unworthy of salvation. "Bring a charge against" (ἐγκαλέω, *engkaleō*) is a technical legal term referring to such a scenario (see Acts 18:38; 23:29). The primary reference is probably to the final judgment, but in a figurative sense we may think of ourselves as being in this circumstance throughout our Christian life.

Who will dare to bring a charge against God's elect? Actually there are any number of accusers who are eager to rise up against us and magnify our sins and destroy our assurance. Chief among them is Satan, whose name means "adversary," and who is also called "the devil," he who will "bring charges with hostile intent" (AG, 180). Thus "the devil" is the slanderer, the accuser, especially "the accuser of our brothers, who accuses them before our God day and night" (Rev 12:10; see Job 1-2; Zech 3:1-2; Luke 22:31). Others eager to accuse us include unbelievers in general (1 Pet 2:12), and certainly anyone we may have harmed at any time during our lives. We may fear that the law of God itself will rise up to accuse us on Judgment Day. And by no means least, our own conscience accuses us with reference to our sinful deeds (2:15).

So what is the point of Paul's question? Not that accusations will never come, but that they will never hold up under the scrutiny of the Judge who will decide our case. None of the charges brought against us will be valid; we need not fear them. Why not? Because we are God's elect, his chosen ones, the ones whom he foreknew and has already predestined to glory (8:29).

"The elect" or "the chosen ones" is a common way of describing believers in the NT.[103] What was said about predestination in 8:29 applies to this concept as well.

---

[103]See Matt 24:22, 24; Rom 16:13; Col 3:12; 2 Tim 2:10; Titus 1:1; 1 Pet 1:1-2.

8:33b-34a It is God who justifies. Who is he that condemns?
(See Isa 50:8-9.) Here the courtroom analogy is most intense. The
subject of justification comes to the forefront again. Earlier (3:24)
we said that justification is a legal or forensic term that refers to a
verdict pronounced by a judge. Specifically as an act, justification is
the judge's declaration that a defendant is innocent, or more precisely, that no penalty or condemnation will fall upon him. When
God justifies us, as the Judge of all he is declaring, "No penalty for
you!" (8:1). This has already occurred for us as believers; it is an
ongoing reality; and it will take place formally with eternal finality
on Judgment Day.

One disturbing thing about the various accusations brought
against us by Satan, by unbelievers, even by our own consciences, is
that they are so often true! We *have* sinned; we *have* done terrible
things. But what the accusers do not take into account is that God
has already justified us in relation to our sins, i.e., he has taken
away their guilt; he has taken their penalty upon himself; he has
broken the connection between our sin and its deserved condemnation; he as Judge has already declared, "No penalty for you!"

Thus the accusers can accuse, but they cannot *condemn*! This is
our "blessed assurance."

On the forensic connotation of "condemn" (κατακρίνω,
katakrinō), see 8:3. The fact that "justify" is used here as the opposite of "condemn" shows that it too is a forensic or legal concept.
See 3:24.

**8:34b Christ Jesus, who died — more than that, who was raised
to life — is at the right hand of God and is also interceding for us.**
This lays out once more the only basis for our justification, namely,
the work of Jesus. Four specific phases of his work are mentioned:
his death, his resurrection, his enthronement, and his intercession
for us.

The first two are past events that are fundamental to our justification and therefore to our assurance (see 3:24; 4:25). The last two
are interrelated and together describe Christ's present and ongoing
role in our justification, a role that began with his ascension.

That Christ is seated at the right hand of God the Father is primarily indicative of his exalted status and honor. The "right hand"
of God is a symbol of his almighty power; that Christ is seated at

God's right hand means he shares in this power (Ps 110; Matt 28:18).

In this context, though, the emphasis is not on the *right* hand or *power* as such, but simply on the close proximity of the crucified and risen Christ to the Father, for the purpose of intercession. This is not the same as the intercession of the Spirit in our prayer life (vv. 26-27). Christ intercedes for us in the sense that he interposes his blood between us and the Father's wrath. As our high priest he presents himself as the sacrifice that has borne this deserved wrath in our place, thus making it possible for us to come to God, to be accepted by him, and to be a part of his intimate family. See Isa 53:12; Luke 23:34; 1 Tim 2:5-6; Heb 4:14-16; 7:25; 1 John 2:1.

8:35 Who shall separate us from the love of Christ? This rhetorical question begins Paul's final celebration of assurance, a crescendo of certainty that finally erupts in a triumphant confession of the all-sufficiency of God's infinite and faithful love. The question is framed in terms of separation: who will separate us from the love of Christ? The rest of the paragraph develops this emphatic answer: NO ONE!

The "love of Christ" is not our love for him but his love for us (v. 37). This is not different from "the love of God that is in Christ Jesus our Lord" (v. 39). This love is not only the subjective love for us within the heart of Jesus, but also all the objective benefits of that love as already bestowed upon us and as promised to us in eternity. Nothing is able to separate us from any of this.

Many persons and many things will try to separate us from his love, i.e., to shake our confidence in his love and tempt us to doubt it and forsake it. Paul has already mentioned sufferings in general (vv. 17-18); here he mentions several specific forms of suffering. None of them, he says, is stronger than Christ's love for us.[104] None of them succeeds as an argument for the proposition that Christ does not really love us after all.

Who shall separate us? **Shall trouble or hardship or persecution or famine or nakedness or danger or sword?** This is not an exhaustive list. These seven things are "a representative few of the

---

[104]Paul knew this from his own experience, since he had undergone most of the things mentioned here. See 2 Cor 11:23-29.

countless ominous circumstances that believers may encounter" in this world (MacArthur, I:510).

"Trouble and hardship" are the same two Greek words used in 2:9 for eschatological penalties. Here they refer to general categories of earthly suffering. "Trouble" (θλίψις, *thlipsis*) refers to pressure, or being pressed and pressured by circumstances. Some think it refers to end-time tribulation, but it should not be limited to this. As MacArthur says, it is "severe adversity in general" (I:511). "Hardship" (στενοχωρία, *stenochōria*) is not much different. It refers to narrowness, or feeling confined and restricted and hemmed in by circumstances. It is probable that the former refers to the external situations that produce suffering, while the latter is the inner mental state of distress resulting from them.

"Persecution" is a more specific form of trouble and hardship. Probably it refers to persecution suffered because of one's belief (Matt 5:10-12; 1 Cor 4:12; 2 Cor 4:9; 2 Thess 1:4). "Famine" can also mean hunger experienced for any reason, especially because of persecution (1 Cor 4:11; 2 Cor 11:27). The same applies to "nakedness," which can mean destitution in general, being "reduced to rags" (1 Cor 4:11; 2 Cor 11:27). "Danger" refers to being in peril or at risk in general, either from natural or personal threats (2 Cor 11:26). "Sword" is symbolic of violence, especially violent death as in war or judicial penalty (AG, 497). To Christians it represents martyrdom (Acts 12:2; see Heb 11:34-37).

8:36 As it is written: "For your sake we face death all day long; we are considered as sheep to be slaughtered." This quote from Ps 44:22 is naturally called to mind from the list of sufferings detailed in v. 35, all of which could result in death. This, along with Matt 5:12 and Heb 11:34-37, shows that such suffering is nothing new in the Christian era but has always been the lot of God's people. The death in view is not so-called "natural" death, but the death of martyrdom.

The NIV translation, "face death," is too weak. The word means "being put to death, being killed." This is happening "all day long." Somewhere, every day, at all times of the day, Christians are being killed because of their belief. We are like sheep for slaughter. This is not a reference to the use of sheep as sacrifices, but to the killing of sheep for food. This is how unbelievers often view believers: we are assigned no real value in society and are fit only for slaughter.

All of these things (vv. 35-36) certainly do not happen to all Christians all the time, but they are always a potential danger. If and when they do happen, certain questions will naturally press themselves upon our consciousness: Where is God? Why is he letting this happen to me? Has he abandoned me? Is he real? Does he really love me? Paul's point is that none of these circumstances and no thoughts such as these are able to eclipse or extinguish the glorious light of God's love that shines forth from the cross.

8:37 No, in all these things we are more than conquerors through him who loved us. Here is Paul's answer to the question in v. 35. Shall any of these things separate us from Christ's love? No! The word is *alla*, the strong adversative often translated "but." Here it means "rather." I.e., rather than these things separating us from Christ's love, we overcome them all. Literally, "in all these things we are more than conquerors!" In the midst of them all and in spite of them all, we emerge victorious.

The word for "to be more than conquerors" is ὑπερνικάω (*hyper-nikaō*). The usual word for "to conquer, to be the victor" is νικάω, (*nikaō*). Here ὑπέρ (*hyper*) is added to magnify the certainty and decisiveness of our victory. We not only defeat every enemy and conquer in every adverse circumstance; we *over*conquer! We do not just survive; we do not just endure. Rather, we win a glorious, overwhelming victory; we prevail completely. To use Hendriksen's word, we are "superconquerors" (I:292). This megavictory occurs not just because we have the inherent strength of conquering heroes. No, it happens because the Holy Spirit empowers us to overcome all spiritual foes (8:13), because God's providence brings good out of all adversities (8:28), and because the knowledge of God's grace through the cross of Christ inspires in us a passion for faithfulness that simply will not be denied.

We overconquer "through him who loved us." This is Jesus (v. 35), and the reference is to his cross. This is shown by the fact that "loved" is an aorist participle, referring to a specific act of love. If in our hearts and minds we keep a firm grip on the meaning and reality of this event, *nothing* can shake us in our faith, assurance, and hope.

8:38-39 For I am convinced that neither death nor life, neither angels nor demons, neither the present nor the future, nor any powers, neither height nor depth, nor anything else in all creation, will be able to separate us from the love of God that is in Christ Jesus our Lord. In these verses Paul completes his answer to the question in v. 35a. He declares that *nothing* will be able to separate us from Christ's love. He switches from first person plural to first person singular, indicating that this testimony is not only truth inspired by the Holy Spirit but also his own unshakable personal conviction arising from the depths of his heart. "I am convinced!" he says. Godet (329) calls this Paul's "shout of victory on the battlefield now abandoned by the enemy."

To make his answer more concrete, Paul reels off a list of ten representative things that cannot separate us from the love of Christ. Eight of these are combined into four pairs. Not every item mentioned is necessarily hostile to Christians, though most have the potential for harm. The main point of the listing is to be as comprehensive and inclusive as possible, to cover the whole range of potential sources of "trouble and hardship." This is accomplished especially by the general pairs, life/death, present/future, and height/depth.

Listed first as not having the power to separate us from Christ's love is the related pair, "neither death nor life." It is natural that death should be listed first, since it has just been in the forefront of concern (vv. 35-36), and since it has "loomed throughout chaps. 5-8 as the great hostile power" (Dunn, I:506). Death, the "Great Separator," scares us because it can come in so many fearsome forms. It is especially threatening in the context of martyrdom.

It may seem strange that "life" is also mentioned as something that cannot separate us from Christ's love. The point seems to be to make these potential threats as comprehensive as possible. Thus "life" includes every possible circumstance that might come upon us before we die, including the things mentioned in v. 35. Thus pairing life and death together "is simply a way of embracing every conceivable condition of humankind" (Dunn, I:507).

The next two items also seem to be a pair, "neither angels nor demons." The second term is not actually "demons," but "rulers" (ἀρχή, *archē*). It could refer to earthly rulers (Luke 12:11; Titus 3:1), but it is also one of Paul's favorite words for angelic beings. As such the KJV usually translates it "principalities." It does not necessarily refer to fallen angels (Col 1:16), but sometimes it does (Eph 6:12; Col 2:15). Though we cannot be sure, that seems to be the connotation here; this is why the NIV translates it "demons."

Though the term "angels" is sometimes used of fallen angels or demons (Matt 25:41; 2 Cor 12:7; 2 Pet 2:4; see 1 Cor 6:3; 11:10), most often it refers to good angels. Thus the NIV translation "angels and demons" seems proper, since pairing these terms in this listing seems intended to cover the whole range of spiritual beings, good and bad.

How good angels can be considered a possible means of separation from Christ's love is somewhat of a puzzle. Men sometimes worship angels (Col 2:18), but good angels always refuse such attempts (Rev 19:10; 22:8-9). Paul poses an hypothetical situation in which "an angel from heaven" preaches a false gospel (Gal 1:8), but if that should happen the angel would no longer be good. We conclude that good angels are included here just to provide a complete spectrum.

The more obvious danger is from demons, who are very active even today in their efforts to thwart God's purposes and to cause believers to stumble (Matt 24:24; Eph 6:10-18; 2 Thess 2:9-10). But Paul's point is that *no* angel, good or bad, has the power to move us away from the love of Christ. Not even Satan himself, and not even Satan's "best shot," can break the grip of the cross upon our hearts.

The next pair, "neither the present nor the future," does not seem to refer to anything in particular but is included to add to the theme of comprehensiveness. Just as with "death and life," so also "present and future" are all-inclusive with respect to those things that might try to separate us from Christ's love. We are tempted to worry about the future because we do not know what it will bring. But this is irrelevant, since we know that it can bring nothing that is able to nullify the power of Christ's love for us.

The next item, "nor any powers," is not in a pair. Since the word can be used for angelic beings (Eph 1:21; 1 Pet 3:22), some think that is its meaning here. But that raises the question as to why it should be listed separately from "angels and demons." A more likely possibility is that here the term is used in its common meaning of "miracles." The NT has several references to demonic, false miracles (Matt 7:22; 2 Thess 2:9; see Matt 24:24; Rev 13:13; 16:14; 19:20). The point then seems to be that no matter how great a miracle someone might perform, if it is related to a false gospel (Gal 1:8), its power is immediately diminished and negated by the greater power of the cross.

Some see "neither height nor depth" as references to pagan concepts of spiritual beings that rule the regions above the heavens and beneath the earth (or below the horizon), but this is unlikely (see Cranfield, I:443). Probably Paul just adds all-inclusive spatial references here, to go with his all-inclusive temporal references to the present and future. "Neither the highest height nor the deepest depth" can separate us from Christ's love (Cranfield, I:443).

The final item is a catch-all category that includes any other possibility that anyone can imagine: "nor anything else in all creation." The love of God as embodied in the cross of Christ looms so infinitely large that no finite, creaturely contingency can hope to overthrow it.

We should note Paul's language very carefully. He says that none of these things in themselves will ever *be able* to separate us from the love of God. None will have the power to do so. This is God's promise to us, and it is the basis for our confidence and hope and assurance of final victory. But Paul does not guarantee us that none of these things will ever become the occasion for our *separating ourselves* from God's love. As is the case with salvation in general, and justification and predestination in particular, so also is our assurance of salvation conditional. It is conditioned upon our own continued trust in the promises of God, which is something that lies within the power of our own free choice.

Some try to avoid this conclusion by pointing out that Paul says *no created thing* can separate us from Christ's love. Since we ourselves are creatures, that must mean that not even we can do anything to separate ourselves from God's saving love (e.g., Moo, I:589). However, the believer's abilities and decisions are not at issue here. It is assumed that we *want* to stay within the love of Christ, and that we are going to make every effort to do so. The point and the comfort of this passage is that no third party, no outside circumstance can destroy the saving relationship between us and God, or separate us from his love. That relationship is between us and God alone. Our ultimate salvation is God's loving will and purpose for us, and it will surely come to pass as long as our faith continues to cling to its one and only hope, the cross of Christ.

It is important to see that the love that is the basis for our unshakable assurance is "the love of God that is in Christ Jesus our Lord." God's love is expressed toward human beings in many different ways, especially in his gifts of creation and providence (Matt 5:43-48). But in the experience of many, these expressions of love are often overshadowed by such things as disease, poverty, and natural disasters. But the love of God embodied in the cross of Christ (John 3:16; 1 John 4:10) is different. It is not affected by contrary circumstances. It *alone* endures as the solid rock upon which our hope and assurance can safely rest.

As a final note, given the crucial role of the cross not only as the basis for our salvation itself but also as the basis for our *assurance* of salvation, it is all the more important to have a right understanding of the meaning of the cross, and all the more imperative to preach and teach and meditate upon what God has done for us through this precious instrument of his love.